THE LOGIC OF LEGAL REQUIREMENTS

The Logic of Legal Requirements

Essays on Defeasibility

Edited by
JORDI FERRER BELTRÁN
GIOVANNI BATTISTA RATTI

OXFORD
UNIVERSITY PRESS

OXFORD
UNIVERSITY PRESS

Great Clarendon Street, Oxford OX2 6DP
United Kingdom

Oxford University Press is a department of the University of Oxford.
It furthers the University's objective of excellence in research, scholarship,
and education by publishing worldwide. Oxford is a registered trade mark of
Oxford University Press in the UK and in certain other countries

First published in 2012
Reprinted 2014

Published in the United States of America by Oxford University Press
198 Madison Avenue, New York, NY 10016, United States of America

British Library Cataloguing in Publication Data
Data available

Library of Congress Cataloging in Publication Data
Data available

ISBN 978-0-19-966164-0

Acknowledgements

We would like to thank Eugenio Bulygin, Andrea Dolcetti, Fred Schauer, and Richard Tur for their great help and steadfast support in projecting and editing the present volume. We also would like to thank all the contributors for their acceptance in participating in the volume and their cooperation during the making of the project.

We acknowledge the financial support of The Spanish Ministry for Science and Innovation, for the project 'Ciencia y proceso judicial: prueba y atribución de responsabilidad' (DER2010-21331-C02-02).

Giovanni Battista Ratti acknowledges the financial support of a Spanish Government 'Juan de la Cierva' Fellowship in Law (University of Girona, 2008–11).

Contents

PART III DEFEASIBILITY AND THE CONCEPTIONS OF LAW

PART IV DEFEASIBILITY AND ADJUDICATION

List of Abbreviations

AGM	Alchourrón, Gärdenfors, Makinson Theory
AI	artificial intelligence
DD	deontic detachment
DDT	defeasible deducibility theory
ELP	Exclusive Legal Positivism
FD	factual detachment
ILP	Inclusive Legal Positivism
LIT	law identification thesis
LNP	logic of normative propositions

List of Contributors

Carlos E. Alchourrón was Professor of the Philosophy of Law and Professor of Logic at the University of Buenos Aires (Argentina).

Manuel Atienza, Professor of Legal Philosophy at the University of Alicante (Spain).

Fernando Atria, Professor of Law at the University of Chile and the University Adolfo Ibáñez (Chile).

Brian H. Bix, Frederick W. Thomas Professor for the Interdisciplinary Study of Law and Language at the University of Minnesota (USA).

Ricardo Caracciolo, Professor of Legal Philosophy at the National University of Córdoba (Argentina).

Bruno Celano, Professor of Legal Philosophy at the University of Palermo (Italy).

Bruce Chapman, Professor of Law at the University of Toronto (Canada).

Pierluigi Chiassoni, Professor of Jurisprudence at the University of Genoa (Italy).

Jordi Ferrer Beltrán, Professor of Legal Theory at the University of Girona (Spain).

Riccardo Guastini, Professor of Jurisprudence at the University of Genoa (Italy).

Juan Ruiz Manero, Professor of Legal Philosophy at the University of Alicante (Spain).

Juliano S.A. Maranhão, Lecturer in Law at the University of São Paulo (Brazil).

Rafael Hernández Marín, Professor of Law at the University of Murcia (Spain).

Daniel Mendonca, Professor of Law at the Catholic University Nuestra Señora de la Asunción (Paraguay).

José Juan Moreso, Professor of Legal Philosophy at Pompeu Fabra University, Barcelona (Spain).

Jonathan R. Nash, Professor of Law at Emory University (USA).

Juan Manuel Pérez Bermejo, Professor of Law at the University of Salamanca (Spain).

Giovanni Battista Ratti, Lecturer in Legal Philosophy at the University of Genoa (Italy).

María Cristina Redondo, Associate Professor of Legal Philosophy at the University of Genoa (Italy) and Researcher at the National Scientific and Technical Research Council of Argentina (CONICET).

Jorge L. Rodríguez, Professor of Law at the National University of Mar del Plata (Argentina).

Giovanni Sartor, Professor of Law at the University of Bologna and the European University Institute (Italy).

Frederick Schauer, David and Mary Harrison Distinguished Professor of Law at the University of Virginia (USA).

Richard H. S. Tur, Benn Law Fellow (1979–2012), Oriel College, University of Oxford (United Kingdom).

Wilfrid Waluchow, Senator William McMaster Professor of Constitutional Studies at McMaster University (Canada).

Legal Defeasibility: An Introduction

Jordi Ferrer Beltrán and Giovanni Battista Ratti***

Defeasibility is a problem which is on the agenda of many fields of knowledge including logic, epistemology, and moral philosophy, to name but a few. In recent years, a great many jurisprudential works have also, more or less directly, dealt with defeasibility in the legal domain.

However, the substantial amount of research on this topic has not yet produced a systematic treatment of the several phenomena referred to under the general heading of 'defeasibility'. In fact, one often has the impression that the use of the same expression to refer to different, though sometimes interrelated, phenomena brings about a number of conceptual confusions. In light of these issues, this book aims to shed some light on the different meanings of 'defeasibility' and clarify the scope of the different 'objects' which are referred to by this expression.

To this end we have invited some of the most prominent legal philosophers in the Anglo-American and Continental traditions to deal with a specific aspect of what is understood by 'defeasibility' in the legal domain,[1] or in philosophical or logical domains which are presupposed by jurisprudents when coping with such a phenomenon. This explains and justifies the structure of the book, as we will see in the following paragraphs.

A. Legal and logical defeasibility

The first part ('General Features of Defeasibility in Law and Logic') is devoted to unravelling the basic concepts related to legal defeasibility, based on the idea that law, or its components, is liable to implicit exceptions, which cannot be specified *ex ante* (viz. before the law's application to particular cases).

The first essay (by Jordi Ferrer Beltran and Giovanni B. Ratti) is devoted to analysing recent trends in legal logic and legal theory and to providing a general reconstruction of the debate on legal defeasibility. With this aim in mind, the paper surveys, in an encyclopaedic mode, the main conceptions of the defeasibility of legal standards under the twofold perspectives of legal interpretation and legal validity. The final part of the paper is devoted to providing a proposal for reconstruction of the relations between defeasibility and validity of legal norms.

The following paper, by Carlos Alchourrón, is the only one which was not written with this collection in mind. In fact, it is a reissue of Alchourrón's paper 'On Law and Logic', which was originally published in 1996. The reasons for this reissue are based on the relevance of Alchourrón's results in dealing with legal defeasibility, and on the

* Professor of Legal Theory, University of Girona.
** Lecturer in Legal Philosophy, University of Genoa.

[1] Here and in what follows, 'Continental' is used, broadly, to denote civil-law legal culture.

fact that many of the contributors to the present collection have these results as their starting point. In particular, Alchourrón's treatment of the pragmatic defeasibility of legal conditionals has proved to be an outstanding contribution to the examination of the sources of legal indeterminacy. It also happens that this part of Alchourrón's work is less known than other research on the logic of belief change and the logic of declarative conditionals, a fact that further convinced us to include the paper in the present volume.

The third essay, by Juliano Maranhão, takes issue with Alchourrón's well-known attack against nonmonotonic logics. The paper surveys Alchourrón's convictions about legal epistemology and argues that they provided the impetus for his opposition to nonmonotonic logics. It also proposes the view that Alchourrón's approach to defeasibility leaves three important aspects aside, which seem to have been endorsed in his final writings: (i) that the legal system is a set of strict conditional rules (not of prima facie rules) which is subject to change into a system containing more refined strict conditional rules; (ii) that within the normative system explicit norms have different epistemic status to derived ones (not all derived norms are valid); (iii) that the defeat results from a creative intervention by the interpreter changing the system of rules into a more qualified and consistent system. One of the highlights of the paper consists in the introduction of a specific revision operator, called *refinement*, which is taken to capture these neglected aspects and provides better representation of the so-called 'epistemic conception' of legal defeasibility.

Essays 6 and 7 deal with defeasibility of reasoning in the deontic domain and the question of whether it may be extended, under certain conditions, to legal reasoning, if this is regarded as a subset of the deontic field. This conceptual possibility—for some others, indeed to be regarded as a normative necessity[2]—is forcefully argued for by Giovanni Sartor in essay 6, while resolutely rejected, on genuine conceptual grounds, by Rafael Hernández Marín in essay 7. Sartor argues that defeasibility is an essential feature of reasoning in general, and legal reasoning in particular. This is mainly due to the fact that legal concepts have to be applied to such diverse domains of instances that they can at best offer a tentative and generic characterization of the objects to which they apply, a characterization which has to be supplemented with exceptions. Defeasibility of legal reasoning also reflects the dialectics of judicial proceedings where each party provides arguments supporting its position, which conflict with the arguments of the other. Hernández Marín holds the opposite view, according to which defeasibility, far from being an essential feature of legal reasoning, is a highly obscure notion, which has no logical ground and must accordingly be rejected. Moreover, Hernández Marín argues that no logic is possible in the normative domain and that no defeasible logic is justified in the descriptive domain: hence, defeasible deontic logic must be regarded as mere curiosity or nonsense.

Frederick Schauer, in essay 4, advocates a 'third way' between the widespread and radical jurisprudential tenets that defeasibility is either a necessary feature of law or an impossible one. Schauer argues that it is a contingent feature of law, depending on the very content of each legal system. More specifically, Schauer argues that the key to the idea of defeasibility is the potential for some applier, interpreter, or enforcer of a rule to make an ad hoc adaptation in order to avoid an absurd or otherwise unacceptable rule-generated outcome. And this implies a very significant conclusion: according to

2 See R.H.S. Tur, 'Defeasibilism', OJLS, 21 (2001), 355–68.

Schauer, defeasibility is not, properly speaking, a possible feature of rules; it is 'rather a characteristic of how some decision-making system will choose to *treat* its rules'.[3]

In essay 5, Jorge Rodríguez discusses at length the pros and cons of regarding legal rules as defeasible, and concludes that, from a properly conceptual point of view, rules cannot be held as defeasible, in the sense that their application is contingent on the non-occurrence of unspecifiable rule-defeaters based on reasons having particular power. Rules' presumptive force, in fact, would always call for an assessment of every member of such a list of unspecifiable defeaters and this would make it difficult (if not simply impossible) to carry out inferences with such rules as premises.

B. Defeasibility in legal interpretation

Part II—'Defeasibility and Interpretation'—aims at disentangling the main relations between the issue of legal defeasibility and the issue of legal interpretation.

In the first paper of this section, Pierluigi Chiassoni analyses in full detail the different meanings which are usually attached to 'defeasibility' in the context of the contemporary jurisprudential debate, and the different 'objects' which are predicated to be defeasible (including e.g. reasoning, norm formulations, concepts, conclusions, norms), distinguishing in particular several kinds of defeasibility of legal norms. In so doing, he disentangles the different relations that defeasibility is said to have with the indeterminacy of law.

The papers by Guastini, Mendonca, and Caracciolo all share a common theoretical basis, much indebted to Carlos Alchourrón and Eugenio Bulygin—two major figures in Continental jurisprudence and deontic logic—and their seminal work *Normative Systems*.[4] The paper by Riccardo Guastini reconstructs the notions of axiological gaps and defeasibility of legal rules as possible products of the meaning-ascribing activities that jurists carry out on legal sources. 'Defeasibility', according to Guastini, is just a novel name for two very well-known techniques of construction: restrictive interpretation, in civil-law legal orders, and distinguishing, in common law ones. Likewise, Daniel Mendonca (essay 11) provides a rational reconstruction of the concept of exception, which is crucial in dealing with the notion of defeasibility, showing the logical form of some intuitive arguments jurists use in tackling rules' negative conditions. On a similar theoretical basis, Riccardo Caracciolo (essay 12), analyses two conceptions of legal defeasibility, propounded by Carlos Alchourrón in his last works, and rejects the plausibility of one of them—the 'dispositional account'—which turns out to have some radically sceptical (and, for Caracciolo, unacceptable) consequences for legal interpretation.

Bix's paper is devoted to enquiring into the connection of philosophical open texture, Hartian open texture, and defeasibility in legal reasoning. Bix, contrary to a relatively widespread view, argues that open texture and legal defeasibility are different phenomena. However, he reaches the significant conclusion that 'defeasible forms of legal reasoning create . . . the same sort of range of available choices that judges face in the Hartian "open texture" of borderline cases'.[5] They are, so to speak, different sources of strong discretion.

[3] F. Schauer, 'Is Defeasibility an Essential Property of Law?', in this volume, ch. 4.
[4] C.E. Alchourrón and E. Bulygin, *Normative Systems* (Vienna: Springer, 1971).
[5] B. Bix, 'Defeasibility and Open Texture', in this volume, ch. 10.

C. Defeasibility and conceptions of law

Part III of the volume is dedicated to one of the most problematic issues in the history of jurisprudence: the connections between law and morality. These connections are examined from the perspective of legal defeasibility and its purported problematic nature for legal positivism.

In essay 13, José Juan Moreso argues that, in minimally developed legal systems, there is a sort of necessary connection between law and morality, which is due to the fact that legal rules are subject to moral defeaters. This, in turn, is due to the fact that a completely formalist or 'opaque' system (which may be found in ancient Roman law, Moreso argues) would contemporarily be regarded as a system flawed with paramount problems of institutional design and implementation.

In essay 14, Manuel Atienza and Juan Ruiz Manero, restating and refining some of the arguments they deployed in their *Theory of Legal Sentences*,[6] advocate for the inherent (nearly necessary) defeasibility of law, on the basis of the idea (originally elaborated by Dworkin) that contemporary law is made on two axiological levels—principles and rules—and that defeasibility is but the 'gap' between these two levels: more precisely, it is the failure of the rule to give a correct implementation to its underlying principle or principles. This would refute legal positivism—or at least exclusive legal positivism in the formulation offered, alternatively, by Raz and Bulygin—for it famously does not admit any reference to moral reasoning in order to identify the content of the law.

A similar tenet is held by Juan Manuel Pérez Bermejo, who enquires into the defeasibility of legal principles and upholds that only a rightly interpreted theory of principles is able to reconcile law's normativity and its necessity for adaptation to change. In so doing, he examines different versions of the principles thesis, eventually opting for what he calls a 'coherence theory' of law, as opposed to 'weight theories'.

Contrary to this widespread view, Wilfrid Waluchow, in essay 15, defends the view that not only does defeasibility (or, to be more precise, the different phenomena this word designates) not pose any serious threat to legal positivism, but also defeasibility, properly understood, may be regarded as a valuable theoretical tool for overcoming the schism between inclusive and exclusive legal positivism. In fact, the Exclusive Positivists—argues Waluchow—may be correct when they say that legal validity is normally, and in the first instance, established by way of non-moral, source-based criteria of validity, whereas Inclusive Positivists are right in holding that legal validity may be defeated or cancelled on moral grounds.[7]

In his paper, Bruno Celano takes up the issue (also referred to by Pérez Bermejo) of the 'particularist collapse' of the defeasibilist theories. Celano analyses the specificationist strategy, which purports to be consistent with the identity assumption, i.e. the thesis according to which a norm, being defeasible, somehow survives the impact of recalcitrant cases. However, Celano shows that, on specificationist premises, the identity assumption withers away. Celano then goes on to distinguish two kinds of exceptions: prima facie and true ones, as a strategy to overcome the conclusion that, when a specificationist strategy is followed, all justified normative verdicts turn out to be particular. According to Celano, norms provide what are *normally* reasons for or

[6] M. Atienza and J. Ruiz Manero, *A Theory of Legal Sentences* (Dordrecht: Kluwer, 1998).

[7] For a metatheoretical analysis of the different relations between defeasibility and legal validity, cf. J. Ferrer Beltrán and G.B. Ratti, 'Validity and Defeasibility in the Legal Domain', *Law and Philosophy*, 29 (2010), 601–26. See also, 'Defeasibility and Legality: A Survey', in this volume, ch. 1.

against certain actions, or certain normative consequences. Norms are defeasible conditionals, which are then liable to true exceptions, when the antecedent is satisfied, under normal circumstances only.

In the concluding essay of this section, Cristina Redondo analyses the question whether reasons for action are, or can be considered, defeasible. Redondo distinguishes between two different kinds of defeasibility—epistemic and ontological—and applies these two concepts to reasons for action. Based on a realist understanding, the idea of a defeasible reason is simply nonsense: for if reasons are facts in the realist sense they cannot be defeasible. A statement in which defeasibility is predicated of a reason would thus be a self-contradictory statement. This is why, according to such a view, sentences such as 'ϕ is a prima facie (defeasible) reason for doing what has been ϕ-ed' must necessarily be interpreted by alluding to an epistemic problem, if we want to avoid contradictions within a realistic stance. Following an alternative, 'constructivist' understanding, defeasibility may instead be regarded not only as a predicate of reasons, but also as an inescapable property of them, since the existence of a reason for a specific action depends on a set of human beliefs and attitudes: this in turn makes it possible to assert without contradiction that something is a reason and is defeasible in itself.

D. Defeasibility and adjudication

Part IV of the volume is devoted to analysing the relationships between defeasibility and legal adjudication, from the perspective of the justification of both the normative and the factual premises.

In an introductory essay, Atria deals with general features of government by general norms, and enquires into the history of ideas regarding general legislation and judicial application. By evoking Hart's dichotomy between formalism and scepticism, Atria revisits some fundamental notions at the basis of contemporary legal systems, and the debates that accompanied their institutional implementation. Atria's paper contains, in its final section, a prolonged criticism of what he calls the 'judge as an automaton model', which he innovatively assigns to formalists and sceptics alike. He goes on to provide a defence of a new model which 'maximize[s] the possibility that all the relevant elements of the particular case before the judge are subject to a scrutiny as close as necessary, and [which] minimize[s] the possibility that when it comes to deciding the case the judge will pursue goals or ends different to giving each their own'.[8]

Richard Tur, in essay 20, offers and discusses in detail several paradigmatic examples of norms treated defeasibly by common law courts and, on this basis, proposes a challenge for contemporary positivist theories: whether any social sources thesis in general or Hart's Rule of Recognition in particular can accommodate themselves to such endemic defeasibilism in adjudication. The answer that Tur suggests is that they cannot, 'for the Rule of Recognition must either strive for greater and greater breadth in order to include all possible sources of override or that the Rule of Recognition must be understood as identifying some but not all relevant legal materials'.[9]

Essay 21, by Jonathan Nash, propounds the opposite view that in adjudication (at least in the US system, often regarded as the paradigm of defeasible-treated standards) norms are regarded, by and large, as indefeasible. In doing so, Nash provides a detailed

[8] F. Atria, 'Legislation and Adjudication', in this volume, ch. 19.

[9] R. Tur, 'Defeasibility and Adjudication', in this volume, ch. 20.

analysis of US jurisprudence, arguing that defeasibility is eminently a context-dependent concept.

Essay 22, by Bruce Chapman, discusses, inter alia, the moral argument that supports the process that private common law adjudication adopts under defeasible rules. According to Chapman, this process provides for interpersonal respect and accountability between the parties in a way that a single stage summary rule does not. Chapman argues that 'in advancing arguments one way or the other under the single stage summary rule, each party looks past the other to the (moral) world and, more particularly, towards some (moral) fact in that world made salient by the rule. *It is as if each party really had no essential role for the other.*'[10] The opposite of this model is the model of defeasible rules, which 'shifts each party's accountability from a world independent of them to a world which (to some extent at least) they construct themselves with the justifiable claims they make upon one another'. Under the model of defeasible rules, the parties are less accountable to what is morally correct or true, and more to what authoritative demands they can justifiably make upon one another, in back and forth fashion, as they construct the rule and set the scope of its final application. In this regard—Chapman argues—'the model of defeasible rules provides more for the parties' joint exercise of a collective or shared rationality under the developing rule than it does for the joint accountability of these parties to some shared reason under a more truthful rule'.[11] This in turn, as Chapman interestingly stresses in the conclusion, would be a powerful argument for considering Hart's positivism as the winning party in the debate with Fuller's or Dworkin's antipositivism.

E. Epilogue: Rejuvenating the 'spirit of Bellagio'

We think that a collection like this, with such skilful contributors dealing with such hotly debated topics, needs no further justification than its index and contents. However, to the stimulating and self-evident qualities of the contributions, we would like to add a 'strategic' reason which has been at the heart of our editing work. This collection is also an occasion for trying to bridge the communication gap between two great traditions of legal thinking, namely the Anglo-Saxon analytical legal philosophy, stemming mainly from the works of Jeremy Bentham, John Austin, and H.L.A. Hart, and the Continental General Theory of Law, whose founding fathers were Hans Kelsen, Alf Ross, Norberto Bobbio, and Genaro Carrió. Defeasibility has been a passionately discussed topic in both worlds, and, despite several widely known differences, one may find in both cultures and the corresponding legal orders that the treatment of legal defeasibility has shown more than one point of convergence, especially regarding certainty and flexibility in decision making based upon rules. This appeared to us to be an opportunity to rejuvenate what we may call the 'spirit of Bellagio', an opportunity which could not be passed by. Let us elaborate.

In 1960 a conference on legal positivism was held in Bellagio, a wonderful town on Lake Como, under the auspices of the Rockefeller Foundation.[12] It was the first time that Anglo-American and Continental jurists came together 'to work towards the clarification of a subject of common interest in the field of jurisprudence'. This happened just two years after the publication of Hart's manifesto *Positivism and the*

[10] B. Chapman, 'Defeasible Rules and Interpersonal Accountability', in this volume, ch. 22.

[11] Ibid.

[12] See the report of this conference in R.A. Falk and S.I. Shuman, 'The Bellagio Conference on Legal Positivism', *Journal of Legal Education*, 14 (1961–2), 213–28.

Separation of Law and Morals and the English version of Alf Ross's masterpiece *On Law and Justice*. In the following years, as an incarnation of 'the spirit of Bellagio', some of the all-time best achievements of legal positivism were published, including Hart's *The Concept of Law*, Bobbio's *Sul Positivismo Giuridico* (On Legal Positivism), Alf Ross's *Validity and the Conflict between Legal Positivism and Natural Law*, Scarpelli's *Cos'è il positivismo giuridico* (What is Legal Positivism), among many others.

This experience, though extremely stimulating and tremendously fruitful, was not repeated for many years and during the years in which the spirit of Bellagio grew dim, Anglo-American and Continental jurists became confined again to their respective domains. So, at the end of the seventies, Genaro Carrió, one of the most prominent members of the 'Analytical School of Buenos Aires' and translator into Spanish of *The Concept of Law*, observed: 'It is dismaying to see that Dworkin's detailed objections to legal positivism, as well as the rich literature that has ensued, have not yet gone beyond the cultural boundaries of English-speaking countries.'[13] As anybody who is even vaguely familiar with present Continental jurisprudence knows, this is no longer the case. Dworkin's works have been widely commented upon and studied, as well as the literature that has stemmed from his evocative remarks. If this has happened, it is also owing to Carrió's challenging words. That said, however, it is worth noticing that many opportunities for common debate have been missed during recent years, and the two legal cultures have for the most part returned to their original separateness.

Whatever the reason for the cyclical separateness between Continental and Anglo-American jurisprudence, it is hard not to note that nowadays an important fracture (mostly of communication) exists between jurisprudents from the two traditions.

The main outcome of this separateness seems to be, in addition to the lack of stimulating projects such as Bellagio's,[14] that many important and original analyses of common topics, which are being studied in both legal cultures, are not considered (or not sufficiently considered) outside the world where they have been elaborated. This volume is an attempt to break this state of affairs, by collecting together some previously unpublished essays all dealing with an issue which is now being debated in both cultures, and by exchanging the main results of such investigations.

The Bellagio conference, of course, was held in the pre-computerized era, when meeting each other face-to-face was almost imperative if one wanted to exchange ideas prior to carrying out purportedly converging enquiries. In the age of e-mail this is no longer an imperative, and this book is primarily the product of a debate carried out by technological means. Fortuitously, however, computers have not yet succeeded in superseding the pleasure and thrill of a 'live' discussion; this book is also the product of a conference on defeasibilism held in Oxford in March 2008, and jointly organized by Professor Richard Tur and the editors of this book, where a collection of works to appear in the present volume were presented and thoroughly analysed in the purest 'Bellagio spirit'.

[13] G.R. Carrió, 'Professor Dworkin's views on Legal Positivism', *Indiana Law Journal*, 55 (1980), 211.

[14] A successful attempt to change this state of affairs was the organization of the 'Neutrality and Legal Theory' Conference at the University of Girona (20–22 May 2010), whose speakers were Robert Alexy, Juan Carlos Bayón, Brian Bix, Eugenio Bulygin, Bruno Celano, Jules Coleman, Riccardo Guastini, Brian Leiter, Jorge Rodríguez, Fred Schauer, Scott Shapiro, and Wilfrid Waluchow.

PART I

GENERAL FEATURES OF DEFEASIBILITY IN LAW AND LOGIC

1

Defeasibility and Legality: A Survey

*Jordi Ferrer Beltrán and Giovanni Battista Ratti**

A. Introduction

The concept of 'defeasibility' seems to have gained a very relevant role in recent jurisprudence. It is commonly held, among jurisprudents and jurists at large, that legal standards are somehow defeasible, that is that they are open to implicit exceptions, which cannot be exhaustively listed *ex ante* and, accordingly, do not provide conclusive, all-things-considered obligations, but rather prima facie ones. In another, closely related, view, inferences drawn within the legal domain are not deductive in nature, but retractable and ampliative, so that they resist unless some more powerful argument is given in favour of their defeasance.

Within this general scope, authors generally agree neither on how defeasibility is to be characterized, nor on what are the exact 'objects' which it is predicated of. Controversy also stems from the identification of the exact sources of this phenomenon. It is not even clear whether this supposed feature of law may be located within the law itself or if it entails a sort of rejection of the separability thesis between the legal and the extralegal. Despite these remarkable differences, most writers generally agree on the fact that the concept of 'legal defeasibility' is central for the description of certain significant aspects of contemporary legal orders.

The notion of 'defeasibility' had a somewhat curious development throughout the twentieth century: it originated in legal and moral terminology, it was then borrowed and elaborated on in the logic of belief revision and conditionals (especially in the field of artificial intelligence) and it again re-entered the moral and legal debate when the authors tried to formalize the discussion on the logical form of legal standards which stemmed from Dworkin's first critique on positivism. The elaboration of this critique (which, under many aspects, misfired) regained new life in Continental analytical jurisprudence when it provided the formal tools for extensive reconsideration of the theory of normative systems, which had been fully developed in the early seventies by Carlos Alchourrón and Eugenio Bulygin in their seminal book *Normative Systems* and since then has been extremely successful, mostly in Continental analytical circles.[1] As this story has hardly been told, and it is probably scarcely familiar to the readership, it is perhaps worth telling at the present occasion. Accordingly, this paper will provide the reader with a genealogical reconstruction of the debate on defeasibility in the legal domain.

Although their genealogy is uncertain, and deserves to be clarified, the theoretical topics dealt with here are surely not unfamiliar to the specialized reader. The

* Jordi Ferrer Beltrán, Professor of Legal Theory, University of Girona. Giovanni Battista Ratti, Lecturer in Legal Philosophy, University of Genoa. We would like to thank Riccardo Guastini and Nicola Muffato, who have discussed with us several aspects of the present paper.

[1] C.E. Alchourrón and E. Bulygin, *Normative Systems* (Vienna: Springer, 1971).

presentation which will be offered, however, may differ in some relevant aspects from presentations that are common in the legal theoretical literature.

Nevertheless, there is a further aspect which has rarely been considered in jurisprudential literature so far and which deserves, in our opinion, to be dealt with here, in order to offer a comprehensive account of the phenomenon under examination: the relations between defeasibility and the concepts of validity and applicability. The last part of our paper will elaborate on this topic.

Consequently, our survey will have the following structure: first of all, we will give a brief characterization of the concept of 'defeasibility' in general and of 'legal defeasibility' in particular (section B). The following section (C) will be dedicated to the substantive analysis of the defeasibility of legal standards. This discussion contains a presentation of Fred Schauer's theory of the defeasibility of legal rules, a reconstruction of the 'defeasibilist turn' of Carlos Alchourrón's last theory (before his untimely passing) and its repercussions on the theory of norms and normative systems that he developed together with Eugenio Bulygin in *Normative Systems*, and an analysis of some features of Andrei Marmor's views on law and defeasibility.

The following two sections of the paper will instead deal with some of the problems that are entailed by an affirmative answer to the question about the defeasibility of the criteria of recognition. More precisely: in section D, we will provide an overview on the question of whether it is meaningful to assert that the criteria for identification of a legal order are defeasible and, if so, what the repercussions on the validity of legal standards are and their possible relations to the applicability of legal standards. In section E, we elaborate on the distinction between validity and applicability of legal norms in light of defeasibility, and propose a novel distinction between internal and external defeasibility of legal standards, based on the difference between the defeat of the normative content of a legal standard and the defeat of its applicability or validity. In the final section, we briefly present some possible future applications of the analytical tools we propose in the paper.

B. 'Defeasibility'

Although it has been widely investigated, mostly throughout the twentieth century, the concept of 'defeasibility' has been known at least from the times of Aristotle, who distinguished between the ideal type of reasoning of deductive logic and the ordinary inferences of everyday life.[2] Deductive logic is of the utmost importance in allowing us to derive, mainly in the scientific discourse, indisputable conclusions from universal sentences. However—as Koons observes—Aristotle held that 'in the practical matters of every day life, we rely upon generalizations that hold only "for the most part", under normal circumstances, and the application of such common sense generalizations involves merely dialectical reasoning, reasoning that is defeasible and falls short of deductive validity'.[3]

However, it is without doubt for the last forty years of the twentieth century, particularly in the field of artificial intelligence (AI), that defeasible reasoning was studied with utmost intensity. As a consequence, many different systems of 'alternative'

[2] In the Preface of D. Nute (ed.), *Defeasible Deontic Logic* (Dordrecht: Kluwer, 1997), VII, it is held that instances of defeasible *normative* reasoning go back to Plato's dialogues. See also F. Schauer, 'Is Defeasibility an Essential Property of Law?', in this volume, ch. 4.

[3] R. Koons, 'Defeasible Reasoning', *Stanford Encyclopedia of Philosophy*, 2009.

logic have been elaborated in order to account for several discourses,[4] which seemed to require something different from the classical logical treatment.[5]

In the field of AI, as well as in the strictly philosophical domain, defeasibility has frequently been dealt with under the heading of 'nonmonotonic reasoning', i.e. literally, reasoning without monotony. Such a kind of reasoning, in fact, involves the rejection of monotony: that is, unlike in classical logic, a certain proposition entailed by a given set of propositions α does not necessarily follow from a set β, which is a superset of set α. Nonmonotonic reasoning is said to improve our reconstruction of common sense and ordinary inferences. This is particularly true of situations where we have an incomplete knowledge of a certain state of affairs and we consequently want to 'allow that a conclusion that is well drawn from given information may need to be withdrawn when we come into possession of further information, even when none of the old premises are abandoned'.[6]

Nonmonotonic reasoning was introduced into the logic debate due to the fact—efficaciously stressed by David Makinson—that classical logic (which is based, inter alia, on monotony) 'was developed in order to obtain a deeper understanding of deduction in mathematics'.[7] However, in other domains, different from pure mathematics, we are generally willing to drop monotony, since our generalizations only hold for normal or typical cases. This happens, in particular, when we draw conclusions from a set of not completely reliable or inconsistent pieces of (supposed) knowledge.[8]

Despite the fact that most authors hold that defeasible logics are formally characterized by failure of monotony, there are also doubts about the failure of *modus ponens*, i.e. that logical rule based on considering the antecedent of conditionals as a sufficient

[4] Cf., e.g., D. Makinson, 'Five Faces of Minimality', *Studia Logica*, 52 (1993), 340: 'It is well known that there are close similarities between the logic of *counterfactual conditionals* (as developed in the 1970s following Stalnaker and Lewis), some versions of *nonmonotonic or defeasible* inference (as constructed in the 1980s in the context of logics for artificial intelligence), *belief or theory revision* (especially in the 1985 paradigm of Alchourrón, Gärdenfors, and Makinson), and *updating* (again, in artificial intelligence literature and especially in recent work of Katsuno and Mendelzon). Similarities can be found at the syntactic level, as resemblances between properties of the operations in question, and also at the semantic level, as resemblances between kinds of model for them.'

[5] It is not our aim here to review such systems: this is a task that, in fact, would require more than an entire volume in its own right. For an introductory overview of different systems of nonmonotonic logic, see G. Antoniou, *Nonmonotonic Reasoning* (Cambridge, Mass.: The MIT Press, 1997).

[6] D. Makinson, *Bridges from Classical to Nonmonotonic Logic* (London: King's College, 2005), 2. In formal terms, we want to abandon the following inferential pattern: 'Whenever $A \vdash x$ and $A \subseteq B$ then $B \vdash x$'.

[7] Ibid., 3. See also F. Tohmé and R.P. Loui, 'Alchourrón's Defeasible Conditionals and Defeasible Reasoning' in A.A. Martino (ed.), *Logica delle norme* (Pisa: SEU, 1997), 14: 'Logic was always considered as a discipline studying the process of *inference*. This notion encompassed deductive as well as non-deductive (or *ampliative*) inference. But in a short period in historical terms, from 1840 to 1910, logic was reduced only to the study of deductive inference, a process that can be explained by the heavy demand of solid foundations required by mathematics.'

[8] G. Antoniou, 'Defeasible Reasoning: A Discussion of Some Intuitions', *International Journal of Intelligent Systems*, 21 (2006), 545: 'Nonmonotonic reasoning is concerned with reasoning about incomplete and inconsistent information. Defeasible reasoning is a family of nonmonotonic reasoning approaches that are based on the idea of defeat among rules or arguments.' R. Morado, 'Problemas filosóficos de la lógica no monotónica' in R. Orayen and A. Moretti (eds), *Filosofía de la Lógica* (Enciclopedia Iberoamericana de Filosofía, 27; Madrid: Trotta, 2004), 327, lists at least four areas in which nonmonotonic reasoning can work as a valuable tool for reconstructing ordinary reasoning: (a) when normal ways of reasoning may fail and their conclusions are consequently retracted; (b) when incomplete information is (wrongly or presumptively) regarded as complete; (c) when from the same pieces of information one can derive conflicting conclusions; (d) when we have to revise our beliefs in light of a changing context.

condition of the consequent.[9] In contrast to the view that both augmentation and *modus ponens* fail, defenders of classical deductive logic have propounded the threefold view that:[10] (a) it is irrational to reject monotony and allow *modus ponens*, since the latter entails (or even boils down to) the former;[11] (b) rejecting both *modus ponens* and strengthening the antecedent involves an almost total loss of inferential power;[12] (c) and, most importantly, defeasibility can be explained by way of a combination of deductive logic and belief revision.

More generally, the debate among defenders and detractors of nonmonotonic logics seems to be predicated on a divergence about the topic of discussion:[13] classical deductive logic is clearly not bound to the ideal of reconstructing everyday, ordinary, reasoning. It is rather a set of inferential tools built to preserve a certain propositional value (i.e. truth) in reasoning. It is evident that in ordinary reasoning—and this is *the* point of defeasibilist theories of logic—we accept as justified conclusions which are invalidly drawn from the point of view of strict deductive logic.

In legal philosophy and deontic logic, the character of the logic of norms has frequently been disputed. Leaving aside the basic problem of finding some solid foundations for a logic of norms (which is far from being resolved), it seems to us worth mentioning the distinction (somewhat seemingly analogous or parallel to the one we have just mentioned) between those logics which have tried to reconstruct certain kinds of deductive validity of reasoning with norms, and those logical systems which have tried to formalize common, everyday, practical reasoning.[14]

The distinction between these two possible approaches to legal reasoning was clearly identified by Norberto Bobbio in his pioneering work dealing with law and logic. There he distinguished between the logic of law and the logic of jurists.[15] The former is an investigation of the (supposed) logical structure and behaviour of legal norms, while the latter is an investigation of lawyers' argumentations.[16] Now, one can fall prey to the temptation to assimilate the logic of law to the application of certain systems of 'classical' deontic logic to the legal domain, and the logic of jurists with some sorts of

[9] For helpful discussion on this point, see D. Makinson, 'Five Faces of Minimality', 360–2.

[10] This is the position of C.E. Alchourrón, 'Philosophical Foundations of Deontic Logic and the Logic of Defeasible Conditionals' in J.J. Ch. Meyer and R.J. Wieringa (eds), *Deontic Logic in Computer Science: Normative System Specification* (New York: John Wiley and Sons, 1993), 44: 'There is no need for a logic of defeasible norms (norms of *prima facie* obligations and permissions) because behind the requirement for such logics, as well as behind the requirement for non-monotonic logics, now in fashion in artificial intelligence, lies a mixture of a standard notion of consequence (or conditional) and the change of our (normative) premises in a dynamic perspective', and E. Bulygin, 'Review of Jaap Hage's "Law and Defeasibility"', *Artificial Intelligence and Law*, 11 (2003), 249: '[Defeasible] arguments imply a change of premises and this can be described in terms of ordinary deductive logic and belief revision.'

[11] C.E. Alchourrón, 'Defeasible Logics: Demarcation and Affinities' in G. Crocco, L. Fariñas del Cerro, and A. Herzig (eds), *Conditionals: From Philosophy to Computer Science* (Oxford: Clarendon Press, 1991), 95ff.

[12] C.E. Alchourrón, 'Philosophical Foundations of Deontic Logic and the Logic of Defeasible Conditionals', 83.

[13] W.V. Quine, *Philosophy of Logic* (Englewood Cliffs: Prentice-Hall, 1970), 80–1.

[14] This distinction is clearly stated by J.F. Horty, 'Nonmonotonic Foundations for Deontic Logic' in D. Nute (ed.), *Defeasible Deontic Logic*, 17: 'Deontic logic was developed, for the most part, by philosophers concerned with valid patterns of ethical and legal reasoning. The study of nonmonotonic logic, on the other hand, was initiated, much more recently, by researchers in artificial intelligence who felt that the logical theories then available could not be used to represent the kind of defeasible generalizations that constitute so much of our commonsense knowledge.'

[15] N. Bobbio, 'Diritto e logica' (1962), reprinted in N. Bobbio, *Contributi ad un Dizionario Giuridico* (Turin: Giappichelli, 1994), 115ff.

[16] T. Mazzarese, *Logica Deontica e Linguaggio Giuridico* (Padova: CEDAM, 1989), 6–8.

defeasible deontic logic or nonmonotonic legal reasoning. But this would be a mistake, since things are much more complex than that.

In fact, there are two tendencies in legal theory that are worth analysing; they can be characterized as follows.

(1) According to what we can call a 'structure-based approach' to the logic of legal standards, such standards have a structure and a logical behaviour which is independent from jurists' interpretative operations. Such logic can be discovered, and by discovering it one is able to disclose the correct logical treatment that each kind of standard requires. Within this broad standpoint, which has a strong 'Platonic' flavour,[17] at least three different views can be singled out: (a) according to the first view, all legal standards are indefeasible, in other words law is only made of standards whose operative facts are sufficient conditions for the normative consequence attached to them; (b) according to the second view, different legal standards are to be distinguished on the very grounds of defeasibility: for some of them are defeasible, while others are not; (c) according to a third view, all legal standards are defeasible.

Before briefly discussing each of these three positions, we must observe that, in literature, one can find some usages of the term 'defeasibility' that run counter to Occam's Razor. The term is, in fact, sometimes used to denote the situation where norms have explicit exceptions, *viz.* exceptions which can be derived from other norms of the system. To say that all norms are explicitly defeasible in the sense that they can be overridden by other norms of the system expresses, of course, a banal truth, for which we already have other legal theoretical terms (such as 'preference among norms', 'hierarchical ordering', and so on). Consequently, to argue that legal rules are defeasible should be understood not as tantamount to making 'the obvious point that legal rules have exceptions, but [to] the stronger one that it is theoretically impossible to enumerate all the exceptions and state all the sufficient conditions for the rule's application'.[18]

Once this preliminary question has been clarified, we can go back to our threefold classification.

(a) The first view—according to which all legal standards are indefeasible—may be taken as maintaining that all legal standards, appropriately formulated in their complete form (containing all their exceptions at a certain given moment), are characterized by antecedents that provide sufficient conditions for the consequent to follow. That is to say that *implicit* exceptions are to be regarded as conceptually impossible. This view has been frequently criticized as a scholastic fiction. What is usually argued is that:[19] (1) perfect conditional norms are not linguistic structures that concretely exist in the legal world, but rather represent the ideal result of the synthesis of many norms belonging to, or applicable in, a certain legal order; (2) the rewriting of the entire legal system in the form of a set of perfect conditional norms can never be completed due to human limitations, both epistemological and practical.

What these critics argue is no doubt correct. However, some qualifications are in order. It is indeed true that human faculties are limited and therefore no lawyer can manage the

[17] Such 'descriptive' models, thus, would not describe, *ex post*, how people normally reason, but, a priori, how logical entities are (presumptively) structured. This way of thinking is often called 'logical Platonism'. Cf. G.H. von Wright, *Norm and Action* (London: Routledge & Kegan Paul, 1963), 4–5.

[18] L.G. Boonin, 'Concerning the Defeasibility of Legal Rules', *Philosophy and Phenomenological Research*, 26 (1966), 371–8.

[19] G. Sartor, 'Defeasibility in Legal Reasoning' in Z. Bankowski et al. (eds), *Informatics and the Foundation of Legal Reasoning* (Dordrecht: Kluwer, 1995), 143–4; R.H.S. Tur, 'Defeasibilism', OJLS, 21 (2001), 361–2.

continuous revision of the antecedents of all the norms which belong to a certain legal order. But this does not entail that it is *conceptually* impossible to rewrite the entire legal order as a set of perfect conditional norms. It can only imply that such an ordering task is not *humanly* possible. However, this is not a reason to reject perfect conditional norms as a powerful tool for theoretical reconstruction: as we will see later on, in fact, jurists are usually interested in small portions of the entire legal system, in order to solve a given practical question. So, if one wants to represent ordinary juristic reasoning with norms, one must take into account that it normally deals with a very limited set of norms, usually reconstructed as strictly conditional norms. And the rewriting of such limited normative systems in the form of a set of perfect conditional norms is not only possible, but also very common in legal literature, and indeed necessary if such systems are intended to provide an applicable solution to legal practical problems.

(b) The second view—defeasibility is the main tool for distinguishing different kinds of standards—has been advocated by many prominent legal philosophers. In particular, many anti-positivistic philosophers have attacked legal positivism on the grounds that it supposedly did not explicate the role that principles (which are considered as essentially defeasible legal norms) played in law and juristic reasoning. Notoriously, this was one of the main points of Dworkin's first attack on positivism.[20] Dworkin's original formulation of the distinction was indeed based on logical considerations: 'The difference between legal principles and legal rules,' he maintained[21] 'is a logical distinction.' Rules, in fact, are applicable 'in all-or-nothing fashion', whereas principles 'do not set out legal consequences that follow automatically when the conditions provided are met'.[22] In other words, principles are inherently defeasible, whilst rules are not.[23] This distinction has been articulated in several manners but each of them has encountered several difficulties. The main complexity seems to be that, since principles can be overridden, by definition, by implicit operative factors, and principles can override rules, it follows that rules also can be overridden by implicit operative factors. If this is correct, the distinction between rules and principles, predicated only on the basis that the latter are defeasible, whilst the former are not, is simply untenable. One solution is that rules are, by definition, totally entrenched (which is tantamount to dropping the premise that principles can

[20] Cf. S. Shapiro, 'The "Hart–Dworkin" Debate: A Short Guide for the Perplexed' in A. Ripstein (ed.), *Ronald Dworkin* (Cambridge: Cambridge University Press, 2007), 26.

[21] R. Dworkin, *Taking Rights Seriously* (London: Duckworth, 1978), 24.

[22] Ibid.

[23] Dworkin's stance is efficaciously summed up by C.E. Alchourrón, 'Philosophical Foundations of Deontic Logic and the Logic of Defeasible Conditionals', 67, in very perspicuous terms: 'Dworkin held that the difference between rules and principles is of a logical nature. Rules apply or do not apply to cases, the answer to their applicability is always of the kind Yes or No. There are no degrees in their field of applicability. On the contrary the applicability of a principle is always a question of degree; one must weigh in each case one principle against others in order to know which one is applicable, since a principle may be overridden in certain cases. In other words *principles are defeasible in their very nature*' (emphasis added). F. Schauer, 'On the Supposed Defeasibility of Legal Rules' in M.D.A. Freedman (ed.), *Current Legal Problems, 51, Legal Theory at the End of the Millenium* (Oxford: Oxford University Press, 1998), 229 fn. 17, observes that Dworkin's distinction is based on a conflation of two different features of legal standards: 'There *is* a distinction between crisp ("Speed limit 55") rules and vague ("reckless driving is prohibited") ones, and there is a distinction between overridable and non-overridable ones. Dworkin's mistake is in assuming that the latter distinction tracks the former, with crispness being the marker for non-overridability. In fact the distinctions cut across each other, for some vague rules ("Do unto others as you would have them do unto you") may be understood as non-overridable, while quite crisp rules, like speed limits, are ordinarily understood, in law and out, as subject to override.'

override rules). This solution too is affected by several shortcomings, the most prominent of which is that it is not a good tool for describing the reality of what happens in the courts, where provisions that at first glance are rule-like are often treated as defeasible (*Riggs* v. *Palmer* is a clear instance of that).[24] Another frequent solution to this problem is to hold that, in spite of appearances, all legal standards are indeed defeasible. To this solution we must now turn.

(c) A first interpretation which holds that all legal standards are defeasible means, inter alia, that no legal standard admits *modus ponens* and strengthening the antecedent. This, in turn, means that no application of legal norms is logically possible or at least theoretically explainable: such a solution to the structural problem at hand implies, thus, a very serious problem for the theoretical explanation of legal application in judicial cases. A second interpretation of the thesis at hand regards all legal standards as potentially overridable in certain cases where they bring about results that are regarded, for some reason, as unsatisfactory.[25] This, in turn, implies that, from this perspective, a determination must be made about when legal standards are indeed *defeated*. Here at least two contrary options have been envisaged: (1) we can count on a set of rationally discoverable ordering hierarchies which determine the defeasance of a certain legal standard in some given circumstances; (2) such a set does not exist or is not completely knowable, and for this reason the applicator has to make a discretional decision as for the defeasance of the legal standard at hand. In the relevant literature on the topic, based on the formalistic view we are discussing, the first option is obviously dominant, although epistemic problems of incomplete knowledge of objective ordering amongst norms are duly considered as fundamental in the characterization of defeasibility as a matter of *implicit* exceptions.

At any rate, and by way of a conclusion of this point, what is important to stress here is that, from the formalistic perspective, we have been examining defeasible logics or reconstructions which favour the idea of the defeasibility of (some or all) legal standards that are as 'Platonic' in flavour as most classical logics are. From such a standpoint, in fact, the former only diverges from the latter in its claim to discover a *different* logical truth, but not for the very quest of such an a priori truth.

(2) According to an opposite stance on law and logic, which we can call the 'interpretation-based account', the different kinds of legal standards that can be identified by analysing common juristic discourse are the product of the interpretation of legal provisions, and the logical treatment which is attached to each type of standard is but the contingent and ever-changing form by means of which jurists manipulate interpreted legal provisions.[26] Here defeasibility is regarded as a prominent interpretative problem.

In recent literature on defeasible logics, this tenet seems to have sometimes been propounded, although under different and somewhat obscure forms, to mark the departure from the common understanding of the logic of legal reasoning. According to the defenders of defeasible deontic logics, for instance, such defeasibilist systems provide an explanation of how conflicting norms are processed, which standard deontic logic cannot offer because of its very nature.[27] This is supposedly so, for standard

[24] 115 N.Y. 506 (1889).
[25] See, for instance, F. Schauer, *Playing by the Rules. A Philosophical Examination of Rule-Based Decision-Making in Law and in Life* (Oxford: Clarendon Press, 1991), 73ff.
[26] G. Tarello, *Diritto, Enunciati, Usi* (Bologna: Il Mulino, 1974), 268ff.
[27] R.P. Loui, 'Alchourrón and von Wright on Conflicts Among Norms' in D. Nute (ed.), *Defeasible Deontic Logic*, 350–1.

deontic logic is taken either (a) to rule out the very possibility of normative conflicts,[28] or (b) not to be able to offer any solution to normative conflicts.[29]

As for the first charge, what is usually argued is that standard systems of deontic logic validate the sentence '$\sim$(Oa & O$\sim$a)' and, for this reason, rule out normative inconsistencies. However, it must be remembered that such a sentence receives different treatments according to its interpretation in terms of norms or normative statements (i.e. descriptive propositions bearing upon norms).[30] In the first interpretation (norms), the sentence at hand is simply taken as an axiom (or as a transformation of the common intuitive axiom 'Oa $\rightarrow$ Pa') for *optimal* normative systems, whereas in the second interpretation (normative statements upon norms), the sentence is understood as providing the definition of a rational norm-giver (which, of course, can be frustrated in *actual* normative systems). It seems clear to us that the first reading is not meant to rule out inconsistencies (it only determines a state of affairs that ought to be satisfied by *ideal* normative systems), whereas the second is manifestly incapable of doing so and not even meant for it. So, standard deontic logic, when properly understood in the twofold interpretations which we have just sketched out, seems to be totally capable of accounting for inconsistencies within normative systems.[31]

The second charge is that standard deontic logic cannot account for the *processing* of normative inconsistencies. Defeasible deontic logics (or, more broadly, nonmonotonic deontic logics) have supposedly supplied successful ways of dealing with inconsistencies in ordinary and juristic reasoning. Common examples of ordinary reasoning are the Tweety problem and the so-called *Nixon Diamond.*

Notoriously, the first example concerns the situation where we commit, at the same time, to the universal sentence 'All birds fly' (in symbols: '(x) Bx $\rightarrow$ Fx') and to the sentence that, Tweety being a penguin, it does not fly ('(x) Px $\rightarrow$ $\sim$Fx) & Pa $\rightarrow$ $\sim$Fa'). It is clear that our heuristic position is one where we have justified reasons to believe that Tweety both flies and does not fly ('Fa & $\sim$Fa') since it is, at the same time, a bird and a penguin ('Ba & Pa'). This complication is usually solved, in theoretical discourses, by the so-called principle of priority of specificity:[32] more specific information defeats more general information.[33]

[28] See, for instance, J.F. Horty, 'Nonmonotonic Foundations for Deontic Logic', 19.

[29] R.P. Loui, 'Alchourrón and von Wright on Conflicts Among Norms', 351.

[30] J.L. Rodríguez, 'Normative Relevance and Axiological Gaps', *Archiv für Rechts- und SozialPhilosophie*, 86 (2000), 151–67.

[31] Another charge against standard deontic logic is that it has some difficulties in explaining conflicts among conditional normative sentences: see R. Hilpinen, 'Conflict and Change in Norm Systems' in A. Frändberg and M. Van Hoecke (eds), *The Structure of Law: Proceedings of the 2nd Benelux-Scandinavian Symposium in Legal Theory* (Uppsala: Iustus Farlag, 1987), 37–49. But, as C.E. Alchourrón, 'Conflicts of Norms and the Revision of Normative Systems', *Law and Philosophy*, 10 (1991), 413–25, has shown, this is also an unjustified criticism.

[32] A sentence with antecedent A is said to be more specific than a sentence with antecedent B, relative to a theory T, if we can derive all of B from A using only the sentences in T, but not vice versa.

[33] It is worth mentioning that, in the discussion of this problem, examples usually introduce other circumstances such as 'x has a broken wing', 'x has its legs, or wings, tied up', and so on. Now, it seems to us that there is a fundamental difference between the exceptions of penguins and the other mentioned exceptions. In the former case, what lacks is the dispositional property of 'being able to fly'. This means that a certain individual, which belongs to the subspecies of penguins, cannot possibly be able to fly (they are not able to fly under any circumstances). In the other cases, what lacks is not the dispositional property of being able to fly, which does not characterize any subspecies, but a contingent feature of a possible (*viz.* not necessary and not impossible) state of affairs (for instance: birds with a broken wing are able to fly if they are cured and they have presumably flown before being injured). The same, with more reason, may be argued for birds with tied-up wings. So, the revision of the antecedent of the universal referring to penguins ends with the introduction of the exception regarding the fact

The *Nixon Diamond* problem is famously instantiated by the following state of affairs: Quakers usually are pacifists; Republicans usually are not pacifists. What about Richard Nixon, a Republican Quaker? Monotonic logics suggest we face an insoluble contradiction in such circumstances, precisely because of monotony, while nonmonotonic logics do not, for their conclusions hold only in normal circumstances. Two main approaches have been propounded in the field of nonmonotonic logic to handle such conflicting sources of information as the *Nixon Diamond*:[34] the so-called 'credulous' one and the 'sceptical' one. According to the credulous approach, one should commit to as many defeasible conclusions as possible, subject to a consistency requirement, whereas according to the sceptical approach one should withhold assent from potentially conflicted defeasible conclusions.

The solving of the first antinomy is, upon first consideration, manifestly similar to the application of the *lex specialis derogat generali* principle for legal reasoning: a more specific rule defeats a more general one (this is used when jurists solve what, in Ross's famous terminology, is a 'total–partial' antinomy). Indeed, according to some defeasible deontic logics, the more specific antecedent of two conflicting norms ought to dominate the more general one.[35] As an account of ordinary legal reasoning, however, it is more than doubtful that the principle of specificity has a general scope as a principle of priority among conflicting norms. In many cases, in fact, the criterion *lex specialis* competes with (and is often defeated by) other criteria, such as *lex superior derogat legi inferiori* and *lex posterior derogat legi priori.*[36] Specifically, the relationships among the criteria for solution of normative conflicts are contingent and changing, and no logic can be built in order to capture the 'very nature' of conflict-solving in normative reasoning, for the simple reason that such a thing does not exist.[37]

What we can do is to try to shed light on the way the three mentioned criteria (and other ones we have not mentioned here) actually work in legal reasoning: as has been accounted for, the relationships among the priority criteria are synchronically manifold and diachronically mutable, so that no logic can descriptively capture a stable usage of precedence among such criteria.[38] It can only prescribe, or suggest, a certain stable systematization of them.

that penguins cannot fly, whereas the revision of the antecedent of universals regarding 'birds with broken wings' or 'birds with tied-up legs' can be endlessly revised due to contingent future facts ('Tweety is cured' or 'Tweety's legs have been untied') which can materialize and trigger such a revision.

[34] G.A. Antonelli, 'Non-monotonic Logic' in *Stanford Encyclopedia of Philosophy* (2010).

[35] See D. Nute, 'Norms, Priorities, and Defeasibility' in P. McNamara and H. Prakken (eds), *Norms, Logics and Information Systems* (Amsterdam: IOS Press, 1999), 214–15; cf. also R.P. Loui, 'Alchourrón and von Wright on Conflict Among Norms', 350.

[36] On the possible relations among the mentioned criteria, see N. Bobbio, *Studi per una Teoria Generale del Diritto* (Turin, Giappichelli, 1975), 113ff.

[37] D. Nute, 'Norms, Priorities, and Defeasibility', 216, admits that, when more than one precedence criterion is taken into account, the relationships that can be envisaged among such criteria, and the defeasible or indefeasible treatment of them, are not easily depicted by a logical model. In this sense, defeasible deontic logics encounter, at a higher order, the same 'problems' that classical deontic logic met at a lower level.

[38] As Guastini has repeatedly shown (see e.g. R. Guastini, *Le Fonti del Diritto. Fondamenti teorici* (Milan: Giuffrè, 2010), 363ff.), the criterion of speciality is commonly used to give a more specific norm priority to a more general one, but it is also used, sometimes, to give alternative priority to one of two rules which connect incompatible solutions to only a subset of the cases that are referred to in their antecedents. The chronological principle is used to cancel *ex nunc* the validity of a norm N1 which has been enacted before norm N2, which has the same hierarchical level as N1 and attaches an incompatible solution to the same set or subset of the cases referred to in the norms' antecedents. Finally, the

The approaches to the second antinomy (a 'partial–partial antinomy' in Ross's terminology) suggested by defeasible logics do not seem to be very promising, for they are either reducible to a deductivist approach or are not able to explain what happens in common, ordinary legal (and especially judicial) reasoning. To hold all the possible (defeasible) conclusions which can be drawn from the same set is viable only under the condition that incompatible results may be considered equally justified. In legal terms, this seems to mean that, when two (or more) incompatible norms may be derived from a certain legal set, the applicator is entitled to deem any of the two (or more) incompatible solutions justified. This is quite a sound idea, even though it runs counter to the views of many legal philosophers who hold that, of two conflicting rules, one must necessarily be invalid.[39] But such an idea does not seem to require any kind of nonmonotonic or defeasible reasoning. On the contrary, the very fact of being able to spot the antinomy is due to the application of deductive, strictly monotonic logic.

In turn, the sceptical approach, consisting in withholding assent from incompatible conclusions, seems to be translatable into a stalemate of legal application, when considered from a jurisprudential standpoint. This of course can be a normal feature for non-evaluative legal science, whose precise task is to expose the possible solutions provided by the law without necessarily choosing one of them. But it cannot be accepted as to the judicial application of law, for no legal decision whatsoever can be taken if both of two conflicting rules, on the grounds of which the case should be legally decided, are held as inapplicable.

Some further, and more general, qualifications are in order here.

In the first place, the logical systems, which have been elaborated in defeasibilist literature, are supposedly designed to account for priority among conflicting norms: that is for *explicit* exceptions. In this sense, they are neither apt, nor meant, to give an explanation to the fact that sometimes norms are treated as having *implicit* exceptions.

Secondly, it must be noted that successful logic models, based on 'classical' deontic logic, have been propounded in order to explain the repercussions of acts of derogation (or rejection) of norms within inconsistent normative systems.[40] So, one cannot say that standard deontic logic does not have any explanation of how normative conflicts are dealt with in practical discourse.[41] The criticism at hand, thus, may be understood

hierarchical principle is used to solve antinomies between norms of different hierarchical levels, by invalidating *ex tunc* the inferior norm.

[39] As is widely known, this is, among others, Kelsen's as well as Dworkin's view.

[40] The main one is, no doubt, the one elaborated by C.E. Alchourrón and D. Makinson, 'Hierarchies of Regulations and Their Logic' in R. Hilpinen (ed.), *New Studies in Deontic Logic* (Dordrecht: Kluwer, 1981). See also, in the same volume, C.E. Alchourrón and E. Bulygin, 'The Expressive Conceptions of Norms'. Perhaps, it is worth recalling that this was one of the main stages in the elaboration of AGM theory, an outstandingly successful theory regarding the rational revision of belief sets, elaborated in the mid-eighties by Alchourrón together with Peter Gärdenfors and David Makinson (hence the name of the theory, after the initials of the authors). Such a theory was originally presented in the seminal 'On the Logic of Theory Change: Partial Meet Contractions and Revision Functions', *Journal of Symbolic Logic,* 50 (1985), 118–39. The possible future move from norms derogation to belief revision had already been noted at 147 of Alchourrón's and Makinson's 1981 paper. AGM's relevance for AI and nonmonotonic reasoning is richly explained in R. Carnota and R. Rodríguez, 'Carlos Alchourrón y la Inteligencia Artificial', *Análisis filosófico*, 26 (2006), 9–52. The analysis provided by Carnota and Rodríguez shows the genesis of Alchourrón's ideas on the topic (from legal theory to beliefs change) and how his works were fundamental in establishing this field of research.

[41] For this reason, it is very surprising to us that L. Royakkers and F. Dignum, 'Defeasible Reasoning with Legal Rules' in D. Nute, *Defeasible Deontic Logic*, 263, ascribe Alchourrón's and

as suggesting that standard systems of deontic logic do not provide a *solution* for antinomies. But such a criticism is clearly off target, since deductive logic is not meant to provide tools for solving normative conflicts; it is only meant to offer tools to detect them. It must also be observed that logic can be applied only when sentences (in this case, normative provisions) have already been interpreted: consequently, logic can only determine which consequences follow from accepting a certain interpretation of legal sources, but it does not say anything (and it needn't say anything) about which interpretation, amongst different possible interpretations, ought to be chosen.

The difficulties of defeasible deontic logics in locating the criticism towards standard deontic logic show a bit of conflation of several problems in reconstructing common or juristic reasoning about or with rules.[42]

Juristic reasoning may be broken down, for theoretical purposes, into three main phases or operations: (1) interpretation; (2) logical development; and (3) ordering.[43] By means of interpretation, jurists move from legal sources to legal norms, thus forming a normative basis. By means of logical development, jurists derive logical consequences from the normative basis, and so are able to detect the possible logical defects, such as gaps and antinomies, which affect the consequences of the normative basis they are handling. It is only with the third operation—i.e. ordering—that jurists deal with gaps and inconsistencies, by bridging the former and solving the latter by means of some priority criteria. It is not clear *where* defenders of defeasible logics locate defeasibility in legal reasoning.

By locating it in phase (2), one may renounce fully developing, from a deductive point of view, a normative basis. But this would make it impossible to spot systematic defects, such as gaps and antinomies. Another understanding, completely different in its theoretical repercussion, may mean that some of the deductive consequences of the normative basis are held not to be valid, or at least not applicable (we will get back to this issue in section D).

To locate it in phase (3) is tantamount to using the term 'logic' in an unusual way, by simply changing the headings under which different juristic operations are accounted for. Development of the logical consequences would be equated with drawing retractable inferences from a certain normative basis, and the 'real logical task' would consist in ordering, according to some preferential criteria, inconsistent or incomplete retractable conclusions. Note that such inferences are regarded as retractable because when they bring about gaps and antinomies, they are rejected and changed in favour of other inferences. But, as it is easy to see, this is only a change of lexicon, not of subject matter.

Makinson's model to defeasible reasoning. This misattribution is probably due to a labelling problem: as mentioned in the text, there is a tendency to call 'defeasible logics' those which deal with the problem of conflicts of norms.

[42] As a matter of fact, the very 'nature' of defeasible logics is controversial. Cf. for instance the following passage from R. Morado ('Problemas filosóficos de la lógica no monotónica', 324) where many of the typical characterizations of defeasible logic are impugned: 'Defeasible reasoning is not necessarily an irrational pattern, nor does it require wrong conclusions or insecure premises. It is an inference which depends on the context and thus may be blocked. Moreover, it does not follow from the fact that rules are revisable (indeed, the majority of scientific rules are such), nor from the fact that it has tacit premises.'

[43] See E. Bulygin, 'Legal Dogmatics and Systematization of Law', *Rechtstheorie*, Beiheft 10 (Berlin: Duncker & Humblot, 1986). In G.B. Ratti, *Sistema Giuridico e Sistemazione del Diritto* (Turin: Giappichelli, 2008), Bulygin's model is refined and eleven different operations usually carried out by jurists are singled out and analysed. Here it is important to stress that further action—i.e. application of a general rule to a given case—is typically carried out by judges, but not by commentators.

If this is so, the idea of defeasible legal reasoning seems to be capable of being accommodated within a traditional setting of metajuristic inquiry, which accepts the hard kernel of standard deductive logic. One can affirm, thus, that in systems of defeasible logic it is not the logic that has changed; it is rather the way of depicting logical tools and locating them in the theoretical reconstruction of jurists' operation that has changed.[44]

The only option left in our threefold model of juristic reasoning is to locate defeasibilism at the level of the interpretation of legal sources. From this perspective, the 'defeasibilist turn' in deontic logic and legal theory probably hides a wide reconsideration of the study of legal interpretation and its importance in legal reasoning. To this point, we will turn repeatedly in the following sections.

C. The legal defeasibility of legal standards

The term 'defeasibility' was first used in the legal studies probably by H.L.A. Hart, who employed it in a paper on 'The Ascription of Responsibility and Rights',[45] to represent legal concepts.[46]

Even if the term was new, the concept was hardly so. It was first introduced into moral thinking in the early 1930s by Sir David Ross who, in criticizing Kant's posture on absolute duties, introduced the concept of 'prima facie' duties.[47] This concept was later formalized by using the idea of normative conditionals which do not admit 'strengthening the antecedent', i.e. conditionals which pose obligations that can be defeated under certain particular circumstances (not exhaustively listed before application to concrete cases).[48]

Years later, as we have already mentioned, this notion reappeared in one of the foundational moments of the contemporary jurisprudential debate: Dworkin's attack on Hart's positivism. Indeed, in this debate, defeasibility of some of the legal standards was used as an argument against Hart. Despite Dworkin's challenge, however, it has been convincingly argued that the notion of a defeasible normative conditional was already present, although under not very clear form, in Hart's *The Concept of Law*.[49] Together with some famous theses on the intensional vagueness of generic terms (i.e. open texture), in fact, there are other passages in chapter VII of *The Concept of Law* that make it possible to envisage a theoretical treatment of what has now come to be known as defeasibility of legal standards. In Hart's treatment of legal standards, one can find a sketch of the *formal* defeasibility of legal standards, when Hart affirms that rules

[44] An analogous idea has been formulated with a catchphrase by C.G. Morgan, 'The Nature of Nonmonotonic Reasoning', *Mind and Machines*, 10 (2000), 347 (whose analysis is concerned primarily with ordinary, and not legal, reasoning): 'The nonmonotonicity of commonsense reasoning is due to the way we use logic, and not due to the logic that we use.'

[45] H.L.A. Hart, 'The Ascription of Responsibility and Rights', *Proceedings of the Aristotelian Society*, 49 (1948–9), 171–94.

[46] R.H.S. Tur, 'Defeasibilism', 356.

[47] W.D. Ross, *The Right and the Good* (Oxford: Clarendon Press, 1930), 19ff.

[48] C.E. Alchourrón and E. Bulygin, 'Norma jurídica' in E. Garzón Vadés and F. Laporta (eds), *El derecho y la justicia*, Enciclopedia Iberoamericana de Filosofía, 11 (Madrid: Trotta, 1995), 146, affirm: 'defeasibility does not depend on the fact that the obligation belongs to a special kind (*prima facie* obligations), but on the form of the conditional that connects the antecedent to the consequent'. For sharp criticisms of Alchourrón's formal reconstruction of prima facie duties, see C.A. Oller, 'Obligaciones prima facie y derrotabilidad', *Análisis filósofico*, 26 (2006), 152–4.

[49] See J.C. Bayón, 'Derrotabilidad, indeterminación del derecho y positivismo jurídico', *Isonomía*, 13 (2000), 97ff.

may 'have exceptions incapable of exhaustive statement' or that 'a rule that ends with the word "unless . . . " is still a rule'.[50] These statements are meant to deny the necessity of that formalistic attitude towards rules which consists in fastening 'on certain features present in the plain case' and insisting 'that these are both necessary and sufficient to bring anything which has them within the scope of the rule, whatever other features it may have or lack, and whatever may be the social consequences of applying the rule in this way'.[51] To treat rules as defeasible (i.e. as providing only contributory conditions for their application) may be *substantively* justified by the combination of two main factors, according to Hart:[52] (a) ignorance of fact; and (b) indeterminacy of aim, i.e. the conjunction of human incapability of predicting all the possible combinations of circumstances which the future may bring and of determining what should be done when such new circumstances arise.

In later jurisprudence, once the topic was clearly targeted, a good deal of clarity was introduced, identifying the question of defeasibility with the above-mentioned issue of the different kinds of conditions which were contained in the antecedents of legal conditionals. At the same time—and this is the point we are going to tackle in this section—the substantive reasons behind the supposed defeasibility of legal standards were also studied.

Many accounts of defeasibility in the legal domain take for granted that (objective) morality is the very source of defeasance of legal norms. Legal norms are sometimes 'disapplied' when they give rise to unjust results, by judges who feel morally bound to do so. And this would entail a failure of the so-called separation thesis, i.e. the thesis according to which the legality of a rule does not depend on its moral value. We can introduce the concept of 'moral defeasibility of legal standards' to refer to this state of affairs.

According to many authors, this feature of legal application is very relevant for legal philosophy since it poses a serious threat to the tenability of legal positivism, which is based on the separation thesis. We do not share this preoccupation though, for the simple reason that positivism is quite capable of accounting for the case when a judge does not apply a norm that she ought to apply according to the law in force because of her feelings of justice and fairness.

Be this as it may, we will not dwell here on such a topic: we will rather tackle the issue of the *legal* defeasibility of legal standards, which has been accounted for (not without certain difficulties, which we will point to in our analysis) by three prominent writers:[53] Frederick Schauer, Carlos Alchourrón, and Andrei Marmor. Let us succinctly examine their views in this order.

[50] H.L.A. Hart, *The Concept of Law* (2nd edn, Oxford: Clarendon Press, 1994), 139.

[51] Ibid., 129. In literature it is disputed whether Hart holds that all legal rules are defeasible or that only some of them are so. The quoted excerpts from *The Concept of Law* seem to support the second view, whereas other quotes (such as for instance p. 270 in 'Jhering's Heaven of Concepts' (1970), in H.L.A. Hart, *Essays in Jurisprudence and Philosophy* (Oxford: Oxford University Press, 1983), where he affirms 'all legal rules . . . are "open"') seem to suggest the first view. For discussion, see J.C. Bayón, 'Derrotabilidad, indeterminación del derecho y positivismo jurídico', 100, and F. Schauer, 'On the Supposed Defeasibility of Legal Rules', 237.

[52] H.L.A. Hart, *The Concept of Law*, 128.

[53] They are generally associated with legal positivism, but such an association is not central for our argument.

1. Schauer's conception of the defeasibility of legal rules

Fred Schauer has extensively elaborated on the formal and substantive reasons which could justify a theory of legal defeasibility.[54] One of the main theses defended by Schauer is that defeasibility is a *contingent*, and therefore not necessary, feature of legal rules. It depends, essentially, on the way the secondary rules of the system provide for this matter.

According to Schauer, moreover, legal rules, as with any other rules, are sensitive to their background justifications.[55] This means that they have the disposition of being defeated by their background reasons (and also, in particularly demanding circumstances, by 'more distant' reasons), whenever such reasons are more powerful than the degree of resistance that the rule itself possesses.

Schauer's (we would say, technical) test for the defeasibility of a legal standard is the following: 'a rule is defeasible when its application is contingent upon the non-occurrence of an unspecifiable list of very good reasons for not applying the rule, such reasons having strength greater than would have been sufficient for those reasons to determine the outcome in the absence of the rule'.[56] This entails that 'legal rules are subject to defeat by the existence of particularly powerful countervailing conditions, and that the list of such particularly powerful defeating conditions cannot and need not be specified in advance, *so long as the requirement of particular power can be specified in advance and is not itself subject to defeat*'.[57]

Clearly, the requirement of objective particular power is what makes it possible to regard a defeasible rule as a genuine rule (in accordance with Hart's tenet that a rule that ends with the word 'unless . . . ' is still a rule).

There is a technical reason which is relevant here: total transparency of rules to reasons makes having a system of rules pointless. 'If *any* injustice is a sufficient condition for an equitable override', writes Schauer, 'then a regime of rules subject to equitable override is extensionally equivalent to a regime of no rules at all in which the decision makers are empowered simply to reach the most just, all-things-considered, outcomes . . . In order for the rules to do the work that rules are expected to do—provide predictability, stability, and constraint on decision-makers—the standard for equitable override of a rule-produced mistake must be one of *extreme* injustice, or *great* inefficiency, or something of that variety.'[58]

This is clearly true: if we want rules to play a role in practical deliberation, we must design a system of decision making which provides that rules may be overridden only in particularly demanding circumstances. Otherwise, rules are totally transparent to the first-order reasons which apply to certain states of affairs, and make no difference in practical deliberation.

Beyond the technical requirement for a successful system of rules, it is not very clear, however, by what means such a power can be objectively measured or identified. In other words, it is not clear in what sense the particular power of reasons can be

[54] The works which will be taken into account here are: F. Schauer, *Playing by the Rules*; 'On the Supposed Defeasibility of Legal Rules'; and 'Is Defeasibility an Essential Property of Law?', in this volume, ch. 4.

[55] F. Schauer, 'On the Supposed Defeasibility of Legal Rules', 232.

[56] Ibid., 238.

[57] Ibid., 239 (emphasis in the original).

[58] F. Schauer, 'Is Defeasibility an Essential Property of Law?', in this volume, ch. 4 at 80 (emphasis in the original).

considered as an 'object' independent from the interpreters' attitudes and choices regarding such a power, an object whose existence can simply be discovered.

A possible hint is given by Schauer's contribution in the present volume: defeasibility depends on 'how some decision-making system will choose to *treat* its rules'.[59] In this sense, a metarule, or a set of metarules, may impose a certain (defeasible or indefeasible) treatment of the other rules of the system. When a defeasible treatment is decided, the technical requirement of the particular power must enter the picture if we want the system of rules not to be coextensive with the set of their underlying reasons. In this context, what is needed is for there to exist a criterion for treatment of other rules—a criterion not necessarily posed by the lawgiver—which is independent from the single interpreter's choices.[60]

A major issue regarding the point under examination is that, among the criteria on how rules must be treated, canons of interpretation must also be taken into account. In many legal orders, in fact, canons of interpretation seem to provide the means both for a defeasible treatment and an indefeasible treatment of lawgiver's rules. Accordingly, the reference to the possible treatment of legal rules provided by the secondary rules on application might obscure the twofold fact that (i) such metarules also are liable to different interpretations, and (ii) that, more often than not, such metarules alternatively allow both a defeasible and an indefeasible handling of primary rules of conduct.

In sum, it seems possible to infer from Schauer's conception that talking about the 'defeasibility of legal rules' is just a somewhat obscure shorthand for referring to different systems of decision making. Such systems form a continuum from having rules totally transparent to reasons at one extreme and completely opaque to them at the other. Within such a context, the requirement of the indefeasibility of the particular power of rules' underlying reasons may be regarded as the technical threshold after which a certain system of rules ceases to have a minimum degree of resistance and reaches the extreme of total transparency to reasons. In turn, such decision-making systems seem to be more dependent upon interpreters' choices than on the lawgivers' mere institutional design.[61] To sum up, according to Schauer, defeasibility would be an eminently interpretative problem, regarding primarily the exegesis of metarules bearing on the interpretation and application of other rules.

2. Alchourrón's views on the defeasibility of legal standards

As we have already mentioned, in much the same years as the development of Schauer's conception, Alchourrón brought about a full-fledged conception of defeasible conditionals, which it is now time to have a look at. However, to completely understand the scope of Alchourrón's views on defeasible conditionals and their impact on Continental analytical jurisprudence, we should briefly present the main theses on norms and normative sets elaborated by Carlos Alchourrón and Eugenio Bulygin in *Normative Systems.*

[59] F. Schauer, 'Is Defeasibility an Essential Property of Law?', 87.

[60] See J. Ferrer Beltrán, 'Sobre la posibilidad del error judicial y los desacuerdos irrecusables en el derecho' in J.J. Moreso, L. Prieto Sanchís, and J. Ferrer Beltrán, *Los Desacuerdos en el Derecho* (Madrid: Fundación Coloquio Jurídico Europeo, 2010).

[61] Schauer himself suggests this understanding of his theory of defeasibility, when he holds that it 'is a way of describing the interplay between a pedigreed subset of rules and the full (and non-pedigree-able) normative universe, such that the former is *treated* by certain decision-makers as presumptively controlling', where the idea of 'presumption' is understood in the non-epistemic sense of 'a degree of strong but overridable priority within a normative universe in which conflicting norms might produce mutually exclusive results' (F. Schauer, *Playing by the Rules*, 204, emphasis added).

In this book, Alchourrón and Bulygin dealt with the classical question of the systematic character of law, i.e. the question whether law is *necessarily* consistent and complete. Their response is negative. But the main point of their publication is that the concepts of completeness and consistency are not to be construed as concepts relative to an *entire* legal order. They are rather regarded as concepts concerning *portions* of the entire legal order, which are cut up by jurists in order to answer legal questions.

They conceive of legal norms as conditional sentences, connecting a generic case (i.e. a class of particular cases) with a normative solution (i.e. the union of a normative operator with a normative content).

Generic cases are identifiable by means of combination of the norms' relevant properties. Relevance is thus a predicate of properties, regarded as the operative factors of the norms, i.e. as the conditions the occurrence whereof make the norms applicable. If relevant properties increase in number, the scope of a norm becomes narrower, and vice versa: if they decrease, the scope of the corresponding norms becomes wider. The sentence by which relevant properties are identified is called 'thesis of relevance'.

According to Alchourrón and Bulygin, a certain property is relevant, within a certain normative system, if: (a) at least one norm of the system mentions such a property; (b) this property (say, *p*) and its complementary (~*p*) have different normative status. This occurs either if they are attached to different normative solutions, or if one of them is connected to a certain normative solution while the other is connected to no solution.

A normative solution, in turn, can qualify a certain action or state of affairs as obligatory, facultative, prohibited, and permitted, this last operator being the primitive one, i.e. the one used to provide definitions for all the others. An obligatory action is that whose commission is permitted and whose omission is not permitted. A prohibited action is that whose commission is not permitted and whose omission is permitted. Finally, a facultative action is that whose commission and omission are both permitted.[62]

A normative system is the set of all the relevant logical consequences that follow from a certain set of norms. Such relevant logical consequences are obtained by applying the rule of augmentation to the relevant norms, i.e. by connecting more specific relevant cases (say: 'p & q') to the solution provided for a less specific case (say 'p').[63]

Completeness and consistency being relational concepts, the question whether there are normative gaps and antinomies in the law must be answered empirically, and not

[62] In symbols: Op = Pp & ~P~p; Php = ~Pp & P~p, and Fp = Pp & P~p. These are called maximal solutions since they deontically qualify both the commission *and* the omission of p, whereas minimal solutions deontically qualify *either* the commission *or* the omission of p. While Op, Php and Fp are maximal solutions, Pp (= Pp ∨ ~P~p), ~Pp (~Pp ∨ P~p), and ~Fp (~Pp ∨ ~P~p) are minimal solutions.

[63] Let us give an easy example: the normative system, which can be extracted from usual rules on unworthy beneficiaries, can be reconstructed, along the lines of Alchourrón's and Bulygin's theory, in the following way. Let 'w' be for the operative fact (*viz.* the property) 'valid will' and 'm' for 'the carrying out of actions against testator's life or physical integrity'. Let 'O' be the normative character 'obligatory', and let 'p' stand for the action of 'inheriting'. Commonly, there are at least three norms which give an answer to the question which beneficiaries are unworthy (the 'universe of discourse' within which the system is developed):

N1: 'If *w* and ~*m*, then ~O~*p*' ('If valid will and no act against the testator, then it is permitted to inherit')

N2: 'If *w* and *m*, then O~*p*' ('If valid will and an act against the testator, then it is forbidden to inherit')

N3: 'If ~*w*, then O~*p*' ('If no valid will, then it is forbidden to inherit').

The normative system, resulting from the complete logical development of these norms, is complete and consistent. Indeed, as the following matrix shows, at least one normative solution is attached to each case (completeness), and no case is connected to two incompatible solutions (consistency).

conceptually: in other words, it is a *contingent* matter whether law is systematically undetermined or not. More precisely, it is contingent upon certain factual circumstances, a determinate class of actions, and certain normative solutions attached by a normative set to the combination of such facts.[64]

There is another theoretical notion which is used in the theory of normative systems and is worth mentioning here, for its importance regarding defeasibilism: that of an axiological gap. By 'axiological gap' Alchourrón and Bulygin mean a case in which the existing normative solution is considered inadequate, from an axiological point of view, since it is drawn without taking into consideration a property that *should* be relevant according to a certain set of evaluations, which are *external* to the normative system under consideration. In other words, the legal system does not draw a distinction, which in the opinion of the interpreter should be, or should have been, drawn. Alchourrón and Bulygin call this sentence a 'hypothesis of relevance', by means of which the properties that *should* be relevant are identified.

It is important to highlight the *external character* which the hypothesis of relevance has in the original formulation of the theory of normative systems, since defeasibilism imports, as it were, an 'internalization' of such a judgement (if not a dissolving of the very distinction between the thesis and the hypothesis of relevance).

As we have mentioned, many of the theorems derived in *Normative Systems* are based on the application of the rule of augmentation (alias strengthening the antecedent, which, in turn, is a property of monotony). Given a certain normative conditional '$p \rightarrow Oq$', any property that is not relevant according to the normative conditional at hand does not change its outcome if it is added to the antecedent. And it is exactly this type of feature of the logical development of normative sets which makes it possible to spot inconsistencies and gaps within a normative system (i.e. a fully logically developed set of normative sentences).

Table 1.1 Unworthy Beneficiary, Normative System 1

Cases/Norms	N1	N2	N3
1. w and m		$O{\sim}p$	
2. w and $\sim m$	$\sim O{\sim}p$		
3. $\sim w$ and m			$O{\sim}p$
4. $\sim w$ and $\sim m$			$O{\sim}p$

However, if we subtract one norm, say N3, from the system, it becomes incomplete as to cases 3 and 4: we call 'normative gaps' in the system those cases which are connected to no solution. Analogously, if we add, say, a norm such as N4 ('If w, then $\sim O{\sim}p$') to the system, it becomes inconsistent with case 2: we call the cases which are connected to incompatible solutions 'normative conflicts' or 'antinomies'. This is easy to see from the following table:

Table 1.2 Unworthy Beneficiary, Normative System 2

Cases/Norms	N1	N2	N4
1. w and m		$O{\sim}p$	$\sim O{\sim}p$
2. w and $\sim m$	$\sim O{\sim}p$		$\sim O{\sim}p$
3. $\sim w$ and m			
4. $\sim w$ and $\sim m$			

[64] Even before, it is contingent upon the interpretation of the norm formulations from which norms are drawn. On this point, see R. Guastini, *L'Interpretazione dei Documenti Normativi* (Milan, Giuffrè, 2004).

This formal apparatus has served as the groundwork for the received view of the reconstruction of juristic systematization in a great many Continental analytical circles from the publication of *Normative Systems* until the early nineties.

In the early nineties, indeed, Carlos Alchourrón became increasingly interested in the study of defeasible conditionals. He published several formal papers on the logic of defeasible normative conditionals, but it is in two less formal papers, published before his premature passing away, that he maintained his more ground-shaking theses, from a legal philosophical point of view.

In the encyclopaedia entry on the concept of a legal rule,[65] co-authored with Eugenio Bulygin, Alchourrón maintained—with a marked change from *Normative Systems*—that most legal standards are defeasible and that, for this reason, they admit neither augmentation nor *modus ponens*. Here, he also defended a 'normality-based' view of defeasibility: (normative) conditionals are defeasible because they hold only for normal circumstances.

In the influential 1996 article 'On Law and Logic',[66] Alchourrón defended the view that legal defeasibility may be productively approached from a pragmatic standpoint regarding the counterfactual intentions of the lawgiver: that is, what the lawgiver would have done if she had considered some circumstances which she could not (or would not) have taken into account. Such considerations on the counterfactual intentions of the lawgiver bring about the defeasibility of legal standards. More precisely, at least three dispositions or attitudes of the lawgiver about the defeat of a certain conditional normative standard 'If A then OB',[67] on the grounds of a certain implicit circumstance C, can be envisaged:[68] (1) the lawgiver may have a disposition to accept both 'If A then OB' and 'If A and C then OB': in this case C counts as an *implicit non-exception*; (2) the lawgiver may have a disposition to accept 'If A then OB' whilst rejecting 'If A and C then OB': circumstance C is thus to be regarded as an *implicit exception*; (3) the lawgiver may have no disposition at all about whether to consider C as an exception (like in case 2) or a non-exception (like in case 1): accordingly, C is *undetermined as an exception*.

The model elaborated in *Normative Systems* seems to be jeopardized by at least three features of defeasible norms, as presented in Alchourrón's papers.

First, the full logical development of a normative set would be pointless: in order to develop a system of norms one should resort instead to a lawgiver's supposed attitudes in enacting the norms at hand. However, since many circumstances would turn out to be undetermined as exceptions, one would derive the conclusion that the complete logical development of a normative basis is hardly possible.

Secondly, since *modus ponens* is not allowed by defeasible conditionals, normative systems would lose most of their inferential power especially regarding judicial application.

Finally, the distinction between thesis and hypothesis of relevance would be obscured (if not completely blurred) by the fact that one should never confine oneself to grasping the literal understanding of a rule formulation and always resort to

[65] C.E. Alchourrón and E. Bulygin, 'Norma jurídica', 144–6.

[66] See C.E. Alchourrón in this volume, ch. 2 at 47. The results which Alchourrón reaches in 'On Law and Logic' are (tacitly) confirmed by E. Bulygin, 'En defensa de El Dorado. Respuesta a Fernando Atria' in F. Atria et al., *Lagunas en el Derecho* (Madrid: Marcial Pons, 2005), as is shown in G.B. Ratti, 'Dos modelos de relevancia normativa' in J.J. Moreso and M.C. Redondo (eds), *Un Diálogo con la Teoría del Derecho de Eugenio Bulygin* (Madrid: Marcial Pons, 2007).

[67] Which reads: 'If A occurs, then it is obligatory that B'.

[68] See C.E. Alchourrón in this volume, ch. 2, at 47.

something beyond it, in order to identify a rule. Consequently, the distinction between a normative gap and an axiological one also becomes fuzzy.[69] No identification of the law would be possible without evaluating it.

These remarks have led commentators to reconstruct Alchourrón's 'dispositional' conception of defeasibility as a threefold metajuristic theory, affirming the following tenets:

(a) The deductive consequences that are necessary to logically develop a certain set of norms are to be conserved, if one wants to preserve their inferential relations, which in turn are required for the explanation of jurists' and judges' reasoning;[70]

(b) 'Dispositional defeasibility' is a heading under which a sceptical view of legal interpretation is hidden.[71] This is suggested, inter alia, by the fact that the difficulties in reconstructing the lawgiver's attitudes about possible implicit exceptions are so serious that they make it almost impossible to carry out a genuinely descriptive detection of the conditions that allow the identification of a norm or 'prevent' its application. Hence, Alchourrón's statement that 'what appears to be a historical investigation hides the political preferences of the interpreter'.[72]

(c) The distinction thesis/hypothesis of relevance, and the related dichotomy normative/axiological gaps, can be preserved insofar as both are related to certain attributions of meaning:[73] the thesis of relevance depends on what is usually called the interpretation 'in force', whereas the relevance hypothesis depends on another, diverging, interpretation. Evaluations about interpretation can be described by the thesis of relevance, whereas the hypothesis of relevance prescribes, or suggests, that other properties should be taken into account. It is important to stress that, unlike in *Normative Systems*, two kinds of hypotheses of relevance are distinguished:[74] (a) external relevance hypotheses, which are formulated by interpreters on the basis of some external evaluations, which do not depend on the rules or reasons that belong to the corresponding legal order; (b) internal relevance hypotheses, which are formulated by interpreters on the basis of other rules or reasons, which are present in the corresponding legal order.

3. Marmor on defeasibility and legal interpretation

The two extremely fruitful theories we have just outlined—Alchourrón's and Schauer's—seem to propose an 'interpretative conception' under the forms of a theory of the relationships among rules and background reasons, or counterfactual attitudes of the lawgiver regarding possible implicit exceptions.

However, in Andrei Marmor's well-known book *Interpretation and Legal Theory*,[75] the possible ties between legal defeasibility and legal interpretation are expressly dealt with. The analysis of Marmor's discussion may prove very useful since its frequent

[69] See M.C. Redondo, 'Reglas "genuinas" y positivismo jurídico' in P. Comanducci and R. Guastini (eds), *Analisi e Diritto 1998. Ricerche di giurisprudenza analitica* (Turin: Giappichelli, 1999), 256.

[70] G.B. Ratti, *Sistema Giuridico e Sistemazione del Diritto*, ch. 7.

[71] R. Caracciolo, 'Normas derrotables. La concepción de Carlos Alchourrón', *Análisis filosófico*, 26 (2006), 156–77.

[72] C.E. Alchourrón in this volume, ch. 2 at 49.

[73] Cf. R. Guastini, 'Defeasibility, Axiological Gaps, and Interpretation', in this volume, ch. 9.

[74] J.L. Rodríguez, 'Axiological Gaps and Normative Relevance'; and *Lógica de los sistemas jurídicos* (Madrid: Centro de estudios constitucionales, 2002), 75ff.

[75] A. Marmor, *Interpretation and Legal Theory* (2nd edn, Oxford: Hart, 2005).

oscillations are a symptom of the difficulty of some legal theories in successfully accommodating legal defeasibility in a general theory of law which regards legal interpretation as an eminently cognitive (and, accordingly, non-creative) enterprise.

The defeasibility thesis is discussed by Marmor as an argument against legal positivism (or, at least, the hard, formalism-oriented, version that he defends). According to Marmor's reconstruction, if all rules are defeasible, they always need to be interpreted (i.e. they can never be immediately and irreflexively understood). But this is unacceptable to positivists, since a foundational thesis of (hard) legal positivism, according to Marmor,[76] is that it 'cannot accept the view that law is always subject to interpretation. It just cannot be the case that every conclusion about what *the law is*, is a result of some interpretation or other'.

Sometimes Marmor, as a consequence of his views on the 'empirical' separation of law and morals, seems to hold a strongly monotonic conception of legal inference:[77]

> When we ask ourselves what it is the legislator sought to achieve by enacting the law, we will always find that certain purposes are manifest in the language of the law itself, as a matter of logic, while others, though they exist, are not. Consider . . . the 'No vehicles in the park' rule. Surely it must have been one of the intentions of the legislator that *if anything is a vehicle it should not enter the park*. The legislator cannot deny such an intention without breaching the rules of language or logic, or what speech-act theorists call the condition of sincerity.

This passage is fundamental to understanding Marmor's views on legal defeasibility. Marmor's words seem to imply that, *as a matter of logic*, legislators must subscribe to the rule of augmentation and, consequently, to indefeasibility. This tenet, in conjunction with Marmor's main thesis that rule formulations, in most cases, can simply be understood in their plain meaning and not interpreted,[78] entails that the circumstances (or properties) which are referred to in the antecedents of legal rule-formulations are to be regarded as *sufficient* conditions for the application of the normative consequent. QED: legal rules are indefeasible, and there is a space for interpretative manipulations only where the lawgiver has spoken with an uncertain voice. Observe that this space, according to Marmor, must be filled by means of resorting to the lawgiver's real or hypothetical intentions.

However, on other occasions, Marmor seems to admit a certain kind of defeasibility for legal conditionals. Marmor in fact asserts that:[79]

> just as it is misguided to presume that unless one can specify necessary and sufficient conditions for the applicability of a concept-word, one's grasp of its sense is in some way incomplete, it is equally misguided to assume that the complete understanding of a rule must remove all possible doubts about its applicability.

This makes it possible that:

> one has a complete grasp of a rule, *if under normal circumstances*, one is able to specify which acts are in accord with the rule, and hence, which would go against it.

But this is exactly the sense in which legal rules are said to be defeasible in that they hold only for normal cases. In this understanding, Marmor's tenet is that the 'prima facie understanding' of the rule *plus* the judgement regarding the fact that we are in *normal* circumstances applying the rule straightforwardly, since the *revised* antecedent of the rule constitutes the set of the conditions which are regarded as sufficient to its

[76] Ibid., 95. [77] Ibid., 127 (emphasis added).
[78] Ibid., 16. [79] Ibid., 117 (emphasis added).

application. And here Marmor has implicitly accepted a revised kind of *modus ponens* and augmentation, which apply to defeasible conditionals. Such a revised kind of conditional shows the conditions for deriving the consequent from a defeasible normative conditional, i.e. when we have the antecedent jointly with all the other implied assumptions (Marmor's 'normal circumstances'). And this entails that, unless we pass from our weak antecedent 'to its function of revision in normal circumstances, we cannot have indefeasible conditionals: but since such a revision function is a variable of mostly evaluative decisions (what is "normal" and what is not) it follows', contrary to Marmor's views 'that the scope of every (indefeasible) rule is the outcome of "interpretation"'.[80]

This is, clearly, a *reductio ad absurdum* of Marmor's main tenet (i.e. legal rules cannot always be subject to interpretation), but it seems to follow from Marmor's own premises, which seem to be, as we have tried to show, contradictory. More importantly for our present discussion, this reduction appears to be a further proof that, by allowing defeasibility into a theory of law, one should be ready to allow for an anti-formalist account of legal interpretation.

Summing up the main results of the analysis we have carried out in this section, we can affirm that introducing defeasibility into the jurisprudential picture seems to have a significant effect on legal theoretical views: it pushes them towards an anti-formalistic view of legal interpretation. This is so because it suggests the idea that different models of legal reasoning are always available to jurists. At least two main models of interpretation can clearly be singled out in the discussion of substantive legal defeasibility we have sketched so far: a formalist, or opaque, model, according to which interpreters must stick to the literal or prima facie meaning of legal sentences (admitted that such a thing exists), and an anti-formalist, transparent, model, which responds to the supposed underlying reasons of legal regulations (or to the real or counterfactual intentions of the lawgiver). The choice of one of these two models—we submit—is the key-stone of the phenomenon to which theorists (more or less consciously) refer when they talk about 'defeasibilism of legal rules'. To this point we will turn later on in our paper. We will now go on to discuss the relations among defeasibility, validity, and applicability of legal standards.

D. Defeasibility and legal validity

In a series of relevant investigations, defeasibility of legal norms is understood as an issue regarding their application.[81] According to this view, a norm is defeasible when it has the disposition not to be applied even though it is indeed applicable. However—as has been argued[82]—every legal norm must be regarded as having such a disposition, at least in those systems which place on applicators peremptory and conclusive powers for

[80] Let it be noted, in passing, that this conclusion should not be treated as a defeat for legal positivism. It may be a defeat for a certain way of regarding exclusive legal positivism, and, in particular, its theory of interpretation. Nonetheless, a more generous theory of legal interpretation, which allows several canons of interpretation into the reconstruction of jurists' practice—a theory which has indeed been elaborated by important positivistic thinkers such as Kelsen, Alf Ross, or Riccardo Guastini—clearly permits the avoidance of self-defeating arguments, such as those defended by advocates of exclusive legal positivism. However, it is important to stress that the defeasibilist turn in jurisprudence has had the beneficial effect of putting interpretation into the central spot of the debate.

[81] For a paradigmatic version on this view, see F. Atria, *On Law and Legal Reasoning* (Oxford: Hart, 2002).

[82] See E. Bulygin, 'Review of Jaap Hage's "Law and Defeasibility"', 247.

the rules to apply. In this sense, even though the rule which ought to be applied to a case is correctly identified, the judge, vested with conclusive decision-making powers, may (legally) decide not to apply it and apply another rule instead.[83]

Even though many researchers have connected defeasibility and application, almost no discussion has been devoted to associating defeasibility with the validity of legal norms.[84] However, it can be argued that, in analysing mainstream twentieth-century jurisprudence, one can find two main questions regarding validity, which are worth being examined under the heading of 'defeasibility', although they have usually not been dealt with under such a term. We will find that different meanings of 'validity', 'applicability', and 'defeasibility' may be singled out and that only by singling them out can one reach a fruitful theoretical explanation of the relations among these three concepts and the complex phenomena they denote.

The first question may be framed in the following way: what logical consequences of the expressed norms (if any) are to be considered as valid law? In fact, the problem of the identification of the legal criteria of recognition (and, as a consequence, of the content of a legal system) may be related to the defeasibility of legal norms. This happens when one considers that the identification of the rules of inference forms part (or can be reconstructed as forming part) of the set of the criteria, which provide the means to identify legally valid rules. Within this context, the main query becomes whether any logical consequence whatsoever of expressly enacted rules is to be regarded as legally valid or, rather, just *some* of them.[85] Clearly, such a query refers to the scope of the set of the criteria for recognition, and chiefly to the possible inclusion of the rules of inference into the set of such criteria.[86]

A first answer to this question maintains that all the logical consequences of expressly enacted rules are legally valid, on the basis of the idea that, unless we accept the rules of inference of classical (monotonic) logic, law, as a normative set, would be completely inert: it would be impossible to qualify reality by means of classifications (i.e. subsume individual states of things under generic categories) and, consequently, law could simply not be applied by judges.[87] In contrast to this view, it has been argued that in order to see derived legal norms as applicable, one does not need to regard them as necessarily valid, insofar as there are norms which impose the application of such derived rules.[88] Moreover, admitting derived rules as valid members of a legal system would render such a system extensionally unidentifiable (unless some relevance

[83] H. Kelsen, *General Theory of Law and State* (Cambridge, Mass.: Harvard University Press, 1945), 153ff.; and R.H.S. Tur, 'Kelsen as a Defeasibilist', address to the conference 'Law and Legal Science', Oxford, September 2010.

[84] Some foundations of such an analysis may be found in J. Ferrer Beltrán and G.B. Ratti, 'Validity and Defeasibility in the Legal Domain', *Law and Philosophy*, 29 (2010), 601–26; and 'Validità, defettibilità e criteri di riconoscimento' in I. Fanlo Cortés and R. Marra (eds), *Filosofia e Realtà del Diritto. Studi in onore di Silvana Castignone* (Turin: Giappichelli, 2008); and G.B. Ratti, 'Regola di riconoscimento e defettibilità', *Analisi e diritto*, (2010), 85–94.

[85] There is, of course, a third possibility, which negates the qualification of 'valid law' to the logical consequences of expressly enacted norms. This view seems to be widespread in Anglo-American jurisprudence: see, e.g., L. Green, 'Legal Positivism' in *Stanford Encyclopedia of Philosophy* (2010).

[86] Such a possibility is strongly rejected by M.H. Kramer, 'Why The Axioms and Theorems of Arithmetic are not Legal Norms', OJLS, 27 (2007), 555–62.

[87] E. Bulygin, 'Lógica deóntica' in C.E. Alchourrón (ed.), 7 *Lógica, Enciclopedia Iberoamericana de Filosofía* (Madrid: Trotta, 1995), 139–40.

[88] See J. Ferrer Beltrán and J.L. Rodríguez, *Jerarquías normativas y dinámica de los sistemas jurídicos* (Madrid: Marcial Pons, 2011), 119.

criterion is provided with the aim of distinguishing relevant and irrelevant consequences from among the infinite consequences a set of norms possesses).[89]

A second answer consists in holding a defeasibilist conception of legal rules. As a matter of fact, recent jurisprudential literature offers at least three different conceptions of legal defeasibility. These conceptions share the common idea that not all the monotonic logical consequences follow from legal rules, but they differ on how the consequences of expressed rules ought to be determined.

A first thesis—which can be dubbed the 'teleological defeasibility thesis'—suggests that we accept as valid logical consequences of expressed rules only those consequences that comply with the alleged rules' underlying reasons.[90]

A second conception—which can be dubbed the 'authoritative defeasibility thesis'—holds that, in order to determine what logical consequences of legal rules can be regarded as valid law, it is essential to determine the *actual* intentions of the lawgiver.[91] As Rodríguez puts it,[92] this second conception 'limits the set of the derived norms to those norms which could be justifiably ascribed to the authority that enacted the norms from which they can be drawn'.

The third conception is Alchourrón's 'dispositional defeasibility thesis', according to which a logical consequence of a norm can be considered valid law only if there would have been, at the time of the enactment, a disposition of the lawgiver to accept it as such, had she thought about the circumstances.

In this sense, divergences about the defeasibility of legal norms (interpreted as a tenet about what logical consequences of legal norms count as valid law) are indeed disagreements about the recognition of valid norms, for they refer to what rules of inference, if any, are admitted by a certain criterion of identification in a legal system. We will come back to this issue later, when dealing with the so-called 'internal applicability' of legal norms: indeed we will have to determine whether both questions (validity of derived norms and internal applicability of expressed norms) are indeed different presentations of the same phenomenon.

The second question we want to mention here is that which has to do with the very defeasibility of the criteria of recognition themselves. Criteria of recognition might be seen as intensional definitions of 'valid law'. To hold that they are defeasible may mean that the properties which are framed in such definitions are not necessary and/or sufficient for legal norms to be valid. And this means, in turn, that legal norms may be valid although they do not possess all the properties which are formulated in the criteria of recognition, and they may be invalid although they possess all these features. We can formalize different states of affairs regarding the defeasibility of such criteria: we can conceive of the set of the criteria of recognition, *qua* conceptual rule, as a biconditional of the form '$(x)\ \phi x \leftrightarrow Vx$' where '$\phi$' denotes the conformity of the norms to formal criteria of validity (i.e. Dworkin's pedigree) and 'V' denotes the legal validity of norms.

[89] See G.B. Ratti, 'Teoria degli insiemi e analisi del diritto' in G.B. Ratti, *Diritto, Indeterminatezza, Indecidibilità* (Madrid: Marcial Pons, 2012).

[90] F. Schauer, 'On the Supposed Defeasibility of Legal Rules'.

[91] See J. Raz, 'Authority, Law and Morality' in J. Raz, *Ethics in the Public Domain* (Oxford: Clarendon Press, 1994), 213.

[92] J.L. Rodríguez, 'Las consecuencias lógicas de las normas' in G. Maniaci (ed.), *Eguaglianza, Ragionevolezza e Logica Giuridica* (Milan: Giuffrè, 2006), 232.

As a matter of course, the biconditional at hand can be broken down into the conjunction of the two following conditionals: '(x) $\phi x \rightarrow Vx$' and '(x) $Vx \rightarrow \phi x$'. By so doing, we may identify four possible options regarding the defeasibility of the criteria.

(1) We do not weaken either of the two conditionals: this means that the criteria are to be regarded as necessary and sufficient conditions for the legal validity of norms (i.e. they are treated as indefeasible).

(2) The first conditional is weakened, but the second is not. We thus obtain '(x) $\phi x > Vx$' and '(x) $Vx \rightarrow \phi x$', which represent the situation where the formal criteria expressly provided by the legal order are necessary but not sufficient conditions for legality.

(3) The second conditional, but not the first, is weakened. Accordingly, we obtain '(x) $\phi x \rightarrow Vx$' and '(x) $Vx > \phi x$'. This means that the formal criteria are sufficient but not necessary conditions of legality.

(4) The two conditionals are weakened, by introducing the corner: '(x) $\phi x > Vx$' and '(x) $Vx > \phi x$'. This means that such criteria are neither necessary nor sufficient conditions of legality.

It must be observed that all the defeasible conditionals used in our formalization can be transformed into material conditions if we add to their antecedents the set of the implicit exceptions (designated by 'E') which prevent the application of the strengthening of the antecedent. Thus we have: '(x) $\phi x \,\&\, E \rightarrow \sim Vx$' and '(x) $Vx \,\&\, Ex \rightarrow \sim \phi x$', which formally state—as we have mentioned earlier—that a norm can be invalid, despite having a legal pedigree, and that it can be valid, despite not having such a pedigree. Of course, the philosophical problem behind this operation is whether the exact identification of the set 'E' is possible or not.[93]

The analysis of the (in)defeasibility of the criteria, in its different forms, proves theoretically very fruitful since it can be used respectively:[94] (a) to explain the possible relations of the defeasibility of the criteria of recognition with the defeasance of rules of conduct and of rules of competence,[95] and (b) to account for different states of affairs which are usually dealt with under the heading of the 'application of legal norms'.

(a) Regarding the first point, we can envisage two different situations. First, it is possible that the criteria for recognition of the system are treated as indefeasible, but provide that all or some of the norms identified by using such criteria are defeasible. Second, it may be the case that the criteria themselves are treated as defeasible. In this case, the defeasible treatment of the criteria for recognition seems to involve the defeasible character of the validity of the norms identified on the basis of such criteria. This is so because, by conceiving the criteria for identification as defeasible, one admits that extralegal reasons may 'cancel' the validity (i.e. the membership of the system) of the norms produced in accordance with such criteria (in favour of the membership of other, more complete, norms).

[93] For discussion, see B. Celano, 'True Exceptions: Defeasibility and Particularism', in this volume, ch. 16.

[94] It also has some significant metatheoretical applications since it allows neatly distinguishing theoretical views depending on how they conceive of the defeasibility of the criteria for recognition. For discussion, see J. Ferrer Beltrán and G.B. Ratti, 'Validity and Defeasibility in the Legal Domain', 619–22.

[95] A norm of competence should be regarded as defeasible when we understand that the definition that it contains provides a set of conditions not sufficient for the validity of the norms enacted on the basis of the competence provided by such a norm of competence.

(b) In jurisprudential literature, the problems of rule application are fruitfully dealt with by means of the distinction between internal applicability and external applicability.[96] Internal applicability of a norm simply consists in the possibility of subsuming a certain individual case under the generic case regulated by the norm itself. Holding the defeasible character of the internal applicability of a norm may be considered equivalent to holding that some of the logical consequences of a norm are not valid, so that its application to the case at hand is prevented.

Conversely, the external applicability of a certain norm may be defined as follows: a norm N1 is said to be externally applicable to a case C, when another norm N2 provides that N1 is applicable to a certain class of cases, of which C is a member. In this context, the defeasibility of the application of norm N1 is equivalent to the defeasibility of the norm N2, which defines N1 as applicable.

E. Validity, applicability, and defeasibility: a proposal

We are now in a position to carry out a conceptual analysis of the relations underpinning the notions of validity, applicability, and defeasibility of legal rules.

In particular, we hold the view that three situations which are usually dealt with under the heading 'defeasibility of legal norms' must be distinguished. For these purposes, let us consider, for instance, a norm N1 which provides that if someone dies without framing a will, then the oldest daughter of the decedent ought to be declared the only and universal heir of the decedent's goods and titles ($\sim W \rightarrow OD$).[97]

(1) Sometimes—as we have previously mentioned—a norm is said to be defeasible in the sense that its validity (i.e. its membership of the legal system) is defeasible. The defeasibility of norms, in this case, refers to the defeasibility of the criteria for identification of the system. To hold that N1 is defeasible in this sense means, actually, that it is the criteria for identification, by means of which N1 is selected as a valid norm of the system, that are defeasible.

(2) Some other times, when one affirms that a norm is defeasible, one means that the external applicability of a norm is defeasible. That is to say that, in spite of the fact that the rule provides a solution for the case under decision (i.e. it is internally applicable to the case), the question whether it must be applied by the judge is not determined once and for all, since its conditions for application contain implicit exceptions whose scope has not been determined. We have already mentioned that the external applicability of a norm N1 depends upon the fact that another norm N2 provides that N1 ought to be applied: for this reason, the defeasibility of the external applicability of N1 is a consequence of the defeasibility of N2.[98] Let us give an example. Let us consider the case in which what is discussed is the legal status of the estate of

[96] The foundation of this distinction is to be found in E. Bulygin, 'Time and Validity' in A.A. Martino (ed.), *Deontic Logic, Computational Linguistics, and Legal Information Systems* (vol. II, Amsterdam: North Holland, 1982); and J.J. Moreso and P. Navarro, 'Applicabilità ed efficacia delle norme giuridiche' in P. Comanducci and R. Guastini (eds), *Struttura e Dinamica dei Sistemi Giuridici* (Turin: Giappichelli, 1996). However, we will use a different definition of this notion: a norm is applicable to a case C, according to a certain legal system S, if, and only if, a judicial decision of application of the law, which is grounded on such a norm, is a justified decision according to S.

[97] 'W' designates the operative fact 'valid will', and 'D' stands for the action of 'declaring the oldest daughter to be the universal heir'. As usual, 'O' is the deontic operator 'ought to'.

[98] Of its internal defeasibility, as we will see later on.

Peter, who passed away recently. A norm of international private law (N2) provides that, for the class of cases S (inheritance without the decedent's valid will), one must apply the norm of the system of the decedent (N1), so that the judge ought to apply N1 to the case of Peter's inheritance.

Now, it can turn out that the norm N2—'S $\rightarrow$ O(Apply N1)'—contains implicit exceptions, so that in not all the cases where S materializes ought N1 to be applied (for instance: if N1 is contrary to the standards of public decency of the system where the judge operates). If such implicit exceptions cannot be exhaustively determined, then we will represent N2 as 'S > O(Apply N1)'. In such cases, N1 is said to be defeasible in the sense that its applicability to the case may be defeated.

(3) Finally, on other occasions, when one affirms that a norm N1 is defeasible, one refers to the fact that its normative content is defeasible. That is to say: what is meant is that the operative facts identified in the antecedent of the norms are only a contributory condition for the normative consequence to follow: the norm's antecedent contains implicit exceptions which may not be exhaustively identified. In this third case, the defeasibility of N1 is neither necessarily a consequence of another norm N2 nor of the criteria for identification of the system. On the contrary, it is the result of the interpretation of N1 in the sense that it allows incompletely determinable implicit exceptions.

It is interesting to point out that, in the first case, the defeasibility of N1 cannot be represented by using the defeasible conditional ($\sim$W > OD), if we want to represent its content. The correct form of representing N1 consists in using the material conditional ($\sim$W $\rightarrow$ OD). This is so for it is not the normative content of N1 that is defeasible,[99] but rather its qualification as a valid norm.[100] In other words, it is not the conditional contained in N1 that is to be weakened, but the other conditional contained in the criteria for identification of the valid norms of the system that will provide that '(x) ϕx > Vx' (for any norm x, if x satisfies conditions ϕ, then presumably x is a valid norm of the system).

Analogously, the defeasibility of the external applicability of a norm N1 cannot be represented by using the defeasible conditional, if we want to account for its normative content. The correct form of representing N1 is by means of the material conditional ($\sim$W $\rightarrow$ OD). This is so because it is not the normative content of N1 that is defeasible, but rather the normative content of N2, which imposes the application of N1 ('S > O (Apply N1')).

For this reason, we will characterize cases 1 and 2, by affirming that the defeasibility of N1 is external. Contrariwise, in case 3, the normative content of N1 is defeasible (what can be represented by the sentence '$\sim$W > OD'). In this occurrence, we can affirm that the defeasibility of N1 is internal.

In order to avoid serious flaws in the analysis of norms the notions of internal and external defeasibility must not be confused. However, they have mutual relations which are worth unravelling. The external defeasibility of a norm N1 affects either its validity or its external applicability and is a consequence of the internal defeasibility of another norm N2 or of the criteria for identification of the system. By contrast, the internal defeasibility of a norm N1 affects its internal applicability, i.e. we cannot determine

[99] By 'normative content' we mean what is provided by the norm.

[100] Indeed, it can be the case that the normative content of N1 may also be represented by a defeasible conditional but this is not due to the defeasibility of the validity of the norm N1, but a combination of the cases 1 and 3.

whether a certain case C can be subsumed under the antecedent of the norm, since it is not a closed antecedent.

In turn, the internal defeasibility of N1 brings about the external defeasibility of the norms derived from it. In other words, if N1 ('$\sim W > OD$') is a valid norm, and if one accepts that the norms which are logical consequences of other valid norms are also valid, then we do not know whether N3 ('$\sim W \& F \rightarrow OD$')[101] is also valid *qua* a logical consequence of N1. This is so because, until the antecedent of N1 is (or is treated as) closed, it is not possible to determine whether N3 is a logical consequence of N3 or not.[102]

Finally, we can say that the internal defeasibility of a norm is the product of interpretation. As a consequence, determining whether N1 is internally defeasible is a doctrinal question, not a theoretical one. When defeasibility has to do with the external applicability of a norm N1, in turn, it is also a consequence of an interpretative decision, but is carried out on another norm—N2—which sanctions the applicability of the former. On the contrary, if defeasibility has to do with the validity of a norm, it must be regarded as a consequence of taking the criteria for identification of the system at hand as defeasible.

F. Some final remarks

Defeasibility—we have seen throughout this paper—has a long history and a somewhat curious genealogy. In our view, recent discussion of this problem has helped clarify that substantive accounts of legal defeasibility are, more or less consciously, bound to emphasize the interpretative character of the operations which underpin the defeasibilist treatment of legal rules. In other words, such a discussion has made it clear that there is no such thing as an objectively defeasible sentence or norm. Defeasibility eminently depends upon the interpretation of authoritative rule-formulations or the construction of precedents. This is what we have called internal defeasibility.

Moreover, it seems possible to identify some problems regarding the disapplication of legal norms as problems regarding the defeasibility of the rules which impose their application. Finally, we found out that in some cases defeasibility in the legal domain relates to the manipulation of the criteria for identification of a legal system, and affects the validity of the norms identified under such criteria. These two different situations have been referred to as external defeasibility.

By way of conclusion, it seems possible to succinctly put forward three possible uses of these notions of defeasibility within the legal domain, and in particular in jurisprudential research.

(1) The defeasibility of legal norms, if understood as a pragmatic tenet of legal interpretation, may be a fundamental tool in order to explain the operations carried out by jurists in order to systematize the law. If we are right, this involves that no nonmonotonic logic is needed in order to account for lawyers' reasoning, since the defeasible aspects of legal reasoning would be completely accounted for in dealing with their interpretative operations;

(2) Distinguishing defeasibility as a question of legal interpretation and as a question of validity or applicability may also prove to be a fruitful strategy for examining some

[101] 'F' designates whatever additional circumstance.

[102] Alternatively, this state of affairs may be explained by affirming that the rules of inference (which allow the derivation of implicit norms from expressed norms) admitted into the system are defeasible.

features of the now fashionable debate about legal disagreements. As a matter of fact, at least some kinds of theoretical disagreements (in Dworkin's broad sense)[103] may be accounted for by means of such notions. On the one hand, jurists, in fact, may be said to engage both in disagreements about the legality of derived rules as valid sources of law, and in disagreements about the meaning that ought to be associated with rule formulations or precedents, by determining whether their literal meaning dominates or it can be defeated by other ascriptions of meaning. On the other hand, what we have called external defeasibility may be useful in disentangling different disagreements regarding the conceptions of legal sources.

(3) Finally, accounting for the possible defeasibility of the criteria for recognition may prove necessary in order to analyse some foundational problems regarding both the 'pragmatic character' of the criteria for recognition and their logical treatment. The analysis of this last point may lead—we submit—to the discovery of some puzzles regarding the existence and the completeness of law, as well as the tenability of those theories which advocate a certain form of 'global defeasibility of legal norms'.[104]

[103] See R. Dworkin, *Law's Empire* (Cambridge, Mass.: Belknap, 1986), 3–6. For discussion, see S.J. Shapiro, 'The "Hart–Dworkin" Debate: A Short Guide for the Perplexed'; B. Leiter, 'Explaining Theoretical Disagreement', *University of Chicago Law Review*, 76 (2009), 1215–50; J.J. Moreso, 'Legal Positivism and Legal Disagreements', *Ratio Juris*, 22 (2009); and G.B. Ratti, 'Los desacuerdos jurídicos en la jurisprudence anglosajona', *Analisi e diritto*, 2009.

[104] See G.B. Ratti, 'Five Faces of the Incompleteness of Law', address at the conference 'How to Build-Up a Legal System', Milan, Bocconi University, June 2010.

2

On Law and Logic

*Carlos E. Alchourrón**

A. Introduction

The role of logic in law has sometimes been overestimated and sometimes underestimated. There are several reasons that can explain these misconceptions. One stems from the idea that logic is concerned with the laws of thought, aiming to describe and to guide the way people argue about different topics. From this perspective the function of logic in law would be the description of different forms of argument displayed to justify legal positions in order to find out how to improve these arguments. This would be a wonderful task, but unfortunately logic is not able to perform it. Logic cannot tell us how to improve our argumentative abilities. It can only show whether and how our conclusions are grounded on the premises used in our arguments. The justification of the conclusion is always a relative matter, since it depends upon the premises considered. Nevertheless, different logics can afford different kinds of justification. An invalid argument can be shown to be valid with a different logical analysis of the statements involved, or from the perspective of a different logic. From the metatheoretical point of view, logic can be used to evaluate the consistency and completeness of a legal system, even though it cannot give us any help in the task of overcoming the inconsistencies or the gaps that may be found in a legal system.

In the history of science logic is intrinsically connected with one of the scientific ideals that characterizes western scientific thought: the deductive or axiomatic organization of a field of research. In a historical perspective the evolution of this ideal is linked with the evolution of geometry. The project of Euclid was to organize the field of all geometrical truths in such a way that from a selection of some of them all others can be logically derived.

The same idea is found in Aristotle's conception of a demonstrative science. The effective realization of this ideal showed how many difficulties it must overcome. It was not until the beginning of this century, in the hands of Hilbert, that Euclidean geometry was completely organized in a deductive form. One of the obstacles stems from our natural enthymematic way of thinking. We usually take for granted, without noticing, many important assumptions that logic may help to identify. Hilbert's axiomatization shows how many unconscious suppositions passed unnoticed for centuries. It is interesting to recall that the first theorem derived by Euclid from his axioms did not follow logically from them. In fact one of the aims of the axiomatic deductive method is to make explicit all the assumptions used in our natural way of arguing. A methodological strategy, closely related to the axiomatic approach, that has proved very fruitful in the history of science, is that of abstracting certain features of a complex reality to build a simplified model of it in order to work with it instead of the richer

* Originally published in *Ratio Juris*, 9 (1996), 331–48. Carlos Eduardo Alchourrón (1931–96) was Professor of the Philosophy of Law and Professor of Logic at the University of Buenos Aires.

reality we are interested in. Examples of this procedure can be found in any science. In political philosophy the abstract models of those theories that work with idealized social contracts constitute instances of the abstracting procedure. The fact is that in an abstract model it proves easier to look for a deductive organization and check for implicit assumptions.

The ideal of the deductive organization is also present in the field of law as well as in legal science (legal dogmatics). In this paper I should like to comment on its possibilities, its political background, its limitations, the kind of conception attached to it as regards the nature of law, and the commitments that follow from it.

Law can be seen as a tool to organize the way of life in a certain society. Certain general patterns of behaviour are necessary to guide the actions that should or can be done. This suggests the convenience of having an explicit formulation of the rules designed to perform this guiding function. Once we have them it is assumed that the particular decisions will be taken in accordance with the relevant rules of the set. In this ideal model the set of rules are the starting points (axioms) for deriving the instructions to follow in each particular concrete situation. I will call the legal conception that stems from this ideal model the conception of the Master System. The ideal is not incompatible with the dynamic nature of law. The system continually receives supplements to update part of its content.

B. The Master System

In legal history the Master System conception is naturally associated with the various codification movements, as well as with their successes and their failures. It is also associated with the rationalistic natural law school of the eighteenth century. Nevertheless, the abstract ideal model is not necessarily committed to many of the putative mistakes of these historical movements.

Its impact on law can be detected in every contemporary legal system. There are several political and theoretical reasons that justify it as an effective ideal. In contemporary society there are at least three principles that have particular significance in relation to the Master System conception. They are:

(A) *Principle of unavoidability*: Judges must resolve all the cases submitted to them within the sphere of their competence. This requirement often appears in positive law in the form of a prohibition against declining to decide a case, and even though each judge is obliged to resolve only the cases within his competence, it is supposed that the competence of all the judges, taken together, is exhaustive. So it is assumed that for each and every possible case there is a judge with competence and the obligation to provide a solution.

(B) *Principle of justification*: A judicial decision requires a ground or reason and the judges must state the reasons for their decisions. Not only is it the unavoidable duty of a judge to resolve all cases submitted to him within the limits of his competence; it is also required of him that his decision should not be arbitrary and that he should give reasons justifying the solution he adopts. The purpose of this principle is to eliminate one of the possible sources of the injustice which might infect judicial decisions without sufficient reasons. This requirement is also almost universally embodied in positive law in the form of obligations imposed upon judges by rules (or codes) of procedure.

(C) *Principle of legality*: Judicial decisions must be grounded on legal norms of the State. This principle is complementary to the previous one: it is held that every decision requires not merely grounds, but grounds of a special kind: they must be legal.

The judge must not go beyond the sphere of the state's law, by appealing to the law of another state or to non-legal (e.g. moral) norms, except in cases where the law itself authorizes him to do so. And even in these cases the ultimate ground for decision will be a legal norm of the system.

The principle imposes a restriction on the selection of grounds, limiting the range of statements which may appear as acceptable grounds. We can summarize the three principles mentioned above by saying:

(D) Judges must resolve all cases submitted to them within the limit of their competence by means of decisions grounded on legal norms of the system. It is assumed that this principle does not impose an impossible obligation. Judges are able to fulfil its requirements. The possibility of satisfying (D) entails the truth of:

(E) In any legal system there are norms that supply grounds for solving every possible case.

This is the Postulate of Completeness (absence of gaps) of legal systems. The above argument shows how the truth of the postulate is assumed behind apparently innocent rules. The truth or falsity of the postulate depends mainly on (i) how the notion of justification is interpreted and (ii) how the elements of a legal system are identified. In the ideal version I am discussing, two conditions must be satisfied in order to provide an adequate justification: (1) the content of a decision should be a logical consequence of the premises that ground it, and (2) the normative premises used in the justification should be general. The only exception admitted to (1) is when the general rules give the judge discretion to take his decision within certain limits, as is the case, for example, with penalties and compensations. The kernel of this notion of justification has suggestive analogies with Carl G. Hempel's theory of explanation of particular facts in empirical sciences. According to Hempel an explanation of an empirical event is a logical deduction whose consequence is a description of the fact to be explained (the *explanandum*) and the premises (the *explanans*) are statements of two kinds: a set of general laws and a set of singular statements describing the initial antecedent conditions. Several adequacy conditions should be fulfilled in every explanation: (i) the *explanandum* should be logically entailed by the *explanans*, (ii) the *explanans* must contain general laws, and (iii) the sentences constituting the *explanandum* must be true. The explanation consists in showing that the phenomenon to be explained is a particular case of a general law. General laws supply the basic explanatory element in every explanation and logic takes the job of linking their conceptual content with what actually is the case. Although empirical sciences do not have an explanation for every fact, the pursuit of scientific investigation is grounded on the belief that there is an explanation for every fact. The principle of universal causation (a version of the principle of sufficient reason) is the analogue of the normative principle of completeness.

As to the identification of the elements of the normative system to be used as grounds in a justification, there are different versions of the theory according to the distinct ways of making the distinction between the so-called formal and material sources of law. The strictest version takes statute law as the only formal source, customs as well as other kinds of norms are considered only when statutes indicate the circumstances in which they have to be taken into account. A strict distinction between creation and application of law would make it pointless to consider precedents as a formal source of law. If a judicial decision follows from a statute, it adds nothing to it and if it does not follow it should not be taken into account because the judge has not fulfilled his duty to apply the law without modifying it. Other versions will also include precedents and customary norms in a subordinate position.

The distinction between normal and material sources of law is closely connected with the definition of positive law. The opinion of the experts, which constitutes so-called legal dogmatics, has a prominent role in some countries but only as a material source. The most controversial issue is the question whether morality is or is not a formal source of law. That it is a material source is beyond question.

The conception is supported by certain political ideals. In the first place it derives from the political doctrine of the separation of powers. More specifically, the separation of the legislative power from the judicial power supplies one of the grounds for this conception. According to this doctrine the legislative power is the main competent authority to specify the general rules to guide and to evaluate people's behaviour within the community. The function of the judicial power is only to resolve particular cases according to the general rules enacted by the legislature. There are several political reasons that ground this kind of separation. In the first place we have the argument from equality. Whenever judges limit themselves to applying the general rules enacted by the parliament, all cases of the same type will receive the same solution. Thus the requirement of the political ideal of formal equality justifies the separation of powers. Then we have the argument from democracy. In those countries in which the members of the parliament are democratically elected, which usually is not the case with the members of the judiciary, a sharp separation allows democratic control of the way of solving disagreements between members of the community. Thirdly we have the argument from certainty and security. Only by means of a strict division of powers are people able to know their rights and duties *in advance* of judicial decisions. Any decision not justified as required is considered arbitrary, in the sense that the adjudicated rights or duties are fixed *ex post facto* by the judge.

Of course, even if it were possible to maintain the sharp separation in the above way, the results do not certify the intrinsic qualities of the solutions adopted. The justice of judicial decisions derives in the model from the justice of the legislated general norms. Moreover, as long as equity requires in some cases a particular solution different from the treatment of standard cases there is no place for it in this theory. The Master System conception has been designed to give satisfaction to the political ideals of security and formal equality, but it cannot guarantee other ideals, such as justice and equity. Since this limitation restricts its importance, we need to see how much of it can be preserved in the light of the constraints of actual practice and other political requirements and look for its impact in the practice of law. The postulate of completeness is one of the conditions that the Master System should satisfy in order to offer the security and objectivity required. Nevertheless, completeness is not sufficient; the system must also be consistent.

The postulate of completeness requires the system to have a normative solution for every case. Quite often it has been said that this is an impossible demand since no one is in a position to know, nor even to imagine, the potentially infinite variety of cases that may occur in a society. In an important sense this is true, but there is an ambiguity in the legal notion of 'case' that may help to understand the scope of the requirement. Thus, for example, we speak about the case of political murder as well as the case of the murder of Mahatma Gandhi or the case of the murder of J.F. Kennedy, of the case of divorce and the case of the divorce of Lady Diana. It is obvious that the word 'case' does not have the same meaning in these phrases. Gandhi's and Kennedy's murders are real events, that happened in a certain place and at a certain moment of time. The expression 'case of political murder' does not refer to any concrete event, it is the mere description of certain properties of a set of events. The property of being a political murder may be instantiated in an unlimited number of concrete occurrences.

In order to remove the ambiguity I will introduce the expressions 'individual case' and 'generic case', respectively, for each concrete particular event and for a class of concrete events that have a common property.

The postulate of completeness is concerned with generic cases. But since metatheoretical notions like completeness impose different constraints in different contexts, the meaning intended here will be introduced with an example borrowed from Argentinian law. It is known as the problem of the recovery of real estate from third-party holders. The problem arises when someone in possession of real estate—which is owned not by him but by someone else—transfers it (by way of sale or gift) to a third party. Then the question arises whether (and if so, in what circumstances) the owner of the real estate may recover its possession from the third party. Or to put the question in other terms: in what circumstances does the third party have an obligation to restore it to its owner and in what circumstances (if any) may he keep it, i.e. refuse to restore it? The legislator made a classification according to three relevant properties: the good faith of the former possessor (the transferor), the good faith of the present holder (the transferee), and the onerous character of the act of assignment (transfer). The legislator gave special provisions for several combinations of the relevant properties, but he left no indication as to how to solve the generic case in which both the transferee and the transferor have acted in good faith and the transfer was onerous.

The general structure of the situation is as follows. For a certain legal problem the norms of the system select as relevant a set of properties. Taking into account the presence or absence of each of the relevant properties, it is possible to construct a set of 'elementary generic cases': that is, cases in which each of the relevant properties is either present or absent. The case in which both the transferee and the transferor have acted in good faith and the transfer was onerous, is, in our example, an elementary generic case. When for each of the elementary cases there is in the system a norm giving an answer to the legal problem in question, the system is complete. When, on the contrary (as in the problem of the third-party holder) no norm of the system indicates how to deal with the normative question in an elementary case, the generic elementary case is a *normative gap* in the system. The class of all elementary cases forms an exhaustive and mutually exclusive classification (a partition) of all the individual cases. Each individual case must belong to one elementary generic case and cannot belong to more than one of them. In this sense, a complete system that gives answers to all elementary generic cases indirectly provides normative solutions to all individual cases.

Although the procedure has been exemplified in relation to a specific legal problem, it should be clear how it can be generalized to take into account the class of legal problems dealt with in a legal system. It is important to emphasize that problems of completeness (as well as problems of consistency) are *relative* to a set of norms and a set of (generic) cases. This relativization allows us to isolate in a system those areas in which there is a normative gap.

Gaps of this kind are called 'normative' because they arise from the fact that the system lacks a general norm to deduce normative consequences for a generic case. Whether the relevant properties are more or less vague is irrelevant for this notion of completeness. Deduction of normative answers for generic cases from general norms of the system is not disturbed by the vagueness of the relevant properties involved. Vagueness can present problems only when we try to subsume an individual case within a generic case.

There is no other way to overcome a normative gap than to extend the normative system, incorporating a new norm to resolve the unprovided-for case. Many well-known arguments provide different forms of filling the gap in the way that is most harmonious with other parts of a legal system. Sometimes an argument from analogy or *e contrario* is the most suitable. On other occasions an appeal to a general principle of law, or the goal of the statute, or the intention of the legislator may supply a more satisfactory way out of the difficulty. The postulate of consistency requires the non-existence of incompatible normative solutions derived from a set of norms for a generic case. Normative solutions provided by the Master System for each generic case must be compatible. Although the relevant notion of compatibility is a main focus of research in deontic logic, I will not discuss the topic, since for the present purpose the intuitive pre-analytic notion is sufficient. It is possible for a generic case to be resolved inconsistently relative to a set of norms and at the same time for another generic case to be resolved consistently by the same set of norms. But in some cases the inconsistency is immediate. An example of this kind of inconsistency is found in the prescriptions of articles 97 and 112 of the Civil Code of Louisiana. According to the former: 'The minor of either sex, who has attained the competent age to marry, must have received the consent of his father and mother.' But article 112 prescribes that 'the marriage of minors, contracted without the consent of the father and mother, cannot for that cause be annulled'. Is the marriage of a minor contracted without the consent of one of his living parents annullable? According to article 112 the answer is clearly negative, but according to article 97 the marriage seems to be annullable since for its validity the consent of both parents is required.

On the standard interpretation, these articles express incompatible norms. But the fact that with a different interpretation the norms expressed by these articles may be compatible shows an important characteristic of the notion of normative consistency: it is a property of the *meanings* attached to normative texts and not of the normative texts themselves. The postulates discussed so far are concerned with certain relations among norms contained in the Master System. The system is a set of norms, not a set of linguistic expressions. By a 'norm' I understand the *meaning* that may be attached to a linguistic expression, not the linguistic expression itself.

Thus since the paragraphs of a statute, a constitution, or a code are linguistic entities, they do not form part of the system. I will refer collectively to the totality of all legal texts as the Master Book. This means that when a paragraph of a statute receives two different interpretations, i.e. when it expresses two different norms, each of the norms forms part of a different Master System coordinated with the same Master Book. Each of the different interpretations of the Master Book gives rise to a different Master System. Only when a Master System is identified, that is, when we work with an interpretation of the Master Book, may we inquire after its consistency and completeness. Independently of its interpretation, it does not make sense to ask, regarding two normative expressions, whether they are consistent or not. On one interpretation they may express compatible norms but on a different interpretation they may be incompatible. A provision which may resolve a generic case under a certain interpretation may be a gap on a different understanding. The interpretations of the Master Book should be empirical. The meanings attached to its linguistic elements must include reference to concrete situations of everyday life. This fact, which is the condition of the possibility of applying the general norms of the Master System, is also the source of most of the uncertainties that legal interpretation must overcome to approximate to the ideal model.

Since the starting point is always the Master Book, the ideal conception requires that there be one and only one clear Master System attached to it. From a theoretical point of view, the ideal of the Master System is the ideal of maximum objectivity. For this reason it is not surprising that enormous efforts have been made to try to reach the ideal without abandoning other political goals. Hart once called the picture of the Master System conception a 'noble dream', recognizing the positive nature of the ideals that lie behind it and at the same time the unrealistic assumptions on which it is based. Most of the unrealistic assumptions derive from the interpretative difficulties of the Master Book.

C. The Master Book

In relation to an ideal such as the present one, there are several dangers. The first is the rationalist illusion of believing that the ideal is realized in some or in all normative systems. The second stems from not noticing that, because there are other ideals that point in different directions, it may not even be convenient to try to maximize its requirements.

The fact that the Master Book is written in ordinary language presents the well-known difficulties derived from ambiguities and vagueness. I will now recall the standard problem of ambiguity to introduce a subject which has not been analysed as much as it deserves: the problem of defeasibility. Legal texts are expressed in natural language. The rules that give meaning to natural language expressions are the starting point of any interpretation. The fact that most expressions are ambiguous, i.e. that they have more than one meaning, is, in an important sense, a virtue of natural languages, since it allows speakers to express a large class of concepts with a restricted vocabulary. In most contexts the plurality of meanings of a term causes no problem in identifying the sense of the sentences in which it occurs. Nevertheless there are circumstances in which semantic or syntactic ambiguities may leave the sense of a normative expression undetermined. Moreover, some words have a technical legal sense different from their ordinary meaning, so that in some contexts it may be doubtful in which of its senses a word has been used. In every process of linguistic communication we must analyse the situation from the point of view of the person who utters a sentence to communicate some conceptual content and from the point of view of the interpreter who tries to grasp the conceptual content communicated. When an ambiguous term occurs in a sentence it may be that the term was not used ambiguously by the utterer—the utterer may have intended to communicate a definite sense with one of the several meanings of an ambiguous term. In such a case the expression was not ambiguous from the point of view of the utterer. Nevertheless it may be ambiguous from the point of view of the interpreter for he may not have sufficient evidence for the meaning effectively used by the utterer. In this case the indeterminacy exists only from the interpreter's point of view. Of course, the ambiguity from the utterer's point of view is independent of the ambiguity of the interpreter's point of view.

This independence of the two points of view has important consequences for identifying a 'creative' element in a process of legal interpretation. To know, for example, whether the interpreter has changed the norm expressed in a normative text, making it more specific or revising it, both points of view should be considered. Whenever an expression is ambiguous from the interpreter's point of view he has, in order to overcome the indeterminacy, no other choice but to select one of the alternative meanings, making use of his evaluative perspective.

Nevertheless, if the expression was not ambiguous for the legislator and the interpreter has selected the same meaning used by the legislator, then the norm expressed by the legislative text is for both, the legislator and the interpreter, the same. Although the interpreter has used in the interpretation his evaluative perspective he has not introduced any modification in the norms of the system. Any decision based on his interpretation is a logical consequence of the pre-existing norms of the system. In this sense his interpretation is not 'creative'. In most cases this coincidence is a consequence of the existence of a common set of basic values shared by the interpreter and the legislator.

In order to know whether an interpretation has modified the law there is no other option but to compare the meanings attributed to a text by the interpreter and the meanings attributed to it by the legislator. It is a well-known fact that more often than not it is very difficult, and in many cases practically impossible, to identify the precise meaning attached to a text by the norm-giver; in particular, when the lawgiver is a corporate body. The communicative model of interpretation faces a substantial task in detecting those changes in the law introduced by judges in their task of adjudication. Even though the linguistic phenomenon of ambiguity does not entail the introduction of an evaluative creative element, it is one of the factors that contributes to create an indeterminacy of the normative system that can be overcome only by an evaluative selective operation. Independently of this standard notion of ambiguity there is a more complicated kind of indeterminacy which is not usually discussed. In artificial intelligence and in logic the problem is known as the problem of nonmonotonicity or defeasibility.

Often, in ordinary language, conditional constructions of the form 'if A then B' are used in such a way that it is not intended to assert with them that the antecedent A is a sufficient condition of the consequent B, but only that the antecedent jointly with a set of assumptions accepted in the context of utterance of the conditional is sufficient for the consequent B. Such is, for example, the case when it is asserted, in relation to a certain gas sample, that its volume will increase if the temperature rises, assuming in the context that the pressure is kept constant. The conditional assertion is defeated when some implicit assumption is not true.

A defeasible conditional can also be defined as one which has implicit exceptions. In the example, a variation in the gas's pressure is an implicit exception that *defeats* the conditional assertion. In relation to a defeasible conditional we may have the truth of 'if A then B' jointly with the falsity of 'if A and C then B'. When such is the case circumstance C is an exception that defeats the conditional 'if A then B'. The above is the standard definition in logic of defeasible conditionals. That is, a conditional is defeasible if the following inference pattern (called 'Strengthening of the *Antecedent*') is logically invalid: from 'if A then B' it follows that 'if A and C then B'. Most of our ordinary-language conditional statements are, in this sense, defeasible. The idea of defeasibility is connected to the notion of 'normality'. We make our assertions for normal circumstances, knowing that in some situations our statements will be defeated. The notion of normality is relative to the set of beliefs of the speaker and the context of utterance. What counts as normal for a person in a certain context may be abnormal for another person or for the same person in a different context.

Most, if not all, normative formulations are defeasible, i.e. they usually have implicit exceptions, i.e. circumstances that defeat the norm though they are not explicitly stated. Even a very simple and clear rule like 'every driver should stop at a red traffic light' may have exceptions not explicitly formulated. For this reason Hart held that rules should be read as ending with a clause like 'unless...' intending to assert that they have an undetermined set of implicit exceptions. Usually our understanding of the rule will allow us to give a list of implicit exceptions as well as a list of circumstances which are not mentioned because they are rejected as exceptions. But the relativity of the notion of normality makes many situations ambiguous from the interpreter's point of view. The above traffic rule may be understood by someone coming from California with the tacit exception 'unless turning right', which would be excluded in European countries. Unless the exceptions are made explicit the conceptual content of the normative expression is left undetermined.

But how shall we identify the implicit exceptions to a normative formulation? How shall we know what meaning is attached to a defeasible normative expression, that is, how shall we know which norm is expressed by that expression? To answer these questions I will use a dispositional notion of defeasibility. Although this is not the only way to deal with the subject, the approach is particularly suitable for the analysis of some problems of legal interpretation.

According to the dispositional approach a condition C counts as an *implicit exception* to a conditional assertion 'if A then B' made by a speaker X at time T when there is a disposition of X at time T to assert the conditional 'if A then B' whilst rejecting 'if A and C then B'. This means that C is an exception to be included in the conceptual content expressed by the conditional, if it is the case that X at time T would have made the exception had he considered the case of having A jointly with C as antecedent to the conditional. On the other hand, a condition C counts as an *implicit non-exception* when there is a disposition of X at time T to assert the conditional 'if A then B' jointly with 'if A and C then B'. This means that C is to be excluded as an exception in the conceptual content of the conditional if it is the case that X at time T would *not* have made the exception had he considered the case of having A jointly with C as antecedent to the conditional. It should be noticed that there may be circumstances in which a condition C is neither an implicit exception nor an implicit non-exception. This is the case when at time T there is no disposition in X to include C as an exception nor a disposition to exclude C as an exception. The exceptional character of C is, in such a case, undetermined. Hence the conceptual content of the conditional is also undetermined in relation to C. So a condition C has three possibilities:

It may be (i) an *implicit exception*, (ii) an *implicit non-exception*, or it may be (iii) *undetermined* as an exception. In legal contexts the dispositional account of defeasibility has some consequences that may seem paradoxical. Suppose that the legislator at the time of enacting a statute did not foresee a certain circumstance C. Of course, at that time he was not in a position to present C as an explicit exception but if it is the case that had he considered C he would have introduced it as an exception, the dispositional account considers C as an implicit exception even at the time of the enactment. In the norm expressed by the statute C is an exception. The explanation of this apparently surprising result is that since we are trying to understand the conceptual content of a speech act we must take into account the utterer's set of factual and evaluative beliefs; this amounts to taking into account his dispositions to react in different circumstances. Thus the purpose of the dispositional account is to fix the conceptual content of normative texts considering the evaluative standpoint of the legislator.

Clearly it is convenient to make explicit what is implicit. Legal science and judicial experience continually perform this task of making explicit the implicit assumptions and exceptions. This attitude follows from the same policy that requires the enactment of a clear statute instead of a customary rule with the same conceptual content. Nevertheless, since unforeseen circumstances by their very nature cannot be made explicit, it seems wise to leave open the formulation of exceptions for those abnormal cases. In this sense Neil MacCormick wrote: 'Notoriously, it would be extremely difficult, perhaps impossible, and for sure the enemy of any kind of clarity or cognoscibility in law, to attempt a formulation of every conceivable precondition of validity in every statement of every rule. So general formulations of rights are apt to leave many background conditions unstated, especially those which arise only in rather exceptional cases.'[1] Nevertheless, as implicit exceptions in a normative text are often made explicit in other texts, the task has sometimes already been performed by the legislator. Systemic interpretation allows us to reconstruct, in such cases, the conceptual content of each of the norms of the system.

The relevance of defeasibility in legal argument can be illustrated by recalling the famous case *The Church of the Holy Trinity* v. *United States*. The Supreme Court of the United States was confronted with a legal disposition that did not make any distinction for a circumstance which was axiologically relevant for the Court. The statute made it unlawful for any person to assist or encourage the importation of any alien into the United States under a contract or agreement made prior to the importation of that alien in order for the alien to perform *labour or service of any kind*. The Church of the Holy Trinity made an arrangement with a British pastor by the terms of which he was to come to the United States and enter into the church's service as a rector and pastor. The circumstance that the contracted person was to serve as a pastor was for the Supreme Court a relevant circumstance even though it was not mentioned in the statute. The Court asserted that it has to be 'presumed that the Legislature intended exceptions to its language . . . The common sense of man approves the judgment mentioned by Pufendorf that the Bolognian law which enacted "that whoever drew blood in the streets should be punished with the utmost severity" did not extend to the surgeon who opened the vein of a person that fell down in a street in a fit.' This statement is a clear recognition of the defeasible nature of legal normative expressions.

It is clear that the normative *text* does not contain any exception. The important question in identifying the existence of a 'creative' element in the Court's decision is whether the norm expressed in the statute's text contains, or does not contain, the exception. For this purpose we have to consider the three alternatives mentioned above.

Let us assume first that the legislator did not in fact consider the particular circumstance of the case, but let us also assume that if he had considered the circumstance he would have made the same exception that was made by the Court. In this case the exception was implicit in the legislative text, and according to the dispositional approach to defeasibility the norm expressed by the text contains the exception as one of its conditions. This means that the norm used by the Court to justify the decision is the same norm that was expressed by the legislator. Although the members of the Court made use of their evaluative perspective they did not introduce any modification into the legal system. The content of the decision follows from the existing norms.

For the second alternative let us assume that the circumstance was undetermined for the legislator. Had he noticed it he would neither include nor exclude it as an exception. Then the interpretation of the Court amounts to a change of the legislative norm. Following their evaluative perspective the members of the Court have enriched the content of the legislative norm by the addition of an exception. But since the exception was not excluded by the legislator the modification is compatible with the previous norm and amounts to supplying a more precise normative content to the statute.

[1] N. MacCormick, 'Defeasibility in Law and Logic' in Z. Bankowski, I. White, and U. Hahn (eds), *Informatics and the Foundations of Legal Reasoning* (Dordrecht: Kluwer, 1995), 103. Editors' note: in the original the reference was to MacCormick's 1991 typescript of the paper referred to in this footnote.

Finally, if the particular circumstance of the case were an implicit non-exception for the legislator because he would have rejected an exception, the Court's interpretation has introduced a norm incompatible with the legislative norm. In the last two alternatives there would be a creative interpretation. The evaluative perspective of the Court would be the source of a new norm. Since defeasibility (or at least the kind of pragmatic defeasibility here considered) is a phenomenon that occurs in a process of human communication, it is not surprising that in legal contexts its discussion is linked to conjectures about the lawgiver's intentions with all the well-known shortcomings of such references. Thus what appears to be a historical investigation hides the political preferences of the interpreter. Nevertheless this historical comparison is necessary to know the kind of fit existing between judicial and legislative interpretation. Defeasibility, more than simple ambiguity, makes the identification of the norms of a legal system very difficult. So it is one of the factors that makes it necessary, in most situations, to introduce evaluative operations and the use of axiological standards in the interpretation of normative texts.

One of the main problems that arises in the application of general norms to individual cases is the classification of an individual case as belonging to one of the generic cases. Jurists usually refer to this problem by the name of *subsumption*. The difficulties of the classification of the individual case may arise from two sources. The first is lack of information concerning some relevant fact. Sometimes we do not know whether or not a concrete fact (individual case) belongs to a class (generic case), because we lack the necessary information; there are some aspects of the fact that we do not know, and this lack of knowledge is the cause of the difficulty in classifying the case. For example, even knowing that every case of transfer is necessarily made with or without consideration, we can very well not know whether the transfer of Peter's house to Andrew has been made with or without consideration, simply because we do not know whether Andrew has paid anything for the house or not. But the difficulty of knowing whether Peter transferred his house with or without consideration may arise from yet another source: the semantic indeterminacy or vagueness of general words. Even with full knowledge of the facts of the case, we may not know whether the transfer was made with or without consideration because we do not know whether the amount of money Andrew gave to Peter for his house is or is not a price in the technically relevant sense. Let us suppose that the amount of money handed over is markedly less than the economic value of the house. In such a circumstance it may be doubtful whether it is a sale or a concealed gift.

Overcoming the uncertainty derived from semantic indeterminacy, which Hart calls problems of the penumbra, requires the use of evaluative standards to justify the interpreter's decision. In a disposition like 'no one shall be criminally liable for an act committed in self-defence', independently of the ambiguities that may disturb its interpretation, significant doubts may arise about whether an act of self-defence was excessive or proportionate to the aggression received. The difficulty may stem from a lack of information about the facts that occurred or, as shown above, from the vagueness of the notion of proportionality. The vagueness of general words implies that sooner or later difficulties will appear in the subsumption of a particular case under a certain category. All general words suffer from some degree of vagueness which may make it undecidable whether some object or situation falls within or outside its field of reference.

In situations of ambiguity the source of the trouble is an excess of meaning. Vagueness on the contrary stems from a lack of sufficient determination of meaning. In both situations the meaning indeterminacy forces the interpreter to perform a selection based on evaluative considerations that may go beyond the immediate linguistic information received by him.

D. Interpretative arguments

Systemic problems (normative incompleteness and inconsistency) as well as linguistic indeterminacies (ambiguity, defeasibility, and vagueness) make the use of evaluative considerations necessary in adjudication. From a broader perspective, evaluative considerations are involved in *every* process of adjudication either in the selection of the norms used to ground the decision or in the identification of the relevant 'facts' of the case at hand. In this sense interpretation is always an evaluative activity. The formalist illusion of the purely deductive model has to be given up. But in order to see the force of the model as an ideal it is convenient to observe the kinds of arguments used to justify the evaluative selections, the elements included in them and the motives that lie behind their use.

There is a group of arguments which are related to the systemic nature of law. Their function is to justify evaluative selections pointing to other elements of the normative system. For example, in an argument from contextual harmonization a statutory provision is understood within a larger scope. Its meaning is identified in the light of closely related provisions of the same statute or of a set of related statutes, showing that the proposed meanings are evaluatively coherent with other sections of the statute or with related sections *in pari materia* of other statutes. Sometimes the argument is strengthened by arguments from general principles of various kinds. Some principles are related to certain institutions. The principles that supply grounds for some dispositions are used to make clear the meanings of other provisions.

Behind these principles lie some inductive operations designed to extend the scope of some norms showing their common evaluative reasons, which may be used to resolve situations not explicitly regulated or whose solution remains uncertain for reasons of linguistic indeterminacy. Systematic arguments from analogy also have this inductive nature. Their function is to extend the evaluative reasons that ground some norms to circumstances that share some common properties in the identification of the generic or individual cases considered. Arguments of this kind are conceptually linked to arguments from precedent. The argument from precedent is designed to show the intersubjective character of the evaluative standpoint used in the interpretation as well as to satisfy the requirement of equality. Of a different nature are arguments from general legal or moral principles. In them, the principle often directly supplies the general norm to justify the resolution of cases unprovided for, or wrongly provided for by specific norms. In other cases the principle supplies the evaluative grounds for the justification of the norm needed for the case.

It is very difficult to make an exhaustive classification of interpretative arguments; the above is only a sample of some recurrent systemic arguments. A non-systemic argument which should be mentioned for its peculiar features is the argument from intention. According to the argument from intention, the interpreter tries to follow the intention of the legislator. The argument has two versions: the 'subjective' and the 'objective'. In the subjective version the decisive element is the historical intention of the author of the legal text or the intention embraced by members of the legislature in the process of legislation. The objective intention is the intention ascribed to the legislature as an ideal rational legislator responsible for enacting that set of provisions in the relevant political circumstances.

In some cases there is sufficient evidence of the subjective intention of the historical legislator. That is the case with the Argentinian Civil Code, which was written by a single man: Dalmacio Vélez Sarfield. The situation is particularly clear because he used to comment in footnotes on the contents of the various paragraphs of the Code. Of course this is not the standard case. Quite often the *travaux préparatoires* do not provide adequate evidence of any particular intention, or they contain so many conflicting statements of intention as to open again a broad range of judicial choice.

In any case, the subjective and the objective version have different purposes. The subjective argument is designed to show a substantial evaluative agreement with the original historical legislator and involves essentially empirical evidence. The objective argument is of a different nature. It is an argument designed to uphold the intrinsic value of the proposed interpretation. For this reason it is assumed that every reasonable person would adopt, in the actual interpretative circumstances, the interpretation that fulfils the objective intention. The argument from objective intention is sometimes used to give prevalence to a current interpretation of some rights instead of the original historical interpretation.

It is clear that the objective and the subjective arguments may ground different and incompatible interpretations. Moreover, the same is the case with all interpretative arguments. Two different principles may point in opposite directions, so that it is necessary to weigh their relative importance for the case at hand. Taking into account different similarities, analogical arguments may support opposite interpretations.

Frequently more than one argument is applicable in a single situation. This might on certain occasions be no more than a case of coinciding arguments, but in some situations their individual strength may be increased by a cumulative effect. Nevertheless, just the opposite may occur: the plurality of arguments may justify rival interpretations. Conflicts between interpretative arguments in relation to cases of the same type are the result of partially incompatible evaluative points of view. So in order to overcome interpretative arguments with opposite results, we need to have some set of normative principles that allows us to interpret legal materials coherently.

Thus we need some pattern that allows us to select between competing results of the use of interpretative arguments. I have described so far some of the interpretative arguments used in the actual practice of adjudication to justify the identification of the required norms. But the subject looks different if we adopt a normative conception of interpretation and adjudication. If we ask not how judges usually justify their selections but how they should interpret legal texts then the answer may differ substantially. From this perspective the most interesting question is concerned with those cases in which there are systemic problems (normative gaps or inconsistencies) or linguistic indeterminacies, that is, those cases in which no explicit rule firmly decides the case either way. Perhaps some judges try to follow the hypothetical subjective intention of the legislator. But is this the right way to solve the problem of adjudication in hard cases? As is well known, Ronald Dworkin has given a negative answer to this question. His positive alternative, in what he calls 'the rights conception', is that judges should identify those norms that best fit the background moral rights of the parties. From this point of view we have a general pattern for resolving the possible conflicts that may arise from different uses of interpretative arguments. All we need to know is which of the competing answers fits the underlying moral rights better. Nevertheless conflicting answers are not completely excluded by the rights conception. Such conflicts may arise from two sources: (i) because two interpreters hold different views about the background moral rights of the citizens, that is when they do not share a common set of moral principles, or (ii) because they have different conceptions of the notion of fitting, that is, when they disagree as to the coherence of the case at hand with the moral rights. Even though moral disagreements and different notions of internal moral coherence are not, as a matter of fact, excluded in the rights conception, the fact that that conception describes an ideal that should guide any process of adjudication entails that it should postulate a privileged moral set of principles, the true moral principles, and a privileged notion of moral coherence.

Hence, since in Dworkin's approach moral principles form part of the law, the completeness and consistency of the Master System appear in new clothes. This shows the enormous force of appeal of the model of the deductive system as an ideal. In the rights conception the model contains not only the formal ideals of completeness and consistency, but also the ideal of justice. I have mentioned Dworkin's approach because it is the most categorical in its conclusions, but I think the deductive ideals of the Master System are present behind most of the theories about interpretative and practical legal arguments. That law should provide a coherent and complete set of answers for every legal case is a theoretical and practical ideal that lies behind many contemporary developments in legal philosophy.

3

Defeasibility, Contributory Conditionals, and Refinement of Legal Systems

Juliano S.A. Maranhão[*]

A. Introduction: Alchourrón's fear of snakes

In the 1990s, deontic logic was in the heyday of nonmonotonic logics, which very soon dominated the mainstream, if not of deontic logic itself, certainly of artificial intelligence and law. Such logics are very appealing to represent *defeasibility* in legal and moral reasoning, i.e. the fact that in legal and moral reasoning some obligations are dropped in the presence of new circumstances (prima facie duties). For instance, it is normally forbidden to kill, but may be permitted if the killer acted in self-defence. They also provide a nice representation of moral dilemmas and normative conflicts where two obligations coexist but may become inconsistent on some particular occasion. For instance, a doctor who is obliged to tell the truth to his patient about his condition and is also obliged to apply his best healing efforts in a situation where he believes the truth will impair the patient's recovery.

Such examples are not easily dealt with within the classical logic where monotonicity holds. If the prohibition of killing is derived using the classical (deontic) consequence relation, it will continue to apply whether the killer acted in self-defence, was smoking, wearing glasses, etc. If there is an obligation to tell the truth about a disease, this obligation is derived whether it will endanger the patient's recovery, the hospital is green, or whatever new circumstance or premise is considered. But the same holds for the obligation to do the best for the patient. In a situation where the truth may compromise recovery, the doctor is committed to tell the truth and not to tell the truth. The problem is that the deontic version of the principle of contradiction, $\neg(Oa \wedge O\neg a)$,[1] leads to the trivialization of the normative system. Hence, monotonicity and the deontic principle of non-contradiction seem to be obstacles to the representation of moral dilemmas.

The characteristic feature of nonmonotonic logics is that the consequence relation (usually represented by the snake $|\!\sim$) fails monotonicity, that is, the principle 'if $A|\!\sim x$ and $A \subseteq B$ then $B|\!\sim x$' is not valid. This means, contrary to classical logic, that some conclusions may be lost with the introduction of new premises, which seems exactly what is requested for the representation of prima facie duties and deontic dilemmas. However, Alchourrón thought otherwise:

> there is no need for a logic of defeasible norms (norms of prima facie obligations and permissions) because behind the requirement for such logics, as well as behind the requirement for nonmonotonic logics, now in fashion in artificial intelligence, lies a mixture of a standard notion of

* Lecturer in Law, University of São Paulo.

1 '$\neg$' is the symbol for classical negation and '$\wedge$' the symbol for classical conjunction.

consequence (or conditional) and the change of our (normative) premises in a dynamic perspective.[2]

According to Alchourrón, the view that defeasibility demands a new consequence relation is a misunderstanding of the classical derivation based on a previous revision of the premises. This claim was acknowledged in the deontic logic community in a paper published in 1993 and was the object of criticism and bewilderment. Loui considered Alchourrón's attack a 'consequence of his fancy for revision',[3] the model he created in co-authorship with David Makinson. In legal philosophy, Peczenik upheld the insufficiency of the AGM model to give an account of the weighing and balancing of reasons that are, according to him, characteristic of legal reasoning.[4]

In 2005, Makinson published a book on defeasible logics, where different ways of generating nonmonotonic logics from classical logic are studied.[5] We read in its preface:

> The book is dedicated to the memory of my former co-author Carlos Alchourrón, who died in January 1996. Despite his fascination with the logic of belief revision he distrusted its neighbor non-monotonic logic, and I could never convince him otherwise. While writing this book, I realized that it is a continuation of our conversations.

Makinson's point seems to be that such a move (first revise, then derive) is a way of generating a nonmonotonic consequence relation, and Alchourrón himself worked on a defeasible conditional, which is nothing but a 'snake' in the object-language of the logic. So why was he so suspicious of snakes?

It is one of the tasks of this paper to answer this question. Alchourrón was certainly *not* claiming that among different constructions of nonmonotonic consequence relations, the one involving revision of the premises should be chosen. His main concern was the philosophical darkness of any nonmonotonic *consequence relation*, deontic or not. For him, the snake *conceals* a change in the epistemic state, and this is poison!

Although this is a general claim for the representation of inferences in any domain of knowledge I will focus the discussion on his convictions about legal theory and the role of legal dogmatics in the description and systematization of norms. Alchourrón's attack may be justified if we go beyond the mathematical level and talk about the philosophical adequacy of the mathematical model with respect to his convictions about epistemology, particularly legal epistemology.

As we intend to make clear, Alchourrón's defeasible conditionals were developed to show the bridge between defeasibility and revision. But, if we are embedded in Alchourrón's concerns, we become suspicious even of his defeasible conditionals. I would like to propose an alternative revision operator, which I call *refinement*, to represent the operation of epistemic change favoured by Alchourrón as the antidote to the concealing snakes.

This paper uses the initial section of one of my papers,[6] where I presented Alchourrón's contributory conditionals and compared them to nonmonotonic logics. It has been updated to reflect the present literature with minor modifications and is useful to

[2] C.E. Alchourrón, 'Philosophical Foundations of Deontic Logic and the Logic of Defeasible Conditionals' in J-J. Ch. Meyer and J.R. Wieringa (eds), *Deontic Logic in Computer Science: Normative System Specification* (Chichester: John Wiley & Sons, 1993), 44.

[3] R. Loui, 'Alchourrón and von Wright on Conflict among Norms' in D. Nute (ed.), *Defeasible Deontic Logic* (Dordrecht: Kluwer, 1997), 348.

[4] A. Peczenik, 'Jumps and Logic in the Law', *Artificial Intelligence and Law*, 4 (1996), 297–329.

[5] D. Makinson, *Bridges from Classical to Non-Monotonic Logic* (London: King's College, 2005).

[6] J. Maranhão, 'Why was Alchourrón Afraid of Snakes?', *Analisis Filosofico*, 26 (2006), 62–92.

make the paper self-contained. Here the novelties are to be found mainly in sections C, D, and E. Section C was completely restructured and rewritten to provide what I understand to be the main elements of Alchourrón's picture of science and particularly the science of law. Section D argues that Alchourrón's contributory conditionals are inadequate as a formalization of the 'epistemic conception' of defeasibility. Section E shows how the refinement operator on bases (sets not logically closed) can cope with the shortcomings of Alchourrón's contributory conditionals. The version of refinement I present is a particular case of an operator I have called conservative contraction.[7] The basic intuition is that this operator replaces the conflicting sentences by weaker and non-conflicting ones within a knowledge system. In section F, I conclude with some comments concerning the logics of defeasible argumentation.

B. Was not Alchourrón snaking?

1. Visiting the nest

Nonmonotonic logics were developed in artificial intelligence to represent inferences under uncertainty. The underlying idea is that an agent who does not have enough information infers based on presumptions of how the world normally is. There are several ways to build a snake, adding implicit assumptions to the (classical) consequence relation and making them vary with consistency constraints. In face of new premises (information) the set of implicit assumptions may be reduced in order to preserve consistency and this is why some conclusions are lost. Makinson distinguishes three basic routes from classical to nonmonotonic logics:[8] (i) *default assumptions*: the addition of a set of sentences to the basic stock of premises with consistency constraints; (ii) *default valuations*: a restriction on the set of valuations of the model in such a way that the restriction varies if new premises are considered; (iii) *default rules*: the insertion of additional inference rules, with consistency checks on its application.

For the purposes of this paper it is sufficient to discuss default assumptions and default valuations, as well as defeasible conditionals that are very close neighbours. So let us pay a very short visit to this nest of snakes.

Classical logic consists of a structure $S=\{\mathcal{A}, \mathcal{R}\}$ where $\mathcal{A}$ is a set of formulas (axioms) and $\mathcal{R}$ a set of inference rules, whereby a consequence relation $\vdash$ between a set of formulas and a formula of the language, and a consequence operator Cn on sets of formulas, are defined in the usual way. A default-assumption logic may be defined within the structure $S_K=\{\mathcal{A}, K, \mathcal{R}\}$, where K is a set of formulas representing the basic assumptions. A *default-assumption consequence relation* $|\!\sim_K$ (alias C_K) is defined as:

> $A \,|\!\sim_K x$ if and only if $A, K' \vdash x$ for all subsets $K' \subseteq K$ that are maximally consistent with A (notation $K' \in (max(K, A))$[9]

Or, using the consequence operator, $C_K(A)=\cap\{Cn(A \cup K'): K' \in (max(K,A))\}$.

Let us call the union of each subset of assumptions within the set A (of beliefs or norms) an *extension*. The definition says that only consequences classically derived from

[7] J. Maranhão, 'Conservative Contraction' in W. Carnielli, I. D'Ottaviano, and M. Coniglio (eds), *The Many Sides of Logic*, series 'Studies in Logic' (London: King's College Publications, 2009).

[8] D. Makinson, *Bridges from Classical to Non-Monotonic Logic*.

[9] $K' \in max(K,A)$ if and only if:

(i) $K' \subseteq K$

(ii) $K' \cup A$ is consistent

(iii) there is no K'', such that $K' \subset K''$ satisfies (i) and (ii).

all possible extensions are accepted. A less radical approach bases the derivation on a selection s of maximal subsets of K which are consistent with A, i.e. $\cap\{Cn(A \cup K'): K' \in s(max(K, A))\}$. To see defeasibility, take $K = \{p \rightarrow \neg f, b \rightarrow f\}$[10] and notice that $\{b\}|\sim_K f$, but it may be the case that $s(max(K,\{b,p\})) = \{\{p \rightarrow \neg f\}\}$ so that not only $f \notin C_K(\{b,p\})$ but $\sim f \in C_K(\{b,p\})$. We may read the example as 'a bird (normally) flies' but 'if the bird is a penguin, then it is not the case that it (normally) flies'.

A second route to defeasibility is semantic. For convenience, in the present paper we will work with possible worlds in a model $M=\{V,[.]\}$ where V is a set of classical valuations (worlds) and [.] is an interpretation function taking us from each sentence to the set of valuations where the sentence holds (or is true). The function [.] satisfies the well-known classical truth conditions. We call $[a]$ the proposition expressed by sentence a. By $[A]$ we mean the set $\cap\{[a]: a \in A\}$. We say that x is a logical consequence of A (notation $A|=x$) if and only if $[A] \subseteq [x]$. To obtain a defeasible consequence relation we have to restrict the set of worlds in which the premises are evaluated (the 'normal' worlds that reflect the normality assumption) and make them vary with changes in the set of explicit premises (the normality assumption is defeasible with respect to the set of premises). In order to do that we use a binary preference relation '$<$' that introduces a partial ordering to the set of worlds within the model $M=\{V,[.], <\}$. We say that w is a minimal element of a set of valuations V if and only if there is no $v \in V$, such that $v<w$. By $min_<[A]$ we understand the set of minimal elements of the proposition $[A]$ under the assumed preference relation. A nonmonotonic consequence relation is then obtained by the following definition:

$$A| \approx_< x \text{ if and only if } min_<[A] \subseteq [x]$$

To check defeasibility, take a model where $V=\{w, v\}$, $[a]=\{w, v\}$, $[b]=\{w\}$, $[c]=\{v\}$ and $<=\{(w, v)\}$. We have that $min_<[a] \subseteq [b]$ and so $\{a\}|\approx_< b$, but it is not the case that $min_<[\{a,c\}] \subseteq [b]$.

Such a nonmonotonic consequence relation corresponds to Bengt Hansson's conditional obligations in his dyadic deontic logic.[11] Hansson's goal was to give a proper account of contrary-to-duty obligations and he interpreted the minimal elements in this semantics as the 'best worlds'. If some circumstance is given, interpreted as a violation of an ideal obligation, you ought to do what is true in all the remaining best worlds ('make the best out of sad circumstances'). He interpreted the relation $\{a\}|\approx_< b$ as a conditional obligation connective in the object-language O(b/a) reading as 'b is obligatory under circumstance a'.

If we index the preference relation to each world where we are evaluating the sentences we get Lewis's counterfactual conditionals. The minimal elements of each relation $<_w$ are here interpreted as the set of worlds w' that are most similar to the actual world w. By $min_w[a]$ we mean the set of minimal elements of $[a]$ under the relation '$<_w$'. Now, a counterfactual conditional $a>b$ is true at a world w if and only if $min_w[a] \subseteq [b]$, therefore behaving quite differently from the classical material implication (here represented by the arrow '$\rightarrow$'). The intuitive reading is that if *a were* true in the (actual) world w then *b would* also be true, since it is true in all most similar worlds in relation to w.

Each similarity relation provides, for each world and proposition, a subset of worlds (the minimal elements) of this proposition. Hence it is clear that the family of similarity relations in Lewis's model may be replaced by a choice function *Ch* having a world and

10 The arrow '$\rightarrow$' represents classical material implication.

11 B. Hansson, 'An Analysis of Some Deontic Logics', *Nous*, 3 (1969), 373–98.

a proposition as argument and a subset of worlds as value. Then we have that $a>b$ is true in a world w if and only if $Ch([a],w)\subseteq[b]$. We may map both approaches if we stipulate for every sentence a and world w that $Ch([a],w)= min_w[a]$, i.e. the choice function 'chooses', for each world and proposition, exactly the minimal worlds of the preference relation. Stipulating suitable constraints on the choice function, or corresponding restrictions on the similarity relation, we get the well-known Lewis logics of counterfactual conditionals V, VN, and VT.[12]

We may specify that the choice function always applies to a single (the actual) world or we may stipulate a constraint on Ch such that $Ch([a],w)=Ch([a],w')$ for all w, $w'\in V$. If we do that there is no need for a second argument (worlds) in the choice function. Lewis calls the systems corresponding to this last constraint 'absolute', getting the counterparts VA, VNA, and VTA of his counterfactual logics.[13] These last systems may be built using Åqvist construction by means of a monadic selection operator f in the object language that corresponds to the choice function on propositions in the model.[14] The counterfactual conditional is then obtained by the definitional abbreviation $a>b = \Box(fa\rightarrow b)$ where $\Box$ is a normal modal necessity operator.

These counterfactual conditionals may be interpreted as deontic conditionals in Hansson's fashion.[15] All these conditionals are nonmonotonic. Their semantics provide a distinguished set of formulas that are theorems of a nonmonotonic logic. Note that restricting the set of valuations has the same effect as adding premises to the antecedent: by restricting the set of worlds we augment the set of propositions that are true in the selected worlds. Therefore, there is a visible translation of the default assumptions approach into the default valuations: $Ch[a]=[\cap\{\{a\}\cup s(max(K,\{a\}))\}]$.

To criticize the snakes, Alchourrón built his logic of *contributory conditionals* in the very neighbourhood of this nest. Let us now visit Alchourrón.

2. Snakes do conceal and this is poison!

(a) Precedents

Although Alchourrón's attack became widely known through papers published in the 1990s,[16] his uneasiness with nonmonotonic consequence relations had already been manifest in two previous works.[17] The first was presented at a conference held in Miami, and the second was published in Italian. These works were provoked by his reading of Hilpinen's paper on normative conflicts.[18] The problem raised by Hilpinen is the existence of norms which do not properly conflict but may generate normative contradictions in particular circumstances. For instance the norms:

N1. Those who commit murder ought to be punished
N2. Minors ought not to be punished

[12] D. Lewis, *Counterfactuals* (Oxford: Blackwell, 1973).

[13] Ibid.

[14] L. Åqvist, 'Modal Logic with Subjunctive Conditionals and Dispositional Predicates', *Journal of Philosophical Logic*, 2 (1973), 1–76.

[15] D. Lewis, *Counterfactuals*, 96–104.

[16] Starting with C.E. Alchourrón, 'Philosophical Foundations of Deontic Logic and the Logic of Defeasible Conditionals'.

[17] C.E. Alchourrón 'Condicionalidad y la representacion de las normas juridicas'; 'Conflictos de normas y revision de sistemas normativos' in C.E. Alchourrón and E. Bulygin, *Análisis Lógico y Derecho* (Madrid: Centro de Estudios Constitucionales, 1991), 267–80 and 291–301.

[18] R. Hilpinen, 'Conflicts and Change in Normative Systems' in A. Frändberg and M. Van Hoecke (eds), *The Structure of Law* (Uppsala: Iustus Förlag, 1987).

According to Hilpinen these norms may coexist as binding in a normative system. However, in the particular circumstance where a minor commits murder the judge is both obliged to punish and not to punish the subject. Hilpinen's point is that the conflict is restricted to this special case and therefore none of the norms needs to be deleted since they continue to provide consistent solutions to 'normal' cases. Hilpinen makes a distinction between normative conflict and normative contradiction applied to conditional norms, and puts forward that in an adequate deontic logic the principle $\neg O(a \wedge \neg a)$ should be valid, but not the principle $\neg(Oa \wedge O\neg a)$, which amounts to the invalidation (in any normal modal logic) of the principle of deontic conjunction $(Oa \wedge Ob) \rightarrow (Oa \wedge b)$.

Alchourrón disagreed with Hilpinen. According to him, the distinction between normative conflicts and normative inconsistency just reveals that a set of norms may be inconsistent given a (possibly empty) set of facts. He saw no reason why we should call the empty case 'contradiction' and the non-empty case 'conflict', and reacted to the idea that, in the former, the system does not need to be revised.[19] In his logic of normative propositions (deontic formulas are interpreted as propositions describing the existence of norms in a system) the principles $\neg(Oa \wedge O\neg a)$ and $\neg O(a \wedge \neg a)$ are both invalid given that there may be normative orders containing inconsistent norms. The case where a minor commits murder may only be consistently solved if we are based on a different normative system where the antecedent conditions of N1 and N2 are modified.

This is already a step towards his later attack. Two points are relevant: first, he did not accept that a system could consistently solve both a general case and another more specific one if it attributes different and conflicting solutions to each of them; second, he did not accept a weakening of the logic to account for such inconsistency, emphasizing that its solution is a matter of decision, not logic.[20]

In that same year Alchourrón approached the problem of defeasibility directly.[21] The departing point was David Ross's concept of prima facie duties. He recognized that the concept is incompatible with the principle of *deontic strengthening of the antecedent* $((b \rightarrow Oa) \rightarrow (b \wedge c \rightarrow Oa))$ given that new facts may cancel existing duties, but restricted the analysis to situations where such facts are *explicitly* mentioned as conditions for the application of another incompatible norm within the system. Then he rejected the adequacy of Lewis's counterfactual conditionals given that its logic satisfies *modus ponens*, which, according to his analysis, should fail in any proper account of defeasibility. His argument is the following:

If one accepts *modus ponens* to detach the consequent of a prima facie conditional $(b > Oa) \rightarrow (b \rightarrow Oa)$, then, given that the consequent of this formula classically implies $(b \wedge c \rightarrow Oa)$, one should also accept $(b > Oa) \rightarrow (b \wedge c \rightarrow Oa)$,[22] and thus admit that no fact c can cancel the obligation contained in the conditional prima facie obligation of doing a under circumstance b.

[19] C.E. Alchourrón, 'Conflictos de normas y revision de sistemas normativos', 301: 'Suppose that α [the normative system] is an inconsistent set under the set of facts F and that the descriptive propositions of F are true. Is it possible that α undertakes its practical role of guiding behavior? I believe that the answer to this question must be negative, because the system has over-determined human behavior, given that all its actions and omissions are demanded.'

[20] This is a conviction Alchourrón inherited from von Wright. See G. von Wright, 'Norms, Truth and Logic' in A.A. Martino (ed.), *Deontic Logic, Computational Linguistics and Legal Information Systems*, vol. II (Amsterdam: North-Holland Publishing Co., 1982), 12.

[21] C.E. Alchourrón, 'Condicionalidad y la representacion de las normas juridicas'.

[22] Note that this is quite different from $(b > Oa) \rightarrow (b \wedge c > Oa)$.

Of course it is perfectly possible to have a consistent system failing to *strengthen the antecedent*, but satisfying *modus ponens*, as in Lewis's systems VW and VC.[23] But Alchourrón's argument actually posits that it is *philosophically or intuitively incoherent* to abandon the first principle while holding the latter.

The addition of *modus ponens* to Lewis's system V, getting VW, is semantically justified on the assumption of the truth of the antecedent of a counterfactual in a particular world where the counterfactual holds. In this case the counterfactual has the truth-value of its consequent, i.e. it becomes a material conditional. But Alchourrón found no intuitive support for this semantic assumption, given that it brings about counterintuitive examples.[24] Indeed, he believed that a counterfactual should not even be evaluated as true or false if its antecedent holds (in this case it is not a proper *counter*factual).

Then he turned to Hansson's dyadic deontic logic where neither deontic strengthening of the antecedent nor deontic *modus ponens* hold, and considered that the cost of Hansson's logic is too high in terms of inferential power.[25] Alchourrón pointed out that in Hansson's system the obligation to punish murderer adults cannot be derived from the set N1–N2, which would be undesirable.

The moral is simply that you shouldn't lose strengthening the antecedent (which corresponds to monotonicity in the meta language of consequence relations). If you do, then you cannot *coherently* hold the validity of *modus ponens* and this was too much for Alchourrón. Indeed, Alchourrón first believed that a logic that failed *modus ponens* would be *misnamed.* At that point, it seemed that Alchourrón was rejecting the very possibility of an adequate formal representation of defeasibility. However, that position was subsequently reviewed, under Makinson's influence, particularly after his influential paper:[26]

> Although I held this view strongly [that every conditional construction should satisfy *modus ponens*], I am now convinced (after Makinson's observation) that there are ordinary language conditional constructions which do not satisfy *modus ponens*, *viz.* defeasible conditionals, because they do not assert sufficient but contributory conditions.[27]

The notion of a contributory condition was formally developed by Alchourrón later. But its seeds were already present in these earlier approaches. According to Alchourrón, intuitively, the reason why we are inclined to believe that murders committed by minors ought not to be punished is that: (i) we identify a conflict of obligations in this case, and (ii) we solve the conflict by giving precedence to N2 over N1.[28] Hence some relevant beliefs about defeasibility became entrenched in Alchourrón's thought: *first*, the defeasibility of obligations is a matter of conflicting duties; *second*, on the intuitive

[23] D. Lewis, *Counterfactuals.*

[24] C.E. Alchourrón, 'Defeasible Logics: Demarcation and Affinities' in Crocco, Fariñas del Cerro, and Herzig (eds), *Conditionals: from Philosophy to Computer Science* (Oxford: Clarendon Press, 1995), 67–102.

[25] 'Nevertheless, the main defect of the system [Hansson's dyadic deontic logic] lies in its loss of inferential power. This happens because together with the undesirable consequences some obvious conclusions disappear, a fact that disqualifies the whole logical system'. C.E. Alchourrón, 'Condicionalidad y la representacion de las normas juridicas', 274.

[26] D. Makinson, 'Five Faces of Minimality', *Studia Logica*, 52 (1993), 339–79.

[27] C.E. Alchourrón, 'Defeasible Logics: Demarcation and Affinities', 98.

[28] 'La argumentación intuitiva muestraque en este caso dos aspectos relevantes hansidotomados en cuenta: (a) que la presentación formal muestraque hay un conflicto de obligaciones en el caso (p&r), y (b) que este conflicto se resuelve porque en este caso la norma (4) tiene prioridad esobrel la norma (3). El que no escapaz de entenderesto, no ha entendido el contenido conceptual del sistema A.' C.E. Alchourrón, 'Condicionalidad y la representacion de las normas juridicas', 276–7.

level, these conflicts are implicitly solved through revision of the normative premises with an underlying classical logic, or at least a logic strengthening the antecedent and satisfying *modus ponens*. Alchourrón's temper would not be satisfied with limiting himself to the diagnosis and he faced the challenge: the result of the enterprise appeared five years later.

(b) Contributory conditionals

In a series of three articles,[29] Alchourrón brought about a representation of defeasibility which he believed to satisfy his philosophical concerns. He developed a general theory of defeasible conditionals, which can be combined with deontic modalities. I begin by presenting the general theory and let the deontic version be discussed in the next section.

Defeasibility was represented in the object-language through a conditional. The conditional should formalize the intuitive notion of a *contributory condition*, i.e. the explicit antecedent is a necessary condition of a sufficient condition for the conclusion. This is so because the antecedent only detaches the consequent in the presence of implicit assumptions, that is, the antecedent together with its implicit assumptions is sufficient for the conclusion.[30]

Hence, the notion of a 'sufficient condition' is the starting point of his construction. He uses S5 strict implication '$\Rightarrow$' ($a \Rightarrow b =_{df} \Box(a \rightarrow b)$, where $\Box$ is S5 necessity operator) given that it translates the notion of logical consequence into the object-language of his logic. Semantically, we regard the strict conditional $a \Rightarrow b$ as true in a world in a model if and only if $[a] \subseteq [b]$. A defeasible conditional is defined in the object-language as a strict conditional with implicit assumptions in the antecedent ($a > b =_{df} fa \Rightarrow b$).[31] Semantically, the choice function *Ch* provides the true condition of the defeasible conditional ($a > b$ is true if and only if $Ch[a] \subseteq [b]$). The novelty with respect to Åqvist's construction is Alchourrón's interpretation of the selection *f* as a revision operator (*fa* represents the joint assertion of *a* with its consistent implicit assumptions). He calls this logic DFT, which he proves to be equivalent to Lewis's VTA.

Given that the set of assumptions must be consistent with the explicit contributory condition, we may interpret *fa* as a revision of a fixed set K of implicit assumptions by sentence *a*, i.e. $fa = *_K(a) = K * a$ satisfying the following *f*-axioms, which corresponds to AGM revision postulates (see Table 3.1).[32]

[29] C.E. Alchourrón, 'Philosophical Foundations of Deontic Logic and the Logic of Defeasible Conditionals'; 'Defeasible Logics: Demarcation and Affinities'; 'Detachment and Defeasibility in Deontic Logic', *Studia Logica*, 57 (1996), 5–18.

[30] The idea of a contributory conditional in terms of a necessary condition for a sufficient condition should not be taken as a definition, but only as a heuristic device to understand the role of the explicit antecedent in the conditional; otherwise, trivially, any pair of sentences *a* and *b* would be related as contributory conditions with regard to each other, given that each is a necessary condition for the sentence $a \wedge b$, which, on its turn, is a sufficient condition both for *a* and *b*. See V. Becher, et al., 'Some Observations on Carlos Alchourrón's Theory of Defeasible Conditionals' in P. McNamara and H. Prakken (eds), *Norms, Logics and Information Systems* (Amsterdam: IOS Press, 1999).

[31] See L. Åqvist, 'Modal Logic with Subjunctive Conditionals and Dispositional Predicates'.

[32] The reader that is familiar with belief revision may be missing the postulates of closure ($K*a = Cn(K*a)$), inclusion ($K*a \subseteq Cn(K \cup \{a\})$), and vacuity (if $\neg a \notin K$ then $Cn(K \cup \{a\}) \subseteq K*a$). To account for the postulate of closure we may interpret *fa* as any finite axiomatization of the theory $K*a = Cn(K*a)$. Postulates of inclusion and vacuity tell us that the simple expansion of a theory by a new proposition is a limiting case of revision. These postulates are absent in the axiomatization of the selection operator *f*. As Becher et al. show, the absence of these postulates makes Alchourrón's contributory conditions avoid Gärdenfors' impossibility theorem. See V. Becher, et al., 'Some Observations on Carlos

Table 3.1

Postulate	Selection operator f	Revision operator $*_K$
Self-deductibility	f1. $fa \rightarrow a$	$a \in K*a$
Equivalence	f2. $(a \Leftrightarrow b) \rightarrow (fa \Leftrightarrow fb)$	if $a \Leftrightarrow b \in Cn(\emptyset)$ then $K*a = K*b$
Consistency	f3. $\Diamond a \rightarrow \Diamond fa$	if $\neg a \notin Cn(\emptyset)$ then $K*a \neq L$
Hierarchical ordering	f4. $(f(a \vee b) \Leftrightarrow fa) \vee (f(a \vee b) \Leftrightarrow fb) \vee (f(a \vee b) \Leftrightarrow (fa \vee fb))$	$(K*(a \vee b) = K*a) \vee (K*(a \vee b) = K*b) \vee (K*(a \vee b) = K*a \cup K*b)$

These axioms are semantically valid given obvious restrictions ø on the function *Ch*, which is a form of generating nonmonotonic logics, as we have seen above. Considering that '$\Rightarrow$' translates the relation of the (classical) logical consequence '$\vdash$' into the object-language we have:

$$\vdash a > b \text{ if and only if } K*a \vdash b$$

The revision operation $K*a$ is defined constructively through a selection of all maximal subsets of K that are consistent with *a*. First we define the operation of contraction $K \div a = \cap s(max(K,\{\neg a\})$, and then we use the so-called 'Levi identity' to define the revision $K*a = Cn(\{a\} \cup K \div \neg a)$. Given that K is a theory and it holds that $Cn (\cup\{\{a\},\cap s(max(K,\{a\})\}) = \cap(Cn(\{a\} \cup s(max(K,\{a\})))$ it follows that:

$$K*a \vdash b \text{ if and only if } a \mid\sim_k b \text{ if and only if } b \in C_k(a)$$

which means that Alchourrón was snaking in the neighbourhood, if not using nonmonotonic logic (both syntactically and semantically).

But the point is that neither is he endorsing this latter step, nor is he endorsing the use of contributory conditionals of the form $a>b$. Does this make sense given that this latter step follows necessarily from the definitions? It does. His efforts consisted precisely in showing the logical 'equivalence' of the revision dynamics to nonmonotonic logics, so that he could conclude, at the logical level: *we do not need snakes.* To illustrate this point, he compared two procedures to analyse the familiar Birds–Penguins example, one by general conditionals, and the other by defeasible conditionals (see Table 3.2):

(1) Birds (*b*) fly (*a*)
(2) Penguins (*p*) do not fly ($\neg a$)

Both procedures avoid the inconsistent and counterintuitive conclusion that penguins, which are birds, fly and do not fly. Given a defeasible conditional where d2 is preferred to d1 we derive the correct conclusion that penguins do not fly. But in Alchourrón's formalization of defeasible conditionals d1 is $fb \Rightarrow a$ and d2 is $fp \Rightarrow \neg a$. Provided that the choice related to fb and fp is given by the equations $Ch[b]=[b \wedge \neg p]$ and $Ch[p]=[p]$ (so that we have $fb \Leftrightarrow (b \wedge \neg p)$ and $fp \Leftrightarrow p$) the procedure that represents defeasible conditionals would be the same as the procedure that uses general (revised) conditionals (we will return to this claim in section D).

As we have seen, Alchourrón abandoned his view that any inference relation or any conditional construction deserving the name should satisfy detachment (*modus ponens*).

Alchourrón's Theory of Defeasible Conditionals' in P. McNamara and H. Prakken (eds), *Norms, Logics and Information Systems* (Amsterdam: IOS Press, 1999).

Table 3.2

General (revised) Conditionals	Defeasible Conditionals
G1. $(b\wedge\neg p)\Rightarrow a$	d1. $b>a$
G2. $p\Rightarrow\neg a$	d2. $p>\neg a$

But the demand for *modus ponens* was still strong at the back of his mind, as we see in the following passages:

I think that we have a natural and spontaneous tendency to understand ordinary language constructions as a way of holding that the antecedent is a kind of sufficient condition of the consequent, the weakest form of which would be material implication. This is equivalent to assuming that conditionals always allow us to detach the consequent in the presence of the antecedent.[33] I see no intuitive reason to have a conditional with *modus ponens* but without strengthening the antecedent, even though I understand the strong psychological tendency to require the fulfillment of *modus ponens* for every conditional construction.[34]

In his construction of contributory conditions, where implicit assumptions related to the antecedent are made explicit and revised in the presence of inconsistencies, he tries to rescue the notion of a sufficient condition in the conditional construction: it does not hold, but we do not lose track of it. With this move, Alchourrón tries to conciliate his understanding of ordinary language defeasible conditionals with his psychological adherence to *modus ponens*.

But note that Alchourrón was not saying that the sentences 'birds normally fly' and 'birds which are not penguins fly' are logically equivalent. As should be clear, he was perfectly aware that defeasibility is concerned with ampliative reasoning. His model of revision is ampliative and defeasible in its dynamics. The procedures (not the sentences) are equivalent, i.e. 'derivation from revisable premises' is the same as 'derivation by default'.

This is what he requires to advance his philosophical argument about adequacy: snakes are dangerous *because they conceal* the dynamics of epistemic change, which is in the very nature of defeasibility.[35] So the philosophical question Alchourrón proposes is: *to conceal or not to conceal?*

C. Alchourrón's epistemic conception of defeasibility

1. The scientific picture

As positivists, Alchourrón and his co-author Eugenio Bulygin are concerned with the scientific grounds of legal dogmatics. One of their main tenets is to make a sharp distinction between the knowledge of what law is (description and systematization of the content of valid general norms) and its critical evaluation according to moral or political standards.

33 C.E. Alchourrón, 'Defeasible Logics: Demarcation and Affinities', 98.

34 Ibid., 101.

35 Alchourrón remarks that when he discusses the procedure that uses defeasible conditionals 'the nature of the total enterprise, which involves a revision of our premises, is concealed, and for this reason might be dangerously misleading'. C.E. Alchourrón, 'Philosophical Foundations of Deontic Logic and the Logic of Defeasible Conditionals', 78.

They propose an abstract model of such descriptive activity inspired by the scientific ideal of an axiomatic system. Under such an approach, the knowledge of law consists in the knowledge of logical consequences of some basic propositions about the content of existent norms (normative propositions).[36] Individual legal decisions are justified to the extent that their content is a deduction from the described general norms.

Therefore, general norms described by legal dogmatics may be taken as explanations (or justifications) of individual decisions, analogously to Hempel's theory of explanation where particular facts are explained whenever deduced from general conditionals together with the description of events.

Just as the ideal pursued by empirical sciences is a consistent and complete explanation of natural phenomena (universal causation), the ideal of legal science is the description of a complete and consistent normative system (completeness and consistency). However, there is an important difference. Given that norms are the result of human acts of will, they may contain inconsistent demands, or may contain gaps, i.e. the normative status (obligatory, permitted, or forbidden) of some regulated action remains undecided in some relevant cases.

The logic of normative propositions (which describe the valid norms) helps identify such defects, but this is all that legal knowledge may do. It is clear that in legal practice the interpreter goes beyond that and eliminates contradictions or integrates gaps to obtain adequate justifications for individual norms. Nevertheless, this does not mean that the normative system is necessarily complete and consistent; it just means that the original system was evaluated and changed by the legal interpreter.

Here lies an important boundary between the cognitive/descriptive and politically evaluative/prescriptive activity. Changes to restore consistency or integrate gaps are part of the prescriptive discourse (the interpreter makes choices), and a proper analysis of the legal practice (distinguishing legal cognition from legal evaluation) should make this point explicit. In his paper 'Normative Order and Derogation' (1982),[37] when the logic of revision was at its birth, Alchourrón emphasized, as its main philosophical implication, that the model makes explicit the choice made by the interpreter between the possible results of a derogation (the indeterminacy problem), which is guided by a hierarchical ordering *concealed* in the activity of integration of the law.

2. Explicit or implicit inconsistencies in the root of defeasibility

The same concern related to derogation is present in his understanding of defeasibility, since the latter would also be the result of an intervention by the interpreter in the system to solve an explicit or implicit inconsistency. Here, the intervention is of a particular sort: instead of cancelling one of the conflicting general statements, the antecedent of one or both of them is better qualified so that their normative solutions apply to different and independent circumstances. Therefore, Alchourrón's analysis of defeasibility is centred on the process of qualification of the antecedent of general norms.

[36] Here I take their work *Normative Systems* as based on a logic of normative propositions describing the content and consequences of the set of explicit norms, given that normative inconsistencies do not lead to trivialization and the distinction between strong permission (explicit authorization) and weak permission (absence of prohibition) which is possible on the descriptive level.

[37] C.E. Alchourrón, 'Normative Order and Derogation' in A.A. Martino (ed.), *Deontic Logic, Computational Linguistics and Legal Information Systems*, vol. II (Amsterdam: North-Holland Publishing Co., 1982), 51–64.

In the case of an explicit inconsistency, such as that obtained by the rules 'killers ought to be punished' and 'minors ought not to be punished', the interpreter should restore overall consistency before the instantiation. For Alchourrón, as we have seen, it is not the case that both may coexist, and in particular instantiations where minors are killers, the former rule does not apply. What happens is that a revised legal system applies consisting of the latter rule and a qualified version of the former according to which 'killers which are not minors ought to be punished'. It is a different rule which is actually valid within the legal system.[38]

But the genuine case of defeasibility that challenges positivism, is that of *implicit inconsistency*. Here a normative solution derived from the general norms is defeated because it fails to satisfy some ideal of justice or the underlying reasons that led to the creation of the norm. In most cases this incoherence will not appear, given that in general the legislator and the interpreter share a common set of basic values. But there may be some hard cases where this is not true. The analysis of these hard cases was the starting point of Dworkin's attack on legal positivism.[39]

Alchourrón believed that the defeasibility of legal norms by moral and political standards would be nothing, but a sort of normative contradiction, this time between the explicit legal norm and the norm which is taken by the interpreter to be implicit under the legislator's intention. Suppose a legal system containing only N1 'killers ought to be punished' and suppose that John kills in self-defence. It is a consequence of this system that killers who act in self-defence ought to be punished, which is the justified normative solution for John's case. The interpreter may consider that this solution offends the moral right of every individual to life, which was the very reason that justified the prohibition on committing murder. This means that only the qualified norm N3 'killers that do not act in self-defence ought to be punished' should be binding.

On account of such cases, Alchourrón and Bulygin make a distinction between the *thesis of relevance* of the system given by the relevant cases in the description of the system, and the *hypothesis of relevance* given by the cases that the interpreter believes ought to be relevant for the system. Therefore, the hypothesis of relevance expresses a judgement about the axiological adequacy of the system.[40] If a condition belonging to the hypothesis of relevance is not present in the system's thesis of relevance, they speak of an *axiological gap*, which is part of the prescriptive, not the descriptive discourse. Bulygin criticizes Dworkin's attack precisely for his failure to distinguish the descriptive from the prescriptive discourse.[41] That is, the principle may be binding on the interpreter and used prescriptively, but it is not part of a description of what law is.

[38] One may not consider this case as authentic defeasibility, referring to it instead as a derogation of the sort '*lex specialis*'. Actually, this particular example is not a prototype derogation given that the resulting normative system keeps a qualified version of the original norm instead of deleting. But it is right that it is not effectively a defeat of the normative system (only an adjustment within its rules). I believe, however, that including explicit inconsistencies in the category of defeasibility was already a way for Alchourrón to make his point. The message is that there is nothing new about defeasibility that would demand a new logic. It is just a case of inconsistency to be solved by the intervention of the interpreter. The only difference presented by the discussion on defeasibility is that the revision is provoked not by a positive norm, but by a norm derived from the evaluations of the interpreter. So the difference may be simplified by distinguishing the revision of an explicit *versus* an implicit inconsistency.

[39] R. Dworkin, *Taking Rights Seriously* (Cambridge, Mass.: Harvard University Press,1977).

[40] C.E. Alchourrón and E. Bulygin, *Normative Systems* (Vienna: Springer, 1971), 156–7.

[41] E. Bulygin, 'Normas, Proposiciones Normativas y Enunciados Juridicos' in C.E. Alchourrón and E. Bulygin, *Análisis Lógico y Derecho* (Madrid: Centro de Estudios Constitucionales, 1991), 169–93.

Jorge Rodríguez claims that the hypothesis of relevance and the axiological gaps should not be immediately identified with the prescriptive discourse, as they may be understood as conveying information about a second normative system that is actually a reconstruction of the *ratio legis* by the legal interpreter.[42] This account gives expression to a well-known argument employed in claims related to axiological gaps according to which the legislator would have provided for a different solution had he considered the unpredicted circumstance.

Alchourrón and Bulygin have remarked, in light of their concern to draw a sharp line between the descriptive and prescriptive discourse, that axiological gaps actually reveal a move from an original normative system to another system with 'more refined cases', where the conditions of application of its norms are better specified.[43] But both authors seem to have later relaxed this view. The different legal systems that are in play in a move from the original to a more refined one were taken by both as 'different levels of analysis' of the same normative system. Defeasibility would be the outcome of the resolution of a conflict between the normative solution provided by the rule and the normative solution given by an inquiry into 'the objective underlying reasons of the rule',[44] or into 'the subjective intention of the legislator'.[45] While Bulygin subscribes to Rodríguez's model, Alchourrón identifies three possible dispositions by the lawgiver, considering a norm '$q \Rightarrow Op$' and an arbitrary factor r not explicitly considered: r is an *implicit exception* (the lawgiver would have *rejected* $q \wedge r \Rightarrow Op$); or r is an *implicit non-exception* (the lawgiver would have *accepted* $q \wedge r \Rightarrow Op$); or r is *undetermined as an exception* (the lawgiver would have neither of the aforementioned dispositions). As Moreso and Rodríguez remark, to avoid an inherent indeterminacy of the legal system (this was Caracciolo's criticism against Alchourrón's dispositional theory), the implicit factor tested against the authority's disposition is only relevant in the first case, implicit exception.[46] The set of consequences of the legal system remains unchanged in the cases of indeterminacy and implicit non-exception. In the case of implicit exception, the original normative solution is dropped from the set of logical consequences.

Given that both Bulygin and Alchourrón ascribe to the interpreter a decisive role in the identification of the 'objective underlying reasons' or of the 'lawgiver's implicit dispositions', both approaches boil down to the admission that the identification of the law may involve justified choices (by the interpreter) among the logical consequences of the explicit rules. That is, maybe only *some* of the logical consequences of explicitly enacted rules are legally valid.[47] And this is an important departure from their conception presented in *Normative Systems* where the legal system is *defined* as the set of logical consequences of propositions describing enacted rules. If the normative system is given by some, but not all the logical consequences of explicit norms, then a distinct epistemic status is attributed to explicit rules in relation to implicit or logically derived ones. This move has an important consequence with respect to Alchourrón's principle

[42] J.L. Rodríguez, 'Axiological Gaps and Normative Relevance', *Archiv für Rechts- und Sozialphilosophie* (ARSP), 86 (2000), 151–67.

[43] C.E. Alchourrón and E. Bulygin, *Normative Systems*.

[44] E. Bulygin, 'En Defensa de El Dorado. Respuesta a Fernando Atria' in F. Atria et al., *Lagunas en el Derecho* (Madrid: Marcial Pons, 2005).

[45] C.E. Alchourrón, 'On Law and Logic', in this volume, ch. 2, 51.

[46] J.J. Moreso and J.L. Rodríguez, 'Estudio Intruductorio: "Carlos E. Alchourrón y la Máxima de la Mutilación Mínima"' in C.E. Alchourrón, *Fundamentos para una teoría general de los deberes* (Madrid: Marcial Pons, 2010), 27–9.

[47] J. Ferrer Beltrán and G.B. Ratti, 'Validity and Defeasibility in the Legal Domain', *Law and Philosophy*, 29 (2010), 601–26.

of *minimal change* of the original normative system, which is also in the core of AGM-like revision logics (we will return to this point in section E).

3. Defeasibility as epistemic revisability

Focusing on a change in an epistemic state about the law (or the world) Alchourrón's tenet is to keep the whole inferential power of the strict conditional. Explicit conditions are sufficient to detach consequences, and through this mechanism individual normative solutions are justified and particular events are explained. Under his epistemology, scientific knowledge (of the world or the law) is essentially composed of a set of general strict conditionals which explain phenomena (events or normative decisions) given the presence of antecedents. Even though he recognizes that there may be implicit assumptions and exceptions within general explanations, it is the very role of science, and in particular of the legal science, to make them explicit.[48]

Hence, there seems to be no place in the scientific discourse for general laws like 'water "normally" turns into steam if the temperature is 100° C' or 'according to Brazilian law, if you kill you "normally" go to jail'. These defaults may be part of everyday common-sense reasoning where conclusions are drawn even if there is uncertainty about actual facts.

However, in the scientific domain, the overall concern regards the *soundness of generalizations*. Actual facts or events are only taken into account as instantiations of general hypothesis. If a generalization fails in a particular instance, e.g. 'John boiled water in La Paz at a temperature below 100° C', then it must be revised by another more qualified generalization, e.g. 'water turns into steam at 100° C if heated at sea level', which is able to explain the failure as well as future events. Now, if after such qualification of the scientific theory, as a matter of fact, we are not sure about the pressure conditions, and still willing to infer *by default* that the water, after being subject to a particular heating, will turn into steam at 100° C, this is a problem related to instantiation, not to the general theory itself.

The same holds for legal science in the reconstruction of the legal system. If, according to the legal system, killers ought to be punished, but under a particular decision John is not punished even though he killed, this decision cannot be justified by the normative system as it stands. Certainly this decision could not be justified by the argument that the killer was John. The justification must be based on some property or circumstance of the case that could be *generalized*, i.e. the same normative solution would be applied to any killer in the same circumstance.[49] For instance, the decision may be justified by the fact that John was attacked by the victim, together with a general rule according to which anyone who acts in self-defence cannot be criminally liable. If this is the justification, the general rule may only be accommodated through a reinterpretation that necessarily changes the legal system. The normative proposition of legal science would then associate a general solution with a refined general hypothesis like 'according to the Brazilian legal system, the killer that does not act in self-defence ought to be punished'. Again, if Peter killed and the judge does not have enough information about the circumstances in which the action occurred, or if Peter's lawyer does not advance a claim of self-defence, then she may presume that this was not the case and 'jump to the conclusion' that Peter should be punished.

[48] C.E. Alchourrón, 'On Law and Logic', 47.

[49] This is due to the moral principle of universalization which is entrenched in a widespread legal ideology according to which every decision should be based on general norms (see the discussion related to this principle in C.E. Alchourrón, 'On Law and Logic').

Note that there is a difference when we consider defeasibility focusing on the *qualification of a conditional*, and when we consider it as making an exception in the *instantiation of a conditional*. Jumping to conclusions or opening exceptions to the general rule is a matter of instantiation, whether we consider that the implicit assumptions related to the antecedent hold or not in a particular case. In this case, the matter is *inferential*, i.e. the exception is admitted within a looser logic where conditionals may fail in some instantiations. By its turn, systematization may be provoked by failure in a particular instantiation, but the problem is how to explain the failure, what may be done by generalizing a relevant property of the exceptional case and qualifying the defeated general conditional. In this second case the matter is epistemic, i.e. it has to do with the revision of our theory to explain phenomena or detach normative solutions. One may also say that in the first case defeasibility has to do with an *exception* in a particular instantiation, while in the second case defeasibility has to do with the *qualification* of explanatory conditionals.

Theories about legal defeasibility often focus their attention on one of these aspects. Those who see defeasibility as a matter of the *application of law* are usually *partisans* of the 'inferential conception'. They emphasize the exception in the instantiation not only due to the identification of a factor in the case at hand which breaks a presumption that is explicit in the rule (explicit exception), but also due to possible unforeseen implicit exceptions that may appear at the moment of application based on the rule's underlying reasons. So they assume an inherent indeterminacy of the law, as a set of prima facie rules and principles of the sort 'if a, then normally, it is obligatory/permitted that b' or 'if a and it is not shown that c, then normally, it is obligatory/permitted that b'.

On the other hand, those who see defeasibility as a matter of *identification of the valid norms* (the justification of legal decisions) are *partisans* of the 'epistemic conception' and emphasize the reconstruction of the legal system as a set of qualified general rules relating normative solution to the presence of relevant factors.[50] In this level of analysis there is no difference at all if a relevant factor is an exception or not because who carries the burden of claiming its presence is not in question (it is in question just in the instantiation). If the factor is an explicit exception it is just a factor relevant in the rule with an indication of the burden of proof for the moment of instantiation. If the factor is an implicit exception then it is just a factor relevant in an interpretative reconstruction which results from a modification of the original system.

Since, according to Alchourrón, the task of science is to provide general and systematized explanations of events or general and systematized normative propositions describing general norms that justify particular decisions, it is the defeasibility as *qualification* that is at stake for him.

Does that mean that under Alchourrón's account (legal) science should make explicit all possible assumptions or implicit exceptions to general conditionals? This seems to be an illusion of certainty that is inadequate for a realistic account of (legal) knowledge.

In fact, Alchourrón agrees that it is impossible to formulate every implicit exception in the interpretation of a normative expression, and that possibly all normative expressions are defeasible in this sense. In one of his last published papers, he quotes Hart by saying that all legal norms should end with a clause 'unless . . . ', and also MacCormick to the effect that the attempt to formulate every conceivable expression would be the

[50] See J. Ferrer Beltrán and G.B. Ratti, 'Validity and Defeasibility in the Legal Domain' for a detailed discussion of defeasibility as a problem of normative validity.

enemy of any kind of clarity or cognoscibility in the field of law.[51] However, agreeing to that just means agreeing with the defeasibility of knowledge, and it does not commit anyone to a conception of knowledge as a set of default rules. I believe that, in Alchourrón's view, knowledge of the world or the law may present itself as certain and complete by means of general strict conditionals *as long as such conditionals can cope with reality*. The defeasibility of knowledge lies in the instability of scientific propositions within the knowledge set, i.e. in the fact that they may be changed and further qualified given surprising observations or the need to justify a conflicting normative decision.[52]

4. What should be explicit in the formal picture of defeasibility?

The discussion above revealed three important aspects of Alchourrón's scientific picture of legal dogmatics that should be captured by the formal representation of defeasibility.

First, he believed that the phenomenon of defeasibility in science carries an intrinsic relation to changes in epistemic states. Defeasibility of a conditional proposition means its susceptibility to qualification (change). Since logical consequence is not an epistemic notion (Alchourrón was not a defender of intuitionist logics) a concealing nonmonotonic consequence relation could not provide a philosophically adequate account of defeasibility.[53]

Second, he also believed that an adequate model of knowledge should consist in a *system* of general propositions that provided sufficient explanations of events or sufficient justifications for particular legal decisions until the system was changed (or subject to deeper analysis of the legislator's implicit dispositions).

Third, an adequate representation of legal knowledge should be restricted to descriptive discourse, making clear the interventions of the interpreter's choices. In later writings, Alchourrón (and Bulygin) accepted that the interpreter's intervention should not be necessarily identified with prescriptive discourse, given that it may be the result of an inquiry into the underlying reasons of the rule (or the legislator's disposition). But such an inquiry may reveal that not every consequence of the general norms is valid (in particular, not every derivation by *strengthening the antecedent* produces valid rules). This means that explicit rules have privileged epistemic status compared to derived ones, and also that the derivation of consequences involves a choice by the interpreter.

Alchourrón believed that by representing defeasibility with contributory conditionals the inherent aspect of change of normative premises would not be concealed, thus satisfying the first tenet above. But, although contributory conditionals keep track of general sufficient conditionals, they are authentic defaults associated with implicit assumptions. A system of contributory conditional rules would not be a system of general sufficient conditionals. Furthermore, defeasibility in this representation would

[51] C.E. Alchourrón, 'On Law and Logic', 46–7.

[52] After exposing the procedure of representation of defeasibility by means of general conditionals, Alchourrón makes the following comments: 'But after the second revision there raises the question: have we reached the right and desired set of premises? Usually we will never be sure to have obtained the desired (much less the right) set of premises, because we are never fully conscious of the infinite set of consequences that follows from any (even from very small) set of premises. For this reason one must be permanently checking the qualities of the premises and be ready to perform as many revisions as their analysis and our experience require.' C.E. Alchourrón, 'Philosophical Foundations of Deontic Logic and the Logic of Defeasible Conditionals', 79.

[53] A similar argument is used by André Fuhrmann favouring revision of an inconsistent epistemic state instead of a paraconsistent logic, i.e. a sub-classical inference relation that handles inconsistent premises without trivialization. A. Fuhrmann, 'Solid Belief', *Theoria*, 63 (1997), 90–104.

be a contingent aspect of each rule and not a (practically unavoidable) property of the system of rules. Therefore, the second aspect of his scientific picture is not adequately captured by his contributory conditionals. Since the implicit assumptions associated with the antecedent are already given, the element of choice (by the interpreter) that causes the change of sufficient conditional rules into new (more qualified) ones is not revealed by his model as well. Clearly, the implicit assumptions are elements to be met or not in particular instantiations, just as in any nonmonotonic logic, which renders his model closer to the inferential conception or to the idea that defeasibility is a matter of application and not of validity of general conditionals. This claim of inadequacy needs a special section for further argument.

D. Do contributory conditionals really fit Alchourrón's scientific picture?

According to the epistemic conception, defeasibility in the scientific domain is nothing but instability of knowledge (about either reality or the law). To be conscious of our limitations to provide general explanations about the world or the law should not hinder our inferences. The *presumption* is that these general conditionals hold and, given the antecedent, the consequence should be detached. Following Alchourrón this is very different from saying that in the presence of the antecedent then *presumably* the consequence should be detached. First we presume we know and within this safe environment we draw inferences as if they were incorrigible. Science should work on this initial presumption. If anything goes wrong, the whole theory should be revised. To make assumptions or presumptions under particular inferences is common-sense reasoning, not science.

In the legal domain, the problem with the 'inferential conception' is that it turns the legal system into a set of prima facie normative solutions. This would affect the very authority of the rules. If we admit 'unless' clauses on rules, opening them to any factor that might be considered relevant according to the 'objective reasons' of the rule we are somehow transferring the authority from the lawgiver to political or moral reasons that grounded the creation of the rule.[54] Alchourrón's theory is, consequently, the result of a struggle to accommodate defeasibility within the 'presumed' authority of law. He only admitted a revision of this presumption in the case of a conflict between the lawgiver's rule and the lawgiver's actual disposition, despite conceding that such inquiry is determined by the interpreter's evaluations.

Although Alchourrón made clear his point about law and science, I believe he was betrayed by his own formalization. After all, Alchourrón's contributory conditionals are *defaults,* and *deontic* contributory conditionals express prima facie rules. That is why, as we have seen, logicians like Makinson were reluctant to understand his fear of snakes.

His formal representation succeeded in throwing light on one aspect of his convictions, i.e. that there is a process of epistemic change involved in defeasible reasoning. But at least two crucial elements are missing: (a) no reference is made to the (theory describing the) legal system as a set of general (strict conditional) rules, but only to assumptions linked to the antecedent of each contributory conditional/rule; (b) the conditional rules are not actually changed into new, more qualified ones: what happens

[54] J. Raz, 'Authority, Law and Morality' in J. Raz, *Ethics in the Public Domain* (Oxford: Clarendon Press, 1994), 210–38; R. Caracciolo, 'Normas Derrotables: la concepción de Carlos Alchourrón', *Analisis Filosofico,* 26 (2006), 156–77.

is that the full statement of the rule shows that it cannot be instantiated if some of its implicit assumptions are contradicted.

Take the example of self-defence within a legal system containing the rule 'anyone who kills (k) another person ought to be punished (p)'. If it is represented as a contributory conditional we have:

R1. $fk \Rightarrow Op$

Now, if the interpreter considers that those who act in self-defence (d) ought not to be punished, in view of the lawgiver's attitude or the objective reasons of the rule, a new rule is taken into account with the content:

R2. $d \Rightarrow O\neg p$

Is there a conflict? Yes, if the consequences of the set of implicit assumptions associated with the operator f do not include $\neg d$.

But the idea of the contributory conditional to cope with this example is that $\neg d$ is an implicit assumption of R1 and, therefore, the consequent of the rule is not detached. That is, fk is intended to represent the set of assumptions A revised by k ($A{*}k$), and if $\neg d \in Cn(A)$, then the set A is going to be contracted by the revision $A{*}k \wedge d$, and nothing guarantees that it would still derive Op. So there is no conflict at all between R1 and R2, and the contributory conditional works exactly like any other nonmonotonic consequence operator: if any of the implicit assumptions is contradicted, the default rule is blocked. The operator f indicates that some revision of the premises took place, and that is why the rule is not instantiated, but there is no move from the identification of an inconsistency towards the qualification of the original conditional.[55] That is to say, there is no epistemic change *provoked* by the new solution given by R2, but just the recognition of an exception whose corresponding presumptive factor was already present in the antecedent of the rule. So maybe the contributory conditionals better represent the instantiation of an explicit exception. However, what would be required, specially to represent implicit exceptions, would be an operator representing an intervention of the interpreter to transform the strict conditional $k \Rightarrow Op$ into another, more refined, strict conditional R1' $k \wedge \neg d \Rightarrow Op$.

Recall that the presumption to be broken should be the presumption of certainty of the theory about the normative system and not the *presumable* detachment of a conditional. However, Alchourrón's formalization makes the detachment *presumable*, given that the antecedent is associated with implicit assumptions. Such assumptions are predetermined: for each conditional you have an associated theory of implicit assumptions. If these conditionals are taken to represent those rules of the legal system, then the procedure to obtain defeasibility is only designed for explicit rules/conditionals and not for derived ones. What is the relation, if any, between the implicit assumptions linked to the antecedent of a rule and those linked to the antecedent of a logically derived rule? If a rule is derived from more than one rule, should we consider that its associated theory of assumptions is the union of the assumptions of each rule used in the derivation? And what if these assumptions associated with different rules are inconsistent?

The idea that defeasibility is a consequence of limited or revisable knowledge of the *corpus* of rules is not captured, given that it is not the legal system that is revised independently of any instantiation. It is the instantiation that is blocked due to a revision.

[55] This is my main divergence from J. Maranhão, 'Why was Alchourrón Afraid of Snakes?'.

To overcome this limitation, one may think of the theory associated with the antecedent as the very legal system composed by general strict conditionals. In this case, consider the legal system $K=\{k \Rightarrow Op, d \Rightarrow O\neg p\}$. Then, we have that $k>Op$, since $Op \in Cn(K^*k)$. In the case $k \wedge d$, however, we have that $(Op \wedge O\neg p) \in Cn(K \cup \{k \wedge d\})$. If according to the underlying deontic logic such normative conflict leads to trivialization, then the set K should be revised to accommodate $k \wedge d$. There might be three alternative results of this revision: $K^*k \wedge d=\{d \Rightarrow O\neg p, k \wedge d\}$, or $K^*k \wedge d=\{k \Rightarrow Op, k \wedge d\}$ or $K^*k \wedge d=\{k \wedge d\}$. The first one would result from the acceptance of the rule $d \Rightarrow O\neg p$ and self-defence as an exception to the general rule that killers ought to be punished.

This was not what Alchourrón had in mind when he talked of implicit assumptions, but it has the advantage of bringing the whole legal system into account; it represents the normative conflict provoked by the introduction of R2 and the change in the normative system. However, this change is the result of an attempt at instantiation, and it has the same effect as the blockage of the rule that was subject to exception (this time deleting it from the remainder set as a result of the revision). We do not have, as Alchourrón envisaged, a change expressing the qualification of the general rule by a new condition. This means that contributory conditionals would represent just reasoning in instantiation of the assumed theory, thus being a logic of exceptions and not of qualification of those general conditionals.

Of course, we said earlier that Alchourrón's goal was to show the bridge between the revised conditional and the defeasible conditional, but in the procedure he favours as the adequate representation of defeasibility there should be a dynamic of change *of the normative system* itself. I believe Alchourrón would be better shielded against Caracciolo's and related positivistic criticisms on the authority of the law if the revision were applied to the legal system itself as composed of strict conditionals, rather than to a legal system of prima facie rules. In the idea of a dispositional theory (or even of objective reasons underlying rules) what is revisable is the interpreter's (legal dogmatics) understanding about what are the authority's choices, not the authority's choices themselves. So everything happens within the epistemic process of the theoretical construction of what Alchourrón calls the 'Master System' from the 'Master Book' of relevant legal texts.

In a nutshell, Alchourrón's logic of contributory conditionals is not a logic of revision, but a nonmonotonic logic based on revision operators, and what he needed to completely represent his philosophical convictions about legal knowledge would be an authentic revision operator applied to a system of general (strict conditional) rules.

E. Refinement of normative systems

1. The refinement operator: internal and global

A revision operator called refinement that qualifies (rather than deletes) one of the sentences of the original set has been developed in three papers.[56] The version I shall present here captures a very simple intuition. Suppose a normative system containing the rule α. Its set of consequences will include $\neg\beta \Rightarrow \alpha$ and $\beta \Rightarrow \alpha$. If in case β this norm is

[56] J. Maranhão, 'Some Operators for Refinement of Normative Systems'; J. Maranhão, 'Refining Beliefs' in J.-Y. Béziau and A. Costa-Leite (eds), *Perspectives on Universal Logic* (Monza: Polimetrica International Scientific Publisher, 2007), 335–49; J. Maranhão, 'Conservative Contraction'.

defeated, because a stronger rule (explicit in the normative system or implicit in the interpreter's reconstruction) $\beta \Rightarrow \neg\alpha$ also applies, then the original rule α should be qualified to the effect that $\neg\beta \Rightarrow \alpha$. So, what happens in this revision process is that one of its derived norms with respect to condition β (namely, $\beta \Rightarrow \alpha$) will be discarded, in accordance with Alchourrón's (and Bulygin's) later conception, which assumed that not all of the consequences of the normative system are valid.[57]

As remarked above, this assumption presupposes that the basic set of explicit norms is not closed by its logical consequences, which implies a revision of the concept of *minimal change* endorsed by Alchourrón. The principle of minimal change has two claims: (i) one should give up norms (beliefs) only when *forced* to do so; and (ii) to derogate a norm (belief) from the system one should delete as few norms (beliefs) as possible to restore consistency.

To see why the principle of minimal change is insufficient to non-closed sets, suppose you believe in the sentence 'water boils at 100° C'. Then you are committed to the belief that 'water boils at 100° C if you are at sea level' and also that 'water boils at 100° C if you are not at sea level'. Later you make a test in La Paz and water boils at a lower temperature. Instead of simply dropping your original belief it would be more reasonable to qualify it, selecting the fact that you were not at sea level as a relevant condition defeating your original belief.

If the set of original beliefs is logically closed and therefore derived sentences have the same status as any within the set, then the change operator will be applied to contract the sentence 'water boils at 100° C if you are not at sea level'. As a consequence, the original sentence 'water boils at 100° C' will be dropped and, given some restrictions,[58] the sentence 'water boils at 100° C if you are not at sea level' will be kept, as wished.

Now, if the set of beliefs is not closed the revision operator must be applied to delete the original sentence 'water boils at 100° C' and, as a consequence, none of its derived beliefs will be kept. Minimality is satisfied in this unreasonable full contraction, given that the original sentence was shown to be false, and it was the only sentence responsible for such falsity. So, according to minimal change, a derived belief/norm has to be abandoned if it loses its support in the set of explicit beliefs/norms (if there is no reason to keep it). This happens because the principle of minimal change applied to non-closed sets has no proviso for the quality or adequacy of derived beliefs to which the agent was previously committed. For instance, no evidence was found in the La Paz test against the derived belief that 'water boils at 100° C if you are at sea level', so why shouldn't it be kept? Instead of minimal change, we should use a stronger principle of conservatism, according to which one is still justified to keep a belief in the absence of a special reason not to (if there is no specific reason to abandon it). We may interpret this principle as saying that we should keep beliefs/norms derived from the original set that were not specifically contradicted.[59]

The internal refinement operator # satisfies conservatism. Provided a normative system Γ of strict conditionals (possibly with empty antecedents) and a norm $\alpha \in \Gamma$ that is challenged by a conflicting conditional $\beta \Rightarrow \neg\alpha$, a function Cn^* selects part of the set of non-tautological consequences of α, i.e. $Cn^*(\alpha) \subset Cn(\alpha) \backslash Cn(\emptyset)$ and the contraction function operates on $\Gamma \cup Cn^*(\alpha)$. The obvious selection given a defeating condition β is $Cn^*(\alpha) = \{\neg\beta \Rightarrow \alpha, \beta \Rightarrow \alpha\}$. Then the operator will contract only the sentence

[57] J. Ferrer Beltrán and G.B. Ratti, 'Validity and Defeasibility in the Legal Domain'.
[58] J. Maranhão, 'Refining Beliefs'.
[59] J. Maranhão, 'Conservative Contraction'. In the particular case of logically closed sets there is no difference between minimal change and conservatism.

Table 3.3

Root-cutting	$\beta\Rightarrow\alpha\notin\text{Cn}\ (\Gamma\#_{\beta}\alpha)$
Success	$\alpha\notin\text{Cn}\ (\Gamma\#_{\beta}\alpha)$
Inclusion	$\Gamma\#_{\beta}\alpha\subset\Gamma\cup\{\neg\beta\Rightarrow\alpha,\beta\Rightarrow\alpha\}$
Core-retainment	if $\gamma\in\Gamma\backslash\Gamma\#_{\beta}\alpha$ then there is $\Gamma'\subset\Gamma\cup\{\neg\beta\Rightarrow\alpha,\beta\Rightarrow\alpha\}$, such that $\alpha\notin\text{Cn}(\Gamma')$ but $\alpha\in\text{Cn}\ (\Gamma'\cup\gamma)$
Preservation	$\neg\beta\Rightarrow\alpha\in\Gamma\#_{\beta}\alpha$

specifically contradicted so that $\beta\Rightarrow\alpha$ is not part of the consequences of the resulting system and the qualified version $\neg\beta\Rightarrow\alpha$ is kept in the set of explicit rules. In other words, given a normative system Γ, a norm $\alpha\in\Gamma$, and a choice of a relevant defeating condition β with respect to α, the *internal refinement* of Γ by α with respect to β (notation: $\Gamma\#_{\beta}\alpha$) satisfies the interesting formal properties emphasized in Table 3.3.

Root-cutting warrants that not all originally derived rules/beliefs are valid, since the derived rule that was specifically attacked by the *defeating* condition has been deleted. *Success* follows immediately from it. *Inclusion* enables the operator to satisfy conservatism. *Core-retainment* is a version of the minimal change principle applied to a set which is larger than the original. It says that only those norms/beliefs that are somehow responsible for the derivation of the *specifically defeated* norm/belief should be deleted. *Preservation* provides the desired qualification of the original norm/belief with respect to the *confirming* condition (which is the negation of the defeating condition).[60]

The internal refinement operator just qualifies the original norm so that its detachment becomes dependent on the *confirming* condition. The complementary move is to incorporate the challenging rule into the set, which detaches the opposite solution in the presence of the *refuting* condition. The definition of such operator is immediate:

Let Γ be a normative system containing the norm α, let $\beta\Rightarrow\neg\alpha$ be a conflicting norm and # the internal refinement operator. Then, the *global refinement* of Γ by $\beta\Rightarrow\neg\alpha$ (notation $\Gamma\bullet(\beta\Rightarrow\neg\alpha)$) is such that: $\Gamma\bullet(\beta\Rightarrow\neg\alpha)=\Gamma\#_{\beta}\alpha\cup\{\beta\Rightarrow\neg\alpha\}$. If the conflicting norm is already present in the normative system, then global refinement collapses into internal refinement $\Gamma\bullet(\beta\Rightarrow\neg\alpha)=\Gamma\#_{\beta}\alpha$.

2. Applying the refinement operator in a normative system based on a logic of normative propositions

In order to represent inconsistent and incomplete normative systems, Alchourrón's logic of normative propositions (LNP) is such that both normative gaps and contradictions are possible. LNP is built by Alchourrón adding the deontic modalities O and P (respectively for obligation and positive permission) to the language of DFT. Since we are going to use refinement operators there is no need for implicit assumptions related to the antecedent, and we may add the deontic modalities directly to the

[60] For details of the construction of refinement and axiomatic characterization see J. Maranhão, 'Conservative Contraction'. In that paper such results are first provided for any choice Cn^* of the set of consequences of the contracted sentence and then refinement is just a special case where the choice selects only a sentence and its complementary (in the sense there defined). The construction is very abstract and its results hold for any theory in any underlying logic whose conditional satisfies decomposability: for any sentences α there are sentences $w(\alpha)$ and $w'(\alpha)$ such that (i) $\{w(\alpha),w'(\alpha)\}\subseteq\text{Cn}(\alpha)$, and (ii) $\alpha\in\text{Cn}(\{w(\alpha),w'(\alpha)\})$. These properties are satisfied by S5 strict conditionals used by Alchourrón as the basis of his logic of normative propositions LNP and also DFT.

language of the normal modal logic S5. Formation rules avoid iteration of deontic modalities, which are given a descriptive interpretation (Oa (Pa) means that the norm demanding (permitting) a exists in the normative system). S5 is enriched by the following axioms:

A1. $\mathrm{O}(a \wedge b) \Leftrightarrow \mathrm{O}a \wedge \mathrm{O}b$
A2. $\mathrm{O}a \rightarrow \mathrm{P}a$
A3. $\mathrm{P}(a \wedge b) \rightarrow \mathrm{P}a \wedge \mathrm{P}b$

and rules of inference:

R1. from $a \Leftrightarrow b$ derive $\mathrm{O}a \Leftrightarrow \mathrm{O}b$
R2. from $a \Leftrightarrow b$ derive $\mathrm{P}a \Leftrightarrow \mathrm{P}b$

Note that the deontic version of the principle of non-contradiction is not a theorem of the logic of normative propositions. Instead we have a definitional abbreviation for normative inconsistencies: *a is inconsistently regulated*: $(\mathrm{O}\neg a \wedge \mathrm{P}a) \rightarrow \mathrm{In}(a)$.

Now we can represent defeasibility as an authentic procedure of revision of a normative system containing strict conditional rules. Take the system Γ containing R1 ('killers ought to be punished'), i.e. $\Gamma = \{k \Rightarrow \mathrm{O}p\}$. The interpreter takes into account R2 the right of anyone to defend her own life ($d \Rightarrow \mathrm{O}\neg p$) thus considering the property d to be a defeating condition for R1. In LNP we have a normative conflict, i.e. $(k \wedge d) \rightarrow \mathrm{In}(\mathrm{p}) \in Cn(\Gamma)$.

This normative inconsistency is the trigger to the internal refinement of Γ by $k \Rightarrow \mathrm{O}p$ with respect to the refuting factor d which is the result of the choice by the interpreter (here given by the choice function Cn^*).[61] As a result, by the preservation property, we will have that $\neg d \Rightarrow (k \Rightarrow \mathrm{O}p) \in \Gamma \#_d(k \Rightarrow \mathrm{O}p)$ and thus $(k \wedge \neg d) \Rightarrow \mathrm{O}p \in Cn(\Gamma \#_d(k \Rightarrow \mathrm{O}p))$. If R2 is an explicit rule then we have that $k \wedge d \Rightarrow \mathrm{O}\neg p \in Cn(\Gamma \#_d(k \Rightarrow \mathrm{O}p))$, solving the original normative inconsistency. If it is a rule derived from the interpreter's inquiry into the objective reason of the rule then we would use global refinement with the result that $\{k \wedge d \Rightarrow \mathrm{O}\neg p, (k \wedge \neg d) \Rightarrow \mathrm{O}p\} \subseteq Cn(\Gamma \bullet (d \Rightarrow \mathrm{O}\neg p))$, generating a new system where the implicit conflict is accommodated.

Hence, from Γ to $\Gamma \bullet (d \Rightarrow \mathrm{O}\neg p)$ we move from a system with strict conditional rules to another, more refined system of strict conditional rules as a result of a creative intervention of the interpreter who selects a relevant conditional defeating the original rule. This means that the global refinement operator does not present the shortcomings of Alchourrón's contributory conditionals with respect to his own scientific picture, and we have a direct representation of defeasibility as epistemic revisability, independently from any defeasible conditionals or prima facie rules.

We said independently because nothing prevents us from using refinement operators on logics such as DFT with contributory conditionals. Not only strict conditionals, but also contributory ones may be refined with obvious adaptations to the refinement function. In this case we would be able to represent defeasibility as *exception* (by defeasible conditionals) and defeasibility as *qualification* in the same logic.

There are some parallels between refinement and contributory conditionals. It is possible to define an even more conservative, nonmonotonic consequence relation or contributory conditional using refinement on the set of implicit assumptions. As we have seen, *fa* may be seen as a revision of a theory K of implicit assumptions $K{*}a$ and

[61] Note that the presence of a *normative inconsistency* does not mean that the theory of normative propositions itself is inconsistent.

the contributory conditional may be taken as $(\wedge K{*}a) \Rightarrow b$.[62] A parallel construction using global refinement would be $(\wedge K\bullet a) \Rightarrow b$. The main difference is that success doesn't hold for global refinement as in AGM revision, which means that one could not jump to conclusion *b* even in the presence of the antecedent *a* without any conflict with the set of assumptions. The jump would only occur in the presence of the antecedent and the relevant chosen condition (which plays the role of the defeating condition in the representation of defeasibility by refinement; here it should be interpreted differently). To recover the jump in the presence of antecedent we could depart from a contraction $(a \wedge K \div \neg a) \Rightarrow b$, which is equivalent to $(\wedge K{*}a) \Rightarrow b$, and use internal refinement instead, which is a more conservative contraction operator, that is $(a \wedge K\#\neg a) \Rightarrow b$. In its turn, contributory conditionals may be seen as the result of refinement operators where the refining choice function Cn^* chooses as defeating factors exactly the negation of those implicit assumptions associated with the antecedent of the conditional. That is, a conditional $(\wedge K{*}a) \Rightarrow b$ would be the result of $\Gamma\#_{\neg(\wedge K)}(a \Rightarrow b)$. So, while contributory conditionals are defeasible conditionals resulting from revision, the internal refinement operator shows exactly what sort of modification of the original system took place to result in a system with more refined conditionals (strict or contributory).

F. A few final words

Alchourrón's convictions about the role of science, in particular the science of the law as descriptive of general norms, led him to view defeasibility as susceptibility to change. Therefore, the formal approach he considered philosophically sound to defeasibility involved the qualification of general conditionals by means of a revision operator. Since he was also convinced that within such formal representation nothing is gained and nothing is lost with regard to the use of nonmonotonic consequence relations, then, he argued, we should take the philosophically sound approach of defeasibility as qualification. Unfortunately, as we have seen here, his formalization, although intended to keep track of the revision process, was just another defeasible conditional more congenial to the inferential conception of defeasibility than to the epistemic conception.

Peczenik has argued instead that logics of defeasible argumentation are philosophically sound to represent legal reasoning.[63] His point is that such logics constitute an adequate representation of the dialectics of advancing arguments for and against a claim, the weighing and balancing of reasons, as well as decisions that jump to conclusions based on general norms and presumptions concerning the facts of the case. Some also believe that this model is incapable of giving an account of the allocation of the *onus of proof*, which is considered essential to the defeasible nature of legal argumentation.

My impression about this debate is that none of the contenders are right, or there should actually be no conflict at all. Maybe the logics of defeasible argumentation better illustrate a process that is focused on reasoning about the instantiation of general norms to particular facts, where the *onus of proof* organizes the arguments for and against a certain claim and allows us to jump to a conclusion (if a claim is not challenged by a counterargument). This is one side of the coin in legal reasoning. But whatever the result of such argumentation, a certain normative solution is justified given some facts that were considered relevant in the process. If new facts are considered relevant so as to

[62] Obviously by $\wedge K{*}a$ we mean the conjunction of the elements of a finite axiomatization of $K{*}a$.

[63] A. Peczenik, 'Jumps and Logic in the Law'.

open an exception to the general norm present in the normative system, this means that the decision can only be justified if a certain change occurs in the normative system. Such reasoning about the underlying justificatory system is the other side of the coin of legal reasoning, which is better represented by the logics of epistemic change.

As remarked above, nothing hinders the representation of both sides of the coin if we use refinement operators on the sentences of Alchourrón's logic DFT. Recent research has also explored the use of revision operators on logics of defeasible argumentation.[64] Just as legal arguers may be contending on a solution for a particular case, they may also be searching for the best legal system, where the preferred solution in that dispute corresponds to an immediate detachment of the refined system. And each norm of the system, or legal system as a whole, may be the result of an argumentation about the validity grounds or its moral adequacy. The interplay between systemic revision and argumentation seems to be a fruitful ground for future research on legal defeasibility.

[64] M. Falappa, G. Kern-Isberner, and G. Simari, 'Belief Revision and Argumentation Theory' in G. Simari and I. Rahwan (eds), *Argumentation in Artificial Intelligence* (Dordrecht: Springer, 2009).

4

Is Defeasibility an Essential Property of Law?

*Frederick Schauer**

Defeasibility is widespread in law. Lawmakers are not omniscient, and accordingly cannot reliably foresee what the future will bring. Situations will thus arise that were not anticipated, and often could not have been anticipated by even the best of lawmakers. This imperfect view of the future is part of the human condition, and as a consequence legal rules, if literally or faithfully followed, will sometimes generate outcomes that are absurd, silly, unfair, unjust, inefficient, or in some other way suboptimal. When such unfortunate consequences occur as a result of the inevitable over- and under-inclusiveness of rules,[1] advanced legal systems commonly provide a mechanism by which legal decision-makers may ameliorate the harsh consequences of necessarily coarse rules. But is it necessary that legal systems do so? Is a legal system that fails to do so not a legal system at all, or less of a legal system, or a defective legal system, because of that failure? To put the question directly, is defeasibility necessary to legality? I have argued previously that the defeasibility of legal rules does not necessarily follow from the defeasibility of language,[2] but even if my argument is sound, defeasibility may still emerge as the necessary consequence not of the nature of language, and not of the nature of rules, but of the nature of law. But does it? Is global defeasibility—the defeasibility of all of the rules of a legal system—an essential component of any non-defective legal system? That is the question that motivates this paper.

I

There are many varieties of defeasibility, and I will leave to others the task of analysing and distinguishing among them in greater detail.[3] Nevertheless, a quick overview of the central idea of defeasibility will usefully provide the prelude for what is to follow.

Historically speaking, we can trace the principle of defeasibility to Plato. In the *Statesman* he offered the reader a conversation between Socrates and the Eleatic Stranger in which the Stranger identifies the inevitable and (to him) undesirable imperfection of general rules:

* David and Mary Harrison Distinguished Professor of Law, University of Virginia. This paper was prepared for the Symposium on Legal Defeasibility held at Oriel College, Oxford, on 8–9 March 2008, and the final version has benefited greatly from the comments of the other participants on that occasion.

1 On the under- and over-inclusiveness of rules, see L. Alexander and E. Sherwin, *The Rule of Rules: Morality, Rules, and the Dilemmas of Law* (Durham, North Carolina: Duke University Press, 2001); F. Schauer, *Playing By the Rules: A Philosophical Examination of Rule-Based Decision-Making in Law and in Life* (Oxford: Clarendon Press, 1991).

2 F. Schauer, 'On the Supposed Defeasibility of Legal Rules', *Current Legal Problems* (M.D.A. Freeman, ed.), 48 (1998), 223–40.

3 A valuable introduction to such an enterprise would be W. Sinnott-Armstrong, *Moral Dilemmas* (Oxford: Blackwell, 1986), usefully distinguishing among overriding, defeating, excluding, and other forms of defeasibility.

[L]aw can never issue an injunction binding on all which really embodies what is best for each: it cannot prescribe with perfect accuracy what is good and right for each member of the community at any one time. The differences of human personality, the variety of men's activities and the inevitable unsettlement attending all human experience make it impossible for any art whatsoever to issue unqualified rules holding good on all questions at all times.[4]

Yet although general laws can thus not guarantee the correct outcome on all occasions, the Stranger recognizes that governance nevertheless requires that general rules be employed:

[T]he legislator who has to preside over the herd... will lay down laws in general form for the majority, roughly meeting the cases of individuals... under average circumstances.[5]

For the Stranger, however, the necessity of governing by the use of general laws does not entail acceptance of the poor outcomes that the generality of laws will sometimes produce precisely by virtue of their generality. When such outcomes do arise, he argues, it would be 'absurd', 'evil', 'ridiculous', 'a disgrace', and an 'injustice' not to provide the necessary correction in each case, and 'nothing would be more unjust' than to fail to do so.[6]

Although Plato in the *Statesman* provided us with the first discussion of the alleged necessity of providing justice-based correction for the flawed outcomes that are inevitably and occasionally produced by general rules, justice-based correction for rule-driven errors is an idea that we now associate most commonly with Aristotle. In the *Nicomachean Ethics* Aristotle too identified the way in which laws by virtue of their generality were incapable of inevitably reaching the best result in every instance, and thus he explained why to him it was necessary that there be 'a rectification of law in so far as law is defective on account of its generality'.[7] This rectification is what Aristotle called *equity*, and Aristotle's claim was not simply that equitable correction of legal mistakes is useful or desirable—rather, Aristotle insisted that equitable correction was compelled by the very idea of justice:

The explanation of this is that all law is universal, and there are some things about which it is not possible to pronounce rightly in general terms; therefore in cases where it is necessary to make a general pronouncement, but impossible to do so rightly, the law takes account of the majority of cases, though not unaware that in this way errors are made. And the law is none the less right; because the error lies not in the law nor in the legislator, but in the nature of the case; for the raw material of human behaviour is essentially of this kind. So when the law states a general rule, and a case arises under this that is exceptional, then it is right, where the legislator owing to the generality of his language has erred in not covering the case, to correct the omission by a ruling such as the legislator himself would have given if he had been present there, and as he would have enacted if he had been aware of the circumstances...

This is why equity, although just, and better than a kind of justice, is not better than absolute justice—only than the error due to generalization.[8]

Aristotle's remarks about equity in the *Nicomachean Ethics* are by no means chance or offhand, for he says much the same thing in the *Rhetoric*:

[4] Plato, *Statesman* 294a–b (J.B. Skemp trans., Bristol, England: Bristol Classical Press, 1952).
[5] Ibid.
[6] Ibid. at 295d–e.
[7] Aristotle, *Nicomachean Ethics* 1137a–b (J.A.K. Thomson trans., Harmondsworth, England: Penguin, 1977).
[8] Ibid.

For that which is equitable seems to be just, and equity is justice that goes beyond the written law. These omissions are sometimes involuntary, sometimes voluntary, on the part of the legislators; involuntary when it may have escaped their notice; voluntary when, being unable to define for all cases, they are obliged to make a universal statement, which is not applicable to all, but only to most, cases; and whenever it is difficult to give a definition owing to the infinite number of cases . . . for life would not be long enough to reckon all the possibilities. If then no exact definition is possible, but legislation is necessary, one must have recourse to general terms.[9]

This is not the place to recount in detail the subsequent history of equitable correction, a history that includes the writings of Cicero in the *Laws*, the development of *aequitas* in Roman law and the power of the Praetors in Rome, and the growth of the courts of equity and then the emergence of a distinctive law of equity in England.[10] And the principal reason for not labouring over the history here is that all of these subsequent developments are variations on the basic theme that we have inherited from Plato and Aristotle—legal rules by virtue of their intrinsic generality will sometimes produce wrong answers, and it is possible for a legal system to create mechanisms and institutions whose job is to correct those wrong answers. When such mechanisms are in place, and thus when individuals and institutions have the power to correct the recalcitrant experiences that are the inevitable consequence of general rules, we can say that the rules of the system are defeasible. Legal rules might be defeated, and good outcomes substituted for rule-generated bad ones, when on a particular occasion faithful application of the rules themselves would otherwise produce the wrong answer.[11]

Defeasibility can be institutionalized in any number of ways. Among the most familiar is the one we have inherited from Aristotle, then Cicero, and then the English, the mechanism by virtue of which some person or institution—the chancellor, for example—has the authority to correct law's mistakes when those mistakes would work an injustice. This is what has traditionally been called 'equity', but the issues are complicated. Initially there is the question of whose job it is to do equity. As equity arose in England, for example, the power to make an equitable correction was separated from the power to enforce, apply, and even interpret the law. Residing originally with the chancellor, and then with jurisdictionally separate courts of equity, the power of

[9] Aristotle, *The 'Art' of Rhetoric* 1374a (J.H. Freese trans., Cambridge, Mass.: Harvard University Press, 1947).

[10] Some of this history is recounted in F. Schauer, *Profiles, Probabilities, and Stereotypes* (Cambridge, Mass.: Harvard University Press, 2003), ch. 2.

[11] I distinguish defeasibility from two different forms of *revisability*. Sometimes when the individual or institution that first made the rule perceives the rule producing a poor outcome, the rulemaker will use this new knowledge to amend, qualify, rewrite, repeal, or otherwise revise the rule. In addition, when the rulemaker has the power both to make a rule and then to apply it, as is often the case with common law decision-making, the occasion of a potentially bad outcome will lead the applier of the rule to rewrite it or remake it in the process of application. Both of these forms of revisability, and especially the latter, can be understood as species of defeasibility, but for purposes of clarity I limit my discussion of defeasibility here to the situation in which the applier of a rule putatively takes the occasion of application not to revise the rule, but instead to make an exception for just the case at hand. In this pure case of defeasibility, the original rule persists in largely unrevised form, save the specific exception that is made for exactly this case. It should thus be apparent that this form of defeasibility is largely a potential characteristic of rules with crisp canonical formulations. When no such canonical formulation exists, either because the rule is vague or because it is a common law rule whose revisability is understood, the interesting questions about defeasibility do not arise. It is no accident that all of the classic examples of defeasibility, some of which will be discussed below, arise in the context of statutes or statute-like regulations. The question of defeasibility is the question whether such statutes should be treated as if they were court made common law rules (see G. Calabresi, *A Common Law for the Age of Statutes* (Cambridge, Mass. : Harvard University Press, 1982), and obviously *that* question does not arise with common law rules themselves.

equitable correction, by being distinct from the law, was not inconsistent with the non-defeasibility of legal rules. The legal rules might work an injustice, but from the perspective *of the law* (in the strict sense, and *not* including courts of equity), there was nothing to be done about it. And in this sense the rules of the law were not defeasible, even though the power of defeat—of equitable override—was granted within an institution that, more broadly, was part of the legal system.

Over time, however, the institution of equity as a discrete system of separate courts and separate procedures has withered in most common law countries. Equity still exists, more or less, but courts of equity and distinct equity-focused institutions and procedures are becoming extinct, even though they have not fully become so yet. But even with the decline of distinct equity jurisdiction and procedure, and arguably because of that decline, common law courts still routinely exercise the power of equitable override, and this is the central form of defeasibility. When application of the law—whether a statute or a common law rule with a widely shared formulation—will produce an unjust result, common law courts often retain or claim the power to set aside the rule or the statute in the service of justice.[12] Sometimes this process of setting aside the rule will be conceptualized as adding an exception to the existing rule,[13] and so Richard Posner has claimed that courts *always* (the word is crucial) retain the ability to add 'ad hoc exceptions' to existing and exceptionless rules.[14] And Posner's claim is virtually identical to Hart's that not only can a rule with an 'unless' clause still be a rule, but also that the list of 'unlesses' cannot be exhaustively specified in advance.[15] Richard Tur's position is similar to Hart's and Posner's, for he too insists that treating rules as defeasible is not merely desirable or useful, and not merely common, but is an essential component of a well-functioning—non-defective—legal system.

There are two qualifications that need to be noted here. First, the power of equitable override—of equity-driven defeasibility—will collapse into a rule-free system of equity if the standards for an equitable override are not higher than the simple fact of the existing rule producing an unjust result. If *any* injustice is a sufficient condition for an equitable override, then a regime of rules subject to equitable override is extensionally equivalent to a regime of no rules at all in which the decision-makers are empowered simply to reach the most just all-things-considered outcome.[16] And the same can be said if we substitute efficiency, utility maximization, fairness, or anything else in the foregoing formula. In order for the rules to do the work that rules are expected to do—provide predictability, stability, and constraint on decision-makers—the standard for equitable override of a rule-produced mistake must be one of *extreme* injustice, or *great* inefficiency, or something of that variety. If defeasibility implicitly incorporates the necessity of the standard for defeat being higher than the standard sufficient for the same considerations to have indicated a result in the absence of a rule, then rules will still have a role to play, but the outcomes the rules indicate will be presumptive and not

[12] See R.H.S. Tur, 'Defeasibilism', OJLS 21 (2001), 355–68. More qualified but to the same general effect is N. MacCormick, 'Defeasibility in Law and Logic' in Z. Bankowski, I. White, and U. Hahn (eds), *Informatics and the Foundations of Legal Reasoning* (Dordrecht: Kluwer, 1995), 99–157.

[13] See A.C. Aman, Jr, 'Administrative Equity: An Analysis of Exceptions to Administrative Rules', *Duke Law Journal*, 2 (1982), 277–331.

[14] R.A. Posner, 'The Jurisprudence of Skepticism', *Michigan Law Review*, 86 (1988), 834–5.

[15] H.L.A. Hart, *The Concept of Law* (2nd edn, P.A. Bulloch and J. Raz, eds, Oxford: Clarendon Press, 1994), 136. See also N. MacCormick, 'Law as Institutional Fact', LQR 90 (1974), 102–26.

[16] See F. Schauer, 'Exceptions', *University of Chicago Law Review*, 58 (1991), 871–904; F. Schauer, 'Is the Common Law Law?' *California Law Review*, 77 (1989), 455–71.

absolute, with the presumption capable of being overridden when the injustice or inefficiency or other suboptimality of the rule-indicated outcome is sufficiently extreme.

Second, it is important to note the difference between a rule that is changed because of a recalcitrant event and a rule that remains unchanged even if the recalcitrant event is dealt with by some form of avoiding the rule-generated, erroneous outcome. When a rule requiring drivers to drive no faster than 60 miles per hour is overridden by the necessity for some driver of rushing an injured person to the hospital, for example, the rule remains unchanged. But when an unexpected event occasions a *revision* of a rule,[17] as is often the case in the common law, the revised rule is not the same as the rule that existed prior to the revision. It may be unique to the common law—or at least definitional of common law method—that rules can be revised in the process of application, but when and how that occurs is not my primary focus here. Nevertheless, it is important to note that changing a rule in order to avoid an erroneous outcome is different from overriding a rule in order to avoid an erroneous outcome, even though both can be understood as forms of defeasibility.

II

The key to the idea of defeasibility, therefore, is the potential for some applier, interpreter, or enforcer of a rule to make an ad hoc or spur-of-the-moment adaptation in order to avoid a suboptimal, inefficient, unfair, unjust, or otherwise unacceptable, rule-generated outcome. Sometimes the method of adaptation may be an equitable override by the same or another institution, sometimes it will be the power to engraft a new exception to a rule in order to prevent a bad outcome, and sometimes it will be the modification of a rule at the moment of its application.[18] At times, and especially as championed by Ronald Dworkin, avoidance of a poor outcome indicated by the most immediately applicable legal rules will be clothed in the language of locating the 'real' rule lying beneath what had only superficially seemed to be the applicable rule.[19] But whatever the method, and whatever the language in which it is described, the consequences are plain: what would have been a poor result had the rule been faithfully followed is avoided by treating the rule as defeasible in the service of larger values of reasonableness, justice, efficiency, common sense, fairness, or any of a number of other measures by which a particular outcome might be deemed deficient.[20]

[17] And see n. 12 above.

[18] I set aside a soft form of defeasibility in which the rule is held to apply, but the sanction for its violation is substantially or totally ameliorated. This approach is the one championed by the mythical Justice Truepenny in Lon Fuller's legendary 'The Case of the Speluncean Explorers', *Harvard Law Review*, 62 (1949), 616–45, and is usefully compared with the opinion of Fuller's own alter ego, Justice Foster, who comes much closer to the idea of genuine defeasibility and who would simply have held the rule not to have applied in that case.

[19] R. Dworkin, *Law's Empire* (Cambridge, Mass.: Harvard University Press, 1986), 16–17. Dworkin's approach sows the seeds of confusion, however, to the extent that he wants to incorporate into the very definition of a rule or statute the full corpus of his entire theory of legal interpretation. Far better is to distinguish what a rule *says* from what it will be understood to *do*, and we can make great gains in clarity by avoiding Dworkin's attempt to collapse this distinction.

[20] 'Faithfully' is perhaps too loaded a term here, and 'literally' might be better, as long as we assume that literal application of a legal rule can include uncontroversial technical meaning and uncontroversial application of subsidiary principles of interpretation.

There is no doubt that defeasible rules are ubiquitous in law. Richard Tur provides numerous examples from English law,[21] and the American legal system furnishes far more.[22] Perhaps most famous these days is *Riggs* v. *Palmer*,[23] a case whose fame is substantially due to Dworkin's efforts, although extended treatment of the case can also be found in the canonical Hart and Sacks materials on the Legal Process.[24] The facts of *Riggs* are well known—Elmer Palmer poisoned his grandfather so as to prevent him from changing his will and consequently eliminating Elmer's legacy—but the important thing to understand is that *Riggs* was not a hard case under the relevant statute. In both the majority opinion of Judge Earl and the dissenting opinion of Judge Gray in *Riggs*, the New York Statute of Wills was understood to be clear—Elmer Palmer was entitled to inherit under the will even though he had murdered the testator. Thus it was the tension between what the statute plainly said and what justice appeared to demand that made *Riggs* a hard case, but it is crucial to distinguish cases like *Riggs*, in which the most obviously applicable legal rule gives an answer but it is a bad one, from cases in which the rules give no answer at all.

When the New York Court of Appeals concluded in *Riggs* that Elmer Palmer could not inherit because of the maxim that 'no man shall profit from his own wrong', it is best understood as having treated the most immediately applicable legal rule as defeasible in the service of justice. It is true that the 'no man may profit from his own wrong' principle is narrower than the full domain of justice, but there are few dimensions of justice—probably no dimensions of justice—that are not instantiated by some common law principle. Although the New York Court of Appeals drew on a concrete legal principle somewhat narrower than justice *simpliciter*, it is most plausibly understood as simply having avoided a potentially unjust outcome by concluding that legal rules are generally defeasible in the service of justice. Much the same conclusion follows when the result that a legal rule generates appears to be unreasonable or ridiculous, even if the nature of the bad outcome is not best described in terms of injustice. In *United States* v. *Kirby*,[25] for example, the defendant was a Kentucky law enforcement officer who had been convicted under a federal law making it a crime to interfere with the delivery of the mail. And that is exactly what Kirby had done. He had unquestionably interfered with the delivery of the mail, but he had done so in the process of boarding a steamboat to arrest a mail carrier named Farris who had been validly indicted for murder by a Kentucky court. The case reached the Supreme Court, where the Court treated the statute as defeasible, holding that it should not be applied where the outcome it literally indicated was inconsistent with the purpose of the statute, inconsistent with common sense, and inconsistent with justice.

If we depart from the realm of the real and enter the domain of the hypothetical, we see the same phenomenon captured in Lon Fuller's famous response to Hart's example of the rule prohibiting vehicles from the park.[26] As is well known, Hart suggested that

[21] See n. 12 above.

[22] I say 'far more' because it is widely believed that legal rules are even more defeasible under American law and practice than they are in Great Britain. See P.S. Atiyah and R.S. Summers, *Form and Substance in Anglo-American Law: A Comparative Study in Legal Reasoning, Legal Theory and Legal Institutions* (Oxford: Clarendon Press, 1987). See also N. MacCormick and R.S. Summers, *Interpreting Statutes: A Comparative Study* (London: Ashgate, 1991).

[23] 22 N.E. 188 (N.Y. 1889).

[24] H.M. Hart, Jr and A.M. Sacks, *The Legal Process: Basic Problems in the Making and Application of Law* (W.N. Eskridge, Jr and P.P. Frickey (eds), Westbury, NY: Foundation Press, 1991), 60–102.

[25] 74 U.S. (7 Wall.) 482 (1868).

[26] L.L. Fuller, 'Positivism and Fidelity to Law—A Reply to Professor Hart', *Harvard Law Review*, 71 (1958), 630–72; H.L.A. Hart, 'Positivism and the Separation of Law and Morals', *Harvard Law*

bicycles, roller skates, and toy automobiles might represent hard cases in the penumbra of such a rule, and thus would be, for him, cases in which the exercise of (legal)[27] discretion was inevitable. These penumbral cases were to be contrasted, Hart maintained, with the straightforward core cases in which the language of rule dictated the outcome, as with, Hart suggested, cases involving ordinary automobiles. But Fuller responded with the hypothetical example of a group of patriots who installed a fully functional military truck in the park as a war memorial. This would clearly be a vehicle, Fuller argued,[28] but just as clearly would it be ridiculous to exclude it from the park on the authority of the 'no vehicles in the park' rule.

As legions of examples resembling *Riggs* and *Kirby* illustrate, Fuller may well have had the best of the empirical argument. That is, if Hart is understood as claiming that the plain meaning of the terms of a rule actually provided a conclusive answer in most or all real cases in real legal systems, and if Fuller is understood as responding that the answer provided by the plain meaning was typically defeasible and never conclusive in well-functioning legal systems, then Fuller's claim appears to be closer to American reality, and possibly closer to the reality in some number of other modern legal systems. Insofar as Fuller was implicitly arguing that American law allowed and possibly even required legal interpreters to prefer the answer indicated by a rule's purpose to the answer indicated by the rule's language when the two came into conflict, he was almost certainly correct.[29]

But Fuller also made a broader claim. For Fuller, it was not merely a contingent empirical matter that legal rules were always or at least typically (and preferably) defeasible in common law legal systems, but also that the defeasibility of legal rules was an essential feature of legality itself, a necessary component of any non-defective legal system, and thus on a par with the other *desiderata* of legality that for Fuller came pretty close to defining law—or at least the ideal of legality—itself.[30] For Fuller, failing to treat a rule like the no-vehicles-in-the-park rule as defeasible was simply to abandon reason, and for Fuller it was of the essence of law that it be reasonable. A system that did not allow purpose-based or reason-based or equitable overrides of the plain indications of a legal rule when necessary to achieve a reasonable outcome was for that reason just so much less of a *legal* system, and perhaps was not even a genuine legal system at all. Indeed, we can understand Fuller's claim in the best light, and without saddling him

Review, 71 (1958), 608–15. See also F. Schauer, 'A Critical Guide to Vehicles in the Park', *New York University Law Review*, 83 (2008), 1109–34.

[27] Hart would not have maintained that all answers were equally good, for he properly recognized that even in the area of legal discretion some answers would be better than others as a matter of policy, morality, politics, or any other legally legitimate but not legally mandated source of non-legal guidance.

[28] Actually he didn't, but he should have. Occasionally in the grip of a radically contextual view of language and meaning, Fuller hinted that maybe the truck/statue was not a vehicle at all. This not only displays a mistaken view about language, but undercuts his own point, for the power of the example for Fuller's purposes resides precisely in the fact that the truck/statue whose exclusion from the park under this rule would be absurd *is* a vehicle, and *is* literally encompassed by the rule.

[29] Hart did later acknowledge that legal systems might well understand the core of a rule in such a purpose-driven way. H.L.A. Hart, 'Preface' in *Essays in Jurisprudence and Philosophy* (Oxford: Clarendon Press, 1983), 8. But this seeming concession is not much of a concession at all, because it simply takes the debate one level back, and that is because we can imagine that even serving the purpose behind a particular rule might produce an outcome inconsistent with the purpose behind the purpose, or with an all-things-considered conception of justice. And at this level there is no reason to suppose that the basic dispute between Hart and Fuller would not still have existed. See F. Schauer, 'Formalism', *Yale Law Journal*, 97 (1988), 509–48.

[30] L.L. Fuller, *The Morality of Law* (revised edn, New Haven, Connecticut: Yale University Press, 1969).

with the view that non-defeasible law is not law at all,[31] by interpreting him as maintaining that non-defeasible law is necessarily *defective* as law, even if the defective law is still law. Just as *any* boat that leaks is defective as a boat even as it remains a boat, so Fuller is best understood as insisting that any legal system is necessarily defective as a legal system, and as law, insofar as it treats its rules as non-defeasible.

III

In evaluating the claim that defeasibility is an essential property of the ideal (or the idea) of legality, we should set the stage by making clear that we can understand what a non-defeasible rule would look like, and how it would operate. As the very existence of a dissent makes clear, it was hardly necessary or obvious that Elmer Palmer should lose in *Riggs* v. *Palmer*. The New York Court of Appeals *could* have said that Palmer would inherit despite the wrong he committed, just as the United States Supreme Court could have concluded that Kirby violated federal law even though he did it for good reason, and even though punishing someone like Kirby was inconsistent with the purpose of the law he literally violated. And some hypothetical judge could conclude that a war memorial made from a functioning military truck was nevertheless a vehicle, and consequently excluded from the park by virtue of the literal meaning of the no-vehicles-in-the-park rule. Such a result might have been condemned as ridiculous, absurd, or, in what is perhaps an even worse condemnation these days, *formalistic*, but that outcome would not have been a conceptual or linguistic impossibility. As long as we accept that words have plain or literal meanings and that those meanings have a context-independent core, and thus as long as we reject (as Fuller did not) the notion that the meaning of a word is entirely a function of the particular context in which it is used on a particular occasion, then we can see that rules—which are written in words—can indeed generate poor outcomes, and we can see that some judge might in fact issue a ruling consistent with that poor outcome.[32]

Indeed, not only can this happen, but in fact it does happen—and with some frequency. Perhaps most dramatic is the fact that *Riggs* v. *Palmer* turns out to be more exceptional than normal, even in the highly anti-formal American judicial system. Although there are other cases in which the outcomes resemble those in *Riggs*, there are also many in which beneficiaries who were in some way or another culpably responsible for the death of the testator were allowed to inherit.[33] In other cases applications of

[31] It is difficult to situate Fuller within the 'bad law is no law at all' tradition, a tradition exemplified by Blackstone and Cicero, but not Aquinas. See generally P. Soper, 'In Defense of Classical Natural Law Theory: Why Unjust Law is No Law at All', *Canadian Journal of Law and Jurisprudence*, 20 (2007), 201–23. Fuller was plainly sympathetic to the view that widespread failure to follow the dimensions of procedural legality he outlined would produce a system not properly called a legal system at all, but with respect to individual components of legality, such as defeasibility, he would more likely have described legal systems without them as defective legal systems than as not being legal systems at all.

[32] I recognize that in some circles this would be considered a controversial (or simply wrong) position, but this is not the place to belabour the standard responses to post-modern theories of meaning. Suffice it to say that without the ability of words to have a contextual or trans-contextual meaning, it is hard to see how we could understand each other, and even harder to explain the compositional nature of language, our ability to understand sentences we have never heard before. We know, absent any context, that 'the cat is on the mat' is about cats and not dogs, mats and not ponds, and about a relationship captured by the word 'on' that is different from the relationship suggested by 'near', 'next to', and 'under'.

[33] Many of them are described in F. Schauer, 'The Limited Domain of the Law', *Virginia Law Review*, 90 (2004), 1909–56.

statutes with arguably suboptimal policy consequences were allowed to stand, as in *Tennessee Valley Authority* v. *Hill*,[34] in which a literal application of the Endangered Species Act mandated the preservation of the habitat of a small, unattractive, and ecologically unimportant fish called the snail darter, even at great cost to the aggregate public welfare as a result of the blocking of an important public works project. And in *United States* v. *Locke*,[35] a statute setting a filing deadline of 'prior to December 31' was upheld even when it resulted in the arguably unfair exclusion of a claim filed on December 31 by someone who assumed, not unreasonably, that the statute really meant to say 'on or prior to December 31'.

Numerous other cases fit this mould, both in the United States and elsewhere, and thus it would be a mistake to describe the defeasibility of legal rules as a universal or even overwhelmingly common feature of decision-making by judges and by the institution we commonly call a 'legal system'. Although legal decision-makers indeed commonly do treat the rules with which they deal as defeasible, just as commonly they do not. They treat the literal or plain language of a rule formulation as conclusive, and thus refrain from adding exceptions at the moment of application, from overriding the indications of the rule in the service of justice or equity or fairness or efficiency, and from modifying the rules at the moment of application. Putting aside for the moment the question whether such non-defeasibility is wise, it is at the very least possible, and indeed it is widespread. Rule formulations have meanings that are distinct from the purposes or background justifications lying behind the rules and are distinct from what the best (or even a good) rule-free outcome in some particular instance would have been. Rules are defeasible to the extent that such rule formulations may be changed at the moment of application for any of a number of reasons, but examples like those above, and countless others, show that rules are often applied as written—treated as non-defeasible—even when what seem to be valid defeating conditions are present. In the contemporary debates about jurisprudential methodology, it is sometimes claimed that identifying the essential features of the concept of law is largely or entirely a descriptive matter, albeit one that for some theorists requires identifying law's 'function or purpose'.[36] From this perspective defeasibility would be an essential property of the concept of law, or of a non-defective legal system, if it were ubiquitous in modern legal systems, and if we could scarcely imagine a legal system without it. But it turns out that neither is the case, and as a descriptive matter it is hard to defend the position that a legal system without widespread and legitimate defeasibility is for that reason not a legal system at all, or is a legal system but necessarily a defective one.

IV

That legal rules are often treated as non-defeasible does not mean that such a course is a wise one. Not does it mean that such a course is consistent with legality in the deeper

[34] 437 U.S. 153 (1978). The case is described and criticized by Dworkin in *Law's Empire*, 20–3.

[35] 471 U.S. 84 (1985). The decision has often been criticized. See, for example, R. Posner, 'Legal Formalism, Legal Realism, and the Interpretation of Statutes and the Constitution', *Case Western Reserve Law Review*, 37 (1986), 179–217; N.S. Zeppos, 'Legislative History and the Interpretation of Statutes: Toward a Fact-Finding Model of Statutory Interpretation', *Virginia Law Review*, 76 (1990), 1314–16. For a rare defence, see F. Schauer, 'The Practice and Problems of Plain Meaning', *Vanderbilt Law Review*, 45 (1992), 715–41.

[36] See, for example, J.L. Coleman, 'Incorporationism, Conventionality, and the Practical Difference Thesis', *Legal Theory*, 4 (1998), 387–95; J. Raz, 'On the Nature of Law', *Archiv für Rechts- und Sozialphilosophie*, 82 (1996), 1–25.

and richer sense, and it is that question that we must now take up. Although legal decision-makers often treat legal rules as non-defeasible, are they right to do so, or is every example of failure to do so also a failure of legality?

The arguments for rules are not unfamiliar, and most of the arguments for rules in general are arguments for treating rules as non-defeasible. If, for example, we (the designers of some decision-making environment) are wary of discretion, and distrustful of judges and other legal decision-makers who might be biased, corrupt, incompetent, ill-equipped for the job, or just very rushed, then we might want to constrain them by rules rather than granting wide discretion. Moreover, when the reasons for constraining decision-makers by rules are at their most powerful, we might not even trust the decision-makers to decide when some application of a rule is ridiculous or absurd, let alone unfair, inequitable, unjust, or inefficient.[37] It is easy to say that it would be absurd to exclude the truck used as a war memorial from the park, but the real question is whether and when some class of officials should be empowered to decide which applications are absurd and which are not. Moreover, rules also serve to allocate decision-making responsibility and therefore effectuate the separation of powers, in the non-technical sense of that term. To treat a rule as non-defeasible, therefore, is simply to decide that some but not other officials will have the power to cancel, override, amend, or modify an existing rule. And insofar as rules also bring the advantages of certainty, predictability, settlement, and stability for stability's sake, treating the rules as defeasible comes at the sacrifice of each of these values, even though of course it brings the potential advantages of fairness, equity, and, in theory, reaching the correct result in every instance.

Thus, once we recognize that it is linguistically and conceptually possible for there to be non-defeasible rules, the inquiry shifts to one about the advantages and disadvantages of treating rules as defeasible. To treat rules as non-defeasible is to accept the possibility—indeed, the virtual certainty over time—of some number of unjust or otherwise erroneous outcomes in particular cases, but that is endemic to the Rule of Law generally. Unless the Rule of Law is simply a synonym for reaching the best all-things-considered outcome, any addition of procedural values, or considerations of stability for stability's sake, or constraints on the decision-maker's discretion—and these are precisely what differentiates the Rule of Law from simply doing the right thing—will also commit the legal system to some number of suboptimal outcomes. And once we recognize this, it turns out that the difference between the non-defeasibility of legal rules and the Rule of Law more generally is simply a matter of degree. Non-defeasibility takes things to an extreme, but it is an extreme broadly consistent with the very idea of the Rule of Law itself.

From this perspective, it becomes apparent that the traditional defences of the necessary defeasibility of legal rules—whether Hart's, or Posner's, or Tur's—mostly rest on a certain view about the powers and abilities of judges. Few people would maintain that police officers, for example, or ordinary bureaucrats, ought to have the power to revise the rules that constrain them when those rules appear to indicate a poor outcome in a particular case. And if that is so, then the view that defeasibility in the hands of judges is required by the Rule of Law while defeasibility in the hands of others is not turns out to be a view about the capacities of judges within particular legal systems. But although it is tempting to celebrate judicial reason in advanced common law legal systems—Lord Coke's glorification of the powers of judges and the artificial

[37] See J. Manning, 'The Absurdity Doctrine', *Harvard Law Review*, 116 (2003), 2387–462.

reason of the law pervades the common law consciousness centuries after Coke's death—it should be relatively non-controversial that this kind of confidence in judicial wisdom is hardly a universal characteristic of every legal system. So long as we can imagine something properly called a legal system in which the power of rule revision and rule override is not entrusted to judges, then we can imagine something properly called a legal system in which defeasibility is somewhat or even largely (as, for example, Jeremy Bentham would have preferred) absent. Moreover, even if we take the position that specifying the central features of the concept of law is at least partially and perhaps largely a normative enterprise,[38] it is far from clear that defeasibility is so plainly normatively desirable in all places and at all times that we should consider it an essential part of the concept of law itself.

V

One less obvious implication of the foregoing is that defeasibility is not a property of rules at all, but rather a characteristic of how some decision-making system will choose to *treat* its rules. The Wittgensteinian maxim that rules do not determine their own applications has become trite, but it reminds us that how a rule will be treated is not something that is inherent in the rule itself. Indulging again the assumption (and belief) that the plain or literal (but not necessarily the ordinary-language) meaning of a rule can indicate an outcome, it is a function not of the rule but of how the rule will be treated whether that indicated outcome is to be taken as conclusive, presumptive, or even, at the extreme, as having no weight in itself, being but a totally transparent (to its background justification, or to the all-things-considered best outcome) heuristic or rule of thumb. The question of defeasibility is not a question about what is *in* a rule, but is rather a question about how what is in a rule, or about how what a rule says, is to be treated, and this is not, and can never be, something that can be determined by the rule itself.

Although it is possible that how the rules of a legal system will be treated will be a function of yet further rules, it might be a useful shortcut to think of the determination of how the indications of a rule are to be treated as a component of the Hartian ultimate rule of recognition. And as such, it is a question of fact and not of law, although what this component of the Hartian rule of recognition *should* be might also be the subject of normative debate, in which the grounds of the debate would necessarily be philosophical, moral, political, and much else, but not themselves legal.

The question of defeasibility is thus exposed as a descriptive and prescriptive one, but not a logical or conceptual one. It is logically and conceptually possible for rules to be interpreted, understood, applied, and enforced according to the literal meaning of the component language of their formulations. Whether in this or that legal system they are in fact so treated is a descriptive question and, it turns out, as the few examples above illustrate, that as a descriptive matter defeasibility is less universal in actual legal systems than we might have thought, even in the legal systems in which we might have most expected it to exist.

With respect to the prescriptive question, whether the literal meaning of a rule formulation will be treated as what the rule indicates, and whether what the rule

[38] See, for example, S. Perry, 'Hart's Methodological Positivism' in J. Coleman (ed.), *Hart's Postscript: Commentaries on the Postscript to The Concept of Law* (Oxford: Clarendon Press, 2001), 311–54. See also R. Dworkin, 'Thirty Years On', *Harvard Law Review*, 114 (2002), 1655–87.

indicates will be treated as conclusive, are questions that cannot be answered by reference to the moral goals of particularized justice. Those goals exist, to be sure, as Plato, Aristotle, and countless successors have argued. But so too do the Rule of Law goals that might be thought of as the goals of generalized justice, or aggregate justice, or systemic justice. And as long as those non-particularistic goals have a place in our moral and prescriptive reasoning, then we cannot conclude—the actual practices of some parts of some common law legal systems notwithstanding—that the defeasibility of legal rules is a necessary part of all legal systems, or that the defeasibility of rules in general is a necessary part of all decision-making environments. Defeasibility may well be a desirable component of some parts of some legal systems at some times, but it is far from being an essential property of law itself.

5

Against Defeasibility of Legal Rules

*Jorge L. Rodríguez**

A. Introduction

Defeasibility has been a widely discussed topic in recent years. The general idea of defeasibility is connected with the notion of 'normality': when we express a conditional assertion, we assume the circumstances are normal, but admit that under abnormal circumstances the assertion may become false. Applying this idea to legal contexts, it might be claimed that legal rules specify only contributory, yet not sufficient, conditions to derive the normative consequences fixed by legal systems, i.e. that legal rules are necessarily subject to implicit and non-specifiable exceptions.

A great number of different claims have been associated with the expression 'defeasibility' in law.[1] Defeasibility has been predicated of legal rules, rule formulations, legal propositions, legal reasoning, and legal systems; has been defended with differences in strength and with a variety of different arguments. One reason that may help to explain these differences rests on the fact that the normative qualification of an action according to a set of norms in a concrete case is *sensitive to variations in context*, variations that can relate either to the *normative* or to the *factual* context. First, the normative solution correlated to a case by a legal rule in a specific situation may be overruled by another rule stipulating a logically incompatible solution, whenever this second solution is preferred to the first. This idea also admits an epistemic version, according to which the normative solutions of a legal system may vary not only when the normative context varies, but also when what changes is our knowledge of the rules in play. Second, normative qualifications are sensible to variations in the factual context, again not just in the trivial sense that whenever the facts of the case are different, the normative consequences may vary accordingly, but also since additional information about the facts of the case may turn applicable to it a certain rule initially judged as irrelevant, or inapplicable a certain rule initially judged as relevant.

In what follows I will restrict the attention to the general and strong thesis that all legal rules are defeasible in the sense that they are open to a set of exceptions incapable of exhaustive statement. I will present this thesis through an analysis of Schauer's ideas on the under- and over-inclusive character of rules (sections B and C). Although I fundamentally agree with Schauer's views, especially with his rejection of this strong defeasibility thesis, I will try to show, first, that under-inclusiveness is not a genuine

* Professor of Law, National University of Mar del Plata. I wish to thank Eugenio Bulygin, Jordi Ferrer Beltrán, José Luis Martí, Giovanni Battista Ratti and an anonymous referee for their useful comments and suggestions on an earlier version of this paper.

[1] In J.L. Rodríguez and G. Sucar, 'Las trampas de la derrotabilidad Niveles de análisis de la indeterminación del derecho' in P. Comanducci and R. Guastini (eds), *Analisi e Diritto 1998* (Turin: Giappichelli, 1999), 277–305, we tried to offer a map of the different alternatives to interpreting this claim.

problem of rules; second, that the differences between over-inclusiveness and defeasibility are broader than those Schauer acknowledges, and third, that the strong defeasibility thesis has the consequence of turning rules into useless tools for practical reasoning. On those grounds, I will consider two different arguments that may and have been held to justify the claim that legal rules are defeasible, based on the difficulties involved in the identification of rules from legal materials (section D). My aim here will be to demonstrate that, in spite of their initial soundness, both arguments fail to validate the conclusion that legal rules are subject to exceptions impossible to state exhaustively in advance. I will conclude these pages with some remarks on the compatibility between legal positivism and the strong defeasibility thesis (section E). Though legal theorists disagree regarding the scope and limits of the sources thesis, I will defend the view that any plausible understanding of it is incompatible with the defeasible character of legal rules, understood in its strong sense; however, legal positivism has several ways to explain, within its own basic commitments, the fact that in deciding particular cases judges sometimes introduce implicit exceptions to the applicable, source-based, legal rules on the basis of non-source-based normative considerations.

B. Under- and over-inclusiveness of legal rules

In his influential book *Playing by the Rules*, Frederick Schauer examines prescriptive rules, pointing out the similarities between prescriptive and descriptive generalizations, while most theorists analysing rules stress the differences between them.[2] On these grounds, Schauer claims that the factual predicate of prescriptive rules is a generalization perceived to be causally relevant to some purpose or justification, and that generalizations limit the number of properties that would be applicable according to the justification in the absence of the rule. Therefore, following Schauer's words, rules operate applying and specifying their underlying justifications, and the factual predicates they contain are probabilistic generalizations that may result in *under-* and *over-inclusiveness* regarding their justifications.

The cases of under- and over-inclusiveness emerge when the generalization that constitutes the factual predicate of the rule fails with respect to its justification. Let us suppose, for instance, that the avoidance of annoying disturbance to the patrons in a restaurant is the underlying justification of a rule such as 'no dogs allowed in this restaurant'. As there can be dogs causing no disturbance whatsoever, the factual predicate of the rule would be over-inclusive, encompassing cases beyond the scope of its background justification. Analogously, patrons might be annoyed by situations different from the presence of a dog in the restaurant. So the factual predicate of this rule would also be under-inclusive regarding the justification generating the rule, as it might not cover cases encompassed by that justification.

Schauer considers that rules have, on the one hand, a factual predicate specifying their scope, i.e. the conditions that give rise to their application and, on the other hand, a consequent prescribing what ought to happen when the conditions specified by their factual predicate are verified.[3] He acknowledges that rules are not usually formulated so that both components may be clearly separated. However, he notes that any rule can be reformulated to take a form such as 'all instances x must (must not/may) p'.

[2] See F. Schauer, *Playing By the Rules: A Philosophical Examination of Rule-Based Decision-Making in Law and in Life* (Oxford: Clarendon Press, 1991).

[3] See F. Schauer, *Playing By the Rules*, 23.

On account of its relevance for what will be said below, it is worth recalling that there are two different ways in which conditional rules can be reconstructed. Following a suggestion by Carlos Alchourrón, these two alternatives can be dubbed, respectively, the *insular conception* and the *bridge conception* of conditional rules.[4] According to the former, both the antecedent and the consequent of a conditional rule lie within the scope of the deontic operator ($O(p \rightarrow q)$). According to the latter, the deontic operator only affects the consequent of the conditional rule ($p \rightarrow Oq$). In the first case, from the conditional rule and the *duty* to perform its antecedent, the duty of the consequent can be inferred, a form of inference which is usually known as *deontic detachment (DD)*.[5] In the second case, from the conditional rule and the *truth* of the antecedent, the duty of the consequent can be derived, a form of inference which is, in turn, usually known as *factual detachment (FD)*.[6] The structure Schauer assigns to prescriptive rules seems to commit him to the bridge conception of conditional rules.

The thesis of the over-inclusive character of prescriptive rules could be broken down into two distinct claims: (a) the factual predicate of a prescriptive rule presents itself as a condition sufficient to derive its normative consequence, and (b) however, there could be cases encompassed by the rule but not by its underlying justification. If in some of those cases of discrepancy the justification overrides the rule, the assumption contained in (a) should be restricted to the weaker claim that the factual predicate of a rule is just a certain kind of *necessary condition of a condition sufficient* for the derivation of the normative consequence provided by the rule.[7]

In Schauer's example, the case of a person who intends to enter a restaurant with a dog that causes no annoyance to the patrons (e.g. a seeing-eye dog, particularly trained to be well behaved) would be an instance that falls within the scope of the rule but outside the underlying justification. If in some of those cases of discrepancy between the rule and its background justification the latter were taken to defeat the former, that would be tantamount to saying that the rule does not correlate the prohibition to enter the restaurant with every case of someone coming with a dog. Entering the restaurant with a dog would not be a condition sufficient for the exclusion, but a necessary condition of a sufficient condition, the sufficient condition being, in turn, coming with a dog with certain additional characteristics that make it annoying for the patrons of the restaurant.

Contrary to this idea, it could be argued that the enactment of a rule does not necessarily rest on a unique justification. Consequently, though a rule may encompass cases which are not covered by a certain justification underlying it, other purposes or reasons inspiring the enactment of the rule could justify its application in such cases. Be that as it may, this argument does not challenge Schauer's thesis that rules are over-inclusive regarding a given underlying justification.

To say that prescriptive rules are under-inclusive as regards their background justification is a much more arguable claim. Again, the thesis may be broken down into two distinct assertions: (a') the factual predicate of a prescriptive rule presents itself

[4] See C.E. Alchourrón, 'Detachment and Defeasibility in Deontic Logic', *Studia Logica*, 57 (1996), 5–18.

[5] *DD*: $(O(p \rightarrow q) \wedge Op) \vdash Oq$.

[6] *FD*: $((p \rightarrow Oq) \wedge p) \vdash Oq$. On the distinction between deontic and factual detachment, see P. Greenspan, 'Conditional Oughts and Hypothetical Imperatives', *Journal of Philosophy*, 72 (1975), 259–76.

[7] In the conditional $((p \wedge r) \rightarrow Oq)$, the antecedent $(p \wedge r)$ is a condition sufficient for the normative solution Oq. As $(p \wedge r)$ propositionally implies p, p is a necessary condition of $(p \wedge r)$. Thus, in $((p \wedge r) \rightarrow Oq)$, p is a necessary condition of a sufficient condition of Oq. See G.H. von Wright, *A Treatise on Induction and Probability* (London: Routledge & Kegan Paul, 1951).

as a condition necessary to derive its normative consequence, and (b') however, there could be cases not encompassed by the rule but falling within its underlying justification. If some of those cases of discrepancy between the rule and its justification were treated according to the latter, the assumption contained in (a) should be restricted to the weaker claim that the factual predicate of a rule is just a certain kind of *sufficient condition of a necessary condition* for the derivation of the normative consequence provided by the rule.[8]

Let us return to Schauer's example. Suppose the case of someone who intends to enter a restaurant not with a dog, but with something equally likely to cause annoyance to the patrons (e.g. a bear). Such a case would be an instance not covered by the rule but within the scope of its underlying justification. The preference for the solution provided by the underlying justification in some of those cases would involve that the prohibition on entering the restaurant is not restricted to dogs. Entering the restaurant with a dog would not be a condition necessary for the exclusion, but a sufficient condition of a necessary condition, the necessary condition being to come to the restaurant with a dog, a bear, or any other annoying thing.

With reference to thesis (a'), Schauer explicitly remarks that the rule's factual predicate could be understood as its hypothesis:

> [F]or prescriptive rules can be formulated in a way such that they commence with 'if x', where x is a descriptive statement the truth of which is both a necessary and a sufficient condition for the applicability of the rule.[9]

However, the assumption that the rule's factual predicate could be understood not only as a sufficient condition but also as a necessary condition of its normative consequence is not properly justified. Schauer himself, who—as previously commented—makes profitable use of the similarities between descriptive and prescriptive generalizations, admits that assuming that the factual predicate is a necessary condition of the consequent seems rather odd as to descriptive generalizations. Schauer states:

> The proposition that philosophers are clever, if taken to mean all philosophers, is falsified by the occurrence of a dim philosopher but not by the occurrence of a clever carpenter. Except in certain special contexts, 'philosophers' is plausibly taken to mean 'all philosophers' but not 'all and only philosophers'. This lack of a logical or linguistic parallel is potentially relevant to thinking about prescriptive rules, for it need not be the case that 'no dogs allowed', as the rule emanating out of a concern with annoyance of patrons, must treat the cases of non-annoying dogs and annoying non-dogs as equivalents.[10]

Nevertheless, Schauer considers that a prescriptive rule requiring x to ϕ is more susceptible to an 'only x must ϕ' interpretation than a descriptive rule stating that x ϕs is susceptible to an 'only x ϕs' interpretation.[11] This may well be correct in certain cases, but then it will be dependent upon contingent interpretative practices, and that does not seem sufficient ground to justify the wide scope of thesis (a'), i.e. that the factual predicate presents itself as a condition necessary to derive the normative consequence of prescriptive rules. Having no basis on the similarities with descriptive rules, the idea that the factual predicate of prescriptive rules may be taken as a necessary

[8] In the conditional $(Oq \rightarrow (p \vee r))$, the consequent $(p \vee r)$ is a necessary condition of the normative solution Oq. As p propositionally implies $(p \vee r)$, p is a sufficient condition of $(p \vee r)$. Thus, in $(Oq \rightarrow (p \vee r))$, p is a sufficient condition of a necessary condition of Oq.

[9] F. Schauer, *Playing By the Rules*, 23.

[10] Ibid., 33, fn. 24.

[11] See ibid., 44, fn. 6.

condition for their normative consequence would require a justification centred on the peculiarities of prescriptive discourse.[12] Unfortunately, far from justifying this interpretation, those peculiarities seem to give a good reason to reject it.

Prescriptive rules do not present themselves in isolation but as members of more or less complex systems of rules. Hence to read the factual predicate of a rule as a necessary condition of its normative consequence would imply that the same action cannot be subsumed under two rules having logically independent factual predicates without producing normative conflicts, even if both rules have the same normative solution. Using again Schauer's example of the 'no dogs allowed' sign in the restaurant, how could a later decision by the restaurant's owner to add another sign reading 'no bears allowed either' cause any possible conflict? However, this will precisely be the consequence of understanding the rule 'no dogs allowed' as equivalent to 'dogs *and only* dogs not allowed', since from such a rule it follows that coming with a bear is allowed.[13]

Be it as it may, my interest here is not so much to emphasize the controversial character of thesis (a'), but rather to remark that, despite the attractive symmetry of Schauer's presentation, the under-inclusiveness of prescriptive rules does not single out any autonomous feature of them. Every piece of meaning expressed by thesis (a') and (b') can be articulated in terms of thesis (a) and (b), and thus underlying under-inclusiveness is dispensable. Understanding the factual predicate of a rule like 'no dogs allowed in this restaurant' as a condition necessary and sufficient for the exclusion of dogs from the restaurant would amount to reading the rule as a complex statement prescribing 'dogs and only dogs not allowed'. Were that interpretation sound, the underlying justification should be read likewise: 'Annoying disturbance and only annoying disturbance not allowed'. Now, the first term of the conjunction constituting the 'no dogs . . . ' rule would then be over-inclusive regarding its justification because it would prohibit the entrance in cases the justification would certainly allow for (e.g. the seeing-eye dog case). The second term of the conjunction constituting the 'no dogs . . . ' rule would then be under-inclusive regarding its justification because it would allow the entrance in cases the justification would exclude (e.g. the bear case). However, the rule 'only dogs not allowed' is equivalent to 'entrance with no dogs permitted'. And the statement that this rule is under-inclusive with respect to the justification of preventing annoying disturbance to the patrons is equivalent to the statement that the rule 'entrance with no dogs permitted' is over-inclusive regarding the underlying justification, because it allows the entrance in cases that would be prohibited by the underlying justification.[14]

[12] In chapter 7 of *Playing by the Rules*, Schauer offers a set of practical reasons to justify taking rules as at least not absolutely transparent regarding their underlying purpose, but those reasons do not justify reading the factual predicate of rules as a necessary—as different from a sufficient—condition of their normative consequence.

[13] Of course, we may think that the rule 'no dogs allowed' was *amended* by the enactment of the rule 'no bears allowed either'. But amendment presupposes that something needed to be amended, i.e. that the previous rule did not allow what the second does, and hence that there was a conflict we have decided to solve interpreting that the second rule must prevail. Therefore, far from being a possible answer to the claim in the text, this reading is tantamount to acknowledge its soundness.

[14] In formal terms, a rule with the structure $(p \leftrightarrow PHq)$ is equivalent to the conjunction $(p \rightarrow PHq)$ and $(PHq \rightarrow p)$. The over-inclusive character of the rule $(p \leftrightarrow PHq)$ means that in the left to right implication, the antecedent has a wider extension than the background justification. The under-inclusive character of the rule $(p \leftrightarrow PHq)$ means that in the right to left implication, the consequent has a more restricted extension than the background justification. But the right to left implication, i.e. $(PHq \rightarrow p)$, may be transformed without loss of meaning into $(\sim p \rightarrow \sim PHq)$, which is equivalent in its turn to $(\sim p \rightarrow Pq)$. Consequently, the statement that in $(PHq \rightarrow p)$ the consequent has a more

Therefore, to predicate the under-inclusive character of prescriptive rules seems to be questionable in two different ways. First, for it needs to assume the controversial claim that the factual predicate not only does ordinarily express a sufficient but also a necessary condition of the rule's normative consequence. Second, for it is reducible, without any loss of meaning, to the over-inclusive character of another rule. Therefore, the truly interesting issue concerning prescriptive rules seems to be their over-inclusive character.

C. Defeasibility and over-inclusiveness

I have previously argued that one of the most complex and discussed issues in deontic logic concerns the way in which conditional norms are to be represented. This problem combines the difficulties which are involved in developing a logic of norms with one of the 'scandals' of logic in general: the nature of conditional statements.

In 1964, Georg H. von Wright proposed a system of logic for conditional norms.[15] This system allowed the following form of inference, known as *strengthening of the antecedent*: the obligation to perform a certain action under condition C implies the obligation to perform it under condition C plus any other. As Geach pointed out, the system is flawed by the difficulty that two logically independent conditions cannot imply contradictory normative consequences within it. This appears, at least at first sight, counterintuitive: there seems to be nothing contradictory in saying, for instance, that murderers ought to be punished, but murderers acting in self-defence ought not to be punished. One of the explored possibilities to avoid this conclusion has been to reject the principle of strengthening of the antecedent as a valid form of inference. However, the failure of strengthening of the antecedent implies abandoning factual detachment as well: from a conditional duty and the truth of its antecedent, the duty of the consequent will no longer be derivable. The failure of both forms of inferences is the distinctive trait of *defeasible* deontic logics, a very popular field of research in recent years.[16] The general idea of defeasibility is connected with the notion of 'normality'. When formulating a conditional assertion, we assume that the circumstances are normal, but admit that under abnormal circumstances the assertion may become false.

The use of defeasible deontic logics (or *nonmonotonic* logics) for the analysis of different aspects of law and legal discourse has undoubtedly led to profitable results. What defeasible deontic logics seek to elucidate is under what restrictive conditions the principles of strengthening of the antecedent and factual detachment may be accepted. But the use of defeasible logical tools in the legal domain has to be clearly distinguished from a substantive thesis that different authors have tried to defend, namely, that for some reason or set of reasons, legal rules *are* defeasible in the sense that all of them are subject to a list of exceptions incapable of exhaustive statement. As I said, this latter idea is the only one I want to challenge in these pages.

The substantive thesis of legal defeasibility was first introduced by H.L.A. Hart in an early paper that later the author refused to reprint.[17] Hart claimed that all legal rules

restricted extension than its underlying justification is equivalent to the statement that in $(\neg p \rightarrow Pq)$ the antecedent has a wider extension than its underlying justification.

[15] See G.H. von Wright, 'A New System of Deontic Logic', *Danish Yearbook of Philosophy*, 1 (1964), 173–82.

[16] See, for example, D. Nute (ed.), *Defeasible Deontic Logic* (Dordrecht: Kluwer, 1997).

[17] See H.L.A. Hart, 'The Ascription of Responsibility and Rights' in A.G.N. Flew (ed.), *Logic and Language* (first series, Oxford: Blackwell, 1951), 145–66. In the Preface of *Punishment and*

should be read as including a clause 'unless circumstances demand otherwise', and so the conditions for their application cannot be specified in advance. Thus, the distinctive sign of legal defeasibility would rest not so much on the existence of overriding conditions restricting the scope of legal rules but on the impossibility of specifying such defeating conditions.

Schauer considers—for reasons I fully agree with—that the thesis that legal rules are in this sense necessarily defeasible appears partly confused, partly superfluous, and partly wrong.[18] After examining and rejecting four previous alternatives, he suggests the following reading of the defeasibility thesis:

> (D5) A rule is defeasible when its application is contingent not only upon the non-occurrence of events specifiable in advance by particular or type, but also by the non-occurrence of conditions specifiable in advance neither by particular nor by type.[19]

There is a plain connection between this strong reading of the thesis of legal defeasibility and the over-inclusive character of legal rules. But this connection is not one of identification. Over-inclusiveness leaves open the question of how a case of discrepancy between the solution indicated by the rule and the one derivable from its underlying justification should be decided. Instead, the defeasibility thesis, under the reconstruction offered by D5, involves that in any of those cases the priority shall be in favour of the outcome contemplated in the justification which underlies the rule.[20] However, as Schauer rightly observes, rules should be capable of serving as reasons for action *qua* rules, i.e. with certain independence from the reasons supplied by their background justifications. Thus, by assuming this strong defeasibility thesis, one is forced to pay the cost of implying the impossibility of assigning normative force to legal rules as such. From this point of view, Schauer claims:

> Unless for some number of at least potential cases the weight of the rule *qua* rule is sufficient to carry the day even in the face of a contrary belief about how this case ought to be decided, the rule is superfluous. If a decision-maker's belief about the particular trumps the force of the rule in every case of conflict between the two, then the rule exists only as a rule-of-thumb.[21]

On Schauer's stance, defeasibility is not a necessary feature of legal rules but a contingent aspect of certain systems of legal decision-making. I fundamentally agree with Schauer on this point. To say that a rule is over-inclusive regarding its background justification solely indicates that it encompasses cases that might not produce the consequence triggered by the rule's justification.[22] However, it is compatible with postulating that in all these cases of discrepancy between the rule and its underlying justification, the normative solution provided by the rule should prevail. On the contrary, claiming that a legal rule is defeasible in the sense under consideration is tantamount to saying that the rule's normative consequence might be overridden even though a certain case falls within its factual predicate. Consequently, a rule may be

Responsibility. Essays in the Philosophy of Law (Oxford: Clarendon Press, 1968), Hart justifies the exclusion of that early paper saying that 'its main contentions no longer seem to me defensible'.

[18] See F. Schauer, 'On the Supposed Defeasibility of Legal Rules' in M.D.A. Freeman (ed.), *Current Legal Problems*, 48 (1998), 223–40.

[19] Ibid., 232.

[20] 'D5, therefore, by denying the possibility that the occurrence of an unforeseen event within a rule's linguistic reach but outside its purpose can justify application of the rule, appears to justify necessary defeasibility only by rejecting the possibility that the rule *qua* rule can be a reason for action independent of the reasons for action supplied by its background justification' (Ibid., 233).

[21] F. Schauer, *Playing By the Rules*, 84, fn. 13.

[22] See ibid., 32.

deemed defeasible on account of its over-inclusive character. This happens when we treat the rule as completely transparent with respect to its background justification in all cases of over-inclusion. However, it might also be the case that a rule is over-inclusive without being defeasible.

The only point in which I do not fully agree with Schauer is the following. Schauer regards the definition of strong defeasibility expressed by D5 as equivalent to:

(D6) A rule is defeasible when its application is dependent not only upon the occurrence of an event lying within the rule's linguistic reach, but upon that event lying within the rule's purposes as well.[23]

He argues that if a rule were only applied when its application were consistent with its background purpose, while being subject to defeat when its application does not serve such underlying purpose, there would be no case in which the rule *qua* rule generates an outcome which is not generated by the underlying justification. Accordingly, the normative force of the rule would simply dissolve.[24]

I believe there is at least one reason to reject the identification between D5 and D6, and to distinguish over-inclusiveness and defeasibility in a much broader sense than the one proposed by Schauer. Were D5 and D6 equivalent, the only grounds to introduce an exception into a legal rule would be its underlying justification. But exceptions to legal rules could derive from sources different from the rule's underlying justification. In fact, Schauer himself writes that, though a rule cannot be conceived of as completely defeasible, for it has to present some degree of resistance to being overruled, we should take care to distinguish two different phenomena. A rule would be inapplicable in virtue of what Schauer calls an *internal failure* when it is not applicable to those cases in which the justification does not apply. A rule would be inapplicable in virtue of what Schauer calls *external defeasibility* when it is overridden by particularly exigent factors external both to the rule and to its justification. Schauer claims that a rule with no resistance to internal failure whatsoever will not deserve, in an important sense, the name of 'rule'. However, being partially opaque regarding its underlying justification and thus having the necessary status to be a rule would be compatible with being overridden by external factors.[25]

When we focus our attention on isolated rules, this distinction between internal and external defeasibility appears to be quite clear. However, as has been pointed out before, rules—and in particular legal rules—do not present themselves in isolation but as part of complex and interconnected systems. And in the face of normative systems, it is not easy to discern between the two different situations, i.e. those in which a rule is inapplicable in virtue of the justification *which underlies that rule*, and those in which the reason for not applying the rule rests on factors which are external both to the rule and its justification, and stems from other rules of the same system or their underlying justifications. The borderline between the two situations will depend on—and vary with—the presupposed criteria for identification of rules. Schauer admits that any case of override can always be reformulated as being outside the scope of the rule.[26] But let us imagine a normative system containing two rules, one stating 'murderers should be

[23] F. Schauer, 'On the Supposed Defeasibility of Legal Rules', 236.

[24] See ibid., 237.

[25] See F. Schauer, *Playing By the Rules*, 117–18. Schauer's distinction between internal failure and external defeasibility is not conceptual but merely contingent, as he observes that it would collapse in a single-valued justificatory system because in such a system the supporting distinction between the justification behind the rule and any other reason cannot be drawn (see F. Schauer, ibid., 118, fn. 8).

[26] See ibid., 90.

punished' and the other providing that 'acting in self-defence should not be punished'. It is really not clear what difference it would make to say that the rule about murderers is externally defeasible in cases of self-defence, instead of saying that the rule about murderers includes an implicit exception restricting its scope to non-self-defence murders.

Regarding normative systems, the distinction between internal and external defeasibility is of some interest only if the qualifications 'internal' and 'external' are taken as predicates of the system as a whole, and not of isolated rules. Along these lines, a rule, which is a member of a certain normative system, will be internally defeasible when the reason for not applying it stems from that very system, whereas it will be externally defeasible when the reason for not applying it stems from extra-systemic considerations (i.e. when it is overridden by rules or justifications belonging to other normative systems). Needless to say, under this understanding the distinction does not justify the assessment of an isolated rule as a germane prescriptive rule or as a mere rule of thumb. This is something Schauer himself seems to acknowledge when he observes that there is little to distinguish the rule that is vulnerable to the inapplicability of its own justification from the rule that is vulnerable to being overridden in virtue of reasons which are external to that rule.[27]

Since the distinction between internal and external defeasibility seems to feature no qualitative aspect, the partisan of the defeasible character of legal rules could reply to Schauer by means of the following line of argument. If a rule may be internally defeasible and still be a rule, it could also be externally defeasible without losing its normative force *qua* rule. Yet this kind of reply, and the defeasibility thesis in general, has to face a deeper predicament in line with Schauer's remarks, though exceeding the realm of exceptions generated by the underlying justifications of rules. Genuinely defeasible rules, in the sense examined here (i.e. those which are subject to an open list of exceptions), are incapable of justifying decisions or actions in any particular case.

In order to derive the normative solution contained in a rule regarding a particular case, two conditions should be met. First, the case must be an instance of the factual predicate of the rule. Second, the factual predicate must operate as a condition sufficient for the normative solution supplied by the consequent of the rule. The connection between the factual predicate and the normative solution of the rule should be strong enough to allow a form of inference like factual detachment. But if legal rules are defeasible in this strong sense, i.e. subject to an open list of exceptions, they cannot validate the form of inference known as strengthening of the antecedent. For, in such a case, the occurrence of the factual predicate of the rule together with any of the exceptions limiting its scope will prevent one from deriving the normative consequence of the rule. And if the strengthening of the antecedent is to be rejected, the same should occur with factual detachment, for the acceptance of the latter implies the acceptance of the former.[28] Therefore, any rule subject to an open list of exceptions allows no inferences whatsoever with respect to any particular instance of its factual predicate,

[27] See ibid., 110–11.

[28] If a conditional connective '>' validates the rule of factual detachment $(((p > q) \wedge p) \rightarrow q)$, since this formula is propositionally equivalent to $((p > q) \rightarrow (p \rightarrow q))$, the conditional '>' would imply the material conditional '→'. And since the rule of strengthening the antecedent is satisfied by material conditional $((p \rightarrow q) \rightarrow ((p \wedge r) \rightarrow q))$, we would obtain by transitivity $((p > q) \rightarrow ((p \wedge r) \rightarrow q))$, i.e. the consequent of the conditional '>' will be derivable from its antecedent in conjunction with whatever proposition that precisely constitutes the rule of strengthening the antecedent (see C.E. Alchourrón, 'Condizionalitá e rappresentazione delle norme giuridiche' in A. Martino and F. Socci Natale (eds), *Analisi Automatica dei Testi Giuridici* (Milan: Giuffré, 1988).

because the possibility of exceptions restricting the scope of the rule cannot be excluded.

The choice between interpreting rules as indefeasible, with the difficulties involved in identifying all their exceptions, and interpreting them as defeasible, and so deprived of almost any inferential power regarding individual cases, has been presented by Soeteman with enlightening clarity. The dilemma Soeteman puts forward is as follows:

> [E]ither we accept . . . that there are exceptions to norms (unconditional as well as conditional) which are not already included in the formulation of the norm, with the consequence that it will no longer be possible to deduce from a norm what we have to do under the concrete circumstance we find ourselves in, or we do not accept this possibility of exceptions (in other words: we only accept exceptions which are already included in the formulation of the norm); the question then is, however, whether we are indeed capable of formulating valid norms.[29]

In what follows, I will try to justify that the second horn of this dilemma does not represent any germane complication concerning legal rules, at least from a positivistic point of view. So far, my intention has been limited to stressing that taking rules as standards that are subject to exceptions which cannot be exhaustively listed, makes them useless tools for practical reasoning. This is so regardless of the source—internal or external—that defeasibility may have. Hence, the problem is much broader than the set of cases of overriding that may be grounded on the over-inclusive character of legal rules. And this problem affects even the weak version of defeasibility that Schauer takes as defensible, according to which legal rules are defeasible when their application is contingent upon the non-occurrence of an unspecifiable list of very good reasons for not applying them, such reasons having strength greater than would have been sufficient for those reasons to determine the outcome in the absence of the rules.[30] For if rules had only this presumptive force, an assessment of every member of such unspecifiable list would be needed in each case of application, and that would inevitably block any possible inference.

D. Defeasibility and interpretation

There is an extended and well-established practice to use legal rules to justify institutional decisions and actions. If the thesis of the defeasible character of legal rules has the consequence outlined in the previous section, then either the thesis is correct but the indicated practice is irrational, or that practice is justified but the defeasibility thesis has to be rejected. Facing these two alternatives, I unhesitatingly choose the second. Nevertheless, I shall not try to justify a general rejection of the defeasible character of legal rules in the limited frame of this paper, a thesis that has been defended with very different kinds of arguments. I simply wish to make a number of points about the more challenging of these arguments.

A first reason that could be used to support the idea that legal rules are subject to an open list of exceptions has to do with the difficulties involved in the identification of legal rules presumably expressed by certain texts or linguistic formulations. The claim of the defeasible character of legal rules may be a way to express the tenet that interpretation of legal texts cannot be restricted to their literal meaning, rendering it necessary to recognize the existence of exceptions which do not appear in their formulations.

29 A. Soeteman, *Logic in Law* (Dordrecht: Kluwer, 1989), 196.
30 F. Schauer, 'On the Supposed Defeasibility of Legal Rules', 238.

Let us suppose the following case, typically presented as an example of defeasibility. A statute in Bologna stated that whoever drew blood in the streets should be severely punished. A barber opens the vein of a person who subsequently falls down ill in the street. Shall the statute be applied to that case? A negative answer could be defended claiming that though the case falls within the scope of the literal formulation of the rule, an implicit exception should be recognized to reach a proper decision in the case at hand. Alternatively, one could say that the statute does not regulate the case of a barber opening the vein of a person to save her life because the purpose of the statute is not to keep Bologna's streets clean. The expression 'draw blood' does not have here its ordinary meaning but a metaphoric one, designed to proscribe duels in the streets of Bologna. Under this reading, the problem would not be that the rule regulates the case with an unfair result, but that the literal interpretation of its terms would be inappropriate.

It is not unusual for legal theorists to force the interpretation of legal rules to present clearly regulated cases as instances not covered by them. Whenever the legal community assumes that a certain case has to be solved introducing an implicit exception which is not present in the literal formulation of a rule, that implies the existence of an interpretative convention assigning legal relevance to additional properties apart from those derivable from legal texts. There could be very good reasons to claim that a certain property, though not explicitly envisaged as relevant by legal authorities when issuing a certain rule, has to be taken as implicitly relevant on the grounds of other formulations issued by those authorities, their 'intentions' or other sources of law admitted as valid. It should be noted, however, that this idea will only support adding certain properties as implicitly relevant. Or, to put it differently, it will only justify the existence of *implicit* exceptions to legal rules, not the existence of a list of exceptions impossible to state exhaustively in advance.

Still, there is a more complex and insightful argument related to linguistic formulations that could be used to justify the defeasible character of legal rules. Those of us with a legal education have a tendency to associate rules with certain linguistic formulations. Although it is generally accepted that legal rules may exist without any canonical formulation—whenever customary rules are accepted as valid law—the vast majority of legal rules are formulated in language as a means to make them public. As Robert Brandom claims, this association between rules and linguistic formulations had prominent defenders, such as Grotius, Pufendorf, and Kant, who identified rules with linguistic expressions of a general kind which determine what ought to be done by explicitly *saying* what ought to be done.[31]

Indeed, the relation between rules and language is more intricate than that. First, rules cannot be so easily identified with certain linguistic expressions even in the event they were thought to come into existence only through the formulation of certain linguistic expressions. No one would accept that the mere fact of the existence of different exemplars of a constitution, each of them formed by a set of linguistic expressions discernible from those which appear in the other exemplars, proves the existence of a plurality of constitutions in a given state. But even recognizing the existence of a single, abstract, constitutional formulation-type despite the plurality of formulation-tokens of that abstract type, a constitution is not merely a set of linguistic symbols or stains on a sheet of paper. What is usually called a 'constitution'

[31] See R. Brandom, *Making it Explicit, Reasoning, Representing and Discursive Commitment* (Cambridge, Mass.: Harvard University Press, 1994), 19. I will basically follow Brandom's ideas to develop this argument.

is what we construe from certain linguistic expressions, not the linguistic formulations themselves.[32]

The fundamental problem in the claim that the formulation of certain linguistic expressions is a condition necessary for the existence of any rule may be presented as follows. Suppose that it has to be settled whether or not a certain linguistically formulated rule applies to a certain case. There are, as it is sound to assume, correct and incorrect applications of a rule, but the criteria for the correct application of a rule involve a normative evaluation that cannot be given by that very rule. In this regard, as stressed by Wittgenstein, applying a rule to a certain case requires an interpretation, and as there cannot be an infinite chain of interpretations to justify the application of any rule, there has to be a way of *grasping* a rule—of understanding its scope—which is not an interpretation.[33]

As Brandom remarks, the moral of these considerations is that the use of linguistically formulated rules presupposes the existence of other rules or norms implicit in practices, which cannot have an explicit formulation in language. Accordingly, the idea of identifying rules with certain linguistic expressions has to be abandoned.[34] These rules, which are implicit in normative practices, play a fundamental role in explaining the way in which explicitly formulated rules operate in practical reasoning.

The failure of the reductionist thesis assimilating rules with explicitly formulated rules, and the acceptance of rules implicit in our normative practices is still silent with respect to the main features of these latter rules. And the answer to this question runs the risk of collapsing into another form of reductionism that Brandom judges as dangerous as the former:[35] to identify rules with regularities of conduct and, thus, lose all possible distinction between what *is* and what *ought to be*. If rules were only relevant to describe regularities of conduct, conforming to a rule would just be producing performances that are regular according to the rule, and so there would be no difference between the way in which, e.g. we are subject to the rule that imposes the duty to pay our taxes, and the way in which inanimate objects are subject to the laws of nature.[36]

There is also a conclusive argument put forward by Wittgenstein against this reduction of rules to mere regularities of conduct. Any set of past performances exhibits a multiplicity of regularities (not just a given regularity), so that a new performance could be judged as correct or incorrect on the grounds of any of such different regularities. This implies that almost any future performance may be judged as regular on the basis of some pattern or regularity identified in virtue of past performances, which is tantamount to saying that there is no criterion of correction whatsoever.[37] Therefore, there should be a way of giving an account of the rules, which are implicit in the normative practice of using those other rules with an explicit linguistic formulation, that does not lead to the collapse of the former with mere regularities of conduct.

[32] On the distinction between norms and norm-formulations, see G.H. von Wright, *Norm and Action: A Logical Enquiry* (London: Routledge & Kegan Paul, 1963), 106.

[33] See L. Wittgenstein, *Philosophical Investigations* (Oxford: Blackwell, 1953), para. 201. Robert Brandom cites an argument with similar implications by Wilfrid Sellars in 'Some Reflections on Language Games' in *Science, Perception, and Reality* (London: Routledge and Kegan Paul, 1963), 321 (see R. Brandom, *Making it Explicit, Reasoning, Representing and Discursive Commitment*, 23–6).

[34] See R. Brandom, *Making it Explicit, Reasoning, Representing and Discursive Commitment*, 20–1.

[35] See ibid., 26–30.

[36] See ibid., 27.

[37] See L. Wittgenstein, *Philosophical Investigations*.

On the basis of this idea (i.e. the necessary existence of rules implicit in normative practices), a new argument in defence of the defeasible character of legal rules could be conceived. Since it would not be possible to express rules articulating exhaustively the criteria sufficient for their correct application, every rule (not just legal rules) would necessarily be subject to an open list of exceptions. Hence, for instance, Juan Carlos Bayón writes:

> [It] is impossible to articulate and make explicit ('codify') a set of rules stating exhaustively when the particular is an instance of the universal, because that would amount to articulating meta-rules for the application of rules, with the consequence of reproducing the problem regarding the application of those meta-rules. Therefore, judgement is irreducible to algorithm, for a complete formulation of explicit criteria for judgement is impossible without an infinite regress. Accordingly, every explicit formulation of norms presupposes a background of other norms implicit in practice, which resist for conceptual reasons to any attempt of exhaustive statement (or codification). A due acknowledgement of this fact should lead us to give an irreducibly open character to any formulation of norms.[38]

Contrary to appearances, this argument is not apt to justify, as a conclusion, the necessary defeasibility of (legal or any other) rules, not at least in the sense that any rule is subject to an open list of exceptions incapable of exhaustive statement. As has been shown above, the only conclusion the argument allows is that, in order to avoid an infinite regress, the criteria for the correct application of rules cannot be completely grasped by rules explicit in language. But this does not mean that they cannot be grasped at all. If they could not be grasped *simpliciter*, the conclusion of the argument would be far more deleterious than the defeasible character of rules: there would be no rules at all. So there is no ground here to justify exceptions to rules, nor, indeed, to justify the open character of such exceptions. For even assuming the impossibility to articulate exhaustively sufficient criteria of application for any rule, this is a problem concerning the *formulation* of rules, not rules themselves. This is precisely the conclusion drawn by Bayón: the open character of any *formulation* of norms. Indeed, the possibility of capturing sufficient criteria of application of rules is presupposed in Wittgenstein's very idea that there has to be a way of grasping a rule which is not an interpretation.

Consequently, the argument which we have just examined may be used to ground the defeasible character of *rule-formulations*, in the sense that it would be impossible to specify sufficient linguistic criteria of application of any rule-formulation. The thesis of the defeasible character, not of *rule-formulations*, but of *rules*, meaning that they are subject to an open list of exceptions incapable of exhaustive statement, demands additional support.

E. Defeasibility, identification, and application of law

In the previous section I have considered and rejected two arguments designed to justify the defeasible character of legal rules. Nevertheless, it seems apparent that the acceptance or refusal of the defeasibility thesis depends crucially upon the way in which the law is conceived. As a consequence, if we are provided with no account of this latter problem, it is hard to reach any definite conclusion on the former.

[38] J.C. Bayón, 'Bulygin y la justificación de las decisiones judiciales: la parte sorprendente' in J.J. Moreso and M.C. Redondo (eds), *Un diálogo con la teoría del derecho de Eugenio Bulygin* (Madrid-Barcelona: Marcial Pons, 2007), 148–9. The English version is mine.

It is well known that legal positivism claims that the existence and content of the law are determined by a set of complex social facts, so that their identification requires no moral considerations. According to the sources thesis, the properties to be taken as legally relevant, and the possible exceptions restricting the scope of legal rules, will always be identifiable from certain social facts. Such an idea, at least at first sight, seems at odds with the defeasible character of legal rules, as this thesis has been defined above. Nonetheless, legal theorists disagree on the exact content of the sources thesis. Accordingly, more than one option should be evaluated.

First, the sources thesis could be understood as implying that the existence of a legal rule depends on a social agreement regarding its correct applications. For example, in his critical evaluation of inclusive legal positivism, Andrei Marmor raises an objection against the idea that determining what the rule of recognition actually prescribes in particular cases could be a matter of moral or political argument.[39] Marmor's point is the following:

> [T]he main flaw in the argument under consideration is that it assumes that there is a potential gap between the convention, which is a rule, and its application, a gap that can be bridged by moral or political arguments. The main reply to this is that there is no such gap. A convention is constituted by the practice of its application to particular cases. It is not the case that we first have a rule formulation, say that convention 'R' prescribes so and so, and then we try to make up our minds how to apply R to particular cases . . . Conventions are what they are, because there is a practice of applying the rule to certain cases; it is the application of the rule which constitutes its very existence. Once it is not clear to the norm subjects whether the convention applies to a certain case or not, then there is no conventional solution to that matter, and at least as far as the convention is concerned, this is the end of it. People can have different views about the convention they would want to have in those circumstances (or how, otherwise they would like to solve the problem they face) but they cannot have an intelligent argument about what the convention *really* requires in those controversial cases. The only reality there is to a convention is the actual practice of its application; a social practice. In the case of conventional rules, there is no gap between the rule and its application, a gap which could be bridged by an interpretative reasoning preferring one application to another. Once the application of a convention is not clear there is no convention on that matter.[40]

According to this version of the sources thesis, legal rules, being conventional, are determined by the practice of their application to particular cases, i.e. legal rules exist as long as there is a convention on how to apply them to particular cases.

A different approach to the sources thesis is offered by Riccardo Guastini. In Guastini's viewpoint, legal positivism only claims that moral considerations are not needed in order to identify normative texts as part of the law, but remains silent on how to interpret such texts.[41] Guastini embraces a sceptical conception of interpretation, according to which legislation is the source of normative formulations (i.e. the symbols expressing legal rules) but not of rules in the proper sense (i.e. the meanings ascribed to such normative formulations through interpretation).

> In a sense, interpretation is the very source of legal rules, since 'it is only words that the legislature utters', and legal texts 'do not interpret themselves'. I mean that law-giving authorities issue not

[39] See A. Marmor, 'Exclusive Legal Positivism' in *Positive Law and Objective Values* (Oxford: Oxford University Press, 2001), 47–70.

[40] Ibid., 57–8.

[41] See R. Guastini, 'Variaciones sobre temas de Carlos Alchourrón y Eugenio Bulygin. Derrotabilidad, lagunas axiológicas e interpretación' in E. Bulygin and G. Palau (eds), *Análisis Filosófico*, Homenaje a Carlos Alchourrón, 26 (2006), 277–93.

meanings (rules), but just sentences, whose normative meaning contents—i.e., the expressed rules—are to be detected by means of interpretation. This is not to say that legal sentences have *no meaning at all* before interpretation. Skepticism claims only that, prior to interpretation legal sentences have no *definite* meaning, since they are liable to different interpretations.[42]

From this point of view, disagreements on the scope and applicability of legal rules never affect the sources thesis, since the latter only refers to rules' formulations and not to rules themselves. Even though a given normative formulation remains constant, whenever the meaning assigned to it varies, the rule changes, and the content of the law changes accordingly. But in spite of such changes, it may well be said that the law exists even in the presence of profound disagreements on its content, since disagreements merely demonstrate that legal texts are responsive to synchronically multiple and diachronically changing interpretations.[43]

The consequences of each of these two versions of the sources thesis in relation to the defeasible character of legal rules are radically different. According to the first version, since the existence of any legal rule is dependent upon an agreement on the application of the rule to particular cases, legal rules must be treated as indefeasible not only at the level of their identification but also in their application. As Marmor explains, under this reading there would be no gap between rules and their applications. In other words, if there is an agreement in the legal community on how to apply a certain rule to a particular case, that will be the legal solution for it. But if there is no such agreement, there will be no solution for the case, and therefore the law, as far as it concerns the case, will be undetermined.

According to the second version, the sources thesis has no implication whatsoever concerning the identification of legal rules, for it exclusively refers to the identification of the relevant legal texts. For this reason, the defeasible character of legal rules now becomes compatible with legal positivism. This is so because there would be no inconsistency in claiming both that legal texts may be identified from a set of complex social facts, and that legal rules, understood as the interpretations ascribed to those texts, are subject to a list of exceptions incapable of exhaustive statement.

In my opinion, however, neither of these two versions of the sources thesis is acceptable. There is an obvious parallel between them and the two reductionist conceptions of rules examined in the previous section. In Guastini's version, legal positivism assigns relevance to certain social facts to identify certain texts, while legal rules will be the result of interpreting those texts. Were that the case, the existence of legal rules would always depend on their linguistic formulation, and this leads to the infinite regress remarked by Wittgenstein's argument. Guastini's sceptical view of interpretation implies that any legal text is open to different possible interpretations, among which there would be no standard of correction. This conception seems unsatisfactory insofar as it does not take into account that, in order to identify the content of legal rules, it is necessary to accept the existence of rules implicit in practice, which do not depend on their formulation in language. Conversely, Marmor's point of view involves assuming the alternative reductionist path: rules would be but regularities. Let us assume that it is the application of a conventional rule which constitutes its very existence. Since the practice is formed by a set of applications compatible with a variety of different regularities, this perspective provides no possible answer to the

[42] R. Guastini, 'A Skeptical View on Legal Interpretation' in P. Comanducci and R. Guastini (eds), *Analisi e diritto 2005* (Turin: Giappichelli, 2006), 139–44 (emphasis in original).

[43] See R. Guastini, *Distinguendo. Studi di Teoria e Metateoria del Diritto* (Turin: Giappichelli, 1996).

Kripkensteinian sceptical challenge.[44] If a rule is but a function of its application to particular cases, and every future application can adhere to some regularity derived from its past applications, rules provide no guidance whatsoever.

We may say that, while Marmor's understanding gives the sources thesis too much potency, Guastini's makes it almost trivial. In fact, against the first interpretation, Dworkin has objected that legal positivism would be unable to explain legal disagreements. If the sources thesis implies that legal rules are conventional in the sense defended by Marmor, lack of agreement on the application of legal rules will always be indicative of the absence of a legal solution. Therefore one should conclude that for legal positivism a rule cannot exist unless there is a complete agreement on its content. On the contrary, the problem of understanding the sources thesis in Guastini's terms lies in turning positivism into an excessively weak conception, compatible with the most naïve version of natural law theories, according to which unjust rules cannot be part of the law. Since justice and injustice are predicates of genuine rules, not of mere texts, this reading of the sources thesis would generate no conflict with the claim that legal rules are necessarily just.

These remarks show that any acceptable version of the sources thesis must occupy a place somewhere between the threshold set by Guastini's view and the upper limit represented by Marmor's position. Legal positivism, we may say, has to find its way between the Scylla of identifying legal rules with mere linguistic formulations and the Charybdis of identifying legal rules with agreements on their application to particular cases.

From the point of view of legal positivism, the conventionality of legal rules—not just of the relevant legal texts—means that their existence is contingent upon the existence of a complex social practice whereby someone's acceptance of a certain rule partially depends on its being accepted by the other members of the group.

Conventionality, understood in this sense, should not be identified with the existence of a social agreement concerning the application of the rule. To say that a rule is conventional in this latter sense is a weaker claim that could include many cases of rules that are not conventional in the former conception, as would be the case whenever there is—what Dworkin calls—an *agreement in conviction*.[45] Let us suppose, for example, that all the members of a certain community consider it morally wrong to torture a child. If it makes sense to speak here of the existence of a rule, such a rule will plainly not be conventional in the first sense, for each member of the group does not accept the rule because of the others' acceptance, but because she thinks it is right to follow it. In this case convergence is accidental. By contrast, if a rule is conventional in the first sense, convergence is a conceptual requisite for its existence.

Consequently, the sources thesis does not necessarily imply that legal rules exist so long as there is an agreement concerning their application to particular cases. Disagreements in the application of legal rules may be the product of a deficient understanding of certain standards of correct application, which are fixed by rules implicit in our normative practices. Thus, the sources thesis being a conceptual thesis about the characterization of the law and not a normative thesis on how certain cases ought to be solved, legal positivism is compatible with a certain amount of disagreement in application. This reading of legal positivism is irreconcilable with defeasibility, at least at the level of the identification of the law. It does not imply, however, that legal rules

[44] See S. Kripke, *Wittgenstein on Rules and Private Language* (Oxford: Basil Blackwell, 1982).
[45] See R. Dworkin, *Law's Empire* (Cambridge, Mass.: Harvard University Press, 1986), 145–6.

should be interpreted as indefeasible on the basis of extralegal considerations in their application to particular cases.

In the sense here explored, defeasibility of legal rules depends on their being subject to implicit exceptions that cannot be exhaustively listed. If this were the case, legal rules would solely provide solutions for normal cases. Accordingly, it would be necessary to evaluate whether those implicit exceptions occur in each instance of application. Under such conception, legal rules will not allow any conclusive solution to be derived for the cases seemingly regulated by them. An argument frequently used to justify legal defeasibility so understood is the following: when enacting rules, legal authorities can only foresee normal cases. It would be impossible to take into consideration every possible characteristic of particular cases to assess their normative relevance or irrelevance. Therefore, legal rules could not be interpreted as indefeasible because that would imply a blind exclusion of the possible relevance of properties of the case which are different from those explicitly taken into account by the lawgiver when enacting certain rules. However, it seems apparent that the singularities of a certain case are not rendered legally relevant or irrelevant only in virtue of some natural property. Their relevance is dependent upon a qualification which can be drawn from certain rules or other normative considerations. In order to justify the introduction of an exception within a rule, another rule with an incompatible solution has to be accepted, as well as a preference selecting the solution provided by the latter in case of conflict. So, the central question here is the following: on the basis of what other rules is it possible to justify the introduction of exceptions, which cannot be exhaustively listed, to legal rules?

Consider the case of two legal rules, both of them identifiable from a certain social source (e.g. the text of a provision of the Criminal Code), one of them punishing whoever performs an abortion and the other exempting from punishment abortions in cases of rape. One way to construe these two rules is to claim that the first is defeasible because it does not state explicitly the rape exception. Yet in this example the exception is clearly identifiable from another source-based rule. Indeed, there is nothing that prevents using the idea of defeasibility here, if defeasibility only means that positive legal rules are liable to those exceptions grounded on other positive legal rules. However, since positive law is the result of a finite set of normative acts, it could not be maintained that the exceptions to rules are incapable of exhaustive statement.

In other words, either the rules that allow introducing exceptions to positive legal rules are identifiable from their source or they are not. In the first case, legal rules cannot be taken as liable to exceptions *incapable of exhaustive statement*, because a thorough examination of positive law will suffice to detect such exceptions, potential problems being merely epistemic. Only in the second case, i.e. when rules justifying the introduction of exceptions to positive legal rules are not source-based, can the open character of the list of exceptions be defended.

In analysing Dworkin's early challenge to legal positivism, Jules Coleman holds that, in order to give a response to Dworkin, legal positivism should explain a fact, not an interpretation of that fact.[46] The relevant fact that should be explained or interpreted is that moral norms often figure as standards to which judges appeal in resolving legal disputes. The interpretation of that fact that Dworkin—among others—offers is that judges appeal to moral norms because they are binding *qua* legal standards, and that they are part of the law because they express an appropriate dimension of justice or

[46] See J.L. Coleman, 'Constraints on the Criteria of Legal Validity', *Legal Theory*, 6 (2000), 171–83.

fairness. Coleman claims that legal positivism does not need to embrace Dworkin's interpretation of such a fact. What legal positivism must explain in terms of its own basic commitments is simply the fact that moral norms do play an important role in adjudication. In Coleman's view, any version of legal positivism has three different explanations of that fact. Moral principles can figure in legal argument:

(a) as discretionary standards;
(b) as binding standards that are not part of the community's law;
(c) as binding standards that are part of the community's law in virtue of their social source.[47]

Following analogous lines, suppose, for the sake of the argument, that when deciding particular cases judges often introduce implicit exceptions to the applicable legal rules, and that such exceptions are grounded on normative considerations that lack until then the appropriate social source (e.g. a moral norm). Not only can the legal positivist give an explanation of that fact, perfectly consistent with his own basic commitments, but indeed he has more than one way to account for it. From a positivistic point of view, the fact that in deciding particular cases judges sometimes introduce implicit exceptions to the applicable, source-based, legal rules on the basis of non-source-based normative considerations, can be regarded as cases where the judge:

(a) infringes her legal duty as imposed by the secondary rules of the system;
(b) uses a discretionary power conferred by the secondary rules of the system;
(c) complies with her legal duty, whenever the secondary rules of the system bind her to take into consideration moral norms for the adequate application of legal rules so as to avoid grossly unjust consequences; or
(d) modifies the legal system, whenever the existing rule of recognition takes the fact that judges use certain rules to justify implicit exceptions to the existing rules as a reason to incorporate those new rules into the system.

It is important to recall that, to the three alternative explanations of the way moral norms may figure in adjudication that any version of legal positivism is able to embrace, Coleman adds another that only inclusive legal positivism may possibly accept: that moral principles are binding standards that are part of the law in virtue of their substantive merits.[48] Analogously, it could be claimed that there is an additional way of explaining, in positivistic terms, the introduction of exceptions to source-based legal rules in particular cases on the basis of non-source-based considerations: whenever judges introduce such exceptions, they do so because they are bound to; they are bound to do so because those normative considerations are part of the law, and they are part of the law because of their substantive merits. I believe, however, that this account of defeasibility is ruled out by any sound reading of the sources thesis, and if inclusive legal positivism—or a certain version of it—is committed to accepting it, there is a strong reason to suspect that inclusive legal positivism is not plausible as an internally consistent form of positivism. Nonetheless, in my view this explanation of defeasibility, excluded by the sources thesis, is but the product of a misunderstanding stemming from the two following facts: first, sometimes judges introduce exceptions to legal rules on the basis of non-source-based considerations that present relevant, substantive merits for the case at hand; second, judges usually have a prima facie duty to justify

[47] See ibid., 174–5.   [48] See ibid., 174–5.

their decisions on legal rules. For this reason, it may be thought that such non-source-based considerations are to be regarded as part of the law because this would explain the reason why judges have to take them into account. The truth is that if a certain consideration has relevant, substantive merits in a certain case, it is *for that reason alone* that judges have to take it into account, regardless of its membership of the legal system.

In the light of the reasons offered so far, legal positivism may hold that legal rules are indefeasible in the sense that all their conditions of application can be identified from a set of complex social facts and, still, accept that the solutions provided by legal rules might be overruled in their application to particular cases by extralegal considerations. From my perspective, Schauer's 'presumptive positivism' should be interpreted along this line. As is known, Schauer takes presumptive positivism to be a descriptive thesis about the character of a pedigreed set of rules within the full universe of reasons decision makers use. However, he also admits that the term 'presumptive' generally refers to the force legal rules have and, more specifically, to a certain amount of force that, unless particularly compelling reasons are believed to exist, legal rules should apply. This gives a normative character to Schauer's position.

> Presumptive positivism is a way of describing the interplay between a pedigreed subset of rules and the full (and non-pedigreeable) normative universe, such that the former is treated by certain decision-makers as presumptively controlling in this not-necessarily-epistemic sense of presumptive. As a result, these decision-makers override a rule within the pedigreed subset not when they believe that the rule has produced an erroneous or suboptimal result in this case, no matter how well grounded that belief, but instead when, and only when, the reasons for overriding are perceived by the decision-maker to be particularly strong.[49]

Insofar as this presumptive force of legal rules is understood as referring to the possibility of overriding their application to particular cases on extralegal grounds in any of the different forms indicated above, presumptive positivism can be taken as compatible with the conceptual positivistic thesis that the existence and content of the law can be identified without recourse to moral considerations. However, it would be completely misleading to say that this presumptive force means that legal rules are defeasible in the sense that they are subject to an unspecifiable list of exceptions.

[49] F. Schauer, *Playing By the Rules*, 204.

6

Defeasibility in Legal Reasoning

*Giovanni Sartor**

In this contribution, I provide a logical analysis of defeasible reasoning. First I introduce the notion of a reasoning schema, and consider how ratiocination proceeds according to the reasoning schemata adopted by the concerned agents. I then distinguish conclusive and defeasible reasoning, and argue that cognitive agents need to engage in defeasible reasoning for coping with a complex and changing environment. I analyse the process of defeasible reasoning, considering collisions of reasons, defeat, preference-based reasoning, and reinstatement, as well as the distinction between rebutting and undercutting. Finally, I consider defeasibility in practical and legal reasoning, and argue that defeasible reasoning constitutes an essential aspect of legal problem-solving.

A. Reasoning schemata and reasoning instances

A reasoning agent proceeds in ratiocination through discrete reasoning steps. Each step is characterized by its preconditions (some mental states already possessed by the reasoner) and its postconditions (some new mental states, to be acquired through performing the reasoning step).[1] Correct ratiocination consists of rational transitions from preconditions into postconditions, namely, transitions taking place according to certain patterns, or *reasoning schemata*, which constitute, and may be validated by, rationality. This idea is developed by the epistemologist John Pollock, whose theory of reasoning provides the basic inspiration for the model here presented.[2] In general, I shall represent reasoning schemata in the following form:

Reasoning schema: *Name*

- A_1; AND ...; AND A_n

—IS A REASON FOR—

- B_1; AND ...; AND B_n

* Professor of Law, University of Bologna and European University Institute.

[1] Here I am considering the sequential component of reasoning, namely, ratiocination, rather than the so-called heuristic component. The heuristic component works in different ways (in making analogies, suggesting hypotheses, etc.) and provides its outcomes to the sequential component. The latter, while being unable to achieve such outcomes on its own, may subject them to its scrutiny. For some observations on this distinction, and on its connections with the usual dichotomy context of discovery versus context of justification, see G. Sartor, *Legal Reasoning: a Cognitive Approach to the Law* (Berlin: Springer, 2005), ch. 2.

[2] See J.L. Pollock, *Cognitive Carpentry: A Blueprint for How to Build a Person* (New York: MIT Press, 1995), and J.L. Pollock and J. Cruz, *Contemporary Theories of Knowledge* (Totowa, NY: Rowman and Littlefield, 1999).

where *Name* is the name of the schema, $A_1, \ldots, A_n$ are the preconditions of the schema (cognitive states the reasoner possesses before instantiating the schema), and $B_1, \ldots, B_n$ are its postconditions (cognitive states the agent possesses after instantiating the schema). I will say that the set of all the preconditions in a schema constitutes its *reason*, and the set of all its postconditions forms its *conclusion*. I will also speak respectively of a *subreason* or of a *subconclusion* to refer to a single precondition or to a single postcondition, that is, to refer to a single mental state contained in the reason or in the conclusion.[3]

Reasoning schemata are *general*, in the sense that they apply to all situations where the reasoner instantiates a certain set of contents, though natural language can express such contents in different ways.[4] Any specific instance of a reasoning schema—any combination of mental states matching the reasoning schema—constitutes a *reasoning instance*. For example, consider the following reasoning schema, named *syllogism*:[5]

Reasoning schema: *Syllogism*

- believing that all *P*s are *Q*s; AND
- believing that *a* is *P*

—IS A REASON FOR—

- believing that *a* is *Q*

Note that the reason of this schema includes two components or *subreasons*:

- the belief in a general proposition, which is usually called the *major premise* of the syllogism; and
- the belief in a particular (individual or concrete) proposition, which is usually called the *minor premise* of the syllogism.

The major and the minor premise are connected by the fact that a predicate (*P*) occurs in both of them. The reasoning schema *syllogism* is instantiated by the following reasoning instance, which embodies its pattern:

[3] This understanding of the term 'reason' corresponds to a common way of using it (my reason for believing *A* is that I believe that *B*, my reason for intending to do *A* is that I desire that *B* and I believe that by doing this I will achieve *C*). However, it does not correspond to the way in which this term is often used in legal theory, namely as a fact justifying a certain action. See J. Raz, *Practical Reason and Norms* (London: Hutchinson, 1975). In the sense in which I am using the term 'reason', a reason is not an external fact, but a cognitive state of the agent, and a reason does not justify an action, but it justifies the adoption of a further mental state, whose adoption is justified according to the procedure of rationality (as long as the agent instantiates the cognitive state constituting the reason).

[4] I shall not address here the issue of whether reasoning schemata are formal or material, namely the issue of whether the applicability of a reasoning schema to a particular set of premises only depends on the logical-linguistic form of such premises (as propositions being conditional or unconditional, universally or existentially quantified, etc.), or whether it also depends on the particular subject matter the premise is concerned with (as propositions expressing empirical facts, expert opinions, legal norms, etc.). In fact, it seems to me that if we have a rich enough *language of thought*, all logically relevant differences in content should become differences in linguistic form. See J. Fodor, *The Modularity of Mind* (Cambridge, Mass.: MIT Press, 1983).

[5] I use the expression *syllogism* since this pattern of reasoning corresponds, in the legal domain, to what is usually called *judicial syllogism*. See J. Wróblewski, 'Legal syllogism and rationality of judicial decision', *Rechtstheorie*, 5 (1974), 33–45. However, I need to remind the reader that the Aristotelian theory of syllogism was not concerned with propositions referring to specific individuals, like proposition (2) and (3) in the *syllogism* schema above. The syllogistic figure which comes closest to that schema would be the Barbara mood, according to which the couple of (universal) premises (1) [all *P*s are *Q*s] and (2) [all *Q*s are *R*s] leads to the (universal) conclusion that (3) [all *P*s are *R*s].

Reasoning instance: *Syllogism*

- believing that all Mondays are days on which there is a flight to Barcelona; AND
- believing that today is Monday

—IS A REASON FOR—

- believing that today is a day on which there is a flight to Barcelona

In the following I am only considering cognitive states represented by beliefs, rather than addressing also non-doxastic cognitive states, such as perceptions in the epistemic domain, and preference, desires, intentions, or wants in the practical domain. However, among the beliefs I also include practical beliefs, such as the belief that something is preferable to something else, that something is a value, or that it is obligatory or permitted to perform a certain action.[6] Therefore, I can omit, in the representation of a reasoning schema, the indication that such schemata concern beliefs as cognitive states of a reasoning agent—rather than the propositions providing the contents of such beliefs—and just indicate the believed propositions. Consequently, the above instance of the *syllogism* schema can be represented as follows (omitting also, for simplicity, the words 'is a reason for' and the name of the instantiated schema):

- all Mondays are days on which there is a flight to Barcelona;
- today is Monday

—THEREFORE—

- today is a day on which there is a flight to Barcelona

Here are two legal examples of normative syllogisms. The first corresponds to the so-called *judicial syllogism*:

Reasoning instance: *Syllogism*

- all thieves ought to be punished; AND
- John is a thief

—IS A REASON FOR—

- John ought to be punished

The second concerns the type of reasoning which is involved in referring to authoritative sources of law, which can be called *meta syllogism*.

Reasoning instance: *Meta syllogism*

- all rules issued by the Head of the Law School are legal (legally valid); AND
- rule [it is forbidden to smoke on the premises of the Law School] was issued by the Head of the Law School

—IS A REASON FOR—

- rule [it is forbidden to smoke on the premises of the Law School] is legal (legally valid)

[6] I will not consider here how practical beliefs connect to non-doxastic conative states. On this point, see G. Sartor, *Legal Reasoning: a Cognitive Approach to the Law*, ch. 3.

While in ordinary syllogisms a rule is used for deriving normative qualifications of people or objects, in meta syllogism a metarule (a rule about rules) is used for inferring properties of rules (more generally, of normative propositions) or relations between rules.

B. The adoption of a reasoning schema

Let us specify what it means for a reasoner to *adopt* a reasoning schema. When saying that a reasoner *j* adopts a reasoning schema, I mean that *j* has a particular inclination, corresponding to, and validated by, rationality: whenever *j* instantiates all preconditions of the schema, then *j* will also tend to instantiate the schema's postconditions. For instance, when saying that *j* adopts schema *detachment*, I mean that *j* has the following inclination: whenever *j* believes both *A* and [if *A* then *B*], *j* will also tend to believe *B*.

I need however to clarify what I mean by *j* having such an inclination. One cannot perform all inferences required by every reasoning schema one adopts; this would lead one to acquire an infinite number of useless cognitive states, and therefore to fill one's head with useless contents. The simplest inference rules of propositional logic are sufficient to lead an overzealous reasoner into such a hopeless condition. Consider, for example, the following schema:

Reasoning schema: *Disjunction introduction*

- *A*

—IS A CONCLUSIVE REASON FOR—

- *A* OR *B*

The inferences that are enabled by schema *disjunction introduction* look obvious: any proposition *A* entails its disjunction with any arbitrary proposition *B* (since if *A* is true, than also *A* OR *B* will be true, for whatever *B*). For instance, a reasoner believing that [today is Tuesday] can safely come to believe that [today is Tuesday OR today is Thursday]. This process unfortunately may continue: as from proposition *A* one infers proposition [*A* OR *B*], from the latter proposition one can infer [*A* OR *B* OR *C*], and so on infinitely.

The impossibility of producing all valid instances of every reasoning schema one adopts is linked to the so-called problem of *logical omniscience*: one cannot derive (and endorse) all implications of one's beliefs. The word 'cannot' in the previous sentence can be read in two different senses. In a first sense, it points to a serious limitation of our cognitive powers: we cannot (are unable to) infer many important truths that follow from what we already know (progressing in the discovery of these truths is the difficult task of mathematicians and logicians). In a second sense, which is the one I am now considering, the assertion that we cannot be logically omniscient rather refers to the futility of a misguided cognitive effort: we cannot (we should not, since it would be silly or unreasonable) derive all useless or trivial implications of our current beliefs.

The way out of the latter problem consists in limiting oneself to performing only those inferences that may be relevant for one's epistemic interests, according to the priorities determined by these interests (and according to the available time and energy). Therefore we cannot view reasoning schemata neither as absolute necessities, forcing one to draw whatever irrelevant conclusions they indicate, nor as pure possibilities, which one can randomly implement or disregard. Reasoning schemata rather express a *necessity* that is *conditioned* to the utility or relevance of their use. Thus, one believing both *P* and [if *P* then *Q*] should acquire belief in *Q* only if one has some interest in establishing whether *Q* holds (and one has nothing more important to do). Otherwise a rational reasoner should refrain from making the inference.[7] Finally, I am presenting only reasoning schemata that are 'rational', in the sense that they pertain to rationality (they indicate ways in which rational cognition proceeds), and are validated by rationality itself, when reflexively applied to the evaluation of its own procedures. Therefore the fact that an agent endorses a reason (the precondition of a rational reasoning schemata) not only leads that agent, as a matter of fact, to endorse the conclusion of the schema, but it also justifies, and guides it to the endorsement of that conclusion: the fact that I currently believe both 'P' and 'IF P THEN Q', not only leads me, as a matter of fact, to believe 'Q', but also justifies me in accepting 'Q', and this justification appears convincing to my rationality itself (as long as I continue to believe both premises, and, in the case of defeasible reasoning, I have no prevailing reason countering such an inference). This justification does not exclude that the belief in 'Q' is false (incorrect). This may happen when the premises (the reason) are wrong: the conclusions I derive from false beliefs, according to correct inferences, are also likely to be false. However, this fact does not make the derivation of such conclusions unjustified, as long as one maintains the belief in their premises (to avoid deriving a false conclusion from false premises, one should retract such premises, rather than refraining from deriving the conclusions they entail). So, the belief in a conclusion may be unjustified, since a mistake was performed in one step of the chain leading the reasoner to that conclusion, but still the reasoner would be justified (on the basis of previous beliefs, and until he withdraws such beliefs) in performing the inference steps in that chain which, taken in isolation, appear to be correct.

C. Conclusive and defeasible reasoning

Two classes of reasoning schemata must be distinguished: conclusive and defeasible ones. The basic difference between the two kinds can be summarized as follows. A *conclusive* reasoning schema indicates a cognitive transition that can operate regardless of any further information the agent possesses, as long as the reasoner instantiates the preconditions in the schema: whenever one endorses the reason of the schema, one may safely endorse its conclusion.

Definition C.1 Conclusive reasoning schema. A reasoning schema R is conclusive if one can always adopt R's conclusions while endorsing R's premises (and one should never reject R's conclusions while endorsing R's premises).

The distinctive feature of a *defeasible* reasoning schema is that it may be defeated by further information to the contrary: the schema indicates a transition that only operates when one has no prevailing beliefs (or, more generally, mental states) against applying the schema or against adopting its conclusions. When one endorses the premises of a defeasible schema but has prevailing beliefs to the contrary, one should refrain from adopting the conclusion of the schema (and withdraw that conclusion if one has already adopted it by instantiating that schema).

Definition C.2 Defeasible reasoning schema. A reasoning schema is defeasible if one should, under certain conditions, refrain from adopting its conclusions though endorsing its premises.

[7] On the connection between reasoning and interest, for an architecture for interest-driven reasoning, see J.L. Pollock, *Cognitive Carpentry*.

In the following sections I shall consider some important aspects of conclusive and defeasible reasoning, analysing their commonalities and differences.

D. Validity and truth-preservation

The strong connection between reason and conclusion that characterizes conclusive reasoning schemata can be linked to the idea of *truth-preservation*. Conclusive inference schemata are truth-preserving: whenever (in any possible situation where) the premises of a conclusive schema are true, then also the conclusions of the schema are true. In other words, it is impossible that the premises of a conclusive schema are true and its conclusions are false.

Definition D.1 Truth-preservation. A reasoning instance R is truth-preserving if necessarily, whenever R's premises are true, then also R's conclusions are true. Similarly, a reasoning schema R is truth-preserving if all R's instances are truth preserving.

Truth-preservation is a very useful and important property, but it does not characterize all rational reasoning patterns. Therefore, it does not delimit the scope of logical reasoning, if by *logic* I mean rational reasoning, or rational ratiocination.

It is true that many authors tend to limit logic to truth-preserving reasoning: they view logic as having the specific function of providing truth-preserving ways of reasoning. Moreover, many logicians refer to truth-preservation by using the word *valid*. For instance, it is said 'an argument is valid if it is logically impossible for all the premises to be true, yet the conclusion false',[8] or, to take another instance, 'an argument is called "valid" when its premises entail its conclusion, in other words, if the premises can't be true without the conclusion also being true'.[9] Correspondingly, it is also said that logic is the study of valid reasoning.

Obviously, there is nothing wrong in using the word *valid* in this specific sense (for which there is a long and very respectable tradition), nor in defining the word *logic* so that it only concerns truth-preserving reasoning. However, these definitions lead people (especially when they are not familiar with formal reasoning and with the technical meaning of logical notions) to the idea that any form of reasoning that is not truth-preserving is 'invalid', in the generic sense of being wrong, arbitrary, or unreasonable. To avoid this connotation sneaking into our discourse (and to avoid confusion with the sense in which the word *valid* is used in the law, for example when discussing legal sources), I shall refrain from using *valid* in the sense of 'truth-preserving' (and *invalid* in the sense of 'not truth-preserving'). This allows us to avoid qualifying all defeasible inferences as being 'invalid': though they are not truth-preserving (it may happen that their preconditions hold, but their conclusions fail to be true), defeasible reasoning schemata are indeed 'valid' or 'sound' forms of reasoning, in the sense of being appropriate ways of approaching certain cognitive tasks.

E. Monotonic and nonmonotonic reasoning

Conclusive reasoning schemata provide for *monotonic reasoning*: the conclusions that can be derived by a reasoner who only uses conclusive reasoning always grow, as long as the reasoner is provided with further input information. More exactly, if a conclusion A can be conclusively derived from a set of premises S_1, then A can also be derived from

[8] M. Sainsbury, *Logical Forms: An Introduction to Philosophical Logic* (Oxford: Blackwell, 2001).

[9] W. Hodges, 'Elementary Predicate Logic' in D. Gabbay and F. Günthner (eds), *Handbook of Philosophical Logic. Volume I: Elements of Classical Logic* (Dordrecht: Kluwer, 1983), 1.

whatever set S_2 results from the addition of further premises to S_1 (from whatever set S_2 such that $S_1 \subset S_2$).

Nonetheless, when one draws defeasible inferences from a set of premises S_1, it may happen that, by adding further premises to S_1, one obtains a set S_2 which does not entail some conclusions one could derive from S_1 alone. Defeasible reasoning schemata license *nonmonotonic* inferences: their conclusions may need to be abandoned when new information is available.[10]

The following reasoning schemata are for defeasible and conclusive syllogism:

Reasoning schema: *Conclusive syllogism*

- all *Y*s are *Z*s; AND
- *x* is *Y*

—IS A CONCLUSIVE REASON FOR —

- *x* is *Z*

Reasoning schema: *Defeasible syllogism*

- all *Y*s are normally *Z*s; AND
- *x* is *Y*

—IS A DEFEASIBLE REASON FOR —

- *x* is *Z*

These are applied in the reasoning instances of conclusive and defeasible syllogism:

Reasoning instance: *Conclusive syllogism*

- all bachelors are unmarried; AND
- John is a bachelor

—IS A CONCLUSIVE REASON FOR—

- John is unmarried

Reasoning instance: *Defeasible syllogism*

- pet dogs are normally unaggressive; AND
- Fido is a pet dog

—IS A DEFEASIBLE REASON FOR—

- Fido is unaggressive

According to the first reasoning instance, when one believes that [all bachelors are unmarried] and that [John is a bachelor], one can conclusively conclude that [John is unmarried]. According to the second instance, when one believes that [pet dogs are normally unaggressive] and that [Fido is a pet dog] one can defeasibly conclude that [Fido is unaggressive]. The difference between conclusive and defeasible reasoning emerges most clearly when one acquires beliefs that contradict the conclusions of one's previous inferences.

[10] On nonmonotonic reasoning, see M.L. Ginzberg (ed.), *Readings in Nonmonotonic Reasoning* (Los Altos, Cal.: Morgan Kaufmann, 1987), which collects the contributions which have originated research in this domain. For an introduction, see also G. Brewka, *Nonmonotonic Reasoning: Logical Foundations of Commonsense* (Cambridge: Cambridge University Press, 1991).

Let as assume, for example, that Mary—who knows that [bachelors are unmarried] and [husbands are married]—after meeting John at a dinner party comes to believe, according to John's statements, that [John is a bachelor]. This leads Mary to believe, according to schema *conclusive syllogism*, that [John is unmarried]. However, the day after a friend tells Mary that [John is Lisa's husband]. This should lead her to conclude, still according to *conclusive syllogism*, that [John is married], which contradicts her belief that [John is unmarried]. At this stage, Mary has no choice but to abandon the premises of one of these inferences. If she sticks to the idea that John is a bachelor, she needs to withdraw the belief that John is Lisa's husband, while if she accepts the idea that John is Lisa's husband, she needs to withdraw the belief that John is a bachelor.

In defeasible reasoning, a different approach is required. Let us assume, for instance, that one endorses all of the following propositions: [Fido is a pet dog], [pet dogs are normally unaggressive], [Fido is a Doberman], [Dobermans are normally aggressive]. According to schema *defeasible syllogism*, this set of premises licenses both of the following defeasible inferences:

- Fido is a pet dog;
- pet dogs are normally unaggressive

—THEREFORE—

- Fido is unaggressive
- Fido is a Doberman;
- Dobermans are normally aggressive

—THEREFORE—

- Fido is aggressive

Let us assume that the second inference here is stronger (more reliable) than the first one. In such a situation, we are not required to withdraw any of the premises of the weaker inference (withdraw the belief that pet dogs are normally unaggressive, or that Fido is a pet dog). We can maintain the premises of both inferences, that is, we can keep on believing both of the following reasons (sets of premises): {Fido is a Doberman; Dobermans are normally aggressive}, {Fido is a pet dog; Pet dogs are normally not aggressive}. However, we shall refrain from deriving the conclusion that [Fido is aggressive].

F. The rationale of defeasibility

Defeasible reasoning schemata, as I have observed in section C, are not truth-preserving: when believing the premises of a defeasible schema, we are led to endorse the conclusions of the schema, though these conclusions are not truth-preservingly implied by our premises (and they may indeed turn out to be false, even when the premises hold true). However, failure to satisfy truth-preservation does not entail logical faultiness. On the contrary, epistemology has come to identify various kinds of sound defeasible inference.[11] Here I list a few of them:

- *Perceptual inference*. Having certain perceptual contents is a defeasible reason to believe in the existence of corresponding external objects. More generally, having a percept with content ϕ is a defeasible reason to believe ϕ. For instance, having

[11] J.L. Pollock, *Cognitive Carpentry*, 52ff.

an image of a red book at the centre of my visual field is a defeasible reason for me to believe that there is a red book in front of me. This conclusion is defeated if I come to know that there are circumstances which do not ensure the reliability of my perceptions (I am watching a hologram).

- *Memory inference*. Recalling ϕ is a defeasible reason to believe ϕ. For instance, my memory that yesterday I had a faculty meeting is a defeasible reason for me to believe that indeed there was such a meeting. This inference is defeated if I come to believe that the supposed memory was an outcome of my imagination.
- *Enumerative induction*. Observing a sample of *F*s all of which are *G*s is a defeasible reason to believe that all *F*s are *G*s. For instance, believing that all crows I have ever seen are black is a defeasible reason to believe that all crows are black. This inference is defeated if I perceive one white crow.
- *Statistical syllogism*. Believing that [most *F*s are *G*s AND *a* is an *F*] is a defeasible reason to believe that *a* is a *G*. For instance my beliefs that [most printed books have even-numbered pages on their left side] and that [the volume on the top of my table is a printed book] constitute a defeasible reason for me to believe that this volume has even-numbered pages on its left side. This inference is defeated if I discover that this volume was wrongly printed with even-numbered pages on its right side.
- *Temporal persistence*. Believing that ϕ is the case at time t_1 is a defeasible reason to believe that ϕ is still the case at a later time t_2. For instance, my belief that my computer was on the top of my table yesterday evening (when I last saw it) is a defeasible reason for me to believe that my computer is still there. This inference is defeated if I come to know that the computer was moved from the table after yesterday evening.

Similar defeasible reasoning schemata may be identified also for practical, and in particular, legal reasoning. For instance, we, as legal reasoners, endorse the conclusion of a rule on the basis of the belief the rule is legally valid and that the rule's antecedent is satisfied. This inference, however, can be defeated either by a stronger rule to the contrary or by showing that the rule at issue is inapplicable. Another typical defeasible inference pattern characterizes teleological reasoning, where we conclude that we ought to adopt a certain plan of action (or the endorsement of a rule), given that it appears that such a plan is able to achieve a certain value, and that its impact on all values at issue is better than the impact of any other plan we have been able to identify so far. This inference, however, is defeated if we discover a different plan which would give a better outcome.

In general, there is nothing strange or pathological in defeasible reasoning. On the contrary, defeasibility is the natural way in which an agent can cope with a complex and changing environment. We do not even need to view defeasibility only in cognitive agents: an agent only endowed with fixed or conditioned reflexes may exhibit a form, or at least an evolutionary antecedent, of defeasible reasoning. Consider a reactive agent having two reflexes r_1 and r_2 such that:

- according to r_1, stimulus s_1 (e.g. tasting good) triggers action a_1 (eat it!);
- according to r_2, stimulus s_2 (e.g. it tastes hot) triggers action a_2 (spit it out!);
- r_2 is stronger than r_1.

Assuming that the strength of each reflex is proportional to its importance for an agent's survival or reproduction, the most useful thing to do (and thus the solution that should have been chosen by natural evolution) when incompatible reflexes are triggered would be to implement the stronger of the two reflexes. Accordingly, when confronted with stimuli s_1 and s_2 (a tasty, but burning bite of food), a well-adapted reactive agent, rather than staying inactive or choosing randomly, will execute r_2 and do a_2 (get rid of the food). Therefore we may conclude that, in a certain sense, reflex r_2 defeats r_1: given only stimulus s_1, the agent would react with a_1, but given the combination of s_1 and s_2, the agent will react with a_2.

Although one may correctly speak of defeasible reflexes, defeasibility acquires its fullest meaning for cognitive agents; for such agents defeasibility consists in having certain cognitive states and withdrawing them when further cognitive results become available. This is what happens, as we have seen in the above pages, in *defeasible ratiocination*: the agent acquires through reasoning certain provisional cognitive states, and later may retract them, as a result of further reasoning.

To refer to the provisional conclusions of defeasible reasoning, usually the qualification prima facie is used. However, qualifying all defeasible conclusions as being prima facie suggests that all results of defeasible reasoning are obtained on the basis of the only information that is immediately available to the reasoner. This suggestion is misleading, since a defeasible conclusion may also be adopted after an accurate inquiry. Possibly a better terminological choice consists in qualifying the outcomes of defeasible reasoning as *pro tanto* conclusions, namely, conclusions which, through being justified on the basis of the information so far considered, may be withdrawn on the basis of further information.[12]

Note that a defeasible belief is not necessarily so strong as to justify acting accordingly. One may be aware that further inquiry may provide reasons against maintaining that belief. In such a case, one may resist acting on the basis of a *pro tanto* conclusion. It will depend on the circumstances of the case, and mainly on the depth of the inquiry so far performed and on the need to provide a quick answer, whether rationality requires jumping from *pro tanto* acceptance into action, or rather deferring action until the issue has been better examined.[13]

Consider, for example, the case of a person who asks his tax lawyer whether he should pay taxes on money he earned abroad. Assume that the lawyer finds a rule stating that money earned abroad should be taxed. However, the lawyer is aware that a number of exemptions exist, concerning different countries and different types of revenue (though she is not aware of the content and the preconditions of such exceptions). Therefore she should tell the client that she only *pro tanto* (namely, on the basis of the information she has so far considered) believes that the money he earned abroad is not taxed. She needs to look further into tax law to provide a sufficiently reliable answer.

G. The logical function of defeasible reasoning schemata

According to the analysis I developed in the previous section, defeasible inference schemata have different, but related, functions.

The first function is that of providing the reasoner with provisional thoughts, on the basis of which one may reason and if necessary act, until one has new information to the contrary. In this spirit, Pollock relates defeasible reasoning to a general feature of human cognition.[14] He argues that normally one starts with perceptual inputs and

[12] This terminology has been suggested by Peczenik in A. Peczenik, *Scientia juris. Treatise of Legal Philosophy and General Jurisprudence—Volume 2* (Berlin: Springer, 2006), section 5.1.3.

[13] The important idea of *rational deferment* goes back to the mediaeval philosopher John Buridan, who was unjustly ridiculed with the famous story of Buridan's ass. See J. Buridan, *Quaestiones super decem libros Ethicorum Aristotelis ad Nicomachum* (1st edn 1513; Frankfurt am Main: Minerva, 1968).

[14] See J.L. Pollock, *Cognitive Carpentry*; and J.L. Pollock, 'Perceiving and reasoning about a changing world', *Computational Intelligence*, 14 (1998), 489–562.

goes on inferring beliefs from one's current cognitive states (one's percepts plus the beliefs which one has previously inferred). Such a belief-formation process must satisfy apparently incompatible desiderata:

- one must be able to form beliefs on the basis of a partial perceptual input (one cannot wait until one has a complete representation of one's environment);
- one must be able to take into account an unlimited set of perceptual inputs.

Defeasibility is the way to reconcile such requirements.

The only obvious way to achieve these desiderata simultaneously is to enable the agent to adopt beliefs on the basis of small sets of perceptual inputs but then retract them in the face of additional perceptual inputs, if those additional inputs conflict in various ways with the original basis for the beliefs. This is a description of *defeasible reasoning*. Beliefs are adopted on the basis of arguments that appeal to small sets of previously held information, but the beliefs can later be retracted in the face of new information.[15] The second function for defeasible reasoning is that of activating a structured process of inquiry, based upon drawing *pro tanto* conclusions, looking for their defeaters, for defeaters of defeaters, and so on, until stable results can be obtained. This process has two main advantages: (1) it focuses the inquiry on relevant knowledge, and (2) it continues to deliver provisional results while inquiry goes on.

A third function of defeasibility is that of enabling our knowledge structures to persist to a certain degree over time, remaining a shared communal asset, while each one of us is constantly exposed to new information, often challenging the information we already have.

We have indeed two basic strategies for coping with the provisional nature of human knowledge. One strategy consists in viewing our persistent knowledge as a set of universal propositions, which may be falsified by any particular fact contradicting them (according to the hypothetico-deductive model described by Popper).[16] When we discover a case where such universal propositions lead us to false (or unacceptable or absurd) conclusions, we must conclude that our theory (the set of the propositions having been falsified) proved to be unacceptable. Thus we must abandon one or some such propositions and substitute them with new universal propositions, from which the false conclusion is no longer derivable.[17] The other strategy consists, on the contrary, in assuming that we must keep our general propositions even when their isolated application would lead us to wrong conclusions. We need to assume that a general proposition only concerns the majority of cases, or the normal cases, so that we can consistently claim that the proposition holds as a rule, while being not applicable in particular cases: the exception serves the rule, or at least, does not damage the rule. To deal appropriately with the anomalous case, then, it is not necessary to abandon the rule or to change its formulation, but rather to assume that the operation of the rule is limited on grounds different from those supporting the rule itself, grounds which may consist of an exception, or of a conflicting rule or principle prevailing according to certain criteria (for instance, a higher, more special, or later norm is traditionally assumed to prevail over a lower, more general, or earlier one). This enables a certain degree of stability in

15 J.L. Pollock, *Cognitive Carpentry*, 40.

16 K.R. Popper, *The Logic of Scientific Discovery* (London: Hutchinson, 1959).

17 On the revision of knowledge in face of change, see C.E Alchourrón, P. Gärdenfors, and D. Makinson, 'On the logic of theory change: Partial meet functions for contractions and revisions', *Journal of Symbolic Logic*, 50 (1985), 510–30; and P. Gärdenfors, *Knowledge in Flux* (Cambridge, Mass.: MIT Press, 1987).

legal knowledge, though it does not exclude the need to abandon a defeasible general rule when it no longer reflects a 'normal' connection; when it is superseded by subsequent information (as in implicit derogation to legal norms); or when it is explicitly removed from the knowledge-base (as in explicit derogation).

H. Collision and defeat

In order to have a first look into the working of defeasible reasoning, let us consider an example that is frequently referred to by epistemologists. Assume that I believe that swans are normally white, and that I am told that there is a swan in the park. This enables the following defeasible inference (an instance of the schema *statistical syllogism*):

- most swans are white;
- the bird in the park is a swan

—THEREFORE—

- the bird in the park is white

However, when I look out of the window, I see that the bird in the park, although being unmistakably a swan, looks kind of pinkish. This prompts the following perceptual inference:

- I am having a pink image of the bird in the park

—THEREFORE—

- the bird in the park is pink

Thus, I am pushed towards conflicting conclusions, supported by competing defeasible inferences (according to the first inference, the bird is white; according to the second one it is pink). Assume that, being a moderate empiricist, I consider the perceptual inference to be stronger than the statistical one. Therefore, I should abandon my *pro tanto* belief that the swan is white and accept (though provisionally) that it is pink. In such a case, we say that the inference concluding that the swan is white is defeated by the perceptual inference according to which it is pink.

Cognitive processes such as the one that we have considered can be explained by introducing two notions: collision and defeat.

Definition H.1 Collision. Let *M* be a reason for adopting *Q* and *M** be a reason for adopting *Q**. We say that that there is a collision between *M* and *M**, when the combined cognitive state which consists in endorsing both of *M* and *M** does not support adopting both of *Q* and *Q**.

When one finds oneself in a collision, one is prevented from performing both colliding inferences. One may be prevented from performing just one of them, or one may be prevented from performing both. Those inferences that are prevented by the collision, are said to be defeated, while the reason that prevents drawing a conclusion is said to be a *defeater*.[18]

Definition H.2 Defeat. Let *M* be a reason for adopting *Q*. Premise *M** defeats (is a defeater for) *M*, if the combined state consisting in endorsing both of *M* and *M** does not support adopting *Q*.

[18] See J.L. Pollock and J. Cruz, *Contemporary Theories of Knowledge*, 195ff.

Table 6.1 Rebutting collision: inference A collides with inference B

Inference A	Inference B
(1) Most swans are white	(1) I perceive the image of a pink bird in the park
(2) The bird in the park is a swan	
(3) The bird in the park is white	(2) The bird in the park is pink

In the example above, mental state *m* (believing that most swans are white and that the bird in the park is a swan) collides with mental state m^* (having the percept that that the bird in the park is pink). State *m* alone was a reason for adopting a *q* (believing that the bird in the park is white), according to *statistical syllogism*. However, the combined cognitive state consisting in believing *m* and having percept m^* is no reason for adopting *q*: because of the defeater m^*, the inference from *m* to *q* is blocked or defeated. The conflict between the two inferences ***A*** and ***B*** originated by the two colliding reasons *m* and m^* is reproduced in Table 6.1 (here and in the following, I shall refer to sequences of propositions—and, in particular, to inferences and arguments—by using symbols ***A***, ***B***, . . .).

I. Collisions and incompatibility

The type of collision exemplified at the end of the previous paragraph (conflict of inferences leading to incompatible conclusion) can be called *rebutting collision*. As a first approximation, rebutting collision can be defined as follows:

Definition I.1 Rebutting collision. There is a rebutting collision between reasons *M* and M^* when

- *M* is a reason to adopt *Q*,
- M^* is a reason to adopt Q^*, and
- *Q* is incompatible with Q^*.

However, only in some cases can incompatibility be assessed by looking only at the directly concerned proposition (more exactly, cognitive states): these are the cases when such propositions would be incompatible in all logically possible situations. For instance, it cannot be the case that Tom both stole a car and did not steal it; nor that Mary both is obliged to repair some damage and is not obliged to do so.

In many other cases, to assess the incompatibility of propositions one needs to consider additional information, concerning meaning connections, causal links, or further facts. For example, to assess that being pink and being white are incompatible states of one and the same object (our swan) one must know that an object cannot have two colours at the same time. Similarly, to know that there is a conflict between the fact that others retain and process one's personal data and one's free self-determination (as affirmed by privacy supporters), much psychological and sociological background knowledge is to be assumed. Finally, to know that low inflation and full employment are incompatible (in a certain economic context) one must have knowledge of economics. Therefore, very often the incompatibility of two conclusions cannot be immediately detected by the reasoner, but is rather the result of finding relevant information and of bringing it to bear through reasoning processes.[19]

[19] For an illuminating discussion, see C. Perelman and L. Olbrechts-Tyteca, *Traité de l'argumentation: la nouvelle rhéthorique* (5th edn, Brussels: Éditions de l'université de Bruxelles, 1988), section 46.

J. Undercutting collisions

Besides rebutting collisions, there is another way in which reasons can collide. This happens when the reasoner has a reason to believe that, in the present circumstances, a reasoning schema does not apply, since under those circumstances the reason of the schema provides no reliable support for its conclusions.

Let us consider a variation of the ornithological example introduced in section H. Assume that I am seeing (or rather having the vision of) a pink bird, and that I come to believe, according to a perceptual inference, that the bird is indeed pink. I notice, however, that there is a beautiful sunset now, throwing red light over all things. I know that red light makes white objects look pink. Therefore, I conclude that it would be unreasonable for me to believe that the swan is pink on the basis only of the fact that it looks pink to me (under the present conditions the pink-looking swan might as well be white). Note that this reasoning does not tell me that the swan is white, since pink objects would still look pink under red light: it only undermines the previous inference, without providing a different conclusion (Table 6.2).

This type of collision (collision between a reason *M*, and a reason *M**, indicating that *M* is unreliable) shall be called *undercutting collision*. More exactly, we can define undercutting collisions as follows.[20]

Definition J.1 Undercutting collision. There is an *undercutting collision* between reasons *M* and *M** when

- *M* is a reason for adopting *Q*,
- *M** is a reason for believing that *M* does not support *Q*.

Under these conditions we also say that *M** *undercuts M*.

For instance, my awareness that there is red light is a reason for believing that the fact that the bird looks pink does not support concluding that it is pink. Such awareness *collides with*, and more exactly *undercuts*, my considering the pink appearance of the bird as a reason for concluding that it is pink.

K. Preference-based reasoning

When one endorses two colliding reasons, one cannot derive the conclusions of both of them: at least one of these reasons is defeated. We may thus distinguish the following two cases:

Table 6.2 Undercutting collision: inference **A** collides with inference **B**

Inference A	Inference B
(1) I perceive a pink bird in the park	(1) There is red light outside
	(2) Perceiving a pink object under red light does not warrant that it is pink
(2) The bird in the park is pink	(3) My perceiving a pink bird does not warrant that it is pink

[20] See J.L. Pollock and J. Cruz, *Contemporary Theories of Knowledge*, 196.

- If one reason, assume R_1, prevails over the other, R_2, we may reject R_2 and endorse R_1 (so that only R_2 is defeated).
- If, on the contrary, neither of the two reasons prevails, and we are not justified in adopting either of them, neither reasons are defeated.

Thus, it appears that a reason R_1 *defeats* a reason R_2, whenever R_1 collides with R_2, and R_2 does not prevail over R_1. When, additionally, R_1 prevails over R_2 (first point above) then R_1 *strictly defeats* R_2 (defeats R_2, but is not defeated by it). Note that the two statements (*a*) [R_2 does not prevail over R_1] and (*b*) [R_1 prevails over R_2] are not equivalent. The first proposition also holds when the outcome of the conflict of the two reasons is a draw (or is undecided), while the second requires that the conflict is positively decided in favour of R_1 (I assume that the prevailing-over relation is antisymmetric).

In a case of rebutting collision, the stronger reason outweighs and strictly defeats its competitor. Consider for example, a recent case that had to be addressed by the Italian privacy authority. It concerned the case of a woman who requested, for health reasons, access to data concerning the DNA of her father (the data was stored in the database of a hospital), who did not give his consent (to her accessing this information). Therefore, the authority needed to balance the privacy-based inference (the father's data could not be provided since sensitive data cannot be communicated without the consent of the data subject) and the inference based upon the right to health (one has a right to obtain what is needed for one's health, such as, for that woman, access to her father's DNA). In such a case the health-based inference was considered to be preferable to the privacy-based inference, so that the latter was viewed as being strictly defeated, and the former inference dictated the outcome of the case.

In the case of undercutting collisions, on the contrary the undercutter prevails since it strictly defeats the attacked reason. This seems indeed the most reasonable way of approaching undercutting. If I have a reason R_1 to believe that the bird in the park is pink, and a reason R_2 to conclude that R_1 is unreliable, I should not conclude that the bird is pink (on the basis of the unreliable reason R_1). Similarly, assume that I find in a law text two rules: a rule r_1, and a rule r_2 saying that r_1 is inapplicable under certain circumstances. If these circumstances are present in the case at issue I should conclude that r_1 is indeed inapplicable, and refrain from deriving its conclusion.

To sum up, when facing a collision, we should reason as follows:

- in rebutting collisions, we should compare the strength of the conflicting reasons, and assume that any reason that is not stronger than its competitor is defeated (only stronger reasons prevail);
- in undercutting collisions, we should assume that the undercutter always prevails.

Let us consider a further example on undercutting. Assume that I have heard two different accounts of the same event, from two friends, John and Mary:

- John tells me *A*,
- Mary tells me NON-*A* (*A* is not the case), and
- I consider both of them to be sufficiently reliable, under normal circumstances (so that I would have believed each one of them, if the other had kept silent).

It seems that I should view the statements of Mary and John as defeating one another, and refrain from forming any belief on the matter (neither *A* nor NON-*A*), unless I can assume that one of the two statements is more reliable than the other. In the latter case,

I should provisionally (defeasibly or *pro tanto*) believe the content of the more reliable statement, and reject the other.

Similarly, assume that I come to know both of the following facts:

- Tom intentionally caused harm to Mary's property by driving into her fence; and
- he acted in a state of necessity, to avoid hitting a child who was crossing the street.

Under such conditions, I should conclude that Tom has no duty to compensate Mary's damage, since the conclusion that he is not liable (having acted out of the necessity of saving a child's life) prevails over the conclusion that he is liable (having intentionally damaged another's property).

This way of reasoning assumes, however, that one has a way of determining what conclusion (if any) is more strongly supported. In some cases, one may do that by adopting mathematical methods. For example, one may use probability calculus, and assume that the strength of each conclusion corresponds to its probability, which can be computed by combining the probabilities of its supporting sub-reasons. Other numerical calculations of the comparative strength of beliefs have also been proposed, which diverge under some respects from standard probability.[21] I cannot here discuss the merit of numerical methods for assessing credibility, which would require us to address the technicalities of probability and statistics. Let us just observe, in general, that there are certain specific legal issues (in particular in the domain of evidence) where numerical calculi can provide appropriate answers. However, these calculi do not provide a generally applicable solution for dealing with incompatible conclusions in moral and legal reasoning. In the law, it is rather the case that one needs to engage in priority reasoning, that is, one needs to bring to bear further information, and decide accordingly which inference prevails. Though this information rarely is numerical, in most cases it enables a sufficiently precise and shareable assessment.

L. Reinstatement

I need to introduce a further idea that explains the characteristic procedure of defeasible reasoning: the notion of *reinstatement*. When a defeater is strictly defeated by a further inference, the inference originally attacked by the defeater may recover its capacity to establish its conclusion.

Let us develop further the pink swan example. As before, assume that the bird of which I am having a pink vision is a swan, so that I would conclude that it is white unless this conclusion was defeated by my perception of its pinkness. Assume also that I realise that the sun is setting, and that the light it is casting makes all white things look pink. My awareness of this undercuts the conclusion that the bird is pink (see Table 6.2). As a consequence of the perceptual inference being undercut, the inference for whiteness is reinstated: I again *pro tanto* believe that the bird is white (being a swan).

Let us consider another example, concerning the difference between rebutting and undercutting. Let as assume that a detective is investigating the violent death of John, of which Mary, John's inconsolable girlfriend, is accused. The detective believes that Mary loved John, but has evidence that her clothes were stained with John's blood. The information he has allows him to build two inferences, which rebut one another: the inference according to which Mary did not kill John, since she loved him (inference *A*),

[21] See, for example, J.L. Pollock, *Cognitive Carpentry*.

Table 6.3 Defeat by rebutting

Inference ***B*** is preferable to inference ***A***	
Inference *A*	Inference *B*
(1) Mary loved John (2) people normally do not kill their loved ones (3) Mary has not killed John	(1) Mary's clothes were stained with John's blood (2) if one's clothes are stained with the victim's blood, then normally one has killed the victim (3) Mary has killed John

Table 6.4 Reinstatement through undercutting

Inference ***B*** is preferable to inference ***A***		
Inference *A*	Inference *B*	Inference *C*
(1) Mary loved John	(1) Mary's clothes were stained with John's blood	(1) Lisa stained John's clothes with blood
(2) people normally do not kill their loved ones	(2) if one's clothes are stained with the victim's blood, then normally one has killed the victim	
(3) Mary has not killed John	(3) Mary has killed John	(2) Mary's clothes being stained with John's blood does not prove that Mary killed John

and the inference that she killed him, since her clothes were stained with John's blood (inference ***B***).

Assume that the detective also believes that inference ***B*** is preferable to (stronger than) inference ***A*** (he gives more credit to chemistry than to psychology). This allows the detective to endorse the conclusion of inference ***B***: at this stage of the inquiry he forms the belief that Mary killed John (inference ***B*** defeats inference ***A***, but inference ***A*** does not defeat ***B***).

However, assume that the detective discovers that Lisa (John's previous girlfriend) tried to frame Mary, by staining Mary's dress with John's blood. Again, this alone would not be a reason to believe that Mary did not kill John, but rather a reason for considering that the inference ***B*** (from Mary's having blood-stained clothes to her being the murderer) is unreliable, and therefore to view this inference as being undercut. Let us consider these three inferences, as shown in Table 6.4.

The latter inference, let us call it ***C***, by undermining inference ***B*** results in reinstating inference ***A***. Thus, we pass from the following situation (the arrow indicates defeat, and goes from the defeating inference to the defeated one):

$$A \leftarrow B$$

where inference ***A*** is strictly defeated by inference ***B***, into the situation:

$$A \leftarrow B \leftarrow C$$

where inference ***B*** is strictly defeated by inference ***C***, and consequently ***A*** is reinstated. Thus given all of ***A***, ***B***, and ***C***, the detective would conclude, according to ***A***, that Mary did not kill John (since she loved him).

A further type of undercutting collision is provided by inferences presupposing that one does not have a certain mental state: these inferences collide exactly with one's

Table 6.5 Undercutting presupposition

Inference *A*	Inference ***B***
(1) If I do not believe that one is guilty, then I presume that one is innocent	(1) I have evidence proving that Mary is guilty
(2) I do not believe that Mary is guilty	
(3) Mary is innocent	(2) Mary is guilty

adoption of that mental state. Such inferences are made when one assumes that, if a certain proposition *A* were true, one would have come to believe *A*, or at least one would possess the information that enables one to infer *A*. This is the rationale of the so-called auto-epistemic logic,[22] which provides one of the theories for negation by failure in logic programmes.[23]

Therefore, when failing to form the belief that *A*, one may conclude that *A* does not hold and reason accordingly. However, when one positively finds that *A* holds, one should abandon inferences based upon the assumption that *A* does not hold. For example, a judge who does not believe that a person is guilty should base his verdict upon the thesis that the person is innocent (*in dubio pro reo*), as shown in Table 6.5.

It may be argued that this kind of situation takes place more generally in the law, whenever a rule makes a certain legal effect dependent upon the fact that certain facts are not shown to hold. This is indeed the typical way of reasoning with legal *presumptions*.[24] Consider, for example, the rule in the Italian civil code, which says that one is presumed to have received a message when the message arrived at one's address, unless one proves that one had no possibility of accessing the message. The judge, according to this rule, will be able to conclude that one has received a message on the basis of the sole fact that the message arrived at one's address, under the assumption that the addressee could read the message. However, if there is evidence showing it was impossible for the addressee to access the message, this conclusion will be defeated.

M. Undercutting in practical reasoning

Undercutting also applies to practical reasoning. The need to act on the basis of defeasible conclusions is particularly apparent when one—pressed by many goals and commitments—needs to quickly find plans and adopt them without further ado (even when one is aware that there may be better plans which one could find, having additional time at one's disposal). However, if a better plan becomes available before action takes place, one should abandon one's previous intention, and adopt the new plan. Consider, for example, the inference leading me to adopt the intention of leaving

[22] R.C. Moore, 'Possible-world semantics for autoepistemic logic' in M.L. Ginsberg (ed.), *Readings in Nonmonotonic Reasoning*, 137–42.

[23] K.L. Clark, 'Negation as failure' in M.L. Ginsberg (ed.), *Readings in Nonmonotonic Reasoning*, 311–25.

[24] See H. Prakken and G. Sartor, 'Formalizing arguments about the burden of persuasion' in *Proceedings of the 11th International Conference on Artificial Intelligence and Law. ICAIL-2007* (New York, NY.: ACM, 2007); H. Prakken and G. Sartor, ' More on presumptions and burdens of proof' in E. Francesconi, G. Sartor, and D. Tiscornia (eds), *Proceedings of JURIX 2008* (Amsterdam: IOS, 2008).

on Monday for Barcelona, since this plan is sufficiently good; it is better than staying at home (the inactivity option), and is better than any plan I have so far considered. This inference gets defeated when I build a plan for leaving on the Sunday before, which allows me to get a cheaper ticket and to make a short visit to the main monuments of the city.

In general, in teleological reasoning one moves from (1) having a goal G and (2) believing that plan (instruction) P_1 is a satisfactory way of achieving G, to (3) intending to realize P_1. However, this inference can be undercut when the reasoner comes to believe that a different plan, let us call it P_2, is better than P_1, as a way of achieving G. The defeat schema seems therefore to be the following:

Defeating schema: *Teleological defeat*

- believing that plan P_2 is a better way of achieving goal G than plan P_1

—IS AN UNDERCUTTING DEFEATER AGAINST—

- using *teleological inference*, for adopting P_1 as a way of achieving G

Assume for example that a judge has so far decided cases on product liability by requiring that customers prove the producers' fault. Assume that the judge adopted this policy since she believed that this was a satisfactory way to induce producers to take care to avoid releasing faulty products. Assume, however, that the same judge now comes across some law-and-economics literature that shows that strict liability provides a stronger incentive to preventing damage to the customer. The judge should then be induced to abandon the fault liability approach in favour of strict liability (for simplicity's sake, in this example I discount the considerations concerning the need that the judge respects legislation or precedents, and coordinates her action with the action of her colleagues, of legislators, and of the citizens).

Here is the corresponding defeat instance:

Defeating instance: *Teleological defeat*

- believing that strict liability is a better way of preventing damage to the customers than fault liability

—IS AN UNDERCUTTING DEFEATER AGAINST—

- using *teleology*, for adopting fault liability as a way of preventing damage to the customers

Another example of this type of defeat is represented in Table 6.6.

Table 6.6 Teleological defeat

Inference *A*	Inference *B*
(1) I have the goal of getting the new book of my friend Henry Prakken (2) plan *p1* (buying it online) is a sufficiently good way of achieving this goal	(1) Plan *p2* (getting a free author's copy) is a more convenient way of getting Henry's book
(3) I intend to implement plan *p1*	(2) the extent to which plan *p1* contributes to achieving my goals does not support its adoption

N. Defeasible reasoning and probability

We may wonder whether defeasible reasoning is the only, or the best, way to deal with incomplete information. In particular, we need to consider the main alternative to it, that is, *probability calculus*, and in particular the versions of probability calculus that are based upon the idea of *subjective probability*. In fact, probability calculus has more solid scientific credentials than any logic for defeasible reasoning, and a rich history of successful applications in many domains of science and practice.

Following the probability approach, the reasoner—rather than facing incompatible beliefs (like the belief that John was driving the car when the car ran over Tom, and the belief Mary was driving the car on the same occasion), and then having to make a choice—would come to the consistent conclusion that incompatible hypotheses have different probabilities (for instance, one would reach the conclusion that there is a 40 per cent chance that John ran over Tom, and a 60 per cent chance that Mary did it). Probabilistic inference, as is well known, determines the probability of an event on the basis of the probability of other events, according to the mechanism of probability calculus: if there is a 80 per cent chance that Tom will have walking problems because of having been run over, there is a 32 per cent chance (40 per cent * 80 per cent) that Tom will have such problems having been run over by John, and a 48 per cent chance (60 per cent * 80 per cent) that he will have such problems having been run over by Mary.

Here I cannot introduce probability calculus, nor discuss the many difficult issues which are related to it (especially when ideas of probability and causation are combined). I shall merely indicate a few issues concerning the probability calculus, which make it inadequate as a general approach for dealing with uncertainty in legal reasoning.

The first issue concerns practicability: often we do not have enough information to assign, numerical probabilities in a sensible way. For instance, how do I know that there is a 40 per cent probability that John was driving and 60 per cent probability that Mary was driving? In such a case, it seems that either we arbitrarily attribute probabilities, or, with equal arbitrariness, we assume that all alternative ways in which things may have occurred have the same probability.

The second issue is a conceptual one: although it makes sense to ascribe probabilities to epistemic propositions, it makes little sense to assign them to practical information. What does it mean that a certain desire (goal) or intention (instruction), has a certain probability? What does it mean that a value, a normative connection, or an obligation has a certain probability?

The third issue relates to psychology: humans tend to face situations of uncertainty by choosing to endorse hypothetically one of the available epistemic or practical alternatives (while keeping open the chance that other options may turn out to be preferable), and by applying their reasoning to this hypothesis (while possibly, at the same time, exploring what would be the case, if things turned out to be different). We do not usually assign probabilities and then compute what further probabilities follow from such an assignment. This cognitive behaviour corresponds to the reasoning skills of which we are naturally endowed. Humans, once they have definite beliefs or hypotheses, are able to develop inference chains, store them in their minds (keeping them unconscious until needed), and then retract any such chains when one of its links is defeated. Conversely, humans are bad at assigning numerical probabilities, and even worse at deriving further probabilities and at revising probability assignments in the light of further information.

Our incapacity for working with numerical probabilities certainly is one of the many failures of human cognition (like our incapability of quickly executing big arithmetical calculations). In fact, computer systems exist which, using complex nets of probabilities (these are called *belief networks* or *probability networks*), perform very well in certain domains by manipulating numerical probabilities much quicker and more accurately than a normal person.[25] However, our bias towards adopting a binary, rather than a probabilistic approach (endorsing one alternative, rather than assigning probabilities to all of them), in the face of uncertainty has some advantages: it focuses cognition on the implications of the most likely situations, it supports making long reasoning chains, it facilitates building scenarios (or stories) which may then be evaluated according to their coherence, it enables linking epistemic cognition with binary decision-making (it may be established that one has to adopt decision *B* if *A* is the case, and NON *B* if *A* is not the case). There is indeed psychological evidence that humans develop theories even under situations of extreme uncertainty, when no reasonable probability assignment can be made.

In a social context a binary approach makes it easier to replicate the reasoning and thinking of other people: one can forecast more easily a binary choice by another than the ascription of probabilities, and such a binary choice can become the focus of social expectations.[26] The limited applicability of probability calculus in the practical domains does not exclude there being various practical and legal issues where statistics and probability provide decisive clues, as when scientific evidence is at issue.[27]

O. The idea of defeasibility in the practical domain

The notion of defeasibility, before becoming the focus of much AI research, was deployed by some epistemologists like John Pollock and Roderick Chisholm.[28] Even before that, however, the idea of defeasibility was frequently applied and sometimes studied in the domain of practical (moral and legal) reasoning.

The word *defeasible* is a traditional legal term, indicating the possibility that a legal instrument is voided in special circumstances. In fact, it is a typical feature of law and morality that they can only offer standards appropriate for normal situations. When exceptional circumstances occur, these standards may need to be put aside.[29] This is well expressed in a famous Aristotelian citation, where defeasibility is considered not a fault, but a natural feature of legal rules:

[25] See, for a short introduction, S.J. Russell and P. Norvig, *Artificial Intelligence. A Modern Approach* (2nd edn, Englewood Cliffs, NJ: Prentice Hall, 2003), ch. 14; and, for a collection of important contributions, G. Shafer and J. Pearl (eds), *Readings in Uncertain Reasoning* (Los Altos, Cal.: Morgan Kaufmann, 1990).

[26] This aspect is particularly emphasized by N. Luhmann, *Rechtssystem und Rechtsdogmatik* (Stuttgard: Kohlhammer, 1974), ch. 6, section 1.

[27] On scientific evidence, see, among others S. Haack, 'Truth and justice, inquiry and advocacy, science and law', *Associations*, 7 (2003), 103–14; and S. Haack, *Defending Science within Reason* (Amherst, NY: Prometheus, 2003), 233ff.

[28] On defeasibility and AI (artificial intelligence), see M.L. Ginzberg (ed.), *Readings in Nonmonotonic Reasoning*. On the notion of defeasibility in epistemology, see J.L. Pollock, *Knowledge and Justification* (Princeton, NJ: Princeton University Press, 1974); and R.M. Chisholm, *Theory of Knowledge* (2nd edn, Englewood Cliffs, NJ: Prentice Hall, 1977).

[29] On defeasibility in the law, cf. among others, T.F. Gordon, 'The importance of nonmonotonicity for legal reasoning' in H. Fiedler, F. Haft, and R. Traunmüller (eds), *Expert Systems in Law: Impacts on Legal Theory and Computer Law* (Tübingen: Attempto, 1988), 111–26; G. Sartor, 'Defeasibility in legal reasoning' in Z. Bankowski, I. White, and U. Hahn (eds), *Informatics and the Foundations of Legal Reasoning* (Dordrecht: Kluwer, 1995), 119–57; N. MacCormick, 'Defeasibility in law and logic' in Z. Bankowski, et al., (eds), *Informatics and the Foundations of Legal Reasoning*, 99–117.

All law is universal, and there are some things about which it is not possible to pronounce rightly in general terms; therefore in cases where it is necessary to make a general pronouncement, but impossible to do so rightly, the law takes account of the majority of cases, though not unaware that in this way errors are made. And the law is none the less right; because the error lies not in the law nor in the legislator, but in the nature of the case, for the raw material of human behaviour is essentially of this kind. So, when the law states a general rule, and a case arises under this that is exceptional, then it is right, where the legislator, owing to the generality of his language, has erred in not covering that case, to correct the omission by a ruling such as the legislator himself would have given if he had been present, and as he would have enacted if he had been aware of the circumstances.[30]

Similarly, Aquinas makes the following precise observation:

[I]t is right and true for all to act according to reason: And from this principle it follows as a proper conclusion, that goods entrusted to another should be restored to their owner. Now this is true for the majority of cases: But it may happen in a particular case that it would be injurious, and therefore unreasonable, to restore goods held in trust; for instance, if they are claimed for the purpose of fighting against one's country. And this principle will be found to fail the more, according as we descend further into detail, e.g., if one were to say that goods held in trust should be restored with such and such a guarantee, or in such and such a way; because the greater the number of conditions added, the greater the number of ways in which the principle may fail, so that it be not right to restore or not to restore.[31]

The very notion of defeasibility is at the centre of the work of David Ross, an outstanding Aristotelian scholar and moral philosopher, who developed a famous theory of prima facie moral obligations. Ross, who endorsed a pluralist form of moral intuitionism, relates defeasibility to the possibility that moral principles are overridden by other moral principles in concrete cases:

Moral intuitions are not principles by the immediate application of which our duty in particular circumstances can be deduced. They state . . . *prima facie* obligations . . . [We] are not obliged to do that which is only *prima facie* obligatory. We are only bound to do that act whose *prima facie* obligatoriness in those respects in which it is *prima facie* obligatory most outweighs its *prima facie* disobligatoriness in those aspects in which it is prima facie disobligatory.[32]

The notion of defeasibility, quite usual in legal practice and in doctrinal work, was brought to the attention of legal theorists by H.L.A. Hart, whose observations anticipate the current debate on the topic:

When the student has learnt that in English law there are positive conditions required for the existence of a valid contract, . . . he has still to learn what can defeat a claim that there is a valid contract, even though all these conditions are satisfied. The student has still to learn what can follow on the word 'unless', which should accompany the statement of these conditions. This characteristic of legal concepts is one for which no word exists in ordinary English . . . [T]he law has a word which with some hesitation I borrow and extend: this is the word 'defeasible', used of a legal interest in property which is subject to termination of 'defeat' in a number of different contingencies but remains intact if no such contingencies mature.[33]

30 Aristotle, *Nicomachean Ethics* (Oxford: Oxford University Press, 1954), 1137b.
31 St. Thomas Aquinas, *Summa Theologiae* (Allen, Texas: Benzinger Bros, 1947), I–II, q. 94, a. 4.
32 W.D. Ross, *Foundations of Ethics* (Oxford: Clarendon Press, 1939), 84–5.
33 H.L.A. Hart, 'The ascription of responsibility and rights' in A. Flew (ed.), *Logic and Language* (Oxford: Blackwell, 1951), 152.

In legal defeasibility two aspects must be distinguished:

(1) the inventive, heuristic reasoning required for understanding the inadequacy of a general rule in a particular context and for stating a corresponding exception or rebuttal;

(2) the structure of the reasoning that takes into account exceptions, rebuttals, and presumptions in order to reach conclusions justified by all available knowledge.

The second aspect does not fall outside logic. Legal defeasibility implies that for justifying a legal conclusion it is normally, but not always, sufficient to select from the available pool of premises a subset supporting that conclusion. In fact, the inference of that conclusion may be defeated, if an exception or an 'unless' clause is satisfied, or if a relevant presumption is found to be contradicted.

P. Defeasibility in legal language

The legislator often explicitly foresees the defeasibility of legal rules by using different linguistic structures. For example, to establish that tort liability is excluded by self-defence or state of necessity, the legislator may use any of the following formulations:

- *Unless clause.* One is liable if one voluntarily causes damage, unless one acts in self-defence or in a state of necessity.
- *Explicit exception.* One is liable if one voluntarily causes damage. One is not liable for damages if one acts in self-defence or in a state of necessity.
- *Presumption.* One is liable if one voluntarily causes damage and one does not act out of self-defence or state of necessity. The absence of both is presumed.

According to all these formulations, for concluding that one must make good a certain damage it is normally sufficient to ascertain that one voluntarily caused that damage, but this inference is defeated if the person turns out to have acted either out of necessity or in self-defence.

By distinguishing circumstances that have to be positively established to derive a certain conclusion from circumstances susceptible to blocking this derivation, the law divides the *burden of proof* between the parties. The plaintiff, who is interested in establishing a certain legal conclusion, has the burden of establishing the supporting circumstances. The defendant, once the plaintiff has succeeded, has the burden of establishing the impeding circumstances. Though defeasibility may not fully explain the dialectics of legal procedures, it provides their logical background.[34]

Q. Defeasibility in legal concepts and procedures

Defeasibility is also an essential feature of *conceptual constructions* in the law. Legal concepts have to be applied to such a diverse domain of instances that they can at best offer a tentative and generic characterization of the objects to which they apply, a characterization which has to be supplemented with exceptions. General legal concepts presuppose defeasibility: the requirement of absolute rigour in defining and applying concepts—the demand that all features which are included in, or entailed by, a concept

[34] For a logical model of the burden of proof, see H. Prakken and G. Sartor, 'Formalizing arguments about the burden of persuasion'.

apply to each one of its instances—would paradoxically run against the very possibility of being 'logical' in the sense of using general concepts.

In fact, even the definitions of the legal concepts that can be found in statutes and codes reflect the stepwise defeasible process of establishing legal qualifications. First a general discipline is established for a certain legal genus (for example, contract), then special exceptions are introduced for species of this genus (like the sale contract), and finally further exceptions may be introduced for specific subspecies (like the sale of real estate). Consequently, when using conceptual hierarchies we must apply to a certain object the rules concerning the category in which it is included only insofar as no exceptions emerge concerning a subcategory in which that object is also included. Defeasibility can be consciously established by the legislator, but it may also result from the evolution of legal knowledge: after a general rule has been established, exceptions are often provided for those cases where the rule appears to be inadequate. This is typically the evolution of judge-made law, where general *rationes decidendi* are often limited by means of *distinctions*, namely, by means of exceptions introduced for specific contexts.

General attitudes of legal reasoning can also be explained and justified as *defeasible presumptions*. For example, interpretation standards and even judicial precedents (*rationes decidendi*) bind judges only defeasibly, in the sense that they should be followed only insofar as they are not overridden by (strong) reasons to the contrary.[35] Even the obligation to apply legislation is considered to be defeasible by many authors, who believe that statutory texts are not legally binding when completely unacceptable from a moral standpoint.[36] Similarly, the due consideration for widespread social attitudes, legal traditions, socially accepted common-sense rules (so much stressed by theorists of argumentation) can be distinguished from blind conservatism only when those factors are given the statute of defeasible presumption. This was also, by the way, the spirit of the principle of inertia advocated by Perelman and Olbrechts-Tyteca, according to which any opinion adopted in the past should only be abandoned when having sufficient reasons to do so.[37] More generally, defeasible endorsement is the appropriate cognitive attitude with regard to what Aristotle calls *endoxa*, meaning any 'opinion held by everyone or by the majority or by the wise—either all of the wise or the majority or the most famous of them—and which is not paradoxical'.[38]

Finally, the procedural aspect of defeasibility also needs to be considered. This aspect concerns the fact that, as observed above, defeasible reasoning activates a structured process of inquiry—based upon drawing prima facie conclusions, looking for their (prima facie) defeaters, looking for defeaters of defeaters, and so on—until stable results can be obtained. Such a process reflects the natural way in which legal reasoning proceeds. This is particularly the case in the application of the law to particular situations, when one has to bring to bear on such situations the different, and possibly conflicting, legal rules that apply to them, and adjudicate the conflicts between these rules. Klaus Günther has affirmed that the application of the law is characterized by a *sense of appropriateness*, intended as the ability to impartially take into consideration all

35 R. Alexy, *A Theory of Legal Argumentation: The Theory of Rational Discourse as Theory of Legal Justification* (Oxford: Clarendon, 1989), 274–9.

36 See A. Peczenik, *On Law and Reason* (Dordrecht: Kluwer, 1989); and R. Alexy, *Begriff und Geltung des Rechts* (Freiburg: Steiner, 1992).

37 C. Perelman and L. Olbrechts-Tyteca, *The New Rhetoric: A Treaty on Argumentation* (Notre Dame, Ind.: University of Notre Dame Press, 1969), 142.

38 Aristotle, *Topics* (New York, NY: Random House, 1941), 104a8–13.

different features of the considered situation, according to all valid rules which may apply to it.[39] Defeasible reasoning can be viewed as a logical model of Günther's sense of appropriateness. The idea of defeasible reasoning is indeed based on the distinction between on the one hand the adoption of general defeasible rules, each of which only takes into account a few aspects of possible situations, and on the other hand the application of these rules to concrete situations, where one needs to take into account all aspects that are relevant according to all applicable rules. Different aspects of the same situation may indeed support contradictory conclusions for that situation, so that a choice has to be made. In fact in the law, as in 'any subject on which difference of opinion is possible, the truth depends on a balance to be struck between two sets of conflicting reasons', the point by which 'truths have reached the point of being uncontested' is far from being attained.[40] Therefore, in legal reasoning the use of *positive logic*, which relates a thesis to its supporting grounds, must be supplemented with critical discussion of the opinion to the contrary, that is, by that *negative logic* which 'points out weaknesses in theory or errors in practice, without establishing positive truths'.[41] Logics for defeasible reasoning have the merit of unravelling exactly the basic structure of Mill's negative logic.

Defeasibility of legal reasoning also reflects the dialectics of judicial proceedings where each party provides arguments supporting his or her position, which conflict with the arguments of the other party. This debate may also be transferred into the judicial opinion that resumes the results of the dispute and determines its output. To justify convincingly a judicial decision in a case involving serious issues, it is not sufficient to produce a single argument, but it is necessary to establish that the winning argument prevails over arguments to the contrary, especially those that have been presented by the losing party. In addition, doctrinal work cannot avoid being contaminated by the dialectics of legal proceedings, since its main function consists in providing general arguments and points of view to be used in judicial debates. In this perspective, doctrinal reasoning may be viewed as consisting in an exercise of *unilateral dialectics*, intended as a disputational model of inquiry in which 'one develops a thesis against its rivals, with the aim of refining its formulation, uncovering its basis of rational support, and assessing its relative weight'.[42]

R. Overcoming legal defeasibility?

Some authors have suggested that the law ought to be recast in a set of consistent axioms, which would lead to compatible outcomes, according to deductive inference, in any possible factual situation. This reformulation of the law would eliminate normative conflicts, and therefore would leave no room for legal defeasibility (at least of the rebutting type). This idea has been affirmed in particular by Carlos Alchourrón and Eugenio Bulygin: the legislator and the doctrinal jurist should combine their efforts towards providing axiomatic reformulation of the law, or at least of particular sections of it.[43] As

[39] K. Günther, 'A normative conception of coherence for a discursive theory of legal justification', *Ratio Juris*, 2 (1989), 155–66; and K. Günther, *The Sense of Appropriateness* (Albany, NY: State University of New York Press, 1993).

[40] J.S. Mill, 'On liberty' in J. Gray (ed.), *On Liberty and Other Essays* (1st edn 1859; Oxford: Oxford University Press, 1991), 41 and 51.

[41] Ibid., 109.

[42] N. Rescher, *Dialectics: A Controversy-Oriented Approach to the Theory of Knowledge* (Albany, NY: State University of New York Press, 1977), 47.

[43] See C.E. Alchourrón and E. Bulygin, *Normative Systems* (Vienna: Springer, 1971).

Euclid developed an axiomatic model of geometry and as modern natural and social science (in particular economics) have developed axiomatic models of their knowledge, so the legislator and the jurist should axiomatize certain domains of the law. By adding to such an axiomatization the description of specific cases (a description to be accomplished in the same language used for the axiomatization), we should obtain a set of premises from which the legal discipline of such cases can be deduced. Accordingly, the model of the deductive application of the law should be extended beyond the so-called judicial syllogism so as to include the whole of predicate logic and deontic logics.

Alchourrón has affirmed that the ideal of the axiomatization of the law should inspire legislation and doctrine,[44] and could contribute to bringing legal studies and scientific method together: as in science the phenomena to be explained, the *explanandum*, should be logical consequences of a set of premises, the *explanans*, containing scientific laws and the description of particular facts,[45] so in law the content of a particular legal conclusion (decision) should be the deductive consequence of a set of premises including both general norms and the description of specific facts.

We need to consider, however, that it is very doubtful whether such a reformulation of the law is always feasible, and, even if it were feasible, it is doubtful whether it would be useful. It is indeed doubtful whether such an axiomatization would really make the law easier to understand and apply. Legal prescriptions would need to become more complex, since every rule would have to incorporate all its exceptions. In addition, such a representation of the law would not be able to model the dynamic adjustment that takes place—without modifying the wording of existing rules—whenever new information concerning the conflicting rules and the criteria for adjudicating their conflicts is taken into consideration. Finally, by rejecting defeasible reasoning, one would lose its capacity to provide provisional outcomes while legal inquiry goes on.

The need to represent the law in ways which facilitate defeasible reasoning does not imply that the current way of expressing legal regulations in statutes and regulatory instruments cannot be improved. Large improvements in legislation techniques on the contrary are required to cope with the many tasks that need to be carried out by modern legal systems. However, such improvements should not aim at producing a conflict-free set of legal rules, just for the sake of logical consistency. They should rather aim at producing legal texts that can be more easily understood and applied.[46] This objective requires a skilful use of the very knowledge structures (such as conceptual hierarchies, specialty, or the combination of rules and exceptions) that enable defeasible reasoning. Such structures are largely used also outside the law, in situations when one has to express precisely ways of dealing with complex and changing situations. For example, conceptual hierarchies (enabling defeasible inheritance) have become a standard programming technique in object-oriented programming (the mainstream programming methodology nowadays), while defeasible reasoning, in the form of negation by failure, provides a core function of logic programming.[47]

Accepting defeasibility in the law has significant implications both for the ways of using legal knowledge and for the structure of such knowledge. On the one hand,

[44] C.E. Alchourrón, 'On law and logic', in this volume, ch. 2.

[45] C.G. Hempel, *Philosophy of Natural Sciences* (Englewood Cliffs, NJ: Prentice Hall, 1966).

[46] T.F. Gordon, 'The importance of nonmonotonicity for legal reasoning' in H. Fiedler, F. Haft, and R. Traunmüller (eds), *Expert Systems in Law: Impacts on Legal Theory and Computer Law* (Tübingen: Attempto, 1988).

[47] For a classical introduction to logic programming, see R.A. Kowalski, *Logic for Problem Solving* (New York, NY: North Holland, 1979).

deductive inference can be complemented with defeasible arguments, supporting their conclusions only to the extent that they are not validly attacked (rebutted or undercut) by further arguments. On the other hand, the picture of the law as conflict-free set of legal axioms can be substituted with a view of its argumentation framework containing conflicting pieces of information as well as the criteria for solving such conflicts. It is important to stress the difference between an argumentation framework and a deductive axiomatic base. While a deductive axiomatic base is consistent and flat, an argumentation framework is conflictual and hierarchical: it includes reasons clashing against one another, reasons for preferring one particular reason to certain others, and reasons for applying or not applying certain reasons given particular conditions.

Both strategies just mentioned, namely representing law as an axiomatic base or representing it as an argumentation framework, may be justified, in different contexts. The first strategy may be appropriate when we want to deepen our analysis of a small set of norms and anticipate as much as possible all instances of their application, finding a precise solution for each of them. The second strategy, however, corresponds more directly to the logical structure of non-formalized legal language (which expresses the law indicating rules and exceptions, principles, preference criteria, etc.), and reflects the ways of legal reasoning, when applied to its peculiar contents: rules and exceptions, different values to balance, different norms implementing different values, standards indicating what norms and values ought to prevail in the case of conflict, etc.

We may transform an argumentation framework into an axiomatic knowledge base whose deductive conclusions include all outcomes which would be defeasibly justified given the argumentation framework (assuming that all the facts of the cases were known). The dialectical interaction between reasons for and against certain conclusions, and grounds for preferring one reason to another, would be transformed into the description of conclusive connections between legal preconditions and legal consequences (the connection which hold*s* on the basis of the given argumentation framework and of the arguments it enables). Flattening legal information in this way, however, entails a loss of information; the deductive knowledge base does not include memory of the choices from which it derives, and therefore it does not contain the information needed to reconsider such choices, for instance, for the purpose of establishing new interpretations. We need to go back to the original argumentation framework when we want to understand the articulation of legal reasoning, and expand or revise its premises on the basis of new information.

Consider for instance the domain of privacy. Here we have (at least under EU regulation) the idea that processing personal data is only admissible for a specific purpose, communicated to the person concerned. Moreover, in general such processing is only admissible when there is consent by that person. These constraints are justified by the need to protect values such as individual self-determination and dignity. However, there is a large set of exceptions to the consent principle, namely different hypotheses when data can be processed without consent. These exceptions are justified by the need to protect competing rights of others, as well as certain social goals. Moreover, we have cases where consent alone is insufficient to make data processing permissible, further requirements being necessary (such as, for genetic data, the authorization of the privacy authority), and for each such exception specific rationales can be found, which guide interpreters in determining the contents and limits of the exception. Finally there may be cases where personal data may be processable, even beyond the explicitly stated legislative hypotheses, on the basis of an authorization by that data protection authority, issued for protecting the rights of others, and prevailing upon the right to privacy. To determine whether the privacy authority has made legitimate use of its powers we need to consider the importance of the values at stake (privacy, freedom of expression, economic freedom, health, etc.) and evaluate whether they have been balanced in a way that respects legal (in particular, constitutional) constraints. We could try to reduce this multi-levelled argumentation framework to a set of flat rules, but we would obtain a representation that is removed from the original legal texts (laws, regulations, authorizations), and whose contents and rationales are much more difficult to grasp.

S. Conclusion

I hope to have convinced the reader that defeasible reasoning is an essential aspect of legal problem-solving, and that the logical structures enabling such reasoning are an essential feature of legal knowledge. There is one last issue to be addressed, to which I will devote some concluding remarks. Can we give to defeasible reasoning a rigorous logical form, so that we can check precisely whether a certain conclusion is defeasibly derivable from a defeasible knowledge base?

The answer, I believe, is positive. Various logical approaches have been devised for modelling defeasible reasoning—default logic, auto-epistemic logic, circumscription, preferential logics, metalogics—and they can be shown to converge towards the intuitive understanding of defeasible reasoning.[48] In legal theory, argument-based approaches to defeasible reasoning—according to which defeasibility results from the interaction of conflicting arguments—have attracted most attention. Among such approaches I take the liberty of mentioning the one developed by Prakken and Sartor,[49] an approach based on ideas common to other argument-based approaches to legal defeasibility.[50] In this model, legal rules and principles are reasoning warrants that—when certain antecedent reasons are available (being provided as part of the input, or as the result of previous inference steps)—support the derivation of legal conclusions. An argument is obtained by constructing a (capsized) tree of warrants, where the top (root) warrant provides the desired conclusion, while the antecedents of conditioned warrants are provided by conclusions of lower warrants in the tree. Such arguments may be attacked (rebutted or undercut) by further arguments. When the attack succeeds, the attacked argument is defeated: this happens when the attacked argument is rebutted by stronger arguments, or when it is undercut. For determining the relative strength of the arguments (as is required in the case of a rebutting attack), we have to appeal to further arguments, telling us which one of the contradictory arguments is to be preferred, on what grounds.

As a first approximation, we can then say that the conclusion of the defeated argument needs to be retracted. However, the picture is complicated by the idea of reinstatement: defeated arguments can be recovered if their defeaters are, in their turn, contradicted by stronger arguments (or are undercut). So, we obtain a model where

[48] See H. Prakken, *Logical Tools for Modelling Legal Argument: A Study of Defeasible Reasoning in Law* (Dordrecht: Kluwer, 1997).

[49] H. Prakken and G. Sartor, 'Argument-based extended logic programming with defeasible priorities', *Journal of Applied Non-classical Logics*, 7 (1997), 25–75; and G. Sartor, *Legal Reasoning*.

[50] See, for instance, T.F. Gordon, *The Pleadings Game. An Artificial Intelligence Model of Procedural Justice* (Dordrecht: Kluwer, 1995); J.C. Hage, *Reasoning with Rules: An Essay on Legal Reasoning and Its Underlying Logic* (Dordrecht: Kluwer, 1997); T.J.M. Bench-Capon, T. Geldard, and P. Leng, 'A method for the computational modelling of dialectical argument with dialogue games', *Artificial Intelligence and Law*, 8 (2000), 233–54; D.N. Walton, *Argumentation Methods for Artificial Intelligence in Law* (Berlin: Springer, 2005); T.F. Gordon, 'Constructing arguments with a computational model of an argumentation scheme for legal rules'.

legal reasoning consists in the dialectical interaction of competing inferences; the outcome of this competition determines what arguments (and consequently what conclusions) will be legally justified in the framework of the available legal knowledge. We are consequently able to distinguish what arguments are warranted, namely, justified with regard to a defeasible knowledge base (having no justified or defeasible attacker), what arguments are overruled (being strictly defeated by a justified argument), and what arguments are merely defensible (being attacked by an argument which is neither justified nor overruled). Recently, the model just mentioned has been extended in such a way as to capture the dialectical allocation of the burden of proof: the party which is shown to be burdened can validly attack an argument of the other party only by providing arguments which are stronger than the argument of the other party, up to the level required by the applicable proof standard.[51] This account can be precisely stated in an intuitive way in the dialectical form of a dispute, where a proponent (the party who advances the initial thesis, namely, the conclusion of the initial argument) interacts with an opponent (a critic), who contests that argument. Both parties use the available knowledge in the best way, using arguments that contrast the arguments of the counterparty. The proponent wins if he always has the last word, proposing arguments that the opponent cannot rebut (using the knowledge available). The opponent wins if she directs against the proponent's argument a criticism to which the proponent is unable to reply. Thus, the idea is that a statement is warranted (relative to a certain body of information) if its proponent can successfully defend it in a dispute, or 'argument game' with an opponent. The reasoner who checks on his own whether a statement is warranted should take both positions, both as the proponent of the thesis and as its critical opponent.[52]

I cannot provide here a deeper analysis of this logical model. What matters for our purposes is that using defeasible reasoning in the legal domain does not entail abandoning logical rigour. On the contrary, it means adopting logical models matching to a greater extent the structures of legal knowledge, the patterns of legal reasoning, and the dialectics of legal interaction.

[51] See H. Prakken and G. Sartor, 'Formalizing arguments about the burden of persuasion'.

[52] See, for instance, H. Prakken and G. Sartor, 'Rules about rules: Assessing conflicting arguments in legal reasoning', *Artificial Intelligence and Law*, 4 (1996), 331–68. For a comparison of different games reflecting different notions of a defeasible consequence, see H. Prakken and G.A.W. Vreeswijk, 'Logical systems for defeasible argumentation', in D. Gabbay and F. Günthner (eds), *Handbook of Philosophical Logic* (Dordrecht: Kluwer, 2002), 218–319.

7

Defeasible Properties

*Rafael Hernández Marín**

A. Impressions about defeasibility

Considerable conceptual obscurity surrounds the topic of defeasibility. I can, therefore, only tentatively put forward the following five theses as representative of the understanding of defeasibility contained in the literature:

(1) The entities that are susceptible of being defeated are, primarily, properties.
(2) A defeasible property is an apparent, but not, or not necessarily, real property.
(3) Although any individual could have a defeasible property, sentences are primarily the individuals that have defeasible properties.
(4) A defeasible sentence is a sentence that has a defeasible property, that is to say, a sentence that appears to have a property without actually or necessarily having it.
(5) A defeasible argument is an argument at least one of whose premises or whose conclusion is a defeasible sentence.

If these theses are correct, the defeasibility of an argument depends on whether its premises or its conclusion have a defeasible property, i.e. an apparent, although not necessarily real property. What I will do, in the following pages, is try to unveil that property.

B. The defeasible properties of the premises of the argument

The premises to which we attribute defeasibility are, in most cases, conditional sentences (or universal generalizations of conditional sentences). One of the obscure points concerning defeasibility is, indeed, how to determine which property of conditional sentences is defeasible and turns the conditional sentence having such a property into a defeasible sentence.

In addition, we need to distinguish between assertive and prescriptive conditional sentences.

1. Assertive premises

Let us consider, in the first place, the following conditional assertive sentence:

[1] If (it rains) then (I will stay at home).

* Professor of Law, University of Murcia. This work has been elaborated in the frame of the research project SEJ2006-12224/JURI, funded by the Ministry of Education and Science of Spain, and FEDER.

Obviously, whatever the context in which this sentence [1] appears, the sense in context, or total sense, of [1] does not coincide with its literal sense, that is, with the sense the sentence has regardless of any context.[1]

However, let us now consider the following conditional assertive sentence, inspired by C.E. Alchourrón's example:

> [2] If (*x* is a gas sample and the temperature of *x* rises) then (the volume of *x* will increase).

Unlike case [1], it could seem, at least at first sight, that the total or in-context sense of sentence [2] does coincide with its literal sense.

And, talking of possibilities, the total sense of [2] could also appear to be coincidental with its literal sense without actually being so. In this case, we might say that the coincidence between the total sense of sentence [2] and its literal sense appears to be, but in reality is not, a property of sentence [2], and that it is therefore a defeasible property of [2]. This could suffice for characterizing as defeasible both sentence [2] itself and the argument wherein [2] is a premise.

One particular case of disparity between the total sense of [2] and its literal sense occurs, although it might seem the opposite, when such disparity is due to the fact that the total sense of the antecedent of sentence [2] contains an additional clause, specifically a negative clause—an exception—which is not included in the literal sense of the antecedent of sentence [2]. Such a negative additional clause or exception, not included in the literal sense but in the total sense of the antecedent of [2], could be 'the pressure of *x* does not vary'. In this case, the total sense of sentence [2] would match the literal sense of the following sentence:

> [3] If (*x* is a gas sample and the temperature of *x* rises and the pressure of *x* does not vary) then (the volume of *x* will increase).

It would then be possible to say that [2] contains the implicit exception 'the pressure of *x* does not vary' and that, therefore, [2] is a conditional with implicit exceptions.

On the other hand, Alchourrón wrote that 'a defeasible conditional can also be defined as one which has implicit exceptions'.[2]

Therefore, and according to Alchourrón's definition of defeasible conditionals, [2] is a defeasible conditional sentence.

A consequence of this definition of defeasible conditional sentences offered by Alchourrón is that the total sense of these sentences, which are sentences that have implicit exceptions, does not coincide with their literal sense, although it might seem the opposite. Therefore, we may say that, according to Alchourrón's definition, in defeasible sentences the coincidence between their total sense and their literal sense is a defeasible property, i.e. an only apparent, but unreal, property of the sentence.

However, when discussing the defeasibility of a conditional assertive sentence like [2], one does not think of the defeasibility of the coincidence between its total sense and its literal sense. One thinks of the defeasibility of its truth, that is to say, one thinks of an apparently, yet not really, true sentence.[3] Thus, a second definition of '(assertive) defeasible conditional' is tacitly introduced: an (assertive) defeasible conditional would

[1] In my book, *Interpretación, subsunción y aplicación del Derecho* (Madrid: Marcial Pons, 1999), 35–52, I expose the distinction between the total sense and the literal sense of a certain sentence and I underlie its significance for the interpretation of legal sentences.

[2] C.E. Alchourrón, 'On Law and Logic', in this volume, ch. 2, 46.

[3] This circumstance can be observed in C.E. Alchourrón, ibid., 45–6.

be, according to this inexplicit second definition, a conditional whose truth is defeasible. In the case of sentence [2], this conditional would be defeasible if its truth were defeated (that is, refuted) because of, for instance, a variation in the pressure of the gas sample *x*.

In this way, the theory about defeasibility of conditional assertive sentences sustained by Alchourrón handles two non-equivalent definitions of defeasibility. Therefore, and as in any other similar case, the theory is contradictory.

So let us suppose, in the first place, that the total sense of [2] does not match up with its literal sense, but with the literal sense of [3], that is to say, let us suppose that [2] means just the same as [3]. In this case, [2] contains an implicit exception. For that reason, and according to the first and explicit definition of defeasible conditionals formulated by Alchourrón, [2] is a defeasible conditional. On the other hand, and since [2] means just the same as [3], the truth of [2] would be defeated by a pressure variation of the gas sample *x* if, and only if, the truth of [3] were defeated by this circumstance. However, the truth of conditional sentence [3] is not defeated by the concurrence of a circumstance turning false the antecedent of [3], such as the pressure variation of the gas sample *x*. Therefore, the same can be said of [2]: the truth of [2] is not defeated by a pressure variation of the gas sample *x*. Thus, according to the second and tacit definition of defeasibility, [2] is not defeasible.

Alchourrón says that, in this example, 'a variation in the gas' pressure is an implicit exception that defeats the conditional assertion'.[4] It must be noticed, however, that if a pressure variation of the gas is an implicit exception in conditional assertive sentence [2], then the latter is certainly a defeasible sentence, according to the first and explicit definition of defeasible conditional. Nevertheless, in this case [2] is synonymous with [3] and, therefore, its truth is not defeated by a pressure variation of the gas, in contrast with what Alchourrón suggests.

Let us suppose now, however, that the total sense of [2] coincides with its literal sense. The temperature of gas sample *x* could rise without an increase in its volume, due to a variation (increase) of the pressure of *x*. It could then be said that the pressure variation of the gas sample *x* shows the falsity of [2], literally understood; and that, thus understood, the truth of [2] is defeated by the variation of the pressure of *x*. For that reason, and according to the second and tacit definition of defeasibility, [2] would be a defeasible sentence. However, in the hypothesis, which we are now supposing, that the total sense of [2] coincides with its literal sense, [2] does not have any implicit exception. Consequently [2] is not a defeasible sentence according to the first and explicit definition of defeasibility.

2. Prescriptive premises

The topic of defeasibility has been transferred with little caution from assertive sentences to legal sentences.[5]

Indeed, like [2], legal sentences are conditional, or synonymous with universal generalizations of conditional sentences. Unlike [2], however, except for rare or debatable exceptions legal sentences are not assertive, i.e. true or false sentences. Therefore, truth is not one of the properties that, apparently or at first sight, could possibly be attributed to legal sentences. That is the reason why truth is not a defeasible property of legal sentences, though it certainly is a defeasible property of assertive sentences like [2].

[4] Ibid., 341. [5] This is what Alchourrón himself does, ibid.

Prescriptive legal sentences have a property, which is analogous to truth in assertive sentences: effectiveness. Nonetheless, when we speak of the defeasibility of legal sentences, we never think of their effectiveness.

It seems to me that when we talk of a legal sentence's defeasibility, we think of the possibility for that conditional, which can be any legal sentence whatsoever, to contain, in Alchourrón's abovementioned terms, implicit exceptions. This implies that, in such cases, the total sense of the legal sentence does not match its literal sense. In short, I believe it is maintained that if a legal sentence is defeasible, then its total sense does not coincide with its literal sense. Additionally, in order to simplify, we can suppose the opposite thesis, according to which whenever the total sense of a legal sentence does not coincide with its literal sense, the sentence is defeasible. This way, and supposing *E* is a legal sentence, the three following expressions are equivalent: '*E* has implicit exceptions', '*E* is defeasible', and '*E*'s total sense does not match up with its literal sense'.

Once the problem of the defeasibility of legal sentences is raised in these terms, it will be necessary to say that some legal sentences are defeasible and others are not. The total sense of defeasible legal sentences does not match up with their literal sense; whereas the total sense of non-defeasible or indefeasible legal sentences matches up with their literal sense. The concrete problem of getting to know whether a certain legal sentence is defeasible or not requires us to find out what is the total sense of the sentence.

On the other hand, the central problem in any case of legal interpretation is determining the total sense of a legal sentence.[6]

Therefore, I agree with Alchourrón when he contemplates the problem of the defeasibility of legal sentences as a problem of legal interpretation.[7]

However, there do not exist general rules allowing us to automatically solve interpretative problems or, more precisely, the problem of determining what is the total sense of a concrete legal sentence. Nevertheless, it is possible to discard some of the ways to pose or to solve the problem.

For example, once it is clarified that the problem of the defeasibility of legal sentences is a problem of legal interpretation, it becomes clear that the problem of the defeasibility of legal sentences has nothing to do with accepting or rejecting legal positivism, in spite of other authors' opinions.[8]

On the other hand, I know no theory in the philosophy of language that holds that the answer to the question whether the sense of a certain sentence *E* is S_1 or S_2 depends on the social consequences of the fact that S_1 is the sense of *E* or the fact that S_2 is the sense of *E*. Analogously, I know no theory in the philosophy of language that holds that the answer to the question whether or not the sense of a certain sentence *E* coincides with its literal sense depends on what the social consequence of the existence of such a coincidence are. For this reason, I hold the view that the existence or the non-existence of the coincidence of total sense and literal sense in a certain sentence (legal or

[6] This is the thesis I maintain in my book *Interpretación, subsunción y aplicación del Derecho*, ch. II.

[7] C.E. Alchourrón, 'On Law and Logic', 341–2.

[8] In my book *Historia de la filosofía del Derecho contemporánea* (Madrid: Tecnos, 2nd edn, 1989), I argue that what is characteristic of the main contemporary jurisprudents, who are usually regarded as legal positivists, consists of two aspects: (a) the rejection of the natural law thesis (i.e. the thesis that it is a necessary condition for the legality of a norm that it complies with the requirements of Natural Law); (b) the defence of an idealist conception of law (i.e. that norms are ideal or abstract entities). According to this characterization of legal positivism (see ibid., 88), there is no connection at all between the acceptance or rejection of legal positivism and legal interpretation. And, since the problem of the defeasibility of legal sentences is a problem of legal interpretation, there is no connection between the acceptance or rejection of legal positivism and the problem of the defeasibility of legal sentences.

otherwise) does not depend on what the social consequences are of the existence or non-existence of such a coincidence. And, since the defeasibility of a sentence equates with the lack of coincidence of its total and literal senses, one must conclude that the defeasibility of a certain legal sentence does not depend on what the social consequences are of the existence or non-existence of such a coincidence.

Alchourrón's treatment of this issue does not seem convincing to me either. Alchourrón specifically confronts the problem of determining when a conditional sentence contains implicit exceptions. His response to this problem is that sentence *E* contains an implicit exception *X* if the speaker who formulates *E* would have introduced in *E* such exception *X*, had he or she considered or thought about it.[9]

This thesis is transferred to legal sentences by Alchourrón himself. So, in order to understand and to evaluate Alchourrón's thesis, we can suppose, recalling a well-known example, that the following sentence is a legal one:

[4] Vehicles shall not enter park P.

Let us also suppose that the entrance of ambulances into the park P is sometimes necessary or advisable (for example, in order to assist someone who is ill); and that the legislator who created [4], had she considered this eventuality, would have excepted ambulances from the prohibition contained in [4]. This amounts to supposing that, had she thought of the abovementioned eventuality and of the exception 'ambulances excepted', the legislator would have formulated, instead of [4], the following sentence:

[5] Vehicles shall not enter park P, ambulances excepted.

According to Alchourrón, the conclusion we can deduce from the described hypothesis would be the following one: [4] implicitly contains the exception 'ambulances excepted'. This means that the total sense of [4] does not match up with its literal sense, but with the literal sense of [5].

Alchourrón's position can be synthesized in the following way. Let us suppose the hypothesis, which I shall call 'H', that if the legislator, author of [4], had thought of the exception 'ambulances excepted', she would have excepted the ambulances from the prohibition contained in [4], that is to say, she would have formulated sentence [5] instead of the sentence [4]. This implies, according to Alchourrón, that [4] implicitly contains the exception 'ambulances excepted', i.e. that the total sense of [4] matches the literal sense of [5].

I disagree with Alchourrón's thesis for the following reasons.

In the first place, I think the conclusion we can deduce from hypothesis H is not that [4] implicitly contains the exception 'ambulances excepted' or that the total sense of [4] matches up with the literal sense of [5]. On the contrary, hypothesis H means that the legislator, author of [4], had she thought of the exception 'ambulances excepted' when formulating this sentence, would have formulated sentence [5] instead of sentence [4]. Additionally, since the finally formulated sentence was not [5] but [4], we must conclude (by *modus tollendo tollens*) that the creator of [4] did not think of the exception 'ambulances excepted' when formulating [4]. On the other hand, if the creator of [4], on formulating this sentence, had meant what [5] means she would have thought of the exception 'ambulances excepted' when formulating [4]. Which leads us to deduce (by *modus tollendo tollens*) that the creator of [4], when formulating this sentence, did not mean what [5] means. Therefore, the total sense of [4], the sense of this sentence in

[9] C. E. Alchourrón, 'On Law and Logic'.

context, does not match the literal sense of [5]. Moreover, the fact that, as we are supposing, hypothesis H is true (i.e. it is true that if the legislator, author of [4], had thought of the exception 'ambulances excepted', she would have formulated sentence [5] instead of sentence [4]) is an indication that, even for the author of [4], the total sense of this sentence does not match the literal sense of [5].

The same idea can be illustrated by means of a different example, clearer than the previous one, so much so that arguments such as the just-developed ones become unnecessary with respect to the following example. Let us suppose that I am in a restaurant and I ask the waiter to 'bring me a sirloin steak, please!'; and, one minute later, I recall that in that restaurant they make a delicious paella, which is one of my favourite dishes. True, if I had recalled this a minute before, I would not have ordered sirloin, but a serving of paella (this is to say, I would not have told the waiter to 'bring me a sirloin steak, please!' but 'bring a serving of paella, please!'). But from this we cannot deduce that the meaning of what I said to the waiter is 'bring a serving of paella!', but quite the opposite.

The total or in-context sense of a certain *sentence E* can depend on any factor comprised in context *C* existing at moment *T*, in which *E* was formulated. The opinions, thoughts, etc., that the author of *E* had at moment *T* doubtless appear among such factors. We can accept the hypothesis that if the author of *E* had had certain thoughts that he did not actually have in *T* and, in short, the context existing in *T* had been different from *C*, the author of *E* would not have formulated this sentence, but a different one. However, this does not affect the sense *E* has in context *C*, wherein it was articulated, in contrast with Alchourrón's view and also with the so-called 'evolutionary' or 'dynamic' theories of legal interpretation.

On the other hand, let us suppose hypothesis H, i.e. suppose that if the legislator, author of [4], had thought about the exception 'ambulances excepted', she would have formulated sentence [5] instead of sentence [4]. Also, let us also suppose Alchourrón was right to say that, having accepted this hypothesis, [4] implicitly contains the exception 'ambulances excepted', in other words, that the total sense of [4] corresponds to the literal sense of [5]. In this case, the total sense of [4] would depend on whether it is true that the author of this sentence would have introduced an exception, had she considered the case. Additionally, if we generalize this thesis, it would be impossible to know, in any case of legal interpretation, what is the total sense of a legal sentence: not only because of the difficulty of getting to know which would have been the thought of the legislator had she considered the possibility of introducing a specific exception in her regulation, but mainly because of the countless possible exceptions. In short, legal interpretation, which consists, as I have mentioned before, of determining the total sense of a legal sentence, would be an impossible task to perform if Alchourrón were right.

True, often the total sense of a legal sentence does not correspond to its literal sense. It may happen, in particular, that a certain legal sentence contains some implicit exception. But the criterion for defining the cases in which a sentence, legal or not, contains an implicit exception cannot be the one Alchourrón formulated.

C. The defeasible property of conclusions of arguments

1. In ordinary arguments

I call 'ordinary arguments' the arguments whose premises and conclusions are assertive sentences.

As we have seen, in the case of (conditional) assertive sentences constituting the premises of ordinary arguments, the defeasible property of such sentences is sometimes considered to be their truth, sometimes the coincidence between their total sense and their literal sense.

However, the property of an ordinary argument's assertive conclusion that we consider defeasible is not its truth, nor the coincidence between its total sense and its literal sense, but its deducibility from the premises of the argument.

The term 'deducible' can be understood, syntactically, as 'derivable' (which is a term we can define by means of clauses expressing rules of derivation or inference), or else semantically, as 'logical consequence' (which is a notion we can define by means of the notion of truth). From now on, I shall use the terms 'deducible' and 'deducibility' in this second sense, i.e. in a semantic sense.

I shall name 'DDT' (*defeasible deducibility theory*) the theory which holds that there are conclusions whose deducibility from a specific set of premises is defeasible. Also, if I correctly understand DDT, what this theory maintains can be expressed the following way.

Let us consider a deductive argument, the premises of which are $P_1, \ldots, P_m$, and whose conclusion is C. This implies that C is deducible from $P_1, \ldots, P_m$. According to DDT, even if C were deducible from $P_1, \ldots, P_m$, it would be possible for C not to be deducible from $P_1, \ldots, P_m, P_n$. DDT holds, thus, that even where a thesis C is deducible from a specific set of premises, if we added a new premise to this set it would be possible for C not to be deducible from the new set of premises. In this case, the deducibility of C from the original set of premises $P_1, \ldots, P_m$ is only apparent, not real, and it is therefore a defeasible property of C. This property or defeasible deducibility of C is called 'nonmonotonic deducibility'. And therefore, this turns the original argument ('$P_1, \ldots, P_m$. Therefore, C', whose conclusion has this property) into a defeasible deductive argument, qualified as nonmonotonic.

In specialized literature, the ideas I have just exposed are usually illustrated through examples such as the following:

> [6] If we were told Tweety is a bird we would draw the conclusion that Tweety flies. However, if we were also informed that Tweety is a penguin, such a conclusion would be defeated and replaced by its negation, i.e. by the affirmation that Tweety does not fly.

Two arguments are mentioned in [6]. The first of them is:

> [7] Tweety is a bird. Therefore, Tweety flies.

The second one is:

> [8] Tweety is a bird; Tweety is a penguin. Therefore, Tweety does not fly.

According to DDT, [7] would be a deductive argument, whose conclusion 'Tweety flies' is deducible from 'Tweety is a bird', its only premise. However, if to this premise we add the premise 'Tweety is a penguin' the conclusion of the original argument, i.e. the thesis 'Tweety flies', is no longer deducible from the new set of premises (on the contrary; according to DDT, what is deducible from the new set of premises is the negation of this thesis, that is, 'Tweety does not fly', as argument [8] shows). For that reason, the deducibility of the conclusion 'Tweety flies' from 'Tweety is a bird' is apparent, not real, and it is therefore a defeasible property of this conclusion. This property or defeasible deducibility is characterized as nonmonotonic deducibility. And, in the same way, argument [7], whose conclusion 'Tweety flies' has the described property, is a defeasible deductive argument, characterized as nonmonotonic.

So much for the account of DDT.

We can begin to comment on this theory by understanding the difference that exists between arguments [7] and [8]. For this purpose, I shall use the expressions 'T-deductive', 'T-deducible', and 'T-deducibility' as abbreviations, respectively, for 'deductive in traditional sense', 'deducible in traditional sense', and 'deducibility in traditional sense', understanding such terms in a semantic sense.

Neither of the abovementioned arguments, [7] and [8], is a T-deductive argument, since in both cases the conclusion is not T-deducible from the premises. This is evident in the case of [7]. However, [8] is not a T-deductive argument either, for 'Tweety does not fly' (the conclusion of [8]), is not T-deducible from its two premises. In particular, it is not T-deducible from the premise 'Tweety is a penguin'. Just like 'Socrates is mortal' is not T-deducible from 'Socrates is a man'.

Nevertheless, [8] could be considered a T-deductive argument, an enthymematic but solid one, implying a true premise: 'no penguin flies'. However, there is no way to turn [7] into a solid, yet enthymematic, T-deductive argument. If we understood in [7] the true premise 'almost all birds fly', the resulting argument ('Almost all birds fly; Tweety is a bird. Therefore, Tweety flies') would not be a T-deductive argument either, since the conclusion would not be T-deducible from the premises. Also, if the premise we understand in [7] were 'all birds fly', the resulting argument ('All birds fly; Tweety is a bird. Therefore, Tweety flies') would now be T-deductive, but not solid, because of the falsity of the understood and added premise.

As far as I am aware, research on these subjects never mentions enthymemes. Therefore, argument [7] must be understood literally. So according to DDT, argument [7], literally understood, would be a deductive argument, although a nonmonotonic one. Additionally, the relationship between 'Tweety flies', the conclusion of [7], and 'Tweety is a bird', the only premise of [7], would be a relation of deducibility, albeit different from T-deducibility, given that, unlike the first one, the latter relationship is monotonic.

I shall name that relation of nonmonotonic deducibility, different from T-deducibility, 'deducibility in a non-traditional sense', in short 'NT-deducibility'. Also, I shall use the expression 'NT-deducible' as an abbreviation for 'deducible in non-traditional sense'. Two questions arise with respect to the described DDT theory: (a) how does DDT understand or define NT-deducibility (remember that T-deducibility, deducibility in traditional sense, understood in the semantic sense, i.e. as a relation of logical consequence, is defined by means of the notion of truth)?; and (b) what is the relation, according to DDT, between NT-deducibility and T-deducibility?

We find an answer to these questions in some of the works on defeasibility which argue something similar to what follows: 'Tweety flies' is a plausible consequence of 'Tweety is a bird', or else, 'Tweety is a bird' is a good enough reason to believe that 'Tweety flies'.[10] These texts suggest the following definition of the NT-deducibility notion: *B* is NT-deducible from *A* if and only if *B* is a plausible consequence of *A* (or if and only if *A* is a good enough reason to believe *B*).

It is worth recalling the lack of precision of the terms 'plausible consequence of' and 'good enough reason to believe', which are used in this definition (these terms are,

[10] See S. Kraus, D. Lehmann, and M. Magidor, 'Nonmonotonic Reasoning, Preferential Models and Cumulative Logics', *Journal of Artificial Intelligence*, 44 (1990), 171.

seemingly, primitive terms of DDT). Although, thus defined, the NT-deducibility relation certainly turns out to be a nonmonotonic relationship, as DDT holds: *B* could be NT-deducible from *A* without being, nevertheless, NT-deducible from *A* and *C* (for *B* could be a plausible consequence of *A* without being, nevertheless, a plausible consequence of *A* and *C*). Moreover, thus defined, NT-deducibility is independent of T-deducibility: the first can exist without the second, as argument [7] shows, and the second can exist without the first, as the principle *ex falso quodlibet* illustrates. This suggests, just as the fact that DDT characterizes both relations as deducibility relations, that they are two species of a single genus.

According to the latter observation, we might consider orienting research as a quest for a generic notion of deducibility, comprehensive of T-deducibility and of NT-deducibility. Nevertheless, there is a fact which prevents us from moving in this direction. It is a fact which reveals that the two relations of deducibility are not two species of a single genus. I am referring to the existence of deducibility relations, such as that between *P* and *P*&*Q*, that are both T-deducibility and NT-deducibility relations. (Notice, in this last regard, that *P* is a plausible consequence of *P*&*Q* and that *P*&*Q* is a good enough reason to believe *P*.)

NT-deducibility, the nonmonotonic deducibility, is a defeasible kind of deducibility. Moreover, just as defeasible truth is only an apparent, not necessarily real truth, defeasible deducibility is only an apparent, not necessarily real deducibility. Furthermore, apparent deducibility, NT-deducibility, and real deducibility, T-deducibility, are not two species of the genus *deducibility*, just as apparent truth and real truth are not two species of the genus *truth*, and just as an apparent horse and a real horse are not two species of the genus horse.

Since T-deducibility and NT-deducibility are not two species of a single genus, when moving from T-deducibility to NT-deducibility, we have not moved from a species of the genus deducibility to a different species within the same genus. What has actually happened, in the words of W.V. Quine, is that there has been a subject change (as would be the case if our discourse, initially concerning philosophers, turns to refer to Europeans, then its subject has changed, and it is not possible to consider philosophers and Europeans as two different species included within one single genus).[11] Therefore, and in order to avoid misunderstandings, we should change denomination, not referring to NT-deducibility as a 'deducibility relation' anymore. Or, to put it in a more rigorous way, we should avoid the term 'NT-deducibility' and similar terms, such as 'logical consequence in non-traditional sense' or 'nonmonotonic logical consequence', for these denominations suggest that this relation, like the T-deducibility relation or relation of logical consequence, has to do with logics while it actually belongs to a different science: be it the theory of probability, or be it psychology, as the terms 'plausible consequence of' and 'good enough reason to believe' respectively suggest.

2. In mixed arguments

A mixed argument is an argument amongst whose premises there is at least one assertive sentence and at least one prescriptive sentence.

The most frequent, or the most frequently mentioned, type of mixed argument in legal and moral philosophy may be illustrated with the following example:

[11] See W.V. Quine, *Philosophy of Logic* (Englewood Cliffs, NJ: Prentice-Hall, 1970), 81.

[9] All citizens must pay taxes (= For any entity *x*: *x* is a citizen $\rightarrow$ *x* must pay taxes);
[10] Pedro is a citizen;
[11] Pedro must pay taxes.

The premises of the above mixed arguments are twofold:

(a) A premise *P* which is a prescriptive conditional sentence, or a universal generalization of a prescriptive conditional sentence, and which is a legal or moral rule. Sentence [9] is an example of such a prescriptive premise *P*.

(b) An assertive sentence *A*, which is a concretion of the antecedent of *P*. The assertive sentence [10], which is a concretion of the antecedent of [9], is an example of assertive premise.

The conclusion of one of those mixed arguments is a prescriptive sentence *C*, such that the conditional sentence $A \rightarrow C$ is a concretion of *P*. The prescriptive sentence [11] is an example of this prescriptive conclusion, since the conditional sentence [10] $\rightarrow$ [11] is a concretion of [9].

Some so-called 'legal arguments', I believe, are mixed arguments of the sort that has just been described. It is true that, despite abundant literature on this subject over the last decades, nobody has specified yet, as far as I know, what is a legal argument and in what sense legal arguments differ from non-legal arguments. Nevertheless it is almost unanimously accepted that the arguments that judges use for justifying their decisions are both legal arguments and mixed arguments, which correspond to the scheme presented above.

In previous work I have criticized this point of view and I have presented an alternative conception of the application of legal sentences and the motivation of judicial decisions.[12] According to this conception, judges neither need to use mixed arguments for applying legal sentences, nor for motivating their decisions. Ordinary arguments suffice for them.

This alternative conception of judicial activity, elaborated within the framework of ordinary logic, is inspired by distrust of (so-called) deontic logic and (so-called) deontic arguments, i.e. arguments whose premises and conclusion are prescriptive sentences, such as the following argument:

[12] Stand up and walk. Therefore, stand up.

In another recent work,[13] I have exposed the reasons for this distrust, which are, in summary, the following.

There exists, in my opinion, no acceptable definition of the semantic relation of logical consequence among prescriptive sentences. This is why we do not actually know what it means to say, for example, that the prescriptive sentence

[13] Stand up

is a logical consequence of the prescriptive sentence

[14] Stand up and walk.

However, we can assume that there exists such semantic definition *D* and that, according to *D*, [13] is a logical consequence of [14]. Guided by definition *D*, we

[12] See R. Hernández Marín, *Las obligaciones básicas de los jueces* (Madrid: Marcial Pons, 2005), chs II and VI.

[13] R. Hernández Marín, 'Los dos dilemas de J. Jørgensen' in P. Comanducci and R. Guastini (eds), *Analisi e diritto 2006* (Turin: Guappichelli, 2007), 143–64.

then construct a system *S* of deontic logic (of propositional deontic logic, let us assume), with the aim of allowing the syntactic relation of derivability in *S* to extensionally coincide with the semantic relation of logical consequence, as this relation is defined by *D*. Let us also suppose that we achieve our objective and that the system *S* of deontic logic (of propositional deontic logic) we have constructed is a suitable system, i.e. correct and complete.

The result will then be that the prescriptive sentence

[13] Stand up

is not only logical but also a derivable consequence, in *S*, of the sentence

[14] Stand up and walk.

Whereby, and by virtue of the metatheorem of deduction, the following expression is a theorem of the system of deontic logic *S*:

[15] If stand up and walk then stand up.[14]

However, this expression [15] is neither a logical truth, nor a truth, nor even a meaningful expression. For that reason, it does not deserve the term 'theorem'.

These remarks justify distrust of the possibility of a deducibility relation, that we might term 'deontic deducibility', between two prescriptive sentences, such as [13] and [14], either understanding this relation of deducibility in the syntactic sense of derivability, or understanding it in the semantic sense of logical consequence.

It should not be a surprise to us that we ought to be suspicious about such a relation of deontic deducibility and, thereby, about the possibility of a deontic logic. As W.V. Quine recalls, like any science, logic searches for the truth;[15] to be precise, and as Quine himself observes, the truth logic looks for is logical truth[16] (a fact C.E. Alchourrón and A.A. Martino ignore when they defend the possibility of a logic without truth).[17] On the other hand, well-formed expressions of deontic logic systems, in particular their 'theorems', are not assertive, true or false sentences but are, at best, prescriptive sentences, if not meaningless expressions like [15]. Therefore, deontic logic can search neither for logical truth, nor even for the truth in general. This implies that there is no place for deontic logic in the sciences, nor in human knowledge. The cultivators of deontic logic have been seduced, as even G.H. von Wright observes, by the similarity between its deontic systems or calculi and ordinary logic systems or calculi.[18] But they have ignored that, although all logical systems are formal systems, not all formal systems are logical systems.

Thus, suspicions about a deontic deducibility relation among prescriptive sentences, different from the ordinary deducibility relation (that is to say, different from the deducibility relation existing among assertive sentences), are justified and have a theoretical explanation.

Those suspicions increase, naturally, in the face of what we could call the 'mixed deducibility relation', i.e. the deducibility relation supposedly existing between

[14] Strictly speaking, [13], [14], or [15] would not be expressions of the system *S*. The system would *contain* formulas symbolizing these expressions.

[15] W.V. Quine, *Methods of Logic* (London: Routledge and Kegan Paul, 1974), 1.

[16] W.V. Quine, *Philosophy of Logic*, xi.

[17] C.E. Alchourrón and A.A. Martino, 'Logic Without Truth', *Ratio Juris*, 3 (1990), 46–67.

[18] G.H. von Wright, 'Deontic Logic: A Personal View', *Ratio Juris*, 12 (1999), 31.

sentence [11] (which is a prescriptive sentence) and the conjunction of sentences [9] (which is a prescriptive sentence) and [10] (which is an assertive sentence).

Distrust peaks with regard to the discourse on a mixed and nonmonotonic deducibility relation, which can be found in some of the theories of legal argumentation devised in later years. According to these ideas, the sequence of sentences [9]/[10]/[11] could be seen as an argument whose conclusion, [11], has a mixed deducibility relation with the conjunction of its premises, [9] and [10], being in such relation to its premises a nonmonotonic one.

This discussion is, however, totally incomprehensible to me. On the one hand, and according to my previous remarks, an ordinary deducibility notion (i.e. among assertive sentences), nonmonotonic and different from the traditional notion of deducibility, is not typical of logic, but of probability theory or psychology. On the other hand, the notion of mixed and monotonic deducibility lacks any theoretical justification, since not even the notion of deontic and monotonic deducibility has theoretical justification. Therefore, I find it flippant to speak of a relationship of mixed and nonmonotonic deducibility, without having previously clarified all of the abovementioned notions, namely: nonmonotonic ordinary deducibility; monotonic deontic deducibility; and monotonic mixed deducibility.

This flippant and careless attitude (towards these matters) is unlikely to engender theoretical contributions worthy of proper interest. On the contrary, what we can expect are contributions to the imperspicuity of an already extremely confusing topic, that of defeasibility.

PART II

DEFEASIBILITY AND INTERPRETATION

8

Defeasibility and Legal Indeterminacy

*Pierluigi Chiassoni**

In the first part of this paper, I will provide a very sketchy analysis of 'legal indeterminacy', pointing out a few basic—and so far as possible—clearly stated, notions.

In the second part, a similar analysis will be attempted for 'defeasibility'.

In the third, and final, part, I will match the outcomes of the inquiries from the two previous parts.

I am aware that this way of proceeding will have the whiff of old-style, ordinary-language philosophy, conceptual analysis. It is a well-known fact, however, that 'legal indeterminacy' and 'defeasibility' figure as two quite elusory butterflies in jurisprudence's garden. That is why I believe something like an entomologist's approach—deeply boring, as it surely is—may nonetheless be of some use.

A. Legal indeterminacy

At the dawn of the twentieth century, learned, context-sensitive, jurists on both sides of the Atlantic denounced indeterminacy—under a variety of headings ('interpretation', 'gaps', 'discretion', 'judicial law-making', etc.)—as a major, necessary, feature of (Western) legal systems. They wished to free legal thinking from the spell of 'formalism'. They turned indeterminacy into a basic issue on the jurisprudential agenda—and a notorious matter of concern for the science of legislation and the theory of the Rule of Law.

I will assume a (useful) theory of legal indeterminacy to be a methodologically aware discourse,[1] purporting to cast light on its subject matter, by dealing with at least the following four issues:

(1) the *subjects* of 'indeterminacy';
(2) the *sources* of indeterminacy;
(3) the *notions*, and *forms*, of indeterminacy;
(4) the *problems* indeterminacy creates for both legal theory and legal politics—for both expository and censorial jurisprudence, to recall a well-known Benthamite distinction.

I will take this frame into account in the following, tentative, analysis of legal indeterminacy. I will deal, first, with the subjects and sources of indeterminacy, i.e. with what is, or may be, said to be 'indeterminate' in law and the factor(s) explaining why that

* Professor of Jurisprudence at the University of Genoa. I wish to thank Riccardo Guastini for many helpful comments upon an earlier version of this paper.

[1] Methodological awareness shows itself, for instance, in the following dispositions: avoiding any confusion between theory and ideology, being aware of the different levels of discourse, having a theory of definition (where lexicographic definitions and stipulative definitions are carefully kept separate), distinguishing between theory and definition, subject of inquiry and method of inquiry, conceptual frameworks and 'the world', etc.

something is, in some sense, indeterminate (A.1). Then, I will define a few, hopefully suitable, notions (A.2).

1. Indeterminacy in law and its sources

When legal philosophers claim that 'the law is indeterminate', or deal with 'law's indeterminacy', their statements seem to refer to a variety of puzzling situations. They may be concerned with one or more of the following subjects:

(1) indeterminate legal *solutions* (*answers, normative consequences*) to (real or hypothetical) cases at hand;
(2) indeterminate *norm formulations* (or *legal sources*);
(3) indeterminate legal *norms* (rules, commands, standards, principles, etc.);
(4) indeterminate legal *concept-words*;
(5) indeterminate legal *concepts*;
(6) indeterminate *interpretative directives* (canons, techniques, methods, rules, codes, etc.);
(7) indeterminate *logical relationships* between legal norms, and between these and the other usual premises of legal reasoning;
(8) indeterminate legal *systems*.

As we shall see in a moment, some of these situations of indeterminacy are—or may be regarded as—*original* (independent, freestanding); while others, by contrast, are—or may be regarded as—*derivative*, i.e. dependent on other indeterminacy situations.

(a) Indeterminate legal solutions

A lawyer may claim (assume, believe, state) that, as to a certain—real or imaginary—case at hand, 'the law is indeterminate', meaning by that, that 'the solution the law provides for such a case is *indeterminate*'.

Such a claim, however, is in its turn indeterminate. It may be understood in at least three different ways.

First, it may be a claim to the effect that 'the law *does* provide *a complete set of alternative solutions* to the case at hand, but it is indeterminate as to *which one* is to be applied'.

Second, it may be a claim to the effect that 'the law provides *two or more competing solutions* to the case at hand, without specifying which one ought to be preferred'.

Third, it may be a claim to the effect that 'the law *does not* provide *any solution at all* to the case at hand'.

If the lawyer is a judge, and at some point in her dealing with a case she finds herself in one of the three situations above, we may talk of the judge as being in a situation of *adjudicative indeterminacy*.

Adjudicative indeterminacy, however, is a derivative form of legal indeterminacy. In fact, as soon as we ask why the solution provided by the law is indeterminate, in one of the three different ways I have just recalled, we are led to consider further situations of indeterminacy.

According to a deductive model of adjudication, the solution to any case at hand is, in fact, dependent on two basic factors: on the one hand, some universal legal norm that is assumed to be relevant to the decision of the case; on the other hand, some statement of fact that allows us to regard the case as clearly included within the scope of the norm.

Indeterminacy may affect both factors: the normative, as well as the factual, inputs of adjudication.

When it affects the (legal) knowledge of the (relevant) facts of the individual case, judges face what has been called—by Carlos Alchourrón and Eugenio Bulygin—a 'gap of knowledge'.[2] In these cases the judge can get no direct or otherwise sound knowledge about whether the defendant or the plaintiff *really* acted in such-and-such a way, as alleged by attorneys and prosecutors. Legal systems usually cure gaps of knowledge by means of closure rules concerning presumptions and the burden of proof. Accordingly, gaps of knowledge do not affect, by themselves, the determinacy or indeterminacy of the legal solution to a case, for their presence, if any, gets cured by suitable 'rules of evidence'. This remark suggests that the indeterminacy of the legal solution to a case is usually directly dependent on the indeterminacy of the normative inputs of adjudication: i.e. on the indeterminacy of 'legal norms'.

Keeping this suggestion in mind, we may now turn to the three adjudicative indeterminacy situations above, to see more precisely what is indeterminate there, and, furthermore, which factor is likely to be responsible for such indeterminacy.

(b) Mutually-exclusive-answers adjudicative indeterminacy

In the first (kind of) adjudicative indeterminacy situation, as you may recall, 'the law *does* provide *a complete set of alternative solutions* to the case at hand, but it is indeterminate *which one* is to be applied'. I will call this situation *mutually-exclusive-answers* adjudicative indeterminacy. How could that be?

The judge has identified a complete set of legal norms from which *one* solution may be provided for the case at hand. For instance, assuming that the case at hand, *a*, may be either C, or non-C (¬C), the judge has identified the following, complete, normative (micro)system made up of two norms: N_1 '$(x)\ (Cx \rightarrow Sx)$'; and N_2 '$(x)\ (\neg Cx \rightarrow \neg Sx)$'. If *a* is C (C*a*), it has the normative consequence S (S*a*); contrariwise, if *a* is ¬C (¬C*a*), it has the normative consequence ¬S (¬S*a*). Unfortunately, these norms prove indeterminate as to the descriptive term that identifies their conditioning facts (namely, 'C'). In these situations, judges face what has been called—again, by Alchourrón and Bulygin—a 'gap of recognition'.[3] Gaps of recognition exist, more precisely, whenever the meaning of some of the descriptive terms in the norms ('valid contract', 'sacrilegious contract', 'vehicle', 'park', 'living will', 'trespass', etc.) turn out to be vague when applied to the facts of the case. Indeed, those facts might be included, as well as not included, within the scope of the norms on the basis of the 'semantic rules' that govern the scope of their descriptive terms. Since, by hypothesis, the guidance offered by semantic rules has run out, there is only one way to cure this form of indeterminacy, if it is to be cured at all (as it ought to be in modern legal systems that forbid *non liquet*

[2] See C.E. Alchourrón and E. Bulygin, *Normative Systems* (Vienna: Springer, 1971), ch. 1.

[3] See C.E. Alchourrón and E. Bulygin, *Normative Systems*, ch. 1. What about a situation where the judge has identified *one* legal norm as relevant (say, through the textual interpretation of a given norm formulation), but this norm proves ambiguous? I consider such a case to be tantamount to a situation of *plurality-of-competing-answers*, and will deal with it in a moment, though under the heading of ambiguous *norm formulations*.

judgments): i.e. by stipulating a new semantic rule (or part of one), addressing that specific event.[4]

We are now in a position to see more clearly *what is* indeterminate, and *why*, whenever a judge faces a gap of recognition—or, in my terminology, a situation of mutually-exclusive-answers adjudicative indeterminacy.

To begin with, any such situation depends, at least prima facie, on the indeterminacy of some *legal concept* and/or of its corresponding *concept-word* in the sentence making up the norm.[5]

The indeterminacy of a legal concept (concept-word), however, is *derivative*: it may be regarded as depending, in turn, on *interpretative directives*. Indeed, one and the same legal concept (one and the same concept-word) may prove vague, say, according to its up-to-date literal meaning (according to its semantic rules narrowly conceived), while, at the same time, it may prove perfectly determinate according to the meaning suggested, say, by legislative history and/or the proper institutional goal of the norm (or its background reasons).

This suggests, in turn, that the original source of the situations of mutually-exclusive-answers adjudicative indeterminacy is to be placed, ultimately, with interpretative directives. It is *their* 'indeterminacy' that usually reverberates on legal sources (in the present case: upon the concept-words contained in norm formulations) and, from there, on the corresponding legal norms, and the connected legal answers to a case.

At this point, however, we need further analysis. 'Indeterminacy of interpretative directives'—in the present case: of directives concerning textual interpretation—is, again, a tricky phrase: for it may refer—either at once, or severally—to at least two different features interpretative tools may show.

On the one hand, by talking of the 'indeterminacy of interpretative directives' one may refer to their *content indeterminacy*: i.e. to the fact that (many, if not all) interpretative directives, as they are handed down by the methodological tradition and juristic literature, usually provide a poor—partial and/or indeterminate—guidance for judges and other interpreters, far from the requirements of the ideal of a rational legal reasoning.[6]

On the other hand, by talking of the 'indeterminacy of interpretative directives' one may also refer to their *systemic indeterminacy*: i.e. to the fact that the set of interpretative directives judges may/ought to apply to (identify and) justify their interpretative outcomes is both *open* (new items may be included; old ones may be discarded, revised, modified, qualified, etc.) and *unordered* (there is no fixed *ex ante* hierarchy among directives and/or their outcomes). Accordingly, each judge is ultimately responsible for the interpretative 'code'—the limited and well-ordered set of interpretative directives—she chooses to apply to decide any single case at hand.

It is worthwhile noticing, before proceeding, that from the perspective of a judge, this kind of adjudicative indeterminacy, due to gaps of recognition, belongs to an intermediate, not to a final, stage of the judge's work. Indeed, it shows up after the

[4] For instance, by stipulating that any deal made on Saturday is a 'sacrilegious contract'; that any trained dolphin, to be used by a child for riding in the park's pond, is a 'vehicle'; that any postcard expressing everlasting love to a city or other place on earth is a (piece of a) 'living will'; that any street like Park Avenue is (part of any) 'park', etc.

[5] I assume norms to be linguistic entities and, quite often, the meanings of norm formulations. This I do without any further commitment as to their ontological status.

[6] From the viewpoint I have adopted in the text, gaps of recognition, as defined by Alchourrón and Bulygin, precisely depend on the partial guidance offered by the single interpretative directive assumed to be paramount: 'Let words be read according to their conventional semantic rules.'

abstract, text-oriented, interpretation of a given norm formulation has already been performed, and it is now time to proceed to its concrete, fact-oriented, interpretation.[7]

(c) Plurality-of-competing-answers adjudicative indeterminacy

In the second (kind of) adjudicative indeterminacy situation, as you may recall, 'the law provides *two or more competing solutions* to the case at hand, without specifying which one ought to be preferred'. I will call this situation *plurality-of-competing-answers* adjudicative indeterminacy. How could that be?

Five puzzling situations may be singled out here: (1) ambiguous norm formulations, (2) generic norms, (3) normative conflicts, (4) explicit gaps, (5) plurality of competing reconstructions of a normative set (legal system).

(1) Ambiguous norm formulations. To begin with, a plurality of competing answers may be the effect of the ambiguity of a single, relevant, norm formulation. The judge assumes that the relevant legal norm for a case at hand may/ought to be derived from a given norm formulation NF_o. NF_o, however, is capable of being read in several alternative ways, leading to a set of alternative (explicit) norms: Int. $(NF_o) = [N_1 \text{ v } N_2 \text{ v } N_1 \ \& \ N_3 \text{ v} \ldots N_n]$.

One source of ambiguity may be the *syntactic* structure of the norm formulation. This is, to my mind, the only truly linguistic sort of ambiguity, so far as legal norm formulations are concerned. It is, though, not a really salient factor of legal indeterminacy, being usually swallowed up within those larger legal-methodological sets of tools we may refer to as interpretative codes.

More often, indeed, the ambiguity of a norm formulation depends on two other, frequently conspiring, factors:

(i) the several, possible, combinations and uses of interpretative directives, along with the several combinations of interpretative resources, or interpretative data, they refer to;

(ii) the so-called juristic theories about legal institutes and other pieces of legal reality—about 'the nature' of interpretation, legal norms, contracts, wills, takings, the Constitution, the basic principles of antitrust law, the Rule of Law, the legitimate scope of legislative discretion, etc.[8]

Both factors cast on norm formulations a distinctive, overriding, *pragmatic* ambiguity—i.e. an ambiguity that depends on interpreters' methodological choices and juristic outlooks, allegiances, and partisanships.[9]

One may wonder about the *scope* and the *degree* of such a pragmatic ambiguity, asking, for instance, such questions as the following: first, whether pragmatic ambiguity is a *necessary* or, rather, a *contingent* feature in the working of our legal systems; second, whether it does concern *every case* or, rather, just *some class of cases*; third, whether, whenever it shows up, it does so in a way that might be regarded as *radical* (*indeterminacy proper*) or, rather, as *mild* or *moderate* (*underdeterminacy*).

[7] For such a two-tier model of textual interpretation, see, e.g. C.E. Alchourrón and E. Bulygin, *Normative Systems*; R. Guastini, *Il diritto come linguaggio* (2nd edn, Turin: Giappichelli, 2006), 145.

[8] On the role of juristic theories, see R. Guastini, *Il diritto come linguaggio*, 142ff. and R. Guastini, 'Defeasibility, Axiological Gaps, and Interpretation', in this volume, ch. 9.

[9] On this account, there is no place for such an independent entry as 'semantic ambiguity': the ambiguity of norm formulations, that is not due to their syntactic structures, is always pragmatic. Indeed, the ambiguity of the literal reading of a norm formulation (which would be usually considered as 'semantic ambiguity') depends on the use of a well-known interpretative directive (the so-called 'literal rule'), which is a move in the complex, practical, game of 'written-law/legal sources construction'.

It is a well-known fact that, within the literature on legal indeterminacy, those issues represent some of the basic problems legal indeterminacy provides for jurisprudents' delight. Here, however, I simply wish to clarify further my position about the pragmatic ambiguity (and indeterminacy) of norm formulations.

I think one should carefully avoid blurring the lines separating two different perspectives an inquiry of *descriptive methodology* may take about legal interpretation and the pragmatic indeterminacy of norm formulations, namely: (i) the perspective of engineering methodology, and (ii) the perspective of sociological methodology.

Engineering methodology inquires into interpretative tools (directives, codes, techniques, canons, etc.) considered in their abstract structures and functioning: i.e. in a way detached from any consideration of convenience, value, and workability in the light of social/legal constraints on their selection and use. From this perspective we may safely claim that, in the here and now of Western legal cultures (civil law and common law countries alike), *every* norm formulation is *technically* liable to pragmatic ambiguity and, accordingly, may give rise to problems of plurality-of-competing-answers adjudicative indeterminacy.

Sociological methodology, by contrast, performs two different kinds of inquiries.

On the one hand, it inquires into the 'authoritative' or 'conventional' interpretative code, if any, obtaining in a given legal experience in a certain temporal frame, paying particular attention to the constraints, if any, that a given society—as a whole, or through qualified sectors of public opinion and professionals—exercises through such a code upon judges and other interpreters of the law, when they choose the methodological tools (interpretative directives and codes) they need for doing their job.

On the other hand, it inquires into each interpreter's standing about the morally and/or legally proper way to perform her task. Here the inquiry concerns the interpreters' own 'conception of the Class of legal reasons', to quote Brian Leiter's words[10]—or, in a different, Continental mood, interpreters' *ideologies* about the law in general, their own legal system, and the proper method for its interpretation, as they are exhibited by the content of their interpretative reasoning. Here, we find each interpreter's basic methodological options and allegiances, if any. From this viewpoint, the interpreter's own tool box may be—and usually is—not tantamount to *all* the interpretative directives, in *all* the several, possible, combinations and uses we find in the realm of engineering methodology. Accordingly, from this perspective, it may well be the case that not every norm formulation is liable to pragmatic ambiguity all the time.

(2) Generic norms. A plurality of competing answers may also feature in the following situation:

(i) the judge has identified a norm—usually a (general, fundamental, basic) *principle*—as the relevant (explicit or implicit) norm to be used to adjudicate a claim;

(ii) the norm, however, is generic ('Let right be done', 'First, do no harm', 'No person may profit from her own wrongdoing', 'Every person is entitled to the

[10] See B. Leiter, 'A Note on Legal Indeterminacy' in B. Leiter, *Naturalizing Jurisprudence. Essays on American Legal Realism and Naturalism in Legal Philosophy* (Oxford: Oxford University Press, 2007), 9ff. and B. Leiter, 'Legal Indeterminacy', *Legal Theory*, 1 (1995), 481ff. See also, e.g. L.B. Solum, 'Indeterminacy' in D. Patterson (ed.), *A Companion to Philosophy of Law and Legal Theory* (Oxford: Blackwell, 1996), 488ff. Leiter distinguishes between 'causal' and 'rational' indeterminacy. A clear statement of the theoretical background of causal indeterminacy is provided by C. Redondo, 'Teorías del derecho e indeterminación normativa', *Doxa*, 20 (1997), 177ff., where she also distinguishes between normative indeterminacy, concerning the deontic status of actions and the solution provided to generic cases within a normative system, and content indeterminacy, concerning the semantic content of previously identified norms in relation to individual cases.

blessings of liberty', etc.) in a way as to allow a plurality of competing specifications in the face of a given real or imaginary case. That is to say, several alternative, more specific, rules (rules of detail, *Konkretisierungen*) may be derived out of it—due to the several types of principle-concretization made available by the methodological tradition.

(3) Normative conflicts. Adjudicative indeterminacy due to the presence, under certain assumptions, of a plurality of competing answers may also be the effect of a different puzzling situation. I mean the situation where:

(i) there is a normative conflict, and

(ii) such a conflict is a *real* conflict: it cannot be settled by resorting to pre-established criteria—i.e. to one, ordered, set of criteria established by an ongoing, authoritative or conventional interpretative code.

Notice that both the identification and the resolution of normative conflicts depend on interpretative directives, though of different sort. Accordingly, even in this situation the original source of adjudicative indeterminacy is to be placed with such directives—and with the individual and collective ideologies that govern their selection and uses.

(4) Explicit gaps. Adjudicative indeterminacy due to the presence, under certain assumptions, of a plurality of competing answers may also be the effect of a further, puzzling situation. I mean the situation where:

(i) there is a normative gap, or more precisely, (what may be called) an explicit gap: available norm formulations, however interpreted, do not provide any (explicit) norm for a case at hand;

(ii) there are several alternative ways of filling up the gap, leading to different outcomes (e.g. by analogical reasoning, *a contrario* reasoning, concretization of fundamental principles, reasoning from the nature of things, etc.);

(iii) none of these ways takes a pre-established, fixed, pre-eminent place above the others, within an ongoing, authoritative or conventional interpretative code. Here again, as in the two previous puzzling situations, the ultimate factor responsible for this kind of adjudicative indeterminacy stays with interpretative directives and their systemic indeterminacy.

(5) Competing reconstructions of a legal system. It may also happen that the content of a legal system is indeterminate: i.e. it is not clear *which* norms make it up, for alternative reconstructions are available.[11] *Salva interpretatione*, this may be the case whenever in a legal system: (i) a norm N_1 has been derogated; (ii) N_1, however, may also be logically derived from a combination of two other norms of the system, say, N_2 and N_3; (iii) the derogating norm, however, does not say anything about whether N_2, or N_3, or both have also been derogated; and consequently, (iv) the system is indeterminate as to the norms making it up, for it may be regarded as containing, alternatively, N_2, but not N_3, or vice versa.

It seems, however, that this example of indeterminacy depends on a gap in the system: i.e. on the fact that a suitable derogating norm is missing. Accordingly, it is tantamount to the example of indeterminacy I considered under the 'explicit gap' heading (heading (4), above).

[11] For such an indeterminacy situation, see E. Bulygin, 'Teoria e tecnica della legislazione' (1st edn 1981), in E. Bulygin, *Norme, validità, sistemi normativi* (Turin: Giappichelli, 1995), 42ff.

(d) No-answer adjudicative indeterminacy

In the third (kind of) adjudicative indeterminacy, as you may recall, 'the law *does not* provide *any solution at all* to the case at hand'. I will call this situation *no-answer* adjudicative indeterminacy. How could that be?

Apparently, we are here at the outer reaches of a legal order. By hypothesis, no possible combination of legal sources and interpretative directives provides the judge with some, either explicit or even implicit, norm, suitable to the case at hand.

Given the rich complexity of legal sources in modern legal systems and, above all, the varieties of combinations and uses of interpretative directives, such a situation appears mostly academic.

2. A few notions and forms of legal indeterminacy

It is time to take stock of the previous analysis. I will try now to single out a few notions of 'legal indeterminacy', corresponding to as many, likely, forms in the legal realm.

A suitable starting point is provided by the variety of the *subjects* of indeterminacy. On such a footing, it is possible to identify not less than four central notions of legal indeterminacy, namely:

(1) adjudicative indeterminacy;
(2) textual indeterminacy;
(3) normative indeterminacy;
(4) methodological indeterminacy.

While dealing with them, a few further, (and to my mind) useful, notions will be considered.

(1) *Adjudicative indeterminacy* (in a broad sense) occurs whenever, in a process of actual or hypothetical decision-making (or, in general, of problem solving: I will not quote this point any more), the law does not provide one determinate solution (answer, normative consequence) to a—real or imaginary, individual or generic—case at hand.

From a sociological point of view, this means, very roughly, that: (a) if the case has already been adjudicated, i.e. is not a case of 'first impression', it has been decided differently in the past and is likely to be decided differently in the future; (b) if the case is a case of first impression it is not possible, on the basis of existing legal materials and the conventional interpretative code, to predict one single legal answer for it.

(2) *Textual indeterminacy* (*sources indeterminacy*) obtains whenever, in a process of actual or hypothetical decision-making, a *norm formulation* proves ambiguous from a syntactic and/or a pragmatic point of view. Such an ambiguity may pertain either to the norm formulation as a whole, or to single expressions—and notably, to single-concept words—within it. In this latter situation, textual indeterminacy (ambiguity) depends on *concept-word indeterminacy* (ambiguity).

(3) *Normative indeterminacy* obtains whenever, in a process of actual or hypothetical decision-making, either of the following is the case: (a) the relevant *norm*—be it an explicit or an implicit norm—proves ambiguous, vague (meaning also 'open-textured'), or generic; (b) there is, at least prima facie, a normative gap; (c) there is, at least prima facie, a normative conflict.

In the first situation, the norm that proves ambiguous may be regarded as the outcome of an inchoate process of norm identification. Indeed, the norm proves capable of different, alternative, readings. Accordingly, one may claim that it is not really *a norm* that has been identified so far in a given situation, but, rather, *a norm-frame*—to echo a well-known Kelsenian idea. And the process of getting one single norm out of it is very much like the process of textual interpretation of some norm formulation (i.e. getting *one* explicit norm out of a given norm formulation).

In the second situation, the norm is indeed one single norm but, unfortunately, it turns out to be vague in certain generic or individual cases at hand. Such a situation of indeterminacy, in turn, cannot depend but on the vagueness of some concept in the norm.

In the third situation, some norms—notably, those we are used to call 'principles'—prove generic, so as to be capable of several alternative specifications (*Konkretisierungen*) as to a given, real or imaginary, case at hand. This type of indeterminacy points, again, to interpretative directives and methodological indeterminacy.

In the latter two situations (normative gaps and normative conflicts), it is doubtful which norm, if any, is to be applied to the case at hand.

(4) *Methodological indeterminacy* obtains in two different, quite often concomitant, situations:

(a) whenever, in a process of actual or hypothetical decision-making, the tools that may be used to justify legal decisions and/or the outcomes of the upward operational stages on which such decisions depend (textual interpretation, norm qualification, norm concretization, gaps filling, etc.) make up *no closed and ordered set* being, contrariwise, an *open, unordered set* of items (*systemic indeterminacy*);

(b) whenever, in a process of actual or hypothetical decision-making, the tools that may be used to justify legal decisions and/or the outcomes of the upward operational stages on which such decisions depend (textual interpretation, norm qualification, norm concretization, gaps filling, etc.) prove, in themselves, indeterminate (*content indeterminacy*).

Three basic sets of tools may be distinguished as follows:

- directives of textual interpretation, ruling over the interpretation of norm formulations (sources-interpretation);
- directives of meta textual interpretation, ruling over such operations as norm qualification (like saying, e.g. that a norm is not 'a simple rule', but a 'principle'), norm concretization, the filling-up of gaps, and the resolution of normative conflicts; and
- rules and forms of logical reasoning, ruling over normative inferences.

Accordingly, within methodological indeterminacy, we may further distinguish two basic varieties: namely, *interpretative indeterminacy* and *logical indeterminacy*, respectively.

From the perspective of sociological methodology, a situation of *radical interpretative indeterminacy* obtains, in a given legal order, whenever *every* norm formulation and/or *every* norm, in that given legal order, is liable to pragmatic indeterminacy—and every solution in whatever adjudicative context is, accordingly, indeterminate.

Contrariwise, a legal order may be regarded as characterized by *moderate interpretative indeterminacy*, whenever the following situation obtains:

(a) some adjudicative outcomes, some norm formulations, and some norms are publicly regarded as determinate, while, at the same time, others are publicly regarded as indeterminate;

(b) society at large, and/or the legal culture and law profession, do not impose on interpreters any strict interpretative code; they only require them to take their interpretative directives, at least in part, from a 'common box' handed down by the methodological tradition—endorsing, in such a way, a form of side-constrained methodological pluralism where only 'extreme interpretations' are not viable, being grossly 'absurd', 'weird', 'wanton', 'arbitrary', 'unreasonable', 'outrageous', etc.;

(c) each interpreter is allowed to choose the interpretative code she thinks proper (she likes), and she may even shift codes from one individual case to another, provided she gets her codes, at least in part, from the box of common tools, and no extreme interpretations are brought about.

I dwelled longer on methodological indeterminacy—and, above all, on interpretative indeterminacy—for one reason. It seems to be, all things considered, the basic, independent form of legal indeterminacy: the one on which all other forms are, more or less directly, dependent.

B. Defeasibility

Though it always enjoyed an undercover presence in (Western) legal thinking, mainly under the heading of the rule–exception issue,[12] the term and subject of 'defeasibility' is a relatively new entry in the jurisprudential realm.

After a first appearance in the late 1940s, due to Herbert Hart's essay 'The Ascription of Responsibility and Rights',[13] defeasibility disappeared for almost 40 years from legal philosophical writings, to gain a new currency, along with studies in deontic logic and artificial intelligence and the law, from the late 1980s onwards.[14]

While some legal philosophers take a sceptical view about it,[15] it seems, nonetheless, that it would be a mistake to dismiss defeasibility simply as a new, currently fashionable, label for well-known, unsurprising, corners of the legal maze. Indeed, defeasibility features as the main character within critical lines of inquiry pointing at some deeply rooted conceptions about crucial issues in law. A tentative list of the targets of the defeasibility turn in legal thinking would include, in my view, not less than eight different views.

A first target is the objectifying conception of the rule–exception relationships. This view sees norms and 'their' exceptions as given, objective, entities in the legal domain. It

[12] See, e.g. J. Bentham, *Of Laws in General* (1791; ed. by H.L.A. Hart, London: The Athlone Press, 1970), 112ff.; K. Larenz, *Methodenlehre der Rechtswissenschaft*, 1979, tr. sp., *Metodología de la ciencia del derecho* (Barcelona: Ariel, 1994), 252–3, 257ff.; F. Schauer, 'Exceptions', *The University of Chicago Law Review*, 58 (1991), 871ff.

[13] H.L.A. Hart, 'The Ascription of Responsibility and Rights, 1948–1949' in A.G.N. Flew (ed.), *Logic and Language* (First Series, Oxford: Blackwell, 1951), 145–66.

[14] Among the forerunners of the 'defeasibility turn' in deontic logic, in the late 1960s, B. Hansson, 'An Analysis of Some Deontic Logics', *Nous*, 3 (1969), 373–98—as reported by C.E. Alchourrón, 'Philosophical Foundations of Deontic Logic and the Logic of Defeasible Conditionals' in J. Meyer and R. Wieringa (eds), *Deontic Logic in Computer Science: Normative System Specification* (London: Wiley & Sons, 1993), 43–84. Another major contribution, in the early 1970s, is L. Aqvist, 'Modal Logic with Subjunctive Conditionals and Dispositional Predicates', *Journal of Philosophical Logic*, 2 (1973), 1–76.

[15] See, e.g. J.L. Rodríguez and G. Sucar, 'Las trampas de la derrotabilidad. Niveles de análisis de la indeterminación del derecho' in P. Gaido, R. Sánchez, and H.O. Seleme (eds), *Relevancia normativa en la justificación de las decisiones judiciales. El debate Bayón-Rodríguez sobre la derrotabilidad de las normas jurídicas* (Bogotá: Universidad Externado de Colombia, 2003), 103ff., 143.

is tantamount to metaphysical realism in law and represents an enduring, though perhaps unconscious, heritage of the age of formalism.

A second target of the defeasibility turn in legal thinking is epistemological realism as to the science of the law. This view regards knowledge in the legal domain as direct, objective, apprehension of fully fledged norms and exceptions, together with legal rights, duties, responsibilities, etc., *out there*; it represents the epistemic counterpart to the objectifying conception of the rule–exception relationships.

A third target of the defeasibility turn in legal thinking is the conditional conception of the logical form of legal norms. This view maintains that legal norms are properly represented as conditional, or hypothetical, normative sentences, where a certain legal consequence (say, the duty to do q: Oq) follows from, or is ascribed to, the set of *sufficient* conditions specified in the antecedent ('p → Oq'; '(*x*) (A*x* → OB*x*)').

A fourth target of the defeasibility turn in legal thinking is (what may be called) the Aristotelian conception of the definition of legal concepts. According to this view, a (proper) definition of a legal concept requires the identification of a set of necessary and sufficient defining properties. This view, however, would be a piece of old-time, pre-Benthamite, conceptualism, owing its present survival to the support from—to quote Hart's words—'philosophers'' truth-functional theory of meaning.[16]

A fifth target of the defeasibility turn in legal thinking is (what may be regarded as) *naïf* norm-universalism. This view amounts, very roughly speaking, to the confident belief in the existence and functioning of *general* legal norms actually and thoroughly controlling people's behaviours, as opposed to the (more modest) perspectives represented, on the one hand, by critical norm-universalism (being content with a net of interlocking, reasonably effective, general norms), and, on the other hand, by outright normative particularism.

A sixth target of the defeasibility turn in legal thinking is the deductive, or monotonic, conception of the logical relationships between legal norms, centred on the so-called law of the strengthening of the antecedent and *modus ponens*.

A seventh target of the defeasibility turn in legal thinking is the linear conception of legal reasoning. This is the cognitive, or psychological, model that represents legal reasoning—and notably, interpretative reasoning—as a simple, linear, forward-going, process, from a fixed set of starting points (inputs, data) to a set of conclusions (outputs); it also represents the cognitive counterpart of the deductive conception of the relationships between norms.

An eighth, and final, target of the defeasibility turn in legal thinking, worthy of being mentioned here, is the so-called separation thesis: there is no necessary connection between law and morals, so that it makes perfect sense to distinguish between the law as it is and the law as it ought to be.

Some of the views above (surely, the separation thesis, the conditional conception of the logical form of legal norms, and the monotonic conception of normative logic, but also some of the other ones, at least in some nuanced version and from a loose, common-sense, perspective) are usually considered as pieces of that influential theory of law which goes under the name of 'legal positivism' or, on the Continent, 'normativism' ('normativistic legal positivism').

16 This line of criticism, as is well known, was put forward by Hart in his earliest jurisprudential essays: H.L.A. Hart, 'The Ascription of Responsibility and Rights' and 'Definition and Theory in Jurisprudence' (1954) in H.L.A. Hart, *Essays in Jurisprudence and Philosophy* (Oxford: Clarendon Press, 1983), 21–48.

Accordingly, the defeasibility turn in legal theory, with its several strands, may be viewed—in a unifying perspective—as the revolutionary attempt to open the way for a new theoretical paradigm in legal thinking: as an intellectual venture fostering a (supposedly) advanced form of *critical, defeasibility-centred, normativism*, that should replace what, by present standards, should be regarded, instead, as the *naïf normativism* dominating such a large part of twentieth century jurisprudence.[17]

As I did with legal indeterminacy, I will assume—as a regulative ideal to my present, very tentative, inquiry—that a useful theory of legal defeasibility (defeasibility in law) would be a methodologically aware discourse, purporting to cast light on its subject matter, by dealing with at least the following four issues:

(1) the *subjects* of 'defeasibility';
(2) the *sources* of defeasibility;
(3) the *notions*, and *forms*, of defeasibility;
(4) the *problems* defeasibility makes for both legal theory and legal politics.

I will take this frame into account in the following, tentative, analysis of defeasibility in law. I will deal, first, with the subjects and sources of defeasibility (B.1); then, I will define a few, hopefully suitable, notions of defeasibility (B.2).

1. Defeasibility in law and its sources

In the scholarly literature, many different things are qualified as 'defeasible', though sometimes the very logical possibility of their being genuinely so qualified is contested.

A tentative survey suggests that while dealing with 'defeasibility in law', or 'law's defeasibility', legal philosophers may be concerned with one or more of the following eleven subjects:

(1) defeasible *facts*;
(2) defeasible *beliefs*;
(3) defeasible legal *concepts*;
(4) defeasible *norm formulations* or *legal texts*;
(5) defeasible legal *interpretations*, or defeasible *meanings*, of norm formulations;
(6) defeasible legal *norms*, rules, principles, standards, etc. (norm defeasibility);
(7) defeasible legal *reasoning*;
(8) defeasible legal *positions*, jural relations, legal entitlements, etc. (status defeasibility);
(9) defeasible legal *arrangements*, like contracts, wills, etc. (arrangement defeasibility);
(10) defeasible legal *claims*;
(11) defeasible legal *conclusions*.

A theory of defeasibility should make clear which subjects—out of the tentative list above—on a closer inspection may be conveniently regarded as defeasible, and why.

Accordingly, in what follows I will briefly consider in turn each one of them, in order to see: *first*, what their 'defeasibility' consists in; *second*, whether, and why, they may, or may not, be suitably considered as 'defeasible'; *third*, which are the factors making them defeasible—i.e. what is, or may safely be regarded as being the source, or sources, of their defeasibility. This inquiry should allow us, in due time, to identify a few, more

[17] It goes without saying, of course, that the very same, supposedly '*naïf*' normativism of the present day is, in its turn, an advanced, sophisticated, form of 'critical' normativism, if compared to the '*naïf*' normativism characterizing jurisprudence in the nineteenth and twentieth centuries.

precise, notions of defeasibility—a few *explicata* out of the bubbling cauldron of intuitive 'defeasibility' *explicanda*.

(a) Defeasible facts

According to Jaap Hage, a first class of defeasibility subjects would consist in the facts of the lawsuits, i.e. the facts making up the individual cases which are the matter of litigation:

> A contract that has come into existence after an offer and an acceptance can be invalidated if one of the parties involved invokes a defeating condition, such as fraudulent misrepresentation, or undue influence. Since this case of defeasibility *concerns the (retro-active) change of the facts*, and *not* our *beliefs* about the facts, we may call it *ontological defeasibility*.[18]

Facts, however, are what they are—and, snobbish scepticism apart, we do know that pretty well since we always, sometimes painfully, run into them. They cannot properly be 'defeasible', i.e. subject to *retro active change*, as is suggested by Hage. Unless, of course, we own a suitable machine through which we, the lucky travellers, may go back in time and fix things up (school grades, marriages, payments, job opportunities, land occupations, auction offers, treasure-troves, etc.) as we like. Accordingly, the only way to make sense of Hage's idea of an ontological defeasibility is to look at it as a metaphor. Indeed, the very words Hage employs suggest this way out: what he is really talking about in the quoted passage above are, in fact, two different, opposing *descriptions* of the grounds of a lawsuit. Plaintiff says: there was offer and acceptance (without fraudulent misrepresentation and/or undue influence). Defendant replies: yes, there was offer and acceptance, but under fraudulent misrepresentation and/or undue influence. Eventually, ontological defeasibility boils down to the revisability—falsifiability—of the descriptions (assertions) concerning the relevant facts of a lawsuit, that have been alleged by the parties, in front of new evidence.

(b) Defeasible beliefs

According to several legal philosophers (J. Hage, J. Rodríguez, G. Sartor, etc.),[19] another, theoretically relevant, class of defeasibility subjects consists of *beliefs*. The beliefs they have in mind may concern several different aspects of any legal experience: the normative status of an action, the normative conclusions following from a given set

[18] J. Hage, 'Law and Defeasibility', *IVR—Encyclopaedia of Jurisprudence, Legal Theory and Philosophy of Law*, December 2004, at 1, italics added and J. Hage, 'Law and Defeasibility', *Artificial Intelligence and Law*, 11 (2003), 221ff. See also G. Sartor, 'Syllogism and Defeasibility: A Comment on Neil MacCormick's *Rhetoric and the Rule of Law*' (Florence, European University Institute, EUI Working Paper Law No. 2006/23, 2006), at 10, for a similar idea of an 'ontic defeasibility': 'there are *facts* [...] that are normally sufficient to determine certain legal or moral outcomes, but can be made irrelevant (undercut) or can be outweighed (rebutted) by further facts [...] when seen from the ontic perspective, defeasibility does not pertain to conclusions or rules, but rather to facts, in the sense of *relevant* aspects of the situation at issue, and it concerns their ability to constitute normative (legal or moral) qualifications and effects'. However, there is no *relevance* at all without some (presupposed) *criterion of relevance*: i.e. some standards according to which certain facts are to be deemed relevant (important, worthwhile considering, etc.) in view of regulating a situation.

[19] J. Hage, 'Law and Defeasibility' (2004), 2 and 'Law and Defeasibility' (2003), G. Sartor, 'Syllogism and Defeasibility: A Comment on Neil MacCormick's *Rhetoric and the Rule of Law*', 11, 'cognitive defeasibility' as the defeasibility of the beliefs concerning ontic reasons (facts) and legal conclusions; J.L. Rodríguez and G. Sucar, 'Las trampas de la derrotabilidad. Niveles de análisis de la indeterminación del derecho', 119ff.

of facts and/or premises, the norms making up a given legal system, the proper justification for some legal conclusion and/or its premises, the proper interpretation of a given norm formulation, etc. Such beliefs are 'defeasible' in the sense that, like the lawsuits' facts-descriptions above, they too would be liable, or open, to revision: to be modified, specified, or utterly discarded, in view of further information which may emerge in the course of the inquiry.

Clearly, beliefs-defeasibility, whatever the subject matter of the beliefs, is *second-order* 'legal' defeasibility: it is not, properly speaking, defeasibility *of* any *legal* item whatsoever, meaning by that things *belonging to*, *being part of*, or anyway *within*, the law.

Furthermore, at least in some cases, it seems to be a typical form of *derivative* defeasibility: our beliefs (knowledge, opinions, views, normative propositions) about some aspects of a legal order are liable to change, for the legal items which they refer to are themselves 'defeasible', in the generic sense of being subject to, liable to, open to, revision and change.

But, of course, beliefs-defeasibility might also be altogether dependent on our own epistemic limitations: something in the law might be perfectly indefeasible, while we would have only tentatively sound beliefs about it.

(c) Defeasible concepts

The claim that legal concepts—or at least, many of the most interesting of them—are defeasible is a well-known contribution Herbert Hart made to contemporary jurisprudence.[20]

There are several ways of reading Hart but, for the present purpose, philological issues will be put aside.

In view of sharpening concepts for juristic use, the thesis of the defeasibility of legal concepts may be accounted for as including the following tenets.

(a) Legal concepts are not suitable objects for definitions purporting to fix a closed list of necessary and, in Hart's words, 'always' sufficient properties.[21]

(b) On the contrary, their defining properties are better conceived of as an *open list*, where paradigmatic properties in paradigmatic cases provide the flexible criterion for analogical extension to further properties in further cases. Accordingly, the logical form of a proper definition of a legal concept should be characterized by an 'etcetera' clause.[22]

(c) Furthermore, two different groups of properties should be considered, and kept apart, in any proper definition of a legal concept, namely: *positive* properties (positive conditions) and *negative* properties (negative conditions).

Positive properties are to be regarded as stating the necessary and *normally* sufficient conditions for a concept to be applied to an individual case (a given set of facts) at hand.

[20] See, e.g. H.L.A. Hart, 'The Ascription of Responsibility and Rights' and 'Definition and Theory in Jurisprudence'; G.P. Baker, 'Defeasibility and Meaning' in P.M.S. Hacker and J. Raz (eds), *Law, Morality and Society. Essays in Honour of H.L.A. Hart* (Oxford: Clarendon Press, 1977), 26–57; N. MacCormick, 'Defeasibility in Law and Logic' in Z. Bankowski, I. White, U. Hahn, *Informatics and the Foundations of Legal Reasoning* (Dordrecht: Kluwer, 1995), 99–117; J. Hage, 'Law and Defeasibility' (2004), 2 and 'Law and Defeasibility' (2003), 221ff; G. Sartor, *Legal Reasoning. A Cognitive Approach to the Law* (Dordrecht: Springer, 2005), 78.

[21] H.L.A. Hart, 'The Ascription of Responsibility and Rights', 148, 149 fn. 1.

[22] Ibid., 147.

This means, more precisely, that they jointly establish a condition *sufficient* for applying the concept to a case, *if*, but *only if*—*once* they have been duly identified (also by saturating the 'etcetera clause', if any) *and* considered as satisfied—*some further conditions* are *not* satisfied instead, for the presence of these negative properties would *defeat* the positive properties, i.e. would make the concept no longer applicable to those very facts. Accordingly, the logical form of any proper definition of a legal concept should also be characterized by an 'unless' clause.[23]

We are now in a position, following Hart, to identify four basic logical forms for the definition of a defeasible legal concept of the sort Hart had in mind:

(1) $(x)\ (Ax\ \&\ Bx)\ \&\ \neg(Dx \vee Ex \vee Fx) \rightarrow Tx$
(2) $(x)\ (Ax\ \&\ Bx)\ \&\ \neg(Dx \vee Ex \vee Fx \vee \ldots) \rightarrow Tx$
(3) $(x)\ (Ax\ \&\ Bx\ \&\ \ldots)\ \&\ \neg(Dx \vee Ex \vee Fx) \rightarrow Tx$
(4) $(x)\ (Ax\ \&\ Bx\ \&\ \ldots)\ \&\ \neg(Dx \vee Ex \vee Fx \vee \ldots) \rightarrow Tx$.

Form (1) reads: 'For any *x*, *if x* is A and B, and *unless x* is D, or E, or F, *then x* is T'.

Form (4) reads: 'For any *x*, *if x* is A, and B, *etc.*, and *unless x* is D, or E, or F, or *etc.*, *then x* is T'.

Form (3) reads: 'For any *x*, *if x* is A, and B, *etc.*, and *unless x* is D, or E, or F, *then x* is T'.

Form (2) reads: 'For any *x*, *if x* is A and B, and *unless x* is D, or E, or F, or *etc.*, *then x* is T'.

Forms (1) and (3) concern *closed-end defeasible* concepts: the set of negative, or defeating, conditions is, by hypothesis, a closed set—no 'etc.' ('and so on') clause holds for these conditions.

Forms (2) and (4) concern, instead, *open-end defeasible* concepts: the set of negative, defeating, conditions is, by hypothesis, an open set—an 'etc.' clause is attached to the set of these conditions.

Leaving aside, at least for the moment, the issue whether, and in which sense, legal concepts (which ones?) are—or should be regarded as—'necessarily' defeasible, the four logical forms above may be considered as presentation tools for the definition of any legal concept whatsoever that, in a process of actual or hypothetical decision-making proves, at some stage of the process, defeasible: i.e. provided with a set of negative, or defeating, defining conditions. The normal situation being apparently, from this perspective, the following: an (assumed) open-end defeasible legal concept gets saturated, as to its open-end defeasibility conditions and in view of its application to a case at hand, in such a way as to be transformed into a (*pro tanto*) closed-end defeasible concept.

What makes legal concepts defeasible? There seems to be a simple answer to this issue. Once we reject Jhering's conceptualist Heaven, legal concepts are just tools worked out by jurists, and continuously rearranged and sharpened by them, to do things in the legal domain. By 'their very nature', they are neither open-end defeasible, nor closed-end defeasible, nor undefeasible. Convenience, juristic theories, and interpretative and definitional attitudes make them what they are.

[23] Ibid., 147, 148, 150. To quote a key passage: 'it is usually not possible to define a legal concept such as "trespass" or "contract" by *specifying the necessary and sufficient conditions* for its application. For *any* set of conditions may be adequate in some cases but not in others, and such concepts can only be explained with the aid of *a list of exceptions or negative examples* showing where the concept may not be applied or may only be applied in a weakened form' (148, italics added). In a later essay, the conditions after the unless clause are classified under two basic headings: *excusing* conditions and *invalidating* conditions: see H.L.A. Hart, 'Legal Responsibility and Excuses' (1958), in H.L.A. Hart, *Punishment and Responsibility. Essays in the Philosophy of Law* (Oxford: Clarendon Press, 1968), 96.

(d) Defeasible norm formulations

Sometimes, legal philosophers seem to identify *norm formulations*—legislative formulations, enacted statutes—as suitable defeasibility subjects:

> any *reasonable approach* to *systemic interpretation* of enacted statutes—claims, for instance, Neil MacCormick[24]—will also *treat legislative formulations as effectively defeasible* since *only providing presumptively sufficient or necessary conditions* as to whatever is enacted.

However, in the very light of their words (e.g. of MacCormick's words), the idea of a defeasible norm formulation appears, at best, misleading. In fact, it rests on a confusion between two kinds of entities that should be kept separate. On the one hand there are norm formulations proper; on the other hand there are norms.

Norm formulations are *syntactic entities*: they are token sentences, belonging to the discourse of a certain legal source, and considered apart from any interpretation whatsoever. They are, indeed, the starting point for processes of legal interpretation: they are the sentences which interpreters, by means of some code of textual interpretation and some set of interpretative resources, translate into one or more explicit norms.

Norms, from this viewpoint, are instead *semantic entities*: they are the *meanings* of norm formulations, or, more precisely, what may be presented, and argued for, as the 'correct' ('reasonable', 'true', 'proper', etc.) meaning of a given norm formulation, according to a set of interpretative directives together with other relevant interpretative inputs (historical data, pieces of scientific information, basic moral values, fundamental legal principles, juristic theories, etc.).

Now, from a conceptual point of view, only semantic entities (in the broad sense I defined before)—namely, sentences that *are*, or are assumed *to be*, *norms*—may be *treated* as providing 'presumptively sufficient or necessary conditions' for some legal consequence. No such treatment is available, contrariwise, for purely syntactic entities.[25]

As a consequence, the idea of a defeasible norm formulation is not to be taken at face value, if it is to make any sense.

Two different, related, readings may be considered.

A. On a *first reading*, the claim that 'norm formulations are defeasible' may be understood as tantamount to the claim that *literal norms are defeasible*. On this reading, it is a claim concerning the defeasibility of those norms that, by hypothesis, represent the literal meanings of some given norm formulations—being, usually, perfectly isomorphic to the latter. So, literal norms—the norms resulting from a literal interpretation of norm formulations—would be defeasible: would only provide presumptively sufficient, or merely necessary but not necessarily sufficient, conditions for some legal consequence. Notice that this claim—as the passage from MacCormick suggests—apparently belongs to a purportedly 'reasonable approach to systemic interpretation of enacted statutes': it belongs, in other words, to a specific *prescriptive* methodology of statutory construction. And it is the very endorsement of such a 'reasonable' methodological outlook (along with its theoretical background) that ultimately accounts for the

[24] N. MacCormick, 'Defeasibility in Law and Logic', 115, italics added.

[25] There are indeed two kinds of norms from this perspective: *explicit* norms and *implicit* norms. Implicit norms are sentences representing norms that, by hypothesis, are not the meaning of any norm formulation, being rather identified by means of certain argumentative processes from one or more explicit and/or implicit norms (e.g. by analogical or *a contrario* reasoning).

defeasibility of the literal norms in a legal order—for their being liable to negative conditions of application imposed, in MacCormick's view, by other norms of the system.

It is perhaps worthwhile noticing here, by the way, that modifications to literal norms, consisting in the adding up of negative conditions for the application of the legal consequence they state, may take, in general, two different forms.

On the one hand, these modifications may be presented, and argued for, as corresponding, say, to some *intentional* or *teleological* reading of the norm formulation itself: in such a case, the literal (*explicit*) norm is being replaced by a different, intentional or teleological, (*explicit*) norm, that is the outcome of a reinterpretation of the relevant norm formulation according either to the (actual, presumed, counterfactual) 'intention' of the lawgiver, or to the 'underlying reasons' of the norm/norm formulation itself.[26]

On the other hand, the modifications to the literal norm may also be presented, and argued for, as the outcome of taking into account *other* relevant *norms* of the same legal system: in such a case, the literal (*explicit*) norm is replaced by an *implicit* norm, resulting from the combination of the literal norm with (pieces and/or consequences of) other norms of the system (I will return to this point later).

In the former case, we may speak of an *internal-interpretative defeasibility* of literal norms; in the latter case, of their *external-* or *systemic-interpretative defeasibility*. The latter case seems to correspond to what MacCormick had in mind in the passage I quoted above.

B. On a *second reading*, the claim that 'norm formulations are defeasible' may be understood as referring to a general interpretative disposition *towards* norm formulations. Namely, to the disposition, that interpreters may choose to adopt, to interpreting norm formulations as sentences expressing defeasible norms—in the two ways above, i.e. internally or externally defeasible norms. From this point of view, we may even talk of norm formulations as 'having the dispositional property' of being interpreted as expressing defeasible norms. Provided we always remember that such a property is, again and ultimately, in the eye of their interpreters.

(e) Defeasible interpretations

Some legal philosophers claim—by way of a theoretical statement belonging to descriptive jurisprudence and, notably, to engineering and sociological methodology (see A.1 above)—that 'interpretations are defeasible'.[27]

[26] See C.E. Alchourrón, 'On Law and Logic', in this volume, ch. 2, 46ff., where he outlines a 'dispositional approach' for the interpretative identification of the negative conditions that may be regarded either as 'implicit exceptions', or as 'implicit non-exceptions', or even as 'indeterminate as exceptions', from the point of the (counterfactual) dispositions of the lawgiver. See, also, J. Ferrer Beltrán and G.B. Ratti, *Validità, defettibilità, e criteri di riconoscimento*, unpublished manuscript, 2008, where, from an interpretative approach perspective (one dealing, I would say, with the 'sources' of defeating conditions), they distinguish between 'teleological' (background reasons), 'authoritative' (lawgiver's actual intention), and 'dispositional' (lawgiver's counterfactual intention) defeasibility.

[27] See, e.g. J.C. Bayón, 'Derrotabilidad, indeterminación del derecho y positivismo jurídico', (1997) in P. Gaido, R. Sánchez, and H.O. Seleme (eds), *Relevancia normativa en la justificación de las decisiones judiciales. El debate Bayón-Rodríguez sobre la derrotabilidad de las normas jurídicas*, 184–5; J.L. Rodríguez, 'La derrotabilidad de las normas jurídicas' in P. Gaido, R. Sánchez, and H.O. Seleme (eds), *Relevancia normativa en la justificación de las decisiones judiciales*, 97ff.; J.L. Rodríguez and G. Sucar, 'Las trampas de la derrotabilidad. Niveles de análisis de la indeterminación del derecho' in P. Gaido, R. Sánchez, and H.O. Seleme (eds), *Relevancia normativa en la justificación de las decisiones*

This claim points, apparently, at two essential features of interpretative practices, as they in fact are here and now.

On the one hand, the *process* of legal interpretation (*interpretation activity*) is, from the viewpoint of its structure, 'defeasible': starting from a given norm formulation and a certain set of interpretative directives and interpretative resources, interpreters identify the (*pro tanto*) all-things-considered correct interpretation (interpretative outcome) of such a norm formulation for a case at hand, as the result of a process where they go through intermediate, tentative, interpretative outcomes, liable to be changed in the light of further information (new interpretative directives, new interpretative resources, etc.). We may also talk of a *retro active* or *feed-back* structure, for it is, up to a certain point, a continuous going back-and-forth from a norm formulation to some norm tentatively identified as one of its meanings. This feature of interpretative *reasoning*—as a cognitive or psychological process—is common to other kinds of reasoning in law, and accounts for their being qualified as 'defeasible', as we shall see in a moment.

On the other hand, the *outcomes* of the process of legal interpretation (*interpretation products*) are, in turn, defeasible: they are liable to be changed—revised, modified, discarded—as further information is added, until the interpreter reaches what she regards as an equilibrium point—for instance, when time has run out and a reasonable amount of 'information' has been 'processed'. At that point, she stays with a final interpretative outcome for the case at hand.

The idea of defeasible interpretations (defeasible interpretative outcomes) is usually conveyed through a language borrowed from cognitive science, centred on the ideas of revisability of beliefs in connection with the constant revisability of the theories (information, inputs) on which such beliefs depend.

This way of looking at legal interpretation is not objectionable in itself; provided, however, that it is not taken to suggest the misleading conclusion according to which interpretation would be a matter of gathering, and neutrally processing, information showing up in a piecemeal, never-ending, way. Indeed, which 'information' shows up, and when, and how to 'process' it, is to a large extent a value-laden, ideologically compromised, discretional undertaking by law's interpreters.

(f) Defeasible reasoning

Quite often, legal philosophers claim that 'legal reasoning is defeasible'.

There are, however, at least two different ways of understanding such a claim, corresponding with two quite different theoretical perspectives.

To begin with, the claim 'legal reasoning is defeasible' may be advanced as a psychological, cognitive-science claim concerning a purportedly essential feature of

judiciales, 116. The very same idea is conveyed by at least two further theories of legal interpretation (two further psychological, or cognitive, models of the process of legal interpretation), where, however, the term 'defeasibility' does not (still) show up. On the one hand, there is the hermeneutic model, centred on the idea of hermeneutic circles. See, e.g. R. Alexy, 'Rechtsinterpretation', 1993, it. tr., 'Interpretazione giuridica' in *Enciclopedia delle scienze sociali* (Rome: Istituto dell'Enciclopedia Italiana, 1993), vol. 7, 416ff. On the other hand, there is the feedback or retroactive model, centred on the distinction between a 'first interpretation' and the several, following 're-interpretations' of the same norm formulation. See, e.g. P. Chiassoni, 'Normativismo semiotico, scetticismo, giochi interpretativi', *Studi in memoria di Giovanni Tarello. Volume II, Saggi teorico-generali* (Milan: Giuffrè, 1990), 241ff. and 'Interpretative Games: Statutory Construction Through Gricean Eyes' in P. Comanducci and R. Guastini (eds), *Analisi e diritto 1999* (Turin: Giappichelli, 2000).

the mental process of reasoning with legal, or legally relevant, data, to get to legal conclusions. From this perspective, legal reasoning is defeasible, not for its being 'legal', i.e. due to some peculiarity of the law-world, but simply for its being a form of human 'reasoning'. Indeed, from a cognitive point of view, all reasoning, as a mental process, is defeasible: it is typically a matter of proceeding through tentative outcomes, liable to be changed, revised, or altogether abandoned, in a further stage of the process, in the light of new pieces of information.[28] As is the case, as we saw above, with interpretative reasoning.

The claim 'legal reasoning is defeasible' may, however, also be made as a claim from a logical point of view: namely, as a claim concerning a purportedly essential feature of the inferences between legal norms, and between legal norms and other premises and conclusions of legal reasoning—considered, here, not as mental processes, but as pieces of justificatory discourses.

Those who make such a claim—like, for instance, Jaap Hage—purport to suggest that classical monotonic logic (centred on the law of the strengthening of the antecedent and *modus ponens*) is not suited to account for legal reasoning, and should be replaced by some form of nonmonotonic logic.[29]

Other legal philosophers however—notably Carlos E. Alchourrón—maintain that what apparently would make 'legal reasoning' defeasible are its basic ingredients—the *legal norms*—and claim, consequently, that there is no need to get rid of monotonic logic to account for normative inferences, provided the logical form of legal norms is suitably changed to accommodate their defeasible character.[30]

In its first, cognitive-science version, the claim about the defeasibility of legal reasoning is true, but trivial: a useful way of conveying what has been clear to many theorists of legal reasoning, well before the rise of the defeasibility turn in legal thinking.[31]

In its second, logical, version, it is a contested claim pointing to what seems to be the gist of the whole matter: the (alleged) defeasibility of legal norms. Before getting to it, however, a few other allegedly defeasible legal items have to be briefly considered.

(g) Defeasible conclusions

Some legal philosophers claim that what should be regarded as really 'defeasible', within the legal domain, are 'legal conclusions'.

Legal conclusions—according to Henry Prakken and Giovanni Sartor—are typically defeasible due to the operation of three factors:

28 According, e.g. to G. Sartor, 'Syllogism and Defeasibility: A Comment on Neil MacCormick's *Rhetoric and the Rule of Law*', 11: 'Defeasible reasoning [is] a structured process of inquiry, based upon drawing *pro-tanto* conclusions, looking for their defeaters, for defeaters of defeaters, and so on, until stable results can be obtained'; see also G. Sartor, *Legal Reasoning. A Cognitive Approach to the Law* (2005) 79; N. MacCormick, *Rhetoric and the Rule of Law. A Theory of Legal Reasoning* (Oxford: Oxford University Press, 2005), 252–3, where reasoning in law is presented as 'arguing defeasibly'; H. Prakken and G. Sartor, 'The Three Faces of Defeasibility in Law', *Ratio Juris*, 17 (2004), 118ff.

29 See, e.g. J. Hage, *Reasoning with Rules. An Essay on Legal Reasoning and Its Underlying Logic* (Dordrecht: Kluwer, 1997), 4ff.

30 See, e.g. C.E. Alchourrón, *Para una Lógica de las Razones Prima Facie*, unpublished manuscript, 1995 and 'Detachment and Defeasibility in Deontic Logic', *Studia Logica*, 57 (1996), 5–18.

31 On this point, see also J.C. Bayón, 'Why Is Legal Reasoning Defeasible?' in A. Soeteman (ed.), *Pluralism in Law* (Dordrecht: Kluwer, 2001), 334–5.

first, the nonmonotonic structure of legal inferences, mirroring in turn the defeasible character of the mental process of reasoning in law ('inference-based defeasibility');[32]
second, the procedural rules concerning evidence ('process-based defeasibility');[33]
third, the choices and evaluations that affect the selection and changes of the 'theories' from which legal conclusions are derived ('theory-based defeasibility').[34]

Apparently, this claim may be considered as parasitic upon the claim concerning the defeasibility of legal reasoning—though it adds some information about the operation, and influence, of procedural rules. It seems we are still dwelling, here, at the margins of the defeasibility issue.

(h) *Defeasible arrangements, positions, claims*

We also frequently run into claims to the effect that 'legal arrangements (e.g. contracts, wills, etc.) are defeasible', 'legal rights (duties, privileges, powers, immunities, etc.) are defeasible', 'legal claims are defeasible', and so on.

Saying that 'legal arrangements are defeasible' is apparently tantamount to saying that they 'can be upset or set aside despite an *initial appearance of validity and durability*'.[35] Legal arrangements, however, are instruments ascribing bundles of legal positions to certain persons. Accordingly, saying that arrangements are defeasible is tantamount to saying that—some, or all, of—the legal positions they granted are liable to be considered invalid, null, void, unenforceable, etc.

Why is that so? Apparently, the following explanation may be provided. Arrangements—and the depending rights, duties, liabilities, etc.—derive whatever validity (legal force) they have from some set of legal norms that regulates them.

Unfortunately, these norms—leaving aside their explicit derogation (and any mistake by the parties and their legal advisors)—may work as Hartian open-end defeasible concepts: they may (be supposed to) have a loose end, through which new negative conditions may be added, which were not considered at the time the arrangement was made, nor could they have been so.

Consequently, arrangements—and their accompanying rights, duties, etc.—are *defeasible* (in the sense of being *liable to supervening invalidity*, i.e. to be later considered invalid, void, etc.), because the norms on which they depend are *defeasible* (in the different sense of being *liable to be saturated with new negative conditions* for the application of their legal consequence).

[32] H. Prakken and G. Sartor, 'The Three Faces of Defeasibility in Law', 118: 'legal *conclusions*, though correctly supported by certain pieces of information, cannot be inferred when the theory including this information is *expanded* with further pieces of information (we use the term "theory" to mean in general any set of premises intended to provide an account of a legal domain)'.

[33] G. Sartor, 'Syllogism and Defeasibility: A Comment on Neil MacCormick's *Rhetoric and the Rule of Law*', 12, where '*procedural* defeasibility' is characterized as 'the defeasibility of the outcomes of legal proceedings, depending to [on] the distribution of the burden of proof between the parties'.

[34] H. Prakken and G. Sartor, 'The Three Faces of Defeasibility in Law', 130, 131, 133: '[*theory-based defeasibility*] results from the evaluation and choice of theories which explain and systematize the available input information . . . different theories of the same legal domain are possible, we need ways of comparing those theories and . . . selecting the most appropriate one . . . the parties in a case, given a shared legal background, develop alternative legal theories, and victory goes to the party who develops the better theory . . . theory-based argumentation, the idea that legal debates consist of the dialectical exchange of competing theories, supporting opposing legal conclusions in the issue at stake [and where] the weaker (less coherent) theory is defeated by the stronger one'.

[35] N. MacCormick, 'Defeasibility in Law and Logic', 99, italics added.

The defeasibility of arrangements, rights, duties, etc. is, accordingly, a *derivative* and, more precisely, a *norm-dependent* phenomenon.

The same conclusion—perhaps with some qualifications—also holds for those rights, duties, etc., that are, at least prima facie, directly ascribed to persons by legal norms (e.g. by constitutional norms, legislative norms, etc.). And, apparently, it would also hold, to conclude, regarding the defeasibility of 'claims': i.e. as to the liability of people's requests for judicial protection of their (alleged) entitlements to be overridden and rejected.

Neil MacCormick, however, apparently takes a different view on the matter:

> Is it *rules* that are defeasible, or *certain formulations of them*, or *claims* made on the basis of such *formulations*, including *legal-doctrinal statements* based on the text of legal 'sources' such as the statute-book or the law reports?...
>
> As with rights, so with rules, it is not the statute nor the precedent that is defeasible in the light of exceptional circumstances relevant to legal principles, when we deal with implicit defeasibility. *It is the claim* based on a particular formulation or interpretation of the rule that is *defeated* in the light of the principle. Thereafter, more cautious formulations of the rule, or doctrinal expositions that draw attention to *exceptions established by case law*, will be called for.[36]

The passage contains many ideas—and, to my mind, also some confusion—very useful to deal with the widespread claims concerning the defeasibility of legal norms. It is to this topic, so far delayed, that I now turn.

(i) Defeasible norms

The standard theory behind the claim that 'legal norms are defeasible' may perhaps be presented, by way of a rational reconstruction, as including the following tenets.

i. Defeasible norms in action

As a matter of fact legal norms, like the legal concepts showing up in their formulations, usually work as defeasible conditionals: they are usually treated by judges and jurists as conditionals the normative consequences of which are subject to 'exceptions', i.e. to *negative conditions* of application.[37]

Negative, or defeating, conditions may be (considered and treated), in turn, either as a closed set or as an open set.

ii. Closed-end defeasible norms

In the first situation, a norm is a *closed-end defeasible norm*. This means that it is assumed to be possible to identify, at any given moment, the *whole set* of its negative conditions of application. This means that, starting from any prima facie norm (say, any norm in its

[36] N. MacCormick, *Rhetoric and the Rule of Law. A Theory of Legal Reasoning*, 252.

[37] Sometimes, legal theorists seem to claim, not that legal norms *usually* are, or are *treated as*, defeasible by jurists, judges, etc. (see, e.g. C.E. Alchourrón, 'On Law and Logic', ch. 2, 46), but that they are *necessarily* so. Consider, for instance, the following passage from F. Atria, *On Law and Legal Reasoning* (Oxford: Hart, 2002), quoted critically by N. MacCormick, *Rethoric and the Rule of Law. A Theory of Legal Reasoning*, 252: 'Hence the rules formulated by legal agencies are always defeasible *for the sake of better pursuing these aims and values* through an appropriately nuanced interpretation of them, and with a regulated discretion in applying them... Defeasibility of rules *is built into* the kind of activity that regulative institutions define through these rules' (italics added). For a sceptical stance on the issue see, e.g. by F. Schauer, 'On the Supposed Defeasibility of Legal Rules', *Current Legal Problems*, 51 (1998), 223–40; R. Guastini, *Variazioni su temi di Carlos Alchourrón ed Eugenio Bulygin. Defettibilità, lacune assiologiche, e interpretazione.*

standard form, corresponding, for instance, to the literal reading of a norm formulation), for instance:

$$\text{PFN}': (x)(\text{A}x \,\&\, \text{B}x \rightarrow \text{OR}x)$$

it is assumed to be possible to identify an *all-things-considered* norm, that contains by hypothesis *all* the negative conditions of application of its normative consequence (in our case: 'OR*x*'), if any:

$$\text{ATCN}': (x)(\text{A}x \,\&\, \text{B}x) \,\&\, \neg(\text{D}x \vee \text{E}x \vee \text{F}x) \rightarrow \text{OR}x$$

This set of negative conditions, furthermore, would be liable to be identified *beforehand*, that is to say, prior to any application of the norm to any individual case.

Notice that the task of identifying, and exhaustively stating, the negative conditions of application of a norm—or, more precisely, of its normative consequence, like, e.g. 'OR*x*'—is an *interpretative* task. Norms do not grow on trees. Accordingly, such a process would usually require two steps:

first, the identification of some set of legal sources (norm formulations), according to some criterion of validity and norm formulations selection (both operations belonging to, though not exhausting, what may be called 'meta textual' interpretation);

second, the interpretation of the identified set of norm formulations according to a selected interpretative code and a selected set of interpretative resources, so as to get a set ('system') of explicit and implicit norms out of it. Such a process has a defeasible structure (see above B.1.(e) 'Defeasible interpretations'), and is typically value-laden, discretionary, and sensible to juristic theories and methodological outlooks.

The closed set of the negative conditions of application of a norm is liable to change, of course. This may depend on two basic factors: on the one hand, a change in the interpretative code and/or in the relevant interpretative resources, leading to different interpretations of the *same* set of legal sources (the same set of norm formulations); or on the other hand, a change in the set of legal sources, due, for instance, to the addition, by normative authorities, of some new piece of norm formulation that may be interpreted as expressing a new, derogation norm.

Accordingly, any change in the closed set of the negative conditions of application of a norm (normative consequence) depends either on methodological indeterminacy, even of a moderate sort, allowing for a plurality of alternative interpretative codes (see A.2, above), or on the dynamic character of legal orders (change of legal sources)—the first of the two factors being in any case paramount, due to the power of interpretative techniques to neutralize the working of new pieces of enacted law.

In light of the preceding remarks, the common-sense notion of a 'closed-end defeasible norm', as a norm the negative conditions of application whereof may be identified *exhaustively* and *beforehand*, if it is to make any sense, has to be redefined, or subject to rational reconstruction, if you like, so as to take expressly into account the fact that closed-end defeasible norms are interpretation-dependent items. This may be done, for instance, along the following lines.

Closed-end defeasible norm: A norm is a *closed-end defeasible norm* if, but only if, relative to *whichever* set of *interpretative inputs* interpreters may select and use in a moment t_0, it is liable to an *exhaustive* set of negative conditions of application.

A set of *interpretative inputs* includes: (a) an interpretative *code* with directives for textual and meta textual interpretation; (b) a set of interpretative *resources*; and (c) a set of *norm formulations*.

Two different kinds of closed-end defeasible norms may be singled out.

On the one hand, there are those norms that are liable to *one* and the *same* exhaustive set of negative conditions of applications. In such, very unlikely here-and-now, situations, a norm may be regarded as a *simple closed-end defeasible norm*.

Simple closed-end defeasible norm: A norm is a *simple closed-end defeasible norm* if, but only if, relative to *whichever* set of *interpretative inputs* interpreters may select and use in a moment t_o, it is liable to the *same, exhaustive*, set of negative conditions of application.

Accordingly, whichever available set of interpretative inputs (*Ii*) is being chosen and used in t_o, the outcome would be the same:

$$N = f(Ii_1 \cdots Ii_n / t_o) = (x)(Ax \mathbin{\&} Bx) \mathbin{\&} \neg (Dx \vee Ex \vee Fx) \rightarrow ORx$$

On the other hand, however, there are also those norms that are liable to *different, alternative*, exhaustive sets of negative conditions of applications, according to different sets of interpretative inputs. In such, very likely here-and-now, situations, a norm may be regarded as a *complex*, or *alternative, closed-end defeasible norm*.

Complex closed-end defeasible norm: A norm is a *complex closed-end defeasible norm* if, but only if, relative to the sets of *interpretative inputs* interpreters may select and use in a moment t_o, it is liable to a plurality of *different, alternative, exhaustive* sets of negative conditions of application.

Accordingly, given the available sets of interpretative inputs, the outcome would be a norm like the following:

$$N = f(Ii_1 \cdots Ii_n / t_o) = (x)(Ax \mathbin{\&} Bx) \mathbin{\&} \neg [(Dx \vee Ex \vee Fx) \vee (Dx \vee Ex \vee Gx) \vee (Ex \vee Hx \vee Lx)] \rightarrow ORx.$$

iii. Open-end defeasible norms

A norm is considered to be an *open-end defeasible norm* whenever the set of its negative conditions of application has a loose end: its members—legal philosophers would say—*cannot* be identified *exhaustively beforehand*.[38]

This does not mean, of course, that when the norm is to be applied to a case, application is frustrated by its (assumed) open-endedness. It means, rather, the following:

(a) the law-applying agencies are (considered to be) *authorized* to determine the norm's set of negative conditions of application, at least for the time being, in front of an individual case to be adjudicated; and

(b) the content of their decisions—i.e. the way they are going to tie up the loose ends of a norm's negative conditions of application—is, by hypothesis, not foreseeable.

[38] According to Bayón, for instance, defeasible norms are norms with 'open-ended character', i.e. 'they are subject to implied exceptions which cannot be exhaustively specified in advance' (J.C. Bayón, 'Why Is Legal Reasoning Defeasible?', 338). The logical form of such a norm would be, for instance, something like the following: '(x) $(Ax \mathbin{\&} Bx) \mathbin{\&} \neg(Dx \vee Ex \vee \ldots) \rightarrow ORx$'.

This point has been made clear by Juan Carlos Bayón in the following terms:

> A *genuine defeasible norm* [i.e. an open-end defeasible norm] leaves the law *indeterminate* as to the very cases *included* in its conditioning facts, so that the judgment about any of those cases *always* requires a *discretional decision among open alternatives* by the law-applying agency.[39]

Adjudication turns open-ended defeasible norms into *pro tanto* closed-ended defeasible norms.

Now, this *pro tanto* closing may happen according to juristic advice and, above all, due to rational justification requirements, in a principled way: that is to say, any 'new' negative condition (as yet unidentified in a judicial decision) is added if, but only if, 'good reasons' may be provided, concerning the 'proper' interpretation of the 'norm' in itself and/or its 'proper' standing within a legal system.

However, if law-applying agencies have such a duty of justification, as is the case in most existing legal orders, then any 'new' negative condition of application of a norm—by hypothesis, *not* included in the *standard formulation* of the norm which a law-applying agency takes as the starting point of its reasoning—is tantamount, from a methodological point of view, to a negative condition that may be identified, and justified, on the basis of a *new* set of interpretative inputs, different from the one(s) on which the standard formulation of the norm, with its negative conditions, depends.

The common-sense notion of an open-end defeasible norm I mentioned above also includes the idea that the new negative condition cannot be 'anticipated' ('stated in advance'). Accordingly, a tentative redefinition of this notion—again, by way of a rational reconstruction—may run, roughly, as follows:

Open-end defeasible norm: A norm, subject to a prima facie exhaustive set of negative conditions of application in a moment t_o, is an *open-end defeasible norm* if, but only if:

(a) a new, further, set of interpretative inputs may be selected and used in a moment t_1, according to which those negative conditions of application are no longer *exhaustive*, for it brings to the fore, and justifies, at least *one* further, new, negative condition of application;
(b) both the resorting to this further set of interpretative inputs, and its outcome, cannot be anticipated in moment t_o.

From the viewpoint of sociological methodology (A.1), the claim that 'norms are open-end defeasible' is true, as to a given legal order, whenever, due to loose interpretative codes and the possibility for interpreters to shift from one code to another, any norm whatsoever, in its present, standard, formulation, may be regarded as liable to a set of exceptions that cannot be stated exhaustively in advance—for, say, the genius of some interpreter, triggered by new situations and/or intellectual progress, may revise current sets of interpretative inputs in such a form as to justify the adding (the 'making explicit' of) a 'new' negative condition.

The claim 'norms are open-end defeasible', however, may also be regarded as part of a prescriptive methodology addressed to (fellow) jurists and judges working in a given legal system. In such a case, it is tantamount to a second-order interpretative directive, running roughly as follows: you may always regard norms as open-end defeasible prescriptions, and

[39] J.C. Bayón, *Derrotabilidad, indeterminación del derecho y positivismo jurídico*, 188: 'una norma jurídica genuinamente derrotable deja el derecho indeterminado en lo que concierne a los casos subsumibles en su supuesto de hecho, de manera que la resolución de cualquiera de éstos requiere siempre una decisión discrecional entre alternativas abiertas por parte del aplicador'.

(re)interpret them accordingly, provided the new exceptions you add to them may be justified according to a reasonable set of interpretative inputs.[40]

By the way, such a prescriptive methodology claim may be contrasted with an opposite methodological option, for closed-end defeasibility, running roughly as follows: you ought to regard norms as simple closed-end defeasible prescriptions, according to the right interpretative code IC_i.

iv. Indefeasible norms?

Sometimes, it is suggested that closed-end defeasible norms are not really defeasible, being rather *indefeasible* norms.

Indeed, so the argument runs, if *every* condition—both positive and negative—has been duly identified and stated, then what we get is a fully fledged, indefeasible, norm. Such a conclusion, however, clearly depends on a different notion of 'norm defeasibility': one that considers the open-endedness of the negative conditions to a legal consequence as a *defining property* of the very concept of a 'defeasible norm'. Such a conclusion would not hold, however, if we use a different concept of a 'defeasible norm': for instance, as along the lines above, meaning by it simply that a norm is *liable to negative conditions* of application.

Only the supreme deities of theoretical and practical expediency may adjudicate the issue. Nonetheless, though open-end defeasibility is surely a more exciting phenomenon, there seems to be no reason, from a conceptual point of view, for wiping from the domain of 'defeasibility' the other—not so innocent—phenomenon of closed-end defeasibility.

v. Open-end, closed-end, explicitly, implicitly defeasible norms

On occasion the distinction I have considered between *open-end defeasible* norms and *closed-end defeasible* norms has been conveyed, apparently, under the heading of the distinction between *explicit defeasibility* and *implicit defeasibility*.

Neil MacCormick, for instance, argues as follows.

(a) Rules-defeasibility may be either 'express', or 'implicit'.

(b) A rule is *expressly defeasible* whenever it has been formulated in such a way as to contain both its positive conditions of (internal) application (say: C_1, C_2, C_3), and some negative condition ('exception' or 'proviso': E_1, for example).

[40] For instance, Richard Tur claims apparently that legal norms *ought to* be considered, and treated, as open-end defeasible norms basically on two counts. First, because of tradition's sake: they have been treated as open-end defeasible standards all the time (at least, in a legal system such as the English common law). Second, because of the superior rationality of such an option: in fact, treating legal norms as indefeasible prescriptions would amount to endorsing a 'flatly formalistic approach to law application'. R.H.S. Tur, 'Defeasibilism', OJLS, 21 (2001), 355–68. Here he also develops a descriptive side, grounded on the following points: (1) Law is best *represented*, most clearly *understood*, and most effectively *taught* as defeasible. (2) Law's defeasibility depends on the *open-ended defeasibility* of legal norms. (3) Legal norms, as open-ended defeasible norms, are better represented and understood—taking stock of Kelsen's, Hart's, and *Critical Legal Studies*' inquiries—as normative conditional propositions, where the normative consequence is subject to a double set of *open-ended defeating (negative) alternative* conditions: (a) 'operative' *exceptions*, that may be either (i) pre-established (explicit, specified), or (ii) *yet to be established* (implicit, unspecified); and (b) *overrides* ('overriding considerations'), i.e. defeating considerations of (i) equity and/or justice, (ii) policy, (iii) purpose, (iv) mercy, (v) rights, and (vi) 'any other "damn good reason" and "compelling objection"' (p. 368). Accordingly, the proper logical form for a legal norm would be something like the following: 'if A, then ought to be B, unless *either* (1) *operative specified or yet-to-be-specified exceptions* ($e_1 \ldots e_n$) *or* (2) *overriding considerations* from the legal system's basic standards/values (*inner morality*) ($oc_1 \ldots oc_n$)'. See also N. MacCormick, 'Defeasibility in Law and Logic', 115 and *Rhetoric and the Rule of Law. A Theory of Legal Reasoning*, 241.

(c) The most interesting cases of rules defeasibility, however, are those where rules are *implicitly defeasible*. This situation obtains whenever *express rules* 'may be subjected to a *fresh interpretation* in the light of some *significant legal principle* in some relatively *unusual circumstances*'. Whenever, in other words, they may be '*trumped* by recourse to some *unstated condition* that is deemed to be *implicitly overriding, given the principles and/or values at stake*'.

(d) Accordingly, '[e]ven in cases of *express defeasibility*, there may be possibilities of *implicit defeasibility* over and above the explicit conditions of defeasance'.[41]

From a theoretical point of view, however, it seems more convenient to consider, and define, the two distinctions as logically independent.

On the one hand, the distinction between *closed-end defeasible* and *open-end defeasible* norms concerns their liability to a closed or an open set of negative conditions of application, taking into account that the identification of any such set is an *interpretative* activity, depending on *methodological options*, and typically rife with leeways and the possibility of reaching different outcomes, both at any given moment, and, above all, in the future (as I have suggested above).

On the other hand, the distinction between *explicit* and *implicit* norm-defeasibility depends on a key distinction from the *general theory of legal norms*: namely, the distinction between explicit norms, i.e. the meaning-contents of authoritative norm formulations, and implicit norms, that are identified by means of logic and/or argumentative techniques from explicit or (other previously identified) implicit norms.

From this perspective, *explicit norm-defeasibility* concerns explicit norms, and is tantamount to their liability to the negative conditions of application that may be read 'within' their norm formulation, by means of suitable techniques of textual interpretation.

Contrariwise, *implicit norm-defeasibility* points to the possibility that, given a certain *explicit* norm EN_1 ('$A \& \neg EC_1 \rightarrow OB$'), with its explicit negative conditions of application ('$\neg EC_1$'), *further* negative conditions for the application of the legal consequence stated by EN_1 ('OB') may show up, that *cannot be read* into its norm formulation (say: 'IC_1' and 'IC_2').[42] This means that the norm EN_1 has to be supplemented with these further, implicit conditions: namely, that it has to be transformed into a derivative implicit norm IN_1: '$A \& \neg(ENC_1 \vee INC_1 \vee INC_2) \rightarrow OB$'.

Notice that the liability of explicit norms to implicit exceptions, in the way just considered, is *not* tantamount to their being liable to an *open* set of negative conditions. These norms may in fact be implicitly defeasible, while at the same time being closed-end defeasible: provided the implicit negative conditions are some closed set, relative to the sets of interpretative inputs interpreters may select and use in a moment t_0.

vi. Norm defeasibility and axiological gaps

Sometimes, norm defeasibility has been regarded as closely connected to another fashionable widget in the jurisprudence toolbox: so-called *axiological gaps*.[43] Indeed,

[41] N. MacCormick, *Rhetoric and the Rule of Law. A Theory of Legal Reasoning*, 240ff., italics added.

[42] The same remarks apply to judge-made and other unwritten law norms, in their standard, established form.

[43] On axiological gaps, the seminal contribution is C.E. Alchourrón and E. Bulygin, *Normative Systems*, x. For the view that 'axiological gaps' are better understood as a sort of normative conflict, see P. Chiassoni, *Tecnica dell'interpretazione giuridica* (Bologna: Il Mulino, 2007), ch. 3.

it has been suggested that defeasibility and axiological gaps are in fact but two sides of the same coin.[44]

This is clearly a metaphoric form of speech. Metaphors are double-edged swords, fatally covering with haze whatever wisdom they convey.

So it may be worthwhile expending a few words on 'de-metaphorizing' the metaphor.

Axiological gaps obtain whenever a norm may be considered either as over-inclusive, or as over-reaching, in the light of some other set of norms, assumed to represent the benchmark for its validity (benchmark standards).

A norm (usually, a simple, explicit, literal norm) is *over-inclusive* when, by hypothesis, in virtue of a certain expression (descriptive term) contained in its formulation, it *also* connects a certain legal consequence to a class of situations which, by the benchmark standards, ought to be regulated *differently*. In this situation, the axiological gap is represented by the presence of a (suboptimal) not-discriminating norm *and* the absence of the (optimal) discriminating norm that is assumedly required by the benchmark standards.[45]

A norm (usually, a complex, explicit, literal norm, or a complex norm resulting from an exclusionary *a contrario* reading of a norm formulation) is *over-reaching* when, in its negative component, it *denies* to a class of situations the *same* legal consequence it provides instead, in its positive component, to the opposite class—whereas the two classes of situations ought to have the *same* legal consequence, according to the benchmark standards.[46] In this situation, which is the exact reverse of the former, the axiological gap is represented by the presence of a (suboptimal) discriminating norm *and* the absence of the (optimal) not-discriminating norm that is required by the benchmark standards.

Now, the idea of norm defeasibility may be used as a tool to remedy the first of the two situations of axiological gap I considered above.

First, it is assumed that the over-inclusive norm is defeasible: subject to negative conditions, that may not appear at a literal reading of the relevant norm formulation.[47]

Second, the over-inclusive norm is reinterpreted in a narrowing-down way, so as to exclude from its scope the class of situations deserving a different regulation. This means that, by means of such a defeasibility-driven reinterpretation of the original over-inclusive norm, a normative gap is created within the system.

[44] See, e.g. R. Guastini, *Variazioni su temi di Carlos Alchourrón ed Eugenio Bulygin. Defettibilità, lacune assiologiche, e interpretazione*.

[45] Consider the following norm formulation at the entrance of a fine arts museum: 'couples allowed'. In its literal reading it may express, from the viewpoint of some set of benchmark standards, an *over-inclusive* norm for, apparently, it allows into the museum *any* sort of couple whatsoever—married heterosexual couples, unmarried heterosexual couples, married homosexual couples, unmarried homosexual couples, inter-species couples, couples of friends, couples of fine-arts-freak cyberdogs, etc.

[46] Consider the following norm formulation at the entrance of a fine arts museum: 'married couples only'. In its literal reading, it expresses what I am calling a *complex* literal norm. Indeed, the norm formulation expresses *two* norms jointly: one positive norm, or positive component of the complex norm ('married couples allowed'), and one negative norm, or negative component of the complex norm (say, 'unmarried couples and singles not allowed'). The same outcome may have been obtained by way of an *a contrario* exclusionary interpretation of the following norm formulation at the entrance of the fine arts museum: 'married couples'. In both cases, from the viewpoint of some set of benchmark standards (say, one set including a certain principle of human equality and/or human dignity), the negative component of the norm might appear sub optimal, and the complex norm over-reaching.

[47] The same remarks would hold, of course, for any 'standard' norm: i.e. for any norm, e.g. a judge-made norm, circulating in a standard formulation.

Third, by means of some gap-filling technique, the normative gap is cured, setting forth a new norm in tune with the benchmark standards.

Defeasibility and axiological gaps (due to over-inclusive norms) are indeed related objects.

However, they should not be confused: indeed, the disease (axiological gaps, as a disguised form of normative conflict) should never be confused with the therapy (defeasibility and the defeasibility technique of reinterpretation).

2. A few notions and forms of defeasibility

Leaving aside defeasible facts and defeasible beliefs, defeasible reasoning, defeasible conclusions, defeasible claims, defeasible legal positions, and defeasible arrangements all point to trivial, contested, or, in most cases, derivative situations of 'defeasibility'.

Indeed, from the viewpoint of the defeasibility and legal indeterminacy issue, the pivotal cases seem to be those of defeasible norm formulations, defeasible interpretations, and, last but of course not least, defeasible norms.

I hope that I have made clear why, to my mind, the claim that 'norm formulations are defeasible' cannot be taken at face value. Suggesting, as you may recall, two alternative readings, both of which share the idea that *norms*—as semantic entities—are properly defeasible objects; while norm formulations, as syntactic entities, may be defeasible, so to speak, only in a metonymical way: i.e. by way of a semantic exchange between the linguistic form and 'its' meaning content.

Furthermore, I have suggested that the claim that 'interpretations are defeasible' is tantamount to claiming that *explicit legal norms* are (or may be) defeasible: for 'interpretations', as this word was used above, is tantamount to the outcome of some interpretative process concerning some norm formulation—an outcome that represents, by hypothesis, a *norm* expressed by that norm formulation.

Consequently, at least for the present purpose, the notion of a defeasible norm seems to be the most relevant, and interesting, to cope with.

Now, I think it may be worthwhile to adopt, as the starting point for a conceptual reconstruction, a basic, generic, (so far as possible) neutral, notion of a defeasible norm. This notion may be something like the following:

Df. 1—*Defeasible norm*: a norm is *defeasible* if, but only if, the normative consequence it states is liable (i.e. may be subject) to a set of negative conditions of application ('exceptions', 'defeaters', 'defeating conditions').

Taking this notion into account, four, more specific, notions may be defined, arranged into two logically independent couples: namely, (1) explicitly defeasible norm, (2) implicitly defeasible norm, (3) closed-end defeasible norm (with the two varieties I considered before), and (4) open-end defeasible norm. These seven notions, together, should provide an elementary conceptual framework for fishing in the river of common sense.

Df. 2—*Explicitly defeasible norm*: an explicit norm is *explicitly defeasible* if, but only if, its normative consequence is liable to a set of negative conditions of application that may be read within its norm formulation by means of suitable techniques of textual interpretation.[48]

[48] A similar notion may be defined concerning judge-made norms, and other unwritten law norms, in their standard formulations, as subjects of interpretation techniques allowing their 'internal' re-interpretation.

Df. 3—*Implicitly defeasible norm*: an explicit norm is *implicitly defeasible* if, but only if, its normative consequence is liable to a set of negative conditions of application that cannot be read within its norm formulation, but derive from other norms of the same legal system.

Df. 4—*Closed-end defeasible norm*: A norm is a *closed-end defeasible norm* if, but only if, relative to *whichever* set of *interpretative inputs* interpreters may select and use in a moment t_0, it is liable to an *exhaustive* set of negative conditions of application.

Df. 5—*Simple closed-end defeasible norm*: A norm is a *simple closed-end defeasible norm* if, but only if, relative to *whichever* set of *interpretative inputs* interpreters may select and use in a moment t_0, it is liable to the *same, exhaustive*, set of negative conditions of application.

Df. 6—*Complex closed-end defeasible norm*: A norm is a *complex closed-end defeasible norm* if, but only if, relative to the sets of *interpretative inputs* interpreters may select and use in a moment t_0, it is liable to a plurality of *different, alternative, exhaustive* sets of negative conditions of application.

Df. 7—*Open-end defeasible norm*: A norm, subject to a prima facie exhaustive set of negative conditions of application in a moment t_0, is an *open-end defeasible norm* if, but only if:

(a) a new, further, set of interpretative inputs may be selected and used in a moment t_1, according to which those negative conditions of application are *no longer exhaustive*, for it brings to the fore, and justifies, at least *one* further, new, negative condition of application;

(b) both the resorting to this further set of interpretative inputs, and its outcome, cannot be anticipated in moment t_0.

If we look at the *sources* of norm defeasibility—i.e. at what makes legal norms liable to explicit and/or implicit exceptions, that may make up *alternative* closed sets at any given moment t, and *open sets* as to the future—the basic factors seem to belong to the realm of interpretation (legal methodology) and juristic theories about the proper way to regard 'the law' and act accordingly.[49]

As we saw earlier, while dealing with 'defeasible norm formulations', *explicit norm-defeasibility* may be regarded, as to its source, as *internal-interpretative defeasibility*. Here, the liability of an explicit norm to exceptions that may be read within its very norm formulation depends on juristic theories about the nature of enacted law and the 'proper' ways to interpret it. And the basic, well-known, conspiring ideas are something like the following:

(a) that enacted law is a *teleological entity*, i.e. something with background reasons that ought to be taken into account while interpreting it—which is an enduring homage to the principle of sufficient reason, as an identifying tract of our basic notions of reason and rationality;

(*b*) that enacted law is an *intentional entity*, i.e. something provided with an author 'meaning something by it' (wishing to communicate something by it), whose

[49] This point is argued for, though in different ways, by several legal philosophers. One of the most original positions is set forth by J.C. Bayón, *Derrotabilidad, indeterminación del derecho y positivismo jurídico*, 182ff., where he explains norm defeasibility (what I would call, roughly, their open- and implicit-defeasibility) by resorting to the idea of a 'closure rule as to relevance', presented as an 'interpretative convention' according to which norms ought to be regarded as liable to explicit exceptions *only*. So that norms are 'defeasible' (in Bayón's sense), when such an interpretative principle is not part of what I would call the conventional interpretative code of a given legal order.

(actual, presumed, counterfactual) intention is accordingly to be given pride of place in its interpretation.

Explicit norms, however, are also (treated as) implicitly defeasible. Again, as we saw above, *implicit norm-defeasibility* may be regarded, as to its source, as *external-* or *systemic-interpretative* defeasibility. Here, the ruling, well-known, ideas run roughly as follows:

(i) legal norms never 'walk alone': they are, contrariwise, (to be regarded as) members of ordered (consistent, coherent, and gapless), dynamic, normative sets;

(ii) accordingly, they are always to be interpreted and reinterpreted taking into account the systemic nature of the law, i.e. by means of the varied set of techniques of systemic interpretation;

(iii) any diachronic modification, by normative authorities, in the set of norm formulations (Alchourrón's 'Master Book') will always affect the normative system (or rather: the several 'Master Systems', again in Alchourrón's words)[50] through the services of an indispensable middle man: interpretation.

C. Defeasibility and legal indeterminacy

From a logical point of view, the relationships between defeasibility and legal indeterminacy may take either of the two following forms:

(1) *identity*: defeasibility is indeterminacy;
(2) *difference*: defeasibility is not indeterminacy, they are different things.

In the latter case, they may be, in turn, either mutually *related* or *unrelated* items. On this footing, three kinds of relationship may be envisaged to hold between them:

(a) defeasibility *depends on* indeterminacy (*defeasibility as a dependent variable*);
(b) indeterminacy *depends on* defeasibility (*indeterminacy as a dependent variable*);
(c) defeasibility and indeterminacy are *independent* in the legal domain (*independence*).

Among legal philosophers, two basic positions have been set forth on this issue.

To begin with, some legal philosophers seem to take the identity view, maintaining that defeasibility is really not (meaningfully) distinguishable from indeterminacy. Indeed, the two concepts would refer roughly to the same, wide, array of well-known, puzzling situations. And—so the argument goes—since the concept of indeterminacy and other related concepts are better-established in legal thinking, there seems to be no need to resort to the new entry defeasibility. Consequently, 'defeasibility' may be dispensed with altogether, without any inconvenience either to legal thinking or to legal practice.[51]

Contrariwise, other legal philosophers maintain defeasibility and indeterminacy to be different notions, referring to different things in the legal domain. Furthermore, they suggest that indeterminacy is to be regarded as a dependent variable of defeasibility.[52]

[50] C.E. Alchourrón, 'On Law and Logic', in this volume, ch. 2.

[51] See, e.g. J.L. Rodríguez and G. Sucar, *Las trampas de la derrotabilidad. Niveles de análisis de la indeterminación del derecho*, 116–18, 143: 'puede darse cuenta de los diferentes problemas que pueden hacer pensar en utilizar la noción de derrotabilidad con relación a las normas jurídicas *sin recurrir a esta idea*'.

[52] See, e.g. C.E. Alchourrón, 'On Law and Logic', 46ff.: 'Usually *our understanding of the rule* will allow us to give a list of implicit exceptions as well as a list of circumstances which are not mentioned because they are rejected as exceptions. *But the relativity of the notion of normality makes many situations ambiguous from the interpreter's point of view*... Unless the exceptions are made explicit the conceptual

Obviously, any meaningful statement about the relationships between such theory-laden things as defeasibility and indeterminacy depends on a clear statement of the conceptual framework one is going to use, and why.

In what follows, by way of conclusion, I will try to connect defeasibility and legal indeterminacy from the viewpoint provided by the several notions I have identified in the two previous sections.

Leaving aside adjudicative indeterminacy, which is a derivative form of legal indeterminacy, and focusing instead on textual indeterminacy, normative indeterminacy, and methodological indeterminacy, the following points may be suggested regarding the defeasibility–indeterminacy relationships.

(1) Textual indeterminacy may depend on norm defeasibility. Indeed, norm defeasibility may be regarded as just *one* factor accounting for the ambiguity of norm formulations: i.e. for their being liable to different readings, so as to express different explicit norms, according to the different sets of interpretative inputs being used. This will happen whenever the same norm formulation may be interpreted as expressing several, alternative, explicit norms, each one characterized by a different set of negative conditions of application.

(2) Normative indeterminacy may depend on norm defeasibility. However, out of the five situations of normative indeterminacy I considered above (A.1 and A.2)—namely, normative ambiguity, normative vagueness, generic norms, normative gaps, and normative conflicts—only normative ambiguity, normative gaps, and normative conflicts may be suitably related to norm defeasibility.

First, normative ambiguity may depend on the possibility of identifying, for a given norm (say, a literal norm), several, alternative, sets of negative conditions of application, according to the ongoing or future sets of interpretative inputs interpreters may select and use. This situation is obviously like the ambiguity of norm formulations.

Second, normative gaps may depend on norm defeasibility. As we have seen above (B.1 (i), *vi*), while dealing with the relationships between axiological gaps and defeasibility, this may happen, from a technical point of view, whenever a normative gap is *created* in order to remedy a (purported) axiological gap. In such situations, an over-inclusive norm (or its norm formulation) is reinterpreted so as to be *not* over-inclusive *any more*, leaving some class of cases unregulated. This means, in different terms, that some negative condition of application is being 'made explicit' here, and is being added to the norm.

Third, normative conflicts may depend on norm defeasibility. Again—and similar to normative gaps—this is so at the level of the identification or, better, not-identification of a normative conflict. For the idea and technique of norm defeasibility may be used, here, to reinterpret a given norm (or its norm formulation) in such a way as to make a prima facie normative conflict disappear—again, by 'making explicit', and adding, some negative condition of application of a norm.

The two latter cases, we may notice, are specific situations where a 'norm' has proved ambiguous.

(3) Norm defeasibility depends on methodological indeterminacy. Methodological indeterminacy affects the scope and degree of norm defeasibility in a given legal order, since it allows for the identification of complex closed-end defeasible norms and open-end defeasible norms. This, in turn, affects the scope and degree of textual and normative indeterminacy in the legal order.

content of the normative expression is left undetermined... Defeasibility, more than simple ambiguity, makes the identification of the norms of a legal system very difficult'; J.C. Bayón, *Derrotabilidad, indeterminación del derecho y positivismo jurídico*.

9

Defeasibility, Axiological Gaps, and Interpretation

*Riccardo Guastini**

A. Introduction

My aim in this paper is to connect systematically a couple of ideas encountered in Carlos Alchourrón's and Eugenio Bulygin's legal theory—*viz.* the idea of axiological gap and the idea of defeasibility—with a sceptical or realistic theory of legal interpretation.[1]

(1) *Axiological gap.* An axiological gap occurs whenever a certain case is regulated by a legal rule but—in the interpreter's opinion—such a regulation is unsatisfactory from an axiological point of view, since the legislature did not take into account a distinction that it should have considered. The interpreter assumes that the legislators decided the way they did because they did not take into account the distinction at hand: should they have considered such a distinction, their decision as to the regulation of the case would have been different.[2]

In other words, an axiological gap is not a case with no legal solution at all, but a case provided with a 'bad' solution.[3] It is clear that this kind of gap does not amount to the absence of any rule whatsoever, since the case is in fact regulated: the rule which is assumed to be missing is a 'satisfactory' or 'just' rule, namely a 'distinguishing' rule, i.e. a rule providing a different ruling in the case which, in the interpreter's view, is substantively different and therefore requires a different verdict.[4]

(2) *Defeasibility of rules.* Any legal rule can be reconstructed as a conditional sentence to the effect that 'if a, then b', the antecedent standing for a class of cases while the consequent stands for a class of legal consequences (such as obligations, permissions, prohibitions, sanctions, validity or invalidity of some kind of act, etc.).[5]

* Professor of Jurisprudence, University of Genoa.

[1] The basic tenets of such a theory can be met in G. Tarello, *L'interpretazione della Legge* (Milan: Giuffrè, 1980); R. Guastini, *L'interpretazione dei Documenti Normativi* (Milan: Giuffrè, 2004); P. Chiassoni, *Tecnica dell'interpretazione giuridica* (Bologna: Il Mulino, 2007); M. Troper, *La théorie du droit, le droit, l'État* (Paris: Presses Universitaires de France, 2001). Cf. also E. Diciotti, *Interpretazione della legge e discorso razionale* (Turin: Giappichelli, 1999).

[2] C.E. Alchourrón and E. Bulygin, *Normative Systems* (Vienna: Springer, 1971), 106ff.

[3] P. Navarro and J. Rodríguez, 'Derrotabilidad y sistematización de normas jurídicas', *Isonomía*, 13 (2000), 61–85.

[4] In this context I am not concerned with the different concept of axiological gap worked out by Rodríguez in J. Rodríguez, *Lógica de los sistemas jurídicos* (Madrid: Centro de Estudios Constitucionales, 2002), 76ff.

[5] This concept of rule is wider than the one assumed by Alchourrón and Bulygin in *Normative Systems*, since it includes sentences which express 'rules' (only) in the sense that they belong to a normative system, although embodying no deontic formula in their consequent.

Many of the normative formulations (maybe every rule formulation) that can be encountered in a legal system are defeasible, i.e. they are subject to implicit exceptions: there are fact situations which defeat the rule although they are in no way expressly stated by normative authorities,[6] in such a way that the legal obligation (or, generally speaking, the legal consequence) settled by the rule does not hold any more.[7]

Defeasibility entails two important consequences: first, the logical rule of the strengthening of the antecedent does not hold for defeasible conditionals; second, reasoning by *modus ponens* cannot be applied to defeasible conditionals.[8] The legal rule 'if p, then Oq' does not necessarily entail 'if p and r, then Oq'. The conjunction of the legal rule 'if p, then Oq' and the statement 'p' does not necessarily entail 'Oq'.

In other words, a defeasible rule is subject to implicit exceptions that nobody can spell out exhaustively in advance, and as a consequence nobody can list in advance the circumstances that are genuine sufficient conditions for the application of the rule.[9] With a view to showing the connection between axiological gaps, defeasibility, and interpretation, I shall introduce a number of fictitious (although not entirely fictitious) examples.

B. Some examples

(1) First example. In a republic ruled by a rigid constitution, a parliamentary form of government, and the judicial review of legislation carried out *a posteriori* by a special Constitutional Court, a constitutional provision grants to the President of the Republic the power of veto over parliamentary acts (i.e. statutes).

Which parliamentary acts are concerned by such a provision? The literal interpretation suggests all of them, both 'ordinary' and 'constitutional' statutes (i.e. statutes providing constitutional amendments), since the text does not distinguish in any way between statutes of different kinds.

Now, let us imagine a jurist arguing, more or less, in the following way.

(a) In the existing constitutional system, where the constitution is (rigid but) subject to revision, two classes of statutes are to be sharply distinguished: 'ordinary' and 'constitutional' statutes. (Such a move is an interpretative technique which can be named 'dissociation' or 'distinguishing'.)

(b) In the existing constitutional system (parliamentary government) the President of the Republic is not the 'head' of the Executive: he or she is rather a 'neutral' power—something like Benjamin Constant's *pouvoir neutre*—whose function is just 'guaranteeing' the constitution, i.e. the ordinary political–constitutional process. (Observe that this is not a strictly interpretative thesis, but rather a 'dogmatic' one—a thesis of so-called 'constitutional theory', if one prefers.)

[6] C.E. Alchourrón, 'On Law and Logic', in this volume Ch. 2, 45ff.

[7] See C.E. Alchourrón and E. Bulygin, 'Norma jurídica' in E. Garzón Valdés and F.J. Laporta (eds), *El derecho y la justicia* (Madrid, Enciclopedia Iberoamericana de Filosofía. Volume XI, 1996), 146. The aforementioned concept of defeasibility refers to *implicit* exceptions; it does not refer to exceptions *expressly* stated by other rules of the same normative system. Cf. M.C. Redondo, 'Teorías del derecho e indeterminación normativa', *Doxa*, 20 (1997), 177–96; and J. Rodríguez, *Lógica de los sistemas jurídicos*, 358, 364ff.

[8] C.E. Alchourrón and E. Bulygin, 'Norma jurídica', 145ff.

[9] J. Rodríguez and G. Sucar, 'Las trampas de la derrotabilidad. Niveles de análisis de la indeterminación del derecho' in J.C. Bayón and J. Rodríguez, *Relevancia normativa en la justificación de las decisiones judiciales* (Bogotá: Universidad Externado de Colombia, 2003), 210.

(c) The function of the veto power is to allow the President to exercise *a priori* control over the constitutionality of statutes, quite different from the *a posteriori* control assured by the Constitutional Court. In particular, the President may use his or her veto power (only) against statutes whose unconstitutionality is self-evident. (This is an interpretive–dogmatic thesis about the *ratio legis*, the *raison d'être*, the aim of the constitutional provision at stake.)

(d) However, problems of constitutionality can only arise regarding ordinary statutes: in no case can a 'constitutional' statute be deemed unconstitutional (except for 'formal' reasons, relating to parliamentary procedure), since any constitutional amendment consists precisely in changing the constitutional text. Hence, in a sense, any constitutional amendment 'contradicts' the constitution (is 'unconstitutional'), but it is authorized to do so. (Such a thesis is entailed by the commonly accepted concept of constitutional amendment.)

(e) Therefore, the constitutional provision concerning the veto power ought to be interpreted as referring only to ordinary statutes—constitutional statutes being excluded. (This is a first interpretive conclusion, deriving from the technique of distinguishing combined with certain dogmatic assumptions.)

(f) The constitution says nothing at all about the veto power over constitutional amendments. (This is a second conclusion deriving from a combination of distinguishing and constitutional theory.)

(g) As a consequence, the President has no veto power over statutes providing constitutional amendments. (This is a further interpretive conclusion derived *a contrario* from the 'silence' of the constitutional text: *inclusio unius est exclusio alterius*.)

This line of reasoning brings about a number of important consequences.

(i) First, by means of the technique of distinguishing, our imaginary jurist created an implicit exception in the constitutional provision at hand. He or she treated it as a defeasible rule—in fact, he or she defeated (in a sense, 'derogated') the rule.[10]

(ii) Second, in so doing, he or she proposed a restrictive interpretation of the provision: its application is now restricted to ordinary statutes (while, according to literal interpretation, it would be applicable to every kind of statute, with no exceptions).

(iii) Third, he or she produced a gap: the constitutional provision now regulates only the case of ordinary statutes, and there is no constitutional regulation at all concerning the veto power over constitutional statutes. Observe that for anyone interpreting that provision according to its literal meaning such a gap is not 'normative' in character, but axiological, since the case of constitutional statutes is actually regulated by the constitutional provision, which—in its literal meaning—refers to any kind of statute with no distinction at all.

(iv) Fourth, our imaginary jurist filled the gap that he or she just created by means of an 'implicit' (although not in a strictly logical sense) negative rule—an example of *Juristenrecht*—according to which the President definitely has no veto power over constitutional statutes.

[10] 'Derogating' meaning in this context the same as defeating, i.e. introducing implicit exceptions into a rule.

(2) Second example. In the same constitutional system the executive—*viz.* the government—is empowered to enact (under certain conditions) 'legislative' decrees, i.e. decrees derogating existing statutes. Such decrees, being provided with *la force de la loi*, like ordinary statutes are subject to the *a posteriori* review of the Constitutional Court. However, a constitutional provision states that the acts of the government are subject to *a priori* control by a special Court of Accounts, enabled to supervise *ex ante* the compliance of governmental acts with statutes, and in particular with the budget as passed—in a 'statutory form'—by the parliament.

Which acts are covered by such a provision? According to the literal interpretation, any act of the executive is covered, since the text does not distinguish in any way among different kinds of acts.

Let us imagine, however, a jurist arguing more or less in the following way.

(a) Two kinds of governmental acts are to be distinguished: legislative and non-legislative acts (by-laws, administrative decisions, and so forth).
(b) Legislative acts, as a matter of course, cannot be required to comply with existing statutes (remember that the state budget is passed in a statutory frame by the parliament)—on the contrary, legislative acts as such are permitted to derogate precedent statutes. They are required to comply only with the constitution.
(c) However, in the existing legal system the control over the constitutionality of legislative acts is within the competence of the Constitutional Court.
(d) Therefore, the constitutional provision at hand ought to be interpreted as referring only to non-legislative acts—legislative acts being excluded.
(e) The constitution says nothing about the competence of the Court of Accounts over the legislative decrees enacted by the government.
(f) As a consequence, the Court of Accounts has no competence at all over the legislative acts of the government.

As in the previous case our imaginary jurist has done four important things:

(i) By means of the technique of distinguishing he or she defeated the constitutional provision, by introducing an implicit exception—i.e. an exception which, according to literal interpretation, does not exist at all.
(ii) In this way, he or she proposed a restrictive interpretation of the provision concerned.
(iii) At the same time he or she created a gap: the constitution does not regulate the power of the Court of Accounts over governmental legislative acts. There is no need to say that for anyone interpreting the constitutional provision according to its literal meaning such a gap is not normative—since the text refers to all the acts of the Executive—but is axiological in character.
(iv) Finally our imaginary jurist filled the gap by a negative rule of *Juristenrecht* according to which the Court of Accounts is definitely not competent to control the legislative acts of the government.

(3) Third example. In the same legal system a constitutional provision states that no act of the President of the Republic is valid if it is not countersigned by the minister who proposed the act.

Literal interpretation: any Presidential act whatsoever ought to be countersigned by the minister who proposed the act. This supposes that every Presidential act requires a minister proposing the act, i.e. a governmental proposal. In other words, there is no act that the President may accomplish except on the basis of a governmental proposal.

Let us imagine, however, a jurist reasoning more or less as follows.

(a) In a parliamentary form of government, the President of the Republic is not the head of the executive—he or she is rather a 'neutral' power whose function is guaranteeing the constitution, i.e. the compliance of the political–constitutional process with the constitution. (This is a dogmatic assumption we have already met.)

(b) Therefore, there must be acts that the President accomplishes in exercising such a function; such acts have no 'partisan'—politically biased—content; hence they do not presuppose or require any governmental proposal.

(c) As a consequence, two kinds of Presidential act should be distinguished: 'substantively' governmental acts (accomplished on the basis of governmental proposals) and 'strictly' presidential acts (without any previous governmental proposal).

(d) The aforementioned constitutional provision does not refer to all Presidential acts—it only refers to substantively governmental acts, while the remaining Presidential acts fall outside its scope.

(e) Therefore, strictly Presidential acts are not regulated by the constitution in any way.

(f) As a consequence, strictly Presidential acts do not require any countersignature.

Once more, our imaginary jurist has done four things.

(i) He or she defeated the constitutional provision at stake by introducing into it an implicit exception which, according to literal interpretation, would not exist.

(ii) In this way, he or she proposed a restrictive interpretation of such a provision.

(iii) The restrictive interpretation enabled him or her to identify a gap: the constitution does not regulate strictly Presidential acts (in connection with the countersignature). From the point of view of anyone preferring a literal interpretation, such a gap is obviously axiological since the constitutional text does not distinguish in any way and refers to Presidential acts without any further specification.

(iv) Finally, our jurist filled this gap by means of a negative rule, created by himself or herself, according to which strictly Presidential acts are not subject to countersignature.

C. Some conclusions

The examples could be easily multiplied—rejecting literal interpretation and defeating rules the way I have tried to show is commonplace in the juristic interpretive game. The examples (although more or less fictitious in character) suggest a number of interesting conclusions.

(1) The examples suggest that the concepts of axiological gap and defeasibility belong not to the theory of normative systems, but to the theory of legal interpretation. Such concepts denote phenomena which arise along the process of interpreting legal texts and depend on juristic (as well as judicial) interpretive strategies. Perhaps it is useful to recall that the logical systematization of the law (in the sense stipulated by Alchourrón

and Bulygin) does not precede, but follows interpretive decisions—no logical inferences are possible from not-yet-interpreted texts; inferences take place from meanings, and meanings presuppose interpretation.

(2) Axiological gaps and defeasibility often look like two faces of the same coin.[11] By defeating a rule one excludes from its scope certain factual situations (which according to a different interpretation would be regulated by that rule). Sometimes, such factual situations appear to be regulated by other rules in the legal system, but in other circumstances this is not the case—they are not regulated by any rule at all. In such a case, there is a gap in the system. Therefore, by defeating a rule, a gap has been produced.[12]

(3) The concept of axiological gap does not belong to juristic (or judicial) language—it belongs to the language of legal philosophy, understood as the logical analysis of juristic (as well as judicial) discourse.

This is to say that the jurist who asserts the existence of a gap—except when speaking in the mood of Bentham's 'censorial jurisprudence'[13]—will never acknowledge that such a gap is an axiological one. On the contrary, he or she will always insist that it is a genuine normative gap, an objective fault in the legal system, independent of any evaluation whatsoever.[14] Nevertheless, if we want to state—at the meta language level, from the 'external' point of view—that the gap at stake is not normative, but axiological, we must presuppose a different interpretation of the same text—different from the one proposed by the jurist who asserted the existence of that gap.

Hence, axiological gaps seem to depend on interpretation in a double sense. On the one hand, they depend on interpretation in the sense that those who assert the existence of an axiological gap presuppose a certain (normally restrictive) interpretation of a given text. On the other hand, they depend on interpretation in the sense that those who state, at a meta language level, that the gap at stake is not normative but axiological in character, presuppose in turn a different (normally literal) interpretation of the same text.

[11] J. Rodríguez, *Lógica de los sistemas jurídicos*, 377ff.

[12] By defeating a rule, an axiological gap is produced. But not all axiological gaps are produced by defeating rules. E.g. in the practice of some constitutional courts, one can find pieces of reasoning like these:

(a) The legislature, while regulating a certain class of cases in a certain way, *did not* regulate in the same way another class of cases which, according to the court, is 'substantively' equal to the regulated one.

(b) The legislature, while regulating a certain class of cases in a certain way, *did not* distinguish, within such a class, two sub-classes which, in the court's view, are 'substantively' different, and therefore require different regulations.

In both cases, we are faced with some sort of axiological gap. In the first case the missing rule is, so to say, an 'equalizing' rule, while in the second case the missing rule is a 'differentiating' one. In both cases the statute at hand is held unconstitutional because of the gap it contains. In the first case, however, no rule has been defeated (and there was no axiological gap in Alchourrón and Bulygin's sense). Cf. G. Parodi, 'Lacune e norme inespresse nella giurisprudenza costituzionale' in P. Comanducci and R. Guastini (eds), *Struttura e dinamica dei sistemi giuridici* (Turin: Giappichelli, 1996), 87ff.; G. Parodi, *La sentenza additiva a dispositivo generico* (Turin: Giappichelli, 1996), 131ff.; J. J. Moreso, *La indeterminación del derecho y la interpretación de la Constitución* (Madrid: Centro de Estudios Constitutionales, 1997), 171ff.

[13] Cf. J. Rodríguez, *Lógica de los sistemas jurídicos*, 82.

[14] I think Rodríguez is right in suggesting that often (maybe normally) the sentences which state the existence of a gap (an axiological one) are interpretive sentences—not sentences aiming at criticizing the existing legal system from an ethical or political standpoint. See J. Rodríguez, 'Lagunas axiológicas y relevancia normativa', *Doxa*, 22 (1999), 349–69.

All of this seems to have a further embarrassing consequence. According to a widespread view, axiological gaps depend on interpreters' evaluations, while normative gaps are 'objective' properties of the law. Things are not that simple, however. If axiological gaps cannot be distinguished from normative gaps independently of interpretation, then one and the same gap (every gap, indeed) can be deemed to be either normative or axiological from different interpretive standpoints.[15] And this means that normative gaps, too, are interpretation-dependent variables: according to interpretation A, a normative gap exists, while according to a different interpretation B, the gap surprisingly disappears, does not exist as a normative gap, and therefore turns into an axiological gap.[16]

(4) The concepts of defeasibility and axiological gaps are (more or less) new in legal-philosophical language, but the phenomena such concepts refer to are the result of a well-known ancient interpretive technique—restrictive interpretation, in which the scope of rules is reduced.

Now, restrictive interpretation is a relational concept: restrictive compared with what? To assert that a certain interpretation is restrictive, one has to presuppose a different interpretation: normally, literal interpretation. However, literal interpretation is still interpretation—less objectionable, perhaps, but not more 'objective' or 'neutral' (value-free) than any other possible interpretation.

Restrictive interpretation, like any other non-literal interpretation, expressly or tacitly supposes the rhetorical argument of *ratio legis*, i.e. the intention—often stated by means of a counterfactual sentence—of the normative authority. More precisely, those who reject literal interpretation assume: first, the existence of a mismatch between what the normative authority said and what it wanted to say (or do); and second, that intention should prevail over the text.[17] The latter assumption is plainly simply a political–juristic ideology. On the other hand, sentences concerning the intention of normative authorities cannot seriously be considered empirical statements: there is no access to the 'mind' of a legislature, especially if it is (as usual) a collegiate organ.[18] And, at any rate, counterfactual sentences have no truth-value.

(5) Restrictive interpretation is the outcome of a particular interpretive technique: the technique of distinguishing (a well-known intellectual procedure of judges in *common law* countries while interpreting precedents).

Such a technique simply consists in distinguishing where the normative authority did not distinguish at all—introducing into a rule 'new' distinctions, i.e. distinctions not made by the normative authority. The interpreter breaks up the class of fact situations mentioned by the text (literally interpreted) and draws two (or more) subclasses aiming at suggesting that such subclasses, being 'substantively' different, deserve different legal consequences.[19] The distinguishing technique is precisely the arguing strategy which allows the creation of axiological gaps and defeating rules.

[15] See M.C. Redondo, 'Reglas genuinas y positivismo jurídico' in P. Comanducci and R. Guastini (eds), *Analisi e diritto 1998* (Turin: Giappichelli, 1999), 256.

[16] 'A provision which may resolve a generic case under a certain interpretation may be a gap on a different understanding' C.E. Alchourrón, 'On Law and Logic', 44. 'An incomplete system (a system with gaps) can be transformed through interpretation . . . into a complete system (a system without gaps)' C.E. Alchourrón and E. Bulygin, *Normative Systems*, 94.

[17] F. Schauer, *Playing by the Rules. A Philosophical Examination of Rule-Based Decision-Making in Law and Life* (Oxford: Clarendon Press, 1991), 74ff.

[18] C.E. Alchourrón, 'On Law and Logic', 45ff.

[19] R. Guastini, *L'interpretazione dei documenti normativi* (Milan: Giuffrè, 2004), 163ff.; E. Diciotti, *Interpretazione della legge e discorso razionale* (Turin: Giappichelli, 1999), 451ff.

(6) Contrary to a widespread view, defeasibility is not peculiar to principles. Principles may possibly be 'intrinsically' defeasible, in such a way that defeasibility is part of the very concept of principle. But one thing is certain: any rule whatsoever can be treated as defeasible. As a matter of fact, jurists do it all the time.

(7) Some legal philosophers suggest that rule defeasibility and axiological gaps depend on the presence of principles within the legal system—rules would be defeated and axiological gaps produced precisely by principles, or, better, interpreters would defeat rules and create axiological gaps in view of applying principles. This is often true. But defeasibility and axiological gaps do not necessarily depend on principles, i.e. there is no logical relationship between them.

Defeasibility and axiological gaps simply depend on interpreters' evaluations, and such evaluations often take the form of juristic 'theories'—'dogmatic' theses framed by jurists in a moment logically previous to interpretation of any particular normative sentence and independently of interpretation.

It should be stressed that dogmatic theses—such as 'In a parliamentary frame of government the President of the Republic is a neutral power, whose function is guaranteeing the constitutional process', 'International custom arises from the consent of states', 'The European legal system and the legal systems of the Member States are mutually autonomous and independent', etc.—are not interpretive sentences: they are not reducible to the standard form of interpretive statements ('sentence S means M'). Sometimes they are but rules—'non-positive' rules, as a matter of course. Sometimes, they are stipulative definitions encompassing value judgements, (hidden) moral or political preferences, and entailing rules. Such definitions orient interpretation and, usually, allow the formulation of 'implicit' apocryphal rules.

Here is one example (a quite clear one). In a very well-known decision—*Marbury* (1803)—the Supreme Court of the USA stated that any written constitution includes (although tacitly) the intrinsic principle according to which 'a legislative act contrary to the constitution is not law'.[20] Such a statement is not an interpretive sentence: there is no rule formulation in the American Constitution which could be construed in such a way. At any rate, the Court itself does not even try and present its thesis as the conclusion of an interpretive reasoning. We are faced with a 'dogmatic' thesis, which directly expresses a rule and allows the Court to draw another 'implicit' rule—the rule which authorizes the Court itself to cast aside (not apply) unconstitutional statutes.

(8) According to Carlos Alchourrón, '[d]efeasibility, more than simple ambiguity, makes the identification of the norms of a legal system very difficult. So it is one of the factors that makes it necessary, in most situations, to introduce evaluative operations and the use of axiological standards in the interpretation of normative texts.'[21]

Such words seem to presuppose: on the one hand, that defeasibility is an objective property of rules, previous to interpretation; on the other hand, that interpretation is—at least in normal circumstances—an operation which does not require evaluations. Evaluations appear to be, in the interpretive process, *not a cause, but an effect* of defeasibility.

This is a somewhat naive conception of both defeasibility and interpretation. Defeasibility does not pre-exist interpretation—on the contrary, it is one of its possible results. And interpreters' evaluations are precisely a cause, not an effect, of rules defeasibility.

[20] *Marbury* v. *Madison*, 5 U.S. (1 Cranch) 137, 2 L. Ed. 60 (1803).

[21] C.E. Alchourrón, 'On Law and Logic', 50.

Just as axiological gaps are not objective properties of the legal system, since they depend on interpreters' evaluations, in the same way defeasibility is not an objective property of rules (or normative sentences). It depends neither on the unavoidable vagueness or open texture of normative authorities' language, nor on the fact that normative authorities are unable to foresee the endless variety of future cases.[22] Open texture, in particular, is an objective and (unremovable) property of any predicate in natural languages, whilst rule defeasibility is the outcome of an interpretive operation.

(9) As a consequence, it makes no sense to ask whether legal rules (either some of them or all of them) are defeasible or not. Rules—or, better, rule formulations, poor devils—are inert, they do nothing: they let themselves be defeated, but do not defeat themselves. Just as beauty is in the eye of the beholder, defeasibility is not in rules, but in the attitudes of interpreters.[23]

(10) The question whether defeasibility is a property of rules or of rule formulations allows a simple answer. A rule formulation is a sentence—not yet interpreted. Defeasibility is a logical property. But before interpretation sentences have no logical property at all—only rules, understood as the meaning contents of normative sentences, can have such properties. Therefore, defeasibility is a property of rules, not of rule formulations.

There is no need to say that defeating a rule—e.g. 'if p, then Oq'—by introducing an exception into it—e.g. 'if p and not r, then not Oq'—amounts to changing the rule, *viz.* substituting the 'original' rule with a different one.

Perhaps the idea that defeasibility is a property of rule formulations arises from the fact that the rules, which are defeated by jurists, are the outcome of the literal interpretation of such formulations—they are 'prima facie rules'.[24] Now, the non-distinction between sentences and their plain (literal) meaning occurs frequently and this is unsurprising, since literal interpretation often amounts to the bare reiteration (without any new wording) of the interpreted text. Nevertheless, literal meaning—even when obvious, and unquestioned—is still a meaning, not a sentence—it depends on interpretation and the key is in the interpretation.

(11) We have to distinguish carefully between (diachronic) defeasibility of rules and the (synchronic, momentary) acts of rule-defeating.

Defeasibility is a dispositional property of any rule whatsoever (understood as the literal meaning of a normative sentence):[25] in other words, any rule is virtually subject to a defeating operation by some interpreter.[26] This amounts to saying that literal

[22] Both (mistaken) ideas can be met in Hart, Carrió, Schauer, and MacCormick. Cf. H.L.A. Hart, *The Concept of Law* (2nd edn, Oxford: Clarendon Press, 1961), ch. VII; H.L.A. Hart, 'The Ascription of Responsibility and Rights', *Proceedings of the Aristotelian Society*, 49 (1948), 171–94; G.R. Carrió, *Notas sobre derecho y lenguaje* (4th edn, Buenos Aires: Abeledo Perrot, 1994), 226; F. Schauer, *Playing by the Rules*, 34ff.; N. MacCormick, 'Defeasibility in law and logic' in Z. Bankowski, I. White, and U. Hahn (eds), *Informatics and the Foundations of Legal Reasoning* (Dordrecht: Kluwer, 1995), 99–117.

[23] Cf. J.C. Bayón, 'Derrotabilidad, indeterminación del derecho, y positivismo jurídico' in J.C. Bayón and J. Rodríguez, *Relevancia normativa en la justificación de las decisiones judiciales* (Bogota: Universidad Externado de Colombia, 2003).

[24] Cf. E. Diciotti, *Interpretazione della legge e discorso razionale*.

[25] C.E. Alchourrón, 'Detachment and Defeasibility in Deontic Logic', *Studia logica*, 57 (1996), 5–18.

[26] Needless to say that sometimes defeating a rule may amount to the infringement of an 'interpretive convention' (J.C. Bayón, 'Derrotabilidad, indeterminación del derecho, y positivismo jurídico'), or—as I prefer to say—may contradict the interpretation 'in force'. See A. Ross, *On Law and Justice* (London: Stevens and Sons, 1958), 108.

interpretation can always be discarded in favour of a restrictive interpretation with defeating effects.

In each given moment, however, any rule can only be either defeated (as the result of an interpretive defeating act) or not defeated.

Whatever the case, however, a defeasible rule, as long as it remains defeasible (i.e. subject to unspecified implicit exceptions), is not useful for deciding cases:[27] it neither allows strengthening of the antecedent nor reasoning in *modus ponens*. Hence it cannot be used as a premise in any normative reasoning. This is why jurists (and judges) do consider rules as defeasible conditionals, but they do not leave them defeasible indefinitely.[28] By defeating a rule, jurists include an exception in it, but the new rule, in its new formulation (with a restricted scope), remains synchronically indefeasible[29]—suitable to function as a premise in a normative reasoning in *modus ponens*, i.e. suitable for application. And—it is understood—diachronically liable to further defeating acts.[30]

(12) The same holds, more or less, for axiological gaps too: in the sense that axiological gaps have but an ephemeral existence.[31] By defeating rules, jurists create axiological gaps. However, they do not do so in view of maintaining (seriously) that the law is—with no remedy—incomplete (or in view of suggesting judges enact *non liquet* decisions). In fact, they immediately fill the gaps they have created by means of new 'apocryphal' rules.

D. A final remark

Is there any relationship between the defeasibility of rules and legal positivism? Prima facie, no relationship at all. Nonetheless, a relationship does seem to exist: it seems that admitting the defeasibility of rules could undermine the main tenet of (methodological) legal positivism.[32]

The argument runs, more or less, like this. Legal positivism claims that the law can be identified independently of any moral evaluation. But, if legal rules are defeasible, their contents cannot be identified without moral evaluations. Therefore, the scientific project of legal positivism is doomed to failure—the identification of law presupposes moral evaluations.

In the first place, such an argument plainly supposes that defeasibility is an objective property of legal rules: a problem 'for interpretation', not an outcome of interpretation. However, as I have been arguing, this is not the case.

In the second place, such an argument is grounded, I submit, on a double confusion.

(i) First confusion. Identifying a certain normative text as a piece of law is something quite different from determining the meaning contents of such a text—what is commanded (permitted, prohibited), to whom, in what circumstances. According to legal positivism, identifying a text as a source of law can be done without any

[27] J. Rodríguez, *Lógica de los sistemas jurídicos*, 361; F. Schauer, *Playing by the Rules*, 116. Hart's idea, often quoted, according to which 'a rule that ends with the words "unless . . . " is still a rule' looks senseless to me. *Tantoque dormitat Homerus*. H.L.A. Hart, *The Concept of Law*, 136.

[28] J. Rodríguez and G. Sucar, 'Las trampas de la derrotabilidad. Niveles de análisis de la indeterminación del derecho', 132.

[29] Alchourrón has made clear that, after the revision of a defeasible conditional, what remains is a strict conditional. C.E. Alchourrón, 'Detachment and Defeasibility in Deontic Logic'.

[30] B. Celano, '"Defeasibility" e bilanciamento. Sulla possibilità di revisioni stabili', *Ragion pratica*, 18 (2002), 223–39.

[31] E. Diciotti, *Interpretazione della legge e discorso razionale*, 454ff.

[32] J.C. Bayón and J. Rodríguez, *Relevancia normativa en la justificación de las decisiones judiciales*.

evaluation. But legal positivism, as such, has nothing to say about the ascription of meaning to such a text. Methodological legal positivism as such is not a—and does not include any—theory of interpretation.

The positivist thesis is quite simple after all: any command of the sovereign is law. And that means that the sovereign's commands need not be just to be law—unjust statutes and constitutions are still law. Legal positivism does not claim more than that.

Besides, in view of determining the normative contents of legal texts, interpretation is necessary. And interpretation usually supposes evaluations. Is there anybody nowadays who seriously maintains interpretation to be a *wertfrei*, value-free, activity?

(ii) Second confusion. The scientific knowledge of the law in force is quite different from interpreting legal texts.

Interpreting legal texts is not simply using received knowledge of the law, but contributing to establish it. If by 'law' we mean not a set of sentences, but a set of meanings, there is no law without interpretation: the law comes from a combination of legislation (in the 'material' sense: production of rules formulations) and interpretation. Hence interpreting is not identifying the law. Rather, it is *a part of the law itself*: an aspect of the object that scientific jurisprudence aims at identifying.

In other words, interpretation is not 'the science of law', but a part of its object. Legal knowledge is a second-order discourse (a meta language) bearing upon interpretive discourse.

10

Defeasibility and Open Texture

*Brian H. Bix**

Introduction

H.L.A. Hart introduced the idea of 'open texture' into Anglo-American analytical jurisprudence. By that concept, Hart referred to the way that the terms in norms (legal and otherwise) can seem certain in a large class of fact situations, but can be uncertain in their application to certain 'borderline' fact situations. Hart's idea of 'open texture' in fact has roots deep in the intricate corners of mid-twentieth century philosophical theorizing about language and meaning, though much of that original understanding of 'open texture' is lost in Hart's borrowing.

Hart's use of the concept was part of an argument against a certain sort of scepticism associated with the American legal realists. In particular, Hart was claiming that in hard cases judges have discretion, but in easy cases there are clear, right answers. This was a middle position between the realists, on one hand, who seemed to argue that judges were never constrained in their decisions, and the object of the realists' critique on the other hand, so-called 'legal formalism', an approach to legal and judicial reasoning which seemed to assert that judges were always constrained. Hart's middle position was generally the same as the conventional view (then as now), that existing law determines the correct answer to most legal disputes, but that judges legislate in hard cases.

'Open texture' was only one of a long list of ideas that Hart introduced to English-language jurisprudence. Hart is also the original source for the idea that legal reasoning is essentially 'defeasible', a form of reasoning distinctly different from conventional logic and reasoning. Though Hart did not develop this idea subsequent to his original suggestion, many other writers have, though there remains some core uncertainty about the nature of 'defeasibility', and the extent to which legal reasoning is in fact essentially defeasible.

This paper examines the connections between these three notions: philosophical open texture, Hartian open texture, and defeasibility in legal reasoning. Section A of the paper will explore the origins of the idea of 'open texture'; section B will look at the way the concept works within Hart's analysis; section C will offer a brief overview of defeasibility before section D compares open texture with defeasibility. The primary conclusion would be that Hartian open texture and defeasibility are, at best, only broadly analogous, in that both create circumstances in which judges have discretion to create new law or exceptions to existing law.

* Frederick W. Thomas Professor for the Interdisciplinary Study of Law and Language, University of Minnesota.

A. Open texture: Waismann and Wittgenstein

Hart borrowed the term 'open texture' from his Oxford colleague, Friedrich Waismann, but it is worth noting how the term changed meaning in the borrowing.[1] Waismann was a member of the Vienna Circle, the group of philosophers and scientists who met to discuss philosophical ideas throughout the 1920s and 1930s. The group was central to the development of 'logical positivism' (a combination of empiricism and verificationism); the group's ideas developed to a great extent in response to, and in combination with, Ludwig Wittgenstein.[2] Waismann was a close collaborator with Wittgenstein for a brief period, and at one point took dictation from Wittgenstein. A planned jointly authored book never came into being, as the views of the two theorists began to diverge too much. Waismann's solo-authored work was meant to be an explanation and application of Wittgenstein's ideas, though Wittgenstein would later distance himself from Waismann's writings, including the writing done to Wittgenstein's own dictation.[3]

Waismann's idea of 'open texture' ('*Porosität der Begriffe*' in the original German)[4] is an application of certain ideas of Wittgenstein that would later appear in Wittgenstein's *Philosophical Investigations*. Section 80 of the *Investigations* reads:

> I say 'There is a chair.' What if I go up to it, meaning to fetch it, and it suddenly disappears from sight?—'So it wasn't a chair, but some kind of illusion.'—But in a few moments we see it again and are able to touch it and so on.—'So the chair was there after all and its disappearance was some kind of illusion.'—But suppose that after a time it disappears again—or seems to disappear. What are we to say now?[5]

Wittgenstein adds, in a later section: 'It is only in normal cases that the use of a word is clearly prescribed; we know, are in no doubt what to say in this or that case. The more abnormal the case, the more doubtful it becomes what we are to say'.[6]

In the above quotations from the later Wittgenstein, the question is of the connection between meaning and unusual circumstances. This raises what might be seen as a fairly conventional issue in semantic theory and the philosophy of language: the extent to which conventional meanings assume usual circumstances, and unusual circumstances may unsettle meaning and understanding. However, it is important to note that in Waismann's text (and in the corresponding works from Wittgenstein's middle period—works chronologically prior to the *Investigations*),[7] the idea of 'open texture' is an offshoot of a more narrow inquiry relating to verificationism. Verification theory equated the meaning of a proposition with what would be needed to verify that proposition.[8] Waismann was considering the question of how material object

[1] H.L.A. Hart, *The Concept of Law* (2nd edn, Oxford: Clarendon Press, 1994), 249.

[2] F. Waismann, *Ludwig Wittgenstein and the Vienna Circle* (Oxford: Basil Blackwell, 1979).

[3] G. Baker, 'Preface' in F. Waismann, *The Principles of Linguistic Philosophy* (ed. Rom Harré, London: Macmillan, 1997), xi–xxiii.

[4] F. Waismann, 'Verifiability', *Proceedings of the Aristotelian Society*, Supplementary volume 19 (1945), 121 n.

[5] L. Wittgenstein, *Philosophical Investigations* (3rd edn, New York: Macmillan, 1968), § 80.

[6] Ibid. § 142.

[7] See F. Waismann, *Ludwig Wittgenstein and the Vienna Circle*; and L. Wittgenstein, *Philosophical Remarks* (Oxford: Basil Blackwell, 1975).

[8] Verification theory also, controversially, claimed that propositions that could not be verified or falsified (e.g. most propositions of religion and metaphysics), were non-sensical. See e.g. A.J. Ayer, *Language, Truth, and Logic* (London: Gollancz, 1936); and F. Waismann, *Ludwig Wittgenstein and the Vienna Circle.*

statements could be translated into sense data. When trying to verify the assertion, 'there is a cat next door', is it sufficient to see the cat, perhaps touch it, and hear it purr?[9] However:

> What... should I say when that creature later on grew to gigantic size? Or if it showed some queer behavior usually not found with cats?... Again, suppose I say 'There is my friend over there'. What if on drawing closer in order to shake hands with him, he suddenly disappeared? 'Therefore it was not my friend but some delusion or other.' But suppose a few some seconds later I saw him again, could grasp his hand, etc. What then?... Have we rules ready for all imaginable possibilities?[10]

'Open texture', in this narrow, philosophical sense (the article will later consider a broader and looser sense in which the term has been used in jurisprudential writings), is connected to a particular set of philosophical ideas from the middle decades of the twentieth century. In particular, Wittgenstein and Waismann had both been, at one time, developing an approach towards language and meaning under which material object statements were made more or less probable, but never completely verified or falsified, by our experiences and sense-perceptions. In the case of both writers, the work was considered in texts that were left unpublished during their lifetimes (and, in Wittgenstein's case, it was clear that he had rejected this approach in moving on to the different approach to language and meaning of the *Investigations*).[11]

In both Waismann's work (and the work of Wittgenstein on which it is based), 'open texture' seems to be not so much vagueness,[12] as conventionally understood, as the mere possibility of vagueness: the uncertainty regarding meaning for logically possible, but realistically highly unlikely, events. The events are so unlikely that it is very improbable that any competent user of the language has even considered how he or she would respond linguistically were the events to occur. For Waismann, 'open texture' reflects an essential fact about empirical terms, and our inability to make their meaning entirely precise or conclusively verifiable.

B. Hart and open texture

As already mentioned, while Hart borrowed Waismann's term, 'open texture',[13] to make a point about the partial indeterminacy of language and (thus) of (legal) rules, his own use of the terms indicates a meaning broader and looser than it had for Waismann.

[9] F. Waismann, 'Verifiability', 121.

[10] Ibid., 121–2.

[11] For Wittgenstein's views, see F. Waismann, *Ludwig Wittgenstein and the Vienna Circle*, 99–101, 158–62, 210–11; L. Wittgenstein, *Philosophical Remarks*, 200–1, 282–97; for Waismann's views, see F. Waismann, 'Hypotheses' in *Philosophical Papers* (Holland: D. Reidel, 1977), 38–59; F. Waismann, 'Verifiability', 119–50. See generally B. Bix, *Law, Language, and Legal Determinacy* (Oxford: Clarendon Press, 1993), 14–17; G. Baker, 'Preface' in F. Waismann, *The Principles of Linguistic Philosophy*, xi–xxiii.

[12] Vagueness is a problem of uncertain borderlines of a category or meaning. 'Bald' or 'tall' are paradigmatic vague terms. Whether vagueness represents an aspect of epistemology or ontology remains highly controversial among philosophers of language.

[13] It seems probable (though not certain) that Hart's related ideas of a 'core of settled meaning' surrounded by a 'penumbra of debatable cases in which words are neither obviously applicable nor obviously ruled out' (H.L.A. Hart, 'Positivism and the Separation of Law and Morality', *Harvard Law Review*, 71 (1958), 607), can be traced to some writings of Bertrand Russell. See B. Russell, 'Vagueness', *Australasian Journal of Psychology and Philosophy*, 1 (1923), 84–92, reprinted in *Collected Papers of Bertrand Russell*, Vol. 9 (ed. John L. Slater, London: Unwin Hyman, 1988), 145–54. Hart

Hart uses the example of a hypothetical statute, 'no vehicles in the park'.[14] He argued that the 'core' meaning of 'vehicle' means that the statute applies unproblematically to a standard car driving through the park. However, when the question comes to someone using roller skates in the park, 'roller skates' are on the 'penumbra' of 'vehicle', and there are thus 'reasons both for and against our use of a general term'; asked to decide the application of this statute in such a case, 'something in the nature of a choice between open alternatives must be made by' the judge.[15]

Terms in the rule will have borderline cases of uncertain application, and thus so will the application of the rule as a whole. On one hand, common law judicial decisions will clarify some borderline cases through new decisions.[16] Once a judge decides (say) that roller skates *are* vehicles for the purpose of the rule, later courts may be bound to follow that interpretation. On the other hand, however, new practices and technologies will throw up new borderline cases.[17] So there will always be a range of cases in which the application of the legal rule is uncertain (at least until a court's decision settles the question).

For Hart, guidance by legislated rule is not that different from guidance by authoritative example (the latter occurs in common law reasoning, where the court's decision favouring one side or the other under certain sets of facts is binding on later courts, but the deciding court's formulation of the guiding rule and justification is not).[18] In each case, there are paradigmatic cases of clear application, but borderline applications that will require some choice to be made by the judge (or other decision maker).

In these discussions, Hart was affirming the conventional view that judges have discretion in hard cases (because the core meaning of terms used in the rule, or the core meaning of the rule itself, has run out). As noted, he was defending this mainstream view against, on one hand, the more radical claims of indeterminacy put forward by the American legal realists, and, on the other hand, certain natural law (and procedural natural law) criticisms of legal positivism.[19]

One can see how in the original context—in the works of Waismann and Wittgenstein—'open texture' refers to a matter of theoretical interest, but is of limited practical application. Open texture is for the extraordinary (cats the size of rooms), not for the merely unusual. What Hart was pointing to was something more mundane, an uncertainty in application that occurs frequently enough for the average reader of *The Concept of Law* to recognize the judicial difficulty Hart is describing.

And though Hart generally speaks of the open texture of particular terms, his intended meaning is somewhat different: the open texture of a term in the context of a particular norm. He frequently used the example of the simple rule, 'no vehicles in the park'. He stated that the average automobile was clearly excluded, because it fell within the 'core meaning' of 'vehicle', but that bicycles and roller skates did not.[20]

does not refer to Russell's work, the way he expressly cites Waismann for the idea of 'open texture' (and elsewhere refers to the works of J.L. Austin and Wittgenstein).

[14] H.L.A. Hart, 'Positivism and the Separation of Law and Morality', 607–11; H.L.A. Hart, *The Concept of Law*, 128–9.

[15] Ibid., 126–7.

[16] Hart also notes that canons of interpretation can reduce, but cannot eliminate uncertainties in interpretation (in part because those canons of interpretation themselves require interpretation). See ibid., 126.

[17] Ibid., 126.

[18] Ibid., 124–8.

[19] L.L. Fuller, 'Positivism and Fidelity to Law—A Reply to Professor Hart', *Harvard Law Review*, 71 (1958), 630–72.

[20] H.L.A. Hart, *The Concept of Law*, 123.

At times, Hart seems to change his focus from the clear meaning (in some cases) and (in other cases) unclear application of particular terms to the clear and unclear meanings and applications of whole rules. Thus, one can find references both to the 'open texture of terms' and to the 'open texture of rules'.[21] To be sure, uncertainty of terms can lead to uncertainty of the norm as a whole, but this is not necessary or universal. An uncertainty in a particular term might be overcome by reading the term in light of other terms in the rule, in light of the rule's purpose, or in light of other, related norms. Hart also switches from focus on the terms themselves to references to the uncertain or incomplete intentions of lawmakers. Whether such a purposive or intentionalist approach to statutory interpretation is required or optimal was, and remains, a controversial topic, well beyond the scope of the present discussion.

Returning to Hart's view of 'open texture': Hart adds that we should not seek, even were it obtainable, rules with no uncertain borderlines. For it is the need, or the possibility, of judicial interpretation at the periphery that gives the legal system useful flexibility, to deal better with future circumstances that had not been foreseen at the time of the original legislation.[22]

C. Defeasibility

In an early work, Hart introduced the idea that legal concepts might be essentially 'defeasible':[23] subject to an analytical structure such that certain criteria justified the assertion of some legal claim (like 'valid contract'), but that claim might subsequently be defeated by the discovery of additional facts.[24] Hart later disowned that earlier article, on the basis that (as he saw it) its main contentions were not defensible,[25] but others have taken up the application of defeasibility to law and legal reasoning.

[21] Ibid., 123–8.

[22] Ibid., 128–130.

[23] The literature on defeasibility since Hart (and prior to this volume) has been extensive: L.G. Boonin, 'Concerning the Defeasibility of Legal Rules', *Philosophy and Phenomenological Research*, 26 (1966), 371–78; P. Helm, 'Defeasibility and Open Texture', *Analysis*, 28 (1968), 173–5; C. Cherry, 'The Limits of Defeasibility', *Analysis*, 34 (1974), 101–7; G. Sartor, 'Defeasibility in Legal Reasoning', *Rechtstheorie*, 24 (1993), 281–316; G. Sartor, 'Defeasibility in Legal Reasoning' in Z. Bankowski, I. White, and U. Hahn (eds), *Informatics and the Foundations of Legal Reasoning* (Dordrecht: Kluwer, 1995), 119–57; G. Sartor, 'Syllogism and Defeasibility: A Comment on Neil MacCormick's *Rhetoric and the Rule of Law*', *Northern Ireland Legal Quarterly*, 59 (2008), 21–32; N. MacCormick, 'Defeasibility in Law and Logic' in Z. Bankowski, et al. (eds), *Informatics and the Foundations of Legal Reasoning*, 99–117; F. Schauer, 'On the Supposed Defeasibility of Legal Rules' in M.D.A. Freeman (ed.), *Current Legal Problems 1998: Legal Theory at the End of the Millenium* (Oxford: Oxford University Press, 1998), 223–40; J. Hage and A. Peczenik, 'Law, Morals, and Defeasibility', *Ratio Juris*, 13 (2000), 305–25; R.H. S. Tur, 'Defeasibilism', OJLS, 21 (2001), 355–68; H. Prakken and G. Sartor, 'The Three Faces of Defeasibility in the Law', *Ratio Juris*, 17 (2004), 118–39; J. Hage, *Studies in Legal Logic* (Dordrecht: Springer, 2005), 7–32; G.A. Antonelli, 'Non-Monotonic Logic' in E.N. Zalta (ed.), *Stanford Encyclopedia of Philosophy*, 2006, (http://plato.stanford.edu/entries/logic-nonmonotonic); J. Stelmach and B. Brożek, *Methods of Legal Reasoning* (Dordrecht: Springer, 2006), 49–63; B. Brożek, 'Revisability versus Defeasibility', *Northern Ireland Legal Quarterly*, 59 (2008), 139–47.

[24] Hart indicated that he was using the term as an extension of an idea from property law, whereby a legal interest in land could be subject to termination or defeat under certain contingencies, but would remain valid if those contingencies did not come about. See H.L.A. Hart, 'The Ascription of Responsibility and Rights', *Proceedings of the Aristotelian Society*, 49 (1948–49), 175.

[25] H.L.A. Hart, *Punishment and Responsibility* (Oxford: Clarendon Press, 1968), v. Tur gives reasons to think that what Hart was disowning was (only) the view that human action generally could be analysed in defeasible terms. R.H.S. Tur, 'Defeasibilism', 356. The articles Hart cites to distance himself from his own earlier work do not call into question the more specific application of defeasibility to legal concepts.

The notion of something being valid presumptively, or for the moment, and then being defeated by considerations later raised (but only if they *are in fact* raised) responds to certain distinctive aspects of legal practice and decision-making, in particular the practices within common law legal systems.[26]

There are different sorts of defeasibility in legal reasoning. One central subcategory is the notion of Equity: creating exceptions to general rules, in their application to particular cases where this is required to avoid (extreme) injustice or absurdity.[27] The basic notion of equitable defeasibility, of seeking exceptions to the literal application of rules, in the name of justice, has been known at least since the writings of Plato and Aristotle.[28] The 'defeating' condition could be one of two different types: a precise doctrinal exception, or a general 'safety valve' exception. The first kind of defeating condition can be found in various doctrinal rules in many legal systems. What is distinctive about this first category is that the courts, in applying these defeating conditions, do not have open-ended discretion, as they do with the second category. For example, a contract is presumptively valid once the main elements (e.g. in American and English law, offer, acceptance, and consideration) are made out, but the court is directed not to enforce the contract if one of the parties then proves the existence of fraud, mutual mistake, or the mental incapacity or underage of one of the parties.[29] These defences to contract enforcement are grounded (historically) in Equity (where, in prior times, the judge might have had broad discretion to grant or refuse the release from legal obligation, on the basis of the judge's view of the 'equities' of the particular case). In modern practice the general equitable concerns have been reduced to (relatively) bright-line rules, leaving judges little to no discretion. If the elements of the doctrinal defence have been made out, enforcement of the contract must be refused.

There are a wide variety of doctrinal contexts, in which this sort of sequence of decision making is present, and it affects also the way we think about the legal standard. Exceptions to the application of rules are too numerous, and frequently refer to circumstances too rare, to be worth incorporating into the main rule. Also, there are practical reasons for placing the burden of proof (and the burden of production) differently: on one party to show that the main criteria have been met for validity, and on the other party to show that the unusual circumstances have been met to show that there is an exceptional, defeating condition. For many writers, it is this structure of characterization, sequential decision-making, and burden shifting, that is described as the defeasibility of legal reasoning.

Examples of the second type of defeating condition described above, the 'safety valve' exception, are the general equitable powers of the common law courts (and, to a lesser extent, the various equitable doctrines and exceptions), and the related power claimed by courts to avoid the literal application of statutes or contractual terms when they

[26] See, for instance, N. MacCormick, 'Defeasibility in Law and Logic'; F. Schauer, 'On the Supposed Defeasibility of Legal Rules'.

[27] As Schauer points out, a legal (or other normative) system cannot allow recourse to equitable overrides too easily or too frequently, or it will lose the benefit (and, indeed, the nature) of governance by rules, benefits that include relative predictability and certainty. See F. Schauer, 'Is Defeasibility an Essential Property of Law?', in this volume, ch. 4.

[28] Ibid.

[29] In all of these cases (and many more), there are complexities regarding what needs to be proven to make the contract void or voidable, and whether the party raising the complaint can enforce the contract despite the doctrinal objection, as well as small but important variations of those rules across jurisdictions, but these need not distract us here.

would lead to absurd or unjust results, or just outcomes clearly contrary to the legal rule's original purpose. Arguably, Ronald Dworkin's favourite case example, *Riggs* v. *Palmer*,[30] fits within this category, when the court refused to apply a general wills statute in a context where the enforcement of a will as written would have resulted in a murderer inheriting from his victim.[31]

Tur argues that there is a comparable 'safety valve' defeasibility in tort law, at least *English* tort law, where an exception may be made to the application of a settled legal rule in the name of 'policy', and in criminal law, where the court or the executive has the authority to reduce sentences in the name of 'mercy'.[32] It is important to notice that, for Tur, his view regarding defeasible legal reasoning is as much prescriptive as descriptive. He simply believes it to be *a good thing* when legal reasoning is sequenced in such a way that there is an option to override a result for justice (or related) reasons, and he believes it unfortunate that what he calls 'positivistic' thinking has reduced the role of such equitable or other overrides in English law.[33]

There is also a different sort of decision making that is often placed within the rubric of 'defeasibility': in common law legal systems, judges usually have the authority to modify legal rules (at least for those legal rules or categories of legal rules developed by courts in the first place—often including most of the legal rules of contract law, property law, and tort/delict law).[34] Thus a party's claim that it has a right under the law may be fully justified under the legal norms and decisions to date, but turn out to be (made) false when the law is (retroactively) clarified or modified when the claim is decided by the court.

It is worth remembering the different effects of different kinds of defeasibility. In the case of Equity (or certain forms of exceptions for policy purposes or to avoid injustice or absurdity), the rule is not (literally) applied to the facts, but the rule otherwise remains valid, to be applied to future cases. By contrast, with common law reasoning, the (perhaps exceptional) facts motivate the judicial decision-maker to *modify* the rule, changing it not only for the case before the court, but for all subsequent cases (until it is modified again).[35]

As discussed above, aspects of the (descriptive) arguments for defeasibility seem strongest within legal systems in which judges have significant power to develop the law, and to modify existing rules. This leads to the question as to whether defeasibility should be seen as a claim about *certain* legal systems, rather than about law (and legal reasoning) in general.[36] As Schauer points out,[37] however much one might consider either equitable exceptions or the modification powers of common law judges to be a good thing, such forms of defeasibility are not universal, nor do legal systems without those characteristics seem unimaginable. A claim that legal reasoning is 'essentially' or 'necessarily' defeasible thus does not seem supportable.

[30] 115 N.Y. 506 (1889).

[31] Schauer makes a similar point about *Riggs* in 'Is Defeasibility an Essential Property of Law?'

[32] R.H.S. Tur, 'Defeasibilism', 362–7.

[33] Ibid., 367–8.

[34] Some commentators emphasize the distinction, creating separate categories of 'defeasibility' and 'revisability'. See, for example, B. Brożek, 'Revisability versus Defeasibility', 139–47. This article will continue the more common practice of treating both as subcategories of defeasibility.

[35] R.H.S. Tur, 'Defeasibilism', 359; F. Schauer, 'Is Defeasibility an Essential Property of Law?'

[36] R.H.S. Tur, 'Defeasibilism', 360.

[37] F. Schauer, 'Is Defeasibility an Essential Property of Law?'

D. Comparing open texture and defeasibility

How should one think about the connection between the idea(s) of defeasibility and those of open texture? Part of the complication of responding to the question is that, as we have seen, there are (at least) two quite distinct ideas that go under the rubric of 'open texture', and 'defeasibility' has been used to cover a fairly broad range of decision making. In the discussion that follows, I will try to narrow the focus, in order to offer some tentative comments on possible connections.

With open texture as narrowly understood by Waismann and other philosophers, there seems to be a kind of defeasibility ('it looks like a cat, but it is nine feet tall', or 'that thing that looks like a chair seems to keep coming in and out of existence'): criteria sufficient to justify a conclusion regarding the application of an empirical term are later defeated by additional evidence. However, 'open texture' in the sense of those philosophers of language, however central it may be to their views on meaning, is peripheral to the concerns of legal theorists, because it only touches on events of extreme rarity.

As discussed above, Hart adapted the concept of 'open texture' to a broader, less precise idea: of when normative terms, or the norms as a whole, are uncertain in their application to borderline cases. Hartian open texture has a very different structure from the type of reasoning that is given the 'defeasibility' label. That label is used where an initial conclusion is warranted, subject to later revision or override when additional facts appear. Thus, there is one solid conclusion, which can be transformed into an equally solid, but contrary, conclusion with more information. By contrast, Hartian open texture is about uncertainty, a range of (equally, or at least comparably) legitimate decisions.

The parallel between the two ideas is that both have been (and are) used to explain and justify judicial discretion and (thus) judicial lawmaking. With Hartian open texture, the terms within the legal norms, and the legal norms themselves, become uncertain, resulting in indeterminate outcomes for novel or marginal cases. In such circumstances, judges must make choices in applying a statute (or other authoritative legal text) to the facts before the court.

Under certain forms of defeasible legal reasoning, courts have the authority either (under Equity or similar ideas) to create an exception in the (literal) application of general rules to a particular case, or (under common law reasoning) to modify the rule itself, and not just for the case before the court, but for future cases as well. In both kinds of defeasibility, there is not, and probably could not be, any sort of bright-line rule about when the judge should create an exception or modification. At best, there is a sense that exceptions or modifications should not be too frequent, at the risk of undermining the whole purpose and benefit of guidance by rules.[38] Thus, defeasible forms of legal reasoning create (when confronting the right sort of fact situation) the same sort of range of available choices that judges face in the Hartian 'open texture' of borderline cases.[39]

[38] F. Schauer, 'Is Defeasibility an Essential Property of Law?'

[39] In Dworkin's terminology, this is judicial discretion both in the 'strong sense' of having choice of which standards to apply, and in the weak sense of using judgement to apply a vague or uncertain standard. R. Dworkin, *Taking Rights Seriously* (rev. edn, Cambridge, Mass.: Harvard University Press, 1978), 31–9.

E. Conclusion

H.L.A. Hart was the original source of the modern idea of defeasibility in legal reasoning, as well as the adaptation for legal reasoning of Friedrich Waismann's concept of 'open texture'. Both defeasibility and Hartian 'open texture' show the dynamism in legal reasoning that is present in many (and perhaps most) legal systems: that judges are necessary adjunct lawmakers, clarifying the legal rules, filling in gaps, and creating modifications or exceptions where necessary to avoid severe injustice or absurdity.

11

Exceptions

*Daniel Mendonca**

I

It is claimed that in natural or ordinary language conditional expressions of the form 'if A, then B' are frequently used in such a way that it is not intended to assert through them that the antecedent A is a sufficient condition of the consequent B, but only that the antecedent A, together with a set of presuppositions accepted in the context in which the conditional is expressed, is a sufficient condition of the consequent B. This is so, for example, when it is stated, regarding a certain gas sample, that its volume will increase if the temperature is raised, assuming in the context that the pressure will remain constant. The conditional statement is defeated when any of the implicit presuppositions is false. Therefore, a defeasible conditional may be defined with a conditional subject to implicit exceptions. In the example, a variation in gas pressure constitutes an implicit exception that defeats the conditional statement. So, in relation to a defeasible conditional, it may be true that 'if A, then B', and false that 'if A and C, then B'. In such a case, the circumstance C constitutes an exception that defeats the conditional 'if A, then B'. But there is a law in logic, called 'strengthening the antecedent', which says that if a condition A entails a consequence B, therefore the same condition A, in conjunction with any other condition C, will also entail the consequence B. The fact of assuming that a conditional is defeasible implies, then, the omission of the law of strengthening the antecedent.[1] And, certainly, many conditional normative expressions, or perhaps all of them, are defeasible: they usually recognize implicit exceptions, in the sense that there are circumstances that defeat the norm, although they may not be explicitly contained in the respective expression.[2]

On that basis, it has even been claimed that all norms are defeasible, and that they should be read as if they concluded with a clause of the type 'unless', assuming they possess an indeterminate set of implicit exceptions.[3] Underlying this thesis is the idea that it always seems possible to argue in favour of an exception to any norm, even if not a single one has been recognized up to that moment. Even if there are no recognized exceptions, the possibility of arguing in favour of an exception not yet recognized is always open to anyone. This is so because law is a practical discipline, which requires a certain degree of flexibility in order to handle situations so far not covered, or changes of

* Professor of Law, Catholic University of Nuestra Señora de la Asunción. The author thanks Professor Ricardo Guibourg (University of Buenos Aires) for his valuable contributions.

1 G.H. Von Wright, 'Conditionality', *Six Essays in Philosophical Logic, Acta Philosophica Fennica*, 60 (1996), 23.

2 C. Alchourrón, 'Sobre derecho y lógica', *Isonomía*, 13 (2000), 23–4.

3 To this effect, see H.L.A. Hart, 'The Ascription of Responsibility and Rights' in A. Flew (ed.), *Logic and Language* (Oxford: Basil Blackwell, 1960), 145–66; and N. MacCormick, 'Defeasibility in Law and Logic' in Z. Bankowski, *Informatics and the Foundations of Legal Reasoning* (Dordrecht: Kluwer, 1995), 99–118.

circumstances not taken into account when the norm was formulated in universal terms. Thus, there would be exceptions *to* the norm which are not exceptions *in* the norm.[4]

In this essay, our purpose will be, precisely, to analyse the different forms that exceptions—both implicit and explicit—can adopt in normative contexts. More specifically, we will try to reconstruct the function that equivalent expressions of the type 'if A, then B, except that C', 'if A, then B, unless C', or 'if A, then B, with the exception of C' perform in such contexts.

II

Let us first consider the case in which a norm implicitly excepts another norm. Let us begin with the following example of the Spanish constitutional regime. According to what is stipulated in Article 14 of the Constitution, Spaniards are equal before the law, allowing no discrimination on account of birth, race, sex, religion, opinion, or any other personal or social condition or circumstance. However, as provided by Article 57.1 of the same body, the Crown of Spain is hereditary for the successors of HM Don Juan Carlos I of Bourbon. This provision also stipulates that succession to the throne will follow the regular order of primogeniture and representation, the first line always having preference over subsequent lines; within the same line, the nearer degree over the more remote; within the same degree, the male over the female; and in the same sex, the elder over the younger. Consequently, although Article 14 establishes the equality of Spaniards on account of birth and sex, Article 57.1 introduces a discrimination into the rules for succession to the Spanish Crown, precisely in terms of both criteria, since it sets the preference for the descendants of the dynastic line over the rest of the Spaniards, that of the firstborn child over the younger ones, and that of the male over the female in the same line of succession.[5] The constitutional doctrine suggests that Article 57.1 introduces an exception to the rule established in Article 14, by which Spaniards are equal before the law on account of sex, except for the purposes of the succession to the Crown of Spain.[6] Presumably, no jurist would find in this set sufficiently serious obstacles to apply those norms when the appropriate circumstances arise. The consequences of these provisions seem to be clear for jurists and for any reasonable interpreter. Nonetheless, as strange as it may seem, it is not easy to formally reconstruct the intuitions which underlie the proposed interpretation.

It seems adequate to think that the norms in question are mere exemplifications of the following diagrams.[7]

$$\text{N1)}\ A \rightarrow OB$$

$$\text{N2)}\ C \rightarrow VB$$

[4] A. Honoré, 'Real Laws' in P. Hacker and J. Raz, *Law, Morality and Society* (Oxford: Clarendon Press, 1977), 108–10.

[5] J. Villaroya, 'Sucesión a la Corona' in O. Alzaga, *Constitución Española de 1978* (Madrid: Editoriales de Derecho Reunidas, vol. V, 1983), 113–14. Part of the doctrine has addressed the point as a possible contradiction, as the preference of the male over the female constitutes a discrimination lacking justification from the point of view of the equality of rights between men and women. See, in that respect, P. Mellado and Y. Gómez, 'En torno a la posible inconstitucionalidad del apartado 1 del artículo 57 de la Constitución española de 1978', *Revista de Derecho Político*, 22 (1986).

[6] L. López Guerra et al., *Derecho constitucional* (Valencia: Tirant lo Blanch, vol. II, 2002), 32.

[7] C. Alchourrón, 'Condicionalidad y la representación de las normas jurídicas' in C. Alchourrón and E. Bulygin, *Análisis lógico y derecho* (Madrid: Centro de Estudios Constitucionales, 1991), 267–9.

Table 11.1 Spanish Royal succession—S1

Cases	S1	
	N1	N2
1) A & C	OB	VB
2) ¬ A & C		VB
3) A & ¬ C	OB	
4) ¬ A & ¬ C		

Yet, some features of this type of formalization are incompatible with the jurists' intuitions. In fact, from N1 and N2 we can simultaneously infer incompatible consequences (OB and VB) when circumstances A and C (A&C) coincide.

The matrix of the system in Table 11.1 (let us call it S1) shows the correlation of cases and solutions in detail.

As it can be observed, N1 and N2 entail conflicting consequences when facing the case in which circumstances A and C (A&C) coincide, since, according to N1, the obligation of B (OB) exists, and, according to N2, the prohibition of B (VB) exists. A way of correcting the formalization proposed in N1 and N2 would be to assume that the problem originates in an inadequate contextual interpretation of the S1 set. From this standpoint, each of the norms composing the set must be interpreted in accordance with the meaning conferred on it by the entirety of the norms belonging to that set. According to that principle, it may be argued that N2 was dictated with the intention of modifying the content of N1, as an exception to N1. Hence, the set should be formalized as expressing the norms N3 and N4, such that:

$$N3)\ (A\&\neg C) \rightarrow OB$$

$$N4)\ (A\&C) \rightarrow VB$$

Observe the matrix of the new system (let us call it S2) in Table 11.2 below.

As these norms do not produce the undesired consequence of imposing conflicting solutions, the difficulty seems to be overcome. This procedure, based on an interpretation according to which a norm excepts another norm, achieves its objective of making the result of the formalization compatible with the intuitive contents of the normative set. The suggested procedure involves two steps: first, the norms for this set must be reformulated, introducing all the exceptions and conditional clauses required by the intuitive interpretation, so the formalization must not introduce non-existent conflicts of obligation; second, only when this task has been satisfactorily accomplished can we

Table 11.2 Spanish Royal succession—S2

Cases	S2	
	N3	N4
1) A & C		VB
2) ¬ A & C		
3) A & ¬ C	OB	
4) ¬ A & ¬ C		

proceed to formalize the norms using the material implication and the deontic operator of the obligation. Although this procedure has unquestioned advantages, it presents the inconvenience that the formulation of each norm within the system must be revised, taking into account the contents of all the other norms.[8]

III

Let us consider, secondly, the case in which a norm is implicitly excepted through value considerations. Our starting point will be the exception jurisprudentially introduced to Article 18.2 of the Spanish Constitution. This provision declares the home inviolable, and establishes that no entry or search may be made without the consent of the householder, a judicial decision or *flagrante delicto.* The Constitutional Court itself has stated that the article in question offers a rigorous protection of the inviolability of the family home by establishing three taxative cases in which entry or search proceeds.[9] But beyond the alleged taxativity, the doctrine admits that the exceptions to home inviolability recognized by the law are essentially four: the householder's consent, the existence of a previous judicial decision, the *flagrante delicto*, and the grounds for justification. In this sense, it is claimed that 'a last exception would be that of the hypotheses which involve grounds for justification (e.g., the state of necessity), not expressly mentioned in Article 18.2 of the Spanish Constitution, but assimilated by STC (i.e. Constitutional Court Decision) 22/1984'.[10] In fact, it has been argued in this decision that 'without consent of the householder or judicial decision, the act is illicit and constitutes violation of the law, except for cases of *flagrante delicto*, and, of course, the hypotheses that generate grounds for justification, as may be the case with the state of necessity'.[11]

Thus, an interpretation sticking to the literal tenor of the constitutional text would contemplate only three relevant situations within the system: consent of the householder, judicial decision, and *flagrante delicto*.[12] Now, with regard to the provision at issue, and in view of the preceding considerations, it would be pertinent to value the system as insufficient on this point. We will expound on this question more carefully. Following Alchourrón and Bulygin, we may use the expression 'relevance thesis' of a normative system regarding the proposition that identifies the relevant properties in such a system, and 'relevance hypothesis' of a normative system regarding the proposition that identifies those properties which *should* be relevant, from some value point of view.[13] Alchourrón and Bulygin employ the term 'axiological gaps' for those cases where the relevance hypothesis does not coincide with the relevance thesis; i.e. when they are regulated and have a normative solution, but the solution turns out to be unsatisfactory because the authority has not taken into account a property which should have been considered (e.g. entering a home in cases of necessity or *force majeure*

[8] It would certainly be desirable that, when passing a statute, the legislator take into account the contents of the other existing norms; if not to facilitate an interpretative task as accurate as the one hereby proposed, at least to avoid unwanted conflicts resulting from his own inadvertence. Yet, it is not a function of the legal science to give the legislator technical instructions of uncertain compliance.

[9] STC 160/1991.

[10] F. Balaguer Callejón (ed), *Derecho constitucional* (Madrid: Tecnos, vol. II, 2003), 148.

[11] STC 22/1984.

[12] See J.J. Moreso and J.M. Vilajosana, *Introducción a la teoría del derecho* (Madrid: Marcial Pons, 2004), 99–103.

[13] C. Alchourrón and E. Bulygin, *Introducción a la metodología de las ciencias jurídicas y sociales* (Buenos Aires: Astrea, 1987), 173–4.

is forbidden within the system). We may say, therefore, that a case C from a universe of cases is an axiological gap in a normative system S if, and only if, the case C is correlated by S with a normative solution, and there exists a property P such that P must be relevant for case C (according to a given relevance hypothesis), and P is irrelevant in S.[14] This would be, precisely, the case of the property relative to the grounds for justification, included by the doctrine and jurisprudence as an additional 'implicit' exception[15] to the rule contained in Article 18.2 of the Spanish Constitution.[16] Such property is not included in the relevance thesis of the constitutional legislator, but it is included in the relevance hypothesis of the Constitutional Court. This mechanism, then, would enable the introduction of implicit exceptions, in terms of value considerations, where they had not been explicitly provided by the legislator.[17]

IV

Let us consider, in the third place, the case in which a norm is explicitly excepted through specific clauses of the type 'except that', 'unless', or 'with the exception of'. This case is, indeed, quite usual in legal practice. For example, Article 15 of the Spanish Constitution establishes the abolition of the death penalty, except for what might be stipulated by military laws in wartime. The doctrine has pointed out with respect to this, that it is not an absolute abolition, but rather an abolition which admits only one exception: during a formally declared war, and as long as it is so stipulated by military penal laws.[18] Let us analyse more carefully, then, the way in which explicit exception clauses with the form 'obligatory A, except that B', or 'if A, then OB, except that C', or similar, operate in normative contexts. Let us begin, then, with the expression 'if A, then OB, except that C'. The expression under analysis might be formally reconstructed as follows:

$$\text{N5)}\ (A \rightarrow OB)\&((A\&C) \rightarrow \neg OB))$$

i.e. 'if A, then OB, but if A and C, then not OB'. It seems pertinent to point out that, strictly speaking, N5 would be a complex norm, made up of a conjunction of two norms (N5' & N5"), namely:

$$\text{N5')}\ A \rightarrow OB$$

$$\text{N5")}\ (A\&C) \rightarrow \neg OB$$

Now, if we were to reconstruct the matrix of the normative system (let us call it S3) configured by N5' and N5", we would obtain the consequences set out in Table 11.3.

In terms of the previously mentioned logical law of strengthening the antecedent, case (1) would show the system's incoherence by providing two different, incompatible solutions (OB and ¬OB) for the same case (A&C). Such incoherence should be solved by determining, precisely, the prevalence of the solution provided by the exception

[14] Ibid., 158.

[15] We use quotation marks in this expression, so habitual in legal discourse, to indicate that it does not strictly refer to a logical deduction: the statement that an exception is implicit in the norm is based, almost always, on a judgement of the observer not exempt from a strong value component.

[16] J.J. Moreso and J.M. Vilajosana, *Introducción a la teoría del derecho*, 111.

[17] On a similar basis, it has been suggested that a distinction should be made between internal and external defeasibility of a norm. See, in this respect, J.J. Moreso, P. Navarro, and M.C. Redondo, *Lliçons de filosofia del dret* (Barcelona: Ediuoc, 2000), 151–2.

[18] J. Pérez Royo, *Curso de derecho constitucional* (Madrid: Marcial Pons, 1999), 332.

Table 11.3 Explicit exception clause N5

Cases	S3	
	N5'	N5"
1) A & C	OB	¬ OB
2) ¬ A & C		
3) A & ¬ C	OB	
4) ¬ A & ¬ C		

with regard to the basic solution. This conclusion suggests that the statement according to which a norm introduces an exception to a norm implies that solutions for both are logically incompatible for a certain case, and that preference is given to the solution of one of them over that of the other one in case of conflict among them. Under this reconstruction, a normative system would not be just a set of norms, but an ordered set of norms.[19]

But once we have granted preference to the solution provided by the exception, the normative system (let us call it S4) might be reconstructed on the basis of the following norm:

$$\text{N6) } ((A \mathbin{\&} \neg C) \rightarrow OB) \mathbin{\&} ((A \mathbin{\&} C) \rightarrow \neg OB))$$

i.e. 'If A and not C, then OB, and if A and C, then not OB', in which N6 would represent a norm made up of a conjunction of two norms (N6' & N6"), such that:

$$\text{N6') } (A \mathbin{\&} \neg C) \rightarrow OB$$

$$\text{N6") } (A \mathbin{\&} C) \rightarrow \neg OB$$

The matrix of the system (let us call it S4) configured by N6 (N6' & N6") would show the consequences shown in Table 11.4.

This reconstruction assumes that the exception was dictated with the intention of modifying the content of the norm, excluding from its scope a particular case (A&C). Under this reconstruction there would be no incompatible solutions in the indicated case, and the problem of the original incoherence would be overcome.

Table 11.4 Explicit exception clause S4

Cases	S4	
	N6'	N6"
1) A & C		¬ OB
2) ¬ A & C		
3) A & ¬ C	OB	
4) ¬ A & ¬ C		

[19] P. Navarro and J. Rodríguez, 'Derrotabilidad y sistematización de normas jurídicas', *Isonomía*, 13 (2000), 75.

V

A variant of the previous case is that in which the exception is introduced through an explicit normative reference.[20] This is the case, for example, of the exception contemplated in Article 115.3 of the Spanish Constitution, which refers to Article 99.5, for the purposes of the established exception. In its paragraph 1, Article 115 stipulates that the President of the Government, after deliberation of the Council of Ministers, and on his exclusive responsibility, may propose the dissolution of the House of Representatives, the Senate, or the Cortes Generales (the Spanish parliament), which shall be decreed by the King; paragraph 3 further stipulates that no new dissolution may proceed before a year has passed since the previous one, except as provided for in Article 99, paragraph 5, which establishes that if, within two months from the first voting for investiture, no candidate has obtained the confidence of the House of Representatives, the King shall dissolve both Chambers and call for new elections with the endorsement of the President of the House of Representatives.

VI

Thus far, we have exposed the mechanism of exceptions in its logical-formal aspect, an approach to which everyday legal discourse attributes limited practical relevance. However, the analysis performed helps reveal a hidden condition of the legal technique: that the observer presumes that the introduction of an exception leads—where the condition for application of the general norm and also the condition of its exception are given—to the second condition prevailing over the first one to determine the normative consequence. Such a procedure does not expressly result from the law, but from the observer's appraisal (usually correct, though not for that reason less conjectural) about the intention of the writer of the norm. This same appraisal still constitutes a decision element contributed by the interpreter, based on certain regularity of the (imperfect) legal technique and with some degree of subjection to the value preference of the interpreter. This last factor may be fully appreciated when the interpreter finds an axiological gap and, directly based on his or her own relevance hypothesis, introduces a new exception under the banner of an 'implicit condition'.

It is relevant to point out, in this context, that whichever the result of the interpretative act in each case, a greater logical accuracy in the use of technical nomenclature would lead to a better clarity of the arguments that may be given in favour of or against each alternate interpretation, and, consequently, to a more intelligible use of the legal reasoning.

[20] It is claimed that a reference clause is, basically, that which indirectly determines the legal consequence of the case contemplated in the norm, through derivation to another norm. However, these reference clauses are considered complete, from a purely formal viewpoint, since they contain a case and a legal consequence, although they acquire full sense only in connection with those norms to which they refer. The reference constitutes, essentially, an adequate technical mechanism to avoid tiresome repetitions. See K. Larenz, *Metodología de la Ciencia del Derecho* (Barcelona: Ariel, 1966), 179–81.

12

Acts, Normative Formulations, and Defeasible Norms

*Ricardo Caracciolo**

I

The starting point of the problem I wish to discuss is the idea of *general norms* that impose duties of action. As is known, as a result of the solution proposed by David Ross for the problem of the conflict of moral duties, it is also accepted nowadays that some—or all—general norms are defeasible and, therefore, some—or all—duties of action are prima facie.

However, in spite of being widely used in the domain of ethics and the theory of law, the idea 'defeasible norm' and the correlative idea 'prima facie duty' must cause some perplexity. This is because they lead to a basic question: that of knowing how a defeasible norm *can* constitute a resolution to the practical question involved in the choice between mutually exclusive alternatives of action. This is equivalent to the question that must be posed regarding the relationship between prima facie duties and conclusive or definitive duties. Incidentally, it is possible to maintain that there is no relation whatsoever between the two types of duty, or between a 'defeasible' norm and another 'indefeasible' one. But it would appear that this would be tantamount to denying any practical relevance to defeasible norms. In this paper I will assume that any plausible explanation of defeasible norms must give an answer to this basic problem. Perhaps the most generalized response to this question indicates that in defeasible norms the conclusive normative solution—the duty with no qualification at all—is subject to *implicit exceptions*, that is, to exceptions not expressed in their content.

In this paper I propose to review and discuss a certain way of understanding this response in the domain of law, namely, that which results from the refined conception of defeasible languages of Carlos Alchourrón, which he called the *dispositional* approach (or conception) of the defeasibility of norms in his article 'On Law and Logic' and which constitutes a *pragmatic* version of defeasibility.[1] This version is especially adequate to provide an account of legal norms that are thought of as results of legislative acts, but which can be extended non-problematically to capture the way in which norms are *accepted* by their addressees.[2] As will be seen, this proposal is based on the systematic use of the distinction between *normative formulations* and *norms*. However, as will be shown, the *dispositional* approach implies a substantial alteration of the original presentation of the *pragmatic* conception of defeasibility. It will be maintained

* Professor of Legal Philosophy, National University of Córdoba.

[1] C.E. Alchourrón, 'On Law and Logic', in this volume, ch. 2.

[2] F. Schauer, *Playng by the Rules. A Philosophical of Rule-Based Decision-Making in Law and Life* (Oxford: Clarendon Press, 1991), ch. 5.

that this change is not plausible in light of reasons that also affect other versions of the defeasibility of norms.

II

What are in question, because the dispositional approach refers to them, are *legal norms* susceptible to being expressed as conditional formulations of the form, for example, N = 'if A then OB', where 'OB' indicates the duty to perform action B,[3] so long as the chain of events A occurs.[4] If that is the case, the duty to perform B, that is, the normative consequent OB can be inferred from N. But this is not possible if N is, or is considered, a *defeasible* norm, because in this case the consequence would be subject to *implicit exceptions*, to negative conditions that are not expressed in the explicit content of the formulation of N. Therefore, with regard to logical calculus, the deontic *modus ponens* rules are not valid here, nor that of the *strengthening of the antecedent*.[5] The formulation 'if A and A1 then OB' cannot be inferred from N if it is a defeasible norm, because –A1 *may* constitute an implicit condition in the conditional that N expresses.

But, within this framework, what in fact are *norms*? There is a direct and clear answer in 'On Law and Logic': norms are the *meanings* of normative formulations. Or, in Alchourrón's words, they are the conceptual contents associated to the expressions of a certain language and of a certain type.[6] Therefore, if indeed there are defeasible norms (legal or otherwise) then there are certain meanings that are defeasible. Alchourrón sometimes seems to suggest this conclusion when he states that:

> Many (if not all) normative formulations are defeasible, that is, they usually possess implicit exceptions that defeat *the norm*, although they are not explicitly stated.[7]

Nonetheless, if one accepts without further inspection what this paragraph says, one would reach a mistaken conclusion. As will soon be seen, according to the general conception of 'defeasibility' accepted by Alchourrón, defeasible norms *cannot exist*.

To prove this one must consider, first, that if it were possible to talk about 'defeasible norms', the *defeasibility* would be a property of *semantic* entities, because norms are the semantic analogy of *propositions*, if one admits that these are the meaning of descriptive linguistic formulations. But it seems that there is no sense in which it can be said that propositions are, or can be, defeated: propositions are true or false and the veritative value that corresponds to every proposition P *cannot* be altered in any way whatsoever or, as is sometimes said, they are eternally true or eternally false. The idea of 'defeasibility' implies the idea that some change is possible, but it seems that no change is possible with regard to propositions. Or, to put it differently, it seems that no other

[3] A controversy exists regarding the logical form of conditional normative sentences. Alchourrón chooses the so-called 'bridge' conception. The deontic operator qualifies the action that figures in the consequent. I shall not discuss this question here either.

[4] Other normative consequences are possible. Here, following Alchourrón, I shall restrict myself to the norms from which duties or obligations are derived. There is no doubt, however, that the considerations that follow may be extended to other defeasible conditionals.

[5] C.E. Alchourrón, 'Detachment and Defeasibility in Deontic Logic', *Studia Logica*, 57 (1196), 5–18.

[6] C.E. Alchourrón, 'Sobre Derecho y Lógica', *Isonomía*, 13 (2000), 20; C.E. Alchourrón, 'On Law and Logic', 44.

[7] C.E. Alchourrón, 'Sobre Derecho y Lógica', 24; and C.E. Alchourrón, 'On Law and Logic', 46, my emphasis.

criterion can be offered (or at least insofar as no such criterion is available) to distinguish 'defeasible' propositions on one hand from 'non-defeasible' ones on the other. However, *beliefs* can be defeated, if by this we mean that the propositions that constitute their contents can, finally, be false. Therefore, supposing this, beliefs are defeated and, if the agent is rational, he or she should modify them. It could be said that the property of 'validity' fulfils the truth function in relation to norms.[8] Then, in keeping with the analogy, one would have to conclude that norms either are valid or are not—that is, are invalid—and this property of each norm N cannot be *modified*, or to put it differently, the validity of N (or its invalidity) cannot be defeated. There is another argument—to which I shall refer further on—which serves to reach the same result, and it derives from the very notion of 'defeasibility' accepted by Alchourrón.

I further believe that he would have agreed with these considerations. But the truth is that, in the philosophical context of his idea of 'defeasibility', this feature *is not located* in the semantic dimension of language. That is to say, it is not located in the domain of norms or of propositions. Rather, what Alchourrón considers defeasible, or not, are conditional formulations, or sentences, or expressions (I shall use these terms as equivalents) with the form 'if A then B', which *must not be* confused with their meanings, that is to say, with the propositions they may express. Or to put it even more accurately, what are defeasible are certain statements that *use* these conditionals, within certain contexts. Which assumes, then, that defeasibility is a feature that may present itself in the pragmatic dimension of language.[9]

Indeed, Alchourrón says, the basic idea of defeasibility results from establishing that, in the everyday use of language, sometimes conditional constructions of the form 'if A then B' do not propose to say that A is a sufficient condition of B, but only that A in conjunction with a set of presuppositions (assumed or accepted by the user of the language) in the context in which the statement is made, are enough for consequent B.[10] This occurs, for example,

> when it is stated, with regard to a certain gas sample, that its volume will increase if the temperature is raised, assuming in the context that the pressure will remain constant... the conditional *statement* is defeated when any of its implicit presuppositions is false.[11]

Likewise:

> A defeasible conditional can also be defined as a conditional subject to implicit exceptions. In the example a variation in the gas pressure constitutes an implicit exception that defeats the conditional statement.[12]

This notion of 'defeasibility', which he associates with the idea of 'implicit exception', is, as is known, widely accepted in the current discussion on defeasible norms,[13] even though, as I shall attempt to show, it is incompatible with the thesis that defeasible norms exist or can exist.

[8] At least in some concept of 'validity'. The discussion regarding different concepts of validity, as well as that which refers to the nature of truth, is not necessary in this essay.

[9] C.E. Alchourrón, 'Sobre Derecho y Lógica', 28; and C.E. Alchourrón, 'On Law and Logic', 49.

[10] C.E. Alchourrón, 'Detachment and Defeasibility in Deontic Logic', 8; C.E. Alchourrón, 'Sobre Derecho y Lógica', 23; and C.E. Alchourrón, 'On Law and Logic', 46. See also C.E. Alchourrón and E. Bulygin, 'Norma Jurídica' in E. Garzón Valdés and F. Laporta (eds), *El Derecho y la Justicia. Enciclopedia Iberoamericana de Filosofía* (Madrid: Trotta, 1996), 145.

[11] C.E. Alchourrón, 'Sobre Derecho y Lógica', 23, my emphasis.

[12] Ibid., 23.

[13] See, for example, J.C. Bayón, 'Derrotabilidad, Indeterminación del Derecho y Positivismo Jurídico', *Isonomía*, 13 (2000), 87–117.

Some observations can be added regarding Alchourrón's proposal. Defeasibility here is s predicate of certain statements—that is, of certain linguistic acts—as of the conditional sentences or expressions that are used in such acts. As these are different alternatives, the question—which in my opinion is relevant—could be asked regarding what the relationships are between the defeasibility of statements and the defeasibility of conditionals. It would seem that, if we remember to place this question at a pragmatic level, the priority corresponds to the way in which language is used. This is because it is obvious that conditional statements of the form 'if A then B' are possible, *without any presupposition whatsoever*, for example, because the speaker believes that if A is reached B is also reached. In this case, it cannot be said that the corresponding conditional has implicit exceptions, that is to say, it is not a defeasible conditional. A different matter is to know whether the proposition expressed in this conditional is true or false. Supposing, in the gas example, that a certain individual x *believes* that the increase in temperature is enough to increase the volume of any sample of gas. In such a case, both x's belief and the proposition that constitutes its content are false, but neither the statement nor the conditional are defeasible. Therefore, the question of knowing whether a conditional expression is defeasible or not *depends* on whether a certain user accepts or not assumptions he or she does not mention. Because only if the answer is affirmative can it be considered that the conditional sentence 'is subject to implicit exceptions'. An important consequence follows from this: there are no *defeasible conditionals*, independent of intentional acts in the use of language. That is to say, there is no such thing as the 'objective defeasibility' of certain sentences.

The following question is to know what the relation is between defeasible formulations and propositions. Or, in the words of Alchourrón, that of knowing what the *conceptual content* expressed in a statement of a user on a particular occasion is. It is evident that any conditional statement actually uttered there corresponds, in all cases, to a conditional proposition of the form 'if A then B', which may be true or false (but not defeasible). But the question of defeasibility is addressed precisely to show that, in certain contexts the statement is carried out under certain assumptions, for example, under the assumption of the absence of a circumstance C (e.g. the variation of the gas pressure). When this is the case, the conceptual content (that is, the proposition expressed in that definite linguistic act) must be *integrated* into the list of all the assumptions admitted by the speaker or, what amounts to the same, of all the implicit exceptions of the corresponding defeasible conditional. The content of meaning here depends, then, not on what is actually *said*, but on what the user of the language *means to say*. If what he or she means to say with 'if A then B' is that A in conjunction with the absence of C is a sufficient condition of B, then the conditional expressing *this* conceptual content is, strictly speaking, 'if A and –C then B'. The 'defeat' of a defeasible statement occurs—says Alchourrón—when one of the implicit assumptions is false, that is to say, when a circumstance assumed as an exception is verified. But this in no way whatsoever implies the falsehood of the proposition expressed in the conditional 'if A and –C then B', which is what the speaker really wishes to state. It can only be said that the conditions are not given for consequence B to occur. In any case, the proposition that is, or is considered false is 'if A and C then B'. There seems to be, then, a certain asymmetry between the defeasible sentences or formulations and their respective conceptual contents. While statements may be defeated, they cannot be directly qualified as true or false if one is to respect the speaker's intention, whereas the respective propositions—those that the user *wishes* to express—are true or false, but cannot be defeated.[14]

III

These ideas constitute the counterpart of the formalism Alchourrón proposes for the logic of defeasible conditionals. To represent, first, the joint statement of the proposition expressed by a sentence A and the set of presuppositions of A assumed by a user, a *revision operator f* is used. Thus—says Alchourrón—if A1, A2, . . . An indicates this set, *f*A symbolizes the conjunction of A with all the assumptions Ai, where i is equal to or greater than 1 and equal to or less than n.[15] This last phrase is really important: it indicates that *f*A is a function that determines a *finite* set. This must be so because for any user of the language x, x can *in fact* only assume a finite set of assumptions (what would assuming an infinite set of assumptions mean?).

Second, the symbol '>' has been proposed to represent the connective of a defeasible conditional. That is, if the conditional 'if A then B' is assumed to be 'defeasible', then its representation is 'A>B'. Once again, what I am interested in emphasizing here is what Alchourrón says about the conditions of truth of defeasible conditionals. So, according to the intuitive idea that he is attempting to formalize—which constitutes his *conception* of defeasibility—a defeasible conditional A>B, used by a speaker x, is true when A in conjunction with the assumptions associated to A, that is to say *f*A, is a sufficient condition for the consequent B. Or what amounts to the same, when a strict conditional whose antecedent is *f*A and whose consequent is B is true. What is more, in Alchourrón's proposal, a defeasible conditional is, by definition, equal to its correlative strict conditional.[16] It follows from this that they express the *same proposition*.

There is no question, then, of truth or falsehood with regard to a defeasible conditional before specifying its revision function, that is, before identifying its strict conditional. A defeasible conditional—of itself—is not proposed to describe world states, according to the speaker's intentions. This, in part, explains why the logic of these sentences is not monotonic. In turn, identifying this strict conditional is *equivalent* to identifying the proposition which, in this context, the speaker actually wishes to express. Therefore, once the proposition has been identified, *there are no implicit exceptions*. In truth, I find no sense in which a conceptual entity, such as a proposition is, can have an implicit content. Indeed there can always be an error regarding the question of knowing what the presuppositions assumed by an individual are and, therefore, it is possible to fail to capture the propositions associated with his or her statements. These assumptions—according to Alchourrón—are linked to the idea of

[14] Since the truth, or falsehood—in the version accepted by Alchourrón—is predicated on the conceptual contents, that is to say, on the propositions and not directly on the formulations that express them, it is inexact to say that 'in relation to a defeasible conditional, "if A then B" can be true and "if A and C then B" can be false'. C.E. Alchourrón, 'Sobre Derecho y Lógica', 23. The same is reiterated in C.E. Alchourrón and E. Bulygin, 'Norma Jurídica', 145. This is because the proposition expressed in 'if A then B' *says* that A is a sufficient condition of B and cannot be true if the one that expresses 'if A and C then B' is false. The exclusion of the rule of strengthening of the antecedent—which prevents the implication relationship—works with regard to defeasible conditionals. But these conditionals, once again with Alchourrón's idea, do not express directly the propositions that the speaker wishes to express.

[15] C.E. Alchourrón, 'Detachment and Defeasibility in Deontic Logic', 9.

[16] Ibid., 9.

what normally occurs, whose content can vary in different contexts and in relation to different individuals. It is an empirical question, similar to that of determining the extent of the terms used by a user in natural language. As Carnap indicates, all that can be proposed for this are fallible hypotheses based on verbal behaviour.[17] But this does not affect the theoretical conclusion relative to the relation between the defeasible conditionals and propositions.

IV

This set of ideas, which reconstructs Alchourrón's conception of *defeasibility*, can be extrapolated to the assumptions of normative languages: especially to defeasible normative conditionals. For this, formalism incorporates the standard deontic obligation operator O as a primitive term, such that O(B) indicates the non-defeasible duty to perform action B. In turn, another operator *d*O is proposed to capture the idea of a defeasible duty. Therefore, *d*O(B) serves to express the defeasible duty to carry out a certain action B or, as it is also named, the prima facie duty B. If the defeasible duty B is conditional, then the corresponding sentence is also defeasible. And the inverse is also valid: if an obligation normative conditional is, or is considered defeasible, then the consequent of the conditional is an obligation or defeasible duty. So that the prima facie duty B, under condition A, is formalized as $(A > OB)$.[18] Nor is the principle of the strengthening of the antecedent admitted in relation to these expressions, nor the rule of derivation of *modus ponens*. This inferential incapacity, in relation to obtaining an unconditional duty, shows that normative defeasible conditionals *are not applicable* because the standard model for applying norms—also accepted by Alchourrón[19]—identifies this with a deductive operation which consists (in part) in using this derivation rule.[20]

Likewise, just as descriptive defeasible conditionals are, so normative ones are formulated under certain unmentioned assumptions. This means that they are subject to implicit exceptions and explains why they are not *directly applicable*. Therefore, according to the considerations above, the norms a user of normative defeasible conditionals intends to express do not result from the explicit content of the corresponding formulations. These conceptual contents—that is, the norms—are the result of a revision f, which selects the assumptions assumed by it or by the individuals who use the language, for example, by a legislator L, on a particular occasion. Once again, here they do not depend on what L said, but on what he actually wished to say. A defeasible normative conditional of the form $(A>OB)$ is defined, then, in terms of a strict conditional whose antecedent is fA (the revision of A) and whose consequent is

[17] R. Carnap, 'Meaning and Synonymy in Natural Languages' in R. Carnap, *Meaning and Necessity. A Study in Semantics and Modal Logic* (Chicago: The University of Chicago Press, 1967). Carnap supposes, to know the extent of a defined term used by a speaker of a language, a defined region of actual objects and, in this measure, a finite set. Further on I shall suggest that the change in Alchourrón's ideas that I propose to revise, implies the same step that Carnap says must be taken to know the intention or the meaning of the same term.

[18] C.E. Alchourrón, 'Detachment and Defeasibility in Deontic Logic', 15.

[19] C.E. Alchourrón and E. Bulygin, *Normative Systems* (Vienna: Springer, 1971), 153ff.

[20] In the words of Alchourrón: 'Another important point regarding the notion of defeasible duty is that from a conditional sentence of defeasible obligation and the truth of its antecedent no unconditional duty may be validly derived. This is so because jointly with the antecedent there may occur a defeating fact that overrules the obligation. Hence, we expect the non-validity of so-called rule of factual detachment or deontic *modus ponens*'. C.E. Alchourrón, 'Detachment and Defeasibility in Deontic Logic', 6. The fact that no duty (neither non-defeasible nor defeasible) can be derived shows that the normative defeasible conditionals are inapplicable.

the non-defeasible duty to perform B, that is to say, OB. This definition shows that the underlying idea is that both conditional formulations have the same conceptual content or, to put it another way, *express* the same norm.[21]

One consequence is that, in the logic of normative conditionals, what Alchourrón calls a 'special form of deontic *modus ponens*' is admitted, allowing for the derivation of a defeasible duty to perform B under condition A, that is to say, of (A>OB), and of the revision *f* of A (*f* A), that is, of A plus all the implicit assumptions, the non-defeasible duty to perform B. So that, finally, the applicable norm is the one expressed in the corresponding strict conditional.[22] This equivalence in the conceptual contents of the two types of conditionals has an important consequence which, I believe, also follows from Alchourrón's conception. It shows, finally, why norms and propositions cannot be defeasible. As 'defeasibility' assumes, by definition, the presence of implicit exceptions, the defeat of a norm (or of a proposition) *should* show the presence of a fact or circumstance that prevents its application (or the descriptive use of a proposition). But norms (and propositions) are *meanings*, that is to say, conceptual contents and there is no sense in which it can be said that a conceptual content has an implicit content. Only formulations allow for the explicit–implicit distinction. Therefore, norms and propositions lack implicit exceptions. From this it follows that neither norms nor propositions can be defeasible.

It is obvious that a *norm* cannot be applied to derive normative consequences before its identification, in the same way that a proposition cannot be used to describe world states prior to its identification. So that the specification of the revision of a certain formulation is equivalent to identifying a norm or, in its case, a proposition. Therefore, showing that a defeasible conditional is defeated by the presence of a circumstance C can be thought of as a step in the identification process, insofar as it indicates that the absence of C is included in the set that results from the revision.

There is, nonetheless, an important distinction that must be made between descriptive defeasible conditionals and normative defeasible conditionals. In the first case, the circumstances or events that constitute their conditions (explicit or implicit) are proposed to describe world states. So their implicit assumptions are descriptive assumptions. What defeats these conditionals is, then, the falsehood of these descriptions, for example the falsehood of the description according to which the pressure of a gas sample has not changed. In the second case, these conditions are events or circumstances that are considered *valuable* for determining the normative consequence, for example the duty to perform a certain action A. Its election is the result of value judgements.[23] Its mention is not merely descriptive. Therefore, its revision function

21 In another paper, Alchourrón says 'a defeasible conditional is a *strict conditional* (which reconstructs the notion of sufficient reason) in whose antecedent figures the *statement of revision*'. C.E. Alchourrón, 'Para una Lógica de las Razones *Prima Facie*', *Análisis Filósofico*, 16 (1996), 114. The italics are CA's; the underlining is mine. However, insofar as a defeasible conditional and a strict conditional are distinct formulations, the identity that Alchourrón indicates must refer to the conceptual contents.

22 Alchourrón says, in relation to this rule of *deontic modus ponens*: 'This principle is very important, for it shows that whenever we have a defeasible conditional duty and also the antecedent *jointly with its assumptions*, the actual duty of the consequent follows. The law makes explicit the cases in which a *prima facie* duty gives rise to an actual duty, showing in this way, a logical interconnection that holds between these two kinds of duties.' C.E. Alchourrón, 'Detachment and Defeasibility in Deontic Logic', 16, CA's italics. There is no doubt that this 'logical interconnection' is a consequence of the fact that a defeasible conditional is defined in terms of a strict conditional, or equivalently, a prima facie duty is defined in terms of a non-defeasible duty.

23 C.E. Alchourrón and E. Bulygin, *Normative Systems*, 11.

must select the result of implicit valuations that must be attributed to the user of normative language, for example, a legislator L. The defeat of a normative conditional occurs when a fact or circumstance that L has valued implicitly as an exception, that is to say, a negative condition, occurs. Once again, this does not mean that the *norm* that constitutes the conceptual content of such a conditional is invalid or non-valid, but that in the absence of a condition it is directly inapplicable.[24]

If the above analysis is correct, in order to preserve the symmetry with the descriptive conditionals, the circumstances admitted as implicit exceptions of the defeasible normative conditional formulated by L must result from L's actual valuations, even though they have not been expressed, for example, because it is assumed that the addressees of the norms produced by share the same value judgements. That is, they *can* receive the normative message he attempts to transmit. This is a condition that ensures the finite character of the assumptions admitted by the user of a language and which corresponds with the notion of *revision* proposed by Alchourrón. Nevertheless, the addressee of a norm N may have a discrepancy with L's value judgements and, consequently, associate value assumptions to the formulation that are different from and even inconsistent with those accepted by the legislator. Which means that—as Alchourrón indicates—the addressee associates with the defeasible normative conditional a norm that is not actually produced by L. It must be remembered that this norm—that is, the one that is expressed in the corresponding strict conditional—depends on this pattern of what L wishes to do. A change in the valuations implies, then, a change in the conceptual contents, that is to say, a change in the norms.[25]

V

As has already been indicated, upon raising the question in relation to legal norms, Alchourrón says in 'On Law and Logic' that:

> [m]any (if not all) normative formulations are defeasible, that is, they usually possess implicit exceptions.[26]

In principle, this statement is surprising. From the point of view of a pragmatic version of defeasibility, the question of knowing which formulations are defeasible and which are not depends on the attitude with which a certain legislator L *uses* normative language. It is therefore a question of fact, which will have to be relativized to each of the corresponding linguistic acts. It may be that what he intended to say is that legislative practice is characterized by this way of producing norms. But it does not seem possible to accept—without further inspection—this incidental empirical generalization of Alchourrón's. Another question is to know whether many or nearly all of

[24] It is normal in the literature to consider only the case of negative conditions, that is to say, the presence of a certain circumstance C as an implicit exception. In such a way that if a conditional of the form 'if A then B' incorporates as an exception the circumstance C, then the strict conditional would be 'if A and –C then B'. But this is not necessary: the defeasible conditional '–A then B' can have as an exception the absence of C, or what amounts to the same, the strict conditional can demand the presence of C. So the formal representation would then have to be 'if –A and C then B'.

[25] A search of the implicit value assumptions is a form of the well-known legal argument that attempts to identify legal norms attending to the 'legislator's intentions', which usually—as Alchourrón also indicates—is a rhetorical form of assigning the interpreter's valuations to legislator L. This is equivalent, if indeed the content of law is a function of legislative intentions—as Alchourrón also seems to assume—to modifying law. C.E. Alchourrón, 'Sobre Derecho y Lógica', 28; and C.E. Alchourrón, 'On Law and Logic', 49. I shall not discuss this idea regarding the content of law in this paper.

[26] C.E. Alchourrón, 'Sobre Derecho y Lógica', 24; and C.E. Alchourrón, 'On Law and Logic', 46.

these formulations destined to integrate the content of law *should* be considered defeasible, from some value point of view, that is to say, that it is better to consider that they are always revisable. Many theorists of law would perhaps be prepared to adopt this thesis. However, it is clear that this idea assumes a sort of 'objective defeasibility' (independent of the intentions of the language user) which does not correspond at all with the pragmatic conception that Alchourrón proposes. His criterion for identifying the content of law that *is*, and not of law that *should be*, consists of considering that legal norms are the result of 'speech acts' and that, therefore, one must bear in mind 'the set of the emitter's factual and value beliefs'.[27] However, as I shall attempt to show immediately, the *change* in the conception of defeasibility that is proposed in this article not only explains this generalization, but also allows us to infer that *all* (and not just some) normative formulations are defeasible.

Be that as it may, the implicit exceptions to the defeasible normative formulation depend—in Alchourrón's conception—on this set of beliefs and, in turn, the *conceptual content*, that is to say, the norm expressed in this linguistic act depends on determining what these implicit exceptions are. Thus, Alchourrón says:

> [u]nless the implicit exceptions have been made explicit, the conceptual content of the normative expression remains indeterminate.[28]

Or what amounts to the same, there is no way of knowing what the norm produced by legislator L is. Therefore, the crucial question is to determine how to identify implicit exceptions, which is equivalent to identifying the *meaning* attributed to a certain formulation.

To answer this question, in 'On Law and Logic', Alchourrón proposes a strategy based on what he calls the 'dispositional notion of defeasibility', which involves an alteration to his original conception. According to this proposal, a certain characteristic or property C counts as an implicit exception to a conditional of the form 'if A then B' if the emitter L, at the time of emission T, has at T the disposition to accept this conditional and, at the same time, the disposition to reject the conditional 'if A and C then B'. This shows, says Alchourrón, that L *would have* formulated exception C if he *had considered* the case of the conjunction 'A and C'. Therefore, the exception of the presence of C *integrates* the conceptual content expressed in the corresponding linguistic act. On the contrary, one must consider that condition C is an implicit non-exception, if at T legislator L has the disposition to accept 'if A then B' jointly with the conditional 'if A and C then B'. Which is the case if he had considered the presence of C irrelevant from the point of view of value. If at time T there is no disposition at all attributable to L with regard to circumstance C, then 'the character of C as an exception

[27] C.E. Alchourrón, 'Sobre Derecho y Lógica', 25; and C.E. Alchourrón, 'On Law and Logic', 47. It is, of course, a version of the classic thesis that privileges legislative intentions for this task of identification. Two arguments are possible against this thesis: the first says that there is no theoretical reason to go further, in this task, than what the legislator actually *said*, if indeed norms are conceptual contents, because the meaning of the language depends on shared, that is to say, public rules and not on subjective components. The second says that legislative acts are, normally, collective actions. A 'collective action' is a theoretical construction which, although it takes into account the preferences of a set of individuals, cannot be attributed to any one of them. Therefore, no one of them is the 'legislator' or 'emitter' of the norms. If this is so, there is no way of knowing the 'intentions' or the 'beliefs' insofar as they are mental states of the legislators, because they simply do not exist. The legislator is also a theoretical artifice. On this point see F. Studnicki, 'On Institutional Decisions', *Archiv für Rechts und Sozial Philosophie*, 57 (1971), 469–84. However, I shall not discuss these objections in this paper.

[28] C.E. Alchourrón, 'Sobre Derecho y Lógica', 24.

becomes indeterminate. Consequently, the conceptual content of the conditional will also be indeterminate in relation to C.'[29] Alchourrón continues, in order to make his idea even more precise:

> Suppose that the legislator at the time of enacting a statute *did not foresee a certain circumstance C.* Of course, at that time he was not in a position to present C as an explicit exception, but if it is the case that, had he considered C, he *would have introduced* it as an exception, the dispositional account considers C as an implicit exception even at the time of the enactment. In *the norm* expressed by the statute, C is an exception.[30]

This implies that, given that at that moment C is normatively relevant for determining the normative consequence, C is a *valuable* characteristic from the point of view of the legislator.[31] The *meaning* of the formulation used in the legislative act depends then on what the characteristics of implicit exceptions are, on one hand, and those that are implicit non-exceptions on the other, according to what the counterfactual value judgements are.

The revision of this paragraph immediately shows the nature of the modification, genuinely substantial, to the former conception of 'defeasibility'. It assumes shifting the criterion of identification of the conceptual content of what legislator L wished to say, according to the value assumptions he actually accepts, to the counterfactual consideration of what he *would have wished* to say if he had valued certain circumstances. It is true that, in one sense, the idea of 'disposition' also fulfils a function in the first version of defeasibility, because if L says 'if A then OB' and actually accepts C as an implicit exception, it can be stated that L is disposed to support the conditional 'if A and not –C then OB'. The disposition here refers *only* to the performance of a linguistic act, supported by its beliefs and value judgements. But the new version incorporates a much more complex class of behavioural disposition: given that, by hypothesis, L has not considered the absence or presence of C at all, what counts is his disposition to effect valuations that he has not yet made. Therefore, given that, by definition, the empirical legislator is not omniscient, there will always be circumstances whose occurrence has not been foreseen. In no case, then, can the *meaning* associated with a certain normative formulation depend on its explicit content, because it will always be necessary to determine for this what the value dispositions are in relation to these circumstances. Which explains why, if this direction is followed, all normative formulations will have to be considered defeasible.[32] This alteration in the conception of defeasibility is, nonetheless, implausible. This leads to a virtual indetermination of the conceptual contents that must be associated with legislative acts and, therefore, with the

[29] C.E. Alchourrón, 'Sobre Derecho y Lógica', 25; and C.E. Alchourrón, 'On Law and Logic', 47.

[30] Ibid.; and Ibid., my emphasis.

[31] With this proposal, Alchourrón eliminates the distinction which—together with Eugenio Bulygin—he proposed in *Normative Systems*, between the 'thesis of relevance', understood as the set of properties that explicitly condition normative consequences, and the legislator's 'relevance hypothesis', understood as the set of properties that the legislator would have valued if he had considered them. C.E. Alchourrón and E. Bulygin, *Normative Systems*, 107.

[32] As it is of no interest here to know what L *meant* to say and only of interest to know what he *would have wished* to say at time T, it might be that, in fact, L has used normative language without any actual assumption at all. This is also an important alteration to the original idea of 'defeasibility'. L's actual value judgements are only indicators of some of his axiological dispositions. But for the new version and according to the following argument, to determine the conceptual content of a certain formulation one must revise *all* of L's dispositions at time T.

impossibility of identifying the content of law, at least in relation to a conception of law that depends on such acts.[33]

VI

This consequence results, first, from what can be called the 'problem of the limit of dispositions'. The idea regarding normative relevance that underlies Alchourrón's new proposal is, no doubt, a version of what is called the dispositional theory of value. In its general formulation a theory of this type should maintain, according to David Lewis:

> [s]omething of the appropriate category is a value *if and only if* we would be disposed, under ideal conditions, to value it.[34]

This is so because, for Alchourrón too, normative relevance, that is, the value of a certain circumstance, does not depend now on actual value judgements, but on dispositions to perform these judgements counterfactually in certain definite conditions. It is not essential for what I intend to show to know whether for Alchourrón these conditions need to be 'ideal'. The minimum needed for a dispositional approach of value is to take into account the circumstances that the legislator has, in fact, not considered. Here it is interesting to emphasize that, according to Lewis's formulation, if there is no disposition of the individual or individuals considered, with regard to 'something in the appropriate category', then the object or circumstance in question is not a value or, if you like, is indifferent to value. As the dispositions are limited, there will always be, then, circumstances or objects or actions that lack value. This would mean—for the discussion proposed in this paper—that they are irrelevant in determining normative consequences. Or to put it differently, if at time T the legislator lacks the disposition to concede value to circumstance C, then its presence or absence would have to be considered indifferent from the point of view of value, according to Lewis's version, because, according to it, the existence of a disposition is a sufficient and *necessary* condition for the *constitution* of value. Therefore, situations of axiological doubt or uncertainty of the agent do not count for assigning value, from his or her point of view. It follows from this that, if it is admitted that only circumstances that L would have valued if he had considered them can be implicit exceptions, the limit of the dispositions should supply a criterion for determining the limit of implicit exceptions. Those that do not constitute implicit exceptions—what Alchourrón calls 'non-exceptions'—would thus simply be the complementary set of circumstances considered valuable and there would be no further distinction to make.[35]

[33] I refer to the idea in law that recognizes legislation as one of its sources. One consequence of this idea is that law *can* change if new normative promulgation acts are performed. But for the mention of 'changes' to make sense, it is necessary for the norms being changed to be identified. If this is not possible, no change is possible, it would seem.

[34] D. Lewis, 'Dispositional Theories of Value' in D. Lewis, *Papers in Ethics and Social Philosophy* (Cambridge: Cambridge University Press, 2000), 68, my emphasis.

[35] All of this counts under the indisputable condition, at least in the context of Alchourrón's conception, according to which the *norms* a legislator L is disposed to produce depend on his value dispositions. Thus, his superficial dispositions to use language in certain ways and not in others would have to be considered a reflection of his value dispositions. If L is disposed to state 'if A then OB' in conjunction with 'if A and C then OB', this shows that he lacks the disposition to value C. But the case in which L does not have the disposition to state 'if A and C then OB' nor the disposition to state 'if A and not –C then OB', it also shows, according to Lewis's formula, that C is irrelevant to L, because there is no disposition to value C.

But Alchourrón does not follow this strategy. As has been indicated above, according to his thesis, if at time T L lacks the disposition to accept the axiological relevance of a circumstance C, or to reject it, its condition as an implicit exception remains definitively indeterminate. Therefore, says Alchourrón, 'the conceptual content of the conditional will also be indeterminate in relation to C'.[36] This is a consequence of the limit of L's value dispositions. It follows that, if the conceptual content that must be associated with a linguistic act necessarily depends on identifying *all* the implicit exceptions of the corresponding defeasible conditional and some of them cannot be identified,[37] then *all* the conceptual content remains indeterminate. This implies that *there is no meaning* that can be attributed definitively to the conditional used in the legislative act.[38] It is therefore inexact to say—as Alchourrón does—that the members of a court of law, when trying a case, can change the legislated norm, according to their own value convictions, if they incorporate as an exception a circumstance whose condition, in this sense, is indeterminate.[39] Because according to his own idea, in such an assumption, there is no such norm that can be modified.

What is more, given the limit of legislators' dispositions, one would have to conclude that in no case can legislative acts produce norms in the strict sense, since there will always be axiologically indeterminate circumstances. It is a notoriously implausible consequence, which could be avoided—as has been indicated—if Lewis's version regarding the dispositional theory of value were adopted, because according to this theory, these circumstances could not be included in the set of valuable circumstances for the legislator, i.e. in the set of normatively relevant circumstances.

Nonetheless, even if it were modified in this direction, this conception of Alchourrón's regarding 'defeasibility' cannot overcome what can be called 'the problem of necessary indetermination'. As has already been indicated, in this conception the conceptual contents of the normative expressions used by a legislator L at a time T depend on L's value dispositions at T, because this explains why he is willing to accept certain circumstances as implicit exceptions. Therefore, in relation to C, it is true that: (1) 'If L had valued C, then C is an implicit exception'. But to know what *all* L's actual dispositions are, it is necessary to consider *all* the possible circumstances because, by hypothesis, the dispositional approach of defeasibility refers counterfactually to circumstances that the legislator *has in fact not considered*. Otherwise, there is no way of knowing what his value dispositions are.[40] The following generalization must therefore be accepted: (2) 'For all circumstances C, if L had valued C then C is an implicit exception'. Which implies with regard to a circumstance C that, if it is true—

[36] C.E. Alchourrón, 'Sobre Derecho y Lógica', 25.

[37] In order to avoid confusion, it should be insisted upon that this impossibility does not result from possible obstacles to knowing the actual dispositions of a legislator, it is a conceptual consequence of the limited character of these dispositions.

[38] Nor could it be said that L's actual dispositions allow one to assign a 'partial meaning' to the normative conditional, because this would have to be understood either as the attribute of the legislative act of a *norm*, regardless of the indeterminate characteristics, against what Alchourrón says, or that it is an incomplete meaning, which is another way of saying that a norm has not yet been identified.

[39] C.E. Alchourrón, 'Sobre Derecho y Lógica', 27; and C.E. Alchourrón, 'On Law and Logic', 48.

[40] The idea according to which the *meaning* that must be associated with the statements used by a speaker depends on his or her dispositions in relation to all possible circumstances is, strictly speaking, analogous to Carnap's methodological proposal to determine the *intention*, that is, the concept, associated with a term used in the practice of a language. According to this proposal—which I shall not discuss here—it is necessary to consider the dispositions of the speakers in relation to all possible objects. R. Carnap, 'Meaning and Synonymy in Natural Languages'.

according to his actual dispositions—that L had valued C, it is also true that (3) 'C is an implicit exception'.

But the possible circumstances do not constitute a finite set. This means that at time T there will always be some additional circumstance in relation to which it is necessary to question what L's dispositions are in order to know if they are an implicit exception or not at time T. The question of knowing what the *meaning* is—that is to say, the norm—associated with a formulation F depends necessarily on being able to draw up a finite list of type (3) sentences. But it is not possible to design such a list.[41] Consequently, it would have to be admitted that the *meaning* of F is *necessarily* indeterminate.[42] As this counts for all formulations, the conclusion is that there is no meaning associated with normative defeasible conditionals.

This is so because what cannot be determined is a finite set that constitutes the *revision* of formulation F. It must be remembered that this revision function is what allows us to know what is the set that represents a sufficient condition of the consequent of a normative conditional. Which leads to another important consequence. For Alchourrón, the normative relevance of a certain circumstance C explicitly mentioned in a normative conditional depends on it constituting a contributory condition, i.e. a necessary condition of a sufficient condition. That is, C is a contributory condition in a normative conditional F, and therefore *relevant* in F if, and only if, there exists a finite set of circumstances K such that (i) K is a sufficient condition of the duty to perform the action mentioned in F, and (ii) C is an element of K. If there is no set K, there is no sufficient condition of the duty and, therefore, the statement according to which C is a contributory condition cannot be justified. Or what amounts to the same thing, it cannot be said that C is relevant, despite its explicit mention in the normative conditional.[43]

This result is theoretically unfortunate, amongst other reasons, because it contradicts the admissible intuition according to which there will always be a *norm*, that is to say, a meaning which, whatever the difficulties in determining it, can be associated with each legislative act. After all, they are intelligible acts. It therefore shows that the modification of the original conception of defeasibility is not acceptable. While the problem of the limit of value dispositions could be overcome, the one that refers to the unlimited character of possible circumstances is far more serious for the so-called dispositional conception of defeasibility. What is needed to deal with it is a criterion for determining a finite set of circumstances which must be considered when establishing the meaning of a defeasible conditional. But it does not seem possible to defend such a criterion, compatible with this conception.

[41] The problem of the indetermination of all the 'possible circumstances' is presented here as an ontological question. But the same result is reached if it is considered an epistemological obstacle, relative to the impossibility of its knowledge.

[42] It must be remembered that it is determining the actual meaning associated with a linguistic act that is being attempted, because that is what results from Alchourrón's conception. Another alternative, which does not lead to this problem, is to answer the much more plausible question of what the meaning of F would have been if L had considered a circumstance C. This assumes that F has actual meaning, independently of L's value dispositions. This option is, incidentally, compatible with Alchourrón's initial proposal.

[43] The explicit mention of C implies, of course, that legislator L has effectively valued the presence of C. It could therefore be argued that its normative relevance results exclusively from this mention. But, by hypothesis, C *is not* a sufficient condition of the duty. It is only relevant if it contributes to obtaining the duty. But if there is no set K, that is, *one* sufficient condition, nor are there any contributing conditions.

Alchourrón himself appears to have considered the problem, and an answer, in suggesting that:

as unforeseen circumstances, due to their very nature, cannot be made explicit, it seems sensible to leave the formulation of exceptions open for *abnormal* cases.[44]

But this proposal only shifts it, without resolving it. First, it is clear that the qualification of 'abnormal' with regard to a certain circumstance C is not enough to count as an exception to a normative conditional. In any case, it is necessary to know what legislator L's actual disposition is with regard to C. Therefore for every abnormal circumstance C, one would have to know what the dispositions were before knowing if it is an implicit exception or not. But the list of 'abnormal' circumstances cannot constitute a finite set *either.*[45] It seems that the only way out might be to propose an external criterion to L's attitudes, according to which a finite set of circumstances could be determined, and then question oneself about his value dispositions, in relation to the components of this set. But this criterion could only result from an *objective* value judgement, in the sense that it must be independent of what L would have accepted or rejected if he had considered these circumstances. It is a value judgement because one must necessarily select a subset of the possible circumstances. But if there were a criterion of this type, one could take a step further and select directly what the relevant normative characteristics are, regardless of the legislators' subjective judgements.[46] It could, however, be asked whether an objectivist proposal of this type—which involves abandoning a pragmatic conception of defeasibility—constitutes a solution to the problem. The answer must be negative, if we are to assume that the domain of value judgements should be made up of all the possible circumstances. Because in this case, as a result of the indetermination of the function of choice, one could not draw up a finite list of exceptions for every final or conclusive duty. Which means—if the argument put forward in this paper is accepted—that it is not therefore possible to associate norms with normative formulations considered defeasible, inside any conception of normative defeasibility which makes use of counterfactual analysis of value judgements to identify norms. So, normative formulations will be not useful to resolve practical problems, because they will not allow one to reach a final solution. It seems, then, that the plausible alternative is to return to Alchourrón's first proposal about general defeasibility.

[44] C.E. Alchourrón, 'Sobre Derecho y Lógica', 26, my emphasis.

[45] The inverse of what happens with the idea of a 'normal' circumstance according to L's own consideration or that of a third party. Because whatever the criterion for normality, the 'normal' circumstances are always a finite subset of all the possible circumstances. This implies that 'abnormal' circumstances, which are the set complementary to the 'normal' ones, cannot constitute a finite set because the possible circumstances are not finite.

[46] I think one can reconstruct in this way what some non-positivist version of law would maintain with regard to the idea of normative relevance.

PART III

DEFEASIBILITY AND THE CONCEPTIONS OF LAW

13

Legal Defeasibility and the Connection between Law and Morality

*José Juan Moreso**

I

One of the most important questions in recent legal positivist literature is how legal adjudication mirrors the positivist law identification thesis, i.e. what are the legal adjudicative consequences of understanding the nature of law in a certain way? And, particularly, whether the identification of law depends on moral considerations or not. Here, I shall defend the position that the identification of law can depend on moral considerations, but it need not depend on them. And I shall try to show that this conception of the nature of law allows us to obtain an adequate image of the adjudication of law, an image which both fits the legal practice and provides us with fruitful theoretical tools.

The fact that the identification of law depends on moral considerations is, obviously, entangled with our understanding of the identification thesis, which is usually presented through certain versions of the so-called social sources thesis, according to which both the existence and the content of the law in a certain society depend on a set of social facts, i.e. a set of actions by the members of that society. The existence of law is not a natural phenomenon, absolutely independent of us. The existence of law is not like the existence of planets and stars. The truth of the statement that the Earth is round does not depend on our beliefs and attitudes; even if all human beings believed the Earth to be flat, it would not be true that the Earth is flat. The roundness of the Earth is a natural phenomenon. On the contrary, the existence of *queues* is not a natural phenomenon. In order to see a row of human beings as a queue, we must share an institutional practice; we must accept certain constitutive rules that define the concept of queue, and certain prescriptive rules that attach certain duties and rights to the position in the queue. The existence of queues is, as it were, *practice-dependent*. They exist, in the sense identified by Searle,[1] as an institutional fact. Thus, even if in a much more complex way, legal systems also have an institutional existence, they are similar to queues and not to planets. It is for this reason that the social sources thesis seems

* Professor of Legal Philosophy, Pompeu Fabra University, Barcelona. I am very grateful to the participants in the Seminar on Legal Defeasibility at Oriel College, Oxford, 10–11 March 2008: Bruno Celano, Bruce Chapman, Pierluigi Chiassoni, Timothy Endicott, Jordi Ferrer Beltrán, Jonathan Nash, Giovanni Battista Ratti, Frederick Schauer, and Richard Tur for their comments and suggestions. For the introduction to the different ways of rejecting the so-called connection thesis I am indebted to Jorge L. Rodríguez and for some suggestions on how to improve my presentation of certain thesis and criticisms I am indebted to an anonymous referee of Oxford University Press.

[1] J. Searle, *The Construction of Social Reality* (London: Penguin Books, 1995).

platitudinous: the existence and the content of the law in a certain society depend on a set of complex social facts.

From the social sources thesis it is possible to derive as a corollary the following thesis, which I shall call the law identification thesis (LIT):[2]

The determination of what law is does not depend on moral criteria or argument.

There are, at least, three ways in which it can be understood.[3] According to the first version, the expression 'does not depend' in LIT is construed as 'cannot depend', that is, it is necessarily the case that the determination of law does not depend on moral criteria. The second version proposes that we read 'does not depend' as 'need not depend', that is to say, it is not necessarily the case that the determination of law depends on moral criteria. In accordance with the third version of LIT, 'does not depend' amounts to 'should not depend'. In this way LIT has a prescriptive reading: it recommends a certain way of identifying the law, a mode which presupposes that what the law is can be identified without resort to morality.

The two first versions of LIT express two interpretations of the separability thesis between law and morality, a core thesis of legal positivism. In J. Coleman's words:[4]

> The two most plausible and distinct interpretations of the Separability Thesis can be expressed in terms of the difference between what in modal logic is called internal and external negation. On the internal negation formulation, the Separability Thesis is the claim that in all legal systems it is necessarily the case that the legality of a norm not depend on its morality or its substantive merits. On the external negation formulation, the Separability Thesis is the claim that it is not necessarily the case that in any legal system the legality of a norm depend on its morality or its substantive merits.

Thus, the *necessary* connection thesis between law and morality can be rejected either by positing that the idea of the connection between law and morality is conceptually *impossible* or that the connection between law and morality is *contingent*. From a modal point of view, a threefold partition of propositions is usually assumed, these being necessary, impossible, and contingent. As a consequence, these positions completely cover the logical space.[5]

[2] See this formulation of the LIT thesis in D. Dyzenhaus, 'Positivism's Stagnant Research Programme', OJLS 20 (2000), 706.

[3] The three ways are presented and analysed by M.H. Kramer, 'Dogmas and Distortions: Legal Positivism Defended. A Reply to David Dyzenhaus', OJLS 21 (2001), 679–80.

[4] J.L. Coleman, 'Second Thoughts and Other First Impressions' in B. Bix (ed.), *Analyzing Law. New Essays in Legal Theory* (Oxford: Oxford University Press, 1998), 265.

[5] Let $\Diamond$: 'possible', and $\Box$: 'necessary', and the predicate L 'legal' and M 'identified by moral argument'. Thus, the *necessary* connection thesis between law and morality can be expressed as follows:

$$\forall x \Box (Lx \rightarrow Mx)$$

and, by Barcan's formula (see, for instance, G.E. Hughes and M.J. Cresswell, *A New Introduction to Modal Logic* (London: Routledge, 1996), 244), amounts to

$$\Box \forall x\, (Lx \rightarrow Mx)$$

and its internal negation:

$$\Box \forall x\, (Lx \rightarrow \neg Mx),$$

which equates with the first version of LIT, i.e. it can never be the case that the determination of law depends on morality or, from the identification point of view, the relationship between law and morality is conceptually *impossible*. On the contrary, the external negation will be:

Supporters of exclusive legal positivism defend the first version,[6] and authors who uphold inclusive legal positivism adhere to the second.[7]

The third version amounts to so-called ethical (or normative) positivism.[8] It can be said that this version conceptually accepts the second version of LIT, but normatively endorses the first version.

II

In this paper I deal with the explanatory capacity that each of the versions of LIT has in order to shed some light on our understanding of the practice of legal adjudication, and in the case of the third version, that of normative or ethical positivism, to the extent that this version is normatively suitable.[9]

But before commencing the analysis of these questions, it is worth pausing to consider that our conception of the identification of law does not determine the answer to the question of legal adjudication; it could be that the identification of law and the adjudication of law are quite distinct matters. It is conceivable that someone could maintain that the law must be identified without resort to morality and, however, still hold that judges should solve legal cases in accordance with morality, i.e. maintain that judges should put the law aside when it is in contradiction with their moral duties. David O. Brink, for instance, asserts that legal positivism and natural law theory should be construed as compatible and

$$\neg \Box \forall x (Lx \rightarrow Mx),$$

an expression logically equivalent to

$$\Diamond \Box x (Lx \wedge \neg Mx),$$

i.e. it is possible that the identification of law does not depend on morality. On the other hand, the second version of LIT implicitly presupposes that it is also possible that the identification of law depends on morality:

$$\Diamond \Box x (Lx \wedge Mx),$$

and the conjunction of the two last logical expressions amounts to asserting that the relation between law and morality is *contingent* on and, therefore, is compatible with legal systems with resort to morality and legal systems without resort to morality.

[6] Mainly J. Raz, *The Authority of Law* (Oxford: Oxford University Press, 1979), ch. 3; J. Raz, 'Authority, Law, and Morality' in *Ethics in the Public Domain* (Oxford: Oxford University Press, 1994), ch. 9; J. Raz, 'Incorporation by Law', *Legal Theory*, 10 (2004), 1–17. But see also S. Shapiro, 'On Hart's Way Out', *Legal Theory*, 4 (1998), 469–508; and S. Shapiro, 'The Difference That Rules Make' in B. Bix (ed.), *Analyzing Law. New Essays in Legal Theory* (1998), 33–64.

[7] See W.J. Waluchow, *Inclusive Legal Positivism* (Oxford: Oxford University Press, 1994) and J.L. Coleman, *The Practice of Principle: In Defence of a Pragmatist Approach to Legal Theory* (Oxford: Oxford University Press, 2001) and my own view in J.J. Moreso, 'In Defense of Inclusive Legal Positivism' in P. Chiassoni (ed.), *The Legal Ought* (Turin: Giappichelli, 2001), 37–63.

[8] As far as I know, the first articulated version of this conception is found in U. Scarpelli, *Cos'è il positivismo giuridico* (Milan: Edizione di Comunità, 1965). More recently it has been defended, for instance, by T. Campbell, *The Legal Theory of Ethical Positivism* (Aldershot: Dartmouth, 1996), J. Goldsworthy, *The Sovereignty of Parliament. History and Philosophy* (Oxford: Oxford University Press, 1999) and J. Waldron, 'Normative (or Ethical) Positivism' in J. Coleman (ed.), *Hart's Postscript. Essays on the Postscript to the Concept of Law* (Oxford: Oxford University Press, 2001), ch. 12.

[9] In this sense, exclusive and inclusive legal positivism do not claim their plausibility from the beneficial moral consequences of adopting one concept of law or another. However, this is precisely the claim of normative positivism. On the beneficial moral consequences thesis see J. Dickson, *Evaluation and Legal Theory* (Oxford: Hart Publishing, 2001), 84–102 and F. Schauer, 'The Social Construction of the Concept of Law: A Reply to Julie Dickson', OJLS, 25 (2005), 493–501.

complementary doctrines. According to Brink, natural law theory endorses two theses: on the one hand, the existence and content of the law depend on true or sound political morality and, on the other hand, a correct judicial decision in any given case must satisfy true or sound political morality. Legal positivism, on the contrary, denies both theses; this means that the existence and content of the law do not depend on true or sound political morality and the correct judicial decision in any given case does not need to satisfy true or sound political morality. However, Brink adds that the first legal positivism thesis, the identification thesis, is compatible with the second natural law thesis, given that this second 'concerns what judges have an all-things-considered obligation to do'.[10]

If the question of legal adjudication depends on what judges should do all-things-considered, then it will be obvious that—to the extent that this is a moral question—the answer must be making decisions which are morally correct.[11] Given that judges are moral agents, when they make decisions that affect the well-being of other persons (as virtually always happens in judicial decisions), they have a moral duty to ground their decisions on moral standards. However, this is not the question which preoccupies us concerning the connection between the law identification thesis and legal adjudication. We are not asking what judges should morally do, but what judges should, in accordance with the law, do and what role morality plays (or should play) in the decisions that judges make according to law. In Raz's words:[12]

> From the fact that the question 'how, all things considered, should the courts decide the case?' is a moral question it does not follow that the question 'how, according to law, should cases be decided?' is a moral question.

III

It could be conceived that the first version of LIT is as follows:

[LIT1] The determination of what law is cannot depend on moral criteria or argument, requires a formalist view of legal adjudication.

According to this interpretation, the legal reasoning used in legal adjudication is technical reasoning which obeys its own rules; legal reasoning is autonomous or isolated, without any reference to moral reasoning. However, this is not the reading propounded by the defenders of exclusive positivism. Raz, for instance, criticizes this conception as follows:[13]

> It is a hard doctrine to sustain. First, there is the question whether the resources of the law are sufficient to provide the resources necessary for the courts both to obey the law and to follow the formalist doctrine. Second, there is the difficulty of reconciling the doctrine with legal practice. Finally, there is the moral issue: is the formalist doctrine morally acceptable?

In fact, Raz believes that formalist doctrines cannot overcome these difficulties: the social sources of law do not determine all the answers to the legal controversies; it is a matter of fact in legal practice that legal adjudication often resorts to morality and the formalist doctrine is not, for Raz, morally acceptable.[14]

[10] D.O. Brink, 'Legal Positivism and Natural Law Reconsidered', *The Monist*, 68 (1985), 377. This seems also the view of T. Spaak, 'Legal Positivism, Law's Normativity, and the Normative Force of Legal Justification', *Ratio Juris*, 16 (2003), 482.

[11] J. Raz, 'Incorporation by Law', 2–7.

[12] J. Raz, 'On the Autonomy of Legal Reasoning' in *Ethics in the Public Domain*, 312.

[13] Ibid., 314.

[14] An argument used, sometimes, against certain understandings of the social sources thesis. J. C. Bayón has called it an 'argument from lack of fit': 'It claims that actual legal practice, as currently developed in countries such as ours, flies in the face of the so-called sources thesis—to wit, the claim

According to Raz, it is the law identified by LIT1 which empowers judges to apply extralegal considerations: 'quite commonly courts have the discretion to modify legal rules, or to make exceptions to their applications, and where they have such discretion they ought to resort to moral reasoning to decide whether to use it and how'.[15] For Raz, therefore, the law is always identified in accordance with LIT1, but judges have discretion to modify it, following moral criteria, when they decide cases. By this reason, Raz divides legal reasoning into *reasoning about the law* and *reasoning according to law*: 'The first is governed by the sources thesis, the second I believe to be quite commonly straightforward moral reasoning'.[16]

In other words, the reasoning according to law is neither autonomous nor isolated but, as it were, *peninsular*.

IV

The second version of the law identification thesis asserts:

[LIT2] The determination of what law is need not depend on moral criteria or argument.

Therefore, according to this thesis it may be that the identification of law depends on moral argumentation, but it may also be that this is not the case. Even though this question is usually associated with the possibility that the rule of recognition includes moral reasons as part of the very criteria of legal validity,[17] it will be sufficient, in the context of this discussion, to take a weaker incorporationist thesis into account: 'the familiar sources of law—like statutes and constitutional provisions—may include moral concepts or considerations'.[18]

In accordance with this interpretation, then, when legal norms incorporate moral concepts or considerations, the law must be identified using these concepts or considerations. Judges should, therefore, apply the law with resort to morality in pertinent cases.

We can now ask whether there is an actual difference here, regarding legal adjudication, between the Razian thesis of reasoning according to law and the adjudication view of inclusive positivism. For both theories, when the law resorts to morality, judges should decide the cases by means of moral argumentation.[19]

Perhaps for this reason, it has been suggested that the controversy between LIT1 and LIT2, the controversy between exclusive and inclusive legal positivism, is a definitional question, which depends on our definition of legal validity. In positivist legal theory, a distinction is sometimes made between two senses of validity: legal validity as *membership*, and legal validity as *applicability*. A norm is valid, in the sense that it belongs to the

that the existence and content of the law is a matter of social fact and then it can be fully determined without resort to moral argument, which is taken to be the very gist of legal positivism. Therefore, the argument concludes, legal positivism is to be modified in order to fit the practice.' J.C. Bayón, 'Derecho, convencionalismo y controversia' in P.E. Navarro and M. C. Redondo (eds), *La relevancia del derecho. Ensayos de filosofía jurídica, moral y política* (Barcelona: Gedisa, 2002), 57.

15 J. Raz, 'On the Autonomy of Legal Reasoning', 319.

16 Ibid., 316–17.

17 As Hart clearly asserts using the term *soft positivism*, in H.L.A. Hart, 'Postscript' to *The Concept of Law* (2nd edn, Oxford: Oxford University Press, 1994).

18 B. Leiter, 'Law and Objectivity' in J. Coleman and S. Shapiro (eds), *The Oxford Handbook of Jurisprudence and Philosophy of Law* (Oxford: Oxford University Press, 2002), 978.

19 For this reason I think that M.H. Kramer is right when he asserts: 'For Raz, adjudication consists in reasoning about the law as well as reasoning according to the law, and thus the Razian judges might decide cases in a manner indistinguishable or virtually indistinguishable from the Dworkinian judges. Though such a practical convergence is hardly inevitable, it is far from impossible.' M.H. Kramer, 'Dogmas and Distortions: Legal Positivism Defended. A Reply to David Dyzenhaus', 682.

legal system S, if and only if it is identified as a member of the system by the criteria of the rule of recognition of the legal system S. A norm is valid, in the sense that it is applicable to a certain case, if and only if there is another norm, belonging to S, which authorizes or obliges the courts in S, to apply it to such a case.[20] In the context of the discussion between exclusive and inclusive legal positivism, J.L. Coleman puts the question in the following terms:[21]

> A better strategy relies on the distinction Joseph Raz emphasizes between legal validity and bindingness on officials. All legally valid norms are binding on officials, but not every standard that is binding on judges is legally valid, in the sense of being part of the community's law. The laws of foreign jurisdictions, the norms of social clubs as well as other normative systems generally can be binding on officials in certain adjudicatory contexts, though they are not part of the 'host' community's law. Judges may be authorized, even directed, by otherwise valid rules to appeal to such principles. They need not be part of a community's law in order for judges to be required to appeal to them in the context of a particular suit. Thus, it does not follow from the fact that judges may sometimes be bound by certain moral principles that those principles are themselves part of the law or are legally valid.

In accordance with this distinction, it could be the case that a moral standard is not part of the law and, nonetheless, is binding on the courts, which have to decide according to it. In this sense, a defender of exclusive positivism could argue in favour of the strong reading of the social sources thesis, even though moral standards are, sometimes, binding on the courts.

Recently, C. Dahlman has insisted on this idea in the following terms:[22]

> There is no conflict between the strong social thesis and the observation that the law sometimes instructs the judge to recognize a norm as a part of the law because of its moral content, since the strong social thesis only concerns epistemic recognition, and the observation that the law sometimes instructs the judge to resort to morality concerns adjudicative recognition.

Nonetheless, there is a way of constructing LIT1 that makes a difference when it is applied to the duties of judges. In standard cases, judges have a legal duty to apply the legal norms identified through the social sources thesis.

According to LIT1, derived from the strong thesis of social sources, when legal norms incorporate moral concepts, judges have discretion. Raz has clearly expressed this view:[23]

> Let us assume, for example, that by law contracts are valid only if not immoral. Any particular contract can be judged to be *prima facie* valid if it conforms to the 'value-neutral' conditions for the validity of contract laid down by law. The proposition 'It is legally conclusive that this contract is valid' is neither true nor false until a court authoritatively determines its validity. This is a consequence of the fact that by the sources thesis courts have discretion when required to apply moral considerations.

[20] See the distinction between these terms in E. Bulygin, 'Time and Validity' in A.A. Martino (ed.), *Deontic Logic, Computational Linguistics and Legal Information Systems* (Amsterdam: North Holland, 1982), 65–82, P. Navarro and J.J. Moreso, 'Applicability and Effectiveness of Legal Norms', *Law and Philosophy*, 16 (1997), 201–19; and J.J. Moreso, *Legal Indeterminacy and Constitutional Interpretation*, trans. by Ruth Zimmerling (Dordrecht: Kluwer Academic Publishers, 1998), 105–15.

[21] J.L. Coleman, 'Incorporationism, Conventionalism, and the Practical Difference Thesis', *Legal Theory*, 4 (1998), 404–5. The origin of this distinction is J. Raz, *The Authority of Law*, 101–2, 119–20. See also W.J. Waluchow, *Inclusive Legal Positivism*, 157, J.L. Coleman, 'Second Thoughts and Other Personal Impressions', 260–1, fn. 19 and 263, fn. 22; S. Shapiro, 'On Hart's Way Out', 506 and M.H. Kramer, 'How Moral Principles Can Enter into the Law', *Legal Theory*, 6 (2000), 103–7. See also J.J. Moreso, 'In Defense of Inclusive Legal Positivism', 41–3.

[22] C. Dahlman, 'Adjudicative and Epistemic Recognition', *Analisi e Diritto* (2004), 231.

[23] J. Raz, *The Authority of Law*, p. 75. See a lucid analysis of this Razian view in T. Endicott, 'Raz on Gaps: The Surprising Part', *Ars Interpretandi. Journal of Legal Hermeneutics*, 6 (2001), 349–71.

If LIT1 implies that whenever the law incorporates moral concepts or considerations judges have discretion (as Raz affirms), then there are good reasons to cast doubts on the plausibility of that thesis. If A signs a contract with B binding himself to kill C within a month, A does not kill C, and B brings an action for breach of contract against A, no lawyer could say that we must wait for the judicial decision in order to know whether the contract between A and B is or is not valid: this contract is void because it is immoral and judges have no discretion in this case. In a similar way, what happens if a constitutional provision specifically excludes cruel punishments and the legislature enacts a norm which attaches, as in Roman Law, the following punishment for parricide (*poena cullei*): the culprit must be drowned in a leather sack together with a cock, a dog, a serpent, and a monkey. Can we say that this is a cruel punishment? I think that all of us would acknowledge that *poena cullei* is a cruel punishment,[24] and, therefore, is unconstitutional. Even though 'cruel' is, without doubt, a moral term, it is applied without any controversy to *poena cullei*, and there is no room here for discretion. Obviously, there is room for disagreement in other cases of application of the concept of cruelty, the cruelty of capital punishment being the most important. In any case, resorting to morality does not necessarily imply judicial discretion.

It seems more reasonable to argue, as LIT2 implies, that when the law incorporates moral concepts, these moral concepts must be used in order to identify what the law decrees. Thus, contrary to Raz's view, the legal reasoning in those cases is not only moral reasoning when it is reasoning according to law, but also when it is reasoning about the law. This is compatible, obviously, with the fact that in some borderline cases of application of this kind of concept, judges have discretion.

As is well known, Raz rejects the incorporationist thesis for reasons related to his conception of authority.[25] This conception will not be analysed here, but I suggest that if the Razian notion of authority has such implausible consequences, perhaps we should try to revise it.[26]

I cannot deal here either with the other question relevant to the feasibility of LIT2 or inclusive legal positivism: whether this thesis presupposes, in order to be suitable, the thesis of moral objectivity.[27]

V

The third version of the law identification thesis can be expressed as follows:

[LIT3] The determination of what law is should not depend on moral criteria or argument.

[24] Precisely for this reason the Romans considered—mistakenly, I think—that this was the deserved punishment for such an atrocious crime.

[25] J. Raz, 'Authority, Law, and Morality'. On the question of the tension between the Razian thesis of the social sources and his thesis of legal reasoning according to law in relation to his doctrine of authority, see F. Atria, 'Legal Reasoning and Legal Theory Revisited', *Law and Philosophy*, 18 (1999), 537–77 and J.C. Bayón, 'Derecho, convencionalismo y controversia'.

[26] It is a suggestion by R. Dworkin: 'Raz thinks law cannot be authoritative unless those who accept it *never* use their own conviction to decide what it requires, even in this partial way. But why must law be blind authority rather than authoritative in the more relaxed way other conceptions assume?' R. Dworkin, *Law's Empire* (Cambridge, Mass.: Harvard University Press, 1986), 429–30, fn. 3.

[27] But see H.L.A. Hart, 'Postscript', 254; K. E. Himma 'Incorporationism and the Objectivity of Moral Norms', *Legal Theory*, 5 (1999), 415–34; M.H. Kramer, *In Defense of Legal Positivism. Law without Trimmings* (Oxford: Oxford University Press, 1999), 152–61 and J.J. Moreso, 'In Defense of Inclusive Legal Positivism', 43–50.

LIT3 presupposes the truth of LIT2, that is to say it presupposes that legal systems can be conceived of wherein the determination of the content of the law depends on moral argument. However, it considers that the core of legal positivism is found in the following normative thesis: the law should be written in such a way that what a law decrees can be identified without resort to morality. Thus, judges could apply the law in a formalistic style, on the basis that they are able to identify the content of legal norms without resort to moral argumentation.

Understood in this way, legal positivism relies on a normative (political and moral) account of the law:[28]

Positivist ideals relate directly to the political justification of prescriptive positivism. The ethics of positivism are concerned with the conduct of those who fill the various roles within a system of government through rules: principally legislators, citizens, lawyers, and judges.

In my view, the defence of ethical (or normative) positivism can be summarized in an argument as follows:

(1) There is a pervasive disagreement on the criteria for moral correction.

(2) In order to respect the moral autonomy of persons, we should govern human conduct through clear and precise rules, which allow us to determine with certainty when certain conducts are legally forbidden.

(1) and (2) imply

(3) If in order to identify the conduct that is legally forbidden, we must resort to a moral argument, then there will be considerable disagreement and, therefore, certainty will be sacrificed and personal autonomy damaged.

Therefore,

(4) The law should be identifiable without resort to morality.

That is to say, there are normative reasons to ban the incorporation of moral concepts and considerations in the law and to strongly recommend LIT1, from a normative point of view.

I agree with the defenders of ethical positivism that something similar to this previous argument is part and parcel of some classical conceptions of legal positivism and also that, even though contemporary accounts of legal positivism are often presented as a set of conceptual theses, this argument underlies implicitly the majority of these versions.

Premise (1) has been clearly defended by many of the adherents to ethical positivism. Tom Campbell, for instance, refers to:[29] 'the pervasive disagreement between members and groups within a politic regarding both the proper ways of making and enforcing decisions which are binding in that society, and the principles and goals which ought to determine the content of these decisions'. Sometimes this thesis carries the

[28] T. Campbell, *The Legal Theory of Ethical Positivism*, 95. Almost forty years ago U. Scarpelli wrote: 'A political choice is inherent to legal positivism, but this choice is a choice for the positive law identified by its formal characteristics, it is a choice for a legal science and practice which, given the positive law, is studied and applied faithfully and independently on any value judgement.' U. Scarpelli, *Cos'è il positivismo giuridico*, 133 (my own translation into English). Recently, also L. Hierro, 'Por qué ser positivista?', *Doxa*, 25 (2002), 272, fn. 6, has also revived Scarpelli's views and demonstrated his agreement with this view.

[29] T. Campbell, *The Legal Theory of Ethical Positivism*, p. 15. See also T. Campbell, 'El sentido del positivismo jurídico', *Doxa*, 25 (2002), 313.

assumption of scepticism (as is the case with H. Kelsen and A. Ross)[30] or, at least, of relativism in morals.[31]

However, it is not necessary to endorse moral scepticism or relativism in order to acknowledge the indisputable fact of disagreement on morals. Even though we accept a place for objectivity in morals, we can acknowledge extensive epistemic difficulties in determining moral rightness and, perhaps, the fact that some moral disagreements are not eradicable.

Premise (2), which insists on the importance of having clear and precise laws, is intertwined with two worthy ideals of political liberalism: first, the ideal of the rule of law, the ideal of being governed by laws, not by men and, second, the separation of powers, with an insistence on the distinction between making law and adjudicating law. In Campbell's words:[32]

> In an ideal Positivist world there would be no such thing as judicial legislation, although there would always be a legislative element in rendering general terms more precise in relation to the complexities of concrete situations. In the non-ideal world we actually inhabit judicial legislation may be the lesser of the two evils.

I do not question that premises (1) and (2) contain a certain amount of truth. However, I am arguing that (1) and (2), correctly understood, even though they imply a weak version of (3), cannot allow us to conclude that the law should be identified without resort to morality.

Regarding (1), I wish only to offer a reminder that, even though the disagreement on morals is extensive, it is not absolute. When the law excludes cruel punishments, it forbids clearly *poena cullei*. When the law authorizes the justified use of force as self-defence, it allows me to defend myself against an attack with a knife. When the law declares void a contract accepted through unjust coercion, it makes invalid a contract that someone has signed under the threat to kill her child. I think that it cannot be seriously argued that whenever the law incorporates those moral concepts in legal norms, judges have discretion and such cases are not regulated by law.

Thus, we must formulate (1) in a different way:

> (1') There is, to a certain extent, a relevant disagreement on the criteria for moral correction.

Premise (2), however, deserves a more detailed analysis.[33] It is indisputable that certainty is an ideal for legal regulation. Legal certainty is a value, but we should identify the reasons for certainty, in order to determine whether they are sufficiently important to defeat any kind of reasons against certainty. Most of the reasons for

[30] H. Kelsen, *Reine Rechtslehre* (Vienna: Franz Deuticke, 1960), 60–71 and A. Ross, *On Law and Justice* (London: Stevens & Sons, 1958), ch. XII.

[31] See, for instance, U. Scarpelli, *Cos'è il positivismo giuridico*, 153, fn. 3. On the other hand, Jeremy Waldron has strongly insisted on the significance of moral disagreement for legal theory: J. Waldron, *Law and Disagreement* (Oxford: Oxford University Press, 1999). Waldron considers the fact of disagreement as a reason to take our public decisions by majority: this is the main link between democracy and disagreement. Given that the disagreement is ineradicable, it is better to take decisions democratically than to give this power to judges. I accept the cogency of this argument in favour of democracy, but if my argument works, then the limited activity of judges is compatible with democracy. See also S. Besson, *The Morality of Conflict: Reasonable Disagreement and the Law* (Oxford: Hart Publishing, 2005).

[32] T. Campbell, *The Legal Theory of Ethical Positivism*, 120. See also the insistence on the importance of certainty in U. Scarpelli, *Cos'è il positivismo giuridico*, 145 and J. Goldsworthy, *The Sovereignty of Parliament*, 271.

[33] I develop here some ideas previously presented in J.J. Moreso, 'Commanducci sobre (neo) constitucionalismo', *Isonomía*, 19 (October 2003), 274–5.

conferring value on legal certainty relate to the value of personal autonomy. One of the faces of personal autonomy is related to the capacity of choosing and carrying out our own plan of life and only clear, precise, and public laws allow us to choose and to plan our life in a reasonable way.[34] But are there reasons to carry this enlightened ideal to extremes? I do not think so, because I consider that personal autonomy also requires that the addressees of rules should argue in favour of the justification of their conduct, when they do not follow these rules. For this reason, legal rules should, in many situations, make it possible to have recourse to the underlying reasons (which are moral reasons) in order to apply them. In this way, for instance, criminal law treats the justifying and excusing conditions, and private law treats the invalidating conditions of certain civil transactions (wills, gifts, contracts, and marriages).[35] A criminal law without justifying conditions would display more certainty than our present criminal systems, but it would be more unjust because our personal autonomy would be weaker. It is more respectful to personal autonomy to allow self-defence against an attack, even though that opens the door to a less certain terrain than the easier one of determining whether an individual has injured another person or not. Now we must determine if the self-defence was legitimate, that is, if it was proportionate, if the attack was not the reaction to a previous unjust provocation, etc. A private law without invalidating conditions would have much more certainty, but it would also be more unjust. If the contracts were not void in the cases of mistake or duress, then it would be clearer (as the *stipulatio* in old Roman law) when we are under a contractual duty. Now, we must determine, for instance, the nature of the mistake, the injustice of the coercion, etc. In brief: honouring personal autonomy, which attaches value to legal certainty, requires making a place for moral argument, even though it sacrifices certainty to some extent. In our moral horizon, there are always values in conflict. How to fit them and weigh them is our task as moral agents. Therefore, the fact that the incorporation of moral concepts into law sometimes diminishes certainty should not necessarily be considered undesirable; on the contrary, often it is the only way to make law more respectful of our moral autonomy.

The same happens with the rules in our daily life. If I want to enjoy a morning of calm work, without being disturbed, in order to, for instance, finish this paper, I can ask my secretary not to put any telephone calls through to me this morning. It is a clear and precise rule, but if the secretary follows it without exceptions, then it could produce ill effects: the President of the Board of Trustees of my University, who wants to talk to me urgently, may not be able to speak to me, or my wife may not be able to tell me that our daughter has been admitted to hospital, etc. For this reason, we do not want secretaries that apply our orders mechanically. Sometimes we formulate explicitly the *defeater*, which makes the rule inapplicable: 'Please don't put any calls through to me this morning, unless it is very important'. This second rule is less precise than the first. Even though some cases are clearly excluded by this second rule (my wife's call, for instance), other cases pose doubts for the secretary, who should exercise judgement in order to apply the rule. However, this second rule respects my autonomy to a greater extent than the first. Someone could still argue that it would be better to formulate a rule that includes clearly all the exceptions. However, this is not possible: there are so

[34] See also J.J. Moreso, 'Principio de legalidad y causas de justificación (sobre el alcance de la taxatividad)', *Doxa*, 24 (2001), 532–5.

[35] The analogy between excusing conditions in criminal law and invalidating conditions in private law comes from H.L.A. Hart, 'Legal Responsibility and Excuses' in H.L.A. Hart, *Punishment and Responsibility* (Oxford: Oxford University Press, 1968), 28–53.

many diverse circumstances that lead to the inapplication of a rule and we cannot enclose them in a canonical formulation without concepts of value.

Thus, my suggestion is that the law introduces moral concepts in a way analogous to the example of the secretary and, with the same arguments, in a justified way. The moral concepts incorporated in the law often work like *defeaters*, permitting certain conduct (self-defence) or forbidding certain regulations (cruel punishments). In my view, even if certainty is sacrificed to some extent, our moral autonomy is defended.[36]

As F. Schauer has argued,[37] the rules always suffer, in relation to the reason that justifies them, their *rationale*, from *under-* and *over-inclusiveness*. A way of partially preserving the advantages of being governed by rules and taking the problem of under- and over-inclusion into account, consists of the incorporation of some *defeaters* to the rules. This means that the rule-applying agencies have recourse to the underlying reasons in some cases, in order to put aside the rule in cases not covered by the underlying reason. It is clear that the inclusion of such *defeaters* affects the *semantic autonomy* of rules and, moreover, diminishes certainty. But this reduction of certainty is balanced by a more suitable justification of the mechanism of applying rules. We could return to the example of the secretary: if we do not include in the rule 'don't put through any phone calls this morning' the clause 'unless it is very important' and we try to specify the circumstances in which the rule should not apply, we will become mired in a casuistry that lead us to the infra-inclusion: there will be circumstances not included in the defeater and not covered by the rationale of the rules. Infra-inclusion in the *defeater* amounts to over-inclusion in the rule.

T. Campbell seems to be aware of these problems when he observes:[38]

> There are problems in the inclusion of vague moral judgment-inviting terms like 'just' and 'reasonable' which encourage extensive judicial discretion. But while it may not be possible to exclude these altogether, they can usually be interpreted as disguised references to accepted standards of conduct in the rules of society at the time, thus incorporating current practice into the law. But, in general, such legislation is undesirably vague and ambiguous in purpose and insufficiently restrictive of judicial legislation. It represents an understandable but regrettable passing of the legislative burden from government to courts.

I have two comments on Campbell's remarks: first, the suggested interpretation of moral *defeaters* as 'just' or 'reasonable' does not seem to me very promising,[39] because in most relevant cases the members of a society will be divided on that point (and some will be rather perplexed). Then we must ask what degree of consensus is required to know whether an evaluative concept is called for. Second, following the adduced reasons, the legislation incorporating moral concepts as defeaters does not seem to me *undesirably vague and ambiguous*, but rather seems to me desirable, even though it necessarily introduces indeterminacy to some extent.

[36] It is obvious that the culture of *constitutionalism* has increased the extent of the incorporation of morality to the law (see, with a positive valuation of the impact of constitutionalism: M. Atienza, *El Sentido del Derecho* (Barcelona: Ariel, 2001), 112–14). However, my argument here does not deal with the normative suitability of constitutionalism, but simply tries to show that incorporationism is a fact of the law of modernity and that this fact is justified from a normative point of view. See, in this sense, F. Laporta, *Entre el Derecho y la Moral* (Mexico: Fontamara, 1993), 61–2. From this point of view, constitutionalism is a special case of incorporationism.

[37] F. Schauer, *Playing by the Rules* (Oxford: Oxford University Press, 1991), 31–4.

[38] T. Campbell, *The Legal Theory of Ethical Positivism*, 119.

[39] See also this interpretation in C.E. Alchourrón and E. Bulygin, 'Los límites de la lógica y el razonamiento jurídico' in C.E. Alchourrón and E. Bulygin, *Análisis lógico y Derecho* (Madrid: Centro de Estudios Constitucionales, 1991), 315–16.

A recent debate on the scope of intuitionism in moral philosophy may be helpful here.[40] The question is as follows: is it suitable to conceive of morals as a set of general principles applicable to particular cases? The generalists answer affirmatively and the particularists negatively. Some generalists not only consider that we should conceive morality as a set of general principles, but also, given that moral properties supervene in certain natural properties, that such principles can be formulated pointing out the natural properties which make a human action morally right or wrong. Utilitarianism, which considers the property of increasing human well-being (or sentient creatures' well-being), is an instance of such generalism, with only one moral principle. Particularists insist on the impossibility of pointing out any natural property, which invariably maintains its contribution to the rightness of human actions.

There is, nonetheless, a third possibility named *thick intuitionism* by McNaughton and Rawling: this refers to non-trivial cases of general moral principles that incorporate necessarily *thick* moral properties. We can preserve the moral principle, which obliges us to keep promises and we can concede that the notion of promise-keeping can be spelled out in non-moral vocabulary. But this moral principle must incorporate some *defeaters* (usually conceived as implicit conditions): 'provided that one's promise is not given under duress and is not an undertaking to do something immoral, then it supplies one with a moral reason to act so as to keep it'.[41] It is worth noting that we can only complete the principle by adding evaluative concepts: 'we have tried to show that there are some reasons for thinking that there might be plausible weak moral principles involving thick concepts, and none involving non-moral concepts'.[42]

Thus, my suggestion is that we should conceive legal regulation in this way: there are good reasons for thinking that we should regulate human conduct in the relevant cases (criminal law, private law, etc.) through clear rules that incorporate *defeaters* formulated in moral terms.

If these arguments are accepted, then premise (2) ('In order to respect the moral autonomy of persons, we should govern human conduct through clear and precise rules, which allow us to determine with certainty when this conduct is legally forbidden') has to be changed to:

> (2') In order to respect the moral autonomy of persons, we should govern human conduct through clear and precise rules, which incorporate *defeaters* with moral content and, which allow us to determine with certainty when this conduct is legally forbidden.

(1') and (2') do not imply (3) ('If in order to identify the conduct legally forbidden, we must resort to moral argument, then there will be a lot of disagreement and, therefore, certainty will be sacrificed and personal autonomy damaged'), but they imply a weak version of (3) as follows:

> (3') If in order to identify legally forbidden conduct, we must resort to moral argument, then there will be disagreement to a certain extent and, therefore, certainty will be sacrificed in order to preserve personal autonomy.

[40] I follow the presentation and the ideas of D. McNaughton and P. Rawling, 'Unprincipled Ethics' in B. Hooker and M. Little (eds), *Moral Particularism* (Oxford: Oxford University Press, 2000), 256–75. Similar conclusions are obtained from R. Holton, 'Principles and Particularisms', *Proceedings of the Aristotelian Society*, suppl. vol. 76 (2002), 191–210; and P. Väyrynen, 'Moral Generalism: Enjoy in Moderation', *Ethics*, 116 (2006), 291–319.

[41] P. Väyrynen, 'Moral Generalism: Enjoy in Moderation', 269.

[42] Ibid., 272.

And most importantly: (1'), (2'), and (3') do not allow us by any means to conclude:

(4) The law should be identifiable without resort to morality.

Given that, and this has been the core of my argument, (2') presupposes rejecting (4).

VI

My conclusions are, then, the following:

(1) From a conceptual point of view, it is suitable to sustain the second version of the law identification thesis, given that it allows us to take into account the indisputable fact that judges often resort to moral argumentation when they solve legal cases. On the other hand, it takes into account this fact without resort to the implausible assumption, developed as complementary to the first version of the law identification thesis, according to which whenever legal rules incorporate moral concepts judges have discretion.

(2) From a normative point of view, even acknowledging the importance of the certainty related to the moral autonomy of persons, it is precisely the moral autonomy that requires sacrificing certainty to some extent in order to make room for the presence in legislation of moral *defeaters*, which allow us a justified application of rules.

Therefore, exclusive legal positivism is unsuitable from a conceptual point of view and, from a normative point of view, there are no good reasons for sustaining ethical positivism.

14

Rules, Principles, and Defeasibility

*Manuel Atienza and Juan Ruiz Manero**

A. An introduction

1. Exclusive Positivism

One of the most distinctive features of any legal theory (or rather, of its underlying general conception of the law) is, in our opinion, its particular way of reconstructing the relationship between the demands of legal norms conceived as guidelines for behaviour and the demands of the underlying values and purposes which those guidelines for behaviour purport to serve.

Thus, in current legal theory one of the possible models in this regard is the so-called *strong* or *exclusive positivism*.[1] Alchourrón and Bulygin's and Raz's legal theories are quite clear examples. Both theories contend that law's regulative dimension can be wholly grasped in terms of mere guidelines for behaviour. Moreover, in their structural approach to norms, Alchourrón and Bulygin regard law as a special set of rules.[2] According to their theory, each legal rule correlates a certain generic case or a certain set of properties to a certain normative solution (an action being either required, forbidden, or permitted). Thus, under this premise, whenever a lawyer faces a given individual case she is merely engaged in checking whether or not its properties can be subsumed within the properties of the generic case set out by such a rule. Insofar as those properties of the individual case fit into one of those rules, it is adequate to claim that the individual case has a predetermined legal solution, namely the solution set forth in the rule within which it is subsumable, i.e. the rule which contemplates the pertinent generic case. When this is not the case, either because there is not such a rule (cases of a *normative gap* or a *normative irrelevance*) or because incompatible rules are at stake (normative contradiction or *antinomy*) or because we doubt whether the

* Professors of Legal Philosophy, University of Alicante. The authors wish to thank Victoria Roca for translating this paper.

[1] See J. Ruiz Manero, 'Algunas concepciones del derecho y sus lagunas' in F. Atria, E. Bulygin, J.J. Moreso, P.E. Navarro, J.L. Rodríguez, and J. Ruiz Manero, *Lagunas en el Derecho. Una controversia sobre el Derecho y la función judicial* (Madrid-Barcelona: Marcial Pons, 2005), 103–26.

[2] The following remarks should be understood as part of what can be called Alchourrón and Bulygin's *classical model*. This model was fully developed in *Normative Systems* and in those subsequent—individual or joint—papers (in fact the vast majority of them) which are further developments of the former. See C.E. Alchourrón and E. Bulygin, *Normative Systems* (Vienna: Springer, 1971). Arguably, Alchourrón's last works on defeasible conditionals would have most probably entailed substantial changes in the original model. Further development of this last point will not be undertaken here. Eugenio Bulygin, in turn, has remained notably loyal to the classical model. See in this respect particularly his contributions to F. Atria, et al., *Lagunas en el Derecho. Una controversia sobre el Derecho y la función judicial.* Juan José Moreso stresses the claim according to which *Normative Systems* should be read as a mere *reconstruction of micro-systems of norms* and then as a piece of work not committed to any particular conception of law. See J.J. Moreso, 'A Brilliant Disguise: entre fuentes y lagunas' in F. Atria, et al., *Lagunas en el Derecho. Una controversia sobre el Derecho y la función judicial.* In Moreso's view, this would be the most fruitful reading of it. However, our presentation of the model of *Normative Systems* herein does not examine the possibility of setting aside the strong positivist conception lying underneath.

properties of the individual case are subsumable within the generic properties contemplated in the rule (*gaps of recognition*), the adjudicatory organ has to decide the case under discretion.

Therefore, according to Alchourrón and Bulygin, two, and only two, mutually excluding possibilities open up: (a) the individual case can be subsumed either within one of the explicit rules of the system or within any other rule logically deducible thereof. Then, the solution for the individual case is legally determined beforehand. Whenever such circumstance obtains, we can correctly and simply say that the case is solved by the law; (b) either—as the second possibility—(b.1) there is no such rule within which to subsume the individual case, or (b.2) one has reasonable doubts whether such a rule exists, or (b.3) there are two competing, mutually incompatible norms within which to subsume the individual case. Those circumstances met, law is asserted to be silent. Hence, the judge's only way to accomplish her duty to solve the case is by resorting to her own absolute discretion; in their own words, she has nothing left but to resort to her 'personal criteria of preference'. For these authors contend that the province of law does not extend past the realm of explicit legal rules and their logical consequences. Thus, either there is a predetermined rule which fits the individual case or strong discretion emerges: in the justification of legal decisions *tertium non datur*.

It should be observed that, according to Alchourrón and Bulygin's legal theory, there is no room for rule defeasibility, since there are no circumstances in which rules can be defeated. The argument runs as follows. Whenever we face a claim according to which a particular individual case has additional properties—besides those generically formulated in the pre-existing rule—requiring special consideration, this should be understood as a mere expression of value disagreement with what law demands, for what law demands is exclusively what is commanded by the pre-existing rule. For instance, under Alchourrón and Bulygin's theory, this would be the proper reconstruction of a case like the famous *Riggs* v. *Palmer*: what the law demanded for this well-known case was solely what was established by the rule under which the case had to be subsumed—that is: the inheritance belongs to the grandson who claimed it. Advocating that he should not be granted the inheritance on the basis that the grandson was the murderer of his own grandfather is only a way of expressing disagreement with what is established by the law.

Raz's view of law certainly differs in several important respects from Alchourrón and Bulygin's. Where the latter engaged in a structural approach to legal norms, conceiving them as rules that correlate cases and solutions, Raz's conception of legal norms is undertaken from the perspective of norms as reasons for action. Thus, Raz advances that all legal norms are *protected* or *exclusionary reasons for action*. Further, those protected or executive reasons are the outcome of certain legal authorities' deliberation on reasons for and against a certain course of action given certain circumstances. Once a legal norm is enacted by an authority, it should be possible for us to understand and follow that norm with no need to reopen the previous deliberative process. This is exactly the reason why they should be understood as protected or exclusionary reasons. Raz's claim is that this is precisely the primary advantage—and its main justification—in having authorities and norms passed by them. Hence, it is for the sake of granting that advantage that Raz strongly contends that 'the identification of a rule as a rule of law consists in attributing it to the relevant person or institution (that is, to a source) as representing their decisions and expressing their judgements'. Further, 'such attributions can only be based on factual considerations', for value argument 'can establish

on the ground of their personal assessment of the best solution considering all the relevant substantial reasons—rather than on the basis of pre-existing norms—then that system will not qualify as law. Such a system—very much like the one imagined by Plato in his *Republic*, namely a system conferring absolute discretion to dispute resolution organs—would not meet the demands generally associated with the terms 'law' or 'legal system'. Of course, it is not only, or mainly, a matter of simple definition (if so, it could always be avoided by a change in the definition). If decisions being adopted by courts on the grounds of a set of pre-existing rules have been part of what is commonly understood by law, this is so since to ground a decision on a pre-existing set of rules has been almost universally considered, throughout history, and for good reasons, the best available structure of justification, not under ideal conditions but under the conditions of the real world.

This last remark should be highlighted. Were we not limited by the real world's constraints, the best justification would be, of course, to resort to all applicable valid reasons considering all the merits of the case. However, under the circumstances of the real world, the choice for a structure of justification in dispute resolution based upon a pre-existing set of rules—consisting mostly of rules of the kind mentioned—is an appropriate choice for different reasons, among which the following four may be mentioned: first, those reasons related to cost reduction in the decision-making process; second, those reasons related to dispute resolution organs that suffer from a deficit of epistemic stock which prevents them from assessing every one of the relevant reasons, and to the mistrust caused by the acknowledged risk of incidental prejudices or biases in those organs' reasoning; third, reasons concerning the allocation of power, i.e. about who should have authority to determine the substantive criteria according to which disputes should be resolved; and fourth, those reasons related to the predictability of dispute resolution organs' decisions and, through them, reasons related to the predictability of the consequences of one behaviour or another by the addressees of those decisions. The predictability of the effects that one's own actions may have on the decisions of the empowered organs is, as some have repeatedly pointed out,[7] a necessary condition for the effectiveness of personal autonomy.

All these are reasons for a rule-based model of law and for a model of justification of court's decisions according to which courts must, at least prima facie, make those—and only those—decisions which can be deductively drawn from the pre-existing rules. Even if all those reasons are strong reasons for that model of law and for that specific model of judicial justification, they are nonetheless not absolute reasons, but reasons requiring to be balanced against other reasons arguing for a different model of law and a different model of justification of judicial decisions: namely, a model which does not regard law only as a matter of rules and which does not contend that to subsume a particular case under a rule is the only way and the last word to be said when decisions by courts must be justified.

Therefore, there are reasons to regard law not merely as a matter of rules but also as a matter of explicit and implicit values and purposes (that is, as a matter of principles, in a broad sense) which the rules are intended to serve. And those very reasons lead us to support the tenet according to which rules can be defeated under the light of certain

[7] Herein we refer to Francisco Laporta and his extense series of contributions culminating in *El imperio de la ley. Una visión actual* (Madrid: Trotta, 2007). On Laporta's ideas and for further elaboration of the lines above, see J. Ruiz Manero, 'Las virtudes de las reglas y sus límites. Una discusión con Francisco Laporta' in F. Serrano and R. Vázquez (eds), *Ciencia jurídica y Constitución. Homenaje a Rolando Tamayo y Salmorán* (México: Porrúa-UNAM, 2008).

principles. The most important of these reasons being the following:[8] if we regard law exclusively as a matter of rules we will have no mechanism at all to avoid serious value flaws in decisions founded upon it, even if those rules were the best possible ones and were applied by the best possible judges. For there is no omniscient legislator who might foresee all possible combinations of properties arising in future cases. Hence, no matter how carefully generic cases are designed, over-inclusion and under-inclusion—two phenomena pointed at by Schauer—cannot be exhaustively prevented. So, we cannot avoid certain cases being (wrongly) included under the scope of certain rules, in spite of clearly not being included within the values and purposes underlying the rule. Neither can we avoid certain other cases that for the same purposes should be included within the scope of certain rules, not being so (wrongly).

However, a decision model solely based on principles or, let us say, a model that could not resort to anything other than values and purposes to ground decisions would increase the costs of decision-making, would render decisions extremely difficult to predict, and would be incompatible with the very logic of separation of powers. This is what makes it clear that, in the history of legal culture, the emphasis has moved, depending on the period and on the legal system, along a continuous range from an extreme where law is regarded exclusively as a set of indefeasible rules—in Regan's terminology,[9] this means to grasp rules as completely *opaque* unlike those principles which give them sense and grounding—and the opposite extreme where rules are taken as merely indicative guidelines for conduct whose application must be excluded—be defeated—on any occasion when they appear incoherent with those principles—in Regan's terminology, to grasp rules as completely *transparent* with respect to those principles. We find that one of the fundamental criteria to evaluate a theory of law is to test its ability to give account of how and at what point along that spectrum the tension between what can be called the pole of rules—connected to predictability and reduction of complexity in decision-making processes—and the pole of principles—connected to coherence of values involved in those decisions—should be articulated and solved.

B. Atypical illicit acts and atypical licit acts

1. Atypical illicit acts

A quite interesting example of this tension between rules and principles is found in what we have called elsewhere *atypical illicit acts.*[10] Under this category we could include illicit acts generated by analogy as well as those other illicit acts under the concepts of 'abuse of rights', 'fraud on the law' (*fraus legis*) and 'misuse of power' (*déviation du pouvoir*).

Illicit acts are actions (in the broadest sense of this term) whose performance entails the violation of regulative mandatory norms, that is, the violation of norms establishing that certain behaviour is obligatory or forbidden. One may infer that so far as permissive norms cannot be violated it is not possible to encounter illicit acts

[8] We are following along these lines Juan Ruiz Manero, 'Las virtudes de las reglas y sus límites. Una discusión con Francisco Laporta'.

[9] Cf. D. Regan: 'Authority and Value: Reflections on Raz's *Morality of Freedom*', *Southern California Law Review*, 62 (1989), 995ff.

[10] See M. Atienza and J. Ruiz Manero, *Ilícitos atípicos. Sobre el abuso del derecho, el fraude de ley y la desviación de poder* (Madrid: Trotta, 2000).

constituted by actions against this sort of norm (clearly, whenever an action and an omission are both permitted, doing the action or omitting it are both licit behaviours). Very much the same occurs with constitutive norms (these norms do not have a deontic qualifier; instead they merely set the conditions for a certain institutional outcome or normative change to occur). Given that mandatory norms can be either rules or principles, there are two kinds of illicit act: typical illicit acts as actions opposed to mandatory rules and atypical illicit acts as actions opposed to mandatory principles.

By 'atypical illicit acts' (legal wrongs) we will refer to those actions which despite being prima facie allowed are, all circumstances considered, forbidden. This change of its deontic status (the turn from permitted into forbidden) occurs by virtue of an argumentative process to that effect. This process leads to the extension of the realm of legal wrongs mentioned above. Two forms or mechanisms of such argumentative process can be distinguished:

Analogy is the first one. There are two kinds of analogy: *analogia iuris* and *analogia legis*. Both involve a weak permission at the level of rules (this means that a particular action is prima facie permitted since it cannot be subsumed within any prohibitory rule). The operation of the deontic status conversion, however, differs from one case to another. In the case of *analogia legis*, the reason for the eventual prohibition—all things considered—rests on the resemblance between the unregulated case and another case or several other cases in which a certain prohibitory rule is involved. The justification for this is that the reasons (the balance of principles) justifying the prohibition in these latter cases also apply in the case that appeared as not regulated. In other words, that balance between principles claims to generate a new prohibitory rule within which the particular act is to be subsumed. In the case of *analogia iuris*, the generation of a new prohibitory rule is directly claimed by the balance among the relevant principles that apply in the case, although no pre-existing prohibitory rule under which other similar cases are to be subsumed is provided by the system.

The second mechanism (which applies in the case of abuse of rights, fraud on the law (*fraus legis*) and misuse of power (*déviation de pouvoir*)) is of particular concern to us. It works as follows. The starting point is the previous existence of an explicit permission. Consequently, the action is prima facie permitted by a regulatory rule. The modification of the deontic status of that particular action occurs as a consequence of the incoherence subsequently manifested between the case subsumed within the rule mentioned and the principles of the system (hence, the case constitutes an *axiological gap* in the system of rules).[11] Here, the balance among principles argues for the generation of a new prohibitory rule within which the case is to be subsumed.

It should be noted that atypical illicit acts pose a situation that differs from a mere situation of conflicting rules or one of conflicting principles. For they presuppose a conflict between rules and principles (abuse of rights, fraud on the law, misuse of power), or between the absence of certain rules and the existing principles of the system (analogy).

[11] The definition of an *axiological gap* here accepted is the following one: 'A case constitutes an axiological gap in a particular legal system if and only if (1) in the system there is a rule that establishes a solution for the case, and still (2) that rule does not consider as relevant a given property which, according to the demands entailed by the balance of the applicable principles in the particular legal system, should be so considered' (Juan Ruiz Manero, 'Algunas concepciones del Derecho y sus lagunas'). Note that this definition is a modified version of Alchourrón and Bulygin's concept of axiological gaps as held in *Normative Systems* for the purpose of adapting this to a principle-sensitive conception of the law.

The existence of atypical illicit acts responds to a demand for coherence (value or justificatory coherence) claimed by any legal system: what is at stake is the demand for a proper fit between the directive dimension of the law and its justificatory dimension; that is, the request for integrity of rules and principles. Some systems (clearly civil law systems) achieve this goal by way of implementing the above mentioned mechanisms: analogy on the one hand, and abuse of rights, fraud on the law, and misuse of power on the other. Analogy plays an important role in other systems (common law systems) too, but their functional equivalent to those other, civil law concepts can probably be found in the technique of 'distinguishing', or in plain resort to principles.[12] In this sense, it may be advanced that the category of atypical illicit acts is general to all developed legal systems due to its significance as a necessary means for sparing us from extreme formalism in the application of the law. For extreme formalism would entail nothing but a sort of value incoherence of legal decisions.

2. Examples of atypical illicit acts

We will not undertake here a thorough analysis of the three concepts mentioned above. Still, we will introduce an 'explanatory definition' and an illustrative—and canonical—example for each of them.

(a) Abuse of rights

'Action A carried out by S under the circumstances X is abusive if and only if:

1) There exists a regulative rule allowing S to do A under the circumstances X. This rule is an element of the network of normative positions in which S is located as a holder of a certain right.
2) As a consequence of action A another—or several—individual(s) suffer(s) an injury or damage D. There is no rule forbidding D taking place.
3) However, D is considered an unjustified damage whenever any of the following circumstances are met:
    3.1) when performing A, either S did not pursue any discernible purpose other than to cause D, or S did A without any discernible serious and legitimate purpose.
    3.2) D is an excessive or unusual damage.
4) The unjustified nature of the damage determines action A to be beyond the scope of those principles underlying the permissive rule mentioned in 1), as well as the emergence of a new rule establishing that under circumstances X' (X plus any other circumstance which might entail either 3.1 or 3.2 being met) action A is forbidden.'

Example: The *Consorcio de la Zona Franca* in Barcelona (as read in a well-known case decided by the Spanish Supreme Court on 14 February 1944) held a government franchise conferred for the extraction of sand from the beaches of the Barcelona seaside. At that time an electric company had a hydroelectric power station placed by the mouth of a river near a beach where the *Consorcio* proceeded to extract sand. This activity caused the destruction of those natural defences that used to protect the hydroelectric

[12] See 'Fraud on the Law—The doctrine of Evasion', *Columbia Law Review*, 42 (1942), 1015ff.; and R. Venables, 'Abuse of Rights in EC Law', *Tax Adviser*, October 2003, 16ff.

power station against river overflows and against storm or sea-tidal effects. As it happens, an especially strong storm took place producing major damage to the hydroelectric power station. Its owner (a corporation) sued for damages. The court gave judgment for the plaintiff.

(b) Fraud on the Law (fraus legis)

'Action A carried out by subject S under the circumstances X is fraudulent if and only if:

1) There exists a regulative rule allowing S to use the power-conferring rule in order to produce, under the circumstances X, result R by performing action A.
2) As a consequence of R, a certain state of affairs E comes into being. According to the balance among those principles justifying the previous permission and other principles of the system, this state of affairs constitutes an unjustified damage or an unlawful benefit. There is no regulative rule forbidding the production of R, although a rule may exist pursuing the avoidance of E.
3) R is a means for E:
    3.1) either in a subjective sense, given that when performing A, S had no other discernible goal whatsoever but to achieve, by means of R, the state of affairs E, being R objectively adequate to produce E.
    3.2) or in an objective sense, given that R is objectively adequate to cause E, even if S had not that particular intention when performing A.
4) The outcome of the balance among those principles mentioned in 2) was powerful enough to generate a new rule establishing that under the circumstances X' (X plus any other circumstances that somehow mean that 2 and 3.1 or 3.2 also take place) it is forbidden to use the power-conferring rule in a way that causes E by means of R. This is the reason why the result R must be considered as invalid to the extent that it leads to E.'

Example: The '*pacto comisorio*' (agreement of rescission) is a contractual clause allowing each party to rescind an agreement whenever the other party breaches it. Under Spanish law, this is not a valid clause if attached by the parties to a pledge loan. Therefore, whenever a pledge, a mortgage, or an *antichresis* in favour of the creditor is granted by the parties in order to secure the payment of a certain debt, in the event the debtor has failed to pay the secured debt by the expiration date the creditor is not allowed to directly appropriate for herself the assets granted as security. In such an event, the creditor is instead legally obliged, in order to satisfy her interests, to follow the corresponding legal proceedings: forced sale of the assets at public auction under judicial control, etc. Sometimes it happens that the parties, in order to (fraudulently) avoid the mentioned prohibition, instead of a pledge loan use the contractual category of 'sale with redemption clause', in which the '*pacto comisorio*' is not prohibited: 'The borrower (A) agrees to sell the lender (B) a certain asset, but he keeps the right to recover it (redemption clause) before a certain deadline (identical to the loan term) and for a certain price (identical to the loan amount); the amount that (B) has lent (A) appears as the price of the sale that (B) must pay. In the event that at the expiration date the debtor–seller has not used his redemption right, then the creditor-buyer irrevocably acquires ownership over it.'[13]

[13] L. Díez Picazo and A. Gullón, *Sistema de Derecho Civil* (Madrid: Cívitas, 1994), Book 1, Vol. 1, 200.

(c) Misuse of power (déviation de pouvoir)

'Action A whenever carried out by a public authority or organ O under the circumstances X constitutes a case of misuse of power if and only if:

1) There exists a regulative rule allowing the public authority O to use the (public) power-conferring rule in order, under the circumstances X and by undertaking action A, to produce a certain administrative action or a legal provision as the result R.
2) As a consequence of R, a certain state of affairs obtains which, according to the balance among the underlying principles of the former permission and further principles of the system, entails an unlawful damage or an unlawful benefit. An applicable regulative rule forbidding the issuing of R (the legal provision in concern) does not exist, though a rule seeking to prevent E from happening may exist.
3) E is a means for R:
   3.1) either in a subjective sense, given that whenever performing A, O did not pursue any discernible purpose other than to achieve, by means of R, the consequence E, being R objectively adequate to E.
   3.2) or in an objective sense, given that E is objectively adequate to cause E, even if O had not that particular intention when performing A.
4) The outcome of the balance among the principles mentioned in 2) is powerful enough to generate a rule establishing that under the circumstances X' (X plus any other circumstance that somehow means that 2 and 3.1 or 3.2 obtained) it is forbidden to use the power-conferring rule in such a way that by producing R the consequence E occurs. Therefore, the result R (the relevant administrative action or legal provision) should be considered (regulatorily) invalid to the extent that it is a means for E.'

Example: In the well-known *Ârrets Lesbats* of 15 February 1864 and of 17 June 1866, the French *Conseil d'Etat* stated that 'if a Prefect uses his power to regulate parking and vehicular traffic in those squares near the train station in order to grant a monopoly to the sole enterprise enjoying a contract with the Railway Company, he commits an act of misuse of power since he has improperly used his powers for a purpose other than one of those promoted by the legislator'.[14] This was a new doctrine at that time. Under the earlier French law, the acts of an authority were invalidated in those cases in which the authority had exceeded the sphere of power granted to it (mere 'excess of power'). These cases, however, meant that the acts of an authority or official body should be invalidated not just in the case of an excess of power, but also whenever they involve a use of the conferred power for a purpose other than those pursued by the legislator.

Therefore, the three concepts comprising the general category of atypical illicit acts (leaving analogy aside) share the following features: (a) there is an action which is prima facie permitted by a rule; (b) either intentionally or not, an injury or damage is caused by that action; (c) the unlawful character of that damage is showed up in light of the balance of the relevant principles of the legal system; (d) the creation, as a result of that balancing, of a new rule limiting the scope of the former rule since the new rule considers as forbidden certain actions that were permitted under the former.

[14] C. Chinchilla, *La Desviación de Poder* (2nd edn, Madrid: Cívitas, 1999), 31.

3. Atypical licit acts

Now, were it tenable to argue for the existence of what we have called atypical illicit acts, it should also be correct to argue for atypical licit acts, namely, those cases in which a behaviour that appeared to be prima facie forbidden by a rule eventually becomes permitted as a result of the balance of the system's relevant principles. So, in the case of atypical illicit acts either a weak permission (i.e when no rule is provided (in case of analogy)), or a strong permission (i.e. when there is a pre-existing permissive rule (in case of abuse of rights, fraud on the law, or deviation of power)) is defeated. In its turn, in the case of atypical licit acts a prohibitory rule is defeated. In our opinion, it would be correct to speak about three different categories of atypical licit acts:

(a) Acts falling *beyond the scope* of a prohibitory rule since none of its underlying reasons apply. For instance: let us consider a rule prohibiting vehicles in the park whose underlying purpose is to privilege the park user's safety over the improvement of traffic flow that would result from the permission of traffic through the park. Assume that a vehicle exhibition is coming up and that for this purpose the vehicles are driven into the park after closing time. This case can be considered to fall beyond the scope of the prohibitory rule since the introduction of vehicles in the park in such circumstances is not a danger to anybody's safety (nor does it affect the traffic flow).[15]

(b) Acts constituting an *exception* to a rule: despite the rule's underlying reasons being applicable, a stronger, extra reason also applies as a ground for the exception. To illustrate this, let us introduce some changes in the example above. Now, an ambulance is driven into the park to rescue an injured person needing urgent medical assistance. The park users' safety could indeed be considered at risk due to the ambulance's speed in the park, but the need to give assistance and save a human life at immediate risk seems to be the prevalent reason under the circumstances.[16]

(c) Cases in which the reasons underlying the prohibitory rule apply to such a low degree that the prohibition becomes unjustified (principle of tolerance). Examples of this might be those situations considered in criminal law as cases governed by the so-called 'principle of insignificance', according to which the acts falling within the scope of a certain criminal rule should remain unpunished to the extent that they injure or endanger a legal good only to a very low degree. This happens in drug-dealing cases whenever the substance in question is dramatically denaturalized (its purity is almost non-existent) or its amount is extremely low.

As for the damage, a key element in the category of atypical illicit acts (abuse of rights, fraud on the law, and misuse of power), we may note that in the case of atypical licit acts such damage either is not produced (in [a]), or is compensated by a superior good (in [b]), or is insignificant (in [c]).

[15] Clearly this example is a mere variation of the one proposed by Fuller in his discussion with Hart: the Second World War truck being driven into the park to place it on a pedestal. See L.L. Fuller 'Positivism and Fidelity to Law—A Reply to Professor Hart', *Harvard Law Review*, 71 (1958).

[16] On the concepts 'ouside the scope' and 'exception', see J. Raz, *Practical Reason and Norms* (Princeton: Princeton University Press, 1990) and Á. Ródenas, 'Entre la transparencia y la opacidad. Análisis del papel de las reglas en el razonamiento judicial', *Doxa*, 21 (1998).

C. Rules' resistance

Several objections have been addressed to this conception of atypical illicit acts and to its underlying thesis on defeasibility of norms.[17] We believe that some of them are due to some misunderstandings. We will not discuss those here: namely, the objection that claims that our approach is far too narrow since it has been developed within the framework of legal positivism entailing a restriction of the scope or strength of the value element for those cases under consideration. These three concepts have also been charged with not being broad enough to fully cover the whole domain of atypical illicit acts. Another objection claims that the cases under consideration could be satisfactorily analysed resorting to rules without necessary reference for this purpose to the category of principles. However, there is an objection addressed by B. Celano which is, in our view, worth considering. B. Celano objects that our approach implies an overvaluation of principles and the correlative undervaluation of rules, to the point that we consider the latter almost irrelevant. The author expresses his thoughts as follows:

> In A&RM's theory, unlawfulness is never entailed by the infringement of a rule (breaking a rule is neither a necessary condition nor a sufficient one of unlawfulness). To establish whether a certain rule-breaking behaviour is or is not unlawful we need to regard the applicable principles. For the very same reason, there are no typical licit acts either, insofar as we understand as such those acts whose lawful character comes from their conformity to rules. Indeed, there is only one decisive factor to establish whether a certain behaviour is lawful or unlawful: namely, its conformity to the demands of the balance of the relevant principles . . . The lawfulness or unlawfulness of the behaviour is therefore independent from its conformity to what is required or permitted by a rule. For the purposes of qualifying a behaviour as legally right or wrong, in A&RM's theory rules are irrelevant.
>
> In A&RM's theory, rules are superfluous: they play no role at all. What depends on rules is just the possibility of ascribing lawful or unlawful behaviours (depending on their conformity or not to the relevant principles) the inconsequential label of 'typical' or 'atypical'.[18]

This is definitely a serious charge. If it were true that in our theory rules appear as 'irrelevant' or 'superfluous' elements of the law, then we should admit that, for that reason alone, our theory fails as a theory that attempts to reconstruct the way in which our legal systems actually operate. It would fail because, in that case, our theory would not be able to give account of a central aspect of our legal practices that no one can deny: that uncontroversial subsumption within rules is the ordinary manner of solving the vast majority of legal cases.

However, we believe that Celano is not right. Our theory does take into account the difference made by the presence of rules and the role they play in legal reasoning. The purpose of our category of atypical illicit (or licit) acts is to give adequate account of the defeasibility of the pre-existing permissive (or prohibitory) rule when the solution to a case that it generates turns out to be axiologically anomalous to an intolerable extent. As explained above, it is a type of reasoning that leads us from the pre-existing rule to a new rule which will eventually ground the solution to the case insofar as it is

[17] Of a special relevance are those appeared in the Italian review *Europa e diritto privato*, 3 (2006) in which the Italian version of *Ilícitos atípicos* is under discussion: *Illeciti atipici. L'abuso del diritto, la frode alla legge, lo sviamento di potere*, trans. by Valentina Carnevale, introduction by Mauro Barberis (Bologna: Il Mulino, 2004). See, among other contributions, those of L. Nivarra, 'Un dibattito palermitano su illeciti atipici', 1019ff.; F.D. Busnelli, '*Illeciti atipici* e il dibattito su regole e principi', 1035ff; C. Castronovo, 'Abuso del diritto come illecito atipico', 1051ff.; B. Celano, 'Principi, regole, autorità', 1059ff.; G. Corso, 'Gli illeciti atipici tra regole e principi', 1087ff.

[18] B. Celano, 'Principi, regole, autorità'.

the result of a balance among the relevant principles of the system. Even if, as a result of the argumentative process, the pre-existing rule is eventually defeated, this does not mean that it plays no relevant role at all during the process.

Perhaps Celano equates too quickly two very different theses. On one hand, is the thesis according to which all rules can be defeated under circumstances that are not fully predictable (were those circumstances completely predictable and the legislator reasonably careful, a rule would never be defeated since it would always include the pertinent exceptions to it). On the other is a completely different thesis according to which the presence of the rule makes no difference at all since it does not present any resistance to the balance of the relevant principles of the system.

We unhesitatingly endorse the first thesis. According to Celano, for the sake of consistency, this commits us to the second thesis too. However, Celano's claim is ill-grounded since it does not take into account that, in situations where rules are in play, not just relevant substantive principles of the system are at stake, but also a different kind of principles—institutional principles—grounding the practice of rule-following (such principles as stability, predictability, respect for allocation of power under the Constitution or under the laws, etc.) are relevant, as we remarked at the beginning of this article.[19]

So, rules are defeated in those cases, and only in those cases, in which the outcome of the balance among the principles that justify a departure from the rule outweighs the outcome of the balance among institutional principles which support the practice of rule-following. To our understanding, this thesis is far from regarding rules as irrelevant or superfluous.

To show how rules oppose resistance we shall give an example of a situation where that departure from the rule is precluded, that is, the rule is not defeated: even though elements (1), (2), (3) of the previous definitions are obtained, element (4) however is not entailed. The reason for this is that the outcome of the balance among the relevant principles does not allow for that step to be taken. Let us consider both a case that could be—though all things considered is not—an atypical licit case, and a case that could be—though all things considered is not—an atypical illicit act.

Spanish traffic regulations (like those of many other countries) include a very rigid prohibitory rule under which it is forbidden to drive faster than 120 km/hr on the motorway. The underlying reasons for this particular rule are quite clear: its purpose is to increase safety and to avoid traffic crashes. Now, what if during a beautiful sunny morning with perfect visibility, on a very long straight stretch of the motorway, with no traffic at all, in a car which is in a perfect state and fully equipped with the newest driving-safety technologies, a driver barely exceeds the speed limit? Should she be sanctioned? The balance among relevant principles undoubtedly entails that she should not. Under those specific circumstances there would be no risk at all (or at least no

[19] In Schauer's words: 'The values secured by rules (e.g. stability, notice, predictability, allocation of power among decision-makers) may themselves occupy a status equivalent to the status of other mid-level principles . . . In other words . . . rule-generating justifications may be equivalent in importance to those substantive justifications external to this rule that may override this rule.' F. Schauer, *Playing by the Rules. A Philosophical Examination of Rule-Based Decision-Making in Law and in Life* (Oxford: Clarendon Press, 1991), 110. Hence, as maintained by Schauer, the resistance opposed by rules against the outcome of the balance among relevant substantive principles is a matter of degree, since 'rule-based decision-making exists only insofar as the instantiation resists continuous modification in the service of its generating justification . . . This resistance need not be absolute . . . For rule-based decision-making to be other than a different name for particularistic decision-making, the rules employed in the former must pre-exist any particular application of them, and must supply some resistance in that application' (p. 84 and note).

higher risk than that of driving on a rainy day, in a worse-equipped vehicle, etc. at a speed below 120 km/hr), so the case would be one where the rule's underlying reasons will not apply. Still, if we appeal against the sanction, we might have some success if we question the proof of the facts (e.g. we challenge the reliability of the speed-measuring instruments), but we will have no chance if we allege on grounds of any of the previous reasons (that is, on the grounds of considering our driving an atypical licit act). Is this so because the appellate authority would be applying the law in a wrong way? We don't think so. It is plausible to think that for several reasons (all of them fairly strong), the balance in this case should entail that the rule should not be defeated. Among those reasons the following are to be noted: the risk of arbitrariness if discretion is conferred upon traffic agents in this matter; negative effects on drivers who might believe that it is permitted to drive faster than 120km/hr under circumstances in which actually (i.e. according to the right balance of principles, when the weighing procedure is rightly accomplished) it is not; etc.

Now, let us elaborate on a kind of behaviour that might be classified under the category of atypical illicit act; particularly, a misuse of power. Under the Spanish law, the *Consejo General del Poder Judicial* (General Council of the Judiciary) has the power to make appointments to the highest positions in the judiciary. In spite of being a highly discretionary power, it has some limits. Probably the most important of them is the constitutional duty to make the appointments by reference to the 'merit' and 'qualification' of the appointees. The situation can be described as follows. The legislative authority thought that the best way for the Council to accomplish its duty to appoint those people really having the highest degree of technical qualification, professional experience, independence, impartiality, and best capable of fulfilling certain judicial policies (those policies decided by the Council but compatible with the Constitution: i.e. women's promotion, a balanced distribution of the geographical origin of Justices, etc.) would be by allowing the Council a broad room for discretion; hence, discretion to pursue lawful goals, in accordance with the Constitution. Nevertheless, the Council has apparently departed from those goals on several occasions. As a result of this, some rejected candidates appealed to the *Tribunal Supremo* (the Supreme Court), successfully in some cases and unsuccesfully in others. The task of the Supreme Court (Third Division) was to control that exercise of discretion. Admittedly, this is a very complex problem.[20] However, we will focus here on just one aspect of it: when power was conferred upon the Council, the legislature stated both that decisions on appointments must be taken by a majority; and that the members of the Council are not required to issue an explicit justification of the content of their vote. That is, there is a rule according to which it is possible to appoint justices without expressing a justification for the vote (hence, without explicitly grounding that crucial moment of the appointment process). This circumstance leads to (or at least favours) justices' appointments according to partisan political sympathies, at the expense of appointments made to fulfil the goals which justified the discretionary power conferred. Would it be right then to consider that this is somehow a misuse of power? Should we claim that the members of the Council ought to explicitly justify the content of their vote (the omission of justification shall then turn from permitted into prohibited) and that otherwise their appointments would be invalid? We don't think so. There are powerful institutional reasons (basically those concerning distribution of constitutional and legal

[20] For a more detailed analysis, see M. Atienza, 'Discrecionalidad y juicios comparativos', *Jueces para la democracia*, 61 (2008), 77–86.

powers) of decisive importance at this point (still, not to the extent that any kind of substantive control by the Supreme Court has to be precluded). To be sure, the regulation of the General Council of the Judiciary is defective in this and other respects. However, this is what the legislature has established; and if the Supreme Court intends to go in this matter 'beyond' what was enacted by the legislature, that will amount to a sort of illegitimate 'judicial activism'.

D. By way of conclusion

As Giovanni Sartor reminds us ('Defeasibility in Legal Reasoning', in this volume), the notion of defeasibility was already used by Hart in 1951 in his analysis of the concept of validity; that is, in the context of the qualification of the states of affairs (normative results) obtained by the use of constitutive rules. Thus, it can be said of a contract that is valid if certain conditions x, y, . . . z are met, provided that no other circumstance x', y', . . . z' suitable to defeat that judgement of validity obtains. The concept of validity (and invalidity) in the context of constitutive rules amounts to the concept of lawfulness (and unlawfulness) in the context of regulative norms: a certain behaviour is lawful (or unlawful) if it is in accordance (or, respectively, does not accord) with what is established by those regulative norms in whose conditions of application x, y, . . . z, the behaviour can be subsumed, provided that no other element x', y', . . . z' suitable to defeat the judgement of lawfulness (or unlawfulness) obtains.

The common distinction between rules and principles in the sphere of regulative norms ought to be understood as follows. Rules establish the conditions that are ordinarily considered sufficient to formulate accordingly a lawfulness (or unlawfulness) judgement, whereas principles operate on a sort of second level of reasoning, often (in most occasions) giving support to the (prima facie or, if you will, *pro tanto*) judgement of lawfulness or unlawfulness established by the rules. In some few occasions though they provide us with reasons to *defeat* the former judgement, thus producing a new rule according to which, whenever circumstances x, y . . . z are met and if any other x', y' . . . z' also arises, then the behaviour in question will turn from being lawful into being unlawful (or vice versa). *Typical* lawfulness or unlawfulness concerns rules (arguably, principles are also at stake, implicitly: still, since the only function of principles here is to back rules up, their role remains rather unnoticed). In its turn, *atypical* lawfulness or unlawfulness takes into account principles whenever these are strong enough to defeat rules—to be more precise, pre-existing rules: one of the primary roles of principles—it must be remarked—is to generate new rules (or to 'reformulate' the pre-existing ones). This is the reason why the contrast between rules and principles, as for the way they operate in legal reasoning, cannot be understood merely in disjunctive terms.

Now, the category of atypical unlawful illicit (unlawful) acts (abuse of rights, fraud on the law, and misuse of power) on which we have focused here, covers not only actions that simply fit the content of a regulative norm (namely, abuse of rights) but also actions that consist in the use of a constitutive norm, a power-conferring norm (fraud on the law and misuse of power). Accordingly, in the first case (abuse of rights), the last part of the definition we propose shows that there is a turn from something being lawful into that same thing being unlawful (that is, something turning from permitted into forbidden); whereas in the other case (fraud on the law and misuse of power) further change takes place: the change from lawful into unlawful entails the change from valid into invalid. With this we are not claiming that judgements of lawfulness/unlawfulness and judgements of validity/invalidity collapse, we are showing how they are connected to each other.

Finally, what we have said in this article constitutes an analysis of certain concepts which should not be considered just as examples of defeasible arguments or defeasible premises (norms), but as examples of the institutionalization of defeasibility in the law. Abuse of rights, fraud on the law, and misuse of power are indeed three legal institutions intended to be structures, a sort of outline for reasoning, provided by the system to make the process of decision-making easier and, to some extent, decisions more predictable in contexts in which mere subsumption within rules is not sufficient should we want to avoid value anomalies. Those are contexts where deductive argumentation only plays a quite minor role. All this reminds us how right Toulmin was when in his renowned book of 1958 *The Uses of Argument* he invited us to regard 'logic'[21]—the term by which he referred to what we rather call today 'theory of argumentation'—as 'generalized jurisprudence'. It is well known that Toulmin advocated in that work for a pragmatic—dialectic—conception of reasoning (which he opposed to the classical model of deductive logic), a more adequate conception to analyse arguments produced in the context of what he called 'rational enterprises' (such as Law, Ethics, Medicine, or Business) and in which defeasibility (as expressed in his concepts of *rebuttal* and *qualifier*) was of particular importance.

21 S. Toulmin, *The Uses of Argument* (Cambridge: Cambridge University Press, 1958).

15

Defeasibility and Legal Positivism

*Wilfrid J. Waluchow**

A. Introduction: the many faces of defeasibility

Is 'defeasibility' a phenomenon that generates trouble for legal positivism? Does it provide good reason to reject positivism in favour of some alternative conception of law? How we answer these questions will depend on a number of factors, not the least of which are what exactly we mean by the term 'defeasible', what it is that is said to be defeasible—the 'object' of defeasibility, as it were—and whether the kind of defeasibility we have in mind is thought to be a necessary feature of the object in question or only something that the object is capable of possessing. A quick survey of the literature on defeasibility reveals quite a range of possibilities—and it is not always clear which of these is in play in any given context. So we will have to be careful in exploring the relation(s) between defeasibility and legal positivism.

When we say that law is inherently defeasible, do we mean that all legal rules (or norms) are in some way defeasible?[1] That only some are? Do we mean that some or all legal rules have this property of necessity? Or only that it is possible for a legal system to have rules of this kind? When we say that a rule is defeasible, do we mean that it is capable of being overridden or outweighed by other rules? By legal principles? By moral principles and values? By any reason that strikes an adjudicator as a good reason not to apply what would otherwise be an applicable rule? Perhaps to say that a rule is defeasible means that someone who normally has an obligation to apply the rule, has in some instance the legal power to *change* it so as to escape its binding force. If so, does the law ever license judges to do this? And if so, may they do so for moral reasons? Often when an author speaks of defeasibility, she means that all (or some) legal rules have built-in exceptions? If so, what precisely does this mean? Is the class of exceptions to a defeasible legal rule a closed set each of whose members has been explicitly stated in the rule, or perhaps somewhere else within the law? Or does it mean something quite a bit stronger than this—that sometimes (or always?) rules are subject to a kind of open-ended defeasibility, that is, subject to exceptions which have not been legally specified in advance, and which perhaps could not be so specified even by the most enlightened of lawmakers? In other words, is the claim that an accurate statement of a legal rule—one which reveals its defeasible logical structure—will always (sometimes, etc.) end, not with a finite list of explicit exceptions, but with the locution 'unless . . . '?[2] Here's another question. When an author speaks of (implicit or explicit) exceptions to legal rules does she mean what Hart once meant when he first raised this particular issue: that

* Senator William McMaster Professor of Constitutional Studies, McMaster University.

[1] Unless the context makes clear that I have more specific meanings in mind, I will use the terms 'rule' and 'norm' interchangeably.

[2] Cf. H.L.A. Hart, *The Concept of Law* (2nd edn, Oxford: Clarendon Press, 1994), 139, where Hart writes 'a rule that ends with the word "unless . . . " is still a rule'.

a complete articulation of a rule will often specify negative conditions—e.g. duress or necessity in relation to murder—which in some way negate the satisfaction of whatever positive conditions it specifies for its application? Does this feature extend to legal artefacts like wills and binding contracts which legal rules help create? Could it extend to the notion of valid law? And finally, when an author says that legal rules are defeasible, does he mean to say, as some theorists contend, that legal rules are always subject to rival interpretations—that what might otherwise appear to be the obvious or correct interpretation of a binding legal rule can sometimes be successfully dislodged by a legally compelling argument supporting some other way of reading the rule? If so, then what's at play here might be described as a kind of interpretative defeasibility.

So there are many very different things we might mean when speaking of law as defeasible. But the story doesn't end here. Sometimes when an author speaks of legal defeasibility, what she appears to mean is not that legal rules are defeasible, but that legal *reasoning* in some way exhibits this property. The two phenomena—defeasible rules and defeasible reasoning—are no doubt closely related to one another, if only because legal reasoning typically involves the application of rules to fact situations, and so to say that legal reasoning is defeasible often means nothing more than that the rules with which legal actors reason are always (or often) defeasible. Nevertheless, it is wise to approach the two phenomena as distinct, if only because we would not want to dismiss without good reason the possibility that, in some case with its particular set of material facts, the legal result required by a non-defeasible rule might nevertheless be one which a legal agent, such as a judge, is not bound to accept. Perhaps, e.g. the rule's answer can be set aside in favour of a competing principle of utmost legal or moral importance. 'How a judge must decide a case' and 'what a valid legal rule requires in that case' are not necessarily the same thing.

So what exactly could it mean to say that legal reasoning is defeasible? Does it mean that there are no incontestable claims, conclusions, or arguments in law? That a legal claim, conclusion, or argument, say to the effect that the defendant is guilty or liable in law, or that a valid contract exists between X and Y, is always subject to legally valid defeat by an opposing claim, conclusion, or argument? Is this a kind of *logical defeasibility* which might lead to rule scepticism and a belief in radical legal indeterminacy? After all, if it's always possible, even in the easiest and clearest of cases, to argue that a legal claim, conclusion, or argument need not be accepted as legally determinative, one might be led to conclude that there really is no such thing as binding law at all—that there are no binding legal rules, and no logically compelling legal arguments based on them, which could possibly determine legally obligatory outcomes. And if this is so, then one might begin to wonder about the viability of the rule of law itself—and about the immense power we would necessarily be placing in the hands of our judges. Or is the idea at play here better expressed by speaking only of a kind of *epistemic defeasibility*—which attaches not to rules, claims, or arguments found in legal practice, but to our knowledge of these things and the degree of certainty which attaches to them? If so, then perhaps all that's being claimed when talk turns to the defeasible nature of legal reasoning is that none of us is incapable of error—that no legal argument we mount will be impervious to challenge, if only via the epistemic chicanery of Descartes' evil genius.[3] If this is all that is meant, then we can readily concede that

[3] Descartes' evil genius appears in the first of René Descartes' *Meditations on First Philosophy*. His powers of deceit are such as to render doubtful the truth of a claim as supposedly simple and certain as that two plus two equals four. Fortunately for Descartes, God comes to the rescue and provides the epistemic assurance Descartes seeks—or so Descartes thinks.

almost every claim, conclusion, or argument in law is inherently defeasible. But then this should come as no surprise. *Any* form of practical reasoning in *any* forum one cares to mention—law, morality, politics, literary criticism, applied philosophy—is in this sense epistemically defeasible. And there is clearly nothing here which distinguishes law as somehow special. And, importantly, there is nothing here which any positivist would wish to deny or which makes trouble for his theory.[4]

It is clear, then, that there are many very different questions and many very different issues in play when the subject of defeasibility in law is brought to the forefront. And so it is impossible to consider the relationship(s), if any, between defeasibility and positivism without first being clear on which type of defeasibility is at issue.[5] Bearing this in mind, and in consideration of the constraints imposed by the space available to me, I propose to limit my focus and proceed as follows. I will begin by introducing and explaining an important distinction between moral and legal defeasibility. I will then attempt to explain the various respects in which law is, for the legal positivist, morally defeasible—and what exactly that means and entails. My next step will be to consider how far a positivist can go in accommodating two claims: first, that legal rules, claims, and arguments are what I call *epistemically defeasible*, and second that these are what I call *logically defeasible*. As we shall see, there is (perhaps surprisingly) much that the positivist can easily accept in the way of both epistemic and logical defeasibility, including the possibility that it may even attach, if conditions are right, to *legal validity*. The precise nature of positivist conditions of validity have, of course, been a controversial subject in recent years. Some positivists, who defend what is now generally called 'Inclusive Legal Positivism' (ILP), argue that among the possible conditions for legal validity accepted by a legal system is that a rule, contract, will, etc., must satisfy certain moral conditions such as compatibility with norms of fundamental fairness or moral equality. Others, who defend what is now commonly termed 'Exclusive Legal Positivism' (ELP) deny this. They insist, for a variety of theoretical reasons having mainly to do with the law's capacity to provide authoritative guidance, that legal validity must always, in all systems of law, be determined by non-moral, source-based criteria. I will close with a few thoughts on whether the notion of defeasibility might provide a novel means of bringing these two sides together in a way which does justice to the insights of each. I suspect that it can.

B. Moral versus legal defeasibility

Legal positivism is often taken—quite mistakenly, I hasten to add—to be committed to a particular theory of legal obligation or duty.[6] This is a theory of obligation well expressed by Bentham's advice 'to obey punctually; to censure freely'.[7] According to this particular rendering of legal positivism, though existing law is always something I am free to criticize or condemn on moral grounds, there nevertheless remains upon me an obligation always to obey it, at least until such time as the law is changed,

[4] This point will be explored in more detail below.

[5] Obviously the same applies with respect to positivism. There are many different varieties of that theoretical orientation and it is not always easy to understand what they have in common or the respects in which they differ from one another. Despite the obvious hazards involved in doing so, I shall take, as my exemplar of legal positivism, the elegant and influential theory defended by H.L.A. Hart in *The Concept of Law*.

[6] I will use the terms 'duty' and 'obligation' interchangeably.

[7] J. Bentham, 'A Fragment on Government' in 1 *The Collected Works of Jeremy Bentham* 221, 230 (Bowring ed. 1859) (preface, 16th para.).

perhaps in response to my moral criticisms. An analogous point is sometimes made in relation to judges and how they should go about deciding cases. Positivism is sometimes thought to entail a theory of judicial obligation requiring judges always to apply existing rules of law, regardless of any injustice which would result from their doing so in particular cases. And this, it is often said, or at least hinted, is enough to discredit positivism as not only a descriptively inaccurate theory of legal practice—judges sometimes *do* set laws aside when these conflict with fundamental moral principles, particularly those associated with the rule of law—it is also revealed to be a soulless, perhaps pernicious, theory unworthy of acceptance by any morally responsible agent. But none of this is even close to being accurate.

The truth of the matter is that positivism in no way entails any such obligations. That the existence of valid law is one thing, its moral merit another thing entirely, is a thesis which stands in easy union with a theory according to which I am morally at liberty, perhaps even required, to disobey valid law when morality demands that I do so. In other words, that legal validity and moral merit are conceptually distinct properties is a fact, according to the positivist, which, *in and of itself*, has absolutely no bearing whatsoever on what, morally, I ought to do. In short, there is nothing in the positivist's theories of law and legal validity which entails any particular theory of moral obligation. And it is crucial to stress that this claim extends to judges and their adjudicative obligations. To be sure, the law itself may explicitly demand that judges apply any and all valid laws, regardless of their views on their moral merit. That is, a system's rules of adjudication may, as a matter of fact, prohibit judges from declining to apply valid laws on moral grounds.[8] It is also true that, morally speaking, the institutional role of *any* judge in *any* minimally just legal system *always* brings with it a special moral duty to apply some laws which are found morally wanting, just as it is the institutional role of any policeman in any minimally just legal system to enforce at least some laws with which he disagrees morally. There are sound moral reasons why judges and policemen should not, given their official roles within a legal system, be at liberty to pick and choose which laws to apply or enforce. These reasons have to do with things like the need for effective, authoritative law within a complex society in which people disagree morally; and the fact (if it is a fact) that someone else, with the authority to do so, has deliberated in good faith about which laws are best to introduce and has decided to introduce the particular law in question, and so on. Despite all this, we must continue to insist on one absolutely crucial point: morality, including the requirements it places on people serving special institutional roles, is not *completely* indifferent to the circumstances in which these people are sometimes called upon to act in discharging their institutional responsibilities. It is not indifferent, for example, to the degree of injustice that might result were a duly adopted, legally valid rule applied by a judge to a particular set of facts. And the same goes for our, sometimes unfortunate, police officer. He is no more under an absolute, unconditional moral duty to enforce each and every law, *come what may*, than a soldier is under an absolute, unconditional moral duty to obey any and all military orders—including, for example, a grossly immoral order to slaughter innocent villagers. In this sense, then, laws are, for both judge and police officer, *morally defeasible*. Indeed, all reasonably just legal systems recognize this inescapable fact, and many, as a result, call on judges (though not police officers) sometimes to *change* or otherwise alter the force or effect of the law so as to avoid applying it in such deeply problematic cases. As all contemporary positivists are happy

[8] On 'rules of adjudication' see H.L.A. Hart, *The Concept of Law*, 96–9.

to assert, the law typically includes the grounds for its own development, reinterpretation, and change in the course of its application to particular cases, including the ones now under consideration—circumstances in which there are overwhelming moral reasons to seek a way to avoid applying a law. In such instances, the law can quite sensibly be said to be not only *morally* defeasible but *legally* defeasible as well, that is, subject to defeat for legally sanctioned moral reasons so as to escape its otherwise binding effect. (We will return to these points later.) But to be clear, even when the law fails to enable a judge to avoid, in some way, the application of a law on moral grounds, the judge always, of necessity, retains the residual moral right—indeed, I would insist, the moral *duty*—not to apply it if doing so would lead to gross injustice. It remains, for him, morally defeasible. Much as a soldier will sometimes reach a stage where his institutional or role-dependent moral duty to obey orders must give way to the more basic, role-independent, moral obligations we all have as responsible moral agents, a judge might find herself morally compelled to violate her institutional, role-relative, moral duty to honour the law she is normally bound to apply. The law cannot strip a judge of her moral autonomy; it cannot expect her to check her moral scruples at the door when she enters the courtroom. It cannot do this any more than it can require us to check our moral autonomy at the door when we enter a civil society governed by the rule of law.

I conclude that there is an important sense in which law always is, of necessity, morally defeasible. This extends to all of us, citizen, policeman, and judge alike, for whom Bentham's prescription to obey punctually may well stand as sound advice—as a useful practical guide or 'rule of thumb' which normally finds its way into what R.M. Hare called our 'intuitive level' of moral thinking.[9] That is, it is a prescription which we are rational to adopt and follow in the normal course of events. But its adoption must always be accompanied by two important caveats: first, the prescription applies only when both our society and its legal system are reasonably just; and second, the obligation to obey, apply, or enforce always remains, at best, and of necessity, prima facie. And in this crucial sense it is a moral obligation that is inherently defeasible—and necessarily so. To think that a positivist must deny this is to mistake his theories concerning legal validity and the nature and structure of legal systems for a very crude theory of moral obligation, one calling for unconditional allegiance and obedience to law. How anyone could saddle morally sensitive proponents of positivism like H.L.A. Hart, Joseph Raz, John Gardner, and Leslie Green with such a monstrous theory really is quite a mystery.[10]

C. Logical and epistemic defeasibility

Sometimes the term 'defeasible' is used to denote a kind of *epistemic defeasibility*—which attaches not to rules, claims, or arguments found in legal practice, but to our knowledge of these things and the degree(s) of certainty we can achieve with respect to them. Essentially, what is being said in such cases is that no claim to legal knowledge is completely impervious to challenge or reasonable dispute. But if this is what is being claimed—that all legal claims to knowledge are in principle contestable—then we can

[9] See R.M. Hare, *Moral Thinking: Its Levels, Methods and Point* (Oxford: Clarendon Press, 1981).

[10] For Hart's views on the moral obligation to obey the law, see *The Concept of Law* and H.L.A. Hart, 'Positivism and the Separation of Law and Morals', *Harvard Law Review*, 71 (1958), 593. See also, J. Raz, *The Morality of Freedom* (Oxford: Oxford University Press, 1988) and J. Raz, *The Authority of Law* (Oxford: Clarendon Press, 1979); J. Gardner, 'Legal Positivism: 5½ Myths', *The American Journal of Jurisprudence*, 46 (2001), 199; and L. Green, 'Positivism and the Inseparability of Law and Morals', *New York University Law Review*, 83 (2008), 1035–58.

readily agree. This will be so even in respect of those cases where no one would seriously entertain a challenge, that is, where the only kind of doubt one could seriously entertain would be founded on radical Cartesian scepticism of a highly speculative sort. But it will also be true in many other cases, including those where a legal official has made an authoritative decision on a genuinely contestable issue. In the latter case, the law may not give us standing to challenge the official's claim legally, say by granting us leave to appeal the authoritative decision, any more than it would in the former case. But it remains true that both the decision, and any claim one might make in dispute of it, is inherently defeasible—that is, subject to the response that the decision-maker got things wrong. In law we never achieve absolute certainty, any more than we do in any other domain of practical reasoning.

But now we face a far tougher question. Do the observations of the preceding paragraph pose any particular problem for positivism? It is difficult to understand why they would, unless one assumes, for some reason, that positivists view law as seriously wedded to the pursuit of absolute certainty as its defining goal or ideal—or perhaps cognate goals like unassailable authoritative guidance or conclusive settlement of disputes.[11] It is easy to see how one might make this assumption, if only because some 'prescriptive' or 'normative' positivists, as they are sometimes called, do seem to view the achievement of a very high level of certainty as one of law's defining goals.[12] And even those positivists who would eschew any such view, do speak of the certainty which law is capable of introducing into our practical reasoning as one of its central virtues. Hart, for example, referred to the 'defect of uncertainty' which inevitably plagues all but the most close-knit of pre-legal societies, and went on to characterize his famous rule of recognition as a remedy for this defect.[13] It is tempting to infer that even a positivist like Hart views certainty as a central goal of legal practice, as part of its *raison d'être*, so to speak.[14] And if we make this inference, then we might be led to view epistemic defeasibility as a serious threat to positivism because that property seems to work against the achievement of absolute certainty. But that would be a mistake. As Hart himself notes, legal systems routinely balance values like certainty, predictability, and stability against competing values, including the need for flexibility at point of application of legal rules so as to avoid morally troubling results. Rules, Hart tells us, are often drafted in very open-textured terms, leaving room for the consideration of contentious background moral reasons when the rules are applied by citizens and judges.[15] Instead of trying to craft detailed, closely textured rules, in a futile bid to achieve an elusive degree of absolute certainty that

[11] On the so-called 'guidance function' of law, see S. Shapiro, 'On Hart's Way Out', *Legal Theory*, 4 (1998), 469; and S. Shapiro, 'The Difference that Rules Make' in B. Bix (ed.), *Analyzing Law* (Oxford: Oxford University Press, 1998). For one among many replies, see my 'Legality, Morality and the Guidance Function of Law' in M. Kramer, C. Grant, B. Colburn, and A. Hatzistavrou (eds), *The Legacy of H.L.A. Hart: Legal, Political and Moral Philosophy* (Oxford: Oxford University Press, 2008).

[12] Prescriptive positivism is a fully normative theory which does not attempt to understand or describe the nature of law or legal systems, but seeks to support recommendations on what sorts of laws we ought to have and what sorts of goals a legal system ought to pursue. On this theory, see T. Campbell and J.H. Gerards (eds), *Prescriptive Legal Positivism: Law, Rights and Democracy* (London: Routledge Cavendish, 2004). Some critics of positivism view this as the only form of positivism worthy of consideration. For Ronald Dworkin's attempt to transform positivism into a normative, 'interpretative' theory of law—and then demolish it so understood—see R. Dworkin, *Law's Empire* (Cambridge: Harvard University Press, 1986).

[13] See H.L.A. Hart, *The Concept of Law*, in particular 91–9.

[14] Once again, see R. Dworkin, *Law's Empire*.

[15] Other methods sometimes used to strike a balance appropriate to the particular context—e.g. tort law versus real estate law—include reliance on variable standards, and the use of common law rules which are developed by judges in a case-by-case manner as new cases are decided.

is simply not possible in the circumstances, rule-creators often employ very open-textured terms like 'reasonable', 'due care', and 'fair'. The measure of uncertainty that is undoubtedly introduced by the use of such inherently contentious, morally laden terms is wisely accepted as a cost worth paying for the sake of these other values. These are values which would be seriously compromised were rule-makers to opt for much more concrete rules in a misguided bid to achieve absolute certainty.

So the fact that law is epistemically defeasible poses no particular difficulty for positivists. It appears to do so only if we saddle them with an over-simplified theory of law's defining ideals or purposes—a theory to which no plausible version of legal positivism is wedded. But this brings us to logical defeasibility. True, we can never achieve absolute certainty in law, even if for some misguided reason we tried to do so. And all positivists recognize this. But what if legal rules are *logically* defeasible? Would the degree of uncertainty introduced by this property be more than any positivist could admit? Do we have here a feature of law which shows the sheer folly of viewing law as positivism proposes? Once again, we must begin by saying 'it depends'. It depends on the kind of logical defeasibility one has in mind. Let's begin with two kinds of logical defeasibility which quite obviously pose no difficulty at all for positivists.

Legal rules sometimes have explicit exceptions. In other words, sometimes there is a finite class of exceptions to a rule each of whose members has been explicitly stated, either in the rule itself, or perhaps somewhere else in the law. In such an instance, one might be inclined to express this point by saying that a full and accurate statement of the rule will end with the word 'unless'. But a far better way to put the point would be to say that a full and accurate statement of the rule will take something like the following form: 'One is forbidden from doing M (defined as A, B, and C), unless X, Y, or Z'. For example, criminal codes often list a number of conditions under which someone can be said to have committed murder (M): S has taken a life (A), has done so knowingly (B), and so on. But typically criminal codes also specify a number of defences—e.g. that one was acting in self-defence (X), or under duress or necessity (Y), that one was suffering from some 'disease of the mind' or subject to an 'irresistible impulse' of some medically recognized kind (Z), and so on. If any of these latter conditions applies, the effect will be to negate or defeat the claim that S has committed murder, even though A through C obtain. S will either be found guilty of a lesser offence, like involuntary manslaughter, or exonerated entirely, as is normal in cases of self-defence. But though the murder rule is subject to these exceptions, it is important to stress that these form a closed set the members of which the law itself specifies in advance. One who sought to express *fully* the rule governing murder would be obliged to include each one of the specified exceptions in her statement of the rule.

A second kind of non-problematic defeasibility is exemplified by the doctrine of federal paramountcy which is sometimes employed in federal states to deal with conflicts between federal and state (or provincial) law. In cases where the two conflict, legal systems routinely give preference to federal law, at least to the extent of the conflict. By this I mean that the state law remains valid and determines results in any other cases in which there is no conflict. In such scenarios, one can quite sensibly say that state laws are always subject to defeat by a paramount federal law. In both kinds of cases—rules with explicit exceptions and cases where rules are overridden because of something like the doctrine of federal paramountcy—we find nothing to give positivists any cause for concern.

But those who say that legal rules are defeasible sometimes mean something quite different from either of these two things. They do not mean that sometimes rules from one authoritative source must give way to rules from a superior source. Nor do they mean that sometimes the full and accurate statement of a legal rule ends with the word 'unless' followed by a closed, finite set of defeasibility conditions. Rather, their claim is that the set of conditions under which any legal rule can be defeated is logically open, so that a full and accurate statement of a legal rule will always take the following form: 'One is forbidden from doing F, *unless*...' Or, if it is a rule which includes explicit exceptions, a full and accurate statement will take something like this form: 'One is forbidden from doing F, unless, X, Y, & Z, *or*...' Here the rule statement includes conditions which have not been specified in advance—indeed which could not be so specified even by the most enlightened of rule-makers. Would this particular kind of defeasibility pose any particular problem for positivism? Once again, we have to begin by saying 'it depends.' If what is at play here is *moral* defeasibility, then as I argued earlier, no remotely plausible version of positivism would deny the claim being made. No positivist denies that we must sometimes decline to obey or apply valid legal norms for compelling, overriding moral reasons. But what if the defeasibility is legal—that is, what if the claim is that any legal rule is always open to *legal* defeat by an open-ended set of competing considerations? Is this more than any positivist can accept? Once again, we need to step back and disentangle a number of different possibilities.

There are a number of different ways in which the force of a legal rule is subject to logical defeasibility, at least two of which we have already considered: (1) a legal rule can have built-in exceptions; and (2) legal rules are subject to being overridden in the manner exemplified by the federal paramountcy doctrine. But as noted, these do not exhaust the possibilities. There are at least three more we need to consider at this stage. Sometimes a legal rule can be *changed* by a judge in such a way as to avoid applying it to the facts of a case. In this instance, the decision to change the rule, so as to avoid its otherwise binding effect, might reasonably be said to be based on a reason triggered by the rule's implicit, open-ended, 'unless' clause. This third type of logical defeasibility involves an actual change in the rule. But what if the rule remains unchanged but is simply not applied? It might be thought that we have here a fourth kind of logical defeasibility—one which attaches, not so much to a rule, but to its force. And finally we have a fifth possibility: that a rule is defeated by being reinterpreted in such a way that it no longer applies to the facts of the case.[16] Let us begin with our first additional kind of legal defeat: defeat by changing rule.

1. Directed powers

As Joseph Raz pointed out in his early response to Ronald Dworkin, legal systems typically provide for their own development. Often they do so by providing the judge with a directed power to change a rule at point of application.[17] This is a Hohfeldian power to change the law coupled with a legal duty to exercise that power when the right circumstances arise. These circumstances often include ones where there are morally compelling reasons not to apply the otherwise applicable law to a particular case. In such instances, the law can quite sensibly be said not only to be morally defeasible but

[16] This way of characterizing things presupposes that there is a stable entity—the rule—which is subject to a new interpretation of it. The rule does not change, but our interpretation or understanding of it does. If we adopt an alternative approach to rules, one which identifies the rule with its interpretation, then this way of escaping the effect of a rule would be a species of the previous type. Were the interpretation to change, the rule would, in effect, change along with it.

[17] On directed powers, see J. Raz, 'The Inner Logic of the Law' in *Ethics in the Public Domain: Essays in the Morality of Law and Politics* (rev. edn, Oxford: Clarendon Press, 1996), 242.

legally defeasible as well, that is, subject to change for legally sanctioned moral reasons so as to escape its binding effect. So what Dworkin took to be a counter-example to the positivist's 'model of rules'—valid laws (as the positivist supposedly must conceive them) being defeated in a case by non-binding, non-legally-valid, principles of political morality—was in actual fact an example of how law itself regulates its own development.[18] Take common law rules, for example. A judge faced with an applicable rule established by a superior court is normally bound by it despite any problematic result to which the rule might seem to lead in the case before him. He is bound to apply the rule even if he would have preferred a different rule, and even if there are reasons of some appreciable weight which suggest that the law could profitably be changed. The need to secure values like certainty, stability over time, predictability, and perhaps fairness to those previously judged on its basis, argue strongly in favour of sticking with an established rule.[19] But if the result of doing so is, say, clearly 'absurd or repugnant', 'irrational', or '*grossly* unfair' (not just *a little* unfair), then the judge will typically be empowered to change the rule so as to avoid that result. It is important to stress that the law does not attempt to spell out the precise conditions under which these results obtain. Rather, it leaves it to the informed judgment of the court to make the decision on its behalf. It is equally important to stress that the law does not, in providing judges with directed powers to change the law in these ways, declare open season on its rules. Not any old reason of whatever importance or weight will serve to engage the directed power to change the law. That is the point behind using phrases like 'grossly unfair' and 'absurd' instead of less dramatic phrases like 'unfair' or 'undesirable'. The former phrases emphasize that the reason must be one of sufficient weight to outweigh all the competing values which argue heavily in favour of consistency with the past. In any event, what we have here is a case of law regulating its own development by the interaction of duty-imposing and power-conferring rules. And there is absolutely nothing in this which should trouble the positivist.

Let us turn now to our fourth form of legal defeat: where the rule remains unchanged, but the rule is simply not applied in order to avoid a result which is in some way troubling. According to Ronald Dworkin, rules, as opposed to principles, are never subject to this kind of defeat. 'If the facts a rule stipulates are given, then either the rule is valid, in which case the answer it supplies must be accepted, or it is not, in which case it contributes nothing to the decision.'[20] Others take the opposite tack: they say that rules are *always* subject to this kind of defeat and are therefore subject to a kind of 'open-ended logical defeasibility'. Both positions are mistaken. The doctrine of federal paramountcy illustrates the error in Dworkin's view. The answer provided by a conflicting state law can be rejected without the rule's invalidity following as a logical consequence. As for the opposite view, that rules are always subject to non-application if there are good reasons to warrant this result, this can't be correct either. As Fred Schauer (and many others) have argued, it is the very nature of a rule that it must be, to

[18] See R. Dworkin, 'The Model of Rules', first published by *The University of Chicago Law Review* (1967) and reprinted in R. Dworkin, *Taking Rights Seriously* (London: Duckworth, 1978). Raz's responses to Dworkin can be found in many places, but see, in particular, J. Raz, 'Legal Principles and the Limits of Law', *Yale Law Journal* , 81 (1972), 823.

[19] These are examples of the kinds of considerations which also support the existence of a special, role-relative, moral obligation on the part of a judge to apply laws with which she disagrees morally. As we saw, however, it is possible, in very hard cases, for these reasons to be outweighed by other moral reasons.

[20] R. Dworkin, *Taking Rights Seriously*, 24. For my critique of Dworkin on this particular point, see W. Waluchow, *Inclusive Legal Positivism* (Oxford: Clarendon Press, 1994), 168–74.

some degree at least, 'entrenched' against rival considerations—otherwise what we have is something other than a rule.[21] It does not follow from this, of course, that a rule must be, as Dworkin seems to suggest, entrenched completely against *every conceivable* background consideration. But there is no denying that it must be entrenched to some degree against some of them. At the very least, background reasons cannot outweigh or override the force of the rule unless, given the particular facts of the case before the judge, they are *especially* weighty or important.[22] What follows from this is that one can sensibly be said to be bound by a rule only if one is not entirely at liberty to refrain from applying the rule (or change it) for whatever reason of whatever weight one cared to mention. For one would not, under these conditions, have a rule at all. And it further follows that were it true that all legal rules are, of necessity, logically defeasible in this very strong sense of the term, then there would be no possibility of ever establishing the rule of law. If one is to have the *rule* of law we need rules by which we are bound in standard, run-of-the-mill cases. So open-ended defeasibility of the kind now being considered would indeed pose a grave difficulty for positivists, who believe that law is fundamentally a rule-governed enterprise. But then this would be true of *any* theorist who viewed law this way—that is, who viewed law as Lon Fuller once characterized it: the attempt to subject human conduct to the governance of rules. And no one, save a few radical rule sceptics, views law in any other way.

This leaves our fifth way in which the force or effect of rules can be subject to logical defeasibility—by reinterpretation. It is sometimes said that legal rules are always subject to rival interpretations. 'Don't like a result dictated by a rule? Provide a different interpretation of it.' If this view is correct, then legal rules end up being subject to the same kind of open-ended defeasibility discussed in the previous few paragraphs—and we have yet another form of radical rule scepticism. But this particular brand of scepticism is no more plausible than the previous ones. To be sure, rules are often subject to rival interpretations, and judges do sometimes choose interpretations which permit them to avoid the kinds of deeply problematic results discussed earlier. But as before, there are limits to this particular avenue of escape, ones which largely follow the lines sketched above: the reason to depart from the standard reading of a rule must be one which the law itself recognizes and which is of sufficient weight or importance to outweigh the competing considerations which argue in favour of sticking with the standard reading. Of course, what I have just said presupposes an important fact: that, for at least most legal rules, it is possible to identify what I have called 'the standard reading of the rule'. But it is just this fact, the sceptic will argue, that must be denied. There are no standard readings in law, just competing interpretations from which judges are at liberty to choose. There is, to employ the now classic terminology of

[21] See F. Schauer, *Playing By The Rules: A Philosophical Examination of Rule-Based Decision-Making in Law and in Life* (Oxford: Clarendon, 1991). According to Joseph Raz, in order for the norm in question to be a rule, it must express an 'exclusionary reason', one which does not simply outweigh other competing reasons (i.e. is not simply entrenched against them to some degree), but excludes at least some of them altogether. But this seems too strong. It takes to be necessary—entrenchment as exclusion—what seems to be only possible. On this see, e.g. S. Perry, 'Judicial Obligation, Precedent and the Common Law', OJLS, 7 (1987), 221. For Raz's theory of exclusionary reasons, see, e.g. J. Raz, *The Authority of Law* and J. Raz, 'Authority and Justification', *Philosophy and Public Affairs*, 14 (1985), 3.

[22] Analogous considerations apply with respect to the judicial power to defeat a rule by changing it. Here too, a completely open-ended logical defeasibility is incompatible with the rule of law. Were judges free in all cases, and for whatever reason struck them as relevant in the case before them, to escape the effect of a rule by changing it, we would have abandoned the rule of law entirely and have substituted a kind of particularist, case-by-case reasoning which dispensed with rules altogether.

H.L.A. Hart, no 'core of settled meaning' surrounded by a 'penumbra of uncertainty'.[23] On the contrary, it is all penumbra. But is this radical view correct? Legal practice suggests otherwise. Most legal systems begin with what, in English law, is called 'the literal rule', according to which legal rules are to be read, so far as possible, in terms of their ordinary, plain meaning. And when the area of law in which the rule figures (e.g. tax law) has developed its own technical meanings to deal with situations ill-suited for description through use of ordinary language, technical legal meaning is what usually governs interpretation. Standard meaning, understood in either of these two ways, is almost always the starting point. To be sure, it is not always the end point. Sometimes a compelling reason or argument of some sort will point towards an alternative reading of the rule. But as before, not any old reason or argument will do. As the court said in *Becke* v. *Smith*:

> It is a very useful rule in the construction of a statute to adhere to the ordinary meaning of the words used, and to the grammatical construction, unless that is at variance with the intention of the legislature to be collected from the statute itself, or leads to any manifest absurdity or repugnance, in which case the language may be varied or modified so as to avoid such inconvenience but no further.[24]

This view was later endorsed by Lord Wensleydale in *Grey* v. *Pearson*:

> the grammatical and ordinary sense of the words is to be adhered to, unless that would lead to some absurdity or inconsistency with the rest of the instrument, in which case the grammatical and ordinary sense of the words may be modified, so as to avoid that absurdity or inconsistency, but not farther.[25]

This 'golden rule' of interpretation, as it is often called, illustrates the crucial points upon which I have been insisting. Legal meaning is typically defeasible, but never in an entirely open-ended way which threatens the rule of law. We must typically start with standard meaning, and this will, in almost all run-of-the-mill cases, be our end point as well. When competing reasons argue for a non-standard reading, these must be legally sanctioned reasons and they must be of sufficient weight or importance to outweigh the many reasons arguing against such a move. Once again, we find nothing which should concern the positivist.

D. Defeasible validity?

Contemporary legal positivism claims that laws exist only when they satisfy certain conditions or tests of validity which have a special social source. Most positivists are happy to say, along with Hart, that these special tests of validity find their footing in a socially constituted 'rule of recognition', a rule derived from the actual practices of legal officials in identifying the valid laws that they are charged with applying, interpreting, or changing (if they have the directed power to do so). Valid laws are those which satisfy these tests for validity contained within the system's rule of recognition. All positivists more or less agree with this particular picture of the nature of legal validity. Where controversy tends to break out is over the precise nature of the tests for validity found within rules of recognition. As I noted earlier, defenders of Inclusive Legal Positivism (ILP) argue that rules of recognition can include decidedly moral conditions—they

[23] See H.L.A. Hart, *The Concept of Law*, ch. 7.
[24] (1836) 2 M&W 195, *per* Parke B.
[25] (1857) 6 HL CAS 61.

might, for instance, include the condition that the rule whose validity is at stake be compatible with norms of fundamental fairness or moral equality. There is nothing in the theoretical commitments of positivism which rules any of this out, say defenders of ILP. Defenders of Exclusive Legal Positivism (ELP) deny this. They insist, for a variety of theoretical reasons having mainly to do with the law's capacity to provide authoritative guidance, that legal validity must always be determined by non-moral, source-based criteria, such as legislative enactment, adoption by a court to decide a case, and so on. But that leaves the defenders of ELP with a puzzle: how to explain the apparent fact that the constitutions of many nation states appear to include moral tests for legal validity. A prime example is the 'due process' or 'equal protection' clauses of the US Constitution. According to those who espouse ELP, these clauses do not, because they cannot, actually express moral conditions of validity; rather, they express moral conditions which trigger the judges' directed power to change the law. The requirement that Congress enact no law which violates due process is not, appearances to the contrary, a condition of legal validity in the United States. Rather, it can only be a moral ground upon which American courts are empowered to invalidate, by their decision to strike it down, what was until that point in time perfectly valid law. So long as the legislation in question satisfied all the relevant, non-moral, source-based tests for legal validity (e.g. it received majority approval in both the House and the Senate, and was not vetoed by the President) then it *was* and still *is* valid law—and this is so even if, as a matter of objective fact, the legislation in question violates due process. It *was* and *is* valid law until such time—if such a time ever comes about—as a judge *makes* it invalid by invoking her directed power to strike it down for due process reasons.

Defenders of ILP are, by and large, unhappy with the directed powers account of a constitution's moral provisions. Their response is that the account falsely characterizes how an act of legislation which violates a constitutional moral provision is often treated; it is not always treated by the legal system as a *candidate for invalidation* by the judiciary. Rather, it is treated as though it *never was* valid law.[26] There is little question that ILP defenders are on to something when they point to the fact that, in some contexts, an enactment or decision which violates a constitutional moral clause is generally taken to be legally invalid, not simply a candidate for invalidation. But it is equally obvious that, until any such enactment or decision is challenged in court and *declared* unconstitutional, it tends to be accepted and practiced as though it were valid law. Indeed, there probably are, at any given moment in time, many such enactments and decisions—acts and decisions which in fact violate a constitution's moral provisions but are never challenged on those grounds. And these are all accepted and practised as valid law on a routine basis. Should I choose, on grounds of due process, not to comply with any such enactment or decision, then in all but the most unusual of cases, the court will, to paraphrase John Austin, reveal the error of my ways by sticking me in jail, seizing my property, or doing to me whatever it is that the law designates as appropriate treatment for one who stands in violation of that particular enactment or decision.[27] So there is a strong inclination to say, along with those who advocate ELP,

[26] It is important to be clear that violation of a moral provision is not always taken to establish invalidity. For instance, courts will sometimes note the violation of a moral provision by an act of legislation but provide the offending legislative body a set time in which to correct the infringement. In such instances, the court in effect suspends the state of invalidity for the set period of time.

[27] 'Now, to say that human laws which conflict with the Divine law are not binding, that is to say, are not laws, is to talk stark nonsense. The most pernicious laws, and therefore those which are most opposed to the will of God, have been and are continually enforced as laws by judicial tribunals. Suppose an act innocuous, or positively beneficial, be prohibited by the sovereign under the penalty of

that so long as the enactment or decision satisfies the non-moral, source-based tests of validity specified in the rule of recognition, it *is valid law*—subject of course to the directed power of a judge to make it invalid by striking it down. But valid nonetheless.

Space prevents me from exploring these deeply contentious points further in any great detail.[28] Instead I will rest content with a few, admittedly sketchy thoughts on whether the notion of defeasibility might help resolve this impasse. Here is the possibility I would like us to consider. Defenders of ELP may be correct when they say that legal validity is normally, and in the first instance, established by way of non-moral, source-based criteria of validity. Do you want to know what stands as valid law in one's community? Ask yourself which rules have a source in legislative enactment, judicial decision, or some other kind of official act recognized as establishing law, e.g. executive order. Normally, this is all one has to consider; and if one rests content in one's life with following rules which derive from these sources, one will be said to have lived up to one's legal responsibilities. However, many legal systems also recognize that some of their laws, duly established in these ways, actually violate important rights of political morality, such as the right to due process or the right to equal treatment before and under the law. And so the decision is made to include respect for these rights as a condition of legal validity, as a condition the violation of which *defeats* the presumed validity of an otherwise valid enactment or decision. We can express this possibility using some of the terms explored above:

R is valid in system S if R satisfies all non-moral, source-based conditions of validity, N, contained with S's Rule of Recognition, unless R violates M1, M2, and M3.[29]

What are the advantages of conceiving legal validity this way in systems with constitutional moral provisions? There are many and here are a few. First, it allows us to make the point that usually, in normal, run-of-the-mill cases, validity follows if non-moral tests are satisfied. And normally, this is all one has to establish if one wishes to know which rules are valid rules of one's legal system. Conceiving of legal validity this way further highlights a point made above when I alluded to Austin: that most legal systems actually require that we (and this includes citizens, judges, police officers, and other legal officials) *presume* validity, and *act* on that basis. They tend to require this at least until such time as violation of a constitutional moral test has been established in a court of law, that is, at least until such time as someone is actually able to defeat the presumption in favour of validity by establishing, in accordance with whatever standard of certainty the system requires, a failure to meet the overriding moral conditions of validity. However, conceiving of validity as a potentially defeasible property in relation to law also highlights, and finds theoretical room for, the important points insisted

death; if I commit this act, I shall be tried and condemned, and if I object to the sentence, that it is contrary to the law of God, who has commanded that human lawgivers shall not prohibit acts which have no evil consequences, the Court of Justice will demonstrate the inconclusiveness of my reasoning by hanging me up, in pursuance of the law of which I have impugned the validity. An exception, demurrer, or plea, founded on the law of God was never heard in a Court of Justice, from the creation of the world down to the present moment.' J. Austin, *The Province of Jurisprudence—Determined and the Uses of the Study of Jurisprudence* (ed. by H.L.A. Hart, Indianapolis: Hackett Publishing, 1998).

[28] For further discussion of these issues, see, e.g. W. Waluchow, *Inclusive Legal Positivism*; M.H. Kramer, *Where Law and Morality Meet* (Oxford: Oxford University Press, 2004); K. Himma, 'Final Authority to Bind with Moral Mistakes: On the Explanatory Potential of Inclusive Legal Positivism', *Law and Philosophy*, 24 (2005), 1–45; and W. Waluchow, 'Four Concepts of Validity: Reflections on Inclusive and Exclusive Positivism' in M. Adler and K. Himma (eds), *The Rule of Recognition and the United States Constitution* (Oxford: Oxford University Press, 2009).

[29] M1–M3 stand for whatever moral conditions happen to be contained within the constitution.

upon by defenders of ILP. Among these are the following: when the violation of a constitutionally recognized moral condition *is* established in a way which defeats the presumption in favour of validity, the conclusion to be drawn and acted on by the court—indeed, the conclusion that *is* typically drawn and acted upon by courts in most legal systems—is not that the offending enactment or decision is ripe for invalidation. Rather, the conclusion drawn and acted on is that the offending measure *never was valid in the first place*—it was invalid *because it violated the constitution.* Legal systems have various ways of giving expression to this way of looking at matters. For example, the person who issued the challenge and who might have been earlier convicted or held liable under the defeasibly valid law will be exonerated. In some systems, e.g. Canada's, he will also be provided with whatever compensation the court deems just and appropriate in the circumstances—just and appropriate because of the treatment he received under a law which has now been shown to have been invalid all along. Conceiving of validity as defeasible in this way allows us to explain all these features of legal practice in a better way than the directed powers account. For recall that, on that account, there was indeed valid law which the defendant violated when he acted (or not) so as to bring the force of the law down upon his head. To be sure, it was valid law which the judge was empowered to invalidate. *But it was valid law nevertheless.* And so we are left struggling to explain why exoneration is the inevitable result and why remedies might be thought appropriate. Why should someone be compensated for violating laws which *were* valid when he acted and which *became* invalid only when the court later struck them down? The directed powers account provides no ready answer. The account on offer here does so without denying the facts of legal practice to which defenders of ELP rightly draw our attention.

E. Concluding thoughts

Defeasibility is a multi-faceted notion. My purpose in this paper has been to explore some of these facets and to ask whether they pose any particular difficulties for legal positivism. My conclusion is this. Not only is defeasibility a notion which makes little trouble for legal positivism, it highlights many key features of legal practice to which positivists have rightfully drawn our attention. It is also a notion which points us in the direction of a solution to one of the thorniest disputes to have divided contemporary positivists over the past thirty-odd years.[30]

[30] I wish to thank Matthew Grellette and Christopher Hinchcliffe for immensely valuable discussion of the issues discussed in this paper.

16

True Exceptions: Defeasibility and Particularism

*Bruno Celano**

A. Introduction

Sometimes, kinds of cases which do in fact fall under the antecedent of a conditional norm are reckoned recalcitrant, i.e. although they fall under the antecedent of the norm we do not wish to allow the consequence to follow. In such cases, we sometimes say that we are abandoning, or discarding, the norm. We concede, that is, that the alleged norm was wrong (or, if you wish, that it was no norm at all). At other times, however, it is claimed that the norm is a defeasible one. Granted, the case at hand is one of those in which the norm is defeated; but this, it is implied, does not amount to a wholesale abandonment of the norm itself. Claims to the effect that a given norm is defeasible, I take it, are different from claims of the former kind, i.e. claims to the effect that an alleged norm is simply wrong (or that it is no norm at all). Being defeasible, the norm somehow survives the impact of such recalcitrant cases. Though somehow revised, amended, qualified, the norm, it is assumed, remains in place: it is still the same norm.

I shall call this 'the identity assumption'. The identity assumption is part and parcel of the notion that some norms are not barely wrong, but defeasible. (This should be taken as a stipulation.)[1] There are various ways of substantiating the identity assumption, corresponding to some main ways of moulding the concept of defeasibility (of norms).

I shall challenge the identity assumption. Or, rather, I shall distinguish two different versions of it, and argue that one of them is hollow. I shall challenge it by reviewing, and rejecting, one of the main ways in which it can be substantiated, namely, a specificationist strategy for dealing with norm conflicts and inappropriate normative

* Professor of Legal Philosophy, University of Palermo. An earlier version of this paper was presented at the workshop on Defeasibilism held at Oriel College, Oxford, on 10–11 March 2008. I am grateful to the participants to the workshop, and to Riccardo Guastini, Giorgio Maniaci, and Giorgio Pino, for comments and criticism.

[1] The term 'defeasibility' designates—in contemporary inquiries dealing with practical reasoning (in morals, law, etc.)—different phenomena (recent attempts at sorting them out may be found in, e.g. J.L. Rodríguez and G. Sucar, 'Las trampas de la derrotabilidad. Niveles de análisis de la indeterminación del derecho' in J.C. Bayón and J.L. Rodríguez, *Relevancia normativa en la justificación de las decisiones judiciales* (Bogotá: Universidad Externado de Colombia, 2003), 115–16; J.C. Bayón, 'Por qué es derrotable el razonamiento jurídico?' in J.C. Bayón and J.L. Rodríguez, *Relevancia normativa en la justificación de las decisiones judiciales*; J.L. Rodríguez, *Lógica de los sistemas jurídicos* (Madrid: Centro de estudios políticos y constitucionales, 2002), 356–99; J. Hage, 'Law and Defeasibility', *Artificial Intelligence and Law*, 11 (2003); E. Bulygin, 'Review of Jaap Hage's Law and Defeasibility', *Artificial Intelligence and Law*, 11 (2003); H. Prakken and G. Sartor, 'The Three Faces of Defeasibility in Law', *Ratio Juris*, 17 (2004). In this paper, my topic is defeasibility of conditional norms, and, thus, of the inferences in which they may occur as premises. This, by itself, doesn't say much, of course. The specific phenomenon that I am concerned with will be apparent from the text.

verdicts (sections B and C). This will lead us to taking a stand in the generalism vs particularism debate (section D). Rejection of the identity assumption leads, when conjoined to an awareness of the phenomena underlying defeasibility claims, to a version of particularism.

Does this particularist stance necessarily involve rejection of any normative generalization? The answer to this question, I shall argue, turns on whether some sense can be made of the notion of a kind of case being 'normal' (section F). Here, a second version of the identity assumption may perhaps be endorsed, thus reviving the defeasibilist project. At the heart of defeasibility claims, so understood, is the idea that norms may be shot through with true, as opposed to merely prima facie, exceptions (section E).

Two caveats are in place here. First, what my argument in this paper is about are norms, not norm formulations (i.e. sentences which are taken to be expressing norms), nor the ways in which we get, from norm formulations, to norms which are taken to be expressed by them. Thus, the issues I shall be dealing with are not issues of interpretation—namely, issues concerning the ascription of meaning to sentences. I grant that much of what is discussed under the heading 'defeasibility in law' may be understood, and properly recast, as a cluster of issues about the ways in which meaning (often, different meanings) may be ascribed to legal sentences.[2] Here, much depends on whether one has a sceptical view of legal interpretation, that is, one leaving no room at all (except in the realm of errors and myths) for the idea of an interpretation of a given norm formulation being the right (or, perhaps, just a wrong) one. If all thoughts of criteria of right and wrong in interpretation are abandoned, if, namely, it is claimed that norm formulations may be interpreted and reinterpreted *ad libitum* so as to draw, from them, opposite conclusions, then no room is left for arguments about whether norms should be taken to be defeasible, in what sense, etc. These issues simply become otiose.[3] In what follows, I am assuming that some such room is left open—that we may sensibly argue about the forms and ways of good and bad inferences involving norms. But I shall not argue for this assumption. Specifically, I do not say anything in defence of the implied claim that, to some extent and in some cases at least, it may be right (or wrong, as the case may be) to claim that norm N is the norm that a given norm formulation expresses. What I am concerned with is the rational reconstruction of (good and bad) forms of inferences involving norms. Thus, the argument is normative (I mean epistemic normativity) throughout.

Second, I shall discuss 'norms' generally, leaving deliberately aside the issue whether we are dealing with either moral or legal norms, or both (or maybe other kinds of norms as well). This is because what I am interested in are abstract relations between normative contents, and the ways it is possible to understand or handle them in the face of the relevant phenomena (i.e. norm conflicts, inappropriate verdicts). *Vis-à-vis* this concern, the panoply of theoretical assumptions required in order to frame our inquiry as one concerning moral rather than legal norms, or vice versa, or the relations between the two—assumptions concerning the nature of law or of morality, or how can law incorporate or refer to morality, or how can morality leave room for the law, and so

[2] R. Guastini, 'Defeasibility, Axiological Gaps, and Interpretation', in this volume, ch. 9. See also J.L. Rodríguez, 'La derrotabilidad de las normas jurídicas' in J.C. Bayón and J.L. Rodríguez, *Relevancia normativa en la justificación de las decisiones judiciales*, 98–9; J.L. Rodríguez and G. Sucar, 'Las trampas de la derrotabilidad. Niveles de análisis de la indeterminación del derecho', 119–20; J.C. Bayón, 'Derrotabilidad, indeterminación del derecho y positivismo jurídico' in J.C. Bayón and J.L. Rodríguez, *Relevancia normativa en la justificación de las decisiones judiciales*, 182–5.

[3] R. Guastini, 'Defeasibility, Axiological Gaps, and Interpretation'.

on—would beg too many questions. Specifically, I am not going to assume that the norms I shall be discussing belong to a normative system, defined by membership criteria, and perhaps including priority rules among conflicting norms. This would to a large extent trivialize the issue and, by the way, when dealing with law or morality, this assumption is, to say the least, troublesome. There is, however, one tenet which is itself deeply controversial and is crucial to my whole enterprise. I shall assume that at least some normative issues (i.e. issues as to whether, for a given antecedent, a normative consequence follows) have a right solution—that there is a right answer to such issues in at least some cases. Nothing will be said to justify this assumption.

B. Specificationism: its promises...

The main phenomenon underlying talk of defeasible norms, the main ground for claiming that some norms are defeasible, is the possibility of conflicts between norms. According to an intuitionist model of the resolution of norm conflicts, what we have to do in such cases is balance the conflicting norms, in order to see which one, in the case at hand, prevails. (What this might mean is, of course, rather obscure.) Specificationism recommends a purportedly different course. When facing a conflict—or, when application of the relevant norm to a given case leads to a verdict we deem inappropriate, or unsatisfactory (this, of course, involves a value judgement)[4]—what we have to do is specify (that is, suitably restrict the domain of application of) at least one of the norms, or the relevant norm, so that, thanks to the inclusion of further conditions within its antecedent (thanks to '*glossing the determinables*')[5] the conflict—or the unsatisfactory verdict—eventually vanishes.[6]

This looks breathtakingly simple, and very promising. Obviously, a sensible specification will have to satisfy some constraints, excluding trivializing or irrelevant moves.[7] But, quite apart from the merits of these requirements, which I am not going to discuss here, the appeal of specificationism lies in what it promises. Specificationism claims to

[4] Whether or not these two hypotheses are in fact different I shall not consider here.

[5] Specification 'narrow[s] a norm by adding clauses spelling out where, when, why, how, by what means, to whom, or by whom the action is to be done or avoided'. See H.S. Richardson, 'Specifying, Balancing, and Interpreting Bioethical Principles', *Journal of Medicine and Philosophy*, 25 (2000), 289.

[6] H.S. Richardson, 'Specifying Norms as a Way to Resolve Concrete Ethical Problems', *Philosophy and Public Affairs*, 19 (1990); H.S. Richardson, *Practical Reasoning about Final Ends* (Cambridge: Cambridge University Press, 1994), ch. 4; H.S. Richardson, 'Specifying, Balancing, and Interpreting Bioethical Principles'; T.M. Scanlon, 'Intention and Permissibility', *Proceedings of the Aristotelian Society*, Suppl. vol. 74 (2000), but see also T.M. Scanlon, *What We Owe to Each Other* (Cambridge, Mass.: Harvard University Press, 1998), 197–202; and T.M. Scanlon, 'Adjusting Rights and Balancing Values', *Fordham Law Review*, 72 (2003), 1478, the latter on the related—but different—issue of 'adjusting', or specifying, institutionally defined rights. For a similar proposal, relying on Alchourrón's understanding of defeasible conditionals, see J.J. Moreso, 'Conflitti fra principi costituzionali', *Ragion Pratica*, 18 (2002); and, for a somewhat hedged version of the claim (which will not be discussed here), J.J. Moreso, 'Cristina Redondo sobre Razones y normas' *Discusiones* 4 (2005) in J.L. Rodríguez (ed.), 'Razones y normas', sect. 4. A parallel suggestion concerning conflicts between moral rights is found in R. Shafer-Landau, 'Specifying Absolute Rights', *Arizona Law Review*, 37 (1995).

[7] H.S. Richardson, 'Specifying Norms as a Way to Resolve Concrete Ethical Problems', 295–7; H.S. Richardson, *Practical Reasoning about Final Ends*, 72–4. These are mainly informal constraints. Formal constraints on specification should parallel the set of formal conditions which, according to Alchourrón, define a revision function for defeasible conditionals. See C.E. Alchourrón, 'Detachment and Defeasibility in Deontic Logic', *Studia Logica*, 57 (1996), 5–18; C.E. Alchourrón, 'On Law and Logic', in this volume, ch. 2; C.E. Alchourrón, 'Para una lógica de las razones prima facie', *Análisis filosófico*, 16 (1996), 113–125. For our purposes, it is not necessary to dwell on these matters here.

be a third way beyond balancing and subsumption, superseding both of them.[8] Thanks to specification, it is claimed, we can overcome conflict, and inappropriate verdicts, through a deeper, more adequate, understanding of the relevant norms.[9] This ensures real progress; we are not merely changing our minds as to what the norms are that we should follow, rather we are refining, qualifying them, on the basis of a deeper understanding of their content.[10] This, it is claimed, is something wholly different from an intuitive balancing of conflicting requirements—an altogether arbitrary procedure, leaving us stuck with abstract, unrefined requirements, liable to come into conflict over and over again. Specification is a reasoned way: the conditions we include within the antecedent of our norms, restricting their scope, count as reasons—reasons why a conflict should be resolved one way or the other, or a novel case distinguished from previous ones, and an inappropriate verdict avoided. Thus, specification brings about an enrichment of our normative outlook, leading us to more finely grained distinctions, refining our normative sensitivity, and our ability to discriminate in matters normative. In order to make specification possible, of course, we have to read our initial norms as defeasible (qualifications such as 'generally speaking', or 'for the most part', 'in most cases', etc. will have to be prefixed to our normative conditionals).[11] They will have to be understood as including *ceteris paribus* clauses: refinement and qualification deploy within the logical space left open by such clauses, sometimes defusing the link between antecedent and consequence. Specificationism is, thus, a species of defeasibilism.

We have to distinguish two main varieties of the specificationist strategy, one claiming that, through specification, we get to contributory norms (i.e. norms stating *pro tanto* reasons), the other claiming that specification leads us from contributory to 'all-things-considered' norms (or, to 'overall' reasons).[12] The former is most plausibly understood as the view that, thanks to specification we move from less specific to more specific contributory norms.

8 H.S. Richardson, 'Specifying Norms as a Way to Resolve Concrete Ethical Problems', 279–80: 'a third, more effective alternative'; 'a third . . . operation'; 'a true third way, rather than just a mixture'; H.S. Richardson, 'Specifying, Balancing, and Interpreting Bioethical Principles', *passim*.

9 The model of specification makes us understand 'how our ethical precepts, many of which are very general and abstract, can reach concrete cases without generating unacceptable conclusions'. H.S. Richardson, 'Specifying Norms as a Way to Resolve Concrete Ethical Problems', 284. I remind the reader (see section A) that my topic is not, specifically, *moral* norms. But there is nothing in the model of specification limiting its scope to the moral domain.

10 Resort to specification 'helps ensure . . . that the reasonable motivation behind the initial, unqualified norm is still captured by what one ends up with'. Ibid., 284. Thus, the notion of specification 'can . . . explain how a moral theory can remain the subject of a more or less stable attachment despite the sort of revision that moral conflicts engender' (ibid.). Specification affords 'the progressive refinement of a theory that remains the same in essentials' (ibid., 298; see also H.S. Richardson, *Practical Reasoning about Final Ends*, 171); 'the model of specification learns from the conflicts it faces, exploiting their friction to push off toward a more concrete and definite understanding of the relevant norms' (H.S. Richardson, 'Specifying Norms as a Way to Resolve Concrete Ethical Problems', 308). Specification is 'a relation between two norms that allows one to trace the significant continuities in a path of revision' (H.S. Richardson, *Practical Reasoning about Final Ends*, 245).

11 H.S. Richardson, 'Specifying Norms as a Way to Resolve Concrete Ethical Problems', 292–3; H.S. Richardson, *Practical Reasoning about Final Ends*, 70–2; H.S. Richardson, 'Specifying, Balancing, and Interpreting Bioethical Principles', 305, fn. 8.

12 The former is Richardson's version (cf. H.S. Richardson, 'Specifying Norms as a Way to Resolve Concrete Ethical Problems', 286–7, 294), the latter Scanlon's (though neither of them uses these phrases). The terms 'contributory' and 'overall', as used here, are drawn from J. Dancy, *Ethics Without Principles* (Oxford: Clarendon Press, 2004).

The identity assumption is part and parcel of specificationism, in both versions. The leading thought in specificationism, it seems to me, is that, in order to solve the normative puzzle we are facing (be it a conflict, or an inappropriate verdict), we have to work out what the relevant norm, or norms, properly understood, involve. What is required, in order to overcome the difficulty, is a better, deeper—more adequate and, therefore, more articulated—understanding of the norm, or of the conflicting norms.[13] The point is sometimes made by distinguishing between a norm, or principle, and its different—more or less adequate, as the case may be—'formulations'.[14] This is emphatically not the distinction between sentences and their meanings (see section A). Rather, a 'formulation' of a norm, in the now relevant sense, is to be understood as a way, one of the many possible ways, of grasping its supposedly complex and finely grained content. One and the same norm may have different formulations: some of them will be mere shorthand, others will capture some of its details. In the process of specification, it is assumed, we do not, in fact, modify the norm, but, rather, its initial formulation; what we are engaged in is amending, refining, the norm's formulation (i.e. our inchoate, partial grasp of its content), in order to put it in line with the norm itself. (The norm is inadequately captured by its current formulation; the latter may be quite simple, the former, understood as its 'underlying idea', is a complex matter.)[15] It is,

[13] Scanlon explicitly emphasizes the identity assumption. T.M. Scanlon, 'Intention and Permissibility', *Proceedings of the Aristotelian Society*, Suppl. vol. 74 (2000), 308, fn. 8. While on Richardson's account, he claims, specification involves 'modifying' conflicting principles, according to his (Scanlon's) view, 'only one principle need be involved' and 'the process [of specification] is typically one of figuring out what the principle requires rather than modifying it'. This, I think, does not do justice to Richardson, in whose view, too, specification amounts to deepening our understanding of our initial norms (see the passages quoted above, nn. 9 and 10). True, Richardson explicitly defines specification as a relation between *two* norms. See, H.S. Richardson, 'Specifying Norms as a Way to Resolve Concrete Ethical Problems', 295; H.S. Richardson, *Practical Reasoning about Final Ends*, 72; H.S. Richardson, 'Specifying, Balancing, and Interpreting Bioethical Principles', 298. But, and this is all that is needed for my argument, it is essential to his enterprise that specification be understood as a way of bringing *the initial norm* to bear on the case at hand. The model of specification he claims (H.S. Richardson, 'Specifying Norms as a Way to Resolve Concrete Ethical Problems',290) 'starts from [the] recognition [that our norms are subject to revision], but establishes a kind of constancy or stability... This stability is essential to the claim that the initial norms are in some way *brought to bear* on concrete cases by means of more specific norms.' Ibid., 291: specification 'licenses us to call a modification... of an original norm still in some significant sense the *same* norm that we started out with'; thanks to specification it is 'not a self-contradiction to speak of modifying a consideration so that *it* applies'; the model of specification lays down 'conditions on the relation between the initial norm or norms and their modifications that explain how the original norms *are* being respected' (all emphases are in the original; cf. also ibid., 297, and parallel passages in H.S. Richardson, *Practical Reasoning about Final Ends*, 170–1). We need specification 'both to allow the development of a stable moral theory and to give us some assurance that the commitment that underlies the initial norm is being appropriately honored'; specification 'lets [the contours of this initial commitment] emerge on reflection' (H.S. Richardson, 'Specifying Norms as a Way to Resolve Concrete Ethical Problems', 292). Specification, in sum, ensures 'stability in the course of revision', ibid. Reading the relevant norms as defeasible ones—i.e. as qualified by clauses such as 'generally speaking', and the like—allows us to understand 'how a norm can be seen as "the same" before and after revision' (Ibid., 293). The identity assumption is rightly envisaged as crucial to specificationist views in R.M. Hare, 'Comments', in D. Seanor and N. Fotion (eds), *Hare and Critics* (Oxford: Clarendon Press, 1988), 263. Richardson overtly acknowledges the 'challenge' posed by Hare ('the challenge I am now addressing of how a norm can be seen as "the same" before and after revision'); his own version of specificationism is supposed to be able to cope with it. H.S. Richardson, 'Specifying Norms as a Way to Resolve Concrete Ethical Problems', 293, fn. 30; H.S. Richardson, *Practical Reasoning about Final Ends*, 71, fn. 2.

[14] See e.g. T.M. Scanlon, *What We Owe to Each Other*, 199: 'succinct verbal formulations' as 'mere labels for much more complex ideas'. A similar idea is mentioned in P. Väyrynen, 'Moral Generalism. Enjoy in Moderation', *Ethics*, 116 (2006), 725.

[15] The phrase is Scanlon's. See T.M. Scanlon, *What We Owe to Each Other*, 199.

thus, *the same norm* that we are supposed to be applying to the case, although, now, better understood, and in a suitably refined formulation.

The identity assumption is what underlies the idea, mentioned a few paragraphs above, that specificationism, in contrast to balancing, ensures (reasoned) progress. Specification does not amount, trivially, to changing our minds as to what the norms are that we should follow. Rather, it brings about a fuller articulation of our normative convictions.

C. . . . and its shortcomings

There is, it seems to me, a simple argument that shows why this strategy fails. I shall call it 'the argument from negative conditions'. It runs as follows.

Our starting point is a norm claiming that when p is the case, C follows. Now, suppose that—as specificationism recommends us to do in the face of conflict—we grant, however, that when p and q is the case, C does not follow. (So that we now acknowledge, *ex post*, that our starting point had to be read as 'if p and not q, then C'.) And we further grant—always following specificationist advice—that, when p, q, and z are the case, C does indeed follow. (So that we now acknowledge, *ex post*, that our previously amended norm had to be read as 'if p and q and not z, C does not follow'). And so on, each time allowing, along specificationist lines, that the addition of a further conjunct may reverse the verdict, i.e. may now show that our previous verdict was right under a hitherto unstated negative condition. My question is, unless we may reasonably conceive of an exhaustive inventory, or list, of all possible conditions p, q, z, w etc. (or properties P, Q, Z, W etc.) which may obtain, and which may make a difference as to whether C follows, and of a full specification of the ways in which such conditions would make a difference (i.e. unless we deem conceivable, and at least in principle epistemically accessible, an exhaustive, ultimate list of all potentially normatively relevant properties or conditions, defining in advance the universe of all possible cases), what sense can be made of saying that, in proceeding as we do, and as specificationism recommends us (thus, in granting exceptions, exceptions to the exceptions, and so on), we are nonetheless going on in specifying—revising, refining, qualifying, amending—one and the same norm? No sense at all, it seems to me.

Further, is the notion of such an inventory and specification a coherent notion at all? No, I think.[16] For two reasons: (1) new, potentially normatively relevant properties may come into existence; and (2) the history of human interactions is intentionally laden.

The first of these two points is, I think, intuitive. (Consider the property of something being a microchip, a nation state, or an academic.) Besides, the meaning of old words may change, so that they come to designate new things. And further, if we allow thick concepts in the antecedent of norms (and I cannot see why we shouldn't, as a matter of grammar, I mean), the point becomes even more obvious.

As to the second point, by saying that the history of human interactions is intentionally laden, and that this makes the notion of a list such as the one envisaged above incoherent, I have in mind two considerations. (1) Practical problems typically arise in

[16] Cf. for a related point J. Dancy, *Moral Reasons* (Oxford: Blackwell, 1993), 67. In the terminology of Alchourrón and Bulygin, such a list may be termed an 'ultimate (normative) thesis of relevance (or hypothesis)'. C.E. Alchourrón and E. Bulygin, *Normative Systems* (Vienna: Springer, 1971), 103–6. (There is no difference, in the present context, between 'thesis of relevance' and 'relevance hypothesis'; ibid., 106. On this last point, see also M.C. Redondo, 'Reglas 'genuinas' y positivismo jurídico' in P. Comanducci and R. Guastini (eds), *Analisi e diritto 1998* (Turin: Giappichelli, 1999), 256.

the course of interactions between a plurality of agents; (2) an action may be described in a plurality of ways, and it is conceived—by the agent herself, or by others—under one or more such descriptions (not necessarily the same).[17] Both phenomena stem from the fact that the mind is endowed with intentionality. I shall consider them in turn.

(1) Practical problems (i.e. problems as to what is to be done in given circumstances) typically involve many individuals. Which properties are relevant in order to determine how one should act, may depend, and often does depend, on the past interaction of these individuals.[18] Often what the present case is, what its normatively relevant features are, does not boil down to what can be read off from its present configuration, but also depends on its history—i.e. on the path along which the relevant individuals have reached the present situation.[19] (Whether the fact that A promised B to phy is, now, a reason for phy-ing may depend on how, in the past, B behaved toward A—or maybe toward C, with whom A, though not knowing him personally, shares some important convictions, such as convictions as to whether, and when, promises should be kept.) The set of all possible combinations of potentially normatively relevant considerations, when account is taken of the path-dependence of cases, cannot be exhausted. This should not be understood in the sense that, due to its complexity, an extremely powerful computer would be needed in order to articulate all relevant possibilities. Rather, this set cannot in principle be exhausted. Human agents have intentionality; intentional states of increasing complexity (intentional states having as their objects other intentional states, and so on), including sets of (both synchronically and diachronically) interlocking intentional states of different levels (e.g. mutual beliefs or common knowledge) may be—and often are—relevant as to what the shape of interaction, and its history, is. (So, for example, A's beliefs about B's, or others', intentions or beliefs, or his hopes about others' future attitudes and behaviour, and so on, may be relevant.) Relations between such states may both be internal—i.e. relating to their content—or causal. (It may be relevant whether B expects A to keep his promise, and this may perhaps depend on what he expects A to expect from him, B, as a consequence of the way in which, as B—perhaps mistakenly—believes, A behaved in a past, similar case; but, maybe, A then behaved as he did in order to induce B to expect him, now, to expect a given behaviour from B, and so on.)

(2) To this it should be added that an action may be conceived, by the agent herself or by others, under an indefinite plurality of descriptions, often different for different individuals.[20] (The agent may not see that what he is doing falls under a certain description, something which may be apparent to some other individual.) There is, it seems to me, no reason to believe that the vocabulary of possible action-descriptions is

[17] G.E.M. Anscombe, *Intention* (Oxford: Blackwell, 1957, 1972), 11.

[18] Needless to say, the argument that follows concerns features which may turn out to be *normatively* relevant. (This is what the list which is at issue in the text is all about, of course.) This dispels a serious misunderstanding, grounding a purported objection against a previous version of the argument (M.C. Redondo, 'Razones jurídicas, Respuesta a Caracciolo, Celano y Moreso' in J.L. Rodríguez (ed.), 'Razones y normas', *Discusiones*, 4 (2005), 150ff.), replying to B. Celano, 'Podemos eligir entre particularismo y universalismo?', in J. Rodríguez (ed.), 'Razones y normas'.

[19] This is the main root for the distinctively particularist idea that there is a narrative dimension in practical rationality.

[20] This point was made, in this connection, by J.J. Moreso, 'Dos concepciones de la aplicación de las normas de derechos fundamentales' in J. Betegón, F. Laporta, J.R. de Páramo, and L. Prieto Sanchís (eds), *Constitución y derechos fundamentales* (Madrid: Centro de Estudios Políticos y Constitucionales, 2004), 491; B. Celano, 'Podemos eligir entre particularismo y universalismo?', 113.

finite. And, obviously, which description is picked out by whom, may turn out to be normatively relevant.

These two factors combine. The history of the present case—the course of interaction between a plurality of individuals—is constituted, *inter alia*, by intentional states (of increasing complexity, etc.); their contents comprise different descriptions of the relevant actions, descriptions under which these actions are known (or, they are expected to be known, or are hoped to be expected to be known, and so on) to some of the agents involved, but perhaps not to others. Under which description a given action falls according to B's lights (or, A believes it to fall according to B's lights, etc.) may matter, as far as the narrative concerning what led to the present situation is concerned. Thus, this plurality of possible descriptions, and of possible intentional states having them as their content, determines (just as it may sometimes make indeterminate) what the normatively relevant shape of the case at hand is.

In sum, human interaction brings about an indefinite plurality of potentially normatively relevant properties, and of relevant histories in which they are instantiated. This multiplicity is non-computable. The notion of the set of all potentially normatively relevant properties, or kinds of cases, is misconceived, just as the notion of the set of all possible novel plots is.

Thus, the claim that, in following specificationist advice, we are specifying one and the same norm proves hollow. It would have some bite, if we could tell what properties have to be *absent* for the norm consequence to follow. This is, however, impossible. Negative conditions cannot be exhaustively enumerated.[21]

The point is not, it should be noticed, that we can never legitimately assume that all relevant negative conditions are satisfied. On the contrary, this is what, more or less sensibly as the case may be, we do all the time. What I am claiming is, rather, that

[21] The argument from negative conditions is close to what Holton takes to be the main (and, according to him, a sound) argument supporting particularism, the 'supersession argument'. R. Holton, 'Principles and Particularism', *Proceedings of the Aristotelian Society*, Suppl. vol. 76 (2002), 196–7. Holton notes that the argument may be blocked by including, in the antecedent of the norm under consideration, a 'that's it' condition (stating that in the case at hand no further properties, apart from those already mentioned in the antecedent of the norm, are normatively relevant, and that no other principle is, either). Thus, by adding 'that's it' as a premise to an inference applying such a norm to a given case, a normative solution for the case will deductively follow (ibid., 199–200). This is, I think, correct. The trouble arises when we notice that inclusion of the 'that's it' clause in the antecedent of the norm amounts to the requirement that all negative conditions be satisfied; and that addition of 'that's it' as a premise in our inference amounts to asserting that they are satisfied. This is, precisely, where the argument from negative conditions shows the main difficulty to be. (It should be noticed that Holton explicitly acknowledges, in the *Abstract* of his paper, that inclusion of 'that's it' clauses in the antecedent of norms amounts to reading them as holding only *ceteris paribus*.) Cf. for a related argument J. Hage, 'Law and Defeasibility', *Artificial Intelligence and Law*, 11 (2003), 237. Hints to the argument from negative conditions may be found in, e.g. J.C. Bayón, *La normatividad del derecho: Deber jurídico y razones para la acción* (Madrid: Centro de estudios constitucionales, 1991) 346–51 (relating to moral norms only); J. Dancy, *Moral Reasons*, 57, 77, 80–1; G. Sartor, 'Defeasibility in Legal Reasoning' in Z. Bankowski et al. (eds), *Informatics and the Foundations of Legal Reasoning* (Dordrecht: Kluwer, 1995), 143; D. McNaughton and P. Rawling, 'Unprincipled Ethics' in B. Hooker and M. Little (eds), *Moral Particularism* (Oxford: Clarendon Press, 2000), 262–3; H. Prakken and G. Sartor, 'The Three Faces of Defeasibility in Law', *Ratio Juris*, 17 (2004), 120 (the 'qualification problem'); P. Väyrynen, 'Moral Generalism. Enjoy in Moderation', *Ethics*, 116 (2006), 725, 736. Its ancestors are in H.L.A. Hart, 'The Ascription of Responsibility and Rights' in A. Flew (ed.), *Logic and Language* (1st series, Oxford: Blackwell, 1951), 147–8; H.L.A. Hart, *The Concept of Law* (Oxford, Clarendon Press, 1961), 125–6, 131,as these passages are illuminatingly read in J.C. Bayón, 'Derrotabilidad, indeterminación del derecho y positivismo jurídico'.

specificationism requires, in principle, listing all negative conditions. And this, precisely, is what cannot be done.

In other words, specificationism, as a strategy for dealing with norm conflicts or inappropriate normative verdicts, is engaged in what M.N. Lance and M.O. Little aptly call the 'usual quest' of theory, 'which is to spend all our time filling in the holes in our generalizations'.[22] The quest proves, as they claim, 'deeply misguided',[23] not because the process never ends (mine, here, is not a claim of the 'we cannot go on ad infinitum' kind), but because it does not even get started in the first place. Negations cannot be enumerated. Thus, all (justified) verdicts turn out to be particular.

The argument from negative conditions leads to the rejection of both versions of specificationism, the contributory and the 'all things considered' ones. As regards the latter, the point is obvious. Achieving a fully specified, 'all things considered' norm, thereby ruling out the possibility of further, unspecified exceptions (apart from those already built into the norm itself) would require us to be in a position to draw a list of all potentially relevant properties of the kind mentioned. And this, we have seen, is misconceived. The former version, too, proves untenable although for a different reason. If what we achieve through specification is still a *pro tanto* reason, it cannot be excluded that the amended norm will itself come into conflict with another norm, thereby showing itself in need of further specification. But if further specification may lead to an inversion, in the present case, of the previously issued verdict (thereby showing, *ex post*, that it was justified only under an hitherto unspecified negative condition), and if—as this version of the strategy maintains—this possibility always remains open (so that we are forced to conclude that our verdicts are justified, whenever they are, under an indefinite and unspecifiable set of negative conditions), then no progress at all is made, it seems, through specification. We were, and still remain, at sea.

I am emphatically not *assuming*, as a (dubiously) self-evident postulate of a sort, that in order to make any progress, we have to be able to get from the contributory to the 'all things considered'. Rather, this is what the argument from negative conditions purports to *show*, that, unless this proves to be a viable move, justified verdicts always hold only under an unspecifiable set of negative conditions. And the move, as we have seen, is not available. To repeat, the worry is not that we cannot go on ad infinitum. This is what we actually do. The problem is, rather, that the supposed progress assured by specification doesn't even get started. Specification does not provide—nor does it purport to provide—*ex ante* guidance as to how our starting points have to be refined (this is a substantive matter).[24] But neither does it provide—nor can it purport to provide—guidance *ex post*, as to how a certain kind of case has from now on to be decided (further specification may, *ex hypothesi*, be called for, thereby reversing our previous verdict, i.e. showing it as holding only under an hitherto unspecified negative condition). So what kind of guidance does the norm (be it in its still-to-be-amended, or its already-amended guise) provide? Once again, all justified verdicts turn out to be particular. Specification only engenders an appearance of progress, where none is made.[25]

[22] M.N. Lance and M.O. Little, 'Defeasibility and the Normative Grasp of Context', *Erkenntnis*, 61 (2004), 453. Lance and Little are addressing, here, 'epistemic theory'.

[23] Ibid.

[24] H.S. Richardson, 'Specifying, Balancing, and Interpreting Bioethical Principles', 302, 305, fn. 4.

[25] I should stress that my argument says nothing about the merits of specificationism (of the contributory variety) as a decision-making procedure in institutional settings, e.g. public policy choices by administrative agencies, or in courts. Specification is advocated as a mode of public deliberation by administrative bureaucracies in H.S. Richardson, *Democratic Autonomy* (Oxford: Oxford University Press, 2002), 104, 227–8, 235, 237–9. Just as, even granted that practical reasoning is basically

All this mandates, I submit, our rejection of the identity assumption. Or, rather, it shows that the first way of construing it is a blind alley.

In spelling out the identity assumption we may wish to say that recalcitrant cases may be accommodated either because they are already provided for, albeit implicitly, by the norm, or because the norm may be refined so as to allow for the recalcitrant case as an exception ('if p then q, except when p and z'). So understood, recalcitrant cases qualify only as prima facie exceptions. On close inspection, or after suitable revision, they turn out to be provided for in the antecedent of the norm. Such a way of dealing with recalcitrant cases does not, I will say, treat them as true (as opposed to merely prima facie) exceptions. It is this way of construing the identity assumption that the argument from negative conditions shows to be hollow. Why not simply say that, in dealing with our normative issue (be it a norm conflict, or a verdict which we deem inappropriate), we are now simply changing our minds, i.e. we are now realizing that the norm we had endeavoured to apply to the case at hand was wrong (or that it was no norm at all), and substituting it with a different one? In fact, when we incorporate, along these lines, an exception in the antecedent of a norm, 'there is no difference between adding an exception to a rule and simply changing it'.[26] Moreover, where does the supposedly deep, qualitative, difference from intuitive balancing of conflicting considerations lie? When, facing a norm conflict, we have to decide which of the two norms is to be modified (in fact, discarded, and substituted with a different, more specific, one), and how or when, facing an inappropriate verdict, we have to decide how the norm's antecedent is to be modified, so that the case at hand does not fall under it any more, what we have to do is, it seems, just balance conflicting normative considerations.[27]

particularist, there may be good reasons for imposing a rule-based decision-making procedure (decision-making by entrenched prescriptive generalizations) on certain classes of choosers, or in certain decisional environments (F. Schauer, *Playing by the Rules. A Philosophical Examination of Rule-Based Decision-Making in Law and in Life* (Oxford: Clarendon Press, 1991), ch. 7; see also F. Schauer, 'On the Supposed Defeasibility of Legal Rules' in M.D.A. Freeman (ed.), *Current Legal Problems*, 51 (1998), 233, 237), so there may be good reasons for proceeding by specification in some institutional contexts.

[26] F. Schauer, 'Exceptions', *The University of Chicago Law Review*, 58 (1991), 893: 'the logical emptiness of the idea of an exception as an analytically distinct concept'; cf. also ibid., 873, and R.H. S. Tur, 'Defeasibilism', OJLS, 21 (2001), 359. This is the root of Alchourrón's dissatisfaction with justification on the basis of defeasible conditionals: so understood, resort to defeasible conditionals is, in fact, belief revision in disguise (on Alchourrón's views about this issue see J.L. Rodríguez and G. Sucar, 'Las trampas de la derrotabilidad. Niveles de análisis de la indeterminación del derecho', 105); J.C. Bayón, 'Por qué es derrotable el razonamiento jurídico?', 265.

[27] This, of course, also depends on how 'balancing' itself is understood. If by 'balancing conflicting considerations' what is meant is staring at the case at hand, and solemnly declaring 'here, N1 overrides N2', period, then of course this would not be a sensible way of proceeding. But this is not a fair picture of what balancing may be taken to be, either. Balancing, as such, is compatible with—and sensible balancing certainly involves—explaining why, as one sees things, in such and such a case N1 should be taken to prevail over N2, i.e. giving reasons as to why, in this kind of case, the former overrides the latter. This, to repeat, is what we do all the time and, as a result, what we get are more specific norms. What is at issue in the text is specificationism's claim to be providing something qualitatively different from this, and to be assuring a kind of progress, of enrichment and rational articulation in our normative outlook, which balancing would be incapable of bringing about. Intuitive balancing, Richardson argues (H.S. Richardson, 'Specifying Norms as a Way to Resolve Concrete Ethical Problems', 283; cf. also ibid., 287–8), lacks 'discursive rationality'. 'The question for balancers' is 'how their weightings have to be explained or justified' (ibid., 282). And, Richardson claims (ibid., 282–3), 'to the extent that the balancing is genuinely distinct from application [i.e. subsumption; ibid., 281] it affords no claim to rationality, for to that extent its weightings are purely intuitive, and therefore lack discursively expressible justification'. The same, however, may be said about the choice, in the face of a conflict, as to which norm to specify, and how. In deciding whether to specify a norm, or which one to specify, and how, what we are doing is, trivially, balancing conflicting considerations (and this,

Or at any rate specificationism tells us nothing different, or more, than this.[28]

Thus, on this reading, the identity assumption proves hollow. Talk of defeasible norms is mere rhetoric. Exceptions are treated as only prima facie ones: they are, in fact, incorporated in the antecedent of different norms. But, does the notion of a defeasible norm allowing for true exceptions make sense? I shall discuss this issue below.

D. From defeasibility to particularism

The argument in the previous section concerned specificationism. Specificationism claims to provide a way of dealing with norm conflicts which is consistent with the identity assumption. This is where its main attraction lies. It has been shown, however, that, precisely on this account, specificationism fails. On specificationist premises, the identity assumption withers away.

This, by itself, does not prove that defeasibility claims in general are incapable of living up to what they promise: that they necessarily fall short of warranting, as they by stipulation (see section A) imply, the identity assumption. Arguments analogous to the one deployed in the previous section can, however, be raised against other versions of defeasibilism. The way specificationism falls short of its promise is paradigmatic, I suggest, of the failures of defeasibilism, in many of its forms.[29]

To illustrate this point let us briefly consider a second, similar way of substantiating the identity assumption, already hinted at in the previous section. This is the claim that *implicitly* exceptions are already provided for by the norm. (This, it seems to me, is what is implied when it is said, as it is often the case, that defeasible norms are norms having implicit exceptions.) The norm's apparent formulation has to be understood, on this reading, as shorthand for a suitably complex counterpart. Its antecedent already contains, albeit in implicit form, the required exceptions. (How so? Maybe because it was the lawgiver's real or counterfactual intention that the norm should not hold for

for all we know, on specificationism's own lights). It is only when balancing is understood according to the (unfair) picture indicated above that the impression arises that specification ensures us something more than that.

[28] According to Richardson, one of the main features of the model of specification, distinguishing it from balancing, is that it goes hand in hand with justification, understood in coherentist terms. Specification can—and should—be practised as a way of improving the coherence and mutual support of our normative convictions (ibid., 300–2, 395, 397; H.S. Richardson, *Practical Reasoning about Final Ends*, 174ff., 185; H.S. Richardson, 'Specifying, Balancing, and Interpreting Bioethical Principles', 302; H.S. Richardson, *Democratic Autonomy*, 110). I have no quarrel with this, provided it is recognized that (1) if we allow (as this version of specificationism does indeed allow, and as the argument from negative conditions demands) for the standing possibility of exceptions to exceptions—or, specifications of specifications, revisions of revisions—coherence and mutual support turn out to be very weak constraints indeed; (2) this feature may be taken to differentiate specification from balancing only to the extent that the latter is given the (unfair) representation mentioned in the previous footnote.

[29] Of course, I have in mind here defeasibility of norms, as described in section A. Different notions of defeasibility, rooted in different concerns such as, e.g. the necessity of reasoning with incomplete information, or the proper ways of allocating the burden of proof, or the representation of knowledge in AI and law research; cf. G. Sartor, 'Defeasibility in Legal Reasoning', H. Prakken, *Logical Tools for Modelling Legal Argument. A Study of Defeasible Reasoning in Law* (Dordrecht: Kluwer, 1997), chs 1–5; J.C. Bayón, 'Por qué es derrotable el razonamiento jurídico?'; J. Hage, 'Law and Defeasibility'. H. Prakken and G. Sartor, 'The Three Faces of Defeasibility in Law' remain unaffected by this argument.

those cases, or for some other reason. Different explanations may be contrived.)[30] This is another main route to identity—thus, to defeasibility—claims.[31] And it, too, is shown to be a blind alley by the argument from negative conditions. Both strategies exhibit the same flaw: they engage us in the inane attempt at 'filling in the holes in our generalizations'. (Exceptions are not *real* holes, they in fact claim, either because they can be presently filled in or because they turn out to be already, albeit implicitly, filled in.)

Where does the failure of specificationism—or, if the suggestion at the beginning of this section is sound, of defeasibilism in many of its versions—leave us? Abandoning the identity assumption, while still allowing for the possibility of norm conflicts or inappropriate verdicts, amounts, I think, to endorsing a kind of particularism.

'Particularism' is an equivocal term, and many different positions may be labelled 'particularist'. This is not the place for sorting out varieties of particularism, their interrelationships, and so on. For our purposes, 'particularism' may be taken to mean what is entailed by the conclusion we reached, through the argument from negative conditions, in the previous section, namely that, when a specificationist strategy is followed, all justified normative verdicts turn out to be particular, i.e. they hold only under an indefinite set of negative conditions. Let us see what this conclusion amounts to.

What may be meant, here, by saying that justified verdicts remain particular is, in fact, two different things, leading to two different notions of particularism. I will list them both, since I believe there is no need, in the present context, to choose one of them and discard the other. The two claims are the following: (1) 'normative verdict particularism', namely, the claim that there are no absolute (i.e. 'all things considered', or overall) norms determining the deontic status of an act;[32] (2) the radical particularist claim ('normative valence particularism') that a feature that is a reason favouring an action in one case may be no reason at all, or even a reason against, in another case (i.e. features may shift their normative valence).[33] The two claims are independent of one another.[34] The two versions of particularism stemming from them are, first, normative

[30] None of them is endorsed here as a viable strategy. Whether such a claim can be plausibly made is a question I simply leave aside. (On what 'implicit' exceptions may be taken to be see J.L. Rodríguez, 'La derrotabilidad de las normas jurídicas', 94–101.)

[31] It was, I think, Alchourrón's way. Alchourrón's is a neat example of what Lance and Little call an 'enthymematic' strategy in dealing with recalcitrant cases (M.N. Lance and M.O. Little, 'Defeasibility and the Normative Grasp of Context', 438; see also M.O. Little, 'On Knowing the 'Why'. Particularism and Moral Theory', *The Hastings Center Reports*, 31 (2004), 37). It should be emphasized, however, that Alchourrón himself was well aware that this was an easy, but Pyrrhic victory over recalcitrant cases (see above, n. 26).

[32] Normative verdict particularism is the generalized form of 'moral verdict particularism', as defined in D. McNaughton and P. Rawling, 'Unprincipled Ethics', 258: 'the claim that there are no absolute principles for determining the overall deontic status of an act'. By 'particularism' is usually meant, in contemporary debates, moral particularism (that is, a doctrine about the behaviour of moral reasons). Since what we are concerned with here are normative structures in general (see section A), particularism will be recast, accordingly, as a doctrine about norms generally.

[33] 'Moral valence particularism': 'there are no properties, apart from the thin moral properties right, wrong, etc., that have universally and counterfactually invariant valence' (ibid., 268). This is, roughly, Dancy's position in *Moral Reasons* and *Ethics Without Principles*. I say 'roughly' because Dancy somehow allows for the possibility of invariant moral reasons, and does not straightforwardly deny that there can be true moral principles. But these complexities need not detain us here.

[34] D. McNaughton and P. Rawling, 'Unprincipled Ethics', 258.

verdict particularism as such; and, second, radical particularism: the conjunction of normative verdict particularism and of the radical particularist claim.[35]

Verdict particularism is, as it were, minimal particularism. It is compatible with there being a multiplicity of *pro tanto* reasons which may, and usually do, conflict with varying strength or weight (and no previously established priority rules, of course), and which on each case have to be balanced against one another (this is, roughly, Rossian intuitionism).

Understood as either claim (1), or as the conjunction of claims (1) and (2), particularism is a position allowing for the following claims: norms can and do in fact come into conflict; when a conflict arises, we cannot but strike a balance, declaring that, in such and such a case, norm 1 weighs more than norm 2—sometimes perhaps substituting N2 with another norm, N2*, more restricted in scope (specification)—the results of such balancing (and substitutions) are, however, open to revision when, as it is allowed, new conflicts arise; no revised norm may be held to be immune to further revision, thus we allow for the possibility that when properties P and Q are instantiated, N1 prevails over N2 (the latter perhaps being substituted by N2*), and that the possibility always remains open that there is a property Z such that, when P, Q, and Z obtain, N2 (or N2*) prevails over N1 (the latter being perhaps substituted by N1*) and so on. The argument from negative conditions entails particularism, in either of these two forms.[36]

Thus, the rejection (via the argument from negative conditions) of specificationism, and of relevantly similar versions of defeasibility claims, leads to particularism. The question is, does particularism (as defined above) amount to avowing that, in fact, no norm is being applied throughout? That, namely, we just see, case by case, what the right answer is? Is there any room left for reliable normative generalizations?

I shall take up this issue in section F. Before attempting an answer to this question, however, we need to pin down a point that emerged in the previous section.

E. Prima facie vs true exceptions

The argument so far has led us to a distinction between two different ways of talking about 'exceptions', in fact, two concepts of an exception.[37]

Exceptions are only prima facie if they may plausibly be understood as incorporated, maybe only implicitly (see section D) in the norms they are exceptions to, i.e. when we may plausibly claim that a proper understanding, or formulation, of the norm would envisage these kinds of cases: properly understood, or properly reformulated, the norm

[35] See ibid., 258–9.

[36] It should be noticed that particularism, as here understood, is not the claim that *individual* cases always escape, because of their inherent complexity or richness, the grip of conditional norms providing normative solutions for generic cases. (The notions of individual and generic case are defined in C. E. Alchourrón and E. Bulygin, *Normative Systems*, 27–30.) This claim is scarcely intelligible, and surely not a consequence of the argument from negative conditions. Rather, it is by virtue of *properties*, or, more generally speaking, features, serving as reasons, that new cases may be distinguished from previous ones—i.e. that a justified verdict may in the present case (a case sharing with the previous one the features that were sufficient reasons for the verdict there) be reversed (so that the previous verdict is now shown to hold under hitherto unspecified negative conditions).

[37] The distinction between these two concepts is somehow adumbrated in R. Dworkin, *Taking Rights Seriously* (London: Duckworth, 1977), 25. It is there entangled, however, in Dworkin's distinction between rules and principles.

provides for them so that, in resolving norm conflicts what we have to do is to ask ourselves 'how the relevant principles . . . are best understood'.[38]

When only prima facie, then, exceptions are nothing but further elements of the antecedent of a norm. That they are taken to be somehow implicit, or that they are formulated as separate items, or as a result of specification,[39] is only fortuitous—in principle, a proper understanding or formulation of the protasis of the norm could, and indeed would, lay them out on the same footing as other conditions.[40]

So, when is an exception a true exception? For a case to qualify as a true exception it must not be already provided for in a reasonably detailed and precise 'unless . . . ' clause attached to the norm. Two points need to be made here.

First, whether such a clause is conceived of as explicit or as merely implicit is immaterial here. When, and to the extent, it can truly and justifiably be claimed that an 'unless . . . ' clause of the required sort is implicitly attached to a given norm, the exception is only a prima facie exception, not a true one. (I am emphatically *not* assuming that such a claim can ever be truly and justifiably made. Maybe not. On this issue, I simply express no opinion.)

Second, the exception is not already provided for in *a reasonably detailed and precise* 'unless . . . ' clause. Obviously, open-ended or abstract clauses such as 'unless phy-ing would be unreasonable in the circumstances', or 'unless the circumstances demand otherwise', 'unless there are very good reasons for doing otherwise', etc. (e.g. promises should be kept 'at least in the absence of special justification'),[41] do not qualify as clauses of the required sort.[42] They can easily be given a particularist interpretation, as allowing for the possibility that some unspecified property, or set of properties, will

[38] T.M. Scanlon, 'Intention and Permissibility', *Proceedings of the Aristotelian Society*, Suppl. vol. 74 (2000), 309. See also ibid., 310: 'plausible moral principles do not merely state general requirements but also incorporate exceptions to these requirements'.

[39] Or even that they are characterized as *non-refutanda* (vs. *probanda*). G. Sartor, 'Defeasibility in Legal Reasoning', 1995), 131.

[40] F. Schauer, 'Exceptions', 872–3 and *passim*; see also F. Schauer, 'On the Supposed Defeasibility of Legal Rules', 227, 231; R. Dworkin, *Taking Rights Seriously*, 25; R.H.S. Tur, 'Defeasibilism', 359–60. In such cases, 'little more than deception is served by employing the language of exceptions'. F. Schauer, 'Exceptions', 895; see also ibid., 898–9. Prima facie exceptions may also be understood as the result of conflicts between non-defeasible norms, when a preference (or a hierarchy) between the conflicting norms is assumed (e.g. because a priority rule, such as *lex specialis*, is presupposed). See J.L. Rodríguez, 'La derrotabilidad de las normas jurídicas', 86; J.C. Bayón, 'Por qué es derrotable el razonamiento jurídico?', 287.

[41] Cf. T.M. Scanlon, *What We Owe to Each Other*, 200.

[42] Or, in other words, what would be required is a 'fairly definite and informative general account . . . of what count as potentially' relevant conditions. P. Väyrynen, 'Moral Generalism. Enjoy in Moderation', *Ethics*, 116 (2006), 737. Cf. G. Sartor, 'Defeasibility in Legal Reasoning', 143; R.H.S. Tur, 'Defeasibilism', 361–2: 'If A is, then B ought to be, unless there is an overriding reason to the contrary': 'one moves from a list of specific reasons, to a general catch-all residual category which unlike a list is not closed and cannot be closed'. A clarification is required here. There is, it seems to me (cf. J.C. Bayón, 'Por qué es derrotable el razonamiento jurídico?', 294), a difference between vagueness, as a feature of general terms, and the open-endedness of clauses such as those mentioned in the text. Contrary to Schauer (F. Schauer, 'On the Supposed Defeasibility of Legal Rules', 231), that exceptions covered by such clauses are 'not specified in advance' is not to be equated with the fact that—i.e. understood as meaning nothing but that—the extension of a vague term or phrase cannot be specified in advance. (This amounts to claiming that the distinction between the two kinds of 'unless . . . ' clauses in the text is not equivalent to, but rather cuts across, the distinction traced by Schauer (ibid., 231), between 'weak' and 'strong non-specifiability', according to whether exceptions can or cannot be specified in advance at least 'by type'. Here, 'type' blurs the important distinction between, on the one hand, the indeterminacy of the extension of ordinary general terms—i.e. vagueness—and, on the other hand, the indeterminacy of open-ended, abstract clauses.)

unexpectedly prove relevant in the circumstances. In order to work out whether such a clause applies to a given case, one has to work out whether applying the consequence would be justified with regard to a wide range of normative considerations. And this sort of judgement, particularists will claim, may, and should, be accounted for along particularist lines.[43]

When is an 'unless . . . ' clause *sufficiently* detailed and precise so as to warrant us in labelling the exception a merely prima facie, not a true one? This, itself, is a normative question, to be answered by working out what 'reasonably' (a *reasonably* detailed and precise 'unless . . . ' clause) amounts to in a given context. We may easily, as usual, give examples falling at the extremes. Often, however, there will be cases in which determining whether an exception is a true or a merely prima facie one will require us to make up our minds about substantive issues. This is the province of *determinatio* of open-ended or abstract clauses, about which I have nothing of interest to say. (I remind the reader that what my argument is about are norms, not norm formulations. Thus, the issues to be dealt with here are not issues of interpretation—remember the caveat spelt out in section A).

True exceptions, then, are not (not even in principle) specifiable, and enumerable, in advance. There are two ways of reading this: (1) E is a true exception if and only if it cannot be provided for in advance; (2) the list of possible exceptions cannot be exhausted. The relevant understanding is the latter. What now turns out to be an unexpected, unprovided-for exception may, from now on, become a settled one; what is left open is the possibility that an exception to this exception will present itself, or, generally, that further exceptions will have to be acknowledged.[44] (Does the former reading even make sense? The only hypothesis I can think of is that of not-yet-existing properties.)

To sum up then, true exceptions occupy a middle ground between two extremes. On the one hand are exceptions already provided for, be it explicitly or implicitly, in the norm through reasonably detailed and precise 'unless . . . ' clauses (i.e. prima facie exceptions). On the other hand is the bare fact of the non-application of a norm. We

[43] Scanlon's suggestion (*What We Owe to Each Other*, 200–1), that we may get to the relevant principle, piercing through its ordinary 'succinct verbal formulation', by considering the 'point' of (that is, by 'understanding the rationale' for) the general requirement the latter expresses (thereby determining whether the present, 'new and difficult', case should count as an exception to the requirement) does not, by itself, weigh in favour of generalism. Particularists will give a particularist account of precisely this way of proceeding. A sort of middle ground is occupied, here, by the notion of principles which relate non-moral features to moral ones (or, conditional norms linking factual antecedents to normative solutions), but do so only by virtue of evaluative or normative riders (in such cases, 'the list of conditions is not open-ended, and it is knowable in advance', but 'the conditions cannot be spelled out in purely non-moral terms'; D. McNaughton and P. Rawling, 'Unprincipled Ethics', 268–72. It all depends on what the relevant evaluative or normative riders are.

[44] It might be argued that true exceptions are what Hart was getting at (H.L.A. Hart, 'The Ascription of Responsibility and Rights', 147–50, and especially in *The Concept of Law*, 135–6: rules have exceptions 'incapable of exhaustive statement'), as these passages are read, and freed from some confusions, in F. Schauer, 'Exceptions', 896–7: 'the way in which rules can be overridden in particularly exigent circumstances and still be rules, even if it is impossible to predict or to specify in advance what those exigent circumstances will be'; and in J.C. Bayón, 'Derrotabilidad, indeterminación del derecho y positivismo jurídico', 163–4, 176–81. See also F. Schauer, 'On the Supposed Defeasibility of Legal Rules', 225: Hart 'made clear that the claim of defeasibility was more than the mere claim that rules can be defeated upon the occurrence of *specified* defeating conditions. Rather, to Hart it was the very *unspecifiability* of the defeating conditions, "the use of the word 'etcetera'," that explained the operation of legal rules.' What I call 'true' exceptions are also the main focus of R.H. S. Tur, 'Defeasibilism', 301ff.; R. Holton, 'Principles and Particularism', *Proceedings of the Aristotelian Society*, Suppl. vol. 76 (2002), see esp. 207, 209, '*exceptio probat regulam in casibus non exceptis*'.

should clearly distinguish, of course, two different issues.[45] The first is how a norm regulates a given case; the second is given that the case at hand falls under the antecedent of the norm, whether the norm is in fact applied or not by a given subject (e.g. a judge) on a given occasion, for whatever reason (because, for instance, the outcome looks unfair or unjust to him, or because he was bribed).[46] The bare fact that a norm is not applied by a given subject on a given occasion is, of course, 'no reason to regard it as defeasible':[47] the case at issue does not, for this reason alone, count as an exception (neither as a prima facie nor as a true one). The notion of a true exception is the notion of an unprovided-for case, C, falling under the antecedent of the norm, in which, nevertheless, the norm consequence does not follow because the norm holds in normal circumstances, or *ceteris paribus*, and the circumstances constituting C are not normal: other things are not equal. It is here, as we shall now see in more detail, that there is room left, in the particularist picture, for reliable, though defeasible, generalizations, and that a second way of understanding the identity assumption gains some plausibility.[48]

F. Default reasons, normal contexts (or, From particularism to defeasibility)

Particularism—especially, radical particularism (as defined in section D)—is a much debated position. One of the objections most often raised against radical particularism is that it does not account for, or even contradicts, an apparently non-dispensable intuition, or platitude, governing moral thought and judgement, namely, that certain features of situations (e.g. that a certain action would cause needless pain to an unwilling innocent) seem to be reasons, as it were, in themselves or in their own

[45] E. Bulygin, 'Review of Jaap Hage's Law and Defeasibility', 247.

[46] 'A judge may correctly identify the applicable legal rule and then decide not to apply it'. Ibid., 247.

[47] Ibid., 248.

[48] One related issue is whether *legal* norms, specifically, are defeasible. Bayón is of course right in pointing out that, when judges decide not to apply applicable legal norms because the outcome is morally unsatisfactory (law and morality being conceived, here, as different, discrete, normative systems), this, by itself, does not show that the relevant norm is defeasible (J.C. Bayón, 'Por qué es derrotable el razonamiento jurídico?', 293–4; see also J.L. Rodríguez and G. Sucar, 'Las trampas de la derrotabilidad. Niveles de análisis de la indeterminación del derecho', 121–2, 144; F. Schauer, 'On the Supposed Defeasibility of Legal Rules', 230; J.L. Rodríguez, 'Derrotabilidad e indeterminación del derecho', 229). The issue is, however, which is the best way of rationally reconstructing the form of legal norms, or of some of them—as defeasible conditionals, or as indefeasible ones. (Why on earth should it be assumed that the burden of proof is on defeasibilists? That, namely, *unless* positive law—explicitly, or perhaps even implicitly?—provides to the contrary, legal norms should be held to be indefeasible conditionals? And, why not read legal norms excluding unspecified exceptions as defeasible? The burden of proof seems to me to be evenly distributed here.) True, the bare fact that judges sometimes decide that the consequence should not be applied in a case which, as it seems, does indeed fall under the norm's antecedent does not answer this question (Bulygin's point in the text). But, on the other hand, the fact—if it is a fact—that true exceptions, not specified in advance (but for open-ended, abstract, or generic clauses), have long been recognized, and are still recognized, as possible (that exceptional circumstances are often recognized as justifying exceptions) in legal culture (e.g. by judges and jurists) in many, or most, or perhaps all legal systems, and that open-ended, abstract, generic clauses of the relevant sort are pervasive in many, most, perhaps all legal systems, may plausibly be taken to justify a defeasibilist reconstruction of at least some legal norms (see R.H.S. Tur, 'Defeasibilism', 307–8; J. Hage, 'Law and Defeasibility', 232–3)—or at least as shifting the burden of proof to the other foot.

right; that is, they seem to be endowed with moral relevance—specifically, with a given (positive or negative) normative valence—by virtue of what they are, not to be made thus relevant by other features of the situations in which they are present.[49] While, on the other hand, other features (e.g. shoelace colour) seem to draw whatever moral relevance they may happen to have in a given situation from other features of the situation. Blurring this difference, it is claimed, amounts to 'flattening the moral landscape'.[50]

This is a serious charge, one particularism should prove able to cope with. Even the most radical particularist should, I think, acknowledge that some reasons look like genuine *pro tanto* reasons: that some considerations seem to have normative relevance in their own right, and that they standardly count in favour of, or against, actions (no special explanation is called for when they do). The device J. Dancy has put forward in order to cope with this phenomenon is the notion of a default reason: some considerations arrive already 'switched on' as reasons in favour of, or against, an action so that when they do so count 'there is nothing to explain'; 'it is only when things are not as they are "default-set to be" that we begin to ask questions'.[51]

Default reasons are an especially tricky issue for radical particularists.[52] What is relevant to our present purposes, however, is a (relatively) uncontentious point. Even if we grant that reasons behave as radical particularists claim they do, even if we grant that all properties may shift normative valence according to context, some room has to be left for the notion of what standardly, or normally happens (as far as which considerations are reasons for which actions is concerned):[53] generalizations about what is a reason for what must be allowed, provided they are read as 'written with the standard case in view',[54] i.e. provided they are understood as relating to what is normally the case—and, thus, as defeasible generalizations.

I have tried to show that some ways of moulding the concept of defeasibility of norms end up in hollow rhetoric; changes in our normative outlook in the face of recalcitrant cases (i.e. norm conflicts, inappropriate verdicts) are all that is at issue. This line of thought leads, I have also claimed, to particularism: rejection of a specificationist understanding of the identity assumption, coupled with an awareness of the phenomena prompting defeasibility claims (that is, recalcitrant cases of the kinds mentioned)

[49] Cf. J. Dancy, 'What is Particularism in Ethics?', ('Cos'é il particolarismo in etica?', Italian transl.), *Ragion Pratica*, 26 (2006), 113–132, on the '"feature-placing" aspect of moral deliberation and reasoning', meaning by this 'the way in which a case can be made for or against an action by starting off with certain features that seem to have a relevance in advance of any consideration of the context'.

[50] S. McKeever and M. Ridge, 'Turning on Default Reasons', *Journal of Moral Philosophy*, 4 (2007). For a similar complaint see D. McNaughton and P. Rawling, 'Unprincipled Ethics', 268, 273. M.N. Lance and M.O. Little, 'Particularism and Anti-Theory' in D. Copp (ed.), *The Oxford Handbook of Ethical Theory* (Oxford: Oxford University Press, 2005), 583.

[51] J. Dancy, *Moral Reasons*, 103, 230; J. Dancy, *Ethics Without Principles*, 112; J. Dancy, 'Defending the Right', *Journal of Moral Philosophy*, 4 (2007), 89, from where the quoted passages are drawn.

[52] See S. McKeever and M. Ridge, 'Turning on Default Reasons'; and Dancy's partial retraction and defence in J. Dancy, 'Defending the Right', *Journal of Moral Philosophy*, 4 (2007), 89–92.

[53] Cf. D. McNaughton and P. Rawling, 'Unprincipled Ethics', 268. Simple normative verdict particularism (as contrasted with normative valence particularism; see section D) may, of course, allow for normative *pro tanto* generalizations (this is the distinctive feature of Ross-style intuitionism). So, when simple normative verdict particularism is concerned, the worry whether particularism allows for reliable normative generalizations is in fact out of place. Both the argument from negative conditions and the distinction between prima facie and true exceptions, although compatible with simple normative verdict particularism, seem to weigh in favour of a somehow stronger form of particularism. And this is the line followed in the text.

[54] The phrase is from ibid., 269.

leads, via the argument from negative conditions, to particularism. But, as we have just seen, radical particularism itself leaves—or at any rate should somehow leave—the possibility open of reliable, though defeasible, generalizations about what is a reason for what;[55] generalizations stating what is normally the case, as far as what is a reason for what is concerned. It is through this notion, normalcy, that we may capture, and make some sense of, the grain of truth in the claim that norms are defeasible.[56]

Let us say, then, that norms state what are *normally* reasons for or against certain actions, or certain normative consequences. Norms are defeasible conditionals liable to true exceptions, i.e. conditionals such that the consequence follows, when the antecedent is satisfied, under normal circumstances only.[57] The crux of the matter is, of course, how is the qualification 'normally' ('in normal circumstances', etc.), to be understood? Here, it seems, normalcy includes, but does not boil down to, the notion of what happens, or holds, 'in most circumstances'.

M.N. Lance and M.O. Little's notion of a defeasible generalization, as one resting on a '(normative) grasp of privileged conditions', hits, I think, the nail on the head.[58] This would be a way of having 'robustly explanatory', illuminating generalizations with true exceptions—or, *mutatis mutandis*, defeasible conditional norms. The problem, however, is still there: how is the relevant notion of 'privileged conditions'—or, what amounts to the same, 'normalcy'—to be understood? Clearly, it cannot be by arbitrary *fiat* that some conditions count as normal ones but, as Lance and Little rightly emphasize, it cannot be a merely statistical matter either.[59]

Lance and Little hint at the possibility of having 'a grasp of the shape of "privileged conditions"',[60] thus developing 'a skill at understanding and recognizing what is

[55] This move from particularism to defeasibility is the theme of M.N. Lance and M.O. Little, 'From Particularism to Defeasibility in Ethics' in Lance et al. (eds), *Challenging Moral Particularism*, (New York: Routledge, 2008). See also M.N. Lance and M.O. Little, 'Particularism and Anti-Theory', 588–91. A hint may also be found in J.L. Rodríguez, 'Introducción' in J.L. Rodríguez (ed.), 'Razones y normas', 22. As Rodríguez rightly points out, particularists will claim that an Alchourrónian revision function for a defeasible conditional is indeterminate (ibid., 24, 25). The notion of a defeasible conditional whose revision function is indeterminate captures part of what talk of generalizations having true exceptions is about. (According to particularists, that is, norms are to be understood as defeasible conditionals liable to true exceptions.) The remaining part is the idea of normalcy, as discussed in the text.

[56] Schauer grants that it is compatible with decision-making by genuine rules that these stay open to reconsideration in 'especially troublesome circumstances'. F. Schauer, 'On the Supposed Defeasibility of Legal Rules', 234. See also ibid., 238–9; and F. Schauer, *Playing by the Rules*, 98, fn. 26 on the 'presumptive force' of rules ('very good reasons', 'an elevated standard of defeat'). This allows for the version of the identity assumption now under consideration (ibid.). See also, in the same vein, F. Schauer, 'Exceptions', 897, about the 'standard of exigency'.

[57] Cf. R.H.S. Tur, 'Defeasibilism', 359; R. Holton, 'Principles and Particularism', 207. That defeasibility of norms should be understood in terms of 'normalcy' (i.e. defeasible norms as norms such that the consequence follows, when the antecedent is satisfied, under normal circumstances only) is often acknowledged, often in passing only. See e.g. G. Sartor, 'Defeasibility in Legal Reasoning', 123; J.L. Rodríguez, *Lógica de los sistemas jurídicos*, 356; H. Prakken and G. Sartor, 'The Three Faces of Defeasibility in Law', 120.

[58] M.N. Lance and M.O. Little, 'Defeasibility and the Normative Grasp of Context'; 'Particularism and Anti-Theory', 589; 'Defending Moral Particularism'; 'From Particularism to Defeasibility in Ethics'. A similar proposal has been put forward by Väyrynen in P. Väyrynen, 'Moral Generalism. Enjoy in Moderation'. I shall not discuss affinities and differences between them (see ibid., 727, fn. 51).

[59] M.N. Lance and M.O. Little, ('Particularism and Anti-Theory', 588; 'Defeasibility and the Normative Grasp of Context', 438, 441, 444, 445) also purport to show that privileged conditions (understood in the relevant sense) may be quite rare. I find their arguments on this score unconvincing.

[60] M.N. Lance and M.O. Little, 'Defeasibility and the Normative Grasp of Context', 452. See also M.N. Lance and M.O. Little, 'Particularism and Anti-Theory', 591.

deviant and normal, what paradigmatic and emendational, what conceptually prior or central'.[61] Such a skill, and its related object (the 'shape' of normalcy) remain, however, rather obscure. As far as I can see, there are two main problems involved.

(1) *Background and shape*. Normalcy, in the relevant sense, is an irreducibly contextual notion, in two respects.
   (a) It cannot be exhaustively spelt out what, in a given case, normal circumstances amount to. (This is the idea underlying the argument from negative conditions, and the point of contrasting true with prima facie exceptions).
   (b) Normal conditions are the context within which norms apply, i.e. they are the background against which normative conditionals properly work. It is only against this background that consequences follow from their antecedents.

This has to be understood by keeping in mind the background–shape relationship in *Gestalt* psychology. In each context, trying to specify what conditions are normal is just like trying to see the background as coming to the fore, showing its shape (just like defining the shape of the background). This cannot be done.

(2) *'Is' and 'ought'*. Normalcy, in the relevant sense, is supposed to occupy an intermediate ground between facts and norms, or between 'is' and 'ought'. The idea of normal conditions is not the idea of a norm, or set of norms (or of a set of facts satisfying them); but nor is it reducible to the notion of a mere regularity, although it includes that. Normalcy is neither rule, nor regularity, but rather something intermediate between the two. And this is awkward. Consider the following two statements:

   Most cases are normal.
   Most of the time (or, usually), things follow their normal course.

   The relevant notion of normalcy only makes sense if these can be understood as meaningful, non-tautological true statements. And I confess that I find this puzzling. Is it (non-tautologically) true that most cases are normal, that usually things follow their normal course? If the argument so far is right, it should be possible to make some sense of statements such as these.

Most of the time, then, things follow their normal course. And it is against this background (i.e. in normal cases) that normative conditionals work—that is, that normative consequences follow from their antecedents—and that true exceptions become possible.

G. Conclusion

I do not wish to claim that, whenever we face a norm conflict, or an inappropriate normative verdict for a given case, what we should do is declare that circumstances are abnormal and that, alas, true exceptions are a standing possibility. That would be ludicrous. Nor is this entailed by the argument so far. Obviously, there is room for specification of our norms, refining the universe of cases which their antecedents incorporate, and for building prima facie exceptions in the antecedents of such revised norms. What I am claiming is that, when this is what we are engaged in doing, talk of

[61] M.N. Lance and M.O. Little, 'Defeasibility and the Normative Grasp of Context', 453.

defeasible norms amounts to mere rhetoric. The identity assumption has no bite, here. We are just revising our normative convictions—changing our minds, more or less sensibly or coherently, as a consequence of balancing conflicting normative considerations.

This, however, should not be confused with a different phenomenon, the emergence of true exceptions to genuinely defeasible norms. This possibility, I have tried to show, is conceptually open. And it is here that the identity assumption can be made sense of, although now in a contextualist framework: defeasible norms remain in place (though their consequences do not follow there) in abnormal circumstances—but which circumstances count as 'abnormal' is a contextual matter. (Defining what is 'normal' would be like seeing the shape of the background.)

The identity assumption, on this reading, rests on a necessarily implicit understanding of what counts as 'normal' conditions, i.e. conditions that usually fit our usual expectations. Most of the time, things follow their normal course and it is against this background that norms can sensibly lay a claim to controlling our behaviour, linking normative solutions (consequences) to kinds of possible cases (antecedents). Against this background of normalcy, true exceptions remain possible but they are, necessarily, exceptional.

It is often said that norm-givers cannot foresee the future. This is true, of course. But what puzzles me most is that they in fact *can*, albeit to a limited extent, foresee the future. Things turn out as usual, most of the time.

17

Principles, Conflicts, and Defeats: An Approach from a Coherentist Theory

*Juan Manuel Pérez Bermejo**

'What was it I said to Lambert about principles? I said there were no general principles, but only special cases; that was stuff, utter stuff!'

F. Dostoyevski[1]

A. Introduction: between regulism and particularism

It is usual to introduce a philosophical issue as a clash of intuitions: several statements on a particular subject that are obviously true, although, upon implementation it appears that they cannot coexist simultaneously. In law, the problem of defeasibility can also be presented as a clash of two intuitions: the first one refers to law's normativity, and the second to its complex and changeable environment.

(a) Law mostly contains general norms that deal with all the particular cases by reproducing their factual descriptions uniformly and without exception.

(b) Law's application is context-sensitive: when they interpret and apply existing norms, legal agents may change their sense and meaning and correct the prevailing ones.

These two statements describe platitudes of our legal practice, and any likely legal theory must give ample recognition to them. However, when we want to reconcile the two assertions, we soon notice that the task seems impossible. From intuition (a), every norm rigidly imputes a legal consequence to a generic case described through a list of fixed properties. Nevertheless, this scenario of firmness and stability is contradicted by another, no less real in which judges reinterpret the understanding of the norm obeyed in the past, and do not apply the legal consequence to particular cases which hitherto fitted that description. On the other hand, intuition (b) allows us to separate a particular case from the norm's factual description through new interpretation of its meaning; however, this decision treats a particular case in a different way to how the same case was treated in the past, thereby breaking the normativist golden rule 'treat like cases alike'.

* Professor of Law, University of Salamanca. I am grateful to my colleagues at the Legal Philosophy Department in Salamanca for their thorough review of this paper, their criticisms and suggestions. I also give thanks to J.J. Moreso, J. Ferrer Beltrán, C. Redondo, H. Bouvier, J.M. Vilajosana, D. Martínez Zorrilla, J.C. Bayón, and P. Chiassoni for their kind comments and remarks.

[1] C. Garnett (tr.), *A Raw Youth* (ebooks@adelaide, Adelaide 2006) III, VI, 2.

This essay searches for an integrative theory capable of reconciling intuitions (a) and (b). It maintains that the best candidate to enact this role is what we call a 'principialist theory rightly interpreted'. Paradoxically, principialist legal theories are often described as incompatible with intuition (a) or, in other words, as 'particularist' theories for which general norms are always 'defeasible'. The purpose of this paper is to rebut these descriptions; it claims that they are based on faulty or unsatisfactory versions of these theories, and lose any credit when they are faced with more convincing interpretations.

Before distinguishing different models of principialist theories, it is necessary to clarify some terms previously referred to with some introductory lines. First, it is convenient to draw up a kind of 'map of coordinates' in order to outline the problems regarding defeasibility; the aforementioned formulations (a) and (b) will be expanded upon, and we will also consider what it would mean to reject either of them (1). Secondly, the meaning and the role of the principialist theories within the context of defeasibility will be briefly discussed (2).

(1) There is a useful way of solving a clash of intuitions: to deny one of them totally. However, one must resist the temptation to do so as this solution is obviously counter-intuitive. Even so, some legal theories have followed this route and dispensed completely with one of the two conflicting sources. Depending on which intuition is ruled out, we can distinguish two different conceptions of law, both radical and hardly admissible because they forget familiar aspects of legal practice.

One will assume that whoever denies intuition (b) shares a 'regulist' conception of law.[2] 'Regulism' describes the law as a fixed list of general rules solving a constrained set of general cases defined through a closed number of relevant properties. The sense or the meaning of any factual description is definitely established combining the relevant properties quoted in its respective norm. The application of law is only concerned with the examination of this strict and closed set of relevant properties: if the properties of a factual description are verified, its legal consequence is mechanically imputed. As an adjudicator of his existing legal system, the judge cannot change the meaning of the factual descriptions either by adding new relevant properties or by ruling others out. These operations could only be justified by using a new legal norm not contained in the fixed list of general rules. However, in regulism, a legal system is identified with a closed list of general rules, and the legal validity of the alleged implicit criteria or underlying reasons is categorically rejected. A regulist theory may confer upon judges discretionary powers to solve the problems of interpretation and application of law when the rule book is exhausted; even so, a regulist theory cannot entitle them to subject to exceptions the general rules of the legal system by using hypothetically implicit or non-positive norms.

These outlines of regulism could capture different legal theories, such as the 'strict conventionalism' described by Dworkin, the 'paleo-positivism' mentioned by Ferrajoli, or the 'entrenched' model of rules distinguished by Schauer.[3] It is precisely in Schauer's depiction where an important point is made explicit: for regulism, rules stand out as

[2] My personal view on 'regulism' is inspired by the well-known category described by Brandom, but it is neither identical nor obedient to the same purposes. See R. Brandom, *Making it Explicit* (Cambridge, Mass.: Harvard University Press, 1994), 18–20.

[3] R. Dworkin, *Law's Empire* (Cambridge, Mass.: Harvard University Press, 1986); L. Ferrajoli, *Derecho y razón*, P Ibáñez et al. trans. (Madrid: Trotta, 1995), 19; F. Schauer, *Playing by the Rules. A Philosophical Examination of Rule-Based Decision-Making in Law and in Life* (Oxford: Clarendon Press, 1991), 42ff.

'uniformizers' or 'stabilizers' of social practice, and their functions rest upon their ability to exclude any claim of exception or speciality. That is why Schauer describes this model as a model of a radical separation of the rules conceived as a fixed list of relevant properties, from all the underlying reasons that could justify any exception or any difference by adding or removing relevant properties. The detachment is radical because the more intense and severe the exclusion of moral or implicit reasons, the more truly and genuinely we witness the nature of rules and normative experience.[4]

Any theory displaying no commitment to intuition (a) embraces a particularist conception of law.[5] For particularists, rules define cases through some limited information expressed by a contingent list of relevant properties. However, dealing with a complex and heterogeneous social practice, we soon learn that any enclosed list of relevant properties can be trespassed on. We must therefore be prepared to admit a continuous flow of exceptions that refute the allegedly necessary connection between the case as it is described in the rule and its legal consequence. The first thesis of particularism says that in the rules there is no factual description we could call invariable. If factual descriptions were invariable, we could take for granted that, as they were verified, the legal consequence imputed to them in the rules would be implemented.[6] Although the general rule '$p \rightarrow r$' can be valid and effective in a large number of contexts, the interpreter may be placed in a context where he will face the relevant property q, of which '$p \wedge q \rightarrow \neg r$' follows. This may lead one to conclude that a simple process of correction or replacement of the old rule for a more complete one has occurred. However, it would be overconfident to suppose that we have simply replaced one rule for another, because the list of potential exceptions is always infinite,[7] and the supposed correcting rule is as defeasible as the corrected one. To take note of any correction would turn the factual description of the rule into an unmanageable and useless book, because it would be amended in the middle of its reading; strictly speaking, this kind of factual description would be a casuistic description of a particular case, and not the premise of a legal reasoning.[8] Particularism stresses the conditions of uncertainty that our knowledge (theoretical and practical) is submitted to, that prevent it from foreseeing the circumstances with which we could generalize fixed factual premises in the rules.[9] Crucially, this incapacity implies the relegation of the status of rules in practical reasoning: if rules are excluded by unexpected exceptions, they cannot be understood as necessary restrictions to our conduct, but simply as auxiliary and

[4] 'We thus see rules as essentially frustrating, exercising their influence by getting in the way'. *Playing by the Rules*, ibid., 87. As far as different models of judicial application of law are concerned, Schauer does not seem to support a pure 'entrenched model' (or a 'rule-based decision-making model'), but a slightly more moderate one ('presumptive positivism'). However, his general considerations about the nature of rules and their working in legal contexts include some remarks which capture the essence of what we call here 'regulism'.

[5] Although more familiar in moral than legal debates, I choose the term 'particularism' because of its prevalence in debates on defeasibility. In legal theory, where its statements are traditional, perhaps it would be more appropriate to talk about a 'casuist' or 'problematic' thought. A valid precursor of this thesis is, e.g. T. Viehweg, *Topik und Jurisprudenz* (Munich: Bech, 1953).

[6] R. Hare, *Freedom and Reason* (Oxford: Oxford University Press, 1963), 18–20; J.J. Moreso, 'Cristina Redondo sobre razones y normas', *Discusiones*, 5 (2005), 74.

[7] J. Dancy, *Moral Reasons* (Oxford: Blackwell, 1993), 81; J. Dancy, *Ethics without Principles* (Oxford: Clarendon Press, 2004), 94–5. As well as infinite, exceptions are of a very assorted nature: they can be *enablers*, *favourers*, *intensifiers*. See, ibid., 52.

[8] J. Hage, *Reasoning with Rules* (Dordrecht: Kluwer, 1997), 6–7.

[9] Thus no property can be 'codified'. M. Little, 'Moral Generalities Revisited' in B. Hooker and M. Little (eds), *Moral Particularism* (Oxford: Clarendon Press, 2000), 289.

sometimes dispensable reasons.[10] Rules do not establish a relationship of imputation or practical necessity between a factual premise and a legal consequence, and they cannot be considered as exclusionary reasons: at most, they formulate either maxims of experience or empirical previsions. Finally, as these rules have been relegated to this auxiliary and epistemical condition, inferential and logical operations arising from the rules will be questioned as being sufficient and even appropriate formulae for solving cases. To a great extent, particularism revitalizes the old saying of topical theories of argumentation according to which jurisprudence is not a science, but a kind of 'art' or 'style' demanding from the interpreter a special sensitivity to capture the particular and distinguishing circumstances of every case.[11] Legal interpreters do not proceed from logical inferences,[12] but from a supposed holistic consideration of the case which disregards the atomistic focus on the particular circumstances and concentrates on the general structure or figure of the case considered as a whole.[13] A solution to a case

[10] In particularism, the role of norms is invoked as a dividing line between a particularism more or less reconcilable with the relevance of general norms (Little, MacNaughton, Celano) and another version described as more radical and norm-destructive (Dancy). These nuances cannot be discussed in this essay. However, it must be mentioned that, generally speaking, the outlines of particularism drawn before can be compatible with both versions. On the one hand, 'soft' particularism is not always so 'soft'. It may emphasize the use of general rules, but does not forget to warn us that these are merely simple and useful generalizations with epistemic value, intellectual assistants always refutable by the circumstances of any particular case, not exclusionary practical subjections. M. Little, 'Moral Generalities Revisited', 295, 298. On the other hand, 'strong' particularists are not always so 'strong'. Dancy, for example, formulates a concept that approaches the idea of rules as revisable assumptions: the *default* reasons. They seem to have a non-contextual value and we can judge them relevant without adding any explanation, solely based on prior experience. See, J. Dancy, *Moral Reasons*, 26, 103; *Ethics without Principles*, 112ff. It is true that Dancy remarks that *default* reasons are not invariable reasons. Undoubtedly, there are differences separating both streams of thought. Dancy jeopardizes even the epistemic contribution of rules when they are understood as a probabilistic tool: our uncertainty towards the potential exceptions prevents us from assigning probabilities and recognizing tendencies. Despite the truth of these nuances, any particularist version sees the role of rules as a 'dispensable crutch for judgment', 'intellectual tools' always open to rectification, and useful assumptions that may be amended according to the circumstances of a particular case. J. Dancy, *Ethics without Principles*, 96–103; J. Wallace, *Ethical Norms, Particular Cases,* (Ithaca and London: Cornell University Press, 1996), 42. For particularism, decisions are not made according to a rule, but to a complete examination of the circumstances of the problem. At most, rules contribute as auxiliary reasons.

[11] T. Viehweg, *Topik und Jurisprudenz*, 95.

[12] J. Dancy, *Ethics without Principles*, 101–9; 154.

[13] J. Dancy, *Moral Reasons*, 101; *Ethics without Principles*, 103. The particularist use of the concept 'holism' is very problematic. First, holism is not a necessary argument for particularism. For its advocates, 'holism' means that moral reasons are not invariable respecting context, but are context-dependent, because they can change according to the specific circumstances of any scenario. M. Little, 'Moral Generalities Revisited', 280; B. Hooker, 'Moral Particularism: Wrong and Bad' in B. Hooker and M. Little (eds), *Moral Particularism*, 13; J. Hage, *Reasoning with Rules*, 116. However, this tenet is not exclusive to particularism, and could be accepted by generalist theories. Likewise we could reject this definition of holism and still support a particularist thesis: 'such an atomist... will simply take an examination of examples to suggest that the things that can be reasons are so many and so diverse that codification is impossible'. S. McKeever and M. Ridge: 'What Does Holism Have to do with Moral Particularism?', *Ratio*, 18 (2005), 13. Second, this use of holism does not fit the most common philosophical usage of the term. In epistemology, 'holism' is classified as a theory of justification for which we deal with problems summoning the whole system of arguments, because the system as a whole is the only possible source of justification. Dancy must disagree with this reading, because he does not recognize any existing previous system. Therefore, the most traditional holistic theories must be, in his interpretation, atomistic theories: Bradley, Bonjour, or Dworkin's theories fit perfectly with his definition of atomism (*Ethics without Principles*, 94). We can therefore understand why some writers are baffled by Dancy's holism and judge it faulty or ill-conceived, and thus defend the traditional and 'invariabilist' version: C. Brown, 'Two Kinds of Holism about Values', *The Philosophical Quarterly*, 57 (2007). Henceforth I will use the term 'holism' as it is used in epistemology and the theory of justification.

does not derive from a logically constructed reasoning, but from a phronetic knowledge; a special sensitivity that enables us to capture the salient or relevant circumstances.[14] As a decision is made, the interpreter cannot 'justify' it in the logical meaning of the term, but he can 'explain' the matter of the affair entirely, and persuade us to accept it as the most appropriate.[15]

To assume that norms are defeasible is to assume the difficulty and, eventually, the impossibility of sustaining intuition (a). Being drastically succinct, defeasibility problems can be introduced from two standpoints: first the validity and obligation of norms and, second, their logical connections. First, the defeasibility of norms means the impossibility of enclosing their validity and obligation scope within a fixed and stable semantic area. Norms seem accurately to define their factual premises combining some criteria and paradigms that, apparently, define their validity and obligation scope in secure terms. However, in their application, norms soon face an unlimited number of exceptions that will encroach on their frontiers: some particular cases will satisfy the factual description of the norm, but will avoid their application; others will not fulfil the description of the norm, although its legal consequence will eventually be imputed to them. The norm is defeated because the perimeter enclosing its validity scope is continuously encroached upon or undermined. When the factual premise is undefined and often subjected to exceptions, it cannot work as a necessary and sufficient condition of its legal consequence, which leads us to the logical dimension of the issue. From the logical point of view, defeasibility problems are described as breakages of some laws of the logic of conditionals. Assuming now provisionally that every norm is a conditional sentence logically symbolized with the formula '$p \rightarrow r$', (p being the factual premise or antecedent and r the legal consequence) defeasibility reveals that strengthening of the antecedent does not preserve the legal consequence: '$p \wedge q \rightarrow \neg r$', ($q$ being the defeater or recognized exception); defeasible conditionals are nonmonotonic, because their conclusions are not preserved, and can be eluded by additional information.[16] In short, to verify the facts described in the factual premise of the norm is not a necessary and sufficient condition for imposing the legal consequence.

From regulism's viewpoint, the aforementioned phenomena would be exceptional and pathological in any developed legal system. However, for particularism, they are in fact familiar and unavoidable, and, being a normal description of legal practice, the 'slippery slope' argument implies that every route of defeasibility leads us all to every particularist thesis, it being impossible to stop at any middle point: if any norm is threatened by an open list of exceptions, its validity scope is not guaranteed; if elementary logical laws such as *modus ponens,* strengthening of the antecedent or monotonicity are normally broken, neither logic norms nor inferential relationships between norms are possible.

(2) After highlighting the two extremes in our map, the question is, is it possible to design an integrative theory capable of reconciling intuitions (a) and (b) without being dragged towards the *Scylla* and *Charybdis* of regulism and particularism? This essay

[14] M. Little, 'Moral Generalities Revisited', 292; J. McDowell, 'Values and Secondary Qualities' in R. Shafer-Landau and T. Cuneo (eds), *Foundations of Ethics* (Oxford: Blackwell, 2007), 137ff.

[15] J. Dancy, *Moral Reasons*, 112–13. Although narrative coherence is sometimes invoked, its particularist version is again peculiar as it rejects a very traditional reason of coherence: to fit with decisions made in the past.

[16] Defeasibility reveals that implication 'does not seem to do the kind of work we ask of implication in a logical setting'. *Modus ponens* is broken too: if p implies defeasibly q, and if we suppose p, the consequence is '$q \vee \neg q$'. N. MacCormick, 'Defeasibility in Law and Logic' in Z. Bankowski et al. (eds), *Informatics and the Foundation of Legal Reasoning* (Dordrecht: Kluwer, 1995), 113–14.

assumes that an integrative position is possible. However, in order to convey the argument more clearly, it is convenient to anticipate a different question: why is a growing interest in normative defeasibility perceptible in current legal theory? Undoubtedly, the answer must be found in the rise of the legal theories we can refer to as 'principialist'. Any theory will be called 'principialist' when it recognizes the existence within the legal system of implicit principles or underlying reasons that can work as valid legal arguments in the interpretation and application of the law. Frequently, the real target in current literature concerning defeasibility is an indictment against principialist theories that accuse them of engendering strong particularist consequences. For example, for Dworkin or Alexy, legal systems are not only sets of rules, but sets of rules and principles. Principles are distinctive norms respecting rules because their validity scope is indeterminate and very general; in some of them, e.g. principles of equality or non-discrimination, the scope is supposed to be so broad that they pervade a large part of the legal system, and could be summoned upon in most of the cases. As well as indeterminate and general, principles are unlisted and innumerable: it is not possible to enclose them in any fixed list because many of them are implicit, and because their interpretation is subjected to a process which may be formulated as 'principles summon more principles', according to which the understanding of a principle must be nourished by the interpretation of others. Because of their generality, several principles are often simultaneously called upon to solve the same case. As they are innumerable and many times implicit, this situation of concurrence can be expected to be normal and regular. We will presume that this compact summary is a faithful reading of principialist theories; the problem is that, from these premises, some theorists believe it inevitable to come to the conclusions that: (a) principles are defeasible and often defeated norms (more specifically, they are defeated every time they are excluded from a case in which they were *a priori* compulsory but were finally displaced by another principle); (b) any priority of principles established by a judge is casuistic and ad hoc: it may be particularly valid for the case at hand, but is not preserved for other cases (in spite of their similarity, new cases may add distinctive circumstances); and (c) if principles are defeasible, the rules are also. In a principialist model, rules are viewed as expressions or determinations of principles. If this is true, any rule will collide with other norms as the principle it expresses or determines is in conflict with other principles. Any rule is always exposed to the influence of principles of justice or morality because the examination of a new case may reveal an implicit and hitherto unconsidered principle prescribing the non-observance of the rule. In these situations, rules must face the conflict with this principle, and the controversy may culminate in the defeat and non-application of the rule.[17] To sum up, a system conceived as an 'order of principles' will also conceive its interpretation and application as a set of particular and casuistic decisions.[18]

The view sustained here is that these particularist conclusions do not follow from the principialist thesis. Moreover, this essay upholds that only a correctly interpreted principialist theory is able to reconcile intuitions (a) and (b), that is, to satisfy normativity and adaptation to change in legal systems by reason of a combination of rules and principles. The term 'correctly interpreted' is essential: undoubtedly, there are ways of presenting a principialist theory showing a clear vulnerability to the symptoms

[17] Defeasibility of principles is introduced through the rules' walls like a Trojan horse. J.C. Bayón, *La normatividad del derecho* (Madrid: Centro de Estudios Constitucionales,1991), 360ff.

[18] F, Schauer, *Playing by the Rules*, 84; C. Redondo, 'Razones jurídicas. Respuesta a Caracciolo, Celano y Moreso', *Discusiones*, 5 (2005), 159.

of defeasibility and to the particularist thesis, and in which the misgivings about the fulfilment of the normative demands expressed in our intuition (a) are explainable. However, there are other descriptions capable of disposing of these problems and explaining the alleged cases of defeat and normative destruction as situations of a different nature.

The remainder of the essay will examine the two possible descriptions of a principialist theory and their competence to evade the particularist frontiers. In the following section, the essay will focus on the description of principialist theories admissibly vulnerable to the defeasibility phenomena and particularist thesis. The essay will underline how these theories willingly admit the dynamics of conflicts of principles and defeat of rules, and their problems of adequacy with legal practice. These theories will be referred to as 'weight-theories'. In the final section, the interpretation of a principialist theory that describes legal practice without resorting to the language of conflict and defeat will be unfolded. An alternative explanation to the current instances of normative defeat will be offered instead. These theories will be termed 'coherence-theories'. Assuming the correctness of these principialist coherence-theories, the conclusion maintains that the defeasibility problem can be better explained in terms of processes of determination and rectification of our norms. These events lack the implications of undermining or destroying our normativity most often highlighted in the literature on the subject. The background to these events is not the truth of the particularist thesis, but the trivial idea of fallibility of our knowledge.

It must be stressed that the essay will be especially concerned with the defeasibility of principles, and will not undertake the thorough and extended analysis necessary to examine defeasibility in rules.

B. Weight-theories

Despite the aforementioned references, an investigation into principles must start by questioning the use of the term 'defeasibility' in this kind of norm. First, principles lack any conditional structure; therefore when discussing principles, we cannot refer to transgressions of some laws of the logic of conditionals. Second, the validity scope of principles is indeterminate, so we cannot verify encroachments upon any delimited frontier around the norm. However, it will be assumed that it is conceptually possible to mention 'defeasibility in principles' by adopting an indirect use of the term:[19] principles would be defeated through the 'ascribed rules' that specify them. A principle like P1 would be defeated in a case when its 'ascribed rule' is defeated in this case. The 'ascribed rule' R1 is the rule that links the closed list of relevant circumstances of the case with the legal consequence defended by the principle P1: the rule is finally defeated because we recognize the competence of a different principle P2, and we apply a different ascribed rule that links the legal consequence defended by P2 to these circumstances. As the ascribed rule R1 is defeated, we would assume that P1 is also defeated in this case. Additional to this conceptual problem is whether the thesis that principles are defeated every time they are excluded from the application of a case (and all the particularist consequences implied) is a true reconstructive thesis of legal

[19] Some scholars even seem to reduce defeasibility of norms to defeasibility of principles: A. García Figueroa, 'La incidencia de la derrotabilidad de los principios iusfundamentales sobre el concepto de Derecho', *Diritto & Questioni Pubbliche*, 3 (2003), 203. Hage's argument is similar when he locates the defeasibility problems in the so-called 'external justification'. J. Hage, 'Law and Defeasibility' *Artificial Intelligence and Law*, 11 (2003), 222.

practice. Obviously, to say that principles are defeated through their ascribed rules implies that the defeated ascribed rule was always obligatory and legally founded in the case at hand. This is the main tenet of the weight-theories, and this section will try to unveil the weakness of this thesis.

To investigate moral principles, even if we are concerned with their working in legal practice, we need to reconstruct a moral theory. However, not just any moral theory is admissible: it must be fitting and suitable to legal practice and, therefore, it must be reconstructed from a legal point of view. This condition forces us to address some cautions of a different nature. The first ones are terminological. Many works on morals, ethics, or meta-ethics use the term 'principle' as an equivalent to the term 'norm', thus blurring any difference between principles and rules. This distinction is essential to us, so what moralists often call 'principles' will sometimes be specified as 'rules' in this article.[20] More importantly, we have to provide answers to some moral controversies, and our answers must suit legal practice. For example, we need to decide whether our values or moral fundamental principles conflict or not. 'Defeat' and 'normative conflict' are concepts that relate: the defeat of any norm is the consequence of its conflict with another normative consideration. Facing a choice between a conflictualist and a non-conflictualist theory of our values, we must choose the theory that best suits our fundamental intuitions on legal practice, and the legal agents' understanding of their own activity. Second, another basic ingredient is the adequate interpretation of the prima facie clause normally linked to moral principles. A 'prima facie' clause and defeasibility are again conceptual relatives, and it is not uncommon to refer to 'prima facie' and 'defeasible' norms as synonyms.[21] As in the issue of conflictualism, the correct interpretation of this clause must be established in the light of legal practice.

Once these conditions are explicitly made, we can identify weight-theories as some descriptions or interpretations of the principialist legal theories according to which legally relevant values or moral principles often undergo situations of conflict in an open list of unpredictable cases. 'Weight-theory' is an ad hoc category with which one will attempt to represent some interpretations of principialism; therefore, it does not designate a list of philosophers and theories that expressly adopt this term or identify themselves with particularism. However, the language and phraseology of Alexy or Peczenik's theories foster these interpretations too easily.[22] Finally, 'weight-theories' is a category in itself concerning principles and values, and that is why, as has been outlined, the following subsections are mainly concerned with the supposed defeats and conflicts of principles (subsections 1, 2, and 3); only at the end the defeasibility of rules will be briefly referred to (subsection 4).

It is a commonplace in principialist theories to stress that the application of principles is not a subsumption, but a weighing or balancing operation. This remark

[20] This use of 'principle' is common in philosophers such as Hare, Dancy, or Scanlon. Inversely, we will not distinguish between 'principles' and 'values'. Although their relationships will not be considered here, it is obvious that these relationships are not in conflict or tension.

[21] J. Dancy, *Ethics without Principles*, 62; B. Celano, '"Defeasibility" e bilanciamento. Sulla possibilità di revisión stabili', *Diritto & Questioni Pubbliche*, 2 (2002), 36.

[22] It is not said that Alexy's theory is particularist. Alexy openly rejects particularism or casuism: R. Alexy, *Theorie der Grundrechte* (Frankfurt: Suhrkamp, 1985), 152. He remarks that what is derived from the balancing of principles are rules, not particular decisions, i.e. general norms, not ad hoc decisions, and he asserts that 'weighing in a particular case and universability are not incompatible'. It is said that the refutation of particularism is more difficult starting from Alexy's theory than from others, and therefore seeing his theory ranked as particularist is not to be unexpected: Maniaci, e.g. terms it 'weak particularism' in G. Maniaci, 'Note sulla teoria del bilanciamento di Robert Alexy' *Diritto & Questioni pubbliche*, 2 (2002), 52ff.

is sometimes followed by a warning: the term 'balancing' works here as a simple metaphor, and not as a proper description of these application processes.[23] However, we have reasons to suspect that terms like 'weighing' or 'balance' hide a more theoretical substance, and are something deeper than simple metaphors. Theories constructed under the influence of Alexy or Peczenik usually agree to adjust the application of principles according to some significant guides for our issue: (a) principles are interpreted as commands of optimization, i.e. values or ideals that must be obtained in the highest possible degree; (b) principles often clash with each other: normally, several principles are summoned upon simultaneously to solve the same case C, and are therefore involved in a situation of conflict or dispute; (c) facing a case like C, the interpreter must 'weigh' the principles in conflict. To 'weigh' means, first, to assign to each principle a weight, a measurement related to its vigour or relevance in C; second, to 'weigh' means to choose as winner of the conflict the principle whose application obtains the highest degree of satisfaction in the values at stake or a lesser degree of frustration in the losing principles;[24] (d) the application of the winning principle P to the case C implies the formulation of an ascribed rule R. This rule specifies the principle P, and imputes its legal consequence to the properties of case C;[25] (e) the validity scope of the ascribed rule R fits strictly the properties of the case C, and can only be applied to identical cases or cases displaying all its relevant properties; (f) the ascribed rule R is *a priori* a definitive rule within its validity and application scope. However, nothing prevents it from being defeated as it faces a conflict with another principle or, simply, as it meets another case that adds to C another relevant circumstance.[26]

Weight-theories assume all these guidelines.[27] For some experts, this description exhibits all the signs of explicit particularism. For Prakken, to found legal conclusions upon the comparative weight of two sets of conflicting reasons 'naturally leads to defeasibility'.[28] However, what we call 'weight-theories' includes more problematic elements. They sustain sentences (a)–(f) upon some theoretical assumptions of our principles and values that are incompatible with their interpretation and application in legal practice. These assumptions include an erroneous concept of validity and obligation of principles (1). This problem will be exposed through the meaning of the term prima facie. They also assume a goal-oriented (2) and a conflictualist (3) moral theory leading to inadequate legal consequences.

(1) For weight-theories, principles are prima facie norms obligatory in an indefinite set of cases. This prima facie clause involves a practical and effective normative value: prima facie norms contain demanding obligations. Because of this obligatory quality,

[23] R. Alexy, *Theorie der Grundrechte*, 82.

[24] Guide (c) represents, drastically miniaturized, the most important criteria involved in the 'proportionality principle', familiar in German jurisprudence and strongly influential in the rest of Europe.

[25] Alexy distinguishes between 'ascribed rules' and 'directly established rules'. R. Alexy, *Theorie der Grundrechte*, 58–60. A directly established rule has the same degree of precision as its principle, because it is equal to the literal interpretation of the disposition proclaiming the principle. However, weight-theory authors admit that directly established rules, precisely due to their broadness, cannot be used to apply principles. C. Bernal, *El principio de proporcionalidad y los derechos fundamentales* (Madrid: Centro de Estudios Políticos y Constitucionales, 2007), 116.

[26] R. Alexy, *Theorie der Grundrechte*, 87ff.

[27] We can find appeals to the weight of principles in many authors (e.g. Hare, Dworkin). However, not all these authors subscribe to conditions (a) to (f).

[28] H. Prakken and G. Sartor, 'The Three Faces of Defeasibility in the Law', *Ratio Juris*, 17 (2004), 122.

competitions of principles are the *locus* of a real normative conflict. If a principle rules prima facie a singular case, this principle embodies a degree of obligation and applicability to solve the case before and after the judicial decision. To presume something as prima facie right is to presume that it is already effectively right, the source of *ab initio* obligations, and entitled to possess the practical effects linked to the term 'rightness'. It is true that, as well as *ab initio*, these obligations can be outweighed and surpassed by others; nevertheless, the outweighed obligation does not vanish for this reason: it is unfulfilled, but this frustration is morally offset by the fulfilment of a more weighted obligation.[29]

The question is whether prima facie clauses may attribute this meaning to principles. From our perspective, we anticipate that the implications of this understanding do not suit the legal practice of principles. Interpretations of weight-theories hold that a principle is a source of an *ab initio* obligation in the judged case, which supposes that this case is included *ab initio* in the validity scope of the principle. However, if the case belongs to the validity scope of this principle or any other entails the *sub judice* problem. We know that the case can possibly belong to the validity scope of a principle P1 due to one, or possibly, several properties of the case, and that is why we take into account this principle as a prima facie principle; however, we are also aware that considering another property, or the light shed by other norms of the legal system, might completely change the nature of the case, and turn our initial ascription of the case to P1 into a mistake. Principles are indeterminate norms respecting the validity scope, and it is precisely this indetermination which brings about the complex tasks of deliberation and judgement developed by courts and judges when they consider principles: to presume the case included in the validity scope of the principle is to presume in it a non-existent precision, a precision that is partially revealed only at the end of the deliberative process. In these situations, we do not know if the case is ruled by the principle and the principle is effectively obligatory; we believe that it might happen, but we do not know this for certain until the end.

Including the case in the validity scope of the principle, weight-theories assert that the prima facie principle is obligatory in the case. This means that all the principles competing to be applied in the same case are simultaneously obligatory, so that prima facie obligations are necessarily conflicting and inconsistent.[30] Finally, weight-theories assume that a prima facie obligation coming from a conflicting principle is actual and demanding because it is legally justified and rests on a legal ground. If this is true, a

[29] Defenders of this thesis are, e.g. R. Audi, 'Intuitionism, Pluralism and the Foundations of Ethics' in *Foundations of Ethics*, 403; D. Brink, 'Moral Conflict and Its Structure' in H. Mason (ed.), *Moral Dilemmas and Moral Theory* (Oxford: Oxford University Press, 1996) 103–4; J. Searle, 'Prima Facie Obligations' in J. Raz (ed.), *Practical Reasoning* (Oxford: Oxford University Press, 1978) 81–4; B. Williams, *Moral Luck* (Cambridge: Cambridge University Press, 1981) 72. As is known, D. Ross's case is more doubtful. See B. Herman, *The Practice of Moral Judgment* (Cambridge, Mass.: Harvard University Press, 1993), 166.

[30] It has been denied that these kinds of obligations are logically inconsistent: P. Foot refers to these cases as cases of 'conflict without inconsistency'. It is impossible to save the moral inconsistency without embracing a view of these obligations in which they are not effective, actual or, simply, not real obligations. Foot's point is based on an analogy between duties and desires. P. Foot, 'Moral Realism and Moral Dilemma', *The Journal of Philosophy*, 80 (1983), 80. Although blessed by academics such as B. Williams, this analogy is doubtful: in T. Scanlon's language, desires are reasons *pro tanto*, because they involve a weight-dimension, and they can be outweighed; but competing moral reasons are not *pro tanto*, but prima facie, and it means that they are not surpassed or outweighed, but annulled and refuted. T.M. Scanlon, *What We Owe to Each Other* (Cambridge, Mass.: Harvard University Press, 1998), 50–1.

weight-theory is forced to maintain that defeated obligations cannot be eradicated, and preserve legal justification and legal vigour after being overridden.[31] Perhaps this view could be upheld in morals, but it is unacceptable in law, where the hypothesis of rights that are recognized by a legal system, accepted as legally compulsory and binding, but finally unprotected or unsatisfied, is out of the question. In short, this interpretation of prima facie clauses does not satisfy the legal domain. Using Brink's vocabulary, the weight-theories' viewpoint supports a 'metaphysical' interpretation of the prima facie clause; this understanding must be replaced by an 'epistemic' view of the clause:[32] the view that is endorsed by coherence-theories.

(2) As principles are innumerable, simultaneously obligatory and prone to conflict, we cannot expect a complete fulfilment of all of them. Instead, principles require us to achieve the values they express in the highest possible degree; in other words, they are orders to optimize or to maximize the values they convey. This means that principles are linked to goals, states of affairs morally preferable or valuable; if they are reasons for our action it is because obedience to them is the way to obtain these outcomes. It also means that we can calculate the weight or importance played by each principle in any singular case because we can fix a mark equivalent to the degree of satisfaction of the value expressed by the principle in the case where it is applied. Choices between principles in conflict are choices between preferable states of affairs according to their values. Assuming all the principles are obligatory, we must maximize them all and minimize their losses. If, finally, we apply one principle in a conflict, and not the others, it is because we obtain a higher amount of the value this principle conveys as well as a lower loss of the values expressed by the defeated principles.[33]

Once again, we face an inadequate description of our most important legal principles and values: the right to live and adhere to any religion, or no religion at all, are not principles that must be satisfied in the highest possible degree, but principles that are either obeyed or not in any particular case in an 'all-or-nothing' alternative. The application of these rights cannot be solved by comparing final outcomes or states of affairs, or fixing degrees of satisfaction. We cannot prove a real appreciation of life and freedom of belief as fundamental values if we attribute to them relative and contextual degrees of importance and demand their respect only if they provide a satisfying global outcome. Far from the model of the kitchen scales,[34] our application of a principle depends on the correct interpretation of its sense or meaning. In other words, our view of our own values does not rest on their relative contribution to final outcomes, but on a theory about their meaning or their *point* that can set all in order and specify in which circumstances they must be decisive.[35]

[31] R. Audi, 'Intuitionism, Pluralism and the Foundations of Ethics', 31.

[32] D.O. Brink, 'Moral Conflict and Its Structure', 104.

[33] R. Alexy, *Theorie der Grundrechte*, 78ff. Some descriptions of weighing are close to the cost–benefit analysis. Alexy describes his criteria as 'none other than an expression of the idea of Pareto-optimality'. R. Alexy, 'Postscript' to R. Alexy, *A Theory of Constitutional Rights* (Oxford: Oxford University Press, 2002), 399.

[34] J. Dancy, *Ethics without Principles*, 105. 'Value commitments . . . are not "scalar": failing to save the life of a rational agent is not half or twice as bad as deception'. B. Herman, *The Practice of Moral Judgment*, 155.

[35] T.M. Scanlon, *What We Owe to Each Other*, 52–4; K. Günther, 'Un concepto normativo de coherencia para una teoría de la argumentación jurídica', *Doxa*, 17 (1995), 291. Although the weighing of principles and use of kitchen scales are often acknowledged as simple metaphors or analogies, some versions take the metaphor very seriously; otherwise, their endeavours to specify the tasks of punctuation and choice of principles through formulae would be inexplicable. Alexy warns us about the purely methodological nature of these formulae, which are far from any mathematical yearning. However, his sketches on weighing actions describe them as scale operations in which the decision is justified in the gain or the loss from applying one or another principle, benefits and losses that must be quantified at

(3) A metaphysical view of the prima facie clause leads us to a conflictualist theory of values.[36] Two rival principles in a case are simultaneously obligatory and, *a priori,* entitled to be applied in this case; the consequence is an open conflict of principles and values.[37] The adopted legal solution, the ascribed rule, is the consequence of this conflict, and its content is calculated in the same way that we calculate the trajectory of a body involved in a crash. The problem is that, in a clash of principles, any legal principle already occupies the space of the problem, and is acknowledged as a legitimate source of binding legal obligations. Therefore, a legal solution proclaims the best right of a principle over the rest, but it does not deny the right and the legally justified status of the rejected thesis. An interesting consequence of these premises is that, in weight-theories, we cannot accept the so-called 'thesis of the right answer' understood in the most orthodox version, emanating from R. Dworkin's theory. For Dworkin, the thesis of the right answer presupposes in every single case the existence in the legal system of one right solution that we can judge as exhaustive and exclusive. He supposes that the reasoning that, in any legal problem, even in the most difficult ones, one side is inevitably right and the other wrong is deeply rooted in our habits of thought.[38] However, in weight-theories, both rival positions are legally grounded, and vouch for rights and legally justified obligations; for them, a legal system does not contain a single, exhaustive, and exclusive answer: there is not one single answer from the point of view of the legal system, but a better answer, or less harmful one, sometimes no answer at all.[39] Of course, our current debate is not which interpretation of the right-answer thesis is correct, but which conception of our values and principles is more consistent with legal practice. Checked against this test, the conflictualist view cannot be satisfactory. It is paradoxical to assume that legal systems ground, justify, and, therefore, acknowledge rights that, finally, are not protected. The sentence 'in the name of the Spanish law I condemn you to *x*, although I admit that Spanish law recognizes the grounds of your claim and the valid rights founded on them' is destructive if we aspire to describe our legal system as an order enjoying a minimum of unity, solidarity, and cohesion. Therefore, the first problem for the conflictualist interpretation of legal principles is to show a diffused picture of our legal systems breaking the less demanding interpretations of unity and consistency.[40] Second, the conflictualist view leads to the

least in an ordinal way, and specified as 'light', 'moderate', and 'serious'. R. Alexy, 'Postscript', 396–412. The mathematical impulse is more visible in other authors like H. Hübmann or G. Lopera, who believe it indispensable to use numerical magnitudes. G. Lopera, *Principio de proporcionalidad y ley penal* (Madrid: Centro de Estudios Políticos y Constitucionales, 2006), 533. Even so, these weight-control formulae suffer from an obvious vagueness. As is known, courts have not been able to contribute with stable criteria to mark conflicting principles. This is visible even in those courts most in favour of balance and proportionality: B. Fassbender, 'El principio de proporcionalidad en la jurisprudencia del Tribunal Europeo de Derechos Humanos', *Cuadernos de derecho público*, 5 (1998), 73; D. Galetta, 'El principio de proporcionalidad en Derecho comunitario', 108.

[36] J. Searle, 'Prima Facie Obligations', 86.

[37] When we solve these cases of competitions of principles, we deal with 'tensions, conflicts or antinomies'. R. Alexy, *Theorie der Grundrechte*, 120.

[38] R. Dworkin, *Taking Rights Seriously* (London: Duckworth, 1977), 290. Alexy brands the Dworkinian thesis as 'absolutist', 'ontological', and 'non-procedimental'. R. Alexy, 'Nachwort. Antwort auf einige Kritiker' in R. Alexy, *Theorie der juristischen Argumentation* (Frankfurt: Suhrkamp, 1991), 412–15.

[39] We refer in these cases to ties: if two sets *a* and *b* of reasons are equipollent or apt to cause a dilemma, there is 'nothing to say about the overall merits of *a* and *b*'. P. Foot, 'Moral Realism and Moral Dilemma', 396; R. Alexy, 'Postscript', 401–2.

[40] In a similar way, F. Müller reproaches Alexy for endangering the principle of unity of the Constitution. See F. Müller, *Juristische Methodik* (Berlin: Duncker & Humblot, 1989), 64ff.

moral paradox that is to command the unfulfilment and non-observance of what is still considered binding and obligatory: although weaker and insufficient, the defeated obligations exist for the specific case, but they are not demanded or enforced, because they are not thought of as decisive. In morals, weight-theorists and defenders of the metaphysical reading of prima facie clauses accept this diagnosis as a normal consequence of the solution of conflicts, and predict as unavoidable a feeling of moral loss, as well as the penitential phenomenon of moral remorse or regret for the outweighed and frustrated demands.[41] In law, to imply that shows of regret must be expected from the legal community as morally appropriate answers, or that this community is burdened with a duty of compensation because of its decision in cases of conflicting principles is ridiculous. However, if we recognize a conflict between legally binding principles in the case at stake, and if we advocate one of the conflicting principles just because its right is a better right (and sometimes only slightly better), we are admitting that the defeated claim is founded upon legal grounds, appeals to some valid rights proclaimed by the legal system for specific cases like the one at stake, and, at the same time, is not protected by law: this is a radical contradiction. To sum up, conflictualist portraits of our existing legal principles and values are inappropriate. Indeed, we know that our principles are limited, and there are hard cases in which they appear to be jeopardized by other values; however, if, eventually, our behaviour is not guided by one of them it is not because this principle has been defeated by a conflicting one, but because our conception of this principle excludes the circumstances of the case from the sense or the meaning we attribute to the principle. Borrowing Scanlon's example, if we employ Beethoven's last string quartets as lift music in our company, the mistake is not to have erroneously weighed music and business: our problem is not correctly understanding the value of music.[42] Therefore, there are not conflicts, but problems of interpretation concerning the meaning of our principles and values: problems that must be solved by a theory able to put them in a coherent order.

The addition of these elements is a theory that has difficulty in avoiding the conclusions of particularism and the thesis that our principles are defeasible even in situations or circumstances where their application seems necessary.[43] Whenever several principles are called on to solve a case, we witness a conflict between principles that are valid and obligatory in the solution of the case, and to not apply one of them can only be understood as its defeat. Principles are removed from cases or areas of social problems included in their validity scope where they are proclaimed as obligatory: this is enough to conclude that, in weight-theories, principles are defeasible norms.

(4) Finally, the aforementioned considerations harm the weight-theories' efforts to find a position integrating regulism with particularism concerning rules. Here, we assume that a 'rule' is the result of interpreting a disposition or an implicit normative sentence that attributes to a norm a concrete and specific factual description consisting of a closed list of relevant properties. This is, for example, the case for the 'ascribed rules' that, in a weight-theory, provide the solution applied to a conflict of principles: the result of specifying the winning principle in a rule whose factual description is equal to the factual properties of the case.

[41] P. Pietroski, 'Prima Facie Obligations, *Ceteris Paribus* Laws in Moral Theory', *Ethics*, 103 (1993), 509; D. Brink, 'Moral Conflict and Its Structure', 105.

[42] T.M. Scanlon, *What We Owe to Each Other*, 85–6, 100.

[43] It has been said that 'weighing' or 'balancing' is an essential ingredient of any particularism. D. MacNaughton and P Rawlings, 'Unprincipled Ethics' in *Moral Particularism*, 260.

In order to deny the particularist appeals and the suspicion of a defeat of the rules, a theory needs to prove that the factual antecedent of the rule is a necessary and sufficient condition for imputing the legal consequence to any case suiting its factual description. In other words, the rule must hold exclusionary powers against any invocation of speciality or exception that could be understood as a defeater. Unfortunately, weight-theories cannot satisfy this condition, because the rules coming from their theoretical framework own an open and provisional factual description.

It could be said that a rule R1 '$p \rightarrow r$' coming from the weighing of P1 and P2 is a definitive rule for the relevant circumstances enclosed in its factual premise '*p*'. However, R1 soon faces a circumstance '*q*', supported by the principle P3 and sustaining its non-observance. This is a frequent and easily expected possibility, because principles are innumerable. More importantly, this likely eventuality would ensure a conflicting scenario, because principles or moral considerations claiming relevance would be understood in a weight-theory as valid and obligatory *ab initio* in the case. The life of rules is normally subjected to conflicts and weight examinations with competing principles. If the rule does not have enough weight, it will not be applied in the case '$p \wedge q$'. This approach leads us to two consequences:

(a) R1 or '$p \rightarrow r$' has been defeated in *q*, and circumstance '*q*' is a proper exception or defeater. Indeed, one could try to avoid the particularist reading of this approach, arguing that '*q*' is not a defeater or exception, but a new ingredient of '*p*' that completes and perfects the factual description; as we have a new understanding of '*p*' or the factual description, we would have obtained a new rule, and replaced R1 by R2. However, this strategy is not appropriate to weight-theories. We must bear in mind that the last process is a scene of normative conflict between several considerations that are recognized as valid and obligatory. That is why, after the examination, R1 is not denied, refuted, or excluded: we still accept R1 or '$p \rightarrow r$' as valid and obligatory in '*p*', although it faces stronger legal titles if we add to '*p*' the circumstance '*q*'. Rules are subjected to exceptions that are external to the factual description of the rule and defeat its application.[44]

(b) As a consequence, to say that '*r*' must be the legal consequence imputed to '*p*' is a provisional and prima facie utterance.[45] As a report on a legal system, it may be only a relative truth, because the rule may clash with other considerations and be applied depending on the weight shown in different contexts. Nevertheless, as an unavoidable conclusion, a rule whose factual description is provisional and open to exceptions cannot work as a necessary and sufficient condition of the legal consequence.

[44] This is explicit in R. Alexy, *Theorie der Grundrechte*, 88–9.

[45] Perhaps to elude these consequences, Alexy's theory and its closest followers are ambiguous when attributing this character. For Maniaci, Alexy's rules are definitive, but they lose this nature when they clash against another rule or principle. 'Note sulla teoria del bilanciamento di Robert Alexy', 51. However, a definitive, but potentially prima facie rule cannot justify a definitive obligation, only a prima facie one. Alexy says that rules are prima facie, but in a different way to principles, because rules enjoy the protection of some formal or institutional principles advocating for them in their conflicts with other principles. Alexy does not deny that rules are only applied in these cases if they face a conflict and show more weight. Formal or institutional principles just represent some extra points in their favour. R. Alexy, *Theorie der Grundrechte*, 87–90. C. Bernal seems to say that rules are both *prima facie* and *all things considered*. C. Bernal, *El principio de proporcionalidad y los derechos fundamentales*, 799. A. Peczenik, however, does not hesitate to classify rules as prima facie norms. A. Peczenik, *On Law and Reason* (Dordrecht: Kluwer, 1989), 80–1.

C. Coherence-theories

Parallel to this analysis, we identify coherence-theories as an abstract construction designed to represent some possible descriptions, understandings, or interpretations of the principialist theories. Although not specifically identified with particular authors, their holistic and coherentist hallmarks are close to the Dworkinian program of 'law as integrity'.

The most obvious sense of this label is that our principles and values are not involved in conflicts: they integrate into a general and coherent order from which they obtain their scope, meaning, and correct interpretation. Obviously, this description seems incompatible with the frequent involvement in many cases of several principles supporting different solutions. However, coherence-theories do not interpret these situations as a challenge to their view: they are not situations of conflict and defeat of principles, but illustrations of a gap in our knowledge concerning their scope and meaning, and occasions to fill it in the light of the other reasons of the system. These theories include an alternative interpretation of the alleged conflicts and defeats of principles that overcome the obstacles pointed to before. This alternative also arises from combining several elements: (1) a view of principles as indeterminate norms; (2) an epistemic interpretation of the prima facie clause; (3) a holistic and coherentist interpretation of the application of principles, according to which the solution to their concurrences is the rule fitting the whole legal system and reconstructing its coherence; (4) finally, the holistic and coherentist framework produces a different explanation to the alleged defeats of rules, which we can only outline here.

(1) It is well known that, for any principialist theory, principles are norms of fundamental importance within the legal system. Their importance is formal or structural, because the architecture or the construction of the system rests on principles, and material, because principles inform the system, and the content of the rules is the expression of one or several principles. Therefore, to acknowledge a principle in the legal system is to acknowledge a compulsory and obligatory norm.

The problem is that we do not know exactly where they must be applied. Their validity and obligation scope is not simply broad: it is indeterminate. It is not possible to determine the factual premise of the principles in an exhaustive, all-embracing way: we cannot display a closed and complete list of general cases and relevant properties to which they must be imputed.[46] Actually, we can assert that some principles (e.g. equality or non-discrimination) cover a large part of the legal system.[47] More essentially, principles are labels or summaries of a complex moral theory by virtue of which they can be specified in a list of rules that are applied to concrete cases. The problem is that we ignore the theory as a complete entity, as well as the content and the reach of the rules that specify the whole content of every principle.[48]

[46] Rules configure their validity scope in a closed way; principles do it openly. M. Atienza and J. Ruiz Manero, *Las piezas del derecho*, 9. Principles lack any 'legalistic precision'. G. Harman, 'Reasons' in *Practical Reasoning*, 111. H. Richardson connects the principles' *looseness* with the Kantian concept of *latitude*, according to which the nature and exact scope of some duties demand a previous work specifying their extension. 'Specifying Norms as a Way to Resolve Concrete Ethical Problems', *Philosophy and Public Affairs*, 19 (1990), 293.

[47] To make it worse, some courts prescribe that, whenever it is doubtful, we must assume the competence of the principle in the singular case: BVerfGE 6, 55 (72); STC 93/1984, FJ5. However, to be indeterminate does not mean to be universal: it is obviously false that any principle must govern all the practical problems. That is why for Richardson ('Specifying Norms . . . ', 292), when the premise of a practical reasoning is a principle, it must be prefaced not by a universal formula ('it is always wrong to lie . . . '), but in a more general way ('generally speaking . . . ').

[48] T.M. Scanlon, *What We Owe to Each Other*, 199.

Due to this status, principles, when considered alone, do not oblige us to perform a set of determinate and concrete actions, or to adopt a set of concrete and specific policies, but encourage us to act through rules or judgements that specify these principles and values. Principles cannot be applied alone, but must be unveiled through a rule that imputes their directive dimension to a set of relevant circumstances. It happens sometimes that we face easy cases where we do not witness concurrences of principles, and we are able to solve the case without conflict, invoking and applying one single principle. However, what we apply in these cases is not just the principle, but a specification of the principle through a rule that imputes the deontic message of the principle to the limited set of relevant circumstances that encompass the case.[49] Cases are solved by rules that are informed by principles and make effective in reality the values expressed by principles.

(2) If we say that a principle P is prima facie obligatory respecting a case C, we mean that we are not completely sure whether the rule that must finally solve C must be a specification of P or any other principle. As principles cover a broad part of a legal system, we can assume that this is a normal and frequent situation: every time we must solve a case, it is normal to summon up several prima facie principles in order to guide us to the solution of the case. A different matter is how easy or difficult it is to prove which principle is the right one. However, generally speaking, a new case usually allows us to invoke several prima facie principles.

In these situations, we face a case C that can be solved with the rules R1 and R2, expressions of the apparent rival principles P1 and P2. If our interpretation is that R1 and R2 are legally valid and obligatory to C, we conclude that our legal system simultaneously holds the validity and obligation of R1 and R2, rules that provide incompatible solutions to C and, therefore, form an antinomy. That would occur frequently: normally, a case allows us to appeal to different principles; to assume that R1 and R2 are valid and obligatory rules is to assume that, many times, every new case discloses an antinomy within the legal system, which would certainly deprive it of any minimal order and coherence. This is reason enough not to suppose that both P1 and P2 can be at any moment simultaneously valid and obligatory in C. The challenge of a case involving several principles is to identify which of the so-called principles applies all-things-considered to it, and which is the most appropriate solution to be found for it within the legal system.[50] If we reason that C is involved in the validity scope of P1, it will be solved by R1, and this leads us to conclude that it was never included in the validity scope of P2.[51]

[49] It can be alleged that we have applied a 'directly established rule', i.e. a rule whose validity scope is equal to the literal interpretation of the legal disposition proclaiming the principle. But, as we have seen, it is also doubtful that one of these rules can be directly applied, because they are indeterminate as principles.

[50] 'In norm logic there is no place for the distinction between simple validity and validity only prima facie'. O. Weinberger, '*Prima Facie* Ought: A Logical and Methodological Enquiry', *Ratio Juris*, 12 (1999), 239. As N. Rescher explains, truth (and, allowing the analogy, normative validity), is not a gradual, but an excluding and exhaustive concept. *The Coherence Theory of Truth* (Oxford: Oxford University Press 1973), 197.

[51] 'Our situation is very different from Abraham's: we are not beholden to two independent sovereign powers one of whom commands freedom of speech and the other of whom commands prosecution for racial insult. On the contrary, we are drawn to each of the rival positions through arguments that, if we were finally to accept them as authoritative, would release us from the appeal of the other one'. R. Dworkin, *Justice in Robes* (Cambridge, Mass.: Harvard University Press, 2006), 111. In Herman's Kantian explanation, the point is not to prove which obligation prevails (there is no more than one legal obligation), but to justify which reason or 'ground of obligation' prevails. *The Practice of*

We can therefore argue that the prima facie clause cannot be interpreted in the metaphysical view assumed by weight-theories, and we must attribute to it a simple epistemic value. If our conclusion is that P2 is not legally valid and obligatory in C, it is meaningless to assume that P2 is binding, legally justified, or entitled to solve C: this is precisely the *sub judice* problem that must be solved in hard cases through a process of deliberation and judgement. During this process, we cannot assert relationships of inclusion between the case and the validity scope of any principle, and can only suppose the prima facie principles as working hypotheses in order to check the conclusions we deduce from them. To take note of a principle as prima facie is to take note of a working hypothesis that could be confirmed, or not. This hypothesis expresses that C could be subjected to a principle, and it is worth considering the reasons supporting this possibility, and contrasting them with the reasons supporting other principles.[52] However, this kind of hypothesis simply adds information about the case, and does not determine its solution.[53] To conclude, the entry in the account of principles and validity hypothesis can only add epistemic reasons, not normative reasons.

Finally, the consequence of including C in P1's validity scope is not that P2's obligations respecting C vanish: deliberation showed that these obligations never existed. Therefore, we cannot say that they are defeated, outweighed, or surpassed; more simply, the hypothesis of their existence has been rebutted.

(3) Weight-theories could still argue that what we have called a process of deliberation and judgement is nothing more than the weighing process they purport to describe, i.e. the process of comparing different weights and obligations. How else could we prove that a case is subjected to a concrete principle, and not to another? The aforementioned argument might sound convincing, however, one might easily be involved in a scenario where a decision must be taken between helping an accident victim or attending an important meeting, or between either denying the right to publish caricatures or denying a considered respect for religious beliefs. These decisions unavoidably require weighing up different obligations and choosing a winner, which supposes a context of conflict.

However, the only admissible message in this argument is that tasks specifying principles can be compared, metaphorically speaking, to tasks of balancing principles. But, accurately described, these tasks neither measure the weight of different principles simultaneously valid in a singular case, nor assume a normative conflict, nor conclude with the defeat of a principle.

As was described in (2), the interpreter starts from a validity hypothesis on several principles respecting a singular case. And, as was seen in (1), a solution to the case

Moral Judgment, 165. See also T.M. Scanlon, *What We Owe to Each Other*, 299. Of course, our explanation is simplified: rules are not usually fostered by one single principle, but several.

[52] Prima facie principles inform us that C includes a morally salient property. However, a trait can be salient, but not determining for the solution. Moral relevance does not mean an acknowledgement of duties. B. Herman, *The Practice of Moral Judgment*, 79.

[53] As Williams expresses, '*prima facie*' must be translated as '*at first glance*', a first glance that can be deceptive. B. Williams, *Moral Luck*, 80. We can reformulate the idea in Scanlon's words: principles are prima facie reasons, but to have a reason is just a fact, not an obligation; we only transform reasons into obligations by showing that they are 'good' reasons. T.M. Scanlon, *What We Owe to Each Other*, 56–7. In Herman's terms, prima facie principles could be identified with the Kantian *grounds of obligation*. For Herman, these grounds are reasons for deliberation, because they delimit the moral deliberation, but, by themselves, they are not reasons for action. *The Practice of Moral Judgment*, 168. N. MacCormick also shares this position in some writings: what is defeated in these situations is not a right, but a claim to a right, one grounded on inadequate or incomplete interpretations of legal conditions to own or to enjoy rights. N. MacCormick, 'Defeasibility in Law and Logic', 102.

comes from a rule that specifies one of the principles taken into account and attributes its legal consequence to the relevant properties of the case. It was also argued that the work of specifying principles consists of reconstructing the meaning and sense of, at least, the principles involved in the case. We need a theory or conception refined enough to reconstruct and put in order the understanding of these principles. An important challenge arising from this theory is the simultaneous explanation of all the principles involved in the case. However, the challenge is in fact more demanding: this theory cannot contradict what we already know about the sense and the meaning of the rest of the principles grounding the legal system; on the contrary, it must be consistent with this knowledge, and show relationships of mutual support with the rest of the reasons admitted by the legal system.[54] We need many concepts in order to have any,[55] and we need many principles in order to understand any. We need a coherence-theory of principles, and we must attribute to this theory a holistic dimension.[56]

An interpreter must check both hypotheses regarding the solution of the case (R1 and R2) with a holistic and coherence test. The aim is to discover which solution leaves the system in coherence, attributing to the different principles grounding the legal system a more complete and harmonious sense and meaning, while also representing the system as a fitting order speaking with one single voice.[57] As we know, a coherence test is complex, and includes several diverse criteria insufficiently explained hitherto. From a Dworkinian explanation, this test controls, on the one hand, the fit or consistency of the rule with the most traditional and customary solutions established by the community's legal practice (mainly statutes and precedents) and, on the other hand, the suitability of the rule to the soundest convictions of justice and morality pervading the legal system and nourishing its political agenda.[58] From other explanations, the test values the consistency with or non-contradiction of other norms, and the cohesion and unity provided to the system as a whole, even at the expense of a relative reform to the system as it existed before.[59] Obviously, we cannot complete a thorough research of the meaning of coherence and its involved yardsticks here. However, we can understand that these criteria do not imply the attribution of more or less weight to some obligations than to others, because coherence judgements are 'all or nothing' judgements: they declare which is the voice with which the system speaks in a case, and which is the piece lacking in the jigsaw formed by its rules and principles;

[54] We would deny an interpretation of a value threatening the validity of another one. In Scanlon's example on morality, we would deny a radical interpretation of equality or neutrality forcing us to adopt this principle in all our private relationships: this interpretation would deny any sensible view of other values, such as friendship. T.M. Scanlon, *What We Owe to Each Other*, 218–19.

[55] R. Brandom, *Making It Explicit*, 89.

[56] Ibid., 89–91; K. Günther, 'Un concepto normativo de coherencia para una teoría de la argumentación jurídica', 291; H. Richardson, 'Specifying Norms as a Way to Resolve Concrete Ethical Problems', 300; T.M. Scanlon, *What We Owe to Each Other*, 68, 214. Only a holistic theory can overcome the problem pointed out by J.J. Moreso: when we specify principles, we resort to norms; but these norms are never specific enough, and they usually include new evaluative and indeterminate concepts. J.J. Moreso, 'Cristina Redondo sobre razones y normas', 76–7. We have summarized this difficulty in the formula 'principles summon more principles'. This formula reveals that, by reconstructing the antecedent of the rules, we call upon a plurality of principles, and all of them must be simultaneously put in order. If the interpreter provides a theory that ushers every principle into a single place, we maximize precision. Paradoxically, to specify requires the broadest possible theory.

[57] H. Richardson, 'Specifying Norms as a Way to Resolve Concrete Ethical Problems', 302.

[58] R. Dworkin, *Law's Empire*.

[59] For other criteria see, e.g. L. Bonjour, *The Structure of Empirical Knowledge* (Cambridge, Mass.: Harvard University Press, 1985); S. Hurley, *Natural Reasons* (New York: Oxford University Press, 1989); N. Rescher, *The Coherence Theory of Truth*.

this role is played by a norm excluding the rest. It is indeed possible that the interpreter decides the validity of one principle against any others by using calculations and operating with numerical magnitudes. This is not to assume that all the investigated principles convey justified obligations respecting the case, though this is more or less justified in each principle. In theoretical knowledge, to demonstrate through a probabilistic proof that a hypothetical cause is the cause of an effect does not imply that the rest of the possible causes were also true, though less true than the finally chosen one.[60] Likewise, to discover that rule R1 shows more inferential connections in the system or leaves in better order our knowledge of principles is not to establish the heavier weight of one of the supposed conflicting principles,[61] but to assert that R1 is the only and excluding solution expressed by the system.

Coherence-theories assume that the problem of the apparent conflict of principles is a conception of our principles still not completely theorized, formulated, or specified; respecting a set of cases or problems, we have not yet ushered the principles into a map, drawing their frontiers and assigning them a specific place, therefore we have to reconstruct their contours, consulting with the rest of the reasons of the system. The so-called 'balancing' operations are a process of deliberation and judgement in which we try to prove which one is the single right solution for the case; which has a justified reason in law, and which does not. The aim is not to establish a scale of weights in the principles involved in the case, but to determine which ones occupy the space or 'hold the field' of the case.[62] Depending on the depth of the research, these operations can be very complex; but complexity does not allow us the evasive strategy of conferring binding reason and legal justification upon every debated thesis and pursuing a gradual solution.

(4) Although this paper is focused on principles, not on rules, these last considerations allow us to outline some sketches on their status obeying a holistic and coherentist model.

Unlike weight-theories, we can interpret rules as definitive reasons exhibiting exclusionary powers. A holistic coherence process bestows upon the rules a moral and epistemic title. They gain a moral title because the solution established in the rule comes from a reasoning that considered the broadest scheme of principles and values legally relevant. There is an epistemic title because, as coherence theories remark in epistemology, processes of investigation are inherently conservative, and researchers presume the rightness of the conclusions in a former process of coherence.[63] As a first consequence, rules are definitive and complete reasons; being supported holistically by the whole scheme of legally relevant reasons, their factual description cannot be conceived as a provisional premise subject to an open list of exceptions, but as a definitive and closed list of relevant circumstances linked to a legal consequence.[64] Second, rules enjoy exclusionary powers against all the reasons of justice and morality

[60] For Rescher (ibid., 197ff.), the higher probability of a cause can be a condition for the discovery of truth, but it does not allow us to establish scales of higher or lower truth, and discuss conflicts of truth, or talk in terms of 'winning' and 'defeated' truths. To confuse validity of principles with some helpful operations to discover the right principle is a mistake analogous to confusing probability with truth.

[61] A traditional criterion of coherence: L. Bonjour, *The Structure of Empirical Knowledge*, 98; T.M. Scanlon, *What We Owe to Each Other*, 222.

[62] B. Herman, *The Practice of Moral Judgment*, 166.

[63] G. Harman, *Change in View* (Cambridge, Mass.: MIT Press, 1988), 48.

[64] For Dworkin, rules contain all the possible exceptions or non-application paradigms. R. Dworkin, *Taking Rights Seriously*, 76–7.

claiming the non-observance of the rules: all the reasons of justice and morality legally relevant were already integrated in the broadest moral theory that justifies the rule;[65] therefore, appeals against basing obedience of the rule on the moral reasons grounding the legal system are founded on an incomplete framework, unjustified and mistaken.

Unlike regulism, a coherence-theory accepts a final non-application of the rule. The aforementioned exclusionary powers are conferred under a condition: the coherence process must have been correctly implemented, and the scheme of reasons supporting the rule must be complete. Even so, we sometimes identify new reasons in the legal system; reasons of justice and morality that are entitled to be legally relevant. More specifically, we realize that our criteria of moral salience have changed: either we have attributed relevance in the past to circumstances that now look neutral, or we did not attribute relevance to circumstances that now seem salient to us. A change in our criteria for moral salience is a reason to re-examine the moral basis of a rule, but not a reason to change the rule. In order to change the rule, it must be proven that the whole set of reasons of the system, now including the new criteria for salience, is badly constructed from a coherence point of view. Furthermore, it must be proven that a new possible rule, unlike the old one, fits or puts in order all the moral reasons of the system. In this case, we prove that the old rule is not the norm that 'holds the field' or represents the legal system in this context. If this condition is satisfied, the old rule R1 is replaced by a new rule R2.

Is it appropriate to describe this process as a typical instance of defeasibility in which the factual description of R1 is defeated by new circumstances or exceptions? As has been shown, the defeasibility of a rule means trespassing upon the frontiers of its validity scope: we can find cases that satisfy its description, but the legal consequence is not applied. We assume that, when a rule is properly defeated, it remains in the legal system,[66] although inadequate as a necessary and sufficient condition of a legal consequence. However, it must be highlighted that this is not the process we have outlined here. In our model, the validity scope of R1 is not violated, but rebutted or rectified, and therefore replaced by another one. The obligation and non-application of the rule within its validity scope are exclusive phenomena: R1 is not applied just when it stops being a rule of the system. If we remember that a rule is the interpretation of a disposition, what we have described is a process of reinterpretation, and the rectification of a rule by another one.

Finally, should we deduce that any rule's life is exposed to an open list of unknown legal reasons disclosed case by case? Is this not an orthodox form of particularism? As previously noted, to invoke the possibility of 'unknown reasons' does not challenge the possibility of sustaining validity and truth in general rules or beliefs; it just expresses the fallibility of our knowledge expressed in these general rules and beliefs, and the possibility of revising and improving it. And this is exactly what is involved in this process. Particularism viewed these episodes as conflicts between the claim of a rule to be applied in a general case '*p*' and the claim of an exception or defeater '*q*' to neutralize

[65] A right principialist conceives the rules as a moral optimum. Regulism is prone to see them as a sub-optimum: F. Schauer, *Playing by the Rules*, 100–2. As well as regulism, the theory here suggested endorses intuition (a) in our Introduction, but with a remarkable advantage: it avoids the relationships of tension, even of frustration (see n. 4) between the rule and the moral reasons underlying its validity scope, so that obedience to legal rules is deprived of all the penitential nuances visible in theories like Schauer's.

[66] J.C. Bayón, 'Why is Legal Reasoning Defeasible?', *Diritto & Questioni Pubbliche*, 2 (2002), 7.

the application of the rule in a particular case or sub-area of its validity scope represented as '$p \wedge q$'. However, the issue at stake is not a conflict between legally justified legal claims: there is only one grounded legal claim, and it is the rule that 'holds the field' or covers the area of problems. When we replace R1 'no entry for vehicles in this park' with R2 'no entry for motor vehicles in this park', we do not solve a conflict between the general duties imposed on any vehicle or '*p*' and the special rights of the peaceful cyclists or '*q*'; we have a better understanding of the law's protection of parks, the meaning of all the values involved, and, finally, the general rule that must govern the problem. It is therefore wrong to deduce that R1 has been defeated in a particular case by attributing relevance or salience to one of its unique and exceptional circumstances. First, if R1 is not applied, this is not due to a particular circumstance working as an exception or defeater: the premise has been the whole legal system, the only possible source of justification in a holistic model. Through this holistic investigation, we conclude that R1 expressed wrongly our moral and political values respecting a social problem, and should be replaced. Second, what we deduce from this premise is not that the circumstance '*q*' defeats the rule R1 '$p \rightarrow r$'; R1 has not been subjected to an exception in a particular case: it has been rebutted and replaced by another general rule R2 '$p \rightarrow r$'. Finally, R2 is not a rule tailored to one case: it is a general rule. Particular cases may be the context in which the wrong moral basis of the rules may be discovered, but they do not exhaust their normative value. Empirically speaking, perhaps we could concede that our books of law are chains of particular cases; but, logically speaking, our books of law are systems of general norms.

18

Reasons for Action and Defeasibility

*María Cristina Redondo**

A. Introduction

The main purpose of this essay is to answer a very general question that may be posed in the following terms: can reasons for action be defeasible? To be sure, any position regarding this issue will entirely depend on how the terms under consideration are understood. Therefore the project will require a careful reflection on both the concept of defeasibility and the concept of reason for action. This essay will primarily be devoted to this endeavour. The first part will be focused on the notion of defeasibility and the second part on two different conceptions of reasons. As we will see, depending on what conception we adopt we will obtain two distinct answers to the initial question.

In order to specify what defeasibility means in this context I will adopt the following strategy. First, I will distinguish two possible approaches regarding defeasibility. It can be said that the first of these leads to a reduction of the problem of defeasibility. According to this position, the expression 'defeasibility' is ambiguous and when we predicate the defeasible character of an obligation, reason, belief, etc. we are making reference to multiple and very different questions. In this approach there is no such thing as *the* problem of defeasibility that can be isolated and dealt with. As a matter of fact, there are many different and independent problems to which we apply the label 'defeasibility'.

In contrast to this first approach, the second one admits that it is possible to delimit a problem of defeasibility not reducible to those that cause it or lead to it. This position attempts to identify a specific concept of defeasibility and articulate a manner of expressing it. However, as we shall see, the answer to the question regarding the nature of the problem is undoubtedly controversial.

In what follows I will try to show that, even though agreement may be reached regarding a common concept of defeasibility, two competing conceptions of this notion remain in play. I will discuss in which of these senses it is possible to say that reasons for action are defeasible. As we will see, it will depend on which presuppositions on the nature of reasons we assume.

B. The reductionist position

It has been stressed that the predicate 'defeasibility' does not single out one specific problem. In point of fact, when we predicate the defeasibility of an item we may be referring to different kinds of difficulties.[1]

* Associate Professor of Legal Philosophy at the University of Genoa (Italy) and Researcher at the National Scientific and Technical Research Council of Argentina (CONICET).

[1] See, for instance, J.L. Rodríguez and G. Sucar, 'Las trampas de la derrotabilidad. Niveles de análisis de la indeterminación del derecho' in P. Comanducci and R. Guastini, *Analisi e diritto 1998* (Turin: Giappichelli, 1999), 283–5.

When defeasibility is predicated of entities like duties, for instance, we are sometimes indicating that the duty so qualified might not be applicable in certain circumstances by virtue of the existence of implicit exceptions. This implies that the complete set of conditions for its application rests partly unexpressed. On other occasions, we could be indicating that the duty that is supposed to govern our behaviour, in certain cases, fails to do so because it has changed over time. In such cases, we are assuming that the defeasible item has a temporal dimension and may not be stable; it could be different at different moments in time. Understood in yet another way, when saying that a duty is defeasible we may be saying that we can identify it in different ways, applying different interpretative rules. At other times, we predicate defeasibility so as to indicate that, from a semantic point of view, the content of a duty is potentially indeterminate. In this case, we are pointing to the well-known problem of open texture, which is an unavoidable feature of general semantic contents. Moreover, 'defeasibility' may stand to express a sort of moral dissatisfaction. By declaring that certain content is defeasible we may be saying that, in a certain class of cases or in an individual case, its application would lead to absurd or extremely unjust results.

As we can see, behind the predicate 'defeasibility' lies a wide range of problems. Actually, those mentioned above are not by any means the only ones; there may be others as well. Even if all of them are classified as cases of defeasibility they do not seem to be instances of a single kind of concern. This suggests that it would be a mistake to believe that 'defeasibility' is the name of a specific kind of property or that all cases of defeasibility can be analysed and treated in the same way.

The position just presented highlights a very important notion. It is true that in all the cases mentioned we are dealing with problems of a very different nature. It is also true that it would be a serious mistake to believe that all *these* problems are part of a single more abstract predicament called 'defeasibility'. Nevertheless, this does not imply that we are unable to identify a specific issue which is referred to throughout this predicate; an issue that is in fact detachable and different from all the problems previously mentioned.

By saying that there is a specific problem of defeasibility we are acknowledging that, even if vastly different from one another, all the difficulties listed above have something in common, i.e. they all make some items defeasible or presuppose that they are defeasible. Explaining what defeasibility consists of does not amount to explaining all those difficulties that lead to it or follow from it. It involves explaining a feature to which all these difficulties, and perhaps not only these ones, are related. By adopting this view, we are not ignoring the possibility that defeasibility is connected to many other different questions such as those mentioned above. Studying these questions we will probably learn more about why an item is defeasible. Nevertheless we will not obtain an account of what defeasibility consists of.

The query I have made at the beginning of this essay presupposes the second approach. That is, it presupposes that we can isolate the concern we are referring to when talking about defeasibility. Even if defeasibility is necessarily intertwined with several issues, it constitutes a definite, separate one as well. Any positive or negative thesis regarding the—possible or impossible—defeasible character of reasons depends on how the specific issue of defeasibility is understood.

C. On defeasibility

Defeasibility is usually predicated upon items such as beliefs, norms, duties, obligations, reasons, etc. That is to say, it is predicated upon entities that have conceptual content.

Taking into account the examples mentioned above, it seems that defeasibility points to a practical problem, a sort of fallibility of the intended referential relation. Consequently, it also points to a corresponding instability regarding how to decide those cases in which the intended referential relation fails.

Although from an abstract or semantic perspective every conceptual content classifies the world into two mutually exclusive and jointly exhaustive groups (the set to which the content applies and its complementary set), in specific cases, and for the various reasons we have already seen, there is always the possibility of doubt arising as to their applicability. In a strict sense, the difficulty is not semantic but pragmatic. Should this conceptual content be applied in these specific circumstances?

Therefore, defeasibility is the typical problem of instability that arises when we apply a concept or a judgement. By saying that certain items like duties, obligations, or reasons are defeasible, we are saying that they do not invariably determine the circumstances in which they apply. In brief, they can fail in their referential purpose of delimiting the specific cases they are supposed to cover or enclose.

It is implied in what has been said that defeasibility affects items having intentional content, i.e. items that are about, directed at, or that represent certain other entities or states of affairs.[2] These items are said to be defeasible insofar as they can fail in this practical aim. It is always possible that those (individual or generic) cases that they are supposed to indicate ought to be excluded from their sphere of applicability on certain occasions.

As we have seen, this typical instability seems dependent on the fact that items having intentional content can be subject to dynamic development (their content may change over time), semantic difficulties (their content may be open-textured, have an implicit facet, or be interpretable in different ways), epistemic problems (we may be in need of additional information in order to identify their content completely), systemic relations (their content may be affected by other contents, with which they are related), moral questions (their content may be liable to substantial criticism), etc. Nevertheless, in all these circumstances we are confronted with the same kind of practical concern regarding the capacity of these items to answer the question of what we should do on a specific occasion. Generally speaking, we could say that in a certain sense the problem of defeasibility amounts to the central question of normativity. That is to say, it relates to the question regarding the possibility of something determining what to do or determining the status of something else. In an even more general but related sense we can say that the problem of defeasibility is the problem of intentionality, the question regarding the possibility of something referring to, or being about something else.

D. Defeasibility. When relevance can be overcome

The *locus classicus* in the analysis of the problem of defeasibility is related to the notion of duty. More precisely, it is the work of David Ross regarding prima facie duties.[3] Independently of the fact that there would certainly be important differences to highlight between duties and other kinds of items on which defeasibility is predicated, as far as the concept of defeasibility is concerned, the two conceptions that emerge from

[2] On the concept of intentionality, see J. Searle, *Intentionality. An Essay in the Philosophy of Mind* (Cambridge: Cambridge University Press, 1983), 1–36. Also, J. Searle, 'Intentionality and its Place in Nature', *Synthese*, 61 (1984), 3–16.

[3] W.D. Ross, *The Right and the Good* (Oxford: Oxford University Press, 1930), 18–47.

this pioneering work can be said to be applicable to any kind of item endowed with conceptual content.[4]

Following this line of thought it is usually stressed that there are two possible understandings that should not be confused. In a first sense, defeasibility makes it possible to express the idea that (a) something has practical import but (b) it is not enough to determine conclusively what has to be done. For instance, saying that ϕ is a defeasible reason we are saying that it is a kind or a category of reason. This means that it is 'susceptible to being overtopped' or 'subject to being surpassed in moral importance'.[5] It can conflict with another reason and be defeated.[6] In this case, defeasibility is a predicate regarding the limited strength of an actual relevant item. Understood in this way, the defeasible character of an item, a reason in our example, can be contrasted, on the one hand, with the property of being an insuperable or absolute reason and, on the other, with the property of being a conclusive one. An absolute reason is one having the highest practical relevance. By conceptual presupposition, it cannot be defeated by any other reason. A conclusive reason, instead, is one that, as a matter of fact, prevails and overcomes all the applicable reasons on a certain occasion. It therefore determines what has to be done, all things considered, in such a circumstance.[7]

In this interpretation, defeasibility is not in itself a very controversial property, especially with regard to reasons. To be sure, according to some conceptions, reasons are not defeasible in this sense.[8] Nevertheless, according to the most usual view they could clearly be so. It seems easy to accept that reasons *have* practical relevance even if they may conflict with other reasons that may prevail over them. In other words, it seems plausible to admit that there is a sense in which reasons could be defeasible.

E. Defeasibility. When relevance can be cancelled

Following the debate on prima facie duties, it is possible to mention a second, much more problematic, interpretation of defeasibility. In this sense, defeasibility makes it possible to express the idea that (a) something seems to have practical import but (b) all things considered, it could turn out not to be so. Saying that ϕ is a defeasible (prima

[4] On these two possible conceptions of the notion of prima facie, see, for instance, J. Searle, 'Prima Facie Obligations' in J. Raz (ed.), *Practical Reasoning* (Oxford: Oxford University Press, 1978), 81–90.

[5] In this sense, 'the status of a *prima facie* moral duty as such has nothing to do with first appearances or tentative identifications', cf. M.H. Kramer, 'Moral Rights and the Limits of the "Ought"-Implies-"Can" Principle: Why Impeccable Precautions are No Excuse' in M.H. Kramer, *Where Law and Morality Meet* (Oxford: Oxford University Press, 2004), 290–1.

[6] According to Susan Hurley, these should be called *pro tanto* reasons. *Pro tanto* reasons 'are not prima facie reasons in the sense that, like rules of thumb, they seem to give reasons to do acts... but may turn out not to when we learn more about the situation'. Cf. S. Hurley, *Natural Reasons* (Oxford: Oxford University Press, 1989), 133.

[7] Regarding the concepts of absolute and conclusive reasons see J. Raz, *Practical Reasons and Norms* (Oxford: Oxford University Press, 1975), 27.

[8] All those positions that do not admit the existence of genuine conflicts between reasons do not accept that reasons are defeasible in this sense. By saying '(ϕ) is a prima facie (defeasible) reason for doing (ψ)' we would not be saying '(ϕ) is simply a reason susceptible of being defeated', but '(ϕ) seems to be a reason'. This way, every conflict between prima facie (defeasible) reasons is only apparent. In fact, when we have reason to do something, there is no room for a rational objection to act so. By analogy with the analysis of wrongdoing proposed by John Gardner, it could be said that a position like this is adopting a 'closure' conception of reasons according to which no action is justified by reasons unless it is justified all things considered. Regarding the closure conception of wrongdoing, see J. Gardner, 'In Defence of Defences' in J. Gardner, *Offences and Defences. Selected Essays in the Philosophy of Criminal Law* (Oxford: Oxford University Press, 2007), 77–89.

facie) reason we are saying: 'at first consideration' ϕ is a reason, but in the light of more evidence, it might actually not be so.[9] This way, we are establishing a contrast between an apparent reason and an actual one. We are not saying that ϕ belongs to a kind or a category of reasons.

Under this perspective, the concept of defeasibility poses a problematic idea. If some data or entities are defeasible in this second sense, this means that they may not be what they appear to be and, as a result, they are in fact helpless in guiding us in our relationship with the world. To point out the defeasible character of something is tantamount to reporting its deceptive character.

The idea is indeed hard to express since by putting it into words we are, in a certain sense, contradicting ourselves. Even if from the beginning I have spoken of defeasibility as something that can be predicated *upon* certain items, the present interpretation would reveal that it is not an authentic adjective modifying nouns such as reasons, duties, and the like. It seems that—as John Searle says regarding the expression 'prima facie'—the word 'defeasible' in this case works as 'an adverbial sentence modifier'.[10] In saying that ϕ is a defeasible reason what we are really saying is 'apparently, or *ceteris paribus,* ϕ is a reason'. In this understanding, 'defeasible' would be used to establish a distinction between appearances and reality, between 'a conditional reason' and 'a reason proper', i.e. a reason that actually exists.

It is important to emphasize that in this case by means of the term 'defeasibility' one is attempting to capture a completely different problem from the previous one. With regard to this I believe it is opportune to follow Searle's advice when he says: 'When any new technical term is introduced in Philosophy without explicit definition, there are at least two questions one must ask of it... The two questions are, what motivates the introduction of the term in the first place and what other terms is it opposed to?'[11] In this sense, firstly, it would be erroneous to think that, in this hypothesis, the attempt is to capture a situation of conflict between duties, obligations, or reasons. Situations of conflict are captured by the preceding approach which, incidentally, presupposes what is in question in this hypothesis, i.e. it presupposes the actual existence of those entities that enter into conflict. When the expression 'defeasibility' is used in this second sense, what we are precisely trying to do is to emphasize that something, which *in principle* is or *appears to be* a specific kind of intentional or normative item (a duty, an obligation, or a reason) might actually *not be* so. In other words, in this perspective, when we speak of a defeasible or a prima facie duty, obligation, or reason, we are establishing an opposition or a contrast between what looks like a duty, obligation, or reason and an actual or real one.

It could be said that defeasibility in this case is connected to all those entities endowed with general conceptual content that attempt to designate a class of cases. These entities may be considered to be tied to a claim to applicability regarding all those classes, subclasses or individual events to which their contents aim to refer. The idea of defeasibility points to a failure in this practical claim. As has been emphasized, even though from a strictly semantic point of view every conceptual content divides the world into two complimentary classes (that which is covered by its scope and another that is excluded from it), such a division may fail. Its concrete applicability in specific

[9] In my view, the difference between these two senses of defeasibility could also be expressed through the distinction between the external and internal applicability proposed in J.J. Moreso and P.E. Navarro, 'Applicability and Effectiveness of Legal Norms', *Law and Philosophy*, 16 (1997), 201–19.

[10] Cf. J. Searle, 'Response' in E. Lepore and R. van Gulick (eds), *John Searle and His Critics* (Oxford: Basil Blackwell, 1991), 389.

[11] J. Searle, 'Prima Facie Obligations', 81.

circumstances could always be justifiably questioned and, likewise, so could the practical import or relevance of the conceptual content.

Both ways of understanding defeasibility have received special attention and are the object of ongoing debate. Considering the fact that they refer to different problems, I believe it is convenient to separate them clearly. As several authors propose, the problem related to the surmountable (*pro tanto*) character that the practical relevance of an entity might have must be distinguished from the question regarding the possible fallible or merely apparent (prima facie) character of that relevance itself.

To sum up, specifically, regarding reasons, if we do not adequately distinguish between these two problems we will be confusing two different discussions. In the first case, defeasibility conveys the idea that the practical import of a given reason may be overcome by the presence of other reasons and, consequentially, even if relevant, it can fail to determine a result. Here, defeasibility points to the problem of the strength of reasons, which can be overridden by conflicting considerations. By contrast, the second discussion refers to the possibility of cancelling conditions. It points to the distinction between a something which is a proper reason and an apparent one. In the first case, by saying that ϕ is a defeasible reason to ψ we are saying that ϕ is a reason, but a surmountable one. That means that, all things considered, it may not be a conclusive reason. In the second case, by saying that ϕ is a defeasible reason we are saying that ϕ *seems* to be a reason but, all things considered, it may turn out not to be a reason at all.

It is interesting to note that the first problem of defeasibility regarding reasons is usually analysed through the idea of balance. The balance of reasons is a kind of practical reasoning in which different relevant considerations, for and against something, are compared in order to determine which ones succeed.[12] The second problem of defeasibility has been thoroughly analysed from a logical point of view by means of non-strict or weakened conditionality. This means that the idea that something is a defeasible item (a duty, obligation, or reason) can be understood in terms of a general conditional sentence that does not follow the rules of classic logic for the strict or standard conditionals. For instance, statements such as 'the fact that S promised ψ is a defeasible reason for S to ψ' or 'prima facie, someone who kills someone else must be sanctioned' have to be analysed in the following conditional way:

1: If someone promises ψ, *then* there is a reason for her/him to ψ.
2: If someone kills another person, *then* there is a duty to sanction him or her.

In the literature on this topic there are two different ways of understanding the meaning of this weakened conditional connective. In other words, there are two ways to understand statements asserting that prima facie or *ceteris paribus* something is the case (in contrast to that which actually is the case).

F. Two readings of the problem of cancelling conditions

If what has been said so far is correct, the idea that some items endowed with conceptual content can have a prima facie status—in contrast to those that have an actual status—amounts to the idea that they can be invalidated by cancelling or nullifying conditions.[13] Nevertheless, the defeasible conditionals that allow us to

[12] Cf. J. Raz, *Practical Reasons and Norms*, 15–48. See also R. Nozick, *Philosophical Explanations* (Cambridge, Mass.: Harvard University Press, 1981), 479–82.

[13] Regarding the different types of reason defeaters see W. Sinnot-Armstrong, 'Some Varieties of Particularism', *Metaphilosophy*, 30 (1999), 1–12.

express this possibility may have two different readings. The first one may be attributed to Carlos Alchourrón when he analyses the notion of prima facie reason.[14] In broad terms, according to this proposal the problem of defeasibility can be expressed through the structure of a general conditional sentence whose antecedent constitutes only a contributory condition in relation to the consequent. The connective of this defeasible conditional, which is represented by means of a corner (>), admits neither the strengthening of the antecedent nor *modus ponens*. That is to say, following the reasoning from this kind of conditional, even if the antecedent obtains, we are not allowed to detach the consequent.

It should be remembered that a contributory condition is a necessary condition of a sufficient condition. That is why this kind of weakened conditional is to be considered equivalent to a strict conditional whose antecedent—consisting of a limited expansion of the antecedent of the weakened conditional—does represent a sufficient condition. The antecedent of this strict conditional is a revision of the preceding one. Specifically, it is to be understood as the conjunction of the original antecedent with all of those implicit presuppositions that allow a sufficient condition to be achieved. Such a revision is represented by adding a revision operator *f* to the original antecedent. Formally, according to Alchourrón's idea, the definition of this defeasible relation is as follows:

$$(\text{Def.} >)\, A > B = (fA \rightarrow B)$$

In other words, a weakened conditional is equivalent to a conditional that, duly completed, does admit the usual laws of strengthening the antecedent and of *modus ponens*: a conditional that allows the consequent to be inferred.

The interesting point in this reading of defeasibility is that it is associated with the notion of contributory condition which, understood as a necessary condition for a sufficient condition, makes it possible to express two especially important ideas. First, by asserting that the antecedent is a merely contributory—not sufficient—condition we are expressing a negative idea: the view that the consequent cannot actually be detached even though the antecedent obtains. For example, if promising to go to your house is a defeasible reason to do so, from the fact that I indeed made a promise, it does not yet follow that there really is a reason for me to go. All things considered, the relevance of this fact might be neutralized by the presence of other circumstances, which are not stated and remain implicit.

Secondly, by stating that something is a contributory condition, a positive idea is also expressed: the presupposition that there exist and it is possible to identify a set of factors that configure a sufficient condition. This possibility is necessarily presupposed because if it be true that the conditional states a contributory condition (for the existence of a reason to do something), it would be so only in relation to that which is considered a sufficient condition (for the existence of a reason to do such a thing). By saying that the conditional expresses a contributory condition, one is implicitly saying that such a conditional expresses in its antecedent a necessary ingredient of a sufficient condition to obtain the consequent. According to Alchourrón, the set of circumstances that would guarantee the inference is partially presupposed. However, it is logically possible.[15]

[14] C.E. Alchourrón, 'Para una lógica de las razones prima facie', *Análisis Filosófico*, 16 (1996), 113–24.

[15] By means of the postulation of limited expansion it is assumed that if the antecedent A is possible, then *f*A (A together with its presuppositions) is also possible. Cf. C.E. Alchourrón, ibid.

Analysed from this point of view, defeasibility makes reference to an epistemic problem. This means that (1) reasons—or any other kind of entity endowed with conceptual content—are not in themselves defeasible entities; (2) in truth, only beliefs or statements that assert or imply the existence of these entities may be revisable or defeasible: for instance, statements like 'promising is a reason to do what has been promised'; (3) these beliefs or statements can be analysed by means of general conditional statements, such as 'if S promises *then* there is a reason for S to fulfil the promise'; (4) a general conditional statement like this is defeasible. Its antecedent expresses only a fragment of a complete sufficient condition, whose relevance may be cancelled if other appropriate conditions do not obtain. In other words, it expresses what only looks like a reason due to the lack of complete information; (5) in such a case the antecedent of the conditional states a contributory condition for its consequent though it has to be revised and completed with all its presuppositions so as to express a sufficient condition. As we know, only in this case, when the antecedent of the conditional obtains will we be able to infer the consequent, and new information will never invalidate this inference.

In a nutshell, when we say that promising is a defeasible reason to do what we have promised, we are on the one hand admitting that the fact of promising does not constitute in itself a reason to act, but on the other hand we are implicitly stating that the fact of promising together with an adequate set of presuppositions does indeed constitute a reason to do what has been promised.

According to an alternative view, when we say that reasons, duties, or other items are defeasible we are not expressing an epistemological difficulty but an ontological one. Like in the former perspective, the statements that identify defeasible entities, for instance, 'promising ψ is a reason to ψ', are analysed through weakened general conditionals such as 'if someone promises ψ *then* there exists a reason to ψ'. Nevertheless, contrary to the previous perspective, it would be a mistake to think that the antecedent of this weakened conditional expresses a contributory condition. This is so because, as has been said earlier, a contributory condition presupposes the possibility of identifying a sufficient condition and, according to this view, in saying that certain entities are defeasible we are precisely saying that this possibility cannot be assured. That is why we use the weakened conditional structure in order to express that it is not possible to identify general sets of circumstances that guarantee the existence of entities of this type. In other words, it is not possible for us to complete the antecedent of the general conditional in order to detach the conclusion.

Following our example, the fact of promising to do something would be a defeasible reason so as to act precisely because every set of conditions that apparently allows us to infer the existence of such a reason would be merely indicative. Undoubtedly, the fact of promising is *commonly* and *normally* a reason for doing what has been promised. However, its relevance may be nullified by the presence of different types of defeaters.[16] That is, the problem is not the lack of information or access to the complete set of general sufficient conditions. The problem is that we could never identify something like a complete set of general sufficient conditions because this does not exist. The fact of promising is not sufficient and it is not even a contributory part of a sufficient condition for the existence of a reason to act in a certain way. And the same should be said with regard to any other fact or circumstance that we might think of as a general condition for the existence of a reason to act. In this reading, the weak conditional that

[16] Cf. J. Dancy, *Moral Reasons* (Oxford: Blackwell, 1993), 67.

serves to express defeasibility not only fails to behave as a strict conditional (which allows the consequent to be inferred from its antecedent), it cannot be completed so as to express a strict conditional. Were it possible to do so, this type of conditional would fail to express precisely that which it is attempting to express: that in fact the existence of this kind of entity cannot be inferred. Reasoning from weak or defeasible conditionals is *nonmonotonic*, which means that conclusions can always be invalidated by additional information.[17]

Thus understood, we can say that (1) certain entities such as reasons—or other types of entity endowed with conceptual content—are in themselves defeasible entities; (2) a statement that asserts or implies the existence of these kinds of entity, such as 'promising is a reason to do what has been promised', can be analysed by means of a general conditional statement, such as 'if S promises to do something then there is a reason for S to fulfil the promise'. In other words, a conditional asserting that under certain conditions the existence of a reason can be inferred; (3) this kind of conditional will *always* be fallible, revisable, or defeasible; (4) it is defeasible in the sense that it only expresses that in all normal worlds in which the antecedent holds, the consequent holds as well; (5) it does not constitute a strict conditional, nor can it be revised or completed so as to express such a kind of conditional. Therefore, any conclusion we can draw from them will always be an unstable conclusion, i.e. it could be invalidated by additional information.

There is manifest disagreement between these two conceptions of defeasibility. This is not the place to defend one position or the other.[18] What is important here is to distinguish the two possible readings in order to answer the specific question regarding whether it is possible for reasons for action to be defeasible. The following section of the paper will be devoted to this subject.

G. On reasons for action

In order to answer the question regarding whether or not reasons for action may be defeasible, we should try to clarify first what reasons for actions are supposed to be. To begin with, reasons for action are usually considered as connected to an evaluative or justificatory role as well as to a motivational or explanatory function. In any case, there are two diverging intuitions regarding the status of reasons that bring about two different conceptions of them. As I will try to show, from one of these perspectives the idea of a defeasible reason is simply nonsense. However, by assuming the other understanding, defeasibility becomes an inescapable feature thereof.

The status and characteristics that these perspectives ascribe to reasons are not independent of the manner in which the distinction between theoretical and practical rationality is drawn. That is why it will be initially necessary to examine this distinction.

The contrast between theoretical and practical reasons may be conceived in different ways. From one point of view, theoretical and practical rationality represent a

[17] Conditional logics are only one of the attempts to model defeasible or nonmonotonic reasoning. They were originally developed for modelling counterfactual reasoning. See H. Prakken, *Logical Tools for Modelling Legal Argument. A Study of Defeasible Reasoning in Law*, (Dordrecht: Kluwer, 1997), 87–95.

[18] In previous papers I have held that only the second interpretation captures the genuine problem of defeasibility. However, if we consider that the two versions are competing conceptions of the same problem, neither of them can be qualified as genuine, except to indicate that we think that it is the correct one or the one that best captures the problem in question.

dichotomy. A theoretical reason is the kind of entity that gives logical support to a conclusion. Only propositional contents—those apt to bear truth value—can be theoretical reasons. In other words, a theoretical reason is any proposition that justifies another proposition.

By contrast, a reason is *practical* insofar as it has capacity to produce a human action. Thus, a practical reason is the kind of entity that can be causally efficacious in leading us to do something. It is something capable of motivating behaviour. Notice that seeing things in this light leads directly to a sceptical stance both regarding the possibility of logical control of practical reasons and the possibility of the practical relevance of theoretical reasons. This is so because, by hypothesis, only theoretical reasons are apt for truth and logical relations, and only practical reasons may move an agent to action. Every time we give a reason in order to justify the truth or falsity of a consideration we remain within theoretical rationality and it does not offer a practical (motivating) reason to do anything. In contrast, it will not be possible to judge any practical (motivating) reason that an agent might have in terms of truth values. Practical reasons can be neither true nor false; they are not the kind of items that can be premises or conclusions of logical reasoning.[19] Instead, they can have causal impact and be instrumentally efficient in producing certain outcomes. Accordingly, to be 'rationally justified' in a practical sense has a very different meaning from that which the same expression has in a theoretical sense. An action or attitude can be practically rational or justified only in an instrumental sense, to the extent that it is a necessary or sufficient means to a certain end. In other words, there is no room for an intrinsic, practical rationality because any evaluation of the *content* of an intentional action or the attitudes that motivate it would be an evaluation in terms of truth values. That is, by definition, it would be a theoretical evaluation.

Taking a different approach, the contrast between theoretical and practical reasons is no longer articulated as a dichotomy resulting in two irreconcilable meanings of rationality. The difference in this case is constructed within rationality understood as a unified human capacity, be it theoretical or practical. As a result, reasons are not in themselves practical or theoretical. Reasons, *sans phrase*, are a basis of justification or explanation in both theoretical and practical domains. To be sure, within this perspective, there is still room to distinguish between theoretical and practical reasons, but this distinction does not express or presuppose that there are two incompatible meanings of rationality.

At any rate, even when rationality is conceived as a unified capacity, it can still be understood in very different ways. Here, I will mention two main conceptions, one related to a realist approach to reasons and the other to an anti-realist or constructivist one.

H. Reasons for action. A realist approach

In a realist approach, the existing reasons are ontologically objective and do not depend on our attitudes, desires, or beliefs. We may *believe* or *accept* that there is a reason for us

[19] In point of fact, a radical sceptical conclusion regarding the possibility of rational evaluation of practical reasons can be avoided by extending the characteristics of theoretical reasons (such as truth or logical consistency), to those psychological states or intentional attitudes that have propositional contents with mind-to-world direction of fit. That is, we can assume that these states follow or mimic the characteristics of their contents that are apt for truth and can be theoretical reasons. For instance, we can evaluate the *performance* of an inference in terms of logical validity or the *belief* or *acceptance* of a propositional content in terms of truth or logical consistency.

to do ψ; however, it is possible that there is no reason at all. So, if we *believe* there is a reason to act in a certain way, we may be wrong. In this case, our action can be *explained* by our subjective attitudes but it cannot be rationally justified.[20] In this framework reasons are considered as primarily connected to a justificatory role. Reasons are facts that count for or against the truth of a proposition. In other words, they are *true* propositions that give support to other propositions; they are truth-justifying considerations.

Within this perspective, more than a gap between theoretical and practical reasons, a contrast should be established between two kinds of questions or assertions that reasons *sans phrase* are apt to justify. It is indeed possible to admit a difference between theoretical and practical domains or spheres of interest and, in this sense, to distinguish between reasons that justify propositions regarding *what is the case* and reasons that justify propositions regarding *what ought to be the case*. A question regarding *what is the case* could be considered a theoretical issue and facts that justify these kinds of propositions theoretical reasons. On the other hand, questions regarding *what ought to be the case* are certainly practical questions and facts that justify propositions of this kind are reasons for action.[21] In a position like this, the motivating or guiding function of reasons for action remains in the background, and can be understood only in relation to their primary justificatory role.[22]

As a consequence of the possible contrast between the existing reasons and our beliefs about them there is, in this view, a further important distinction to be made regarding reasons, both in theoretical and in practical domains. This distinction refers to those reasons that justify what *is*, or *ought to be*, the case, on the one hand, and those reasons that justify our *believing* that something is, or ought to be, the case, on the other. Naturally, we are always talking of justificatory reasons but we are asked to distinguish two independent questions. On a particular occasion, there may be reasons to *believe* that p is, or ought to be, the case, and in such a case we are justified in *believing* that p is, or ought to be, the case. However, in the same situation there may not be reasons for justifying the proposition 'it is the case that p', or 'p ought to be the case'. This implies that we may be *justified* in believing an *unjustified* proposition. On the other hand, we may *not be justified* in believing a *justified* proposition. What is of importance here is that we should keep these two questions separate. Particularly, regarding practical questions, we should not confuse *reasons for believing* that we ought to act in a certain way with *reasons for acting* in such a way.[23]

[20] Taking this into account, we can see that the expression 'practical reasons' may be ambiguous. On the one hand, it could refer to justificatory reasons regarding what ought to be done (i.e. reasons for action) but, on the other hand, it could refer to motivating factors, which explain but do not justify actions. Even if reasons for action are necessarily practical reasons, practical reasons are not necessarily reasons for action; they may be motivating, explanatory reasons.

[21] To be sure, under which conditions there exists a reason for action is something that depends on a substantive moral theory regarding what reasons there are, how we identify them, and the like. According to the moral theory we assume, we will identify existing reasons in different ways.

[22] I think this position can be attributed to Joseph Raz. See J. Raz, *Practical Reason and Norms*, 17–19.

[23] This poses a problem regarding the status of those reasons for accepting a proposition. According to the classification proposed, they have to be considered *reasons for belief* and not *reasons for action*. This is so because they justify an epistemic attitude towards a proposition that may be wrong. However, unless we adopt an ad hoc—and certainly misleading—reconstruction, the *acceptance* of a proposition is something we can *do* on the basis of reasons, that is, it can be a kind of rational *action*. In this sense, reasons for accepting a proposition are *reasons for (a specific kind of) action*. In sum, reasons for accepting a proposition can be seen as reasons for belief or reasons for action. At the same time, both

The point I want to emphasize is that by assuming this contrast between *reasons for action* that justify a practical proposition (regarding what ought to be done) and *reasons for believing* or *accepting* such a proposition, this position assumes a realist approach with regard to reasons for action. From this point of view, the existence of reasons for or against an action is independent of the fact of our beliefs in their existence, even if these beliefs are justified.

Returning to our initial question, we should try to determine in what sense, if any, reasons so understood can be defeasible. As we know, one possibility is to interpret defeasibility as indicating an ontological problem. In this reading the statement 'ϕ is a prima facie reason for A to ψ' means that ϕ is normally a reason for A to ψ, but *it can turn out not to be so.* Furthermore, it presupposes that it is not possible to identify a general sufficient condition for there to be a reason for A to ψ.

However, from this realist approach, a reason for action is an ontologically objective fact. If a fact understood in this way designates that which is indeed the case, independently of our beliefs, and the concept of defeasibility indicates that which may not be the case; it is impossible for this kind of fact to be defeasible. In other words, understood as an ontological problem, defeasibility cannot be a problem of reasons. In this sense, a statement asserting the defeasible character of a reason would be a self-contradictory statement. In a position like this, sentences such as 'promising is a prima facie (defeasible) reason for doing what has been promised' must necessarily be interpreted as alluding to an epistemic problem. What is identified as a defeasible reason is in fact only a—contributory—part of the set of sufficient conditions for there indeed to be a reason. As we know, this idea can be expressed through a weak conditional statement like 'if we promise, *then* there is a reason to do what has been promised'. In this conditional some information is missing, or, which amounts to the same, the fact explicitly stated in the antecedent (i.e. the act of promising) will only allow us to obtain the consequent once it has been duly completed.

Concisely, in a realist conception, if there are reasons for actions, they cannot be ontologically defeasible. What may be so are our beliefs or statements about their existence, where this means that such beliefs or statements are incomplete.

I. Reasons for action. A constructivist approach

From a different point of view, it is only relative to human intentionality that a state of affairs in the world can be seen as a reason for action. In this sense, the existence of reasons depends on the agent's beliefs and attitudes. They are part of an observer's reality, a constructed world, ontologically subjective.[24] In this approach, rationality is seen as a capacity that cannot be distinguished from all those other abilities of *doing* something *intentionally* in a broad sense: the capacity to think, to speak, to perceive, etc.[25] As with the previous approach, here there is no principled distinction between practical and theoretical reason. But, in this case, theoretical reason is a branch of practical reason: '[it] . . . is that branch of practical reason that concerns reasons for accepting, recognising, believing and asserting propositions'.[26] In this view, both

justificatory reasons regarding what we *ought to do* and justificatory reasons regarding what we *ought to accept* about what we ought to do should be considered reasons for action.

[24] See J. Searle, 'Prima Facie Obligations', 120.

[25] Cf. J. Searle, *Rationality in Action* (Cambridge, Mass.: MIT Press, 2001), 22–4.

[26] See, J. Searle, 'Prima Facie Obligations', 120.

theoretical and practical reasons are considerations that count for or against something we can do intentionally.

I will not analyse this conception of reasons in detail. Nevertheless, in order to answer the question posed at the outset, it is interesting to highlight some relevant points. First and foremost, in this perspective reasons are not seen as truth supporters. The main function of reasons is not to justify propositions but to explain other facts. Specifically, reasons for action explain human actions. According to John Searle: 'The varieties of explaining relations correspond to the indefinite varieties of explanations one can give for phenomena . . . The explaining relation includes making something happen, causing, necessitating, making more probable, *justifying*, bringing about, doing something for the purpose of or for the sake of . . . and others.'[27] Consequently, for this position, not all reasons are facts, particularly not all reasons for action. One may be mistaken about facts (i.e. our action can be unjustified) but one can still have reasons for acting in the way one acts. In other words, one can still offer an explanation.

For instance, let's suppose that it is going to rain. According to the previous perspective, this fact, even if I am justified in believing that it is not going to rain, is a reason for carrying an umbrella. Alternatively, in the present conception, it is my belief that it is going to rain which is my reason for carrying an umbrella regardless of whether or not it is true.[28] From this point of view, beliefs and other intentional states may be reasons for action even if they are not justified. This is so because the primary function of reasons is to explain why someone acts in certain way and not why something is the right thing to do. Justification (i.e. the answer to the question why something should have been done or is a good thing to have been done) does not always state the reasons that the agent acted upon.[29]

It is clear that these two approaches propose different conceptions of what a reason for action is. However, using different language, both talk about the same thing. What for the previous position are reasons for action (i.e. facts that justify an action), in the present perspective are facts that explain why that action is the right thing to do. Certainly, according to this second position, facts could also be reasons for an action, but this depends on whether they can act as motivators and have a role in the explanation of that action. At the same time, what for this conception is a reason for an action can certainly also justify it (for example the existence of an obligation). But this is so only as long as the reason that explains the action is, at the same time, what explains why this action was good or correct.

It follows that, for the present understanding, reasons for action can be facts, but not all reasons for action are facts. 'The formal constraint on being a reason is that an entity must have propositional structure and must correspond to a reasons statement . . . All reasons are factitive entities . . . Thus, the fact that it is raining, my belief that it is raining, my desire that it rains, and my need that it rains can all be reasons.' According to Searle, reasons 'can also be propositional structured entities that are neither facts nor intentional states, entities such as obligations, commitments, requirements, and needs. This feature of the ontology of reasons explains the syntactical feature that reason

[27] Emphasis added. See J. Searle, ibid., 105.

[28] Actually, it is a reason because it is part of a total reason that includes, for instance, my desire to be dry and a further belief that with the umbrella I will be able to remain dry. See J. Searle, ibid., 115.

[29] Searle distinguishes between justifications and 'justificatory explanations' which are a subclass of explanations. Justifications are not explanations of why an act has occurred. For example, I am justified in carrying my umbrella if it rains, even though it is not the reason why I am carrying it. See J. Searle, ibid. 115.

statements require a "that" clause or other equivalent form, which will express a whole proposition.'[30] Thus, reasons are not necessarily facts, but they are all 'factitive' in the sense that they have a structure specified by a 'that' clause.

Finally, it should be added that according to this approach, there can be internal and external reasons for action. In any case, both kinds of motivators are factitive entities in the sense mentioned above. For instance, the hope that..., the fear that..., the ambition that..., etc. are internal reasons. Needs, obligations, responsibilities, etc. are in turn external reasons.

Things being thus, reasons for action are entities of a kind that 'exist only because we believe them to exist'.[31] They may be epistemically objective but they are always ontologically subjective. Strictly speaking, this theory holds that entities of this kind exist if, and only if, a precise set of social conditions obtains.[32] Continuing with our example, it is possible that the fact of promising constitutes a necessary piece of a sufficient condition to assert the existence of a reason to act. In this sense, like in the previous approach, a statement such as 'promising constitutes a prima facie reason to do what is promised' can be analysed by means of a weak conditional sentence such as the one proposed by Alchourrón. In this case, what we are saying is that promising does not guarantee the existence of a reason; nevertheless, jointly with a set of presupposed conditions, it does allow the existence of a reason to be inferred.

However, this constructivist conception of reasons also leaves open the possibility that reasons in themselves may be defeasible entities. If the existence of a reason for a specific action depends on a set of human beliefs and attitudes, in contrast to what happens in a realist conception of reasons, it is perfectly possible to assert without contradiction that a reason is ontologically defeasible. Being the result of collective intentionality and the attitudes of agents, reasons cannot avoid having certain characteristics determined by their subjective metaphysical status. In this sense, for instance, no one denies that this kind of entity may clearly exist at a given moment but may change with the passage of time. Moreover, it might not just be unstable from a temporal point of view, but as a matter of fact, at a given moment its very existence may be something unfixed or undetermined. In such a scenario, we should accept that an assertion like 'promising constitutes a reason to do what is promised' only expresses something that is usually or commonly so.

It could be thought that from the fact that promising is not in itself a sufficient condition for the existence of a reason to act in a certain way it does not follow that a set of sufficient conditions does not exist. And this is true. The problem is that, according to this perspective, the sufficient conditions for there to be a reason to act will always depend on a set of subjective attitudes and a collective intentionality. In this sense, *any* set of circumstances that we might consider a sufficient condition for the existence of a reason to do something will present the same kind of problem: it may be questioned as not sufficient to infer the existence of a reason.

In other words, in a constructivist conception, a statement in which defeasibility is predicated on a reason is not a self-contradictory statement and, therefore, could well be true. What is more, even if sufficient conditions for the existence of a reason to act in a particular way are deeply ingrained, there is nothing to prevent them from being

[30] Cf. J. Searle, ibid., 103–4.

[31] Cf. J. Searle, *The Construction of Social Reality* (London: Penguin Books, 1995), 1.

[32] According to Searle, in order to explain the existence of these social facts, three elements are required: the assignment of function, collective intentionality, and constitutive rules. See J. Searle, ibid., 13–29.

questioned. This is why defeasibility is not just a contingent possibility regarding reasons. By virtue of their subjective nature, it is an inescapable or unavoidable trait that they exhibit.

If the previous analysis is correct, we can conclude that when reasons for action are conceived as facts different and independent from our attitudes and beliefs, the identification of something as a prima facie (defeasible) reason can only be understood as pointing to an epistemic problem, a lack of information regarding what constitutes a sufficient condition for the existence of a reason. However, if a sufficient condition obtains the resulting existence of a reason is not defeasible. By contrast, when reasons for action are conceived as part of a social or constructed reality, the identification of something as a prima facie (defeasible) reason could also be understood as pointing to an ontological problem. Under these conditions the defeasibility of reasons is an inescapable possibility resulting from their intentional, perspectival status.

PART IV

DEFEASIBILITY AND ADJUDICATION

19

Legislation and Adjudication

*Fernando Atria**

A. Introduction

Few issues have been more persistently discussed in contemporary legal theory than adjudication or, more precisely, what can be called the judicial process and its relationship to (legislated) law. Legal theory's prolonged soul-searching exercise in this regard is part of a more general effort to come to terms with a legacy of 'formalistic' legal thinking. Indeed, if the nineteenth century was the century of codification and its by-product, a 'mechanic' and rigorously 'formalistic' understanding of interpretation, the twentieth century was the century of the reaction to 'formalism'. As is usually the case with such 'reactions', however, 'nineteenth-century formalism' quickly became a catchphrase rather acritically identified with a caricature. In fact, and even though the twentieth century produced a plethora of theories and positions to fill the space vacated by 'nineteenth-century formalism', so that it is difficult to say that there is a dominant, 'mainstream' account, there is a rather surprising consensus regarding the 'formalism' to which these positions understand themselves to be reacting. I take the following description to be representative:

> one of the crucial points suggested by thinkers of the Enlightenment for the political and legal organisation of government is the separation between legislative power, the power to create new law, a political power *par excellence*, vested in a parliament comprised of representatives of the people, on the one hand, and a judicial power, purely technical, vested in professional judges, in charge of applying the laws passed by the legislative power.[1]

In the extraordinarily influential words of Montesquieu, the judge was to be 'no more than the mouth that pronounces the words of the law'[2] (an idea that appears in a passage the subtlety of which is usually ignored, and to which we shall return below). This view of the judicial process was, in turn, supposedly based on a rather unrealistic view of (legislated) law: the idea that in it a solution to any conceivable case was to be easily, 'mechanically' found. And few things have kept legal scholars busier, at least since the publication in 1899 of François Gény's *Méthode d'interprétation et sources en droit privé positif*, than to demonstrate that this nineteenth-century view is, and was all along, utterly unrealistic.[3]

It is reasonable for us to be highly sceptical about this idea. The nineteenth century is particularly significant, from the point of view of legal theory, because it is the century in which the modern idea of law became self-conscious. In other words, it became

* Professor of Law, University of Chile and University Adolfo Ibáñez.

[1] E. Bulygin, 'Creación y aplicación del derecho' in F. Atria, et al., *Lagunas en el Derecho. Una controversia sobre el derecho y la función judicial* (Madrid: Marcial Pons, 2005), 30.

[2] Montesquieu, *Spirit of the Laws* (orig. edn 1752; London: G. Bell & Sons, 1914), XI.6.

[3] I will use the Spanish version: F. Gény, *Métodos de Interpretación y Fuentes en Derecho Privado Positivo* (orig. edn 1899; Madrid: Reus, 1925).

embedded in institutions that were consciously designed to give expression to a modern idea of law. A modern idea of law begins with the claim that law is will, not reason, and because of that it is contingent and, as any human artefact, not necessarily perfect. It would be rather schizophrenic if together with the affirmation of the artificiality and contingency of law we were to find an unbridled optimism about (legislated) law as a perfect system. If we look more carefully at this issue, we shall find precisely the contrary: not this unbridled optimism, but jurists clearly aware of the fact that law cannot solve all cases (at least in the sense in which it would be necessary for it to ground a 'mechanical' conception of adjudication). How can we explain, then, that legal scholars so aware of this problem created institutions that relied so heavily on an assumption they knew to be false?

Academic folklore replies: because of the opinion that French revolutionaries had about the performance of the pre-revolutionary judiciary. Mauro Cappelletti, for example, gives this as a (contributory) explanation of the origin of the idea of parliamentary supremacy:

> In France it must be traced back, in part, to a deeply felt popular revulsion against the abuse of the judicial office by the higher courts of justice under the *ancien régime*. These courts . . . asserted their power to review acts of the sovereign, refusing to apply those found to be incompatible with the 'fundamental laws of the realm' . . . Those judges were so deeply rooted in the feudal regime that they found any liberal innovation unacceptable . . . The popular feelings against [these judges] were well justified, and this justification is reflected, albeit in a veiled form, in that celebrated work, *De l'esprit des lois* . . . Quite understandably, given the kind of judges of the time, an enlightened Montesquieu preached that the judges should be entrusted with no political power at all: 'There is no liberty . . . if the power to adjudicate is not separated from the legislative and the executive powers'.[4]

Although this is an implausible explanation for such an extraordinarily lasting and deep effect, there is no need to deny the facts on which it is based. Instead, I intend to ignore it and consider the possibility that the 'formalist' turn may be explained in terms of a tension internal to the modern understanding of law, a tension that, moreover, explains the distinction between legislation and adjudication. If this explanation is valid (be it as a complement or alternative to Cappelletti's), then we will be in a position to note that the problem faced by French revolutionaries when trying to translate their ideals into institutions is still very much present, even if their solutions seem unacceptable to a contemporary eye.

As we shall see, what is discussed today under the heading of 'defeasibility' will be at the centre of this tension. Legally speaking, this shows that, contrary to what contemporary discussions might suggest, the problem of defeasibility can only be understood when considered under an institutional light.

B. Arbitrariness to a degree of perfection

We begin with Jeremy Bentham's criticism of the common law tradition. This development brings into sharp relief the institutional dimension of defeasibility because of two different reasons: on the one hand, Bentham was a strong supporter of the codification movement; he thought that common law was the problem, and legislation was to be the solution. On the other hand, the problem of defeasibility (and thus the

[4] M. Cappelletti, *The Judicial Process in Comparative Perspective* (Oxford: Oxford University Press, 1989), 191–2.

problem of legislation, i.e. the authority of general rules in particular cases) is, or so one could think, particularly acute under a utilitarian theory such as Bentham's. Additionally, if we are to follow Bentham, we can take advantage of the fact that the groundwork for such an undertaking is already available in the form of Gerald Postema's *Bentham and the Common Law Tradition.*[5] We can begin, therefore, by noticing an apparent contradiction that Postema finds in Bentham's criticism of the common law. According to Postema, it seems as though for Bentham, common law adjudication involves both mindless imitation and judicial manipulation of fictions and abstract formulas of 'natural law' and the like, governed only by judicial whim and 'sinister interests'.[6] According to Postema, the contradiction is not with Bentham but with common law. The problem was that it could not provide a *sustainable* equilibrium between (in Hart's words), 'the need for certain rules . . . and the need to leave open, for later settlement by an informed, official choice, issues which can only be properly appreciated and settled when they arise and are identified'.[7] Unable to reconcile these conflicting demands, *common law* 'was doomed to swing, pendulum-like, between the opposite poles of arbitrariness and rigidity'.[8] Postema refers to this constant movement as the 'paradox of inflexibility', but since it is not a paradox (and if it were, it would be of flexibility as much as of inflexibility), I will label it 'the cycle of adjudication'.

Postema describes the cycle as it develops in three stages. In the first stage, characterized by judicial decisions without a rule of *stare decisis*, the *common law* is arbitrary: each judge decides each case according to his or her opinions. Since there is no rule of precedent, judicial decisions 'cannot begin to serve the goal of security which is the basic function of law'.[9] As a reaction to the arbitrariness of this first stage, the second stage begins when a rule of *stare decisis* is introduced. Now, past decisions are binding for present judges. But if the problem in the first stage was arbitrariness, the problem in the second becomes that of excessive rigidity. The rule of *stare decisis* stiffens adjudication, causing what Bentham called the 'unaccommodatingness' of *common law.*[10] Even if the rules 'aim at utility', they will 'either fall short of the mark or overshoot it';[11] they are, to use the useful language popularized by Frederick Schauer, either over-inclusive or under-inclusive.[12] Since judges and the legal profession, having experienced (in the first stage) the irrationality of judicial arbitrariness, appreciate and value the goal of certainty sought by the inflexibility of *stare decisis*, they are willing to ignore the injustice it can cause, in some cases, as the price to be paid for a rational system of adjudication. This explains 'the hardness of heart which is a sort of endemical disease of lawyers'.[13] The same reasons that provoked the movement from the first stage to the second one, that is, the ones that justified the adoption of the rule of *stare decisis*, make legal professionals 'accustomed even to heap miseries on the heads of those by whom [they] know them to be unmerited', because they do it 'for the sake of that

[5] G. Postema, *Bentham and the Common Law Tradition* (Oxford: Clarendon Press, 1986).

[6] Ibid., 279ff.

[7] H.L.A. Hart, *The Concept of Law* (orig. edn 1961; Oxford: Clarendon Press, 1994), 130.

[8] G. Postema, *Bentham and the Common Law Tradition*, 280.

[9] Ibid. This is the moment of 'barbarous law', 'in which the judge is suffered, and obliged by physical necessity, to act without any pre-existing rule'. J. Bentham, *Rationale of Judicial Evidence* (orig. edn 1827, Edinburgh: William Tait, 1843), 310.

[10] J. Bentham, *Of Laws in General* (London: Athlone Press, 1970), 194 fn. 1.

[11] Ibid.

[12] F. Schauer, *Playing by the Rules: A Philosophical Examination of Rule-Based Decision-Making in Law and in Life* (Oxford: Clarendon Press, 1991).

[13] J. Bentham, *Of Laws in General*, 194 fn. 1.

universal good which consists in the steady adherence to established rules'.[14] Bentham noticed that this is an unstable state of affairs. And it is unstable for the reasons explained by Rudolf von Jhering, in section 50 of the second volume of his monumental *The Spirit of the Roman Law*. Jhering observed that, while the partial wrong that judges do in particular cases, when they decide on formal grounds, is clearly visible, the contribution these formal decisions make to the maintenance of a practice of constant adherence to rules is much less notorious, although not less real:

> Everybody points out the shortcomings [of formalism] but nobody notices its benefits, which are purely negative . . . One case, and one case only, that displays the inadequacies of form, like one testament declared to be void, one law-suit lost because of a formal problem, is more painful and notorious than thousands of cases in which, for the normal run of things, form has fulfilled its fundamental function.[15]

The 'hardness of heart' is accepted as a necessary companion to legal form, and legal form is, in turn, a necessary condition for the eradication of the characteristic arbitrariness of the first stage of the cycle. The fact that the formality of the decision is a condition for the eradication of arbitrariness is what Jhering meant when he said that the 'sworn enemy of arbitrariness, form is liberty's twin sister'.[16] This provides strong justification for the formalism of the second stage, indeed so strong that it makes tolerable the injustice produced in ('recalcitrant')[17] cases wrongly decided, as long as the memory of the first stage is still alive. But this is the reason for the instability: as the memory of the first stage begins to fade away and the rule of *stare decisis* moves from being a radical innovation to being an obvious part of legal orthodoxy, the valuable achievement that it represented begins to lose its urgency. Then the public pressure to avoid heaping misery on the heads of those who do not deserve it will become progressively stronger. This second stage ends when the public pressure to avoid substantively unjust decisions becomes strong enough to justify deviation from the legal form. Then, the third stage of the cycle begins:

> But when at length the eyes of the public have to a certain degree opened, the evil which has been the result of their [judges'] thus treading in one another's steps in some cases of quibble, has become so palpable and grossly mischievous—giving impunity, for example, to murderers, because some word has been miswritten or left unwritten by somebody,—when things have come to this pass, not only allowance but applause has been bestowed on a departure.[18]

Then the pendulum returns to the moment of arbitrariness, though aggravated: now there is not only arbitrariness, but 'arbitrary to the point of perfection', because now the judge 'finds himself at perfect liberty to give or to refuse impunity to the murderer, at pleasure: if he refuses it, liberality is his word; if he gives it, *stare decisis*'.[19] This is the 'double fountain' principle with which Bentham mocks Lord Mansfield's idea that the *common law* 'makes itself pure by drinking from the fountain of justice'. Now the judge may drink 'at pleasure' from both the fountain of *stare decisis* and from the fountain of

[14] Ibid.

[15] R. von Jhering, *El Espíritu del Derecho Romano* (orig. edn 1852–65, Granada: Comares, 1998), 647 (L 2 §50).

[16] Ibid., (L 2 §50).

[17] See F. Schauer, *Playing by the Rules*, 39ff.

[18] J. Bentham, *Justice and Codification Petitions* (orig. edn 1827, Edinburgh: William Tait, 1843), 478.

[19] Ibid.

discretion (he may, to put it in our terms, decide according to substance or according to form).

Now, 'without danger either of punishment at the hands of the law, or so much as censure at the hands of public opinion, [the judge] can give success to plaintiff or to defendant, according as he happens to feel inclined'.[20] For Bentham, the common law was the problem, and large-scale legal reform was the solution. This reform could only be codification: 'No otherwise than by codification can the reform here prayed for—or any effectual reform in any shape—be carried into effect.'[21] Bentham believed that legislated law could break the cycle of adjudication because, unlike judicial decisions, legislated rules could be 'sufficiently broad in scope and sufficiently precise in formulation' to avoid or reduce dramatically the possibility of recalcitrant cases.[22] Postema generalizes and provides a structural explanation of the cycle's development: 'the judge is charged with both tasks of protecting the security and certainty of the law—since there is no other effective source of legal rules—and at the same time maintaining some sensitivity to the demands of justice and particular utility of each case'.[23]

The cycle of adjudication, with its progressive succession of stages of formalism and arbitrariness, has a strict correlate in legal theory. As H.L.A. Hart claimed:

> In some legal systems at some periods it may be that too much is sacrificed to certainty, and that judicial interpretation of statutes or of precedent is too formal and so fails to respond to the similarities and differences between cases which are visible only when they are considered in the light of social aims. In other systems or at other periods it may seem that too much is treated by courts as perennially open or revisable in precedents, and too little respect paid to such limits as legislative language, despite its open texture, does after all provide. Legal theory has in this matter a curious history; for it is apt either to ignore or to exaggerate the indeterminacy of legal rules.[24]

It is remarkable that, despite his declared intention of avoiding this 'oscillation between extremes',[25] Hart was unable to escape from it. His intended way out was the notion of open texture. But there is a systematic ambiguity in Hart's use of the notion of open texture in chapter 7 of *The Concept of Law*.[26] Sometimes open texture is a property of words and concepts in natural languages (open texture = vagueness, which reflects a characteristic of words and concepts in natural languages), and at other times it is a feature of the way in which it is reasonable to understand legal rules (open texture = inadequacy, which reflects our relative 'ignorance of fact' and 'indeterminacy of aim').[27] In terms to be introduced shortly below, the open texture of rules sometimes amounts to what Savigny called 'laws of undetermined or incomplete expression' and sometimes to what he called 'laws of improper expression'. In the first case, Hart becomes a formalist: to use an example he often used, it is possible that the word 'vehicle' has an area of open texture, so that it is unclear if the legislative decision to exclude vehicles from the park applies to bicycles, tricycles, prams, and the like. However 'if anything is a vehicle, a motor-car is one',[28] therefore Fuller's case (in which a group of veterans were planning to use a motor car in a war memorial in the park) is an easy case, and the veterans' plan must

[20] Ibid.
[21] Ibid., 439.
[22] G. Postema, *Bentham and the Common Law Tradition,* 282.
[23] Ibid., 283.
[24] H.L.A. Hart, *The Concept of Law*, 130.
[25] Ibid.
[26] For exegesis and quotes, see F. Atria, *On Law and Legal Reasoning* (Oxford: Hart, 2002), 89–94.
[27] H.L.A. Hart, *The Concept of Law*, 128.
[28] Ibid., 126.

be declared against the rule by a 'Hartian' judge. Here, Hart's theory would suggest deciding as a formalist, who refuses to consider (as long as the legislative expression is to be applied to a 'core' instance of its meaning, however inadequate that application might be) the social ends pursued by the rule. Nevertheless, if, to avoid formalism, Hart were to abandon this understanding of the idea of open texture and embrace the second possibility, then the appeal to the rule will no longer be enough to decide the case (any case!), and it will be necessary, in addition, to show that the rule-based solution strikes an adequate balance among 'competing social needs'. It is difficult to deny that the question of whether the rule strikes, *vis-à-vis* the case, a proper balance between those 'needs' is what Hart himself would have called a 'fresh judgment' (= a decision not already contained in the rule to be applied). In Hartian terms, this is rule-scepticism because it means that a 'fresh judgment' mediates between the rule and each case of application. We can see Bentham's cycle of adjudication at work: disappointed absolutists become rule-sceptics, only to transform into disappointed sceptics (frightened by the arbitrariness of the first stage), becoming then formalists, and so forth. Thus, chapter 7 of *The Concept of Law* accurately identifies Bentham's cycle and, hoping to solve it, does nothing but reproduce it.

Is the cycle of adjudication a riddle that can be solved, or is it an unavoidable part of the human condition? To answer this question we must return to Postema's idea that the cycle appears because the judicial process is expected to serve two ends: it must secure, on the one hand, the predictability of judicial decisions and the certainty of law and, on the other, that legal solutions to particular cases will satisfy some level of appropriateness. Bentham (as interpreted by Postema) believed that the riddle could be solved with the introduction of a new source of validity, i.e. legislation, norms valid because they are formally posited. Hence, judicial decisions could rely on the fact that the legislator would give rational solutions to particular cases, freeing judges from the second goal of the judicial process. All judges would then need to do would be to secure the predictability of judicial decisions and the certainty of law. Whether or not the content of the solution given to the case was adequate would be beyond his jurisdiction. What is usually called the 'revolt against formalism' can be seen as the final realization that Bentham's faith in the rationality of legislation as the solution to the cycle of adjudication was mistaken. Indeed, the history of continental legal positivism proved that legislation was to reproduce rather than solve the problem, making the judge as blind to the particularities of the concrete case as the *common law* did, according to Bentham.

The distinction between legislation and adjudication, I believe, can only be discussed fruitfully when the problem it aims institutionally to address is correctly identified. And the problem is the cycle of adjudication, the conclusion that twentieth-century legal theory seems to have drawn from Bentham's (and, generally speaking, codification's) failure: that there is an irreducible opposition between deciding according to law and giving adequate solutions to particular, concrete cases. The cycle is an alternation in the relative importance of these opposite goals: times of formalism (emphasis on certainty at the price of judges heaping miseries on the heads of those by whom they know them to be unmerited) are followed by times of de-formalization (less heaping but more judicial arbitrariness) which leads to 'arbitrariness to a degree of perfection'.

As will be explained in the pages that follow, a full understanding of the distinction between legislation and adjudication consists in regarding it as the institutional solution to this dilemma. The solution to the dilemma is possible by making the application of abstract, legislated rules probably sensitive to the particularities of the case at hand without having to pay the price of denying the authority of law.

C. Modern law and the cycle of adjudication

The same academic folklore that explains the subordinate position of the judge in French post-revolutionary law assumes that this position rested on the assumption that 'law is always complete and coherent in the sense that it provides one answer and only one answer to any legal problem'.[29] Twentieth-century legal theory, as discussed above, rejected this assumption in order to free itself from the 'formalism' that it implied. Indeed, in our post-Kelsenian times we are used to understanding the distinction between adjudication and legislation (in Kelsen's terms) as a purely quantitative one with minor theoretical importance (this shows the inner link, astutely discovered by Hart, between formalism and rule-scepticism). What gives plausibility to this idea, so alien to our institutional cultures, is the belief that legal theory ascribes to nineteenth century legal thinking, i.e. that any non-quantitative distinction between adjudication and legislation had to be a distinction between applying the law and creating it. But this, of course, requires Bulygin's assumption. Once we abandon this assumption, the fact that the distinction between making and applying the law is not correlative to judicial and legislative institutions is not a reason to deny that there is a qualitative difference between these two powers.[30]

1. Mouthpieces of the law

It is true that Montesquieu, as we have seen, thought that the judge ought to be 'the mouth that pronounces the words of the law'. But it is wrong to ascribe to him the idea that (legislated) law always provided an appropriate solution to any particular case. Indeed, the 'mouthpieces' passage discusses precisely this issue:

> It is possible that the law, which is clear-sighted in one sense, and blind in another, might, in some cases, be too severe. But as we have already observed, the national judges are no more than the mouth that pronounces the words of the law, mere passive beings, incapable of moderating either its force or rigor. That part, therefore, of the legislative body, which we have just now observed to be a necessary tribunal on another occasion, also is a necessary tribunal in this; it belongs to its supreme authority to moderate the law in favour of the law itself, by mitigating the sentence.[31]

This passage occurs in the context of Montesquieu's attempt to spell out the implications of the principle of separation of powers. He claimed that it was subject to three exceptions. The second of these exceptions is the one that is important for us now. What made it necessary was that since judges were the mouth that pronounces the words of the law, the fact that the law could not provide reasonable solutions to all conceivable cases was problematic: 'It is possible that the law, which is clear-sighted in one sense, and blind in another, might, in some cases, be too severe.' We need to subject this particular phrase to close scrutiny because it contains an extraordinarily important idea. It is that law is clear-sighted and blind at the same time. It is blind because, prima facie, it neglects any property of a particular case that is not relevant. Article 9 of the Chilean Labour Code, for example, states that, '[i]f the employer does

[29] E. Bulygin, 'Creación y aplicación del derecho', 30.

[30] The relevance of the distinction between creating and applying the law in regard to the judicial role is one of the issues discussed in F. Atria, E. Bulygin, J.J. Moreso, P. Navarro, J.L. Rodríguez, and J. Ruiz Manero, *Lagunas en el Derecho* (Madrid: Marcial Pons, 2005).

[31] Montesquieu, *Spirit of the Laws*, XI.6.

not timely exercise the right vested in him by this Article, the lack of a written contract will constitute a legal presumption that the content of the contract is the one claimed by the worker'.[32]

According to article 4, if (a) there is an employment relationship but (b) no written contract, and (c) if the employer has not let the *Inspección del Trabajo* know about the worker's refusal to sign the contract, then the worker will be believed as to the content of the (oral) contract. If (a), (b), and (c) obtain, the law is blind to further properties of the case. But it is not only blind, it is also clear-sighted since it is precisely *because* it is an unwritten labour contract and *because* the employer has not exercised the right vested in him by article 9 that the worker ought to be believed. An oral contract will usually be more difficult to prove than a written contract. If general contract law were to apply, that additional burden would affect both parties equally, making it more difficult for both of them to prove their claims. Article 9 expresses the legislative decision that the relative positions of employer and worker are not like those of the parties under the general rules of contract law for (broadly speaking) two reasons: because during the employment relationship, the position of the worker is such that he cannot be expected to force the employer to put the contract in writing and because, once the employment relationship has been terminated, the employer will be in a better position to assume the contingency of proving what is difficult to prove. Precisely he who has the greatest control over the formalization of contractual terms is benefited by the lack of form. This is a characteristic circumstance of labour relationships, justifying (or at least this is the meaning of article 9) a rule that burdens the employer with the risks that, in absence of such a rule, would in law be equally shared by the parties. Now the formalization of the employment relationship is in the immediate interest of the party who has the greatest control over it and, because of this, it becomes likely. The law, in its clear-sightedness, aligns the interest of the worker and the interest of the employer so that its goal can now be achieved without coercion.

We need to distinguish between the 'operative facts' of the rule (abc) and the conditions that justify a rule with just those operative facts (the asymmetry between employer and worker mentioned in the last paragraph; let us call them 'd'). The law is blind because d is not part of the rule. The question about the applicability of the rule is decided not according to whether it is fair to believe the worker (i.e. whether d obtains), but according to the form of the relationship among the parties (abc). A rule justified by a given set of conditions (d), but the application of which is not conditional on them, may seem irrational. But the irrationality is mere appearance: in fact, it is because the application of article 9 does not depend on the fact that d obtains, that article 9 can be easily applied by the parties and contribute to defining a practice in which workers' rights are effectively protected. Blindness and clear-sightedness are, then, two sides of the same coin: law is not blind and clear-sighted. It is clear-sighted *because* it is blind. Law's blindness and clear-sightedness are nothing, in other words, but one and the same thing; law's *formality*, which excludes the consideration of everything irrelevant and thus makes possible a decision on each and every case, according only to what is relevant. But, says Montesquieu, the law, blind and clear-sighted as it is (or clear-sighted because it is blind, as we have seen),

[32] If the worker refuses to sign the contract, the employer must notify the *Inspección del Trabajo* (the government's labour protection agency), who will in turn require the worker to sign. If the worker still refuses, he can be fired without compensation. This is the right to which the provision quoted in the main text makes reference.

can be 'too severe', so that it is necessary 'to moderate the law in favour of the law itself'.[33] Montesquieu is not referring here to the excessive severity of a general rule, like the excessive severity of a law that imposes the death penalty. In this case, to moderate the law is to repeal it. It would not be a case of 'moderating the law *for the law itself*', but instead a case of moderating the law for justice's sake. Excessively severe laws must undoubtedly be repealed, but because they are unjust. It is also undoubted that the power to repeal laws that are unjust because they are 'too severe' belongs, in this sense, to the legislator, not as an exception to the principle of separation of powers, but as an application of it. Thus, I take it that Montesquieu is *not* referring to cases such as these, i.e. not to cases in which justice demands that a given general rule be repealed or modified, but to those cases in which a given rule is, when applied to the case, too severe *from the point of view of the rule itself*. In a case recently decided by the Chilean Supreme Court, a worker whose contract was unwritten was the respondent company's CEO, who avoided writing the contract on purpose in order to avail himself of the presumption in article 9. After having been fired (because of fraudulent behaviour), he sued his former employer, demanding a salary that, according to the evidence presented by the parties, amounted to 150 per cent of the compensation originally stipulated. He claimed that since there was a labour relationship and no written contract, article 9 was applicable (the court understood that the available evidence was not strong enough to defeat the legal presumption, although without the presumption, it would have been enough for the defendant to carry the day. This might be incoherent, but we can ignore it now; let us proceed accepting the court's understanding.)

Here the law is too severe since part of what the law is blind to is that this is not the typical case regulated by labour law. The main assumption in article 9 (and in all labour law) is the asymmetry between worker and employer, an asymmetry that labour law seeks to correct through rules like article 9. Of course, this rule is unacceptable in a general contract law, in which the law maintains its neutrality among the parties. Nor does article 9 intend to permit or aid the worker in committing fraud against his employer. However, in *Sterndorf* v. *Manaplast* it was, in bad faith, being used just for this purpose, and so we can say that in this case, the breadth of article 9 of the Labour Code should be moderated, not because the presumption it contains is unfair, but because deciding *this case* according to that rule would be *against that rule*. Article 9 must be moderated for its own sake.[34] Montesquieu's second exception to the principle of the separation of powers concerned cases of this kind and, Montesquieu continued, since the purpose was to correct a law that did not limit its application as it should, it had to be corrected by whomsoever had the authority to create it and modify it. And so Montesquieu recommended (and was followed by French revolutionaries, with little success, as we will see) the creation of a parliamentary commission to which the judge could refer the problem, suspending the procedure in the meantime. It is important to note that in Montesquieu's view, granting a parliamentary commission the power to moderate the law for the law itself was an *exception* to the principle of separation of powers. But why

[33] NB: the *Spirit of the Laws* uses here 'loi' rather than 'droit' so that, if we keep in mind that they are used by Montesquieu in the context of legislation, the phrase could be recast as 'to moderate the rule in favour of the rule itself'. The expression as it appears in the main text glosses over a crucial point, which will be explained presently.

[34] Nothing in the argument depends on the reader agreeing with me on this point of Chilean labour law. What will be crucial will be the difference between criticizing article 9 because of its unfairness (because it is, for example, partial to the worker while it should be impartial) and criticizing it as applied to this case.

was it an exception? If moderating the law for the law itself was a proper exercise of legislative power, then it would, in principle, correspond to the legislative power. Indeed, the two other cases discussed in Book 9 of *The Spirit of the Laws* are truly exceptional in that one power is given the authority to do something that would, in principle, correspond to another. Thus, in the first case, 'a part of the legislative body' is called in to adjudicate particular cases:

> The great are always obnoxious to popular envy; and were they to be judged by the people, they might be in danger from their judges, and would, moreover, be deprived of the privilege which the meanest subject is possessed of in a free state, of being tried by his peers. The nobility, for this reason, ought not to be cited before the ordinary courts of judicature, but before that part of the legislature which is composed of their own body.[35]

In the third case, the executive power is called upon to 'have a share in the legislature'. The executive power, pursuant to what has been already said, ought to have a share in the legislature through the power to reject laws; if it did not, it would soon be stripped of its prerogative. And should the legislative power usurp a share of the executive power, the executive would be equally disabled. 'If the prince were to have a part in the legislature by the power of resolving, liberty would be lost. But as it is necessary he should have a share in the legislature for the support of his own prerogative, this share must consist in the power of rejecting.'[36] The power to moderate the law for law's sake, then, is as judicial as the power to convict the rich and powerful and as naturally part of the province of the judge as it is part of the province of the legislator to change its mind and refuse to do something it had previously considered doing. It is, therefore, an inherently judicial power that must nevertheless be transferred to the legislative power.

We must now consider the reason why this exception is justified. Montesquieu does not explain it but assumes it; if judges are the mouth that pronounces the words of the law, this power cannot be given to them. To understand the reason that justifies this exception, it may be useful to look at Friedrich Carl von Savigny's influential *System of Contemporary Roman Law*, written in the middle of the nineteenth century.[37] In chapter IV of the *System*, Savigny discusses the problem of legal interpretation. Section 35 is dedicated to the breakdown of 'legal interpretation in its normal state', which may happen for two reasons: 'First, indeterminate expression, when the law does not contain any concrete thought; secondly, improper expression, the meaning of which contradicts the true thought of the law.'[38] Concerning 'laws of indeterminate (or incomplete) expression', Savigny explains: 'The law's incomplete expression has the exact character of an interrupted discourse that leaves, therefore, its sense in suspense; as for example a law that were to require witnesses for some point and failed to specify their number.'[39] On the other hand, a law has 'improper expression' when

> [i]t gives a clear and determinate meaning, but different from the true thought of the law. Seeing this contradiction the question is asked as to which one must prevail; now, the word being the means and the thought the object, the former should be subordinated to the latter. A coherent relation between the two must be established and, to achieve this, the expression must be corrected.[40]

35 Montesquieu, *Spirit of the Laws*, XI.6.
36 Ibid., XI.6.
37 I quote from the Spanish edition, F. von Savigny, *Sistema del Derecho Romano Actual* (orig. edn 1840, Madrid: F. Góngora y Compañía editores, 1878).
38 Ibid., 155.
39 Ibid.
40 Ibid.

We have already mentioned a case of improper legal expression: article 9 of the Chilean Labour Code in *Sterndorf* v. *Manaplast*. There the problem was that the law's true intention was not to benefit the CEO who, in abuse of his powers, kept the contract unwritten in order to sue afterwards and avail himself of the legal presumption. The intention of the law did not benefit the plaintiff, although its expression in fact did. The expression was, therefore, improper. Legal interpretation in both of these cases had to correct the defects of the law. But since they are different defects, the corrections they require are also different. The defect of incomplete expression 'must be corrected in all cases and offer no danger at all'. It must be corrected in all cases because as long as it remains uncorrected, no law can be applied. The defect of improper expression, on the other hand, 'is more delicate to treat and requires greater precautions'. The general form of the correction of the improper expression is to 'rectify the expression' so as to 'harmonize form and thought'.[41] The reasons why the problem of improper legal expression gives rise to more serious issues than that of incomplete legal expression are elegantly explained in a passage that deserves to be quoted in full:

> The procedures through which an improper expression is corrected differ from those used to fix an indeterminate expression. First, a determined thought is assumed to exist underneath a defective expression; this relation does not admit, as indetermination, of logical proof, and must be established by reference to history and is, for this reason, less certain, admitting of degrees. Another circumstance increases the difficulty of this matter: the expression is the most immediate and more natural sign of thought, and the latter is precisely not objected to in the present case. Indeterminate expression demands necessarily the solution of interpretation because without it there is no law nor expression to be applied; here, on the contrary, the letter of the law gives us a clear sense that can be applied to the case. Lastly, concerning indeterminate expression, the operation that identifies the defect is different from the one that corrects it. Here the two operations are the same. Indeed, we judge the expression to be improper by comparing it with the real thought of the law; therefore in order to identify this impropriety we need be aware of the thought, in which case we have already found the solution.[42]

Laws of incomplete expression have a *logical defect*, one that can be ascertained by anybody. Of course, the judge will need to have discretion to complete the expression; but this discretion will be limited by the fact that its outer limits are, in this sense, public. Insofar as the judge is exercising his discretion within these limits (self-policing because they are public), the authority of the legislator is not challenged; if the incomplete law is not completed, no law can be applied. And furthermore, the question of whether or not the law is indeed incomplete is, in principle, neutral as to how it should be completed: the distinction can be made, at least in principle, between the question of whether or not there is incompleteness in the expression and what is, therefore, the best way for the judge to complete it using his discretion.

When the issue is, on the contrary, that of improper expression, things are considerably different. Here we deal with a law (like article 9 of the Chilean Labour Code) that contains a clear and determined expression, one that is 'defective' because it is contrary to its thought. The option that was previously excluded, that of applying the law regardless of its defect, is now open; the case can indeed be decided according to the original expression. If this is problematic, it is because deciding according to the expression would not show due respect for the authority of the legislator; but disregarding the expression would be a challenge to that authority if the expression is not improper. And defects as to improper legal expression do not correct themselves, for the identification of

[41] Ibid., 160. [42] Ibid., 160ff.

the defect is not neutral as to the solution. Savigny's problem here was ironically identified by Lon L. Fuller, who tried to show that he was aware of the risk contained in his understanding of law as a 'purposive enterprise':

> Fidelity to law can become impossible if we do not accept the broader responsibilities . . . that go with a purposive interpretation of law. One can imagine a course of reasoning that might run as follows: This statute says absinthe shall not be sold. What is its purpose? To promote health. Now, as everyone knows, absinthe is a sound, wholesome and beneficial beverage. Therefore, interpreting the statute in the light of its purpose, I construe it to direct a general sale and consumption of that most healthful of beverages, absinthe.[43]

Savigny agrees with Fuller: under the guise of harmonizing thought and expression, the judge may replace the legislator's thought because in dealing with these cases, it is not always clear '[w]hether the thought that is the result of our interpretation is really the legislator's thought or the thought that the legislator ought to have had, in which case the interpretation would be correcting not the expression, but the thought itself'.[44]

We can now return to Montesquieu. It will be remembered that the question posed at the start of this section was why giving to parliament the power to moderate the law, for law's sake, is an exception to the principle of the separation of powers. It is no exception to this principle that the legislator exercises legislative powers; what is exceptional is that it exercises non-legislative powers. We can now say that underlying Montesquieu's argument is the idea that the power to adjudicate naturally includes the power to correct improper legal expression, which must, however, be given not to the judge but to the legislator. The reason for this exception is that, if judges can correct an improper legal expression, it will be unlikely that judges will decide according to law. The risk is that the judge, claiming to correct the expression's inappropriateness, will be free to modify the law, transforming it into the law he would have liked the legislator to dictate.

It is interesting to note that neither Montesquieu nor Savigny considered laws of incomplete expression to be a serious problem. Montesquieu did not think that this problem merited a further exception to the principle of separation of powers, and we have seen that Savigny thought that the incompleteness of the expression 'offers no danger whatsoever'. However, both noticed the subversive potential implied by giving judges the power to correct improper legal expression (subversive, that is, of the position that defines the judge in a modern legal system). The reason why this is worth noting is that twentieth-century legal theory claimed to have abandoned Montesquieu's conception of adjudication, not because it realized that the judge could not but face problems of improper legal expression; on the contrary, twentieth century legal theory rejected Montesquieu's views because of incompleteness of expression (vagueness) rather than improper expression (defeasibility). Thus, for example, Hart would call 'formalism' a 'vice' if we consider formalist the judge who '[e]ither does not see or pretends not to see that the general terms of the rules are susceptible to different interpretations and that he has a choice left open uncontrolled by linguistic conventions. He ignores, or is blind to, the fact that he is in the area of the penumbra and is not dealing with a standard case.'[45] Here the vice is not its blindness to the possibility

[43] L.L. Fuller, 'Positivism and Fidelity to Law—A Reply to Professor Hart', *Harvard Law Review*, 71 (1958), 670.

[44] F. Von Savigny, *Sistema del Derecho Romano Actual*, 162.

[45] H.L.A. Hart, 'Positivism and the Separation of Law and Morals' in H.L.A. Hart, *Essays in Jurisprudence and Philosophy* (Oxford: Clarendon Press, 1983), 49–87.

that the linguistic expression used by the legislator is in contradiction with its intention, but to the fact that, given the limits of natural languages used to express legislative decisions, 'linguistic conventions' turn out to be incomplete, leaving a space for the judge to decide with discretion.[46]

For Hart, then, the possibility of laws of incomplete expression proved formalism to be a vice. He believed that authors like Montesquieu and Blackstone were to blame for this erroneous vision of the judge as an automaton. As we have seen, this is undeserved, at least concerning Montesquieu. Just like Savigny a century later, Montesquieu was not worried about the strictness with which judges should apply laws of incomplete expression. Granted, Montesquieu did claim that, '[i]n republics, the very nature of the constitution requires the judges to follow the letter of the law; otherwise the law might be explained to the prejudice of every citizen, in cases where their honour, property, or life is concerned'.[47] But this idea, as we have seen, cannot apply to cases of incomplete expression, in which there is no law to apply. Montesquieu's advice is clearly applicable to cases of improper expressions and its message is to deny the judge the power to correct them. We have seen that this is not a consequence of a particularly formalistic view of the judicial process, but a conclusion to be reached in spite of the fact that, in principle, this is part of the judicial power. The reason to deny judges this power was, in other words, not that it did not belong to the judicial 'province'; it was exceptionally denied even though it belonged to it. Ergo, the reason was institutional, not conceptual.

2. Judicial institutions

Let us remember the academic folklore: the reason why French revolutionaries assigned the judge a subordinate position was the resentment they and the French people in general felt regarding superior courts' pre-revolutionary practices. This position was further justified by the assumption that the law always contained an answer that the judge could mechanically apply. This second idea was not, *pace* this folklore, part of the movement of codification. The idea of mechanical jurisprudence that evolved on the coattails of the codification process was not the consequence of a theory of law based upon the naive belief that law always had an answer to every conceivable problem. The problem was how to give institutional form to the idea that law is valid, not because of its reasonableness, but because it is a declaration of will. This modern idea of law required a distinction between the act of declaring a given will and the act of applying a will that has already been declared. The vexing question in cases of improper expression is: if the judge is subject to law, what is he to do when the legislator's expression is in contradiction with his decision? Savigny's answer appears, in principle, convincing: 'the word being the means and the thought the object',[48] it seems that only form's fetishism could justify a preference for the means when they contradict the ends, for the legislative

[46] I believe the same could be said of Kelsen's rejection of the idea of the judge as an automaton. See, for example, Troper, who claims that 'the main criticism' of the theory according to which 'judicial decisions are the result of syllogistic reasoning the major premises of which is the law, particular facts being the minor premise' is that 'the norm that the judge applies is not given to him. He has to create it.' See M. Troper, *Por una Teoría Jurídica del Estado* (Madrid: Dykinson, 2001), 76. Troper is using the expression 'creation' here in a way similar to that of Savigny, i.e. for the completion of the incomplete expression: 'this choice, generally called "interpretation", consists then in the determination of the meaning of the text. That is to say, of the "applicable norms"' (ibid., 77, my emphasis).

[47] Montesquieu, *Spirit of the Laws*, VI.3 (this seems to be the passage to which Montesquieu refers in the 'mouthpieces' passage).

[48] F. Von Savigny, *Sistema del Derecho Romano Actual*, 160 f.

expression when it contradicts the legislative thought. This is true 'in principle'. But of course the problem is to distinguish between cases in which the judge corrects the expression to serve the 'spirit' of the law and cases in which, under the excuse of correcting the expression, the judge is changing the law. This problem constitutes the subtext of article 19 of the Chilean Civil Code; 'when the sense of a law is clear, the letter of it is not to be disregarded under the pretext of pursuing its spirit'.

The wording of article 19 is telling: the problem is not that the judge is able to correct the letter of a law in pursuit of its spirit; the problem, rather, is that the judge is able to use *the pretext* of pursuing the spirit of the law in order to decide against it. And the institutional problem is that the distinction between these two possibilities is formless whereas the power to do the former would in fact give judges the power to do the latter. And this problem was then particularly acute because the moment of codification was precisely the moment when an idea that seems obvious to us *now* acquired self-consciousness: that law is valid because it is willed and not because it is intrinsically rational. The movement of codification had to create institutions that made judges' subjection to (legislated) law not only possible but probable, when the traditional judicial understanding of their function saw the (posited) law as a guide and not as a norm ('the rule flows from law, not law from the rule' as the Digest stated).[49]

It is highly anachronistic, then, to say that, at the beginning of the nineteenth century, an arrogant and defective theory of the legislator's omnipotence had become dominant, one in which the judge had to become an automaton because everything a judge needed to decide the case was previously foreseen and adequately configured in law. This fails to see that the problem was that of creating institutions that could redefine the judicial function as an office subject to (legislated) law, even though (a) the law could not foresee every situation and, accordingly, adequately solve each application case and (b) the judicial function's traditional understanding of itself was such that if the judge was given the power to amend the law's expression, it was most likely that this would reinforce the idea that judges' duty was not that of deciding according to posited law, but to give each their own using posited law as a guide, as rules of thumb.

In order to see how this problem was confronted, it is useful to look at the institutions that were created to give form to the modern idea of law under these two conditions. The first institutional form was the *référé législatif*, according to which judges were authorized in some cases, and obliged in others, to ask the legislator for the solution of some interpretative problem. The second was the *Tribunal de Cassation*, originally conceived less like a supreme court and more like, so to speak, a legislative policeman in charge of 'watching over, overseeing, even inspecting the application of law';[50] the power to legislate included the power to control the way in which laws were applied. In fact, as a member of the parliamentary commission said when presenting the bill that created this Court: 'The power to enact the law naturally implies the power to watch over its observance. In fact what follows strictly from principle, if it were possible, is for illegal judicial decisions to be annulled by decree.'[51]

The *Tribunal de Cassation* must be understood in the context of the idea of judicial independence, which, in turn, means nothing but subjection to law. These two ideas

[49] See below, n. 78.

[50] F. Gény, *Métodos de Interpretación y Fuentes en Derecho Privado Positivo*, 77.

[51] Le Chapelier, reporting to the National Convention (25 October 1790), in ibid., 76ff. The *Convention Nationale* had the power to annul decisions of the *Tribunal de Cassation*: F. Gény, *Métodos de Interpretación y Fuentes en Derecho Privado Positivo*, 44 fn. 4.

are two sides of the same coin: in order for the judge to decide with strict subjection to law, he must not be subject to anything else. Thus, if judicial independence from the Assembly must be guaranteed, and if the *Tribunal de Cassation* was an Assembly's agent, then the problem was not to secure the independence of the *Tribunal* from the Assembly (it does not make sense to claim the independence of an agent from its principal), but that of judges from both the Assembly and the Tribunal. To this end, the jurisdiction of the *Tribunal de Cassation*, was doubly limited: on the one hand, it had the power to void decisions only when they went against an explicit legal expression; on the other hand, if it declared a judicial decision to be void for this reason, the case was to be remanded to a different judge so that it could be decided again. Note, however, that the new judge was not bound by the interpretation relied upon by the *Tribunal* in order to annul the sentence. In fact, it could insist on the interpretation rejected by the *Tribunal*. This was necessary for judges to be subject to law alone, and not to the will of the *Tribunal*.

The *référé législatif*, on the other hand, could be facultative or mandatory. The facultative *référé* gave judges what Bentham called 'suspensive power'; if the law turned out to be insufficient, the judge could suspend the trial and defer the case to the Assembly's consideration, which decided on the insufficiency. The mandatory *référé* was related to the situation mentioned above in which the *Tribunal de Cassation* was obliged to annul the decision of a case for the second time (since the judge to whom the case was remanded after the first annulment had decided in a way that was still considered against the law by the *Tribunal*). Gény believes that the introduction of the *référé* in both its forms and the *Tribunal de Cassation*, 'evidently implied that in the legal sphere the law (*loi*) was always sufficient for everything, and that the interpreter was not authorized to search for principles beyond'.[52] Nonetheless, this seems a hasty conclusion. The first idea Gény reads in these institutions makes them incoherent. If 'the law is always sufficient for everything', what is the point in permitting a court to suspend the trial for the Assembly's decision on the law's insufficiency? In fact, the institution of the *référé* may be used as evidence to claim precisely the opposite; precisely because the law is not always sufficient for everything, it is necessary to allow, or even demand, that legislative opinion be consulted.

However, the institutional imagination of the French revolutionaries was not enough. Thus, these two institutions were not effective and did not last long. The *référé legislatif facultative* was abrogated by article 4 of the *Code Civil* (1804), which adopted the opposite solution: the 'principle of inexcusability', according to which the judge was forbidden to give a *non liquet* decision. The *référé législatif obligatoire* was eliminated in 1837, when it had already become obsolete. In the end, the *Tribunal de Cassation* itself evolved from its original function as a legislative agent to a much more judicially self-conscious one: to standardize the interpretation and application of legislated law and to secure equality before the law. For our purposes, what is particularly relevant are the reasons why these two institutions failed to achieve their goals, as explained by Gény himself. We can distinguish two types of reasons for this. The first is what we might call external compromises. Sometimes, a given goal can be pursued in a certain way only at the expense of other, also important goals; the second is that of contradiction, when pursuing a goal becomes, at some point, self-defeating in that the more the goal is pursued, the farther away it gets. According to Gény, reasons of the first kind caused the abolition of the *référé législatif* in 1837:

[52] Ibid., 79.

Especially during the time in which the power to interpret was given to the legislative bodies (rather than the Conseil d'État),[53] they were busily engaged in more urgent matters, and felt repugnance when they had to busy themselves with these issues arising from individuals' private interests. Additionally, the clearest consequence of the *référé* was a notorious delay, highly prejudicial for the parties to the case.[54]

This does not show that the *référé* was contradictory, but only that its normal operation affected other important goals (increasing the delay in the conduction and resolution of trials, forcing legislative bodies to dedicate time and effort to serving private interests). When external reasons press upon an institution, the conflict is solved through a judgment of relative importance. Is the function that the *référé* fulfils important enough to justify the damage done to the parties by the inevitable delay? This type of conflict easily leads to the cycle of adjudication: the closer the memory of the problems that the new institutions purport to solve is, the easier it will be to accept contingent costs. However, in the particular case we are now discussing, Gény claims not only that the *référé* was problematic because it affected other legislative goals, but also that it was contradictory, i.e. self-defeating:

> As a matter of pure theory [a consensus quickly emerged] that the *référé législatif*, established with the goal of maintaining the separation between legislative and judicial powers, was contrary to its own end, and in reality sacrificed the latter to the former, insofar as it gave a legislative body authority to pass judgment on a particular case, which by nature corresponded to the judicial power.[55]

The reasons for the contradictory nature of the *référé* can be generalized: the argument assumes that since the legislator has exclusive competence to decide A or B at Time 1, if in Time 2 its decision turns out to be ambiguous between A and B, the decision as to how this ambiguity should be resolved is equally legislative in character. The argument assumes, in other words, that the fact that in one case the decision is taken at Time 1 and in the other it is taken at Time 2 is irrelevant from the point of view of the kind of decision it is. But this is not so: at moment 2, the legislator knows the direct impact that the decision will have on a particular case, something unknown at moment 1. It is unlikely that the decision at Time 2 will not take this information into account. Gény's point is unassailable: it is an instance of deciding a particular case and that is not an exercise of legislative power. As we shall see, the categorical nature of Gény's objection shows one of the conditions under which democratic legislation is possible (= only if the abstract decision is taken independently on any particular case of application).

The importance of this idea, I hope, will become clearer as we proceed. For now, we may observe that it has a considerable methodological consequence. In fact, if Gény's argument (and its generalization) is correct, then the decision about what must be read in the legislative decision (if A or B) is a legislative decision in relation to the kind of *question* decided; but at Time 2, it can be no longer understood as legislative, and this is for the same reason why it is problematic to give the judge the power to correct law's improper expression; because at Time 2, the institutional conditions that make legislation probable no longer obtain. Although other institutional solutions may be imagined, this means that they will have to be solved by the judge. So the judge will have to decide not only the judicial question about the parties' rights and duties given the applicable norms and the circumstances of the case, but also the legislative question

[53] That is, until Nivose VIII (December 1799).

[54] F. Gény, *Métodos de Interpretación y Fuentes en Derecho Privado Positivo*, 83.

[55] Ibid., 84.

of what the applicable rule is (at least regarding the choice between A or B). And the reason why he will have the power to so decide is institutional, not theoretical; the judge must solve this issue not because, according to its type, it is properly judicial in nature, but *in spite of the fact* that it is not so. This implies that we cannot characterize the judicial function by looking at the legal configuration of judicial organs in one, many, or all legal systems, for this would not allow us to discriminate between powers that are vested in judges because they are properly judicial in nature and those that are given to the judge in spite of their not being of a judicial nature. But it must seem odd to say that legal concepts get their content from something other than posited law. This might suggest a kind of pre-modern argument for a natural law of concepts. This point should be answered before we proceed. Thus, in the next section we shall take a detour into the theory of legal concepts, a detour that will allow us to better understand the references, in the paragraphs above, to powers being legislative or judicial 'in nature'. We shall see, moreover, that such a detour will turn out to be crucial to the understanding of legal institutions, their form and structure, and (above all) the relations between them.

D. Legal concepts: between function and structure

The argument so far has shown that because of institutional reasons (be they the need to make external compromises or to avoid contradiction), it might be impossible to arrange legislative or judicial institutions as if the arrangement, in each case, could proceed directly from first principles. This means that it should not be surprising to find that courts or legislatures or executives have powers that would not naturally correspond to them. But what sense can we make of this idea, to wit, that there are powers or attributes that correspond to the 'nature' of an institutional body? If such a body, like a court or a legislative assembly, owes its existence to constitutive rules, what could it possibly mean to say that there are powers that correspond to them (in a pre-institutional sense, would not this have to be?)? The answer to this question is a theory of the pre-institutional nature of institutional concepts. This pre-institutional nature is what is usually referred to as 'substance'. A theory of the pre-institutional nature of institutional concepts is necessary, then, to the understanding of legal institutions; we shall see that they have to be described as (more or less successful) attempts to give form to formless ideas. A theory of the pre-institutional nature of institutional concepts includes an explanation of the institutional move; what is the deficit of the non-institutional concept so that it requires institutionalization?

To begin with, we may say that X's nature is that by virtue of which X is X. But this is not enough. Saying that X has a nature is not only saying there is something by virtue of which it is X. In addition, it implies that something is, so to speak, inside X ('internal' to X), i.e. not reducible to something extrinsic to it. Thus, if there is such a thing as 'human nature', this is because there is something by virtue of which humans are humans and that this is not reducible to conditions external to them (this is the reason why Marxism has traditionally understood—erroneously—that historical materialism and the notion of human nature are incompatible).[56] The idea that legal concepts have a nature, i.e. that there is something by virtue of which they are what they are, and that whatever that is, it is intrinsic to them (i.e. does not depend on something extrinsic to them, such as a contingent legislative declaration), is today discarded as a relic of

[56] See G. Cohen, *Karl Marx's Theory of History* (Oxford: Clarendon Press, 1979), 151.

pre-modern law. It is easy to understand why: if modern law is contingent, if 'three correcting words of the legislator [are enough to turn] entire libraries into waste paper',[57] it seems that 'property', for example, is whatever the legislator says property is.

It is an attitude such as this that explains the curious path followed by twentieth century legal theory in matters related to what we are discussing here. The judicial process has no 'nature' because the judicial process is whatever the legislator says it is: but then the pre-eminence given to legislated law was put into question; the reason why it was thought to be crucial was that it determined the content of judicial decisions; and this was soon seen as formalistic. What was important was to look at whatever it was that was decisive in determining the content of judicial decisions, and legislative declarations have no pre-eminence. This justified a 'realistic' methodological turn: what legal theory had to explain, as long as it was descriptive rather than normative, was what law actually was, and not what it ought to be according to a theorist's desires or ideology. Observing, therefore, what judges 'really do', and ignoring the 'myths' inherited from the nineteenth century, it was possible to note that the idea that judges decide according to formal rules and formal rules alone was false. Posited law was only one of the considerations that judges followed when passing judgment, and sometimes not even the main consideration. This led to the replacement of the issue of judge's subjection to legislated law with a question about the characteristics of judicial decision (i.e. is the judicial decision entirely reducible to the judge's will or is it 'constrained' by independent criteria and, if that is the case, what are these criteria?). The 'realist' or 'descriptive' point of view, concerned with 'describing law as it is', caused the legislative power and legislative function to become theoretically unimportant. Usually they were treated as mere historical accidents that implied nothing in relation to the concept of legislation or the nature of judicial process because there were no such things. Thus, legal theory in recent decades has been obsessively concerned with judicial discretion and the relationship between law and morals in adjudication, with little or no reference to the problem of legislation and the legislative function.

But as we have seen and shall see in more detail, it is impossible to understand the idea of the judicial process without understanding its relationship to legislation. The judge's position as we know it is qualitatively different from the pre-modern judge's position. With the modern idea of law that can be artificially created through a declaration of will emerges the idea of the judge as independent and subject to law. And, as we shall see, this is not an historical coincidence: on the contrary, it means that in order to understand the idea of judicial power, we need to understand its relationship to legislation. But this, in turn, is impossible unless we can distinguish, from among the things judges 'do', what they do because it is inherent to their function (i.e. what they do *qua* judges) from what they do in spite of the fact that it does not correspond to their function. This may be generalized in relation to legal concepts. Legal institutions can only be understood as giving form to formless ideas. But the form is not (it cannot be) entirely transparent to substance (otherwise it would be pointless), and thus institutional forms do not correspond perfectly to the ideas they attempt to formalize. It is important, therefore, to understand the limits of legal form, and this is the reason why last section's discussion of the failure of the *référé* was important.

Michael Moore has suggested that it is useful to distinguish different kinds of concepts. According to Moore, there are three such kinds: natural, nominal, and

[57] J.H. Von Kirchman, *La Jurisprudencia no es Ciencia* (Madrid: Centro de Estudios Constitucionales, 1983), 29.

functional.[58] *Natural* kinds 'not only exist "naturally" (i.e. without human contrivance) but also have a nature to them that gives the essence of the kinds', like water or gold. *Nominal* kinds 'are simply a set of individual things that share no nature save a common name used to refer collectively to the class', like the set of things called *Figueroa Street* in Los Angeles. Finally, a *functional* kind 'like a natural kind has a nature that each instance of the class shares, but the nature is functional and not structural'. Moore's example of a functional kind is 'stomach': anything that sufficiently fulfils the function of processing food (in a certain way) is a stomach, regardless of its structure.[59] Moore's purpose in introducing this typology is to show that law is a functional kind, and that this idea, correctly developed, leads to a natural theory of law. According to Moore, a natural theory of law claims (i) that moral facts exist and (ii) that law's validity (i.e. the validity of law as a normative order as well as a particular law and a decision in a particular case) depends on its corresponding to those facts.[60] As I do not want to go that far (indeed I believe that a proper understanding of the relationship between function and structure prevents a conclusion such as Moore's, as we shall see below), I believe I can clarify the way in which I will adopt Moore's labels. In the sense in which these words will be used here, kinds are defined either by something internal to them (natural kinds) or external to them (nominal kinds). What is internal to natural kinds may be their form or structure (structural or formal kinds) or their function (functional kinds). Nominal kinds, by definition, have no nature: there is nothing internal to them by virtue of which they are instances of the kind.

Our point at the end of the previous section concerning the legislative and the judicial functions can be expressed now by saying that 'legislation' and 'adjudication' cannot be purely nominal kinds. They have to be, therefore, natural kinds. But what kind of natural kind? They could be structural or formal kinds: then they would be defined, as water, by their structure. An example of such an explanation is Mauro Cappelletti's attempt to identify 'the nature of judicial process'; a nature that would distinguish it from other processes, particularly the legislative one. What defines the judicial process, Cappelletti claims, is '(a) its connection with cases and controversies, hence with "parties", and (b) the impartiality of the judge'.[61] From these two central features of the nature of judicial process follow three rules that, taken together, define the judicial process: *nemo iudex in causa propria*, *audiatur et altera pars* and *ubi non est actio, ibi non est jurisdictio*.[62] An act, then, belongs to the class of judicial acts, according to Cappelletti's explanation, when the procedure through which it is performed may be classified as 'judicial', that is to say when the three requirements listed above have been met to a sufficient extent: 'A judge who decides a case not brought to him by a party; who does not give the defendant a reasonable opportunity to defend himself; or who decides his own case, might still wear the judicial robe and call himself a judge, but he is no longer a judge.'[63]

A structural explanation of the nature of the judicial process like Cappelletti's must answer two objections: the first one is incidentally noted by Cappelletti himself,

[58] M. Moore, *Placing Blame* (Oxford: Oxford University Press, 1997), 19–23.

[59] Ibid., 20.

[60] M. Moore, 'Law as a functional kind' in R.P. George (ed.), *Natural Law Theory* (Oxford: Clarendon Press, 1994), 188–242.

[61] M. Cappelletti, *The Judicial Process in Comparative Perspective*, 31. Notice the fact, mentioned above, that no reference to judges' subjection to posited law appears here.

[62] Ibid., 31ff.

[63] Ibid., 34.

who observes a trend towards the 'judicialization' of legislative and administrative procedures:

To be sure, there is, in some Western countries, a most accentuated trend today to 'judicialize', as it were, the legislative and the administrative processes. 'Hearings' of the conflicting interests have been introduced in these processes; instruments (including entrenched bills of rights and binding rules of legislative and administrative procedure) have been adopted to protect minorities or under-represented majorities against partisan action by legislatures, executives and administrative agencies; and 'impartiality' has been preached, even (more or less rhetorically) mandated, to the political branches as well. Yet the fact remains that those characteristics are typical of the judicial process, so much so that one speaks of 'judicialization' of the non-judicial processes.[64]

But, of course, the question could be turned on its head: why should we call this trend a judicialization of non-judicial procedures? Why wouldn't we say that these procedures are no longer non-judicial and are actually judicial procedures, precisely insofar as they become characterized by the notes that define the judicial process? If, in spite of this 'trend towards judicialization', these procedures are still 'political' in a relevant sense, this must be because Cappelletti's three formal requirements do not define the judicial process or specify its nature. There is something by virtue of which these procedures remain political even if they have adopted the judicial structure. This can only make sense if the judicial process is not a structural kind.

And if the concept is not structural, what are we to make of Cappelletti's claim that these forms are characteristically judicial? Would we have to say that Cappelletti is simply wrong? We shall see that this is a crucial point concerning any functional theory of legal concepts: though the concept is functional, not structural, there is a non-contingent connection between function and structure.

The problem with Cappelletti's concept of judicial process is common to theories that consider legal concepts as structural kinds: it is usually the case that the chosen structural features are correlated with instances other than those of the concept involved. Moore discusses this problem by reference to the idea that 'criminal law' is a structural class, defined by punishment.[65] If that is the case, the crucial question for a theory of criminal law is to characterize the concept of punishment. If it is structural, then it is utterly meaningless to say that something shares the structure of punishment but is not punishment. But this would imply a rather odd theory of criminal law; it is difficult to distinguish, for example, looking at structure alone—between a fine and a tax and a civil damages award. If there is no such structural distinction, the conclusion would have to be that criminal law includes tax law and the law of civil liability (or, by reference to our previous example, that Cappelletti's judicialized 'political' processes are now judicial). To avoid this conclusion, one may want to deny that taxes are an instance of punishment. But to say this, it is necessary to look beyond structure, to function; they are not punishments because they do not perform the function of expressing blame. This leads to a functional concept of criminal law and tax law (and the law of civil liability, etc). What characterizes each is 'the distinctive ends of [each] not [their] distinctive means of attaining them'.[66]

The second objection against a structural account of legal concepts appears when we try to determine which structural features are relevant, and why that is the case. Cappelletti's answer appears at times to assume that 'judicial process' is a nominal kind because he seems to think that in order to justify his list of structural features, he can rely on nothing more than an appeal to the past: 'Factual experience rather than sophisticated theories demonstrates this point. And historical experience indicates quite

[64] Ibid., 32. [65] M. Moore, *Placing Blame*, 25. [66] Ibid., 22.

clearly that the "nature" of the judicial process, far from being characterised by the process's non-creativity, is characterised by (a) its connection with cases and controversies, hence with "parties", and (b) the impartiality of the judge.'[67]

But if what is relevant is 'factual experience' and factual experience alone, then it seems that the concept is not, after all, structural but nominal: it seems to be an appeal to what *has been called* (by whoever is relevant here) 'judicial process'. But this, of course, does not make sense—Cappelletti cannot believe that the judicial process is whatever is called 'judicial process', since if that were the case, the whole attempt to find its 'nature' would be radically empty; nominal kinds are defined by their lack of a nature. How, then, can the selected list of structural features be justified? Cappelletti hints at something that is more than mere factual experience; it is an experience that reflects 'millennia of human wisdom'.[68] This suggests a functional concept; the 'wisdom' referred to is wisdom as to the fact that a process characterized by the features he identified is the best way to serve the goals pursued by the judicial process. But, of course, if the selected list of structural features is justified in a functional way, the concept turns out to be functional, not structural.

We can generalize the argument of the last paragraph: legal concepts cannot be structural kinds. What in a given context might look like a structural concept may eventually turn out to be either a nominal or a functional kind. This is a consequence of the fact that legal concepts are institutional concepts and they do not have a pre-institutional structure. A structural explanation of any legal concept will dissolve into a nominal or functional explanation as soon as the particular structural features that define the class are in need of justification. When referring to structural concepts such as water, for example, the answer (to the question of why this rather than that particular structural property) lies in the fact of the existence of water as something independent of our theories of water, so it is possible to point to the thing called 'water' and show that the chosen structural features are the ones that truly constitute its nature. Unlike wates, however, legal concepts are theory-dependent: as we have seen, the idea that it is possible to understand the judicial process simply by looking at 'what judges do' has no content at all. Therefore, the structure chosen will have to be justified by referring either to a fact external to the thing (e.g. convention, and then the concept will be nominal) or to a fact internal to the object (its function, and then the concept will be functional). There is no sense to the idea that structure can be justified by structure. The claim that legal concepts cannot be structural concepts is the content of Ronald Dworkin's usually misunderstood 'semantic sting' argument. Dworkin claimed that a theory like Hart's was a semantic theory because it purported to uncover the basic criteria followed by lawyers and judges and lay people that govern their use of the word 'law'.[69] Hart and his followers complained that this was a gross mischaracterization; that Hart himself had argued against semantic theories:

Questions such as those I have mentioned, 'What is a State?', 'What is law?', 'What is a right?', have great ambiguity... But if, in the effort to free them from this risk of confusion with other questions, we rephrase these requests for definitions as 'What is the meaning of the word "State"?', 'What is the meaning of the word "law"?', 'What is the meaning of the word "right"?', those who ask are apt to feel uneasy, as if this had trivialized their question. For what they want cannot be got out of a dictionary, and this transformation of their questions suggests it can. This uneasiness is the

[67] M. Cappelletti, *The Judicial Process in Comparative Perspective*, 31. The last part of this passage was quoted above, text accompanying n. 61.

[68] Ibid.

[69] R. Dworkin, *Law's Empire* (London: Fontana, 1986), 33–5.

expression of an instinct which deserves respect: it emphasizes the fact that those who ask these questions are not asking to be taught how to use these words in the correct way.[70]

But Dworkin's point was deeper than this. And the terminology used above helps to explain it; if law is not a functional kind, it must be a structural or a nominal kind. Hart seems to have thought that it was a structural kind ('law as the union of primary and secondary rules'), but when it comes to institutional facts, structural explanations are always inconclusive and eventually reveal themselves to be either functional or nominal. This can be seen from any attempt to ground a purely structural explanation of law as the subject matter of legal theory. Joseph Raz, for example, has tried to defend such an account. He begins by rejecting both the 'semantic approach' (which understands legal theory as the attempt to uncover the hidden rules of the use of the word 'law' and related words) and the lawyer's perspective (according to which 'law' is whatever 'is appropriate for courts to rely upon in justifying their decisions', which seems to be at least an instance of a 'functional approach'). He then defends the view that legal theory must take an 'institutional approach', which 'strives to present an analysis of a central political institution which... should be accepted as the analysis of law'.[71] But the central question then becomes, as above, that of identifying the 'central political institution' and of differentiating it from other political institutions and other institutions generally. Indeed, Raz goes on to single out courts as the institutions crucial to understanding this major political institution ('it is entirely plausible to regard the notion of law as bound up with that of a judicial system').[72] He subsequently goes on to characterize courts by reference to three features: they deal with disputes with the aim of resolving them, they issue authoritative rulings, and they are bound to be guided, at least partly, by positivist authoritative considerations.[73]

But isn't it highly implausible to consider this to be the 'starting point for further critical reflection'?[74] The three characteristic features listed above identify not only what are usually called 'courts', but also administrators and even legislative organs. Shouldn't the starting point be whatever explains whether this is important? Should we look for structural features to distinguish courts from administrators, or should that distinction be declared theoretically irrelevant? What about the distinction between criminal courts and civil courts? Indeed, the idea that the courts 'deal with disputes with the aim of resolving them' is more natural in the context of civil courts than criminal courts because sometimes the fact that the defendant is willing to assume criminal liability does not do away with the need for the judicial decision. Does this show that civil courts are better examples than criminal courts of a judicial organ, or is it irrelevant?

The answer to these questions cannot be structural, for they will have to rest, ultimately, on a non-structural explanation, be it nominal or functional. Dworkin's point was that a nominal answer was no answer because in that case, there would be nothing to say about law or about the idea of courts and we could only talk about 'law' and of 'courts', i.e. about the words and their conditions of use. But (and this was

[70] H.L.A. Hart, 'Definition and Theory in Jurisprudence' in H.L.A. Hart, *Essays in Jurisprudence and Philosophy* (Oxford: Clarendon Press, 1983), 21–48.

[71] J. Raz, 'The Problem About the Nature of Law' in J. Raz, *Ethics in the Public Domain* (Oxford: Clarendon Press, 1994), 188.

[72] Ibid., 188ff.

[73] Ibid., 189.

[74] Ibid., 188.

Dworkin's original point, right then as it is now) this denies that law has meaning.[75] For this reason, the question now is not to offer nor examine an argument for the claim that legal concepts are nominal kinds. That would be a negative conclusion, a form of what Dworkin called 'internal scepticism': it is the consequence of a failure of interpretation, the failure to find a functional or structural explanation for legal concepts. We now have reason to believe that legal concepts cannot be structural kinds. But can they be functional kinds? We have to attempt to develop such a theory of legal concepts and if we fail, we can consequently say that legal concepts are nominal kinds. This article represents the beginning of this endeavour.

Assuming then, for now, that concepts such as adjudication and legislation are functional kinds, we must return to the relationship between structure and function. The argument just stated is that structural explanations of legal concepts will eventually dissolve into functional explanations, i.e. that legal concepts cannot ultimately be structural concepts. The first step will have to be an explanation of the expression 'ultimately'. To discuss this issue, we can go to Moore, who distinguishes two functions that the nature of a concept (structural or functional) must fulfil. The first is ontological and the second is that of individuation. As regards the ontological dimension, the structure or the function gives us *a definition*; it allows us to explain what the concept is. As regards the question of individuation, the structure or the function is then used to identify the members of the structural or functional class. Moore believes that the solution to the ontological problem *is* a solution to the individuation problem: 'When we have answered our ontological question of what kind of kind an area of law might be we will also have placed ourselves in a position to answer the individuation problem. If an area of law is a functional kind, then any law that serves the function essential to that area will be part of that area of law.'[76]

It is important to understand why this conclusion is correct in one sense and incorrect in another. This ambiguity is what the above use of the word 'ultimately' was meant to convey. We have seen that legal concepts cannot be structural kinds: they are either nominal or functional kinds. But, crucially, from this it does not follow that there is no space in legal thinking for structural kinds. Legal concepts are not ultimately structural, but there is space for a structural concept of (say) criminal law. Moore seems to believe that if a concept is functional, it must be immediately functional. In law, this denies the fundamental role of structures (of form). Structures mediate between function and individuation. What is individuated according to the function is a structure, and the members of the class are individuated structurally. 'Legislation', for example, is a functional concept. Legislation's function is to identify 'our' (the citizens') norms, so that to be subject to them is not to be subject to an alien will (i.e. oppression). If the concept were immediately functional, we would have to conclude that decisions formally presented as laws (i.e. adopted by the competent organ and procedure) are not laws if they are not an exercise of self-government. But this would mean that the law has no authority. The identification of law could be subject, for example, to the objection of false conscience: those who voted in favour of the law believed that it was what they wanted, but they do not know what they really want (this is, for example, the neo-liberal argument for labour-law reform: the workers think they want legal protection, but that is only because they do not

[75] The argument later developed in *Law's Empire* was previously presented in an article tellingly called 'Legal Theory and the Problem of Sense'. See his contribution to R. Gavison (ed.), *Issues in Contemporary Legal Philosophy. The Influence of H.L.A. Hart* (Oxford: Clarendon Press, 1989).

[76] M. Moore, *Placing Blame*, 22.

understand what is best for them. If they did know, they would see that increasing labour protection makes the workforce more expensive and thus increases unemployment). Legislation could never decide anything since its validity would always depend on its fulfilling its function to a sufficient degree. Therefore, 'law', in the sense of norms that claim authority and are thus binding on judges, the police, and citizens, is a functional concept (i.e. defined by its function), but one that is individuated not by reference to the function but to a structure functionally individuated. This allows for the partial autonomy of structural concepts (they are only ultimately functional, but most of the time there is no need to get to the ultimate nature of things). This is a consequence of the fact that law is not only a normative system, but also an institutionalized one. And institutionalization implies formal concepts (structures) and distribution of competencies; the fact that concept X is functional does not imply that whoever has the competence authoritatively to decide whether X is the case also has authority to decide it functionally. It is, in fact, not only possible but also usual that an official have legal authority to enforce X, but has to defer the decision of whether X applies to somebody else; this means that the official has no authority functionally to individuate X and must act on a structural individuation of it (= 'X is the case because someone with the authority so to declare, has decided that X is the case', and regardless of the fact that it functionally is or is not the case).

But in the end, the concept is functional, not structural. The tendency to think that the structural individuation of legal concepts excludes their being functional concepts is what is called 'formalism' (in a pejorative sense). The problem (law's improbability, we may say) is that function and structure are necessary, but they do not yield the same results (what is functionally a piece of legislation might not be so, structurally speaking). Mediating institutions solve this improbability since they are institutions that understand themselves functionally, but whose function is performed structurally. The problem of mediating institutions is that their normal working, blind to their function, tends to exclude the functional dimension (= 'formalism'), an exclusion that causes, in reaction, the abandonment or devaluation of the structure's crucial function (= arbitrariness). What we previously called the 'cycle of adjudication' shows this tension as it is played out in modern law. Moore's claim that function is decisive at both the ontological and the individuation level is a form of 'functional atomism' (because he believes that the conception of law as a functional kind implies that each member of the kind must fulfil that function). The argument here is that law's intelligibility assumes something we may call 'functional holism' (because the function individuates a structure and the structure individuates each member, which may become a structure because it has the adequate structure and not because, individually considered, it performs the function).

This was, in fact, our initial problem: the institutional form of the judicial process made necessary the recognition of judicial powers to non-judicial organs (the case of the *référé*). From a functional point of view, these powers are judicial in nature (the fact that they are vested in the legislative assembly is not decisive as to their nature). A theory of the judicial process must proceed, so to speak, in two steps: first, it must find the function that defines the judicial process and then it must understand the relationship between such a function and a given structure. The relationship between function and structure is that structure makes probable what is improbable (correct performance of function). Gény's point against the *référé* (that it was against its own purpose) can be understood now as a case of contradiction between function and structure: the structure not only failed to make more likely the correct performance of the function, but it actually made it unlikely.

E. Legislation and jurisdiction

1. To each their own

I want to begin with the old idea that law means giving to each their due. If this idea is to remain useful, we cannot understand it as it is presented in the *Digest*, i.e. as a definition of (the function of) law. This is because in this sense, it is a pre-modern concept of law, one without space for the modern idea of legislation, the self-conscious creation of new general and abstract legal norms. Therefore, if this idea is to remain relevant in understanding modern law, we must use it to characterize the (function of the) judicial process rather than law itself (and we will have to say about Roman law that it was a 'judicial' law in the sense that it was seen as progressively emerging from particular decisions. What emerged from these decisions was later systematized in the form of rules, but these rules were not like modern rules of law, they were what Rawls called 'summary rules'.[77] That is the reason why Romans could say rules, *regulae iuris*, did not create law but summarized it: 'a rule is something that briefly describes how something is. Law does not flow from the rules, but rules flow from law', says the *Digest*).[78] Giving to each their due means, in other words, giving to each what, according to valid and applicable rules, is his or her right. In modern law's conditions, there can be no adjudication without legislation. 'Modern law's conditions' are what J. Habermas and others have called a 'post-metaphysic' condition, that is to say, a condition in which nature and tradition no longer have direct normative force.[79] The function of nature and tradition in pre-modern law is now fulfilled by positive law, the 'sovereign will' in the terms of article 1 of the Chilean Civil Code. In the context of this article it is impossible fully to develop this idea, so we shall have to be brief here.

If in modern law the law is understood as will so that its validity is procedurally and not substantively determined, we cannot say the same about judicial decisions. Without going into the dispute of whether judges create or apply law, what a judge does is adjudication insofar as it aims to declare the rights of each party; a judicial decision claims validity insofar as it is a correct application of antecedently existing law. In other words, the judge's decision claims to be an application of law currently in force, not the creation of new law. This explains the need for justification characteristic of judicial decisions. It is not enough that an official simply declare his conviction that X follows from currently enforceable law. He must publicly offer the reasons why it does follow because the fact that X follows from currently enforceable law is internal to a judicial decision in the sense that it grounds its validity. This justification requirement does not exist regarding, for example, legislative decisions. The fact that legislative decisions need not be explicitly justified reflects the fact that they do not claim to be valid as correct applications of currently enforceable law. Within the legal system the law is valid because it is valid. If a litigant objects to the validity of a law for substantive reasons, the judge can simply point to its formal

[77] J. Rawls, 'Two Concepts of Rules' in S. Freeman (ed.), *John Rawls. Collected Papers* (orig. edn 1955, Oxford: Clarendon Press, 1999;), 20–46.

[78] 'A rule is something which briefly describes how a thing is. The law may not derive from a rule, but a rule must arise from the law as it is.' By means of a rule, therefore, a brief description of things is handed down and, as Sabinus says, is, as it were, 'the element of a case, which loses its force as soon as it becomes in any way defective' (Paul D. 50.17.1). On this, see F. Atria, *Law and Legal Reasoning*, 150–60.

[79] J. Habermas, *Between Facts and Norms* (orig. edn 1992, Cambridge, Mass.: Polity Press, 1996).

validity. If he objects that the judicial decision does not follow from enforceable law, the judge owes him an explanation.

The reason why it is wrong to define the judicial office by reference to the idea of law application is that not all law-applying decisions aim at giving each his or her due. After Kelsen, it is hard to deny that every act that is part of law's chain of production, with the only exception of the foundational act, is a law-applying act. Therefore, there is no coextension between giving each his own and applying law. But not every act has the point of administering justice in this sense or, in what amounts to the same, of applying the law without a goal other than giving each their due. Under the conditions of modern law, however, the opposite is true; giving to each their own necessarily assumes deciding according to law because the institution of legislation is the structural means of identifying the norms that are the citizen's. This shows the internal connection between the idea of giving each their own and the application of law, and also the improbability of adjudication. By the 'improbability' of adjudication I mean the tendency of institutions, whose function is to give each their own, to do something other than give each their own. The institutional organization of judicial office can be understood as the necessary means to, as much as it is possible, *neutralize* these sources of improbability, thus making jurisdiction probable.

2. Legislation and its function

According to article 1 of the Chilean Civil Code,

> a law is a declaration of the will of the sovereign which, given in the form prescribed in the constitution, is mandatory, prohibiting or permissive.

Note that this is a functional and structural definition. Functionally speaking, a law is the will of the sovereign. But it is not individuated by reference to the sovereign, but by the fact that it has been adopted according to the procedural rules contained in the Constitution. This is an application of the idea, developed above as an objection to Moore's functional atomism, that the fact that a concept is a functional kind does not imply that function immediately supplies an individuation test. A judge might think that a formally valid law is no law in the functional sense because it is not the will of the sovereign but a factious will, but he would not be acting as a judge if he were to declare that because of this it is not valid law. When it comes to individuation, structure is prior to function. But function is prior to structure in the sense that it is a condition of the intelligibility of structure.

What can it possibly mean to say that a law is 'the will of the sovereign'? After all, 'the sovereign' is 'the people' (or 'the nation') and it is difficult to say that collective entities like 'the people' or 'the nation' have mental states. This point, of course, requires further clarification, but here we can say this: the will of the sovereign is whatever goes in the interest of the sovereign; the will of the sovereign in a democratic state is whatever goes in the interest of all. Yet, of course, to say that a decision goes in the interest of all is not to say that it goes in the immediate interest of everybody. A decision to ban smoking is justified insofar as it reflects the proper balance between the immediate interests of smokers and non-smokers. The claim that it is in the interest of everybody is not reducible to the claim that it is in the immediate interest of each, but to the claim that it (a) takes all equally into account and (b) is impartial between the interests of everyone.

This (perhaps too) blunt statement was necessary to identify something, at least provisionally, as the function of legislation. The next step of the argument looks at structure. The structural feature of legislative decisions that I want to focus upon now is that they are abstract conditional statements; given certain conditions, some legal consequences follow: if abc, then d.

Each of the antecedent's terms (a, b, and c) is a *property*.[80] A property is a feature of a state of affairs that may be true or false. A group of properties identifies a *case*. The consequent may be called a 'solution' (which commands, forbids, or allows the performance of an action). Note that both cases and solutions may be *generic* or *specific*: a generic case is a group of properties, while a specific case is an existing state of affairs in the world. A specific case 'corresponds' to a generic case when it is a state of affairs of which the properties defining the generic case are true. Thus, legislative decisions correlate generic cases with generic solutions. Connecting now the two things that we have already noted, the passage of a law according to which 'when abc, then d' means that the legislator has decided that it is in everyone's interest that the (generic) case identified by properties abc be correlated with the (generic) solution d. It seems that from the above explanation of legislation, the following account of the judicial function follows: judges must declare whether a particular state of affairs corresponds (or not) to a generic case correlated by a law with a generic solution and, therefore, whether it must (or must not) be correlated with the specific solution corresponding to the generic solution contained in the law. Twentieth-century legal theory rejected this understanding of judicial office (the judge as an automaton). The reason for this, as we have seen, was the possibility of incomplete expression; since posited rules are full of gaps, ambiguities, and antinomies, the idea that the correlation between the generic and the specific case can be thought of as the (merely cognitive) process of 'finding' whether the (generic) properties are true of the case, is 'a myth'.

If the argument contained in the first section of this article were correct, this is a case of reaching a correct conclusion for wrong reasons. It is obvious that in cases of obscurity, gaps, or contradiction, the judge cannot mechanically apply the law since there is no law to be mechanically applied. It is, however, perfectly possible to endorse the 'mechanical' vision of law application and claim that, in some cases, it is impossible. The point, in other words, that laws are sometimes of incomplete expression does not warrant the rejection of the judge-as-automaton theory; to accommodate it, all that is necessary is to admit that not all that judges *do* is exercise judicial powers. Curiously enough, in discarding the idea of the judge as an automaton for this reason, twentieth century legal theory actually endorsed a mechanical approach to the application of law. Hart (for example) and the nineteenth-century formalists are not in disagreement when it comes to explaining what it is to apply the law to a particular case: the disagreement appears when we ask whether this is all judges do (Hart would then claim that this is impossible in areas of penumbra). Their disagreement is not, in other words, a disagreement about what it is to apply the law. They disagree as to whether this is always possible. Hence, the academic folklore mentioned above: since there is agreement as to what counts as applying the law, what explains the rejection of nineteenth-century formalism must be found somewhere else; this is solved by ascribing to the nineteenth-century jurist the extravagant belief that, precisely when the law began to be understood as the contingent will of the sovereign, it began to be thought of as something perfect! Once this implausible belief is ascribed to the jurists of the codification movement, the contemporary legal theorist can loudly reject it.

[80] Here I adopt the useful terminology introduced by C.E. Alchourrón and E. Bulygin, *Normative Systems* (Vienna: Springer, 1971).

If we are to abandon the idea of the judge as an automaton while holding to the idea of fidelity to law, what needs to be revised is precisely the understanding of what counts as 'applying' law to a case; what, oddly enough, is common to nineteenth and twentieth century legal theory.

3. The form of law

We go back now to the two observations above about legislation: legislation correlates generic cases with generic solutions, and its institutional meaning is that it constitutes a declaration of the sovereign's will (that is to say, of what becomes everybody's interests). That both things are related is not accidental; the point of structural features that define the legislator as a constituted power have, as their point, to make probable that whatever is passed as a law becomes everybody's interest and it is obvious that one of the main aspects of this is that the decision must be abstract. This is not, of course, the only condition. The aim of making sure that decisions are in the interest of all when adopted through a procedure that can filter out particular interests goes a long way towards explaining not only gross, but also some minor aspects of, the legislative process and the legislative organ: its composition, its modes of action, its rules of debate and opportunities for decision, etc. However, it is the first condition (that legislative decisions are abstract in the sense that they correlate generic and not specific cases and solutions) that is key. It implies that the legislator could only have decided that the abstract decision was in everybody's interest. And the problem is that from the fact that it is in everyone's interest (i.e. it is justified, it is the will of the people) that the generic case be correlated with a generic solution it does not follow that every case whose description corresponds to the generic case is a case in which the generic solution becomes the interest of everybody.

The problem has been discussed at length in moral and legal theory. It has appeared under different labels, but it is always the same: the (possibility of the) distinction between act utilitarianism and rule utilitarianism; the plausibility of a 'situational ethic' and the problem of ethical particularism in general; the distinction between rules and principles; the defeasibility of rules, etc. In all of these cases, the problem is always the same, that is, the relationship between a generic case correlated by a rule with a generic solution and the question of whether that immediately implies a solution to a relevant specific case. It might be useful to consider one of the instances of this controversy. Kant and Benjamin Constant discussed the consequences of accepting a generic norm such as 'thou shall not lie'.[81] The fact that the norm 'thou shall not lie' is valid means that it works in everyone's interest. Using the terminology of discourse ethics, which provides an especially adequate context for this discussion, we may express this condition of validity of a general norm in the form of a principle of universalization 'U': a norm can claim to be valid if it can meet with the approval of all affected. Now, Constant asked himself, what if the secret police of a terrorist regime appear at my door inquiring as to the whereabouts of a friend who has gone into hiding? Kant's point was that from the fact that the norm against lying was a justified norm there followed an 'unconditional' duty not to lie. To say that there is a valid norm according to which 'thou shalt not lie' is to say that the command 'thou shalt not lie' works in everybody's

[81] I. Kant, 'On a Supposed Right to Lie from Philanthropy' in I. Kant, *Practical Philosophy* (Cambridge: Cambridge University Press, 1996). B. Constant, *Curso de Política Constitucional* (Madrid: Taurus, 1968).

interests, and from that it follows (so Kant claimed) that telling the truth becomes everybody's interest in each possible case of application, including Constant's case. But this is clearly unwarranted. It is one thing to say that it is in everybody's interest that we have an obligation to tell the truth, and it is something else to say that I have a duty to tell the truth in Constant's case. The former means that 'thou shalt not lie' can be grounded on reasons that give the same weight to the interests of each; the latter means that, given the particular circumstances of the case, the application of the norm to it takes into due account the way in which the norm affects the interests of all actually involved.[82] The problem in the former case can be solved by reference to abstract reason and in the latter case by the idea of impartial application.

The problem is that this distinction threatens to make the principle U irrelevant. This was probably the reason that led Kant to hold the implausible view that the duty to tell the truth is unconditional in the sense in which he so claimed against Constant. The problem could be described by saying that when the (abstract) reasons to ground the norm against lying were considered, we failed to notice the possibility of a case like Constan's; had we considered it, we would have phrased the norm differently. To compensate this deficit, we may go back to the abstract norm and modify it, adding an exception to it (like 'lying is permissible if it is necessary to save the life of an innocent person unjustly persecuted by the secret police of a terrorist regime'). This, of course, solves our present problem, but fails to guarantee that it will not arise in the future, by reference to a different unusual case. To avoid having to modify the norm each time an unusual case presents itself, we might be inclined to add to the norm a generic exception (like 'lying is permissible when it is correct, all things considered, to lie'). But then the norm becomes redundant, in a rather obvious way: one has the duty to tell the truth when it is correct to tell the truth not because there is a norm to that effect, but because it is correct. In one of two different ways, therefore, to solve the problem of 'recalcitrant' cases seems to rob norms of their normativity: in the former case, because from the fact that no (explicit) exception is applicable to the case at hand, we could not conclude that the rule is to be applied (the case could be a novel 'recalcitrant' case); in the latter, because in order to know that the rule applies, we need independently to establish that acting according to it is correct, in which case the rule comes too late to contribute to the decision.

Constant's point was that in order to conclude that one has the duty to lie in the circumstances he was discussing, it was not necessary to deny the general validity of the norm against lying. It is reasonable to understand the rule against lying as forbidding, say, the telling of a lie in order to manipulate someone into doing something for one's immediate profit. The norm against lying expresses our understanding that lying in normal cases such as this would show lack of respect for the other as an end in itself. In order to do this, we need not pause to consider, for example, how the would-be liar plans to invest the resources thus obtained. But it is not reasonable to understand that the decision contained in the norm refers to cases like Constant's; the norm does not express a decision in cases such as this, for while the interests of each involved have been considered by reference to normal cases, the question of what is in the interests of everybody in special cases like Constant's has been left as open as it was before.

In terms of discourse ethics, this means that the principle of universalization, to be workable, must be broken up into two principles: one controls the justification

[82] For an insightful discussion of the distinction between application and justification see K. Günther, *The Sense of Appropriateness* (Albany: SUNY, 1993), *passim*.

(validity) of norms and the other controls the application of norms. The first one understands the idea of impartiality behind U in a universal and reciprocal sense ('Have the interests of all those affected by the norm been equally considered?'), while the other understands impartiality in an applicative sense ('Is the norm whose application we are discussing one that treats the parties' interests impartially when applied to the case?'). It is important to note that, although the idea is the same (impartiality), it appears in a sufficiently different way in each principle, so applying one is not reducible to applying the other.[83] This point is relevant because it shows that the necessity of opening an application discourse does not imply denying what was decided in the corresponding justification discourse. Justification and application differ in their content, i.e. in what is subject to discursive determination:

> In reality, it may often seem as if justification and application discourses could not be separated analytically, from one another... This objection does not hold true; it arises as a result of the appearance that those arguments which are relevant in application discourse are also relevant in justification discourses. But the criterion according to which their relevance is judged are different in both discourses. Whereas in justification discourses it is exclusively a matter of the generalizability of articulated interests independent of a particular situation, in application discourses it is precisely a question of situation-specific interests, which are unimportant for the validity of a norm.[84]

This distinction between justification and application provides the key to understanding the institutional distinction between legislative and judicial power. It also shows why the idea of the judge as a 'mere' applicator of law is not defective because judges sometimes do something different from applying the law (in cases of incomplete legal expression, for example), but for the more important reason that it fails to understand what applying the law is. We can now say that the problem with the automaton is not that it is sometimes impossible, but that it does not apply the law to the particular case; instead, it reiterates the universality of the law in the particularity of the case.

At this point we can go back to Savigny's distinction between incomplete and improper legal expression. The focus is now on the latter, which will provide us with a clue to understanding the nature of the judicial function. Two points should be noted. The first concerns the way in which Savigny refers both to improper and to incomplete expression as 'defects of law'. But this common language disguises a further significant difference. Incomplete expression is a property of a general norm ('on its face', as they say in American law), while improper expression is a property of a norm as applied to a case. It would be strange to say that the norm 'thou shalt not lie' is an improper expression. It seems more proper to say that the expression of the norm is improper in a case like Constant's. Incomplete expression is a defect of the general norm, while improper expression is a consequence of a particularity in the case. The problem of incomplete expression is that the (abstract) legislative decision is incomplete; in other words, it is a problem appreciable *in abstract*, with no reference to any case whatsoever. The cases in which the issue is discussed provide the institutional opportunity to face the problem, but the problem exists before the cases. The same does not happen with improper expression. Here the problem is not in the abstract legal norm but in the case; what we should say is that the expression, applied to the case,

[83] Thus, one can have a justified norm the application of which is inadequate (see the discussion in the main text) and a non-justified norm the application of which is adequate. An example of the latter case is something like racist contract law in Nazi Germany, as applied to a case in which none of the parties was a victim of persecution or discrimination.

[84] K. Günther, *The Sense of Appropriateness*, 124.

solves it in an improper way, and solves it improperly not because *the law* is defective, but because *the case* is special. An improper expression is not abstractly improper: it is improper facing the facts of the case.

The second point to be noted is that, *pace* Savigny, the improper expression is not, as the incomplete expression, a defect of the law. The conscious creation of general and abstract norms (i.e. legislation) would be impossible if the passing of a law implied the claim that the correlation between generic cases and solutions contained in it were presumed to hold true for each and every case in which the abstract properties obtain. If that were the claim, legislation would require (to put it in Hart's terms) a level of clarity of purpose and knowledge of the world that is incompatible with the human condition.[85] Moreover, this would probably require that the law use a language so specific and precise that it would be difficult for citizens to understand. This, of course, does not mean that the problem cannot be considerably reduced by a careful drafting of legislated rules; it only implies that the aim cannot be to avoid improper expression so that when they arise, we cannot say that they are cases in which laws proved to be defective.

But this point is not given full weight when the argument is presented as if it were grounded solely on the legislators' volitional and cognitive deficits, howsoever important they might be. It also has to do with the function of legislation, that of ascertaining what works in the interests of all. Legislation as an institutional fact becomes necessary as a consequence of the improbability of its function being 'naturally' (i.e. non-institutionally, spontaneously) performed. What makes improbable the ascertaining of what is in everybody's interests is the way in which common interests and factious interests are confused in the political process. They are confused not because it is hard to tell them apart, but because the distinction is purely substantive. A political demand (as opposed to, say, military or economic pressure) is defined by the claim that it becomes the interests of everybody. Of course, the fact that it *claims* to go in the interests of everybody does not mean that it actually does. Political deliberation, be it institutionalized in legislative procedures or informal as public opinion, performs a filtering function, filtering, that is, the particular interests so that (it becomes probable that) political decisions serve common interests. Hence, politically speaking, identifying a position on a given issue as one that serves particular, and not common interests, is the same as refuting it. The institutional question, therefore, is 'how can the legislative process be structured in order for it to be successful in discriminating among propositions that are in everyone's interest and propositions that claim to be in the common interest, but actually serve factious interest?'

A complete answer to this question is a theory of legislation. Here the point is only to connect these considerations with the abstract and general character of the legislative decision. Recall the point above that the *référé* was contrary to its own end. At this point it was stated that the fact that the legislator correlates generic cases with generic solutions and does not deal with specific cases and solutions was central. We can now see why. If the decision is a decision about the solution of a generic case, this means that a decision or proposal of legislative decision must be formulated in language that makes it more difficult (i.e. more improbable) to identify factious interests in order to serve them. This end is also served by the fact that legislative decisions are not taken immediately by the citizens, but by their representatives (failure to see this point leads to the mistaken view that representative democracy is 'second-best', that the ideal form

[85] H.L.A. Hart, *The Concept of Law*, 128ff.

of democracy is direct democracy). The fact that the legislator decides no particular case as well as the fact that the legislator is not just a speaker for the (particular) interests of his or her (local) constituents are not shortcomings of really existing democracies; they are institutional mechanisms that pursue the goal of making democratic self-government probable.

4. Adjudication, legislation, and the citizen's dignity

Now we can pull together the threads of the argument. Recall Bentham's criticism of the common law. In his view, the system of precedent (in that it forces the judge to decide not as he thinks is correct given the facts of the case, but according to past decisions) leads to 'acting without reason, to the declared exclusion of reason, and thereby in declared opposition to reason'.[86] The judge might think that it is reasonable to declare the defendant's action 'permitted', but there is a precedent according to which it must be declared 'prohibited'. There might be reasons behind precedent, as there are reasons behind the judge's opinion. Precisely what the judge cannot do is to directly address the issue of which set of reasons is stronger. Instead of discussing what is really crucial to the decision, i.e. whether it is rational to punish the defendant, the judge can and must discuss a different issue, a *formal* one, i.e. is this case covered by past precedents? To Bentham, this was the wrong question to ask. He thought that this way of reaching a decision was tantamount to deciding *arbitrarily*.

This is not, of course, the place to discuss the substance of this argument, whether or not Bentham's criticism of the common law was fair to it.[87] We may wonder, however, whether a similar objection is applicable to the judge whose function is to decide according, not to precedent, but to legislation. We have already seen that Bentham answered this question negatively because he thought that legislation would put an end to the irrationality of the common law. But we have also seen that in this sense, his hopes were somewhat exaggerated because codification led to a kind of formalism that was rather close to the formalism of common law. As P.S. Atiyah has shown, the real target of Bentham's criticism seems to be the position of a judge who must decide according to rules and not according to what is rational. And now our question must be 'if the judge passes judgment against him, can the defendant complain that he has been mistreated because the judge could not discuss the rationality or reasonableness of the (abstract) prohibition according to which he was punished?'

In a 'normal' case, the answer is trivially negative: the decision is not arbitrary (not for that reason anyway) because the issue was excluded from the jurisdiction of the judge as a consequence of the fact that it had already been decided: it was discussed and decided by parliament that in normal cases, what is in everyone's interest is X. The defendant's complaint is not really a complaint against the arbitrariness of the judicial decision, but against the fact that the judge accepts that the decision about the legality of his action is not the judge's decision. Note that the decision that the judge defers to the legislator is not related to the *specific* case, but to the *generic* case. And what is decisive here is which organ (the legislator or the judge) is in a better institutional position to solve the generic case. The answer again is obvious. If the answer holds, the defendant's complaint may be easily answered; it is not that the substantive

[86] Bentham, quoted in P.S. Atiyah, 'Form and Substance in Contract Law' in *Essays on Contract* (Oxford: Clarendon Press, 1984), 93–120.

[87] See generally ibid.

considerations according to which his case was decided have not been considered, but that they were considered by the legislator. The formal ('exclusionary') reasons that justify the judge's lack of competence to discuss the substantive reasons are institutional means of protecting the competencies assigned to organs that, because of their different configuration, are in a better position to decide the question about the justification of those rules, i.e. to decide what is in everyone's interest.

But things are considerably different when the case is one of improper expression. The defendant's complaint here will not be that the judge failed to consider the reasons justifying the correlation between the generic case and the generic solution, he will claim that his case is special so that the solution of the generic case, howsoever justified it might be, does not impartially take his interests into account. It fails to do so because the legislator did not consider cases like the particular case under discussion, but decided by reference to normal, typical cases. Since (or insofar as) the case is an abnormal one, nobody has decided it: the legislator did not consider what was in everybody's interests in a case like this, and the judge, if acting as an automaton, will refuse to raise the exclusionary veil and look at the reasons behind the abstract norm. Now Bentham's critique reappears with all its force: the decision is arbitrary because no one has decided that this action deserves sanction *in those circumstances*; the defendant's interests were never considered by anybody, neither the legislator nor the judge. The problem is not that the legislator decided the case unfairly. *The legislator has not decided the case*; the legislator has taken a decision that reflects his judgement about how the interests of everybody must be served in normal, typical cases. After weighing and balancing all the conflicting interests, it is in everyone's interest that the action X be prohibited. But an unusual, atypical, abnormal case is one in which different interests are involved. The legislator has decided nothing in respect of this weighing of these different interests.

Now we can, at last, formulate the main objection to the idea of mechanical application of law. If this idea is defended (as the nineteenth-century jurist did, *pace* the folklore), accepting, in principle, the possibility of laws of improper expression, then we must say that they did so as a sort of *trade-off*: if the judge were to have the power to correct the improper expression, the risk is that, 'under the pretext' of doing so, the judge will modify the law; if judges do not have this power, the risk is that of heaping miseries on the heads of those by whom we know this to be unmerited. A choice is necessary, or so the argument goes, because both risks cannot be avoided. The first risk is that democratic self-government become impossible or unsustainable as long as judges will not be bound to law if they do not believe it to be substantively correct (i.e. they will not be bound to law); the second risk is deciding on a person's life, property, or liberty by reference to a law that does not take his interests into account. A choice for 'mechanical' application of law pays the price of heaping unmerited miseries upon the heads of some to make democratic self-government possible. And those upon whose heads miseries are heaped and known to be unmerited are then used as a means to make democratic self-government institutionally possible.

Thus, political life is impossible without oppression. This is the way in which I believe it is useful to understand the dilemma faced by the codification movement: if law is an expression of will, then that will can only be our will; any other solution is heteronomy, i.e. oppression. If the judge can correct the improper legal expression, there is no way in which he can be prevented from using this power as a pretext and changing the law when he does not like it. There is then no subjection to our will but to the judge's. But if, in order to avoid this heteronomy, we bind the judge to law's expression, then we oppress (i.e. use instrumentally) those who, in cases of inappropriateness of legal expression, see their rights affected with no consideration for their interests. Their interests are the price we pay for our democratic freedom.

Since the judge applies the law, the judge *qua* judge cannot question its validity. This was always the most powerful argument for the idea of 'mechanical' judges. Indeed, it is a premise that must be preserved after doing away with the idea of the judge as an automaton. We have seen that this understanding of the judicial process must be rejected, but we must accept the premise from which it starts. The conclusion to be rejected follows from the premise to be preserved only with the help of a minor premise that must also be rejected: that applying the law is nothing but repeating its expression, replacing its universal quantifier ('for all X') by an indexical expression ('this X'). In other words, under the conditions of modern law (i.e. law as something artificially made), legislative and judicial power must be understood by reference to each other. The idea, so common to recent legal theory, that the judicial function can be understood without reference to legislation can only make sense as an attempt to provide a structural explanation of the concept of a judge. But as we have seen, structural explanations of legal concepts are impossible: they reveal themselves to be, at the end, either functional or nominal explanations. A functional explanation of the idea of a judge must begin by noticing the division of labour between judges and legislators. This is too prominent a feature of all modern legal systems to be irrelevant. Furthermore, it must explain the notorious structural differences between them. The structural differences are so significant and so uniform across different legal systems that they must correspond to a difference in function. It is a form of division of labour that corresponds, as we have seen, to the breaking down of the principle of universalization into two: one of justification of norms and one of application of norms.

The institutional form of the legislative power aims at making it probable that whatever decisions manage to get through the legislative process reflect the interests of everyone involved in typical cases. That is why legislative bodies are always assemblies that claim to represent, at least in principle, all citizens. The legislator need not consider any particular case; it considers the norm whose justification is at issue from the point of view of the reasons that may be offered for and against it. Indeed, the consideration of particular cases during the legislative process usually makes it less, rather than more, probable that a decision that is structurally legislative (because it was adopted through the legislative process) will be functionally legislative (in everybody's interests).

When the issue is that of applying to a particular case a norm that has been justified (i.e. posited through the legislative procedure), there is no reason to go back to the question of whether it becomes the interests of all. This is the point made at the beginning of this section: the legislative decision cannot be revised by the judge (*qua* judge) because the structure of the judicial process is not one that makes it likely that through it what is in the interest of all will be correctly determined. The judicial function is defined not by the need to decide on general norms, but on concrete cases. For the judge (*qua* judge), the question is what is owed to the parties. Why is this improbable so that institutional form is necessary? The answer lies in the very idea of a judge: we have seen that this office is required by a full recognition of the dignity of the citizen, which immediately implies that they cannot be used as means. It is improbable that the official called 'judge' will decide the case as a judge, i.e. without pursuing some goal beyond that of giving each his due. It is at this point that we can go back to Cappelletti's structural characterization of the judicial process and note that those structural features (to which the features generically labelled 'judicial independence'—i.e. subjection to law—must be added) can be understood as an institutional means of ensuring (making probable) that when the moment comes for a particular case to be solved by the application of a general rule, the possibility will be there for the citizen to ask an official to look at his particular case and decide it without any goal beyond that of ascertaining what is owed to that citizen. This is the reason why judicial institutions are designed (a) to maximize the possibility that all the relevant elements of the particular case before the judge be subject to a scrutiny as close as necessary, and (b) to minimize the possibility that when it comes to deciding the case, the judge pursue goals or ends different from giving each their own. This is the important insight behind the idea of *res ipsa loquitur* ('the thing speaks for itself'). This expression is absurd if it is understood to imply that things have, so to speak, immanent normativity. Things and facts obviously get their institutional significance from institutional rules, and in this sense, they do not *ipsae loquuntur*, speak for themselves. But having this (important) caveat in mind, it is possible to understand that the sense of this aphorism is to underscore the fact that the judge must let himself be struck by the singularity of the case. In a metaphoric, yet not imaginary, sense, judicial power consists in *letting the facts speak*, in attending to the case in order to appreciate it in its own terms and decide it according to the law of the citizen. The argument of this article could be seen as a development of the meaning of this last sentence. The normal understanding of these issues seems to imply that there are two different ways of conceiving judges and the judicial function, depending on whether one begins with the idea of application of law or that of administration of justice. The point of this paper has been to show that, under the conditions of modern law, these two seemingly contradictory views can be integrated (indeed, can only be understood if integrated).

20

Defeasibility and Adjudication

*Richard H.S. Tur**

'Into every tidy scheme for arranging the pattern of human life, it is necessary to inject a certain dose of anarchism.'

(Bertrand Russell, *Sceptical Essays*).

'The life of the law has not been logic; it has been experience.'

(O.W. Holmes, *The Common Law* (1881), 1).

A. Goldilocks

I start with the imperfectibility of rules and what I call my 'Goldilocks' thesis: 'even the most carefully drafted rules fail to achieve perfect fit. However painstakingly drafted, a rule may include some cases which morally should be excluded and it may exclude cases which morally should be included. Rules are either too wide and hard or too narrow and soft, frequently both and never, like the porridge or the bed in the fairy tale, "just right".'[1]

Acknowledging the imperfectibility of rules raises a question about what to do in 'hard cases' (in the sense of an unwelcome result rather than any defect of rules), such as *R (on the application of Pretty)* v. *DPP* which concerned a married couple's wish that the husband assist the severely disabled wife (who was suffering from an incurable illness and enduring great pain, discomfort, and distress) end her own life,[2] notwithstanding the clear words of the Suicide Act 1961. The English courts and the European Court of Human Rights did not treat this as a defeasible rule; quite the reverse. To my mind there is something fundamentally wrong in saying to such a person, 'Well you have had a miserable time and morally we quite see that you should be allowed the assistance you seek in ending your own life, but you know, the greater good of society requires that you should continue to suffer for fear of being a bad example—hard cases make bad law'. Morally, society simply should not use someone like this unfortunate woman as a means only and not as an end in herself. Nor may society 'impose an excessive burden on the individual'.[3] This has been judicially reasserted recently with some emphasis.[4]

* Benn Law Fellow, Oriel College (Oxford). Whereas I take sole responsibility for this submission, I am extremely grateful to all participants in a 'Defeasibilism Workshop' in Oxford in March 2008 for their generous and helpful comments; and to Jordi Ferrer Beltrán and Giovanni Battista Ratti who are the moving spirits behind the collection of essays to which mine is a modest contribution and whose intellectual support and friendship I sincerely value.

[1] R.H.S. Tur, 'Legislative technique and human rights: the sad case of assisted suicide', *Criminal Law Review*, (2003), 3–12.

[2] [2001] EWHC Admin 788; [2002] 1 All ER.

[3] *International Transport Roth GmbH* v. *Home Secretary* [2002] 3 WLR 344, 365 *per* Simon Brown LJ, citing *James* v. *UK* (1986) 8 EHRR 123, 144–5.

[4] *Huang* v. *Secretary of State for Home Department* [2007] UKHL 11, at para. 19.

B. Justice?

The question naturally arises as to what might or should be done in the face of such rule-generated injustice? Law and legal systems can do something or nothing. I advocate doing something. Not everyone agrees. One robust, even heroic, response is to do injustice in order to preserve certainty, or to further important social policy. For example, according to Lord Hoffmann, 'the IAAF's system for the control of drug abuse is plainly draconian. It carries the risk of grave injustice to an athlete if a laboratory test should be wrong... I think that the IAAF adopted its system... in the belief that although it might sometimes cause injustice in the individual case, it was necessary in the wider interests of the sport.'[5] This raises questions of trade-off: how much individual injustice is tolerable in a system of rules? For some, and I agree, 'a sound rule must not be applied so rigidly that it becomes a denial of justice'.[6] Yet in the *Pretty* appeal all the judges, including the author of the splendid aphorism just quoted, applied section 2(1) so rigidly as to deny justice.

C. Rules rule, unless...

I draw two conclusions from these examples. First, even allowing that 'justice' may function (as manifestly it does) as an overarching adjudicative category of defeasance overriding rule-determined outcomes, it need not do so and it is no part of a defeasibilist's approach to law and legal systems that judges must defeat rules where rule-application generates injustice. The defeasibilist's descriptive claim is that judges sometimes do this and do it commonly enough for it to be flagged as a salient feature of law or legal systems. The defeasibilist's prescriptive claim is that judges should do it more and more openly, as being consistent with judicial vocation to do justice. The defeasibilist's may also be a conceptual claim but that argument is beyond the scope of this paper.

D. The practical effect of legal theories

My second interim conclusion is that there is no reason to suppose that all judges adopt or deploy the same legal theory and that there is good reason to suppose that the theory of law adopted tacitly or expressly by judges impacts on their decisions. In this, as in some other jurisprudential matters, I follow Lon Fuller.[7] To my mind, Lord Hoffmann is a devotee of 'ethical positivism', that is a conception of law that opposes the intercession of moral deliberation in the identification or application of law.[8] It therefore does not surprise that his view in *Modahl* privileges certainty over justice, as he puts it, 'in the interests of sport'. But there are judges who take a different view of their role. They adopt what has been aptly called a 'recourse role'.

[5] *Modahl* v. *British Athletic Federation Limited*, *The Times*, 23 July 1999.
[6] *R (on the application of Pretty)* v. *DPP* [2002] 1 All ER 1, para. 77, *per* Lord Hope.
[7] L. Fuller, 'The Case of the Speluncean Explorers', *Harvard Law Review*, 62 (1949), 616–45; see, too, P. Suber, *The Case of the Speluncean Explorers: Nine New Opinions* (London and New York: Routledge, 1998).
[8] T. Campbell, *The Legal Theory of Ethical Positivism* (Aldershot: Dartmouth, 1996).

E. Recourse role

A recourse role is a role that enables the agent to take action in situations where the role's prescribed ends conflict with its prescribed means.[9] The end or objective of adjudication may be 'doing justice'; the means are 'applying rules'. Sometimes, perhaps more often than some legal theorists or judges are willing to concede, these are in conflict. Recourse roles provide for such situations by establishing conditions under which the agent may be justified in undertaking actions that depart from the primary role requirements. Recourse roles extend a liberty in handling role obligations. The judicial duty to 'apply the law' may be taken—and is taken by some judges and legal theorists—to be 'exclusionary'[10] or 'all-or-nothing'[11] and not susceptible of override on moral or common sense grounds, or otherwise.[12] This 'recourse' approach to judicial decision-making parallels moral decision-making, in which the choice between conflicting obligations is left to the agent as a responsibility of the role. Of course a role need not necessarily be structured like this but it can sometimes be that moral dilemmas occurring within the role are part of the role itself. What is at issue is how might we characterize the judicial role?

The notion of a recourse role may be more fully developed by considering it (and the theory of law of which it is an element) as an alternative to each of two extremes in legal thinking. First, what I shall call 'legalism' sanctifies following the rules without question, celebrates the rule of law and fidelity to law, and leads to a conception of good judges, good lawyers, and good citizens as 'subsumption automatons'.[13] This is what some American legal realists have referred to as 'rule-fetishism'.[14] Secondly, what I shall call 'anarchism' (or wild-card discretion) sanctifies the moral conscience of the sovereign individual, celebrates agents who always do their best according to their own lights, and leads to a conception of good judges, good lawyers, and good citizens as creative, questing, untamed, free spirits. This second approach exhibits a high degree of rule-scepticism. Both extremes are equally unreal and equally dependent on an inapt conception of what a 'rule' is and of what 'acting in accordance with a rule' might be.

As an alternative to both extreme approaches (said by critics, perhaps unkindly, to be conjoined in Hart's conception of law) consider a role that both requires conformity to its rules *and* extends a liberty to deviate from its rules in appropriate circumstances. Consider, that is, a role that 'is structured to allow the role agent to evaluate the consequences of adhering to the role's prescribed means in terms of the role's prescribed

[9] This discussion draws heavily on M.R. Kadish and S.H. Kadish, *Discretion to Disobey* (Stanford: Stanford University Press, 1973), 35–6 and revisits and develops ideas discussed in R.H.S. Tur, 'Medical Confidentiality and Disclosure: Moral Conscience and Legal Constraints', *Journal of Applied Philosophy*, 15 (1998), 15–28.

[10] J. Raz, *Practical Reason and Norms* (London: Hutchinson, 1975), esp. ch. 1.2.

[11] R. Dworkin, *Taking Rights Seriously* (London: Duckworth, 1977); B. Simpson, 'The Common Law and Legal Theory' in W. Twining (ed.), *Legal Theory and the Common Law* (Oxford: Blackwell, 1986), ch. 2.

[12] For example, the dissent in *Riggs* v. *Palmer* 115 NY 506, 22 NE 188 (1889) and the majority *Tennessee Valley Authority* v. *Hill* 437 US 153 (1978).

[13] See M. La Torre, 'Formalism and Anti-Formalism in Modern Law—State Law and Beyond' in W. Krawietz, N. MacCormick, and G.H. von Wright (eds), *Prescriptive Formality and Normative Rationality in Modern Legal Systems—Festschrift for Robert S. Summers* (Berlin: Duncker & Humblot, 1994), 647–72, esp. 658, attributing this phrase to Regina Ogorek.

[14] J. Frank, *Law and the Modern Mind* (New York: Coward-McCann, 1930, 1949), 81, 283; F.S. Cohen, 'Transcendental Nonsense and the Functional Approach', *Columbia Law Review*, 3 (1935), 809–49.

ends'.[15] A judge, on such a view, should always ask not only what the legal rules require but also if the rule-determined outcome is acceptable in terms of value and sense. The presumptive nature of the primary obligations of the role—here, to apply the rules according to their (literal or ordinary) meaning—are such that one requires an overriding or compelling reason, 'damn good reason',[16] to deviate. The rules of a role are tried and tested and have a toughness or 'stickiness' that is not easily overridden,[17] but they also have a cultural contingency that renders them properly open to continuing review by role agents. What we can see here, then, is still an obligation to comply but no longer the absolute obligation pre-supposed by legalists and anarchists alike. What we can see is an obligation equipped with a liberty. That is a distinct conception of obligation. If there is a defeasibilist theory of law, it would be defeasibilist all the way through.

F. Exceptions and overrides

A major issue in jurisprudence is the nature and logical status of the legal proposition. Here I take as a point of departure the 'canonical form of the norm', that is, 'if A is, then B ought to be'.[18] If this is taken at face value it produces a highly legalistic account of judicial process that is descriptively inaccurate and normatively unappealing.[19] For example, a judge (Justice Gray) would be required either legalistically to grant a felonious beneficiary an inheritance under the will of a murdered testator or to act anarchically outside the law in order to do justice (Justice Earl).[20] This alternative has seemed unattractive to many, not least (in different ways) to Herbert Hart and to his successor at Oxford, Ronald Dworkin.

Hart's solution has great attractions for me. He observed that 'to argue in this way is to ignore what rules are in any sphere of real life. It suggests that we are faced with the dilemma: "Either rules are what they would be in the formalist's heaven and they bind as fetters bind; or there are no rules, only predictable decisions or patterns of behaviour." Yet surely this is a false dilemma. A rule that ends with the word "unless . . . " is still a rule.'[21] This is a basis of my own idea that law may be best understood as open-ended, defeasible, normative, conditional propositions, that is in the form, 'if A is then B ought to be, unless . . . '. The unless clause falls to be filled in, depending on which area of law is under consideration, by equity (contract), policy (tort), mercy (criminal law), rights and derogation (constitutional and administrative law), and purpose (statutory interpretation). This account of law seeks to be faithful to what judges do in the creative development of legal doctrine over time, not only in common law and constitutional adjudication, but also in the application of statutes.

Kadish and Kadish observe that 'we may say that the legal system extends to the judge a liberty to interpose his own judgment in place of the rule' and they cite the following judicial outburst, reported in 1966, as 'not at all untypical': 'This is ridiculous law, passed in the heat of passion without any thought as to its real consequences. I absolutely refuse to send to prison for twenty years a young boy who has done nothing

[15] M.R. Kadish and S.H. Kadish, *Discretion to Disobey*, 61.

[16] Ibid., 62.

[17] See F. Schauer, 'The Jurisprudence of Reasons', *Michigan Law Review*, 85 (1987), 867.

[18] M. Golding, *Philosophy of Law* (Englewood Cliffs, NJ: Prentice-Hall, 1975), 39; and see H. Kelsen, *The Pure Theory of Law* (Berkeley: University of California Press, 1967).

[19] See R. Dworkin, *Taking Rights Seriously*, and R. Dworkin, *Law's Empire* (London: Fontana, 1986).

[20] The *locus classicus* is *Riggs* v. *Palmer* 115 NY 506 (1889).

[21] H.L.A. Hart, *The Concept of Law* (Oxford: Clarendon Press, 1961), 136.

more than sell a single marijuana cigarette to a buddy. The law was not intended for such cases. I have been accused of usurping commutation and pardon powers. This is not true. I simply will not give excessive sentences and where the legislature leaves me no alternative, I will lower the charge or dismiss altogether.'[22] Clearly, this judge's view of the judicial role is consistent with that role being understood as a recourse role and with rules of law (even statutory rules) being understood as subject to defeasance for good reason. Moreover, this I take to be a 'defeasance proper', albeit intellectually crude, in that it is override, not exception. As is well-understood a rule plus exception is logically equivalent to a rule once the exception is moved from the *apodosis* to the *protasis*. Indeed, I believe that exclusive legal positivism (and perhaps 'presumptive legal positivism')[23] may have a vested theoretical interest in seeking to (mis)represent overrides as exceptions.

The approach I favour does not rest content with identifying the judicial role as recursive. It also suggests that lawyers and citizens, too, have some margin of appreciation such that when they encounter a legal rule ('if A is then B ought to be, full-stop'), they are to follow it *unless* there is very good reason not to do so. This engages their critical reflective qualities. Of course, those who deviate from the basic rule do so at their own risk and there is no guarantee that the legal system will accept their reason as compelling, but there is some reason to suppose that the law does acknowledge the existence of such a recursive attitude to its rules and that legal change may flow, in part, from the moral pioneering involved. It seems to me that an understanding of a citizen's role in a democratic legal system is enhanced by application of the notion of a recourse role. 'The self-professed aim of modern education is to "liberate" people from prejudices and traditional forms of authority. Educated people are said not to obey authority blindly, but rather learn to think for themselves.'[24] If there is a defeasibilist theory of law, it would be a theory of law not only for judges. There is a popular view that Hart's was a theory of law and Dworkin's a theory of adjudication and that they never actually engaged, but passed by each other as ships in the night. My own view is that every theory of law worthy of the name, entails a theory of adjudication. Defeasibilism in adjudication is informed by and speaks to a defeasibilist theory of law.

G. Law against the law, generally

Part of the argument is that law permits internal challenges. Kadish and Kadish helpfully illustrate their 'discretion to disobey' thesis with a discussion of an effort over many years to obtain a decision on the constitutionality of a Connecticut statute passed in 1879 making it a crime to use contraceptives or to assist others in their use.[25] About 65 years ago, a physician challenged the validity of the statute on the grounds that it prevented him helping several patients whose life would be threatened by childbearing. This challenge reached the court under a declaratory procedure which provided for a judicial determination of rights and duties. The court however held that the physician lacked standing (*locus standi*). His patients would have had standing but

[22] D.J. Newman, *Conviction: The Determination of Guilt or Innocence Without Trial* (Boston: Little, Brown & Co., 1966), 178.

[23] F. Schauer, 'Formalism', *Yale Law Journal*, 97 (1988), 509; and F. Schauer, 'The Jurisprudence of Reasons', *Michigan Law Review*, 85 (1987), 847.

[24] F. Fukuyama, *The End of History and the Last Man* (New York: Avon Books, 1992), 116.

[25] M.R. Kadish and S.H. Kadish, *Discretion to Disobey*, 102–6.

the physician could not assert their rights and was not asserting that any of his own rights were infringed by the statute.[26]

Twenty years on another physician's challenge reached the court.[27] This time the claim was that the statute infringed the physician's own right to practise medicine and he was joined by two of his patients who claimed that the unavailability of contraception presented a risk to their health. Once again the court contrived not to decide, this time on the basis that there was no 'ripened controversy' in that no one was actually facing criminal prosecution. Indeed, perhaps only one prosecution had ever been initiated under the statute. This history, plus the fact that condoms were widely available for sale in Connecticut drugstores, suggested to the court that the physician's scruples were 'academic' and that his 'personal sensitivity' about obeying the law did not change the fact that in reality he had nothing to fear.

The physician therefore established and advertised a public birth control clinic in direct violation of the statute and when later prosecuted, invoked the constitution in defence. This time unquestionably there was both standing and ripeness, and the court, reaching the merits, held the statute unconstitutional and quashed the physician's conviction.[28] Here it was necessary to break the law in order to test and modify it. Would we say that the physician was a morally good or a morally bad physician or citizen? My own view is that it is certainly the right and possibly the duty of everyone to resist unconstitutionally exercised public power and conscientiously to disobey pernicious laws on moral and religious grounds. That the legal system appears to accommodate such a conditional attitude to its laws appears to me to be a powerful reason for respecting the law. But respect is an attitude very different from either craven, slavish obedience or from anarchical, unthinking, knee-jerk rejection of all law. What I am advocating is a 'critical reflective attitude' (rather different from what Hart meant by that phrase) to the law's requirements and a readiness to test them where they appear to conflict with professional or personal morality.

Lest it be thought that this conclusion turns upon the very special constitutional arrangements enjoyed by Americans and having no obvious counterpart in the United Kingdom (other than 'rights lite' under the European Convention on Human Rights which has been cautiously incorporated into domestic law by virtue of the Human Rights Act 1998), I turn to the celebrated case of *Gillick* v. *West Norfolk and Wisbech Health Authority* (1985).[29] Mrs Gillick, a Catholic mother, objected to the policy of the health authority in providing contraceptive advice or treatment to underage women, without parental knowledge or consent. She sought an assurance that no such advice would be given to her four daughters while they were under 16 years of age without her prior knowledge and consent. When no such assurance was forthcoming Mrs Gillick sought a declaration that the policy was unlawful and adversely affected her rights as a parent. The House of Lords held that a woman under 16 did not lack the legal capacity to consent to contraceptive advice, examination, and treatment, provided in the clinical judgement of the appropriate health care professional, she had sufficient understanding and intelligence to know what was involved.

Welcome as this decision may have been from a secular and rational perspective, it represents a change in the law—it could no longer be said that children remained in the complete control of their parents—and that change was won by pioneering spirits

[26] *Tileston* v. *Ullman* 318 US 44 (1943).
[27] *Poe* v. *Ullman* 367 US 497 (1961).
[28] *Griswold* v. *Connecticut* 381 US 479 (1965).
[29] [1986] AC 112.

willing to risk criminal sanction in pursuit of their moral mission to deliver the health care in the best (medical) interests of the patient. And the risks were serious. One dissenting judge took the classical view that Parliament had for the past century regarded sexual intercourse by a man with a woman under 16 as a serious criminal offence by the man though not by the woman even though she might have initiated the activity or encouraged the man to do the act.

Consequently, those providing contraceptive advice and treatment to underage women might have been prosecuted as secondary participants in serious crime. However, the majority wisely held that the bona fide exercise by a doctor of clinical judgement must be a complete negation of the guilty mind which is an essential ingredient of the relevant crimes. I regard the American example as illustrating that law enforcement agencies may exhibit a resource role in that there were so few prosecutions under the legislation as to be negligible and *Gillick* illustrates the recourse role of the judiciary in England. However, neither example takes us to the crucial point. Although defeasibilism is comfortable with judicial review of primary legislation under a Bill, Convention, or Charter of Rights ordinarily the outcome is 'rule change' or invalidation, generally, whereas the debate, as I understand it, takes *override* as potentially a serious challenge to established theories of law. Fascinating as it is, *Gillick* is also a 'rule change' case and not an instance of defeasibilism in adjudication.

H. Law against the law, particularly

As a further illustration of the recourse role and of the defeasibility of apparently exclusionary rules, I turn again[30] to the widely unknown case of Dr Biezanek,[31] a mother of six, a niece of the incomparable novelist Graham Greene, who became in 1963 Britain's first Catholic doctor operating a birth control clinic, and who was acquitted by a Liverpool jury in 1993 on a charge of supplying cannabis to her adult daughter as treatment for a serious and intractable disease. The trial judge ordered that no details of the daughter's disease be published but since the condition was one amenable to treatment by cannabis as, in Dr Biezanek's words, 'the only drug which alleviated the symptoms' it may not be too difficult to guess. Dr Biezanek had formerly opposed the recreational use of cannabis and had even thrown her daughter out but she had since been persuaded by an article about American doctors seeking to make it available on prescription for so-called 'intractable illnesses'. Since it could not be prescribed in Britain she had asked her daughter how to obtain supplies and she had then bought cannabis from dealers and administered small doses to her daughter three times a day. Dr Biezanek's defence included the notion that she followed a 'higher law' and that she risked becoming a criminal because of her moral conscience. Her lawyer explained that Dr Biezanek considered her conduct 'the right and proper thing'.

Dr Biezanek's case did not change the law generally, but she was acquitted by a jury nullifying the plain letter of the law presumably on moral grounds, in response to the merits of her 'defence'. Dr Biezanek's case is helpful to my argument that not only judges, lawyers, and doctors, but also citizens may enjoy a recourse role in that the facts straddle the line between someone acting in a professional capacity and someone acting solely as a citizen.

[30] R.H.S. Tur, 'Rule of Recognition' in *The New Palgrave Dictionary of Economics and the Law*, Vol. 3, (London: Macmillan, 1998), 386–9; and R.H.S. Tur, 'Medical Confidentiality and Disclosure', 15–28.

[31] *The Times*, 20 October 1993.

For Hart, the rule of recognition is 'the *proper* way of disposing of doubts as to the existence of the rule... [and]... for conclusive identification of the primary rules of obligation'. But it is not clear that the rule of recognition operated in the same way for the various actors in Dr Biezanek's case in that presumably the police, the prosecutor, and the judge understood the possession and supply laws to apply even to the extreme facts of the case whereas the accused, herself, and at least some of the jurors took a different view. It seems fairly obvious that the various actors approached the question of the identification of primary obligations under the criminal law in different ways and that, rather than any mechanical application of one officially accepted rule of recognition, the various actors adopted and applied different principles of acceptance. The question for an addressee of such a rule is not so much about the rule's existence but whether one is free to act on one's own judgement. That is a question which the rule receiver must answer prior to any official determination and 'rules of recognition do not provide the answer but principles of acceptance do'.[32] It is not so much a question then of whether the rule of recognition itself is subject to defeasance but what sort of legal theory would emerge were the rule of recognition thus reconceptualized.

These several accounts and examples of law against the law, generally or particularly, illustrating the legally endorsed moral nullification of law appear to me to be descriptively accurate over a wide range of law and normatively appealing not only to democratic citizens but also to professionals such as doctors and lawyers whose role involves testing the law on moral grounds and who should be ready to do so, if but only if, they believe on the good-faith exercise of professional or personal judgement that the outcome mandated by the literal application of the legal rule is unacceptably inconsistent with the moral mission of their professional role, or their conception of what it is to be a citizen.

I. Justice again

Cases such as *Henningsen* v. *Bloomfield Motors* present defeasance as potentially sweepingly wide.[33] Mr Henningsen had bought a car under a contract which included a term limiting the manufacturer's liability exclusively to repairing defective parts. The court however agreed with his argument that the manufacturer should not be protected by the term and should meet medical and other expenses of those injured in a crash even though there was no statute or common law rule in support. The court relied on the following ringing dictum: 'Is there any principle which is more familiar or more firmly embedded in the history of Anglo-American law than the basic doctrine that the courts will not permit themselves to be used as instruments of inequity and injustice'. 'Justice' deployed as such an overarching category of defeasance in adjudication appears to me seriously to challenge the descriptive accuracy of contemporary legal positivist accounts of law and to lead to heroic defences such as legal positivism being neutral or inert in adjudication.[34] One might reasonably wonder quite what the point is of such a very 'thin' theory of law.[35]

[32] M.R. Kadish and S.H. Kadish, *Discretion to Disobey*, 192.

[33] 32 NJ 358, 161 A, 2d 69 (1960).

[34] J. Gardner, 'Legal Positivism 5½ Myths', *The American Journal of Jurisprudence*, 46 (2001), 199–227.

[35] K. Greenawalt, 'Too Thin and Too Rich: Distinguishing Features of Legal Positivism' in R.P. George (ed.), *The Autonomy Of Law: Essays on Legal Positivism* (Oxford: Clarendon Press, 1996), ch. 1.

In the real world of adjudication, however, legal theories may actually impact on judicial decisions, for good or ill. For example, in *Great Peace Shipping Ltd* v. *Tsavliris Salvage (International) Ltd*,[36] the Court of Appeal appears to have been influenced by an exclusive positivist legal theory in renouncing the cogent and coherent reasoning of Steyn J in *Associated Japanese Bank* v. *Credit du Nord*.[37] *Great Peace* has its admirers and its detractors. Those who defend it see it as (re-)establishing 'one law of mistake and not two'.[38] Those who criticize it, as I do, see it as seeking to remove a desirable flexibility born of equity, inconsistently with a defeasibilist conception of law and adjudication, and then illogically proposing to restore flexibility by statute.[39] Ronald Dworkin correctly observes: 'According to most lawyers' views of the strict doctrine [of precedent] in Britain, the Court of Appeals [sic], which is just below the House of Lords in authority, has no choice but to follow its own past decisions'.[40] In *Great Peace*, however, the Court of Appeal refused to follow its own past decisions in three leading cases,[41] thus adopting defeasibilism in judicial process whilst seeking to exclude it from an aspect of the substantive law of contract.

Justice cannot, however, be treated as the sole category of defeasance, seductive though that view may be. Consider the remarkable case of *Wilson* v. *First County Trust*.[42] Here Mrs Wilson borrowed £5,000 against her BMW 318 convertible from a pawnbroker for a period of six months. There was an additional 'document fee' of £250 and with interest at an eye-watering annual percentage rate of 94.78 per cent, the total amount payable to redeem the car was £7,327. Upon the loan not being repaid the pawnbroker (a two-man company) sought repayment, which failing the car would be sold. The resourceful Mrs Wilson instituted proceedings in the county court on the alternative grounds that the agreement was unenforceable by virtue of section 127(3) of the Consumer Credit Act 1974 because it did not contain all the prescribed terms, which failing, the agreement should be reopened as grossly extortionate. She failed on the first point (on the basis that the 'document fee' was held correctly to have been included in stating the loan to be for £5,250) but succeeded on the second, the judge reducing the rate of interest such that she was left with £6,900 to pay to redeem her car. This she did in December 1999.

However, she subsequently succeeded in the Court of Appeal almost a year later on the basis that the £250 'document fee' was held by that court not to be 'credit' within the meaning of the Act. It followed that the agreement was unenforceable and First County Trust were ordered to repay £6,900 to Mrs Wilson, with the overall result that she 'was entitled to keep her loan, pay no interest and recover her car'.[43] This seems like a blatant case of unjust enrichment and overly harsh on the lender. Moreover, the Court of Appeal floated the possibility of section 127(3) being incompatible with Article 6(1) of the European Convention on Human Rights and Article 1 of the First Protocol to the Convention. This led to an adjournment and the addition of the

[36] [2003] QB 679; and see more generally, P. Suber, *The Case of the Speluncean Explorers: Nine New Opinions*.

[37] [1989] 1 WLR 255.

[38] E. McKendrick, *Contract Law* (7th edn, Basingstoke: Palgrave MacMillan, 2007), 308.

[39] At para. 161 of the report. Justly does McKendrick observe the irony in lamenting the loss of flexibility by those responsible for that very loss (ibid., 307).

[40] R. Dworkin, *Law's Empire*, 25.

[41] *Solle* v. *Butcher* [1950] 1 KB 67; *Grist* v. *Bailey* [1967] Ch 532; *Magee* v. *Pennine Insurance Co* [1969] 2 QB 507.

[42] [2003] UKHL 40.

[43] Paragraph 6 of the law report.

Secretary of State for Trade and Industry as a party. In May 2001 the Court of Appeal held that the inflexible exclusion of a remedy by section 127(3) prevented the court from doing justice in the case, and was disproportionate to the legitimate policy objectives of consumer credit legislation. The court declared the section incompatible with the Convention. The court also held the section incompatible with the rights guaranteed by the First Protocol.

The Secretary of State took an appeal to the House of Lords. By this time neither of the original parties were involved. Some motor insurance companies and the Finance and Leasing Association intervened, as did the Speaker of the House of Commons and the Clerk of the Parliaments. The House of Lords considered many complex issues, including retrospectivity and adverting to Hansard as an aid to construction of statutes, and it also addressed the important issue of unjust enrichment and whether the lender has a separate restitutionary claim against the borrower for the return of the money lent. The Court held that the lender did not. Lord Nicholls stated, 'the lender is intended to be left without recourse against the borrower in respect of the loan. That being the intention of Parliament, the lender cannot assert at common law that the borrower has been unjustly enriched.'[44] Lord Hoffmann's dicta in another case about section 127(3) are cited with approval: 'It was not open to the court to say this consequence is unjust and should be reversed by a remedy at common law'.[45] This is surprising. Ordinarily the common law endures after the passing into law of a statute unless the statute expressly abolishes it and plainly the Consumer Credit Act 1974 does not expressly negate any other pre-existing common law remedy available to the lender. So the House of Lords disapplied the normal presumption of statutory interpretation without, as it seems to me, providing sufficiently compelling reason for doing so.

More importantly the House of Lords reversed the Court of Appeal on the incompatibility of section 127(3) with the Convention. This is surprising because the deep and wide injustice is recognized. Lord Nicholls acknowledged that 'Parliament was painting with a broad brush. The unattractive feature of this approach is that it will sometimes involve punishing the blameless *pour encourager les autres*. On its face, considered in the context of one particular case, a sanction having this effect is difficult to justify.'[46] With respect, it is not difficult to agree with this. Indeed the matter was considered by the relevant Committee which reported in 1971, 'it offends every notion of justice or fairness that because of some technical slip which in no way prejudices him, a borrower, having received a substantial sum of money, should be entitled to retain or spend it without any obligation to repay a single penny'.[47] Despite all this Lord Nicholls has 'no difficulty in accepting that in suitable instances it is open to Parliament, when Parliament considers the public interest so requires, to decide that compliance with certain formalities is an essential prerequisite to enforcement of certain types of agreements. This course is open to Parliament even though this will sometimes yield a seemingly unreasonable result in a particular case. Considered overall, this course may well be a proportionate response to a perceived social problem.'[48] Then again, it may well be disproportionate and there may be more effective and fairer ways to achieve the legitimate state interest that is prayed in aid. In any event, this case, though problematic in a number of ways, illustrates that public policy may be so potent

[44] At para. 49 of the law report.
[45] *Dimond* v. *Lovell* [2002] 1 AC 384, 397–8.
[46] At paras 72 and 73 of the law report.
[47] Report of the Committee on Consumer Credit (Cmnd 4596) vol. 1, p. 311, para. 6.11.4 (1971).
[48] At para. 74 of the law report.

a category of defeasance as to trump even the normal judicial commitment to doing justice. It is of course easy to disagree with the House of Lords in *Wilson*. Underlying the decision, as it seems to me, is a commitment to Parliamentary sovereignty and a rigid, rules-based approach to legal reasoning which may be more yesterday's than tomorrow's legal paradigm.[49]

J. Overruling

Hart thought that 'the result of the English system of precedent has been to produce, by its use, a body of rules of which a vast number, of both major and minor importance, are as determinate as any statutory rule. They can now only be altered by statute.'[50] Of course that was originally written before the *Practice Statement (Judicial Precedent)*:

> Their Lordships regard the use of precedent as an indispensable foundation on which to decide what is the law and its application to individual cases. It provides at least some degree of certainty upon which individuals can rely in the conduct of their affairs, as well as a basis for orderly development of legal rules. Their Lordships nevertheless recognise that too rigid adherence to precedent may lead to injustice in a particular case and also unduly restrict the proper development of the law. They propose therefore to modify their present practice and, while treating former decisions of this House as normally binding, to depart from a decision when it appears right to do so. In this connection they will hear in mind the danger of disturbing retrospectively the basis on which contracts, settlements of property and fiscal arrangements have been entered into and also the especial need for certainty as to the criminal law. This announcement is not intended to affect the use of precedent elsewhere than in this House.[51]

This is a remarkable development and so obviously defeasibilist. Ordinarily the House of Lords will follow its own decisions for all sorts of good reasons but exceptionally it will depart from that when justice or the proper development of the law requires it. Legal commentators differ on the significance of this development, some suggesting that it has been used but rarely although ten instances or thereabouts in its first quarter century is not insignificant.[52]

K. Prospective overruling

My own take on the Practice Statement is that overruling will remain relatively rare unless and until the House of Lords adopts prospective overruling.[53] There is an obvious and serious constraint on judicial law making and law changing, namely retrospectivity. It would be wrong to disappoint the legitimate expectations of parties by changing the rules upon which they relied after the event. Judge-made law is always retrospective and this constrains judicial activism. Accordingly, prospective overruling

[49] R.H.S. Tur, 'Resources and Rights: Court Decisions in the United Kingdom' in R. Rhodes, M. P. Battin, and A. Silvers (eds), *Medicine and Social Justice: Essays on the Distribution of Health Care* (New York: Oxford University Press, 2002), 156–68.

[50] H.L.A. Hart, *The Concept of Law*, 131–2.

[51] [1966] 1 WLR 1234.

[52] See further J.W. Harris, 'Towards Principles of Overruling—When Should a Final Court of Appeal Second Guess?', OJLS, 10 (1990), 135.

[53] See R.H.S. Tur, 'Prospective overruling' in P. Cane and J. Conaghan (eds), *New Oxford Companion to Law* (Oxford: Oxford University Press, 2008), 950; R.H.S. Tur, 'Varieties of Overruling and Judicial Law Making: Prospective Overruling in a Comparative Perspective', *Juridical Review*, (1978), 33–64; and R.H.S. Tur, 'Time and Law', OJLS, 22 (2002), 463–88.

has not been popular with English judges and commentators. However, there may have been something of a sea-change relatively recently.

Lord Hope observed:

> The question then is whether it can ever be consistent with the exercise of its judicial power for the House to declare that a decision which it takes which changes the law is not to affect events or things done in the past but only events or things done in the future. While I recognise the force of Lord Goff's argument to the contrary in *Kleinwort Benson Ltd* v. *Lincoln City Council* [1999] 2 AC 349, I think that it would be unwise to say that the power to do this can never be available in any circumstances. The speeches that were delivered in *R* v. *Governor of Brockhill Prison, Ex p Evans (No 2)* [2001] 2 AC 19 show how reluctant your Lordships have been to engage in this debate. It is no doubt true that in almost every case that can be imagined the exercise of the judicial power will require the House simply to declare what the law is, with the inevitable result that it will apply to other comparable cases whenever the events occurred. But it is not possible to predict the future with complete confidence, and it seems to me that the question whether this technique should be adopted remains an open one.[54]

He added:

> Where the future may lead us we cannot tell. So, like my noble and learned friend Lord Nicholls of Birkenhead, I would not rule out the possibility that in a wholly exceptional case the interests of justice may require the House, in the context of a dispute about the state of the common law or even about the meaning or effect of a statute, to declare that its decision is not to operate retrospectively.[55]

As with the Practice Statement, so with these dicta: they are defeasibilist through and through though we have yet to encounter a case in which the House of Lords actually overrules for the future only.

L. 'Provocation ping-pong'

Although precedent in English law is not now so rigid as previously, every first-year law student knows that the House of Lords is the court of highest authority and that its decisions are binding on all lower courts, including the Court of Appeal. Moreover, it is universally understood that whereas decisions of the House of Lords are binding, those of the Privy Council are merely persuasive. Until very recently any student who suggested otherwise in a law examination would have been likely to fail. Nonetheless these apparently fixed and unalterable rules of judicial process and adjudication have now also succumbed to a defeasibilist interpretation in the English legal system. The doctrine of provocation is not perhaps English criminal law's finest achievement. Indeed the doctrine has been a focus for controversy in and out of the courts and in *the latter context has been referred to as* 'ping-pong'.[56] *R* v. *Smith (Morgan)* involved a fatal stabbing during an argument about the deceased's alleged theft of the defendant's carpentry tools.[57] At the murder trial the defendant pleaded provocation, relying on evidence of a mental condition which had the effect of reducing his powers of self-control below that of an ordinary person. The trial judge ruled that the defendant's mental condition was a characteristic to be attributed to the notional reasonable man

[54] *National Westminster Bank* v. *Spectrum Plus Limited* [2005] UKHL 41, at para. 71.

[55] At para. 74 of the law report.

[56] C. Withey, 'Provocation Ping-Pong' *New Law Journal*, 156 (2006), 258–9 and 299–300; and see [2006] QB 58 at para. 40.

[57] [2001] 1 AC 146.

when determining the gravity of the provocation, but not to the loss of self-control. The Court of Appeal allowed the defendant's appeal and substituted a manslaughter verdict, on the basis that no distinction was to be drawn as to the relevance of the mental condition in assessing the gravity of the provocation to the notional reasonable man and his reaction to it. This was duly upheld in the House of Lords by a bare majority.

In *Attorney General for Jersey* v. *Holley* a specially assembled, nine-judge Privy Council considered in effect whether the House of Lords decision was wrong and decided by a majority of six to three that it was.[58] Lord Nicholls introduced the matter thus:

> This appeal from the Court of Appeal of Jersey calls for examination of the law relating to provocation as a defence or, more precisely, as a partial defence to a charge of murder. Jersey law on this subject is the same as English law. In July 2000 the House of Lords considered the ingredients of this defence in . . . *R* v. *Smith (Morgan)* . . . The decision of the House in that case is in direct conflict with the decision of their Lordships' board in *Luc Thiet Thuan* v. *The Queen* [1997] AC 131. And the reasoning of the majority in the Morgan Smith case is not easy to reconcile with the reasoning of the House of Lords in *R* v. *Camplin* [1978] AC 705 or *R* v. *Morhall* [1996] AC 90. This appeal, being heard by an enlarged board of nine members, is concerned to resolve this conflict and clarify definitively the present state of English law, and hence Jersey law, on this important subject.

One peculiarity of the case was that the Privy Council should feel it appropriate to sit as it were as an enlarged appeal court to review a decision of the House of Lords. Another peculiarity was that the Attorney-General of Jersey undertook not to seek to restore the defendant's conviction for murder which had been quashed by the Jersey Court of Appeal on the basis of the law as stated in *R* v. *Smith (Morgan)*. So there was no real controversy to be adjudicated, the effect on the appellant being the same whatever decision the Privy Council reached. There can be no doubt that the Judicial Committee of the Privy Council consisting of nine of the twelve Lords of Appeal in Ordinary set out definitively to clarify English law on a particular issue, unusual though that obviously is.

The next case to note is *R* v. *James and Karimi*,[59] where the Court of Appeal chose to follow the Privy Council and not the House of Lords, stating 'in effect, in the long term at least, Holley's case has overruled the Morgan Smith case'.[60] Moreover, it was the nine Lords of Appeal in Ordinary who sat in Holley's case who have departed from the established approach to precedent. Accordingly, the Court of Appeal was bound to prefer the Privy Council decision to the earlier decision of the House of Lords on the same issue. The court refers to the justification for departing from well-established rules of precedent and then sets out in some detail the conditions under which it is proper to depart from so central a rule of judicial process and adjudication:

> What are the exceptional features in this case which justify our preferring the decision in Holley's case to that in the Morgan Smith case? We identify the following. (i) All nine of the Lords of Appeal in Ordinary sitting in Holley's case agreed in the course of their judgments that the result reached by the majority clarified definitively English law on the issue in question. (ii) The majority in Holley's case constituted half the Appellate Committee of the House of Lords. We do not know whether there would have been agreement that the result was definitive had the members of the Board divided five/four. (iii) In the circumstances, the result of any appeal on the issue to the House of Lords is a foregone conclusion.[61]

[58] [2005] 2 AC 580. [59] [2006] QB 588.
[60] At para. 39 of the law report. [61] [2006] QB 588 at para. 43.

The court added:

> We doubt whether this court will often, if ever again, be presented with the circumstances that we have described above. It is those circumstances which we consider justify the course that we have decided to take, and our decision should not be taken as a licence to decline to follow a decision of the House of Lords in any other circumstances.[62]

This is a quite startling illustration of defeasibilism in judicial process and adjudication.

M. From adjudication to legal theory?

How might all these examples, and many others, be theorized? The challenge is whether any social sources thesis generally,[63] or Hart's rule of recognition in particular,[64] can accommodate itself to such endemic defeasibilism in adjudication. The susceptibility of legal rules to override generates a problem for the Hartian construct. Either the overriding elements, such as justice or policy, are 'law' or they are not. If they are 'law', they must be identified by the rule of recognition as such or it must be candidly admitted that non-legal materials not only feature in legal arguments but sometimes have greater weight in determining outcomes than do legal materials. It then follows that the rule of recognition must either strive for greater and greater breadth in order to include all possible sources of override or that the rule of recognition must be understood as identifying some but not all relevant legal materials. But neither an over-inclusive nor an under-inclusive rule of recognition will convince critics of legal positivism in that, if over-broad, the separability of law and morals thesis is undermined and, if too narrow, there is a lack of descriptive fit with the linguistic practices of the community. Not only American Legal Realists regard what judges do in court as ordinarily being 'law' even if they sometimes leave law behind and deploy wholly moral reasoning. This latter point is one to which Hart might have been particularly sensitive in that his theory was embedded in the linguistic philosophy of its day, using, as Professor J.L. Austin put it, 'a sharpened awareness of words to sharpen our perception of the phenomena'.[65]

N. Conclusion

In this paper I have offered various examples of defeasibility in adjudication, sufficient to justify the conclusion that it is a salient feature of some legal systems. Moving from description I have acknowledged that defeasibility is normatively appealing to me. Perhaps it suffices to defend defeasibilism as a descriptively accurate, normatively appealing, methodological precept claiming only that 'law is best represented, understood, and taught in the form of open-ended, defeasible, normative conditional propositions'.[66] Clearly much still remains to be done to move forward to a defeasibilist theory of law. Opponents are ready to decry that suggestion on the basis, they claim, that defeasibility is neither analytically a necessary feature of rules nor conceptually of

[62] [2006] QB 588 at para. 44.

[63] J. Raz, 'Legal Positivism and the Sources of Law' in J. Raz, *The Authority of Law* (Oxford: Clarendon Press, 1979), ch. 3.

[64] See R.H.S. Tur, 'Rule of Recognition', 386–9.

[65] H.L.A. Hart, *The Concept of Law*, vii.

[66] R. H.S. Tur, 'Defeasibilism', OJLS, 21 (2001), 355–68.

legal systems. On the basis that no rule can exhaustively determine the conditions of its own application, it does not seem necessary to concede that defeasibility is not analytically a feature of rules. Moreover, whatever the antonym of 'defeasible' is, say 'indefeasible', it is not conceptually a necessary feature of legal systems either, although the all-or-nothing or fixed conception of rules is widely associated, rightly or wrongly, with the exclusive legal positivist theory of law to which defeasibilism may be a viable alternative.[67] Obviously developing that challenging thesis would take the author well beyond the kind invitation to comment on defeasibility and adjudication.

[67] T. Campbell, *The Legal Theory of Ethical Positivism.*

21

Legal Defeasibility in Context and the Emergence of Substantial Indefeasibility

*Jonathan R. Nash**

Commentators have long debated the extent to which defeasibility permeates legal argument. An inference drawing a conclusion from a proposition is 'defeasible' if there is some other proposition that, if taken in conjunction with the original proposition, undermines or casts doubt upon the conclusion drawn by the inference.[1] Thus, for example, the statement 'impossibility renders an otherwise enforceable contract unenforceable' renders defeasible the statement 'a written contract formed upon a meeting of the minds and an exchange of consideration is enforceable'. From the perspective of the common law, legal precedent is defeasible to the extent that it may be overturned. Legal philosophers such as John Dewey[2] and H.L.A. Hart[3] have argued that legal statements are inherently defeasible.[4]

The theoretical debate over whether legal propositions are universally defeasible has important real-world implications. If indeed all legal propositions are defeasible—if all constitutions can be amended, statutes repealed, and judicial precedents overridden—then law may seem to be reduced inexorably to what Felix Cohen described as 'transcendental nonsense'.[5] Such an understanding of law is inconsistent with notions

* Professor of Law, Emory University. I benefited greatly from a presentation of this paper at a 'workshop on defeasibilism' held at Oriel College, Oxford University in March 2008. I am also grateful to Elizabeth Glazer and Robert Schapiro for comments on earlier drafts, and to Bruce Chapman, Oscar Chase, Kyron Huigens, Daryl Levinson, Saul Levmore, Mark Movsesian, Lori Nash, and Richard Tur for helpful suggestions and conversations. Many thanks to Katherine Nachod for outstanding research support, and to Jeffrey Brooks, Keith Kendall, and Kenneth Leonczyk for excellent research assistance.

[1] A more complete and precise definition and discussion of defeasibility appears below. See section A.

[2] See J. Dewey, 'Logical Method and Law', *Cornell Law Quarterly*, 10 (1925), 22. ('No concrete proposition, that is to say one with material dated in time and placed in space, follows from any general statements or from any connection between them').

[3] See H. L. A. Hart, 'The Ascription of Responsibility and Rights', *Proceedings of the Aristotelian Society*, 49 (1948–9), 173–83, reprinted in A. Flew (ed.), *Logic and Language* (1st Series, Oxford: Blackwell, 1951), 147–54, noting and explaining 'the defeasible character of legal concepts'.

[4] There are other examples. See, e.g. B.S. Jackson, *Law, Fact, and Narrative Coherence* (Roby: Deborah Charles, 1988), 45. '[L]egal concepts are inherently defeasible: their application, residing as it does in human hands, is always subject to the decision not to follow normal semantic constraints . . . every act of adjudication involves an act of creative interpretation'); see also R.H.S. Tur, 'Defeasibilism', OJLS, 21 (2001), 355: 'I seek . . . to present and defend the suggestion that law is best represented, most clearly understood, and most effectively taught in the form of open-ended, defeasible, normative, conditional propositions.' Frederick Schauer believes this view is in fact widely held. See F. Schauer, 'On the Supposed Defeasibility of Legal Rules' in M.D.A. Freeman (ed.), *Current Legal Problems* (1998), 225–6.

[5] See generally F.S. Cohen, 'Transcendental Nonsense and the Functional Approach', *Columbia Law Review*, 35 (1935), 809.

of government functioning by 'rule of law.' It may undermine the legitimacy of the law, which ultimately might render the law impotent.

In this essay, I argue that the extent to which law is defeasible is heavily contextual. In order properly to understand different conceptions of defeasibility, it is important to locate the context in which different conceptions are offered. In particular, there is the question of the background against which one should judge whether a legal proposition is defeasible. The choice of background informs one's conception of 'defeasibility'. First, one can consider defeasibility of legal propositions and legal reasoning purely in the abstract,[6] with no system of law in place. Second, one can consider defeasibility against the background of an established legal system but one that need not continue in perpetuity. Third, one can consider a functioning legal system that, it is assumed, exists and will continue to exist indefinitely, but where legal rules can be changed by the legislature or by the courts (ultimately under the universal rule of recognition). Last, one can consider the portion of an existing legal system (that exists and will continue to exist) that has evolved sufficiently that changes to the legal rules contained therein are highly unlikely to occur (if indeed they ever do).

I argue that Dewey's and Hart's competing conceptions of defeasibility lie in the third and fourth backdrops just described. I will further argue that the better conception is the one that lies in the fourth backdrop—where more evolved legal concepts lie. These more evolved legal concepts rest on legal assertions that typically are unlikely to be defeasible. As such, I argue that the fourth backdrop offers at least a state of 'substantial indefeasibility'. An area of law features substantial indefeasibility when a substantial number of legal rules in that area are perceived to be indefeasible either absent action by the legislature or otherwise by extenuating circumstances. The notion of substantial indefeasibility builds upon the Hartian idea of a sizeable 'core' where the proper interpretation of legal assertions is undisputed; it requires in addition that a legal assertion in that core be perceived to be indefeasible absent legislative interference or some overriding reason why the legal assertion should be subject to defeasance.

Substantial indefeasibility rescues legal reasoning from devolving into 'transcendental nonsense', as Cohen suggests. Moreover, it accords with a 'punctuated equilibrium' view of law and legal evolution.

[6] Because his thesis in 'The Ascription of Responsibility and Rights' is broader than simply the question of defeasibility, Hart devotes considerable time to the question of whether statements such as 'my father made his will yesterday' are true or false. See H.L.A. Hart, 'The Ascription of Responsibility and Rights', 157. Hart suggests that, even if the will does not comply with governing law and so is not valid, '[w]e should... hesitate to say it is' false. Ibid.

My analysis here is narrower. I focus on defeasibility in the context of legal propositions. Given this focus, the question arises when, for my purposes, the statement 'my father made his will yesterday' will qualify as a legal proposition. Must a court in fact rule on whether or not the purported will is in fact valid? This would seem to generate far too limiting a definition of legal proposition. On the other hand, should the question of whether the sentence is a legal proposition turn on whether the speaker in fact *believes* the document in question to be a legally valid will? This would seem to produce a definition of 'legal proposition' that may be both over-inclusive and under-inclusive, since whether the speaker considers a will to be valid is not determinative of whether the will in fact is valid.

Rather, the better approach seems to be to treat the statement 'my father made his will yesterday' as a legal proposition to the extent it can be understood to assert the meaning 'my father made a document, that the courts would recognize and enforce as a legally valid will'. In effect, then, the core legal proposition is that 'the document is a legally valid will'. Thus, specific legal propositions with which we shall be concerned—in the language of Dewey—are statements about whether persons or things meet the criteria for some legal status (whether that status be, e.g. legally valid will, legally enforceable contract, liability for negligence, etc.). These legal criteria are set forth in general statements of law.

I also argue that, to the extent that perceptions of commentators and courts reflect its existence, substantial indefeasibility is a prominent feature of US jurisprudence. Since common law systems, of which the US system is an example, are said to be more susceptible to defeasibility than other systems, the existence of substantial indefeasibility in US law strongly suggests that the phenomenon is vital in other jurisprudences as well.

To make the point under US law, I rely in large measure on jurisprudence under the law of federal *habeas corpus*, and under private litigation to vindicate constitutional violations allegedly committed by state officers in their official actions—known as 'section 1983 litigation' based upon the statute that authorizes it. Under statute and common law, *habeas* jurisprudence directs that federal courts leave intact state criminal convictions against subsequently recognized constitutional violations except to the extent that *then-existing* case law made the alleged constitutional violation apparent. Similarly, section 1983 jurisprudence affords state officers immunity from suit unless it can be shown that, at the time their actions were undertaken, the fact that those actions violated the Constitution was clearly established. These rules allow us to infer that Congress and the courts understand substantial swaths of law to be substantially indefeasible.

I proceed in this essay as follows. Section A briefly elucidates the concept of legal defeasibility. Section B describes how the concept of defeasibility will vary with the context of the relevant legal setting in which it is examined. Section C provides evidence of substantial indefeasibility in US jurisprudence. Section D briefly concludes.

A. The concept of defeasibility

Before setting forth the various backdrops against which one might consider defeasibility, it is important and enlightening to consider in more depth the basic definition and concept of the term. Given propositions P, Q, and R, the inference (P = > Q) is defeasible if and only if there exists some proposition R that is logically consistent with P such that P and R together defeat the original inference, i.e. if ~[(P ∧ R) = > Q]. John Pollock offers a more formal definition of a 'defeater' (in the example, R is a defeater for the proposition that P implies Q).[7] He proceeds to distinguish two categories of defeaters. R is a 'rebutting defeater' of (P = > Q) if and only if R is a defeater that provides a reason for believing ~Q. By contrast, R is an 'undercutting defeater' if and only if R is a defeater that provides a reason for denying that P wouldn't be true unless Q were true, i.e. for believing that ~(P = > Q). In short, a rebutting defeater directly contradicts the purported conclusion Q, while an undercutting defeater raises doubt about the connection between P and Q which originally warranted the inference (P = > Q).[8] Examples of rebutting defeaters in law would be duly enacted statutes or decisions of high courts that overrule prior precedent and set a new legal standard. Examples of undercutting defeaters would be court decisions that, though they do not directly overrule prior precedent in a given area, are of sufficient relevance that they cast doubt on the continued validity of the prior precedent.

The notion that the inference (P = > Q) is defeasible is equivalent to the notion that the inference is not universally true. In this form, the relevance of defeasibility to legal reasoning becomes clear. The paradigm for legal reasoning is to begin with what purports to be a generally applicable statement or rule of law (P), apply that rule to

[7] J.L. Pollock, 'Defeasible Reasoning', *Cognitive Science*, 11 (1987), 484.
[8] Ibid., 485.

certain facts (F), and then to reach a conclusion (Q)—symbolically $(P \wedge F) => Q$. To the extent that any inference drawn from P, the purportedly generally applicable statement of law, in fact is defeasible, then P is not generally applicable. Let us say that a proposition (as opposed to an inference) is itself defeasible if there exists some inference that can be drawn from the proposition that is defeasible. With this terminology in place, it is clear that every legal proposition is either defeasible or universally applicable; it cannot be both. Thus, the claim advanced by Dewey and Hart (in 'The Ascription of Responsibility and Rights') that all legal propositions are defeasible is equivalent to the assertion that there is no universally applicable legal proposition.

B. Conceptions of defeasibility

To what extent and in what way(s), then, are generally applicable statements of law defeasible? It is in answer to this question that different conceptions of the concept of defeasibility in legal reasoning emerge, for the answer depends upon the legal backdrop against which we consider the question.

1. In the abstract

First, let us examine purportedly general legal statements and their defeasibility completely in the abstract, i.e. with no preconceived notion of what form the legal system must take or what its rules must be—indeed outside the realm of any particular legal system. Here, it is clear (unless perhaps, as discussed below, one is a natural law adherent) that all purportedly general legal assertions are indeed defeasible. Thus, any inference drawn from a purportedly general legal assertion is defeated by the statement 'there is no legal system against which to judge the validity of the purportedly general legal assertion on which the inference in question rests'.

A question arises whether this defeater is a rebutting defeater or an undercutting defeater. A moment's reflection reveals that it is neither. It surely is not a rebutting defeater since it does not contradict the conclusion reached by the defeated inference and recommend a different, correct conclusion. Nor can it be said to be an undercutting defeater, since it does not draw into question the connection between the purportedly general legal statement and the conclusion. In effect, it defeats the inference—and the general legal statement—by suggesting that the entire enterprise represented by the inference is meaningless since there is no legal system. In this sense, the defeater in effect represents a legal positivist critique of natural law; because there is no law in the absence of a legal system, legal reasoning in such a setting is wholly without meaning.

The foregoing categorization of this lone defeater as neither a rebutting nor an undercutting defeater is enlightening. Rebutting and undercutting defeaters both are, to use Dworkinian language, internally sceptical statements in respect of the defeated purportedly universal legal assertion.[9] That is, they both rely upon the legal system in which the universal legal assertion resides to level their criticism of, and to defeat, the universal legal assertion. By contrast, the defeater here is externally sceptical. Indeed, as Dworkin predicts, a person who rejected this defeater—presumably a natural law adherent—could respond to the defeater only by relying on his or her own moral belief in and reliance upon natural law. This categorization of the defeater is, on reflection, consistent with a positivist view of law.

[9] See, e.g. R. Dworkin, *Law's Empire* (London: Fontana, 1986), 141.

2. In the context of an existing legal system which may not persist

Now consider a more realistic setting: there is an existing legal system[10] but one that is subject to wholesale replacement.[11] Here, again, all purportedly universal legal assertions are defeasible. Even if an assertion of law P were said to be settled as generally applicable under the then-existing legal system, one could respond that, tomorrow, a new legal system could take the existing system's place, and that new system might reject the assertion P that the original system espoused. Thus, the statement 'a new legal system has replaced the old one' ('Statement R') would defeat almost any inference one might otherwise claim generally to draw from P (except perhaps the identity P = > P). To the extent that the new system of law in fact established an assertion of law W that directly contradicted P, then Statement R would be a rebutting defeater of P = > Q for many conclusions Q. However, even if the new legal system contained no such assertion of law W that directly contradicted P, Statement R would still be an undercutting defeater of P = > Q for most conclusions Q, since Statement R at least would draw into question the logical connection between P and Q by making the continued validity of P subject to question. After all, there simply is no reason that any one legal rule must be a part of every conceivable legal system in exactly the same form.[12]

It is appropriate to distinguish defeaters here from defeaters in the first setting considered above—i.e. purely in the abstract. In both situations, all purportedly universal legal assertions are defeasible, but here the defeaters are either undercutting or rebutting defeaters, while in the abstract the defeaters are external defeaters. In Dworkin's terms, the defeaters here are internally sceptical; they operate within the context of the (soon-to-be-defunct) legal system. This distinction is logical since here, as opposed to the abstract setting, we are operating within existing (though perhaps changing) legal institutions.[13]

[10] By 'legal system', I mean to refer to a continuing system of laws, not to the continuation of a particular government. Cf. Z. Elkins, T. Ginsburg, and J. Melton, *The Endurance of National Constitutions* (Cambridge: Cambridge University Press, 2009).

[11] One might question the extent to which a traditional legal system is required. Compare, e.g. H.L.A. Hart, *The Concept of Law* (2nd edn, Oxford: Clarendon Press, 1994), ch. 4, arguing that international law does not conform to traditional notions of law and legal systems, with J. Goldsmith and D. Levinson, 'Law for States: International Law, Constitutional Law, Public Law', *Harvard Law Review*, 122 (2009), 1791, arguing that domestic constitutional law and international law share foundational uncertainties.

[12] In some sense, the point is analogous to debates in the philosophy of language over the importance of context to meaning. Cf. H.E. Smith, 'The Language of Property: Form, Context, and Audience', *Stanford Law Review*, 55 (2003), 1125–57, explaining the parallels between meaning, context, and audience scope in language and law.

[13] An analogy to the emergence of legal property rights may be instructive here. A common explanation offered by property law theorists for the emergence of property rights is that government-enforced property rights are required because, in their absence, people cannot agree to share property or otherwise to respect others' rights in property. See John Locke, *2nd Treatise*, §§31, 36–8, 45–8, 123–4. On this account, property rights are needed to avert the 'tragedy of the commons'. See G. Hardin, 'The Tragedy of the Commons', *Science*, 168 (1968), 1243. As a consequence, people create governments to create enforceable property rights in order to avoid this problem. However, this account suffers from a contradiction: if (by assumption) people cannot agree to respect property rights, why should we expect the same people to have agreed to create a government? It is on this basis that Carol Rose suggests that the population of people that undergirds the traditional account—a population of self-interested individualists who cannot agree—must be mediated by some people who are inclined to agreement and cooperation. See C.M. Rose, 'Property as Storytelling: Perspectives from Game Theory, Narrative Theory, Feminist Theory', *Yale Journal of Law and the Humanities*, 2 (1990), 43–53.

Recasting this story in terms of defeasibility, property theorists emphasize that government is needed to render property rights indefeasible (to whatever extent they are in fact indefeasible). What is missing from the property theorists' account is explicit recognition that the existence of the government is itself

3. In the context of an existing legal system that will persist indefinitely

It is appropriate now to consider defeasibility of legal reasoning against a much narrower background: where the legal system is assumed to exist and never to pass out of existence. I should specify that I do not mean thereby to assume that the legal rules under the legal system are set in stone and cannot change. Rather, I mean only to assume (using Hart's nomenclature) that the ultimate rule of recognition does not change.[14]

Again, all purportedly universal legal assertions seem subject to defeat. For example, if one considers as the generally applicable legal proposition 'a contract is legally enforceable if there is offer, acceptance, and mutual consideration'. Even were that statement indeed indefeasible under the set of legal rules in effect at one time, it would be defeated for example by the statement 'the legislature has enacted a provision that removes the requirement of consideration for contract'.

What possible forms might defeaters take under this conception of defeasibility, and how would they be characterized? One category of defeaters would be legislative enactments that alter generally applicable statements of law. Examples of such defeaters that actually have come to pass would include the enactment by state legislatures of the Uniform Commercial Code or Statutes of Fraud in the field of contract law. These defeaters would change directly the governing law and, as such, would qualify as rebutting defeaters. Similarly, court decisions that overturn prior precedent, thereby altering the governing law, also would qualify as rebutting defeaters.[15]

Undercutting defeaters would also be a possibility. For example, a decision by a court in a related area that cast doubt on the general applicability of a statement of law would qualify as an undercutting defeater.

At first blush, there seems to be little if any difference between this situation and the previous one: it seems that any inference drawn from any generally applicable statement of law is defeasible under this conception—whether by rebutting defeaters, undercutting defeaters, or both. This is not the case, however. Since this conception of defeasibility assumes that the legal system itself remains intact and that the ultimate rule of recognition is constant, the statement 'a legally enforceable contract is what the ultimate rule of recognition says it is', is not defeasible.[16]

Does the indefeasibility of such statements contradict Dewey's or Hart's claims? Probably not, since, as discussed below, this was not the setting in which either of them

defeasible, and the very forces that render property rights defeasible—and therefore of dubious value—in the absence of government may conspire to render the government defeasible (or to preclude the formation of the government in the first instance).

For further discussion of the creation and durability of property rights in the light of defeasibility, see n. 39.

[14] See H.L.A. Hart, *The Concept of Law*, 91.

[15] Also along these lines, the Restatement (Second) of Contracts specifically contemplates that new laws that make it illegal for a party to perform under a contract discharge the obligation of that party so to perform. See Restatement (Second) of Contracts §261 ('Where, after a contract is made, a party's performance is made impracticable without his fault by the occurrence of an event the non-occurrence of which was a basic assumption on which the contract was made, his duty to render that performance is discharged, unless the language or the circumstances indicate the contrary'); ibid. §264 ('If the performance of a duty is made impracticable by having to comply with a domestic or foreign governmental regulation or order, that regulation or order is an event the non-occurrence of which was a basic assumption on which the contract was made').

[16] Cf. R.P. Loui, 'Hart's Critics on Defeasible Concepts and Ascriptivism' in *Proceedings of the Fifth International Conference on Artificial Intelligence and Law* (1995), 29–30, noting that the assertion 'a *contract* exists *if and only if* there was a *contracting* and it was *effective*... cartoons the issue, but it does provide necessary and sufficient conditions, trivially, by remigrating the defeasibility').

was discussing defeasibility. Moreover, to the extent that it was, both would probably rely on the apparent need to 'remigrat[e]' the defeasibility as support for their claims.[17]

4. In the context of a legal system that will persist indefinitely, and of legal rules that have well-established cores

Last, we turn to the most narrow conception of defeasibility—defeasibility against the backdrop of a legal system that is assumed to continue forever, and where it is assumed that neither the legislature nor the courts will take any action affirmatively to *change* the governing law. By this I mean that the concepts of law with which we deal are mature ones, with comparatively small frontiers or penumbra located at the distant perimeter of large cores of decided meaning. Courts are called upon to clarify the law. The law thus can continue to evolve. However, the elements of claims and the available defences are well established—even if ambiguity may remain as to whether they are fulfilled on particular facts. It is assumed that the legislature will not change the rules, and the highest court in the jurisdiction will not overrule prior precedent. Thus, courts are called upon solely to interpret existing law.

Even if one assumes that the legal system is established and constant and that no fundamental changes are made to a purportedly general statement of law, courts still may be faced with 'difficult' cases, i.e. cases where the courts may be called upon to apply existing legal standards to new and unfamiliar factual scenarios. Legal concepts and their accompanying, purportedly universal statements of law *evolve* over time. Different legal concepts are at different stages of evolution in our own legal system. One would describe the concept of 'enforceable contract' as highly evolved, while the legal regime created by, say, the Americans with Disabilities Act of 1991 is far less evolved.[18]

It is well to restate this assertion in Hartian terms. All legal concepts have frontiers, i.e. cases that raise questions that are 'open-textured' under existing precedent.[19] A legal concept that is comparatively less evolved will have an 'open-textured' frontier that is close to the core of the concept. By contrast, the 'open-textured' frontier of contract law is well beyond its core.

Let us consider legal concepts—and accompanying, purportedly general statements of law—that are comparatively less well evolved. The issue here is that elements of claims and the available defences (comparable problems would arise for power-conferring legal concepts) are not fully identified. Thus, any inference drawn from a statement to the effect that 'the owner of a business is liable to an individual under [for example] the Americans with Disabilities Act if the individual can establish all the elements of a claim under the Act, and the owner cannot establish entitlement to any applicable defence', would be defeated by the statement 'the high court has identified a new element of a claim under the Act [or a new defence that is applicable]'. In this example, the defeater is a rebutting defeater. It also may be possible to have undercutting defeaters in the form of decisions on related or analogous, but not identical, issues by courts that may cause persons analysing cases—in particular, judges—to question whether existing prior precedent remains vital and valid.

Jurisprudence under the Americans with Disabilities Act thus could not be said to have advanced to the 'evolved' setting described in this section (B.4). By contrast, it

[17] See n. 16.

[18] As an example of continued dispute over the proper application of the statute, see C.R. Sunstein, 'Cost–Benefit Analysis Without Analyzing Costs or Benefits: Reasonable Accommodation, Balancing, and Stigmatic Harms', *University of Chicago Law Review*, 74 (2007), 1895, where Cass Sunstein criticizes a recent federal court Americans with Disabilities Act decision authored by Judge Richard Posner.

[19] See H.L.A. Hart, *The Concept of Law*, 128–31.

seems fair to say that basic contract law (if not, for example, contract law under the UCC, the Uniform Commercial Code) has advanced that far. Prior precedent is quite established—it is rarely if ever overruled or cast in doubt.[20]

How realistic—and how bright—is the distinction between this setting, and the setting described in section B.3, above? Contract law is as good an example as any of a well-developed area of law, and it seems unlikely now that courts *on their own* would introduce new elements or new defences applicable in contract law. While there surely are social forces that may call for new applications of contract law—consider the growth in importance of electronic agreements, i.e. contracts made over the internet—it seems likely that courts faced with such forces simply will interpret *existing* contract law in the face of these social forces, leaving it to the legislature to provide for truly new rules to govern in these new areas of application.[21] (Consider the recent effort to generate uniform legislation governing contracts made over the internet under state and federal law in the United States, and in the European Union.)[22]

Of what use is the distinction between the settings described in sections B.3 and B.4? The answer is that they highlight differences in both Dewey's and Hart's approaches to defeasibility. In fact, Hart—in 'The Ascription of Responsibility and Rights' and *The Concept of Law*—and Dewey—at different points in *Logical Method and Law*—both suggest different conceptions of defeasibility. These different conceptions, I will argue, correspond to the settings described in sections B.3 and B.4.

The strongest defeasibility argument lodged by Dewey is his statement that '[n]o concrete proposition, that is to say one with material dated in time and placed in space, follows from any general statements or from any connection between them'.[23] Read literally, this statement suggests that there are no indefeasible, universal legal assertions, even in the setting described in section B.4. As Scott Brewer has demonstrated, however, Dewey's literal claim collapses under its own weight on the horns of a dilemma.[24] Moreover, the balance of Dewey's paper does not push his claim as far as the excerpted statement standing alone might suggest. In particular, Dewey concedes that 'antecedent assurance' is 'large wherever social conditions are pretty uniform, and when industry, commerce, transportation, etc. move in the channels of old customs. It is much less wherever invention is active and when devices in business and communication bring about new forms of human relationships.'[25] In effect, the different settings described in sections B.3 and B.4 herein mirror Dewey's distinction. Thus viewed, Dewey's thesis is not that any universal statement of law is always subject to defeat, but only that universal

[20] Frederick Schauer makes a similar distinction; see F. Schauer, 'On the Supposed Defeasibility of Legal Rules', 234–7, although he believes that '[t]he claim of necessary defeasibility appears most plausible with respect to the model of common law decision-making', ibid. at 236. I believe instead that the relevant distinction is stability in the law, which may be a function of numerous factors, including whether the area is subject to common law decision-making but also, for example, the comparative legal maturity of the area. Cf. R.D. Friedman, 'Logic and Elements', *Notre Dame Law Review*, 73 (1998), 591: '[P]resumptive implication is compatible with the idea that, *at least in some areas of the law*, full implication of th[e] more stringent type is an impossibility' (emphasis added).

[21] Cf. J.L. Goldsmith, 'Against Cyberanarchy', *University of Chicago Law Review*, 65 (1998), 1202: 'People transacting in cyberspace do things that would be regulated by state, national, or international law if they occurred in person or by telephone or mail'; J.R. Nash, 'A Context-Sensitive Voting Protocol Paradigm for Multimember Courts', *Stanford Law Review*, 56 (2003), 149.

[22] See generally M.H. Dessent, 'Digital Handshakes in Cyberspace under E-SIGN: "There's a New Sherriff in Town"', *University of Richmond Law Review*, 35 (2002), 943.

[23] J. Dewey, 'Logical Method and Law', 22.

[24] S. Brewer, 'On the Possibility of Necessity in Legal Argument: A Dilemma for Holmes and Dewey', *John Marshall Law Review*, 34 (2000), 26–31.

[25] J. Dewey, 'Logical Method and Law', 25.

statements of law may be defeated by legislative enactments or by fundamental shifts in law—in other words in the setting described in section B.3, not section B.4.

This account is consistent with the analysis Hart provides in *The Concept of Law*. Hart argues that most legal questions with which courts are faced fall within a well-defined core.[26] While all legal issues have penumbra that are open-textured and open to interpretation, that does not mean that the universal legal assertions that undergird these issues must be defeasible. Indeed, on the contrary, Hart's account of a well-defined core protects these assertions from defeat, for the existence of an open-textured penumbra as to specific application of a general legal assertion does not make the general assertion's necessary and sufficient conditions less certain.

The account given by Hart in *The Concept of Law* does not mesh with Hart's earlier direct analysis of defeasibility in 'The Ascription of Responsibility and Rights'. There, Hart asserts that, in accordance with Dewey's single-statement, strong assertion of defeasibility, no universal legal assertion is indefeasible.

Hart's argument in 'The Ascription of Responsibility and Rights' rests on the problem he perceives in representing 'heterogeneous' defences as necessary and sufficient conditions of a claim.[27] This argument is faulty. There is no reason that, if defences can be enumerated (even if they be heterogeneous), the absence of those defences cannot be stated as necessary and sufficient conditions for a claim to succeed. After all, just as defendants generally must establish their entitlement to defences, plaintiffs generally have the burden of establishing the elements of a claim. There simply is no reason for a theory of reasoning and for a conception of defeasibility to turn on whether a particular condition must be proven by the plaintiff or defendant.[28] In other words, if heterogeneous defences present a problem, so too should (or at least could) heterogeneous elements to be established by the plaintiff.[29]

Consider a universal assertion of enforceability of contract. Assume—as this section (B.4) does—that there is no change to the overarching governing law. How, then,

[26] See H.L.A. Hart, *The Concept of Law*, 131: '[T]here is no single method of determining the rule for which a given authoritative precedent is an authority. Notwithstanding this, in the vast majority of decided cases there is very little doubt'; ibid., at 139, legal rules generate a 'core of certainty'.

[27] Ibid., 150.

[28] Bruce Chapman suggests that the distinction that Hart draws between elements of a claim and defences is justified on the ground of defeasibility's 'path-dependent nature'. B. Chapman, 'Law, Incommensurability, and Conceptually Sequenced Argument', *University of Pennsylvania Law Review*, 146 (1998), 1509. By this he means that, '*until* some factual evidence of the defeating conditions is forthcoming, [a] concept simply *does* apply to the facts already at hand'. Ibid. Thus, for example, a contract may be enforceable until such time as an action to enforce it is time-barred. Compare, in this regard, the discussion in n. 6 about the extent to which the statement 'my father made a will yesterday' is a legal proposition and is false if it does not meet the governing legal standard.

True though Chapman's basic point may be, I do not believe that it accords with Hart's view in 'The Ascription of Responsibility and Rights', since it in no way turns on the heterogeneity of defences that Hart emphasized in that article. Moreover, I would point out again that, along the lines of the discussion in the text, there is no reason that Chapman's point should be confined to defences. Just as a contract that is enforceable may later become unenforceable because a defence becomes available to a party, so too a document that is not at one point yet a contract because one of the elements of contract has not been met (say acceptance of an offer) may become an enforceable contract when that element is met. In other words, compliance with affirmative elements of claims can also be seen as path-dependent.

[29] See R.P. Loui, 'Hart's Critics on Defeasible Concepts and Ascriptivism', 27, describing approvingly Feinberg's characterization of 'defeasibility as the source of shifting burdens'; see also J. Feinberg, 'Action and Responsibility' in M. Black (ed.), *Philosophy in America* (London: George Allen and Unwin, 1965), 136: 'The notion of defeasibility . . . is inextricably tied up with an adversary system of litigation and its complex and diverse rules'; G.P. Baker, 'Defeasibility and Meaning' in P. Hacker and J. Raz, *Law, Morality and Society* (Oxford: Clarendon Press, 1977), 33: 'Given the procedural rules for English law, we can determine . . . the burden of proof.'

could the statement 'a party to a contract can enforce the contract against the other party if and only if the party seeking to enforce the contract establishes by a preponderance of the evidence that the elements of an enforceable contract are met, and the party against whom enforcement is sought does not successfully assert by a preponderance of the evidence any applicable defence' be defeasible? (A full and accurate statement would list each of the elements and applicable defences.) Hart suggests in 'The Ascription of Responsibility and Rights' that defeasibility necessarily arises from the fact that some defences 'destroy altogether the claim that there is a contract, so that it is void *ab initio*',[30] while others render the contract 'merely "voidable" at the option of the party concerned',[31] and others 'merely extinguish the right to institute legal proceedings, but [do] not otherwise affect the existence of the contract'.[32] Why cannot this be addressed by adding as necessary and sufficient conditions for an enforceable contract 'if the defendant is unable successfully to assert that the contract is void as against public policy'; 'if the defendant cannot establish that he or she entered into the contract while intoxicated or, if he or she can establish that, he or she opts nonetheless to be bound by the contract'; and 'if EITHER the defendant cannot establish that an action to enforce the contract is time-barred OR the defendant has in any event affirmed the continued validity of the obligation after the time to enforce the contract would otherwise have run out'? Hart acknowledges that such a strategy exists, but in a footnote dismisses its effect as 'vacuous'.[33] Michael Bayles, on the contrary, thinks the approach sound.[34] And it appears that Hart himself later came around to this position.[35]

The susceptibility to defeat of purportedly universal legal assertions in the setting described in this section (B.4) lies if at all not with problems of enumerating all possible defences or exceptions to a legal definition, but with the possibility that the contours of legal concepts are inherently complex, even as their peripheries extend farther and farther out from their cores. This problem can arise as well from positive elements of legal claims, as from defences. For example, consider the common example of a statute that bans 'vehicles' from a park. Obviously, one element of the prosecution's claim in a case alleging a violation of the statute is that a 'vehicle' was involved. A problem may arise if the proper scope of the definition of 'vehicle' *continues forever* to raise troubling and unclear questions. In other words, as judges continue to find that some items qualify as 'vehicles' because they meet conditions sufficient to fall within the definition, and other items do not because they lack conditions that are held to be necessary to fall within the definition, the contours of the definition of 'vehicle' remain as jagged as they were when the first cases questioning the definition arose. (A helpful analogy may be to fractal theory, which suggests that a coastline looks equally jagged whether viewed from orbit around the earth or from a relatively short distance above the coastline.)[36] As Hart explained in a later piece, '[i]ndeterminacy springs from the fact that it is impossible in

[30] H.L.A. Hart, *The Concept of Law*, 149.
[31] Ibid., 150.
[32] Ibid.
[33] Ibid., 152 fn.1.
[34] See M.D. Bayles, *Hart's Legal Philosophy: An Examination* (Dordrecht: Kluwer, 1992), 12: '[A]bsence of the defence seems to be a positive condition'.
[35] See R.P. Loui, 'Hart's Critics on Defeasible Concepts and Ascriptivism', 26 (quoting and citing later works of Hart).

Relying on the assertion that '[w]ork on default reasoning, defeasible reasoning, logic programming, and argument, has shown that the difference between positive and negative conditions is crucial.' Ronald Loui adheres to the notion that defences are distinct from elements. Ibid.

[36] For explication, and discussion of the application of fractal theory to legal citation networks, see D.G. Post and M.B. Eisen, 'How Long is the Coastline of the Law? Thoughts on the Fractal Nature of Legal Systems', *Journal of Legal Studies*, 29 (2000), 545.

framing general rules to anticipate and provide for every possible combination of circumstances which the future may bring'.[37]

Whether or not an endless decision tree will grow out of a purportedly universal legal assertion is an empirical matter. Whether or not they *must* occur in *all* such cases (which would have to happen for Dewey's and Hart's broad defeasibility claims to be true) seems to be highly questionable. At least for some legal assertions, it seems likely that the penumbra that Hart speaks of is far enough from the core of the assertion and well defined enough that an infinite chain will not raise.[38] However, the answer cannot be resolved in the abstract.

In any event, however, even if these infinite chains indeed occur in respect of all purportedly universal legal assertions, I submit that, nonetheless, the distinct settings described in sections B.3 and B.4—based as they are on Hart's description of a core of settled meaning in *The Concept of Law*—remain important. This is because I believe it would remain relevant and meaningful to speak of legal assertions that are substantially, if not wholly, indefeasible.[39] By this I mean that mature legal concepts with a well-

[37] H.L.A. Hart, 'Problems of the Philosophy of Law', 6 *Encyclopedia of Philosophy* (Paul Edwards, ed. 1967), reprinted in H.L.A. Hart, *Essays in Jurisprudence and Philosophy* (Oxford: Clarendon Press, 1983), 103.

[38] One might think, in this regard, of the provision in the US Constitution governing amendments to the Constitution—US Const. Art. V. Article V includes a provision that shields from possible amendment a state's right to 'equal Suffrage in the Senate' absent the state's consent otherwise. Ibid. Some have argued that Article V cannot itself be amended. See, e.g. D. Linder, 'What in the Constitution Cannot be Amended?', *Arizona Law Review*, 23 (1981), 722–5. See also ibid. at 733 (suggesting that Art. V 'cannot be amended to so as to create any new limitations on the amending power'). For discussion of other possible limitations on the power to amend the Constitution, see, for example, J.R. Vile, 'The Case Against Implicit Limits on the Constitutional Amending Process' in S. Levinson (ed.), *Responding to Imperfection: The Theory and Practice of Constitutional Amendment* (Princeton: Princeton University Press, 1995), 213, arguing that the Constitution's implicit limits on Art. V 'wisely protect liberty by guarding against the transient whims of the majority'); C.A. Kelbley, 'Are There Limits to Constitutional Change? Rawls on Comprehensive Doctrines, Unconstitutional Amendments, and the Basis of Equality', *Fordham Law Review*, 72 (2004), 1487; A. Vermeule and E.A. Young, 'Hercules, Herbert, and Amar: The Trouble with Intratextualism', *Harvard Law Review*, 113 (2000), 760 fn.160, identifying Akhil Amar's 'implicit assumption that constitutional amendments should be read to cohere with all other parts of the document'; J. Mazzone, 'Unamendments', *Iowa Law Review*, 90 (2005), 1754–801, discussing pre-Civil War substantive limits on Art. V; ibid. at 1805–12, arguing that certain amendments to the Constitution impose substantive limits on future amendments.

As compared to constitutional provisions, statutes are generally understood to be less durable. Nonetheless, some commentators argue that certain statutory regimes attain 'super-statute' status, which status renders them virtually impossible to repeal. See W.N. Eskridge, Jr and J. Ferejohn, 'Super-Statutes', *Duke Law Journal*, 50 (2001), 1215ff.

[39] An analogy to the emergence and durability of legal property rights may be instructive here. As I indicated above, see n. 13, a common explanation offered by property law theorists for the emergence of property rights is that government-enforced property rights are required because, in their absence, people cannot agree to share property or otherwise to respect others' rights in property. This traditional account has been criticized because it fails to explain how the very people who are unable to agree to respect one another's property rights can agree to give rise to a government that will protect property rights. See ibid.

Now, instead of considering the story of the creation of property rights, let us consider instead the durability of property rights once they are created. Now the standard account suggests that the persistence of government is for property rights to endure. If this is so, then we should expect at least many property rights to enjoy substantial indefeasibility. In fact, much of the property literature suggests something even broader: property rights are ubiquitous, and extend across culture, class, and—most important for our purposes here—type of legal system. See J.R. Nash, 'Packaging Property: The Effect of Paradigmatic Framing of Property Rights', *Tulane Law Review*, 83 (2009), 694–707, describing this literature, and critiquing the point; compare *United States* v. *Percheman*, 32 U.S. (7 Pet.) 51, 86–7 (1833) (Marshall, J.) ('[I]t is very unusual, even in cases of conquest, for the conqueror to do more than to displace the sovereign and assume dominion over the county. The modern usage of nations, which has become law, would be violated; that sense of justice and of right which is acknowledged and felt by the whole civilized

established core of settled meaning are defeasible only in the distant penumbra, and necessarily in comparatively minor ways.[40] Thus, while it may be true that all universal legal assertions are, logically, defeasible, that conclusion does not have the devastating effect on legal reasoning that some—such as Felix Cohen—would suggest. Cohen is simply wrong that all legal reasoning is nothing more than 'transcendental nonsense',[41] since most mature legal assertions are at least 'substantially indefeasible'.

Cohen suggests that at bottom courts do not reach reasoned conclusions, but rather that they decide upon a functional outcome and then assemble legal language—that Cohen refers to as 'transcendental nonsense'—in support of that conclusion. Cohen asserts that courts could as well reach the opposite conclusion, and assemble 'transcendental nonsense' in support. If, however, as I argue, most mature legal assertions are at least 'substantially indefeasible' and if the extant legal system consists of enough mature legal assertions, then Cohen's objection is not of great concern, playing a role only at the distant and limited periphery of legal concepts.

It remains to construct, by proceeding backward through the various possible backdrops of defeasibility we have considered, a truly indefeasible universal statement of law. The logic in constructing such a statement in this way becomes evident when one realizes that (with the exception of the first backdrop—that of law in the abstract), each backdrop has been a proper subset of the one that preceded it. In other words, the available defeaters in section B.4 are a proper subset of those available in section B.3, which in turn form a proper subset of those available in section B.2. Thus, an indefeasible universal legal assertion might be (in reality, spelling out all the applicable elements and defences): 'A contract is enforceable by a party if and only if (i) the party seeking enforcement can establish all the elements of a contract; and (ii) the party against whom enforcement is sought cannot establish entitlement to any defence; provided that the elements and defences referred to in prongs (i) and (ii) are determined in accordance with (iii) the governing rule of recognition (iv) under the then-existing legal system'. While the foregoing in practice may do little other than to point out that what most lawyers and judges (and likely laypeople) would call 'universal' statements of law are in fact defeasible, this approach accords nicely with a 'punctuated equilibrium' view of law.[42] Although legal assertions well may be defeasible over time—whether

world would be outraged, if private property should be generally confiscated, and private rights annulled. The people change their allegiance; their relation to their ancient sovereign is dissolved: but their relations to each other, and their rights of property remain undisturbed... A cession of territory is never understood to be a cession of the property belonging to its inhabitants. The king cedes that only which belonged to him. Lands he had previously granted were not his to cede') with *Johnson* v. *M'Intosh*, 21 U.S. (8 Wheat.) 543 (1823) (Marshall, J.) (holding that Native American property rights were largely, though not entirely, extinguished by European conquests). If that is indeed the case, then it seems that property rights are heartily indefeasible—that is, they often survive even from governmental system to governmental system.

[40] But see F.M. Bloom, 'State Courts Unbound', *Cornell Law Review*, 93 (2008), 512: 'Many legal terms are wrapped in hopeless "open-textured" uncertainty.'

[41] See F.S. Cohen, 'Transcendental Nonsense and the Functional Approach', 809.

[42] The concept of the 'punctuated equilibrium' originated in the biological sciences as a description for the process of evolution. See E. Lee, 'The Public's Domain: The Evolution of Legal Restraints on the Government's Power to Control Public Access through Secrecy or Intellectual Property', 55 *Hastings Law Journal*, 91 (2003), 172 fn. 397. For applications of the concept to legal settings, see, for example, ibid. at 172–4; W. Dean Burnham, 'Constitutional Moments and Punctuated Equilibria: A Political Scientist Confronts Bruce Ackerman's *We the People*', *Yale Law Journal*, 108 (1999), 2237. Cf. L.A. Cunningham, 'The Common Law as an Iterative Process: A Preliminary Inquiry', *Notre Dame Law Review*, 80 (2006), 747, describing how the common law can evolve yet still feature periods of remarkable stability.

because of changes to the actual governing legal system, or because changes in circumstances over time warrant changes to particular legal rules—many if not most evolved legal rules are in fact indefeasible, or at least substantially so, over extended periods of time.[43]

C. Evidence of substantial indefeasibility in US jurisprudence

In the previous section, I advanced the claim that many—in fact, a substantial portion of—legal statements in mature legal systems are substantially indefeasible, meaning that, though they may technically be defeasible, they are well enough established that absent extraordinary circumstances they will not be subject to defeasance. While this is at heart an empirical claim that would be quite difficult to validate, I offer in this section some evidence that the claim is accurate.

I focus on US jurisprudence in this undertaking. I do so in part because of my familiarity with it, but also in great part because it is in large measure a common law jurisdiction and it has been suggested that common law decision-making is generally even more defeasible than civil law decision-making.[44] Thus, signs of substantial indefeasibility in US jurisprudence would suggest its existence and perhaps ubiquity in other legal systems as well.

Consider first the views of commentators. Richard Friedman has argued that logic plays a significant role in legal reasoning and discourse.[45] In particular, he finds the jurisprudence of issue preclusion susceptible to analysis using indefeasible rules of classic logic.[46] Friedman does not contend that all of law may similarly be treated. He notes that 'a certain entropy in rules, or at least in many rules' may 'tend to break down their sharp edges' and thus to render them less susceptible to helpful representation by symbolic logic.[47] And he also highlights the usefulness of defeasible logic to

[43] Cf. S. Brewer, 'Exemplary Reasoning: Semantics, Pragmatics, and the Rational Force of Legal Argument by Analogy', *Harvard Law Review*, 109 (1996), 1018, discussing the conception of 'deductive defeasance', under which '"defeasing" decisions... are best reconstructed from a logical point of view as changes in the law, as reflected by changes in the logical structure of analogized and disanalogized legal rules, rather than as the addition of new premises to a perpetually open-ended premise set (as in inductive arguments)'.

[44] See, e.g. F. Schauer, 'On the Supposed Defeasibility of Legal Rules', 236: 'The claim of necessary defeasibility appears most plausible with respect to the model of common law decision-making.' See also E.H. Levi, *An Introduction to Legal Reasoning* (Chicago: University of Chicago Press, 1951), 19: 'It is customary to think of case-law reasoning as inductive and the application of statutes as deductive. The thought seems erroneous but the emphasis has some meaning.' Cf. J.A. Lovett, 'On the Principle of Legal Certainty in the Louisiana Civil Law Tradition: From the Manifesto to the Great Repealing Act and Beyond', *Louisiana Law Review*, 63 (2003), 1397, arguing that Louisiana jurisprudence exhibits the tension inherent between the certainty generally associated with civil law on the one hand, and equity and flexibility on the other; but cf. R.H.S. Tur, 'Two Theories of Criminal Law', *Southern Methodist University Law Review*, 56 (2003), 801–2, 'Codification, for all its aspirations and pretensions, cannot entirely, if at all, abolish history, ethics, and sociology'; L. Grossman, 'Langdell Upside-Down: James Coolidge Carter and the Anticlassical Jurisprudence of Anti-Codification', *Yale Journal of Law and the Humanities*, 19 (2007), 149, arguing that nineteenth-century American opponents of legal codification did not hold monolithic views of the logical structure of American common law.

[45] See R.D. Friedman, 'Logic and Elements', *Notre Dame Law Review*, 73 (1998), 575.

[46] See ibid. 577–81. Richard Tur is not so sanguine that the English scheme of *res judicata* is indefeasible, although he allows that, as compared to other forms of *res judicata* issue preclusion is the better candidate for that status: '[T]here is a degree of diffidence and uncertainty as to whether *res judicata* is defeasible in both its guises or only in respect of issue estoppel.' R.H.S. Tur, '*Res Judicata* and Theories of Law', *Oxford University Commonwealth Law Journal*, 1 (2001), 127.

[47] See R.D. Friedman, 'Logic and Elements', 587.

understand certain aspects of legal discourse.[48] Still, his success in applying classic logic to the area of issue preclusion lends credence to the notion that some legal concepts may properly be viewed as indefeasible, at least for extended periods of time.

Frederick Schauer's views suggest that the extent to which an area of law is substantially indefeasible turns on the extent to which the law in the area rests on a 'model of formality' or a 'model of adaptability'.[49] As he explains, both these models are 'plausible, and both are found to a greater or lesser degree in most of the world's legal systems'.[50] He further notes that most areas of law rest upon some hybrid of the two.[51]

Henry Smith has suggested an economic rationale as to why law might tend to evolve with extended periods of stability, and hence indefeasibility. He draws an analogy between defeasibility of inference and legal defeasibility. He explains that:

> [r]esolving ambiguities or assessing the strength of defeasible inferences is easier with more background knowledge of context; and imposing the burden of using context on wide audiences without background knowledge raises processing cost in two ways. First, such audiences are not likely to have this background knowledge at low cost. Second, the number of those incurring this cost can also be large.[52]

By similar logic, then, defeasible legal rules can have high costs. As Smith explains:

> Th[e] notion of [legal] defeasibility has informational implications similar to the defeasibility of inference in interpreting any communicative act. To the extent that information drawn from a communication (for example, a claim, a legal rule) is defeasible, processing it will be more costly. Determining to what degree to pursue nondefeasibility will depend in part on the nature and size of the audience.[53]

The potentially high costs associated with broadly applicable defeasible legal rules suggest that the law should evolve to minimize their occurrence. This, then, lends economic support to the hypothesis that settings such as those described in section B.4—that is, settings in which persisting relative stability renders many legal rules substantially indefeasible—should be common.

The question of whether law is seen to be substantially indefeasible is ultimately one of perception. To verify the claim that a substantial portion of US law is seen to be substantially indefeasible, I shall consider the views of the courts as expressed through judicial opinions and practice, and also the views of the Congress as expressed through legislation.

Courts in the United States generally adhere to the doctrine of *stare decisis*.[54] Succinctly put, *stare decisis* requires courts, subject to certain exceptions, to follow as

[48] See ibid. at 587–97. In particular, he suggests that traditional logic—and, therefore, indefeasibility—will in general apply more readily to settings where the law is expressed as a rule as opposed to a standard. See ibid., 587.

For a discussion of the applicability of logic to law, see H. Bavli, Note, 'Applying the Laws of Logic to the Logic of Law', *Fordham Urban Law Journal*, 33 (2006), 937.

[49] F. Schauer, 'On the Supposed Defeasibility of Legal Rules', 237.

[50] Ibid.

[51] Ibid. ('Just as the common law is willing to sacrifice some of th[e] virtues [of formality] to get *this* case right, so might other systems be willing to sacrifice some of the virtues of act-based optimization in order to achieve other goals').

[52] H.E. Smith, 'The Language of Property: Form, Context, and Audience'.

[53] Ibid., 1178 fn. 255. Cf. S. Shavell, 'On Optimal Legal Change, Past Behavior, and Grandfathering', *Journal of Legal Studies*, 37 (2008), 37–8: '[L]egal rules should be more stable than would apparently be appropriate, that is, appropriate were past behavior not taken into account'.

[54] For discussion of the question of the application of *stare decisis* to nonjudicial actors, see 'Symposium, *Stare Decisis* and Nonjudicial Actors', *Notre Dame Law Review*, 83 (2008), 1147. For discussion of the cognate question—the extent to which nonjudicial actors may provide precedents for courts (and other public authorities)—see M.J. Gerhardt, 'Non-Judicial Precedent', *Vanderbilt Law Review*, 61 (2008), 713.

precedent earlier court decisions and holdings.[55] *Stare decisis* can be horizontal and vertical. Under horizontal *stare decisis*, a court that issues a holding is bound in future by that holding in future cases, unless the holding is overruled by that court or by a higher court.[56] Under vertical *stare decisis*, a decision by a superior court binds all inferior courts in the judicial hierarchy.[57]

The doctrine of *stare decisis* accords with the general notion of substantial indefeasibility; holdings of courts are presumed to remain law. Indeed, they only lose the force of law once they are validly and legally overruled. Still, there are several objections that one might raise to reliance upon *stare decisis* as evidence of substantial indefeasibility in the US common law system.

First, one might object that the doctrine of *stare decisis* is not absolute. For example, the Supreme Court has on occasion justified overruling prior precedent when it concludes that the prior precedent is 'unworkable'.[58] It also has occasionally been suggested that decisions issued by close votes (say 5–4) are less robust and entitled to less precedential weight than decisions issued by wider majorities.[59] On the basis that legislative recourse provides an escape valve for undesirable statutory interpretation, the courts have indicated that decisions interpreting statutes are entitled to greater *stare decisis* effect than are constitutional decisions.[60] Finally,

[55] See J.R. Nash and R.I. Pardo, 'An Empirical Investigation into Appellate Structure and the Perceived Quality of Appellate Review', *Vanderbilt Law Review*, 61 (2008), 1749–51.

[56] See ibid., 1750. Though in theory it could, horizontal *stare decisis* has not been held to extend such that a court is bound by holdings of co-equal courts, that is courts that are of equal level in the judicial hierarchy. See ibid. at 1750 fn. 13.

[57] See ibid., 1750.

[58] See, e.g. *Payne* v. *Tennessee*, 501 U.S. 808, 827 (1991) ('[W]hen governing decisions are unworkable..., "this Court has never felt constrained to follow precedent"' (quoting *Smith* v. *Allwright*, 321 U.S. 649, 665 (1944))). For a critique of the unworkability doctrine, see, for example, Lauren Vicki Stark, 'Note, The Unworkable Unworkability Test', 80 *N.Y.U. L. Rev.* 1665 (2005).

[59] See, e.g. *Payne* v. *Tennessee*, 501 U.S. 808, 829 (1991) (justifying the overruling of earlier Supreme Court decisions in part on the grounds that they were decided by 'the narrowest of margins, over spirited dissents challenging the basic underpinnings of those decisions'); cf. M. Rosenfeld, 'Comparing Constitutional Review by the European Court of Justice and the US Supreme Court', *International Journal of Constitutional Law*, 4 (2006), 639, noting that a 5–4 US Supreme Court decision is 'a binding opinion without seeming authoritarian', and discussing an example of the court overruling an earlier controversial decision decided by 5–4 vote); but see M.J. Gerhardt, 'The Role of Precedent in Constitutional Decision Making and Theory', *The George Washington International Law Review*, 60 (1991), 113: 'It would disrupt our legal system severely for anyone on or off the Court to treat a 5–4 vote with a vigorous dissent as a rule of law entitled to less respect from the Court and other government decision-makers than any of the Court's other constitutional law decisions'.

[60] See, e.g. *Neal* v. *United States*, 516 U.S. 284, 295–6 (1996); see also A. Coney Barrett, 'Statutory *Stare Decisis* in the Courts of Appeals', *The George Washington International Law Review*, 73 (2005), 317, observing, and criticizing, similar practice by the lower federal courts; cf. K.A. Bamberger, 'Provisional Precedent: Protecting Flexibility in Administrative Policymaking', *New York University Law Review*, 77 (2002), 1272, arguing that ordinary *stare decisis* should not apply to court interpretations of statutes issued before the agency with administrative responsibility for the statute has had a say, in order to preserve administrative flexibility. For debate over the constitutional status of the *stare decisis* rules governing constitutional decisions, compare, for example, M. Stokes Paulsen, 'Abrogating *Stare Decisis* by Statute: May Congress Remove the Precedential Effect of *Roe* and *Casey*?', *Yale Law Journal*, 109 (2000), 1535, arguing that Congress may alter such rules, with R.H. Fallon, Jr, '*Stare Decisis* and the Constitution: An Essay on Constitutional Methodology', *New York University Law Review*, 76 (2001), 570, arguing for constitutional status of such rules. See also D.L. Shapiro, 'The Role of Precedent in Constitutional Adjudication: An Introspection', *Texas Law Review*, 86 (2008), 947–56, demonstrating through an example the difficulties Supreme Court Justices face in applying *stare decisis* to constitutional decisions. Cf. M.J. Ryan, 'Does *Stare Decisis* Apply in the Eighth Amendment Death Penalty Context?', *North Carolina Law Review*, 85 (2007), 847, noting that lower courts have applied, and arguing that they should apply, different *stare decisis* rules in Eighth Amendment death penalty cases.

stare decisis rules don't always extend horizontally[61] or vertically as one might expect.[62]

These limits on *stare decisis* doctrine are orthogonal to the argument here, however. My point is neither that some legal propositions are entirely indefeasible nor that every legal proposition is substantially indefeasible, but only that many legal propositions are

[61] Consider that federal district judges are not bound by decisions of other district judges in the same district. See J.R. Nash and R.I. Pardo, 'An Empirical Investigation into Appellate Structure and the Perceived Quality of Appellate Review', 1750 fn.13; cf. J.R. Bartels, 'United States District Courts *En Banc*—Resolving the Ambiguities', *Judicature*, 73 (1989), 40, identifying *en banc* district court hearings in 38 reported decisions and unpublished decisions from 1928–89.

Construing horizontal *stare decisis* more broadly, courts do not generally see themselves as bound by decisions issued by sibling courts of co-equal stature in the judicial hierarchical structure. Thus, for example, federal courts of appeals do not understand themselves to be bound by decisions issued by sister circuits. See, e.g. J.R. Nash and R.I. Pardo, 'An Empirical Investigation into Appellate Structure and the Perceived Quality of Appellate Review', 1750 fn.13. (Indeed, it seems that the Supreme Court relies upon so-called 'circuit conflicts' in deciding which legal issues are ripe for review. In some sense, the absence of horizontal *stare decisis* among circuits allows issues to percolate up to the Supreme Court for review. See S. Estreicher and J. Sexton, 'A Managerial Theory of the Supreme Court's Responsibilities: An Empirical Study', *New York University Law Review*, 59 (1984), 717–20.The limited nature of horizontal *stare decisis* is also demonstrated by the limited extent to which state courts are bound by federal court decisions on questions of federal law. On the one hand, state courts are bound by Supreme Court precedent on federal law; see, e.g. R.A. Schapiro, 'Interjurisdictional Enforcement of Rights in a Post-Erie World', *William and Mary Law Review*, 46 (2005), 1408: 'The US Supreme Court stands as the ultimate interpreter of federal law, reviewing issues of federal law that arise in lower federal courts or in state courts', and also by any decisions on federal law by a higher-ranked state court whose decisions would ordinarily be binding upon the state court.

Lower federal courts' interpretations of state law might be persuasive, but are not binding. See *Lockhart* v. *Fretwell*, 506 U.S. 364, 376 (1993) (Thomas, J., concurring) ('The Supremacy Clause demands that state law yield to federal law, but neither federal supremacy nor any other principle of federal law requires that a state court's interpretation of federal law give way to a (lower) federal court's interpretation. In our federal system, a state trial court's interpretation of federal law is no less authoritative than that of the federal court of appeals in whose circuit the trial court is located'); *State* v. *Mechtel*, 499 N.W.2d 662, 666 (Wis. 1993) ('It is clear... that determinations on federal questions by either the federal circuit courts of appeal[s] or the federal district courts are not binding upon state courts'). Cf. *State* v. *Knowles*, 371 A.2d 624, 627–8 (Me. 1977) ('[E]ven though only a decision of the Supreme Court of the United States is the supreme law of the land on a federal constitutional issue, nevertheless "in the interest of developing harmonious federal–state relationships it is a wise policy that a state court of last resort accept, so far as reasonably possible, a decision"' of the federal court of appeals within the geographic circuit of which the state lies on a federal constitutional question (quoting *State* v. *Lafferty*, 309 A.2d 647, 667 (Me. 1973) (Wernick, J., concurring))). But see R.H. Fallon, Jr, D.J. Meltzer, and D.L. Shapiro, *Hart & Wechsler's The Federal Courts and the Federal System* (5th edn, Foundation Press, 2003), 481, describing a 1995 Congressional bill that would have made a decision by a federal court of appeals on federal products liability law binding (absent modification by the Supreme Court) on all courts of any state lying within the geographic reach of the circuit, citing S. 565, 104th Cong., 1st Sess., §3(E), 104th Cong. Rec. S. 3978–80.

One might think that, the general rule that state courts are not bound by lower federal courts notwithstanding, a state court might consider it pointless to resolve a case differently than would a federal court when the federal court might enjoy the chance to review the state court decision collaterally. Even here, however, state courts have adhered to the rule that they are not technically bound. In *People* v. *Santamaria*, 884 P.2d 81 (Cal. 1994), the California Supreme Court, considering a prisoner's appeal, reached an interpretation of federal law at odds with a determination of the relevant law earlier reached by a panel of the Ninth Circuit on a *habeas* appeal by a California state prisoner. The state high court explained that, by virtue of the federal courts' *habeas* review authority, '[w]e... have the situation that, although normally federal circuit court decisions are not binding on this court..., here they have the power to effectively overrule our decision.' Ibid. at 92 (citations omitted). The state court stuck to its interpretation and concluded by 'urg[ing] the federal courts to reconsider that decision if and when the issue is again before them in light of our analysis of state law and... subsequent [Supreme Court and court of appeals] decisions...' Ibid. at 93 (citations omitted).

[62] The application of vertical *stare decisis* poses a problem in the setting of bankruptcy appeals, insofar as certain appeals from bankruptcy courts may be heard by either the federal district court or (with the consent of the parties) the circuit's bankruptcy appellate panel. See J.R. Nash and

substantially indefeasible. The relevant point, then, is that *stare decisis* acts to cabin a court's discretion to overrule prior precedent. That, in turn, will tend to foster substantial indefeasibility.

Second, one might point out that there are some cases that never gain *stare decisis* effect. First, many courts issue so-called unpublished opinions that, by their own terms and under court rules, lack precedential effect.[63] We might say that unpublished opinions are 'defeasible by design'.

Second, the vote by which a multimember appellate court decides a case sometimes dictates that the case not be given *stare decisis* effect. Tie votes do not set any precedent.[64] Decisions not issued by a quorum of the court are without any effect, including precedential effect.[65] And sometimes judges on a multimember court in a

R.I. Pardo, 'An Empirical Investigation into Appellate Structure and the Perceived Quality of Appellate Review', 1761–2. There is contention as to whether the decisions of federal bankruptcy appellate panels that hear certain appeals from bankruptcy courts are binding precedent on the bankruptcy courts within that circuit. Compare, e.g. *Philadelphia Life Ins. Co.* v. *Proudfoot* (*In re Proudfoot*), 144 B.R. 876, 879 (B.A.P. 9th Cir. 1992) ('[B]AP decisions originating in any district in the Ninth Circuit are binding precedent on all bankruptcy courts within the Ninth Circuit in the absence of contrary authority from the district court for the district in which the bankruptcy court sits'); *Life Ins. Co. of Va.* v. *Barakat* (*In re Barakat*), 173 B.R. 672, 676–80 (Bankr. C.D. Cal. 1994) (concluding that BAPs bind bankruptcy courts on matters arising in core proceedings even though district courts do not), *aff'd on other grounds*, 99 F.3d 1520 (9th Cir. 1996) with *Ore. Higher Educ. Assistance Found.* v. *Selden* (*In re Selden*), 121 B.R. 59, 62 (D. Ore. 1990) (stating that BAP decisions bind only those bankruptcy courts sitting in the district out of which the appeal arose), with *Daly* v. *Deptula* (*In re Carrozzella & Richardson*), 255 B.R. 267, 273 (Bankr. D. Conn. 2000) (rejecting the argument that substantial motivation of Congress in creating BAPs was to generate a uniform body of bankruptcy law within the circuits; concluding that there is no principled reason why decisions of a BAP should have more precedential authority than those of district courts; and finding it odd and unseemly, if not unconstitutional, for a BAP—comprised of three Article I judges—to be generating for bankruptcy judges, and perhaps also for district judges, the law of the circuit until the circuit court had spoken); *In re Virden*, 279 B.R. 401, 409 n.12 (Bankr. D. Mass. 2002) (same).

Vertical *stare decisis* is also an issue for the United States Tax Court, insofar as appeals from that court lie with the federal court of appeals in which the taxpayer resides. The tax court has held that, to the extent it disagrees with an opinion issued by a federal court of appeals, it will follow the court of appeals' rule only in cases where the appeal will be heard by that court of appeals. See *Golsen* v. *Comm'r*, 54 T.C. 742, 757 (1970), *aff'd*, 445 F.2d 985 (10th Cir. 1971). It appears, however, that the tax court's justification for this practice is grounded not in the notion that it is bound by *stare decisis*, but rather in the practical concern that to proceed otherwise would simply guarantee reversal by the court of appeals (which is of course bound by its own rule). See ibid. at 757 (attributing the practice to the desire for 'efficient and harmonious judicial administration').

63 For criticism of the practice, see, for example, D.R. Cleveland, 'Overturning the Last Stone: The Final Step in Returning Precedential Status to All Opinions', *Journal of Appellate Practice and Process*, 10 (2009), 61.

For examination of the distinction between the American and English practices, see L. Faircloth Peoples, 'Controlling the Common Law: A Comparative Analysis of No-Citation Rules and Publication Practices in England and the United States', *Indiana International and Comparative Law Review*, 17 (2007), 307.

64 See J.R. Nash, 'The Majority That Wasn't: *Stare Decisis*, Majority Rule, and the Mischief of Quorum Requirements', *Emory Law Journal*, 57 (2009), 855–6.

65 See ibid., 839–49; cf. J.R. Nash, '5th Circuit's Shameful Disappearing Act', *The National Law Journal*, 12 July 2010, at 34 (critiquing the Fifth Circuit in *Comer* v. *Murphy Oil USA*, 607 F.3d 1049 (5th Cir. 2010), *mandamus denied sub nom. In re Comer*, 79 U.S.L.W. 3128 (U.S. 10 January 2011), for vacating a panel decision based upon a vote of a quorum to grant *en banc* rehearing, but then dismissing the appeal when the quorum dissipated once a judge who had voted in the *en banc* poll recused herself). A separate question arises as to whether, and if so to what extent, precedential effect attaches to a decision joined by a number of judges that, while it constitutes a majority of judges hearing the case, does not constitute of a majority of judges authorized to sit on the court and hear cases. For discussion, see generally J.R. Nash, 'The Majority That Wasn't: *Stare Decisis*, Majority Rule, and the Mischief of Quorum Requirements', 869–87.

multi-issue case will decide a case in such a way that the vote of the judges on the outcome differs from the result one would obtain if one summed up the vote of the judges on an issue-by-issue basis and in fact decided each issue on that basis.[66] Such cases are called cases of 'doctrinal paradox', in reference to the intractable difficulties such cases pose to lower courts, and subsequent panels of the same court, when they try to determine the proper precedent to follow.[67] We might refer to all these types of cases as 'inherently defeasible': the very makeup of the votes that generates them renders them immediately defeasible.

The existence of inherently defeasible decisions does not per se undermine the notion of a substantially indefeasible jurisprudence. The fact is that such decisions do not arise very often.[68] And, to the extent they from time to time occur, many jurisdictions take steps to mitigate the problem; New Jersey, for example, authorizes the appointment of lower court judges to sit on cases heard by its supreme court in order to avoid ties.[69] To the extent these problems arise in lower or intermediate courts, moreover, higher courts also might mitigate these problems by choosing to review such cases.[70] In the end, the possibility of a few decisions out of many being defeasible is clearly not a per se threat to a measure of indefeasibility that turns, by definition, on substantiality.

The problem of holdings that are 'defeasible by design'—that is, unpublished decisions—poses a different problem, albeit one that also is not insurmountable for a claim of substantial indefeasibility. Unlike inherently defeasible decisions, decisions that are defeasible by design are quite numerous. Indeed, some courts classify the majority of their decisions as unpublished.[71]

To see that the phenomenon of unpublished decisions is not inconsistent with substantial indefeasibility, consider that the genesis of unpublished decisions seems to have been a desire to conserve judicial resources. By agreeing that only some opinions handed down will be binding precedent, the judges on a court can focus their resources on deciding, and perfecting opinions in, cases that will, so to speak, 'really matter' going forward. In this sense, then, not only is the notion of unpublished decisions that lack precedential value not inconsistent with substantial indefeasibility, it is designed to

[66] See J.R. Nash, 'A Context-Sensitive Voting Protocol Paradigm for Multimember Courts', 79–82.

[67] See ibid., 95–135.

[68] With respect to the number of cases of doctrinal paradox, see J.M. Rogers, '"I Vote This Way Because I'm Wrong": The Supreme Court Justice as Epimenides', *Kentucky Law Journal*, 79 (1991), 439, cataloguing all the occurrences; J.M. Rogers, '"Issue Voting" by Multimember Appellate Courts: A Response to Some Radical Proposals', *Vanderbilt Law Review*, 49 (1996), 997–9; but see D.G. Post and S.C. Salop, 'Issues and Outcomes, Guidance, and Indeterminacy: A Reply to Professor John Rogers and Others', *Vanderbilt Law Review*, 49 (1996), 1082 fn. 35, using a stylized example to show that, on not implausible assumptions, doctrinal paradoxes will arise in '[a] nontrivial proportion of cases'. With respect to cases with tie votes, see R. Black and L. Epstein, 'Recusals and the "Problem" of an Equally Divided Supreme Court', *Journal of Appellate Practice and Process*, 7 (2005), 85–6, presenting data showing that an even panel of Supreme Court Justices heard cases (and thus a tie theoretically could have resulted) in only 19.35 per cent of cases, and that in only 6 per cent of those cases 'did an actual tie result'; ibid. at 87–94, presenting data and concluding that 'discretionary recusal does not appear to lead to an appreciable increase in either equally divided Courts or plurality opinions'.

[69] See E.A. Hartnett, 'Ties in the Supreme Court of New Jersey', *Seton Hall Law Review*, 32 (2003), 735.

[70] See J.R. Nash, 'A Context-Sensitive Voting Protocol Paradigm for Multimember Courts', 157.

[71] See, e.g. M. Hannon, 'A Closer Look at Unpublished Opinions in the United States Courts of Appeals', *Journal of Appellate Practice and Process*, 3 (2001), 201, '[C]urrently more than 79 per cent of federal circuit court opinions are unpublished.'; ibid. at 202 tbl. 1, presenting annual summary statistics.

enhance it. Courts that issue large numbers of cases face the reality that some cases will contradict one another.[72] The escape valve of unpublished decisions allows judges on a court the freedom to focus on, and develop, a limited set of cases and holdings that will really tend to be indefeasible.[73]

The consistency of unpublished decisions with substantial indefeasibility also can be seen by considering the two classes of cases that tend to comprise unpublished decisions. First, and the notion of unpublished opinions seems to have arisen with this use in mind, courts determine that some cases simply do not announce new rules of law such that they are worthy of publication.[74] Since cases of this nature do not, by definition, break new ground, one would expect them neither to defeat other cases nor to be likely to be defeated in the future by other cases, at least as to major, established points of law. The second class of cases consists of cases that do raise novel issues of law but novel issues that, for one reason or another, the judges on the court are reticent to decide definitively at that time.[75] Here, of course, there is a substantial probability that a subsequent holding might overrule the earlier unpublished case. But in some sense the court avoids, or at least ameliorates, that possibility by leaving the first decision unpublished; leaving the decision unpublished renders it, in some sense, null for *stare decisis* purposes. Thus, the fact that the first decision is unpublished avoids the need to say that the second decision defeated the first; instead, the second decision—which presumably will decide the issue definitively and will be published and thus enjoy *stare decisis* effect—will, one might expect, enjoy substantial indefeasibility, while the first decision is technically just a nullity.[76]

[72] See P.M. Wald, 'Changing Course: The Use of Precedent in the District of Columbia Circuit', *Cleveland State Law Review*, 34 (1986), 480: 'Inevitably, [court of appeals decisions] are not all consistent'; see also *McMellon* v. *United States*, 387 F.3d 329, 332–4 (4th Cir. 2004) (*en banc*) (noting that, while the issue of conflicting panel decisions was 'fairly uncommon' before the court, it was prudent to develop a precedential rule to address such situations).

[73] See, e.g. *Hart* v. *Massanari*, 266 F.3d 1155, 1176 (9th Cir. 2001) ('No doubt the most serious implication of [a] constitutional rule [that bars unpublished opinions] is that it would preclude appellate courts from developing a coherent and internally consistent body of case law to serve as binding authority for themselves and the courts below them'); *Symbol Techs., Inc.* v. *Lemelson Med. Educ. & Res. Found.*, 277 F.3d 1361, 1368 (Fed. Cir. 2002) ('Courts contribute to the growing imprecision, uncertainty and unpredictability of the law by issuing repetitive opinions on subjects that have been thoroughly irrigated'); A Rep. of the Comm. On Use of App. Ct. Energies of the Advisory Council on App. Justice, No. 73–2, Standards for Publication of Judicial Opinions 6 (1973) ('Unlimited proliferation of published opinions constitutes a burden and a threat to a cohesive body of law'); The Hon. Boyce F. Martin, Jr, 'In Defense of Unpublished Opinions', *Ohio State Law Journal*, 60 (1999), 191–3: '[J]udicious use of unpublished opinions gives greater emphasis to those that are published'. For a critique of this argument, see, for example, R.B. Cappalli, 'The Common Law's Case Against Non-Precedential Opinions', *Southern California Law Review*, 76 (2003), 781–4. For discussion of the effect of no-citation rules on courts' precedential practices, see J. Allen, 'Just Words? The Effects of No-Citation Rules in Federal Courts of Appeals', *Vermont Law Review*, 29 (2005), 591–603.

[74] See P.M. Wald, 'Changing Course: The Use of Precedent in the District of Columbia Circuit', 500: 'Perhaps the most frustrating way courts deal with unpopular precedent is by evading the precedent in a judgment without opinion or in an unpublished memorandum.'

[75] See ibid.

[76] There is a limit to how much weight the fiction of an unpublished decision being a nullity can bear. Perhaps this is the reason that the practice of unpublished decisions draws the ire of many commentators, see n. 63, and the reason that the focus of criticism tends to be on unpublished decisions that fall in this class of cases (i.e. cases that do announce new rules of law). See P.M. Wald, 'Changing Course: The Use of Precedent in the District of Columbia Circuit', 500 ('Perhaps the most frustrating way courts deal with unpopular precedent is by evading the precedent in a judgment without opinion or in an unpublished memorandum'); see also *United States* v. *Edge Broadcasting Co.*, 509 U.S. 418, 425 fn. 3 (1993) ('We deem it remarkable and unusual that although the Court of Appeals affirmed a

Even if we accept that neither the limits of *stare decisis* nor the existence of inherently defeasible decisions nor the existence of decisions that are defeasible by design is inconsistent with the notion of substantial indefeasibility, there still remains the question of how broadly case holdings are construed. Common law courts are notorious for distinguishing, without overruling, earlier case precedents.[77] So, too, do they sometimes announce new elements for claims, new defences against claims, and sometimes even new rules altogether. If this practice is widespread and pernicious, then even a strong doctrine of *stare decisis* will not save the notion of substantial indefeasibility. Put another way, a setting where precedential effect is great but decisions are interpreted narrowly does not seem conducive to substantial indefeasibility.[78]

My view is that, while these practices surely occur, and occur with great frequency in some areas, nonetheless the dominant perception (if not the reality) is that many areas of law remain substantially indefeasible. To see this, let us consider an area of law notorious for constitutional common law rulemaking: the area of constitutional criminal procedure. This is an area where the United States Supreme Court has, from time to time and with varying frequency, announced new rules of law. The question has arisen, however, as to whether these new rules should apply retroactively. It is in the answer to this question given by the Supreme Court, and then the Congress, that we shall see the strength of the perception of substantial indefeasibility.

The Court has developed what it calls a 'new-rule jurisprudence' with respect to the retroactivity of new rules of criminal procedure. The new-rule jurisprudence draws a distinction between cases heard on direct appeal from state court, and cases in which petitioners pursue post-conviction relief in federal court by seeking a writ of *habeas corpus*.[79] In *Teague* v. *Lane*,[80] Justice O'Connor announced the general rule that,[81] subject to limited exceptions,[82] 'new constitutional rules of criminal procedure will not be applicable to those cases which have become final before the new rules are

judgment that an Act of Congress was unconstitutional as applied, the Court found it appropriate to announce its judgment in an unpublished *per curiam* opinion').

77 For example, Richard Tur suggests that it is not uncommon in English practice to consider that '[t]he temporal effect of "not following" or "departing from" (like "distinguishing") an earlier decision is not inevitably retrospective, and may well be prospective only, whereas the temporal effect of overruling, properly so-called, is both prospective and retrospective'. R.H.S. Tur, 'Time and Law', OJLS, 22 (2002), 477. He comments that the English common law thus 'achieves by stealth, and quite cleverly, an effect akin to that of prospective overruling by appropriate deployment of the "not following" technique. In so doing, however, it shows that some of the descriptive and normative objections to the declaratory theory [of law] ... are well founded.' Ibid., 488.

78 See C.R. Sunstein, 'Foreword: Leaving Things Undecided', *Harvard Law Review*, 110 (1996), 25–8, discussing the connection between *stare decisis* and minimalist jurisprudence.

79 Federal *habeas corpus* review of state court criminal convictions is authorized under 28 U.S.C. §2254. Though the Supreme Court has never held that the new-rule jurisprudence applies to petitioners seeking post-conviction relief of *federal* court criminal convictions, see 28 U.S.C. §2255 (authorizing such post-conviction proceedings), many lower federal courts have assumed that it does. E.g. *Danforth* v. *Minnesota*, 552 U.S. 264, 281, n.16 (2008).

80 489 U.S. 288, 301 (1989).

81 Justice O'Connor was joined by only three Justices on this point, thus making these statements not technically a holding of the Court. Subsequent case law made clear, however, the vitality of the approach set out in *Teague*. See, e.g. *Penry* v. *Linaugh*, 492 U.S. 302, 313 (1989).

82 Exceptions apply where the new rule is either (i) one that renders types of primary conduct 'beyond the power of the criminal law-making authority to proscribe', 489 U.S. at 311, or (ii) a 'watershed' rule that 'implicate[s] the fundamental fairness of the trial', ibid. at 311–12.

announced'.[83] Here, a case becomes 'final' once the criminal defendant has exhausted his or her direct appeals. The general rule of *Teague* thus means that new rules of criminal procedure cannot apply, and cannot be announced, in *habeas* proceedings.

Teague's general rule requires courts to categorize rules of criminal procedure as either 'new' or not. Here, Justice O'Connor's opinion explains: 'In general . . . a case announces a new rule when it breaks new ground or imposes a new obligation . . . To put it differently, a case announces a new rule if the result was not *dictated* by precedent existing at the time the defendant's conviction became final.'[84] As the court elucidated in a subsequent case:

The *Teague* inquiry is conducted in three steps. First, the date on which the defendant's conviction became final is determined . . . Next, the *habeas* court considers whether 'a state court considering the defendant's] claim at the time his conviction became final would have felt compelled by existing precedent to conclude that the rule [he] seeks was required by the Constitution.' [*Lambrix* v. *Singletary*, 520 U.S. 518, 527 (1997)] (quoting *Saffle* v. *Parks*, 494 U.S. 484, 488 (1990) (alterations in *Lambrix*). If not, then the rule is new.[85]

The *Teague* 'new-rule' regime provides considerable support for the notion of substantial indefeasibility. To see this, it is of paramount importance for us to observe that inherent in the 'new-rule jurisprudence' is that there are not only 'new rules', but also 'old rules'. The new-rule jurisprudence means that convictions based upon old rules will not be upset (subject to limited exceptions) by most claims to entitlement to the benefit of a new rule. Put another way, the old rules are indefeasible with respect to cases that become final before a new rule that would defeat them, or the results in those cases, is announced.

This limited indefeasibility is not, however, a strong form of substantial indefeasibility. After all, the fact remains that the general legal propositions embodied in the old rules may well be subject to defeasibility, only not retroactively in a limited class of cases.

To conceive of the broader support that the new-rule jurisprudence offers for substantial indefeasibility, consider that the new-rule jurisprudence assumes that it is possible to isolate the state of the law at the time of criminal conviction and to deduce results that follow logically from it—or, to put it in the language of *Teague*, to determine whether the relief sought by the criminal petitioner was '*dictated* by precedent existing at the time the defendant's conviction became final'.[86] Consider also that the new-rule jurisprudence is not an absolute bar against federal *habeas* relief; post-conviction relief will, presumably, sometimes be available. But for post-conviction relief to be available, it must be the case that it is possible for 'old rules' to apply in different settings without becoming 'new rules'. One might be tempted to think, given the view

[83] 489 U.S. at 310.
My point here is not to defend *Teague* and its new-rule jurisprudence on the merits. Indeed, the decision and doctrine have received considerable criticism. See, e.g., L. Meyer, '"Nothing We Say Matters": *Teague* and New Rules', *University of Chicago Law Review*, 61 (1994), 423; S. Bandes, 'Taking Justice to its Logical Extreme: A Comment on *Teague* v. *Lane*', *Southern California Law Review*, 66 (1992), 2453. Rather, my point is that, whatever its merits, the adoption and continuing workability of *Teague* turn on the perception that assertions of constitutional criminal law are often substantially indefeasible.

[84] 489 U.S. at 301. The court made clear in a subsequent case that, even where the court described its holding in one case as '"controlled" by a prior decision', the court's holding could still be a 'new rule' if the outcome was 'susceptible to debate among reasonable minds'. *Butler* v. *McKellar*, 494 U.S. 407, 415 (1990).

[85] *O'Dell* v. *Netherland*, 521 U.S. 151, 156 (1997).

[86] Ibid.

of the common law as evolving judicial decision by judicial decision, that a claimant's attempt to invoke the benefit of an existing legal rule in a distinct factual setting might be characterized as invoking a 'new rule'.[87] The 'new-rule jurisprudence' makes clear that that will not be the case.[88]

The fact that it is understood that 'old rules' may apply in new settings without automatically morphing into new rules reveals the perception that 'old rules' have considerable play in them before they reach their limits. This perception is at odds with the view that the common law involves a 'case-by-case' evolution with each case a step in that evolution. The perception, instead, accords well with a 'punctuated equilibrium' understanding of common law evolution. And it accordingly sees old rules under a presumption of substantial indefeasibility.[89]

[87] An analogy to this view might be drawn to a controversial challenge to the 'law of trichotomy' in mathematics that identifies all real numbers as either positive, negative, or zero. The challenge relies upon the fact (at least as of today) that there are numbers whose full decimal expansion is, while theoretically calculable, unknown. The number π is such an example; we know that π is a transcendental number whose decimal expansion is infinite. While we could theoretically determine every digit in π's decimal expansion, there is currently (and presumably there may always be) insufficient computing power and resources to do so.

Remaining with the number π, let us define π^* thus. Let n represent the final decimal digit we can today determine in π's decimal expansion, and then let x be the value of $(n + 100)$th digit. Note that x has a value, but we cannot today determine it. Let us now define π^* as exactly the same as π, except that the $(n + 100)$th digit sees x (the $(n + 100)$th digit in π itself) replaced by y where y is set equal to either (i) 9 if $0 \leq x \leq 4$ or (ii) 0 if $5 \leq x \leq 9$.

Now let $\alpha = \pi - \pi^*$. From the definition of π^*, we can tell that α will be positive if $0 \leq x \leq 4$, and negative if $5 \leq x \leq 9$. We cannot, however, tell which is the case, since by definition x lies beyond our current computational power. The challenge to the trichotomy of real numbers asserts that, insofar as we cannot determine whether α is positive or negative, then it falls into none of the three categories, i.e. it is neither positive, negative, nor zero. See P.J. Davis, R. Hersh, E. Marchisotto, and G. Rota, *The Mathematical Experience* (Boston: Birkhäuser, 1995), 412–13.

One can see the analogy between this challenge to the law of trichotomy and old and new legal rules: The trichotomy of real numbers as positive, negative, and zero can assign only numbers we can definitively determine. In this capacity, it functions analogously to an 'old rule'. It would seem that application of the law of trichotomy to other numbers—including α—would be 'dictated' by application of the 'old rule' and thus would not be an instantiation of a 'new rule'; indeed, this approach is broadly consistent with the view espoused in *Teague*. On the other hand, if the challenge is valid, then one might see the categorization of α as application of a 'new rule'.

It is worth mentioning that the challenge to the law of trichotomy has numerous detractors. See ibid. at 412 ('Most mathematicians, when presented with this example, violently reject [the] conclusion'). Cf. K. Chang, 'In Math, Computers Don't Lie. Or Do They?', *New York Times*, 6 April 2004, at F1 (noting debate within the mathematics community as to the validity of proofs of mathematical theorems that are achieved using computer calculations).

[88] That is not to say that it will always be easy for a court to discern when a claimant is in fact invoking an old rule albeit in a different factual setting, or is rather asserting a new rule. Consider, for example, the opinions of the United States Court of Appeals for the Fourth Circuit in *Turner* v. *Williams*, 35 F.3d 872 (4th Cir. 1994). There, all three members of the panel voted to deny relief to the *habeas* petitioner. But two panel members voted so on the grounds that, while the relief sought was under an 'old rule', the argument was meritless. A third panel member concurred only in the judgment, opining that the relief sought would have required announcement of a 'new rule' and thus was beyond the power of the court to grant. See ibid. at 904 (Luttig, J., concurring). The majority's opinion numbered 28 pages in the official reports; the dissent's 16 pages. (The concurring judge's position was ultimately vindicated in *O'Dell* v. *Netherland*, 95 F.3d 1214, 1222–3 (4th Cir. 1996), *aff'd*, 521 U. S. 151 (1997).)

[89] It is interesting to note that the 'new-rule jurisprudence' is itself defeasible. First, to the extent that defeasibility turns on exceptions to the general rule, the general rule of 'new-rule jurisprudence' is subject to certain exceptions. See n. 82 and accompanying text; but see *Teague*, 489 U.S. at 313 ('Because we operate from the premise that [new rules of criminal procedure that qualify as watershed rules] would be so central to an accurate determination of innocence or guilt, we believe it unlikely that many such components of basic due process have yet to emerge'). Second, the court recently held that

Congress evidently shares this perception; it has seen fit to codify a version of the *Teague* 'new-rule' test.[90] The resulting statute 'precludes relief on *habeas* petitions unless (absent an unreasonable factual determination) the state court adjudication of the petitioner's claim "resulted in a decision that was contrary to, or involved an unreasonable application of, clearly established Federal law, as determined by the Supreme Court of the United States".'[91] While the court has held that the statute does not obviate the need for federal courts to apply the *Teague* standard—and thus that the statute and *Teague* do not precisely overlap[92]—still the point remains that Congress, like the court, is of the view that old rules exist, that old rules deserve some quantum of indefeasibility, and most important that old rules can apply in new factual circumstances without thereby morphing into new rules.

In addition to 'new-rule jurisprudence,' the judicial treatment of qualified immunity to section 1983 cases for government officials also provides support for the perception that some areas of law at least are seen to be substantially indefeasible. Section 1983 is a provision of federal law that empowers individuals to bring suit against state officials for violating individuals' federal constitutional and statutory rights while acting under colour of state law.[93] Section 1983 suits are often brought by people who claim to have had their constitutional and statutory rights violated by the police.

The courts have limited certain public officials' susceptibility to section 1983 suits by rendering them sometimes immune from suit.[94] In determining entitlement to immunity, courts today apply a purely objective test:[95] '[G]overnment officials performing discretionary functions, generally are [immune from civil suit] insofar as their conduct does not violate clearly established statutory or constitutional rights of which a reasonable person would have known'.[96] In conducting this inquiry, courts must determine, 'not only the currently applicable law, but whether that law was clearly

state courts remain free not to follow the 'new-rule jurisprudence' and to apply new rules retroactively in state post-conviction proceedings as they (or presumably state legislatures in setting out rules for the state courts to follow) see fit. See *Danforth* v. *Minnesota*, 128 S. Ct. 1029 (2008). Third, one might consider that (i) the fact that *Teague* does not have a lengthy pedigree, see *Teague*, 489 U.S. at 299–305 (describing the court's treatment of retroactivity of rules of criminal procedure before *Teague*) combined with (ii) the fact that *Teague* did not immediately attract a majority of the court (Justice O'Connor's opinion was for a plurality, though it was later adopted by majority opinion, see n. 81) and remains unpopular today in some quarters, make *Teague* a reasonable candidate for being overruled at some point. In any event, the fact that the 'new-rule jurisprudence' may one day be overturned and is in any event defeasible is orthogonal to my argument. My only point is that the perceptions underlying the existing 'new-rule jurisprudence' are consistent with a view of rules of constitutional criminal procedure as being substantially indefeasible.

90 See Anti-terrorism and Effective Death Penalty Act of 1996 (AEDPA), Pub. L. No. 104–132.

91 28 U.S.C. §2254(d)(1) (as amended by AEDPA §104(3)).

92 *Horn* v. *Banks*, 536 U.S. 266, 272 (2002) (*per curiam*) ('The AEDPA and *Teague* inquiries are distinct... Thus, in addition to performing any analysis required by AEDPA, a federal court considering a *habeas* petition must conduct a threshold *Teague* analysis when the issue is properly raised by the state').

93 See 42 U.S.C. §1983.

94 Immunity from suit is even more powerful than an affirmative defence; it precludes a trial altogether, let alone liability. Thus, claims of immunity are typically determined at the start of a case, and a denial of immunity is (contrary to the usual federal rule that appeals may occur only upon a final decision in a case, see 28 U.S.C. §1291; Nash, note 21, at 84–5 (noting the general rule)) immediately appealable. See *Cohen* v. *Ben. Indus. Loan Corp.*, 337 U.S. 541, 546 (1949) (recognizing limited possibility of appealing final collateral orders even where there is no final order for the entire case).

95 E.g. *Mitchell* v. *Forsyth*, 472 U.S. 511, 517 (1985) (noting that the Court's decision in *Harlow* v. *Fitzgerald*, 457 U.S. 800 (1982), 'purged qualified immunity doctrine of its subjective component'); see *Harlow*, 472 U.S. at 815–17 (discussing and criticizing the previous regime entailing examination of objective and subjective factors).

96 *Harlow* v. *Fitzgerald*, 457 U.S. 800, 818 (1982).

established at the time an action occurred'.[97] So-called 'qualified immunity' extends, then, to state officials who, though they in fact have violated someone's constitutional and statutory rights as those rights are understood today, did not violate those rights under the law as in effect and interpreted at the time of the alleged violation.

Much like 'new-rule jurisprudence', then, the 'clearly established' standard for determining entitlement to qualified immunity presumes both the existence of an 'old' legal regime and the possibility of the 'old' regime establishing certain statutory and constitutional rights, and also that rules under the 'old' regime may apply in different factual settings without losing their status as components of the 'old' regime. In short, then, the perceptions that underlie the 'clearly established' standard are consistent with an expectation of substantial indefeasibility of the relevant statutory and constitutional rules.

D. Conclusion

In this essay, I have endeavoured to establish that the scope of defeasibility varies with context. I have also argued that, even if defeasibility itself is rare or non-existent, substantial indefeasibility will be a standard feature of a mature legal system. I have also presented evidence of the widespread existence, and of the perception of the widespread existence, of substantial indefeasibility in US jurisprudence. The existence of substantial indefeasibility in a common law system strongly suggests its existence in other legal systems as well.

[97] Ibid.

22

Defeasible Rules and Interpersonal Accountability

*Bruce Chapman**

A. The puzzle of defeasible rules

At first glance it is hard to know what is meant when someone says: 'Well, that's the exception that proves the rule!' An exception hardly seems supportive of its rule; if anything, the exception seems to qualify the rule and to take it down a peg. Far from *proving* the rule, an exception appears to render it less of a rule. Certainly it gives the rule less scope. It may even leave us thinking that the rule could be vulnerable to more exceptions, that it is less rule-like than we originally thought.[1]

On the other hand, there is the sense in which an exception *presupposes* the rule. Without the rule there is no exception. Not that they must always travel together, of course. We can, at least in principle, have rules without exceptions. But we cannot have exceptions without rules. Rules are conceptually prior to exceptions; the two are essentially sequenced concepts.[2] So, there is a moment, maybe only the briefest of conceptual moments, when *every* rule must stand free of *any* exceptions. Perhaps this is the sense in which the very idea of an exception proves the rule. And it proves the rule in a particularly robust way. Far from proving the mere coexistence of the rule with the exception, it seems to prove the rule's *priority*, a moment when the rule is alone and without exceptions.

Still, there is the nagging feeling that, in a more substantive and important way, exceptions are not friendly to the rules they except. In the end, after these brief conceptual moments have passed, and the exception has done its work, the original rule has less application than it had before. Some might even say that the original rule is now gone and a new rule stands in its place. We have not so much added an exception to the original rule as changed it altogether.[3] Where the old rule, confidently and without qualification, announced that '$p \rightarrow q$', that is, that in circumstances or class of cases p consequence q follows, the new rule admits from the outset that q only follows if we add the qualifier that limits the antecedent circumstances to the smaller class of cases (p *&* *not-r*). So, the rule, properly stated, is '(p *&* *not-r*) $\rightarrow q$'. This new rule, in one

* Professor of Law, University of Toronto.

[1] A more complete version of the saying, sometimes trotted out to make better sense of it, is: 'the exception proves the rule so far as matters not excepted' (or in Latin, '*exceptio probat regulam de rebus non exceptis*'; see *Black's Law Dictionary*). But this version fares only slightly better than the original. 'Matters not excepted' are at best untouched by the exceptions; they are hardly proved by them. Worse, the possibility of further exceptions, even to matters *so far* not excepted, is suggested. So the puzzle of proof by way of exceptions remains.

[2] For discussion of essentially sequenced concepts, see B. Chapman, 'Law, Incommensurability, and Conceptually Sequenced Argument', *University of Pennsylvania Law Review*, 146 (1998), 1514–20.

[3] See, e.g. F. Schauer, 'Exceptions', *University of Chicago Law Review*, 58 (1991), 893.

stage, has absorbed or blended in the exceptional circumstances *r* (by negating them in the antecedent) and now stands by itself, more complicated perhaps, but *more accurate* in its offering a more complete statement of the antecedent conditions for the application of the rule.[4]

This is not to say that it will always be easy to articulate this more complicated single-stage summary (or 'blended') rule. Sometimes it will be hard to find the right words.[5] Suppose (to use a well-worn example) that someone proposed the rule that there should be no vehicles allowed in the park.[6] Almost immediately it will be thought that not all vehicles are to be included in the prohibition. Emergency vehicles (e.g. ambulances, fire trucks), disarmed but otherwise still operative vehicles used as war memorials (e.g. a vintage armoured car mounted on some pedestal), and, possibly, roller skates, need not be included. However, it will be difficult to come up with the one word that captures all vehicles but these, and easier to articulate the rule as 'no vehicles are permitted in the park except when (or unless) the vehicle is an emergency vehicle, an inoperative military vehicle used for a war memorial, etc.'. Moreover, the 'etc.' might be important too, indicating that our list of exceptions is not exhaustive of all the exceptions that we will eventually need to add to the general prohibition; it might simply be too hard to think of all those possibilities right now.[7] So the limited availability of certain linguistic tools or concepts might force us to articulate the general rule as subject to an exception, or an 'unless' clause, and our bounded imaginations might require that we keep the list of exceptions open by adding an 'etc.' at the end. But the argument will persist that, despite these limitations, with each addition to the list of exceptions we have progressed towards a more accurate or truthful statement of what the rule actually requires. It will be said that the original rule, far from being *proved* by these added exceptions, is nothing but a pretender encountered along the way to this more complete truth.[8]

[4] This appears to be Ronald Dworkin's view of the relation between exceptions and rules; see R. Dworkin, *Taking Rights Seriously* (London: Duckworth, 1977), 25 and text at n. 34.

[5] F. Schauer, 'Exceptions', 873–5.

[6] For an account of this famous example and its origins in the debate between Herbert Hart and Lon Fuller, see F. Schauer, 'A Critical Guide to Vehicles in the Park', *New York University Law Review*, 83 (2008), 1109.

[7] The difficulty of precisely stating in advance all the possible exceptions that might apply to the rule was conceded by Hart; however, he did not think that this undermined its status as a rule: 'A rule that ends with an "unless" clause is still a rule.' See H.L.A. Hart, *The Concept of Law* (Oxford: Clarendon Pree, 1961), 136.

[8] Of course, there are those who criticize this blended model of rules and exceptions. For example, while Frederick Schauer might accept all this as an *account* of what exceptions really are, he has objected that, nonetheless, there is a real danger of the rule *qua* rule disappearing as these sorts of exceptions are added. For if, as seems likely, we are adding exceptions to the rule in light of what is required by our understanding of the background purpose or reason for having the rule, then the rule is doing no real work as a guide to what we should do in any particular case. Rather, in each case we are simply looking *directly* to that background reason or purpose in order to decide what to do. The rule, together with its various exceptions, is merely the output of our labours, not a very useful input into them. But Schauer thinks rules *are* useful inputs into our decision-making. Just as there are reasons that justify the particular rules that we have, so there are reasons for having rules as such. According to Schauer, rules provide for stability, protect reliance, economize on the costs of decision-making, and avoid the most serious risks of error that accompany more particular decision-making. They also serve to allocate decision-making power (both intertemporally and interpersonally) and are helpful to achieving coordination. So while there is the background reason for having the particular rule, a reason which, strictly speaking, will call for exceptions to be written into the rule as particular circumstances require, there are also reasons to have rules as such, reasons that call for caution in adjusting the rule in this particularistic way. See F. Schauer, *Playing By the Rules. A Philosophical Examination of Rule-Based Decision-Making in Law and in Life* (Oxford: Clarendon Press, 1991), 137–66.

Those who argue for the special nature of defeasible rules are likely to resist this last, single-stage, summary-form characterization of what they see as an essentially multi-staged idea. They will argue that there *is* a *prior* rule '$p \rightarrow q$' and *it* is defeasible if (and only if) the exceptional circumstance r is added. Defeasibility is a property of the original rule, something that happens to it and which it (somehow) survives if the exception does not arise.[9] So we have a two-staged sequence that allows, first, for the rule '$p \rightarrow q$' and, second, for the (possible) exception to the rule 'p & $r \rightarrow$ *not*-q'. Admittedly, this is a little mysterious. Normally, in the logic of conditionals we think that the sufficiency of p for q cannot be lost if one adds a further proposition r; this is the logical requirement that goes by the name of 'strengthening the antecedent'. However, it is now widely recognized that the formal logic of defeasibility does not admit this requirement; indeed, as the present discussion suggests, defeasibility is more or less defined by its denial of it.[10]

But it is one thing to offer a definition or formal logic of defeasibility; it is quite another to motivate the idea. Further, our discussion also suggests a cluster of more substantive questions: can there be a *real* difference between, on the one hand, bringing an exception to bear on the original rule at some second stage, so that the rule is less general in its final application than it was before, and, on the other hand, writing the exception into a new and different rule from the outset so that, under this more complicated articulation, the new, one-stage, summary rule has an extensionally equivalent scope of final application? In the end, does this not come to the same thing? Indeed, is this not what we mean by an extensionally equivalent, final application of the two rules, one entirely new, and the other the original but with an added exception, the stuff of defeasibility? Where could we find a difference that could possibly matter if, in prospect, there is no real difference in the scope (or final application) of these two structurally different sorts of rule?[11]

Maybe there is some room for a difference *before* we get to the final application of the rules. After all, because they are conceptually sequenced ideas, we have already opened up the possibility, indeed the necessity, of at least a conceptual moment between the first-stage rule and its second-stage (added) exception. This conceptual space cannot exist for the newly written, more complicated rule which, in its single-stage summary form, simply absorbs the exception because, at that moment at least, it is exception-less. However, the conceptual space is possible within a two-stage defeasible rule and this space could provide for a difference that matters.

Of course, this difference will not matter to those who care *only* about the final, extensionally equivalent scope in the application of the two structurally different rules. Having a moment along the way to that result, a moment between the rule and its exception, will only matter to those who are moved by how, or *the process through which*, we get to this same final result. But notice this: if these process theorists care enough about living the conceptual moment between a rule and its exception, then they might go further. They might even be prepared to live with some *limitation* that this process brings to the final application or scope of their original rule, together with

[9] H.L.A. Hart, 'The Ascription of Responsibility and Rights' in A. Flew (ed.), *Essays in Logic and Language* (Oxford: Basil Blackwell, 1960), 148, emphasizing that a defeasible rule or concept 'while subject to termination or "*defeat*" in a number of different contingencies... remains intact if no such contingencies mature' (emphasis in the original).

[10] See, e.g. J. Hage, 'Law and Defeasibility', *Artificial Intelligence and Law*, 11 (2003), 221–2.

[11] F. Schauer, 'On the Supposed Defeasibility of Legal Rules', *Current Legal Problems*, 51 (1998), 227.

its added exception, as compared to the new, more complicated, single-stage exceptionless rule. In other words, if concerns for process matter enough, then the final result under the two-stage defeasible rule might be (tolerably) different from that under a single-stage summary rule.

No doubt those who are sceptical of defeasible rules will continue to find all this quite mysterious. Is it *really possible* to live within the conceptual moment that exists, *logically*, between a rule and its exception, to live, as it were, within the interstices of defeasible legal rules? And is it plausible to suggest that having a moment there is a *valuable* part of some process of rule application, valuable enough, indeed, that some might be prepared to live with a more modest final application of the rules than they would otherwise choose to support more completely if they did not have this high regard for actually going through a two-stage process?

In this paper I hope to convince the sceptic that the answer to both these questions is 'yes' and that these answers say something about the positive authority of legal rules and the claims made under them. However, answering the first question affirmatively is the easier task. Let us consider it first.

B. Living with defeasible rules: pleadings, defences, and partial truths

The possibility of living for a moment in the logical space that exists between a rule and its exception arises when one individual makes a claim under some rule, typically a claim against another individual, and this claim, if properly and authoritatively made out, will be successful if the individual against whom the claim is made offers no effective reply. The reply, in its turn, makes use of what are (new or established) exceptions to the rule. This simple process, so characteristic of the pleadings, presumptions, and defences that we observe between plaintiffs and defendants in private common law litigation, expresses the structure of a two-staged defeasible rule.[12] It does so because the plaintiff making his claim, while hostage (ultimately) to the possibility of a reply from the defendant, is not required to address that possibility under the initial rule that supports his claim. At this stage, therefore, the rule *does* take the simple form '$p \rightarrow q$'.

It is the reply, or defence, to the claim that introduces the exceptional circumstances *r*. These exceptional circumstances might exist, but it is the defendant's obligation, *and right*, to introduce them *or not* as she sees fit. If she chooses not to introduce them, then the initial claim, authoritatively asserted by the plaintiff under the rule '$p \rightarrow q$', simply carries the result *q* with it. On the other hand, if the defendant does offer a reply *r* and, further, is successful in offering this reply, then the result *not-q* will be the result under the exception (or exception rule) '(p & r) $\rightarrow$ *not-q*'.

Thus, the single-stage, more complicated, summary rule '(p & *not-r*) $\rightarrow q$', while not strictly *inconsistent* with the two-stage defeasible rule made up of '$p \rightarrow q$' and '(p & r) $\rightarrow$ *not-q*', obscures an essential part of that two-stage process.[13] There is an intermediate moment in this process, a moment that could persist *depending upon what the defendant (effectively) chooses to do*, where it might be that both *p* and *r* are true and yet *q* holds. That is what is provided for under the first stage of the defeasible rule '$p \rightarrow q$', even as it

[12] Of course, the process could go on, under some rejoinder to the reply, to express a three-stage defeasible rule. This complication is ignored here. For discussion, see R. Epstein, 'Pleadings and Presumptions', *The University of Chicago Law Review*, 40 (1973), 559–61.

[13] For discussion of how the summary rule obscures the defeasible nature of rules, see H.L.A Hart, 'The Ascription of Responsibility and Rights', 150.

awaits the possibility of reply under the exception '$(p \,\&\, r) \rightarrow$ *not-q*', and what, unhelpfully, the more complicated, single-stage, summary rule '(p & *not-r*) $\rightarrow q$' is silent about.

Moreover, there is some reason to think that the more complicated, single-stage, summary rule is not only unhelpfully silent about the (intermediate or persistent) possibility that both p and r are true and yet q holds. More seems to be at stake. For recall that the claim to superiority that the more complicated, single-stage, summary rule makes is that it offers a *more* truthful account of what is actually required under the rule. Where the rule '$p \rightarrow q$' pretends to the truth, the argument goes, the real (more qualified) truth is to be found in the rule '(p & *not-r*) $\rightarrow q$'. That is, not all circumstances p are sufficient for q; only those circumstances p, qualified by *not-r*, are. So while we can have both the rule '$p \rightarrow q$' and the rule '(p & *not-r*) $\rightarrow q$' together without *logical* contradiction (indeed, the two together exemplify what is required by 'strengthening the antecedent'), and where it *could* be that both rules are true in just the way that this logical coherence of the two rules allows,[14] the difference between the two rules is that *in fact* they *do* not purport to offer equally faithful accounts of what (in the end) can truthfully be claimed under the rule.[15] Rather, the single-staged summary rule purports to offer a truth that the first-stage defeasible rule does not.

This brings us to our second question, namely, whether it is *valuable* to have a moment between a rule '$p \rightarrow q$' and its exception '$(p \,\&\, r) \rightarrow$ *not-q*' as part of some two-stage process of defeasible rule application. However, we now have a better sense of the burden that must be met in offering an affirmative reply to this question. For now we know that the more complicated, single-stage, summary rule '(p & *not-r*) $\rightarrow q$', and individual claims made under that rule, purport to be truthful in a way that initial claims made under the defeasible rule do not, even if the latter concede that they are subject to the possibility of reply or correction at some second stage in the process. Is there some value in making room within our private common law processes for these less-than-perfectly-truthful initial claims? It is to a discussion of this possibility that I now turn.

C. The value of defeasible rules: justifiable claims and interpersonal accountability

In the process of private common law litigation, for example in a negligence claim or a claim for breach of contract, the plaintiff typically bears the initial burden of proving that he has been wronged by the defendant. If the plaintiff meets this legal burden, then the defendant is at risk of being found liable if in turn she does not meet the burden of offering some sort of reply or defence. However, for the burden to shift to the defendant in this way, the plaintiff need not prove his case with certainty. Rather, it is enough if he can prove his case 'more probably than not', that is, on a balance of probabilities.[16]

[14] Suppose that all *ps* really are *qs*. Then that subset of *ps* that are qualified by not being r (i.e. the *p-not rs*) will also be *qs*.

[15] That the different claims under the first-stage rule '$p \rightarrow q$' and the second-stage reply rule '$(p \,\&\, r) \rightarrow$ *not-q*' can be *rationally* integrated (or, at least, integrated without contradiction), even if they cannot be equally accountable to some independent truth, will be important for our later discussion when we show that defeasible rules are more properly construed as the product of the collective rationality of the parties' interlocking claims, and not the stuff of reason (or truth) under some (more accurate) summary rule.

[16] A higher standard of proof (say, proof beyond a reasonable doubt) might be required of the state in a criminal law prosecution of some accused. But the more even, balance-of-probabilities standard

However, it is important also to appreciate that the plaintiff has the burden of proving his case more probably than not on the basis of *direct* evidence (that is, evidence that, arguably and credibly, arises out of the particular circumstances of the case as the plaintiff represents it). Mere statistical or circumstantial evidence, typically, will not suffice. If the plaintiff cannot produce any direct evidence on some matter that is essential to the proof of his case (for example, that the defendant's negligence actually caused his loss), then the plaintiff is said to be non-suited, that is, the case is dismissed without any requirement that the defendant say anything in reply. Moreover, and this is the crucial point, such a plaintiff might be non-suited for inadequate direct evidence on the matter even if it can be shown that, *statistically*, it is more likely than not, say, that the defendant's negligence *is* the cause of the plaintiff's injury. A much discussed example will help to illustrate the point.[17]

Suppose that the plaintiff has been out cycling at night and has been injured by a negligently driven bus forcing him off the road. Unfortunately, there are no witnesses to the accident and, while the plaintiff can show that there is little doubt that a negligently driven bus was the cause of the accident, he cannot prove which of two bus companies might be the one involved. As it happens, however, 90 per cent of the buses that drive that particular route are operated by the Blue Bus Company. The question is whether the plaintiff can make use of this statistical truth to prove his case that it was more likely than not (i.e. that it is 90 per cent likely) that an employee driver of the Blue Bus Company negligently forced him off the road and, therefore, that Blue Bus should be vicariously liable for his injury.

While controversial amongst academic commentators, it is quite clear that the courts will overwhelmingly reject a merely statistical basis for the plaintiff's claim against Blue Bus.[18] If this is all the plaintiff can offer, that is, if he can offer no direct evidence identifying Blue Bus as the wrongdoer, he will be non-suited. Indeed, we can strengthen the example somewhat to show how much more powerful direct evidence is for the plaintiff proving his case than is statistical evidence. Suppose, for example, that (in contrast to the first hypothetical) there was a witness to the accident and that this witness says that it was a bus from Red Bus Company that caused the accident. Red Bus is the company that operates the remaining 10 per cent of the buses on the route. While this is not as statistically likely as the involvement of Blue Bus, the plaintiff can show that his witness is very reliable. Under environmental conditions very like those that prevailed on the night in question, from the same distance as she was from the accident that night, this witness can correctly pick out the colour of the bus in 80 per cent of these simulated test cases. On this sort of direct evidence, it is likely that the plaintiff will be able to establish a prima facie case against Red Bus even though, *as a strict statistical matter*, it is still true, even taking into account this direct evidence and its reliability, that Blue Bus (not Red Bus) was more likely than not the bus company involved.[19] So, not only is it true that the courts will not defer to mere statistical

that is characteristic of a private law action is thought to reflect better the equal standing of the two parties in such actions. This difference is not important for the purposes of this discussion.

[17] Variations of this example are discussed in J.J. Thomson, *Rights, Restitution and Risk: Essays in Moral Theory* (Cambridge, Mass.: Harvard University Press 1986), ch. 13; and in F. Schauer, *Profiles, Probabilities and Stereotypes* (Cambridge, Mass..; London: Belknap, 2003), ch. 3. The examples are based on the case *Smith* v. *Rapid Transit Inc.* 317 Mass. 469, 58 N.E. 2d 754 (1945).

[18] *Smith*; see F. Schauer, *Profiles, Probabilities and Stereotypes*, for academic discussion and for further support that this would indeed be the courts' approach to the problem.

[19] This is a basic application of Bayes's theorem. Using the background probabilities, and assuming that 100 buses pass by, the 80 per cent reliable witness will say 'it is red' in 8 out of the 10 cases where a

evidence if that is *all* that is on offer, but, further, the courts will not allow statistical evidence to weigh all that heavily against direct evidence if *both* are on offer. The plaintiff must meet, and will be accepted as meeting, his burden of proof on the basis of direct evidence even if the statistical evidence suggests otherwise. The real question is why this should be so.

The answer, it seems, is this: what matters in law is not so much what *is* true, but rather what one party can *justifiably say* to another is true. The latter, at least, is what carries the plaintiff's initial claim past the initial burden of proof and what calls for the defendant's reply. Of course, truth will not be entirely irrelevant to what one can justifiably assert as true. Wild and implausible claims to the truth (say, by *unreliable* witnesses) will rightly be dismissed and not require a reply from the other party. But the mistake is in thinking that the level of justifiability that one reaches in one's assertions of the truth somehow tracks, faithfully and monotonically, the actual likelihood of that assertion being true.

This approach to the problem is not peculiar to legal assertions or claims. Suppose, for example, that you have bought a lottery ticket.[20] The winning ticket has been chosen at random but not yet announced. (This is assumed here to ensure that there is now a fact of the matter, i.e. something about which we can make assertions that are now either true or false.) The chances are one-in-a-million that the number on your ticket stub has been drawn and that you have won. While under these probabilities I am justified in *believing* that you have lost, even in *saying* that I believe you have lost, I am not justified, just because of the very high probability of its being true, in *saying* that I *know* that you have lost.

Nor is what is missing for such a claim to knowledge simply that I need some higher probability support for making it. In fact, a *lower* probability of truth, based on a different kind of information, might well justify my asserting that I know you have lost. Suppose, in a slight variation on the example, that you have entered a different lottery where the chances of your winning are much better, say, one-in-a-thousand. But I have observed that your ticket was not actually placed in the ticket drum from which the draw was taken. Now, while I am a very reliable witness, I am not infallible; so there is a remote chance, say 1 per cent, that I might be mistaken about this observation. Therefore, there is a 1 per cent chance that (despite what I think I saw) you might still have that one-in-a-thousand chance of winning. This means that your chance of *losing* the second lottery is 99,999 out of 100,000 (i.e. 1 – (1/100 x 1/1000)). This is not as high as the chance of your losing the first lottery at 999, 999 out of a million. Yet, because I base my claim to knowledge about your chances of losing the second lottery on something more than a mere statistical likelihood, namely, that I observed your ticket failed to get into the drum for the draw, I can justifiably claim that I know (as much as anyone can claim to know something) that you will lose in this second lottery in a way that I cannot in the first.

This suggests that there is nothing particularly unusual in the law making room for justifiable claims under rules that are 'less probably true' than some alternative rule that, because more qualified, actually offers a more truthful form of the generalization. What matters, it seems, is not what is true, nor even what is most likely to be true, but what a person can justifiably say is true. The latter, and not so much the former, is what carries

Red Bus goes by and 'it is red' in 18 of the 90 cases that a Blue Bus goes by. So the probability that the bus actually is a Red Bus, given that the witness says 'it is red', is 8 out of 26, or less than a third.

[20] J.J. Thomson, *Rights, Restitution and Risk*, 234–42.

the plaintiff, as much as any person making a claim, through the first stage of his case and which calls for the defendant's reply.

Now, in reply, the defendant might have (the greater) truth on her side. That is, while the rule '$p \rightarrow q$' might be adequate as a (first-stage defeasible) rule justifying the plaintiff's initial claim, the defendant might be in a position to offer the qualifier *r* and win *not-q* under the second-stage rule '(*p & r*) → *not-q*'. So the exchange of claims might eventually work itself towards the (greater) truth that is captured by the single-stage summary rule favoured by the defeasibility sceptic, namely '(*p & not-r*) → *q*'. But, again, what will matter for the justifiability of the defendant's reply, just as for the justifiability of making claims more generally, will not so much be the greater truth of her claim, but what she can *justifiably say* is true. This, as we have seen, is something quite different.

Further, we can now understand why, under the two-stage defeasible structure, it is possible for an intermediate moment to persist where both *p* and *r* are true and yet *q* holds. For if what matters in a process of making claims and counterclaims is not (ultimately) what is true, but what a party can justifiably say or claim is true, then it will matter crucially that the parties, along the way to this truth, actually *make* the claims and counterclaims that they do. For that is what is presupposed in a process focused on justifiable *claims* to truth rather than truth itself. But then this leaves open the possibility that both *p* and *r* are true and yet *q* holds. For it is possible that the defendant, with the greater truth on her side, might simply choose not to offer the reply, or make the claim, *r*. Or, perhaps it is that she has the statistical truth of *r* on her side, but can make no such justifiable claim on the basis of direct evidence. This would simply be a case of her confronting the same difficulty as the plaintiff who, in making an initial, first-stage claim, is non-suited in the Blue Bus problem. Either way it is the *authority* (or not) that the defendant (and only the defendant) has to make a justifiable counterclaim *r*, together with the *fact that she actually exercises that authority*, and not the truth of *r* as such, that will determine whether, when both *p* and *r* are true, *q* will hold.

The use of the word 'authority' in the last sentence reinforces two distinct but equally important points that have been implicit in the discussion to this point. First, if a party has the authority to make the claim he or she does in some litigation process, then, as already suggested, he or she exercises the claim (or not) as a matter of right.[21] It would not do, for example, if the rest of us together, or any one of us on our own (even the particular party against whom the claim is made), simply attended out of some personal sense of duty to whatever it was that this party might want, or need, in exercising that claim. The claim and, more specifically, the *exercise* of the claim by the claimant, must be the source of the obligation we feel.[22] Now, this suggests that we might not (yet) feel the burden of the claim upon us '*just* because he said so'; but the burden or obligation we feel (to reply, if not to act) is at least *partly* explained just by the fact that he said so. In this respect it is *source-based* in precisely the way that models of authority typically suggest.[23]

[21] More accurately we should say it is a matter of 'power', not right, as it is the exercise of the claim, if effective, that puts the respondent under a duty either to meet the claim or to offer a reply. But the duty does not exist prior to, nor independent of, the exercise of the claim.

[22] In this respect, the account of defeasible rules being developed here supports 'recourse theory'. For discussion of how this theory differs importantly from the theory of corrective justice precisely because it makes the process of claim and counterclaim central to private law adjudication, see J. Solomon, 'Equal Accountability Through Tort Law', *Northwestern University Law Review*, 103 (2009), 1765–1822.

[23] See F. Schauer, 'Authority and Authorities', *Virginia Law Review*, 94 (2008), 1931–61.

But the second point takes us that one step further. There is a sense in which an authoritative claim by one party upon another *must* arise '*just* because he said so'. For if the authority *only* has a claim on us because he has a good *reason* for making the claim, and it is this background reason that really obligates us, not the claim itself, then the claimant's role is less essential. At most the claimant, and his claim, is an *epistemic* authority for us; what he says offers good guidance for knowing what, or where, the applicable background reasons are. We are not following the directive of the authority 'just because he said so', that is, just because he is the relevant authority. Rather, we are following the directive, or at least feeling the burden of an obligation to reply, 'because (i) he said so *and* (ii) what he says (usually) is a very good indication of what the relevant reasons are'. In other words, the obligation we feel is not so much source-based as content-dependent. But if this is what grounds the claimant's authority, then we are really only beholden to the background reason to which the epistemic authority, and the claim he makes, is a useful guide. We are, in effect, treating this authority as an instrument for that purpose (a bit like a thermometer reliably telling us the temperature), and not respecting the authority as something with a *content-independent* (authoritative) standing to make claims upon us. As Stephen Darwall has argued, such an epistemic authority, if it is an authority at all, really has no dignity.[24]

Now suppose that we had a single-stage summary rule in place, '(*p & not-r*) → *q*', the one that (as the defeasibility sceptic suggests) most accurately reflects the true moral scope of the rule. It is tempting to think that we might propose such a rule because we only want to see claims advanced under a rule if the rule is the most accurate or truthful reflection of what the reason of the rule requires, all things considered. If that were so, then claimants, and those responsive to claimants, would all appear to be beholden to the background reason or moral truth of the rule *and not to each other* in the way that models of (source-based, content-independent) authority make possible. Beyond offering an epistemic guide to what is required by the background reason of the rule (the one that best reflects the whole moral truth of the matter), there would be nothing especially valuable in having the actual assertion of any claim under the rule.

It must be conceded that, while this is a tempting interpretation of the single-stage summary rule, it is not the only one. It is possible that under such a single-stage summary rule we could be providing for the special authority (and dignity) of the claimant. After all, we could concede, as envisaged in the first point emphasized above, that it really does matter that the claimant actually make the claim against some respondent. It is not enough, we might say, that those against whom the claim is made feel the obligation as a duty to (the whole) moral truth, treating the claimant, and his claim, as a mere epistemic authority or guide for where those duties lie. We could say that, even under this single-stage summary rule, we *are* operating with a source-based, content-independent approach in the way that is required under respect for authority as such. What matters is the assertion of the claim itself, not merely what is evidenced by the background reason of the rule by such an assertion.

But notice that while we would have preserved the authority of the claimant under this interpretation of the single-stage summary rule, we would have preserved that authority, and the special dignity and respect that goes with having it, *unilaterally*. Only the initial claimant under the single-stage summary rule (the one that captures the whole moral truth of the rule in one step) would have any of the authority and respect

[24] S. Darwall, *The Second-Person Standpoint* (Cambridge, Mass.; London: Harvard University Press, 2006), 13–14.

that goes with making claims under rules against another party. The advantage of a two-stage defeasible rule, by contrast, is that it provides for interpersonal or bilateral respect, that is, for the respect that goes with having the authority to make the first-stage claim *and* the respect that goes with having the authority to make a second-stage counterclaim or reply.

Nor is the difference here just to be found in the fact that more parties (i.e. two rather than one) have authority and the respect that goes with having it. As Darwall has argued, the making of a claim against another party provides second-personal *reasons* for that party to act in response to that claim.[25] But this means that the claim presupposes that the second party is the sort of being who *can* act on reasons, a status or capacity that commands respect on its own.[26] So there is a kind of confirmation or reinforcement of the status that the first claim presupposes of the second party in the respect that goes with that party having an authority of her own to make counterclaims in reply. Moreover, the authority of the second party to make counterclaims reciprocates and affirms in the first party his status as a being capable of acting on reasons, a capacity that calls for the same sort of respect that is accorded to him as an authority to make *his* (initial) claims.

This reciprocal confirmation is lacking in the model of unilateral authority under a single-staged summary rule. There, at best, the defendant or second-party respondent can only *deny* the initial all-encompassing claims of the plaintiff under the summary rule. She has no authority to make claims, or to offer affirmative defences or replies, of her own under an independent, second-stage, exceptional rule. So, in contrast to the two-stage process that exists under defeasible rules, a process that knits the parties together in a self-confirming exchange of mutual respect, the process that begins and ends with the plaintiff making a unilateral claim under a single-stage summary rule only half-heartedly asserts respect for the responding party, the defendant, and, as a consequence, only receives a half-hearted confirmation of the status of the initial claimant, the plaintiff, in return.

D. The positive authority and collective rationality of defeasible rules

This discussion suggests that there is a moral argument that supports the process that private common law adjudication adopts under defeasible rules. This process provides for interpersonal (or, in Stephen Darwall's terms, *second*-personal) respect and accountability between the parties in a way that a single-stage summary rule does not. The latter, even if it accommodates the possibility of respectful argument (i.e. around an initial all-encompassing claim and a subsequent denial of that claim), holds each party accountable to what is (morally) true for them under the rule, that is, what (again, in Darwall's terms) is a *third*-personal reason for each of them. In a sense, in advancing arguments one way or the other under the single-stage summary rule, each party looks past the other to the (moral) world and, more particularly, towards some (moral) fact in that world made salient by the rule. *It is as if each party really had no essential role for the other.* And, even if we recognize the special authority of the initial claimant to *start* the argument by actually making a claim against some other party (i.e. if we recognize that

[25] Ibid., 20–2. Later I will argue that the making of a claim does not so much provide 'reasons' for the respondent (to act or reply) as it does make a demand on the respondent's rationality. See text following n. 28. But both sorts of claim (on reasons or rationality) presuppose the same sort of capacity in, and respect for, the respondent, the point that is essential here.

[26] Ibid.

it is the fact that he actually makes his initial authoritative claim, and not just the truth of it, that is the source of all subsequent discussion between the parties), the argument *from this point on* holds each party accountable not so much to each other, and each other's claim, as to a moral truth in the world which, while common to them, stands independent of each party and what each party claims.

The model of defeasible rules, by contrast, shifts each party's accountability from a world independent of them to a world which (to some extent at least) they construct themselves with the justifiable claims they make upon one another. Now, sometimes this can seem to be quite liberating. The plaintiff, for example, is not hostage to the statistical truth of his claim, but only to what he can justifiably claim is true. As we have seen (in the case of the alleged but unlikely Red Bus accident), this can allow for a claim by the plaintiff that he would not be able to make if he was limited to what was more likely to be true as a statistical matter. Of course, the defendant could be forgiven if she were to think of all of this as *less* liberating. For this easier claim by the plaintiff could form the basis upon which the defendant is finally held responsible (unless, in turn, she can offer some sort of justifiable reply). However, while this is true, the defendant needs to remember that the plaintiff cannot use a mere statistical truth to launch an initial claim against her; that is the effect of the plaintiff being non-suited against Blue Bus in the case as originally presented. So it is unclear what the *combined* effect under the model of defeasible rules is for the *net* accountability of any one party to another.

What is clear is that under the model of defeasible rules, the accountability of the parties to one another is *more of their own making* (together). Under the law, they are less accountable to what is morally correct or true, or what the most morally correct or true legal rule might demand of them all things considered, and more accountable to what authoritative demands they can justifiably make upon one another, in back and forth fashion, as they construct the rule and set the scope of its final application. In this respect the model of defeasible rules provides more for the parties' joint exercise of a collective or shared rationality under the developing rule than it does for the joint accountability of these parties to some shared reason under a more truthful rule. This last point is worth emphasizing as it suggests, somewhat surprisingly perhaps, that the model of defeasible rules (as opposed, say, to the more familiar 'model of rules')[27] might be closer to the arguments of the legal positivist than it is to those of the natural law theorist. However, to see this clearly, we first need to say something about the difference between reasons and rationality.[28]

Reasons attend to a relation that should exist between an attitude (e.g. a belief, intention, desire) that an individual has and some fact about the individual's situation.

[27] This is, of course, Dworkin's characterization of positivism; see R. Dworkin, *Taking Rights Seriously*, chs 2 and 3. Defeasibility is typically thought of as taking a step away from positivism (and its model of rules) towards something more like Dworkin's model of principles. But the argument here is that the model of rules and the model of principles have more in common than is usually appreciated, and the model of defeasible rules comes closer than either to a source-based account of legal obligation, at least in the context of adjudication.

[28] The discussion of reasons and rationality that follows owes much to the recent work of John Broome. See J. Broome, 'Normative Requirements', *Ratio*, 12 (1999), 398–419; J. Broome, 'Are Intentions Reasons? And How Should We Cope with Incommensurable Values?' in C.W. Morris and A. Ripstein (eds), *Practical Rationality and Preference: Essays for David Gauthier* (Cambridge: Cambridge University Press, 2001), 98–120; J. Broome, 'Normative Practical Reasoning', *Proceedings of the Aristotelian Society*, Suppl. vol. 75 (2001), 175–93; J. Broome, 'Practical Reasoning' in J.L. Bermudez and A. Millar (eds), *Reason and Nature: Essays in the Theory of Rationality* (Oxford: Clarendon Press, 2002), 85–112; and J. Broome, 'Reasons' in R.J. Wallace, M. Smith, S. Scheffler, and P. Pettit (eds), *Reason and Value: Essays on the Moral Philosophy of Joseph Raz* (Oxford: Clarendon Press, 2004), 28–55.

In the case of theoretical reason, for example, that *p* is true is a good reason for believing *p*. In practical reason, that the building is burning is a good reason for forming the intention to leave it. Rationality, by contrast, goes to the relation that should exist between these attitudes themselves. Theoretical rationality, for example, requires that you not believe both *p* and *not-p*. And practical rationality (e.g. means–ends rationality) might require that you not (i) intend to accomplish some end *E*, (ii) believe that the only means to accomplishing *E* is to intend the means *M*, and (iii) not intend the means *M*.

Moreover, these requirements of both theoretical and practical rationality are *strict*; that is, they hold regardless of the content of (or reasons for) *p*, *E*, and *M*. In this respect they are stronger than the requirements of reasons which might only hold *pro tanto*, that is, as a matter of weight. For example, that the building is burning might be a good reason for forming the intention of leaving it, but it does not strictly require that intention. This fact, and the reason which is provided by its being a fact, might be outweighed by another fact, for example, that you could save someone from the fire if you did not form the intention of leaving the building straight away.

However, while the requirements of theoretical and practical rationality are stronger in holding strictly rather than merely *pro tanto*, they are weaker in this sense: they hold only *relative* to one another. That is, unlike reasons, they do not detach and apply to any one of the different attitudes in particular. Thus, in the means–ends rationality requirement mentioned earlier, that you have the primary intention in (i), and the belief in (ii), gives you no particular *reason* to have the derivative intention in (iii). Your belief in (ii) might well be false, for example, and a false belief in (ii) can give you no particular reason to have the derivative intention in (iii) even if rationality might require such a derivative intention *if* (now as a relative matter) you have the intention in (i) and (continue to have) the (false) belief in (ii). For if you have both the intention in (i) and the belief in (ii), but you do not have the derivative intention in (iii), then you are not, strictly, as you should be *as a matter of rationality*, and even if some *reason* supports the fact that you do not have this derivative intention in (iii).

By now enough has been said about reasons and rationality to explain why the model of defeasible rules provides more for the parties' joint exercise of a collective or shared rationality under the developing rule than it does for their joint accountability to some shared reason under a more (morally) truthful rule. After all, recall that each claim and counterclaim is authoritative for the other party, not because it is true, that is, not because there is some (greater *pro tanto*) reason in the world for believing it (even as opposed to not believing it), but merely because of the (source-based, content-independent) fact that the authority actually *makes* that claim *as an authority*. (Of course, the claim, to be authoritative, must pass some minimum threshold of credibility, for example, that it be supported by a *reliable* witness; the point is that it need not be, nor even be consistent with, the most credible claim that could be made, say, as a purely statistical matter.) This, and only this (i.e. 'just because he said so'), is what calls for an authoritative reply if the initial claim is not to carry the day. And the reply, presumably if it *is* a reply, will offer an (again, minimally credible, but not necessarily the most credible) *answer* to that claim. That is, it will build on, and be relative to, the rationality (not the reason) of the initial claim. Thus, together with the initial claim, the reply will set the final scope of application of the multi-staged defeasible rule. In this way it is the claims as laid down by the parties themselves, and how these rationally relate to one another (not to how the world is), which finally gives order to the terms of their interaction.

But this tells us that the authority of a defeasible legal rule for the final result under it is a matter of the shared rationality for the parties of their own *positive* claims, not some independent (moral) reason. That is, the final authority of the rule supervenes on what *in fact* is claimed and counterclaimed as a matter of legal process under the rule (as it develops and matures), and not what is (morally) true for the parties apart from those claims. Nor *could* it be otherwise if we are to provide for the interpersonal respect and accountability that such a process of claim and counterclaim provides. For even if we attempted to include interpersonal respect and accountability as some part of the whole moral truth of a single-staged summary rule, it would be self-defeating to attend to *that* moral truth as something to which the parties were jointly accountable as a matter of reason, not rationality. For if the parties were to attend to this moral truth as a matter of reason, then again they would be looking past one another to what reason demands of them as a third-personal truth and not towards each other as a matter of interpersonal (or second-personal) respect and accountability. Far from faithfully attending to this moral truth, this would be to undermine it. This particular moral truth can *only* be achieved if the two parties jointly work out the final scope of the defeasible rule that binds them as a matter of (second-personal) shared rationality, not as a matter of their joint accountability to some (third-personal) moral reason.[29]

Does any of this have a bearing on the debate between legal positivism and natural law theory? Consider again the rule that announces that there are to be 'no vehicles in the park'. This is, of course, the rule that was at the centre of the debate between Hart and Fuller on the separation of law and morals. Hart originally conjured up this rule to argue that, while there might be hard cases in the 'penumbra' of the word 'vehicle' (say, 'bicycles' or 'roller skates'), something which might call for judicial interpretation and discretion as to what the law 'ought to be' in such cases, there would nevertheless also be 'core' cases (say, the ordinary family sedan out for a Sunday drive) that would be clearly covered by the word 'vehicle' and, therefore, clearly within the scope of the rule or the law 'as it is'. Prohibiting the latter from the park, Hart meant to argue, would be illustrative of the possibility of a *morality-free legal act*,[30] and this was all that he needed

[29] This also suggests that even if there are competing claims that eventually need to be 'weighed' against one another as the parties develop the scope of the rule that rationally orders their interaction, the weighing cannot take place in some space that is external to them or their claims. Again, this would be to hold the claimants accountable to some (third-personal) reason or moral truth of the matter rather than to each other. However, claims *can* be weighed in a way that avoids such third-personal accountability. Under proportionality analysis, for example, the force of each claim is measured according to how high it is *on its own scale* and this is compared to how high the other claim is *on its scale*. The claim with the higher proportionate claim on its own scale 'outweighs' the other. But there is no common (commensurable) space in which both scales operate (as in the more usual cost–benefit or utilitarian analysis that turns on a commensurable cardinality across the two scales). The judgement of greater proportionate effect that some decision might have on the one claim as compared to the other will be invariant, for example, to whatever weights different judges bring to the different scales (again, unlike in the more usual cost–benefit or utilitarian analysis, where the different weights will have a determinative effect on how the two scales are compared). These different weights can only have that sort of (commensurable) significance where the different claims and counterclaims are accountable to moral truths (or relative weights) in a world independent of the claimants. In a world where the claims are only accountable to each other (and not some third-personal reason) the weighing of the claims must be invariant to those weights, as it is under a proportionality analysis. For an example of how this plays out when the claims of individual, constitutionally protected rights are defeasible in the face of counterclaims arising out of a pressing and substantial state interest, see the Canadian case, *R.* v. *Oakes* [1986] 1 SCR 103. Under *Oakes* individual rights are defeasible and, interestingly, the *Oakes* test finishes with a proportionality comparison. For further discussion of proportionality in the context of defeasibility, see B. Chapman, 'Law, Incommensurability, and Conceptually Sequenced Argument', 1492 fn. 10.

[30] F. Schauer, 'A Critical Guide to Vehicles in the Park', 1114.

to make his point against the natural law theorist who, Hart suggested, would have us believe that *all* such acts must *always* attend to what moral reason demands.

It was in response to this claim for core meanings independent of moral purpose that Fuller offered up his example of the military vehicle mounted on a pedestal to be used as a war memorial. While this was clearly a vehicle, it was surely not so clear that it was meant to fall under the rule's general prohibition. So, by way of this example, Fuller meant to insist that, contrary to Hart's argument, it would always be necessary to consult the background moral reason or purpose of the rule to know exactly what cases were covered by it. It was the reason for the rule, and not the core meaning of the word 'vehicle', that would allow us confidently to claim that the family sedan (the easy case) was within the rule and the war memorial was not. Legal rules, and claims made under them, could not operate independently of these background moral reasons for the rule. Without some such consultation of this background reason, any legal rule, and any claim under that rule, would be senseless and, therefore, defective as law.[31]

We need not come to any final assessment here as to whether Fuller or Hart had the better of this debate. What is most interesting for the present discussion is that for Fuller the rule is always to be understood in light of its background reason or purpose. Hart, as we have already observed, seems more open to going forward with what the rule, and its core meaning, prescribes unless (or until) the rule confronts some reason not to. Thus, Fuller, as the natural law theorist in this debate, seems to be committed to the single-stage, reason-based, defeasibility of rules, the very thing that I have argued defeasible rules should not and cannot attend to if they are to serve the value of interpersonal accountability and respect. By contrast, Hart's account of the defeasible rule, while not obviously motivated by a concern for interpersonal accountability, is at least open to the possibility of containing that value.[32]

Interestingly, something of the same difficulty is confronted by another of Hart's key protagonists in the debate over positivism, Ronald Dworkin. Dworkin also lumbers positivism with a 'model of rules', a model, he says, that is incapable of accommodating what rule-appliers really need to sensibly decide hard cases, namely, principles. Principles, says Dworkin, have a logical structure different from rules. They operate much like the *pro tanto* reasons mentioned above, inclining a decision in one direction rather than another according to some weight that the principle brings to bear on what is at issue in the decision. However, closer to the strict requirements of rationality, rules are more categorical, Dworkin says, necessitating a particular decision if they apply at all: 'Rules are applicable in all-or-nothing fashion. If the facts a rule stipulates are given, then either the rule is valid, in which case the answer it supplies must be accepted, or it is not, in which case it contributes nothing to the decision.'[33] Does this leave any room for exceptions? Dworkin goes on:

> Of course a rule may have exceptions... However, an accurate statement of the rule would take [these exceptions] into account, and any that did not would be incomplete. If the list of exceptions is very large, it would be too clumsy to repeat them each time the rule is cited; there is, however, no reason in theory why they should not all be added on, and the more there are, the more accurate is the statement of the rule.[34]

[31] F. Schauer, 'Is Defeasibility an Essential Property of Law?', in this volume, ch. 4.
[32] H.L.A. Hart, 'The Ascription of Responsibility and Rights'.
[33] R. Dworkin, *Taking Rights Seriously*, 24.
[34] Ibid., 24–5.

Thus, there can be exceptions to a rule, but only in the very limited sense made possible by the (by now familiar) single-stage summary rule that seeks, ideally, to blend all exceptions into the most accurate statement of the rule.

Dworkin's point, ultimately, is to argue that legal principles (like 'no person should profit from his own wrong') do not accommodate exceptions in this way. Indeed, principles, unlike rules, do not even purport to set out 'rule-like' (antecedent) conditions that make their application necessary in some case. So, according to Dworkin, if principles play an essential role in the adjudication of hard cases (in the way he suggests they must), and if principles (with their dimension of weight) cannot be accommodated within the (all-or-nothing) model of rules, then the model of rules provides an inadequate account of adjudication.

But if principles are akin to *pro tanto* reasons, then Dworkin's argument *against* the model of rules is effectively an argument *for* defeasibility as accountability to (the balance of) true moral reasons. But, again, this is to commit defeasibility to a set of principles that, because they do not attend to the ('just because they said so') authority of the claims and counterclaims of the affected parties, cannot accommodate the value of interpersonal accountability and respect that comes out of a purely *rational* (and interpersonal) accommodation and integration of these different claims. Of course, neither can the model of rules that seeks to incorporate all that is morally true in one single-staged summary rule, the model that Dworkin rejects in favour of his model of principles. But this is to ignore the possibility that between the model of principles and the model of rules is the model of *defeasible* rules, the one, arguably, that Hart originally had in mind. This is the model which I have sought to illuminate in this paper, and it is the only one, it seems, that gives appropriate expression to the interpersonal accountability and respect that we value so much in law and adjudication.

Index

The manufacturer's authorised representative in the EU for product safety is Oxford University Press España S.A. of El Parque Empresarial San Fernando de Henares, Avenida de Castilla, 2 - 28830 Madrid (www.oup.es/en or product.safety@oup.com). OUP España S.A. also acts as importer into Spain of products made by the manufacturer.
Printed and bound by CPI Group (UK) Ltd, Croydon, CR0 4YY
14/09/2026
02216306-0014